GUN CONTROL
AND THE CONSTITUTION

GUN CONTROL AND THE CONSTITUTION
Sources and Explorations
on the Second Amendment

Edited with an Introduction by

Robert J. Cottrol

RUTGERS
THE STATE UNIVERSITY OF NEW JERSEY
SCHOOL OF LAW

Garland Publishing, Inc.
New York & London
1994

Library of Congress Cataloging-in-Publication Data

Gun control and the Constitution : sources and explorations on the Second
   Amendment / edited with an introduction by Robert J. Cottrol.
      p.   cm.
   Includes bibliographical references.
   ISBN 0–8153–1666–6 (pbk. : alk. paper)
   1. Firearms—Law and legislation—United States.   2. United States—
Constitutional law—Amendments—2nd.   I. Cottrol, Robert J.
KF3941.A7G86   1994
344.73'0533—dc20
[347.304533]   94–15079
                                                                   CIP

Printed on acid-free, 250-year-life paper
Manufactured in the United States of America

CONTENTS

GENERAL INTRODUCTION

Controversies in Constitutional Law began as a series in 1992. The goal of the series is to provide teachers, scholars, and students with a convenient access to the law, debates, and scholarly literature surrounding major constitutional law questions. By conveniently gathering this material in one place, this series allows users to quickly become familiar with the arguments and issues surrounding a particular constitutional controversy.

Gun Control and the Constitution was one of the first publications in Controversies in Constitutional Law. Initially *Gun Control and the Constitution* was a three volume hardback series. That series has attracted a good deal of attention in the scholarly community, just as the problem of gun control attracts attention in the political community.

Indeed, the subject remains controversial and current. The debate over the meaning of the second amendment and the public policy issues surrounding that debate remains vigorous. In the 1993 Virginia gubernatorial election gun control was a major issue, and may have helped decide the outcome in a number of state and local races. As I write this foreword President Clinton is signing the Brady Bill that requires a waiting period for the purchase of handguns. This is the most significant gun control legislation since World War II. Clearly the question of gun controls remains a significant political and legal issue. It is quite likely that the recently passed gun control legislation will be in the courts. The issue will certainly remain in the public press.

Professor Cottrol's one volume paperback allows scholars, teachers, students, and the general public to have greater access to the cases and scholarly literature surrounding this controversy. The materials in this volume suggest the range of the debate over the origin of the Second Amendment and over public policy that might stem from that Amendment. Neither Professor Cottrol's introductory essay nor the cases, government reports, and articles in this volume are likely to end the debate. Indeed, the goal of this series is to stimulate the debate and encourage students and the general public to participate in the debate.

INTRODUCTION

THE SECOND AMENDMENT: INVITATION TO A MULTI-DIMENSIONAL DEBATE[1]

"A well regulated Militia, being necessary to the security of a free State, the right of the people to keep and bear Arms, shall not be infringed."[2]

The contemporary debate over the Second Amendment is one of the more intriguing controversies in American constitutional discourse. Few issues excite greater passion. It is a staple of editorial and op-ed writers in the popular press. It is the subject of a vast polemical literature by political partisans on both sides of the often acrimonious gun-control debate. Noted legal scholars have recently termed the Second Amendment "embarrassing" and "terrifying." Former Chief Justice Warren Burger has indicated his belief that the amendment's inclusion in the Bill of Rights was a mistake, a rare public admission on the part of a Supreme Court justice concerning the supposedly sacrosanct Bill of Rights. Conservative columnist George Will and liberal New York Congressman Major Owens have urged repeal of the provision guaranteeing a right to keep and bear arms.

Some see the amendment as a guarantee of political freedom, a hedge against a potentially tyrannical government. This position cuts across familiar ideological lines. It has been embraced, in varying degrees, by the reputedly conservative National Rifle Association, liberal constitutional scholar Sanford Levinson, and retired Army Colonel-turned-syndicated-columnist Harry Summers. Others, including former Chief Justice Burger, conservative former Supreme Court nominee Robert Bork, and, of course, various gun-control advocacy groups, generally believed to be politically liberal, see the Second Amendment as having been wrongfully used as a tool to combat needed public safety and anti-crime measures.[3]

Oddly enough, this often rancorous exchange has suffered a curious neglect from those we normally turn to for constitutional interpretation, the legal academy and the courts, particularly the United States Supreme Court. The nation's highest tribunal has only seriously addressed the issue in three cases: the most recent of these, *United States v. Miller*,[4] is over fifty years old. With the Second Amendment we have a scholarly debate that members of the academy have been generally reluctant to join, an historical controversy more faithfully attended to by partisans on different sides of the gun-control debate than by professional historians, an arena of jurisprudence from which the nation's highest court has been largely absent.[5]

This controversy, unlike the debate over almost every other provision of the Constitution, occurs at the most fundamental level. It is a debate over basic meaning. Briefly stated, the modern debate over the Second Amendment is part of the larger gun-control debate, the extent to which that constitutional provision was intended to limit the ability of government to prohibit or severely restrict private ownership of firearms. It is a debate fueled, in part, by the fear generated by this nation's high crime rate, including an average of 20,000 homicides committed annually with firearms. The debate is further fueled by the presence of firearms in roughly half the households in the country, many of them owned for protection.[6]

This debate has produced two familiar interpretations of the Second Amendment. Advocates of stricter gun controls have tended to stress the amendment's militia clause, arguing that the purpose of the amendment was to insure that state militias would be maintained against federal encroachment. Advocates of this view, the collective-rights theory, argue that the framers' sole concern was with the concentration of military power in the hands of the federal government. Opponents of stricter gun controls have tended to stress the amendment's second clause, arguing that the framers intended a militia-of-the-whole, or at least a militia consisting of the entire able-bodied white male population. They argue that this militia-of-the-whole was expected to perform its duties with privately owned weapons. Advocates of this view also urge that the militia clause should be read as an amplifying rather than a qualifying clause, that is that, while maintaining a "well-regulated militia" was a major reason for including the Second Amendment in the Bill of Rights, it should not be viewed as the sole or limiting reason, and that other reasons, including a right to individual self-defense, were also included in the framers' contemplations.[7]

This introduction will not settle this controversy. It is not intended to do so. In my view the individual-rights theorists have made the better historical case, but I would urge readers to draw their own conclusions by reading the works selected for this volume and other studies that explore the Second Amendment. Few people come to this issue without some prior views on the subject and I freely confess my inclinations in favor of the individual-rights view, both as a matter of historical interpretation and for some of the policy reasons indicated in the article that I co-authored with Raymond T. Diamond, reprinted in this volume. All of that having been said, this introduction is divided into two parts. The first part, "Arms and Rights: From Medieval England to Modern Mean Streets," outlines the history of the notion of the right to keep and bear arms in English and, later, American law and culture, both before and after the adoption of the Second Amendment. Some of the ground covered should be familiar to students of this controversy, though I hope this essay might advance the conversation particularly through a discussion of state constitutional law, the contribution that body of law has made and might yet make to the jurisprudence of arms and rights, and through a thorough exploration of the principal United States Supreme Court case on the subject, *United States v. Miller.*[8]

In the second part of this introduction I would like to suggest that the debate over the Second Amendment should expand beyond the familiar partisan precincts of the current gun-control debate. It will always be a part of the gun-control debate and I would not attempt to argue that either those who see the Second Amendment as an irrelevancy, needlessly impeding necessary public safety measures, or those who argue that the Second Amendment safeguards a fundamental freedom should stop trying to persuade either the lay public or academic and legal specialists. But this is a debate that goes much deeper than the gun-control debate, as important as that debate is. The Second Amendment raises intensely important questions for students of political philosophy and constitutional theory, questions that have been neglected too long by the academy. I hope the second part of this introduction can at least pose these questions and help create a more multi-dimensional debate.

ARMS AND RIGHTS: FROM MEDIEVAL ENGLAND TO MODERN MEAN STREETS

If the right to keep and bear arms has become a matter of strident controversy in late twentieth-century America, this was not always the case. For much of American history, this right was extolled as fundamental, a bedrock constitutional principle that could not be denied free people. This widespread agreement occurred in part because of the frontier conditions that existed in colonial America and persisted throughout much of the nineteenth century. The consensus also came about because of the role private arms ownership played in achieving American independence, particularly in the early years of the Revolution. The often violent and lawless nature of American society also helped contribute to the widespread view that the right to possess arms for self-defense was fundamental.

But the Second Amendment and the right to keep and bear arms cannot be understood solely through an examination of American history. Like other sections of the Bill of Rights, the Second Amendment was an attempt to secure what was believed to be an already existing right. The framers of the Bill of Rights did not believe they were creating new rights. Instead they were attempting to prevent the newly formed federal government from encroaching on rights already considered part of the English Constitutional heritage.[9]

To understand the Second Amendment it is necessary, in part, to understand the framers' world and their view of the right to bear arms as one of the traditional "rights of Englishmen." The English settlers who began to populate North America in the seventeenth century were heirs to a tradition over five centuries old, governing both the right and duty to be armed. They were also heirs to an English distrust for professional armies and police forces, a distrust that was formally expressed at least as early as the signing of the Magna Carta. At English law, the idea of an armed citizenry responsible for the security of the community had long co-existed, perhaps somewhat uneasily, with regulation of the ownership of arms, particularly along class lines. The Assize of Arms of 1181 required the arming of all free men. Later statutes would even require villeins to have arms in order to be prepared to participate in the defense of their communities. Lacking both professional police forces and a standing army, English law and custom dictated that the citizenry as a whole, privately equipped, assist in both law enforcement and military defense. By law all men between 16 and 60 were liable to be summoned into the sheriff's *posse comitatus*. All persons were expected to participate in the hot pursuit of criminal suspects, the "hue and cry," supplying their own arms for the occasion. There were legal penalties for failure to participate. The maintenance of law and order was a community affair, a duty of all citizens.[10]

And all able-bodied men were considered part of the militia and were required, at least theoretically, to be prepared to assist in military defense. The law required citizens to possess arms. Towns and villages were required to provide target ranges in order to maintain the martial proficiency of the yeomanry. Despite this, the English discovered that the militia-of-the-whole maintained a rather indifferent proficiency and motivation. By the sixteenth century the practice was to rely on select bodies of men intensively trained for militia duty, rather than to rely on the armed population at large.[11]

Although English law recognized a duty and a right to be armed, both were highly circumscribed by English class structure. The common people partici- pated in the defense of their communities, but the law at times regarded them with suspicion as a group capable of mischief, mischief towards each other, towards their betters and towards their betters' game. At times the notion of arms distributed amongst the population at large was also regarded as potentially subversive. Restrictions on the type of arms deemed suitable for common people had also long been part of English law and custom. Game laws had long been one tool used to limit the arms of the common people. The fourteenth-century Statute of Northhampton restricted the ability of people to carry arms in public places. A sixteenth-century statute designed as a crime control measure prohibited the carrying of handguns and crossbows by those with incomes of less than one hundred pounds a year. Catholics were also subject to being disarmed as potential subversives after the English Reformation. Although recent research indicates that the various class and religious discriminations did not rise to the level of total prohibition of arms ownership, the notion of qualifying the right to own and carry arms by social condition co-existed with the English notion of arming the population at large.[12]

The need for community security had produced a traditional duty to be armed at English law, but it took the religious and political turmoil of seventeenth-century England to help transform that duty into the modern notion of a political right to keep and bear arms. The attempts by Stuart Kings Charles II and James II to disarm large portions of the population, particularly Protestants and suspected political opponents, met with popular resistance and helped implant into English and later American constitutional sensibilities that the right to possess arms was of fundamental political importance. These efforts led to the adoption of the Seventh Provision of the English Bill of Rights in 1689:

> "That the subjects which are Protestants may have arms for their defence suitable to their conditions and as allowed by law."[13]

By the eighteenth century, the right to possess arms, both for personal protection and as a counterbalance against state power, had come to be viewed as one of the fundamental rights of Englishmen on both sides of the Atlantic. Sir William Blackstone, whose *Commentaries on the Laws of England* greatly influenced American legal thought both before the American Revolution and well into the nineteenth century, listed the right to posses arms as one of the five auxiliary rights of English subjects without which their primary rights could not be maintained:

> "The fifth and last auxiliary right of the subject, that I shall at present mention, is that of having arms for their defence, suitable to their condition and degree and such as are allowed by law. Which is also declared by the same statute . . . and is indeed a public allowance, under due restrictions, of the natural right of resistance and self-preservation, when the sanctions of society and laws are found insufficient to restrain the violence of oppression."[14]

A few words with respect to Blackstone are in order here. His importance with respect to the question of the right to keep and bear arms, and indeed a number of other issues, should not be underestimated. Written between 1765 and 1769

(Volume I was published in 1765), *Blackstone's Commentaries* played an influential role in teaching late eighteenth-century American lawyers the rudiments of the common law. The role of his commentaries as the foundation of many an American lawyer's legal education increased in the early nineteenth century. I have argued that with respect to the issue of the right to keep and bear arms it is important to consider not only Blackstone's potential influence on the framers of the original Constitution and Bill of Rights, but also his influence on the framers of the Fourteenth Amendment, many of the principal proponents of which intended to apply the Bill of Rights to the states.[15]

Although Blackstone's discussion of the "Fifth Auxiliary Right" is often mentioned within the context of the Second Amendment debate, his relevance to the debate does not end there. Blackstone was aware of the evolution of the English militia from a body of the whole people to the more select body instituted under James I. He expressed a concern that military forces should come from the people and not be a distinct class.[16]

Blackstone also had interesting views on hunting, which he regarded as a natural right, albeit one that the state could restrain. He also expressed the view that many of the game laws of Europe, although ostensibly enacted either to preserve species or to discourage idleness among agricultural workers, were really designed to disarm the common people: " . . . For preventing of popular insurrections and resistance to the government, by disarming the bulk of the people: which last is a reason oftener meant, than avowed, by the makers of forest or game laws . . . "[17]

American commentator St. George Tucker, who used Blackstone's observations as an occasion to contrast what he believed was the somewhat anemic right to bear arms under English law with its more robust American counterpart, made the following observation:

> "Whoever examines the forest, and game laws in the British code will readily perceive that the right of keeping arms is effectually taken away from the people of England. The commentator [Blackstone] himself informs us, "that the prevention of popular 'insurrections and resistance to government by disarming the people is a reason oftener meant than avowed by the makers of the forest and game laws.' "[18]

Incidentally it would appear that Tucker had somewhat misread Blackstone. Blackstone's reference to game laws as a device used to disarm the populace appeared to be more a discussion of Continental and not British game laws. Whatever the case, Tucker's observation coincided with the general American view that the right to bear arms was considerably more robust in America than Britain. Tucker contrasted the British and American rights by observing:

"The right of the people to keep and bear arms shall not be infringed. Amendments to C. U. S. Art. 4, and this without any qualification as to their condition or degree, as is the case in the British government."[19]

If some five centuries of English experience had transformed the duty to be armed for the common defense into a right to be armed, in part, to resist potential political oppression, a similar evolution in thought had occurred in the American colonies between the earliest seventeenth-century settlements and the American Revolution. Early English settlement in North America had a quasi-military character, an obvious response to harsh frontier conditions. Leaders of settlements often held the title of militia captain, reflecting both the civil and military nature of their offices. In order to provide for the defense of often isolated colonies, special effort was made to insure that white men, capable of bearing arms, were brought into them.[20]

Far from the security of Britain, often bordering on the colonies of other frequently hostile European powers, colonial governments viewed the arming of able-bodied white men and the requirement that they perform militia service as essential to a colony's survival. The right and duty to be armed broadened in colonial America. If English law qualified the right to own arms by religion and class, those considerations were significantly less important in the often insecure colonies of early America. If by the seventeenth century the concept of the militia-of-the-whole was largely theoretical in England, in contemporary America it was the chief instrument of colonial defense. While the English upper classes sought to restrict the ownership of arms on the part of the lower classes as a means of helping to enforce game laws, any significant effort to restrict hunting in North America with its small population and abundant game would have been considered absurd. From the beginning, conditions in colonial America created a very different attitude towards arms and the people.[21]

Race provided another reason for the renewed emphasis on the right and duty to be armed in America. Britain's American colonies were home to three often antagonistic races, red, white and black. For the settlers of British North America, an armed and universally deputized white population was necessary not only to ward off dangers from the armies of other European powers, but also to ward off attacks from the indigenous Indian population that opposed the encroachment of English settlers on their lands. An armed white population was also essential to maintain social control over blacks and Indians who toiled unwillingly as slaves and servants in English settlements. This helped broaden the right to bear arms for whites. The need for white men to act not only in the traditional militia and posse capacities but also to keep order over the slave population helped lessen class, religious and ethnic distinctions among whites in colonial America. That need also helped extend the right to bear arms to classes traditionally viewed with suspicion in England, including indentured servants.[22]

The colonial experience helped strengthen the appreciation of early Americans for the merits of an armed citizenry. The experience of the American Revolution, of course further strengthened that appreciation. The Revolution began with acts of rebellion by armed citizens. And if sober historical analysis reveals that it was actually American and French regulars who ultimately defeated the British and established American independence, the image of the rag-tag, privately equipped militia successfully challenging the British Empire earned an enduring place in American thought and helped shape American political philosophy. For the generation that authored the Constitution, it reinforced the lessons their English ancestors had learned in the seventeenth century. It helped revitalize Whiggish notions that standing armies were dangerous to liberty. It helped transform the idea that the people should be armed and that security should be provided by a militia-of-the-whole from a matter of military necessity into a political notion, one that would be embodied in the new Constitution.[23]

This view that an armed population contributed to political liberty as well as community security found its way into the debates over the Constitution and is key to understanding the Second Amendment. Like other provisions of the Constitution, the clause that gave Congress the power to provide for the organizing, arming and disciplining of the militia excited fears among those who believed that the proposed Constitution could be used to destroy both state power and individual rights. It is interesting, in light of the current debate over the meaning of the Second Amendment, that both Federalists and anti-Federalists assumed that the militia would be one that enrolled almost the entire white male population between the ages of 16 and 60 and that militia members would supply their own arms.[24]

But many feared that the militia clause could be used both to do away with the state's control over the militia and to disarm the population. Some expressed fear that Congress would use its power to establish a select militia, a body of men chosen from the population at large who would receive special military training and would perform almost all militia duties somewhat similar to the modern National Guard. Many viewed this select militia with as much apprehension as they did a standing army. The English experience of the seventeenth century had shown that one could be used to disarm the population at large. Richard Henry Lee of Virginia expressed the fear that it might be so used in the American colonies.[25]

Other critics of the new Constitution reflected the fear that without an armed population and a broad-based militia, the newly empowered federal government could turn despotic. Anti-Federalists in Pennsylvania called for a right to bear arms for self defense, state defense, defense of the United States and for hunting.[26] A letter dated January 25, 1788 and traditionally attributed to Richard Henry Lee argued for a broad-based militia, and against the enlistment of a select militia. This letter reiterated the notions that a select militia would be as dangerous to liberty as a standing army and that arming the population at large was essential to the prevention of tyranny:

> ". . . A militia when properly formed, are in fact the people themselves, and render regular troops unnecessary . . . First, the constitution ought to secure a genuine and guard against a select militia by providing that the militia shall always be kept well organized, armed and disciplined, and include, according to the past and general usage of the states, all men capable of bearing arms; and that all regulations tending to render this general militia useless and defenseless, by establishing select corps of militia, or distinct bodies of military men, not having permanent interest and attachments in the community be avoided . . . These corps, not much unlike regular troops, will ever produce an inattention to the general militia; and the consequence has ever been, and always must be, that the substantial men, having families and property, will generally be without arms, without knowing the use of them, and defenseless; whereas, to preserve liberty, it is essential that the whole body of the people always possess arms, and be taught alike, especially when young, how to use them; nor does it follow from this, that all promiscuously must go into actual service on every occasion. The mind that aims at a select militia, must be influenced by a truly anti-republican principle . . ."[27]

In their efforts to answer critics of the Constitution Alexander Hamilton and James Madison addressed the charges of those critics who argued that the new Constitution could destroy both the independence of the militia and deny arms to the population. Hamilton's responses are particularly interesting because he wrote as someone who was openly skeptical concerning the military value of the militia-of-the-whole. The former Revolutionary War artillery officer conceded that the militia had fought bravely during the Revolution, but he argued it proved no match when pitted against regular troops. Hamilton urged the creation of a select militia that would be more amenable to military training and discipline than the population as a whole. Despite this he conceded that the population as a whole should be armed.[28]

But if Hamilton gave only grudging support to the concept of the militia-of-the-whole, Madison, author of the Second Amendment, was a much more vigorous defender of the concept. In *The Federalist Number 46* he left little doubt that he saw the armed population as a potential counterweight to tyranny.

> " . . . Let a regular army, fully equal to the resources of the country, be formed; and let it be entirely at the devotion of the federal government: still it would not be going too far to say that the State governments with the people on their side would be able to repel the danger. The highest number to which according to the best computation, a standing army can be carried

in any country does not exceed one hundredth part of the whole number of souls; or one twenty-fifth part of the number able to bear arms. This proportion would not yield, in the United States an army of more than twenty-five or thirty thousand men. To these would be opposed a militia amounting to near half a million citizens with arms in their hands, officered by men chosen among themselves, fighting for their common liberties and united and conducted by governments possessing their affections and confidence. It may well be doubted whether a militia thus circumstanced could ever be conquered by such a proportion of regular troops. Those who are best acquainted with the late successful resistance of this country against the British arms will be most inclined to deny the possibility of it. Besides the advantage of being armed, which the Americans possess over the people of almost every other nation, the existence of subordinate governments, to which the people are attached and by which the militia officers are appointed, forms a barrier against the enterprises of ambition, more insurmountable than any which a simple government of any form can admit of. Notwithstanding the military establishments in the several kingdoms of Europe, which are carried as far as the public resources will bear, the governments are afraid to trust the people with arms . . . [29]

This desire to maintain a universal militia and an armed population played a critical part in the adoption of the Second Amendment. It is also important to remember that firearms ownership, for self-defense and hunting, was widespread with few restrictions, at least for the white population. The Second Amendment, like other provisions of the Bill of Rights, was designed to prevent the newly created federal government from encroaching on rights that were then enjoyed. It is significant that the universally accepted view of the militia, at the time, was that militiamen would supply their own arms. One year after the ratification of the Bill of Rights, Congress passed legislation reaffirming the notion of a privately equipped militia-of-the-whole. The act, titled "An Act more effectually to provide for the National Defence by establishing an Uniform Militia throughout the United States," called for the enrollment of every free, able-bodied white male citizen between the ages of 18 and 45 into the militia. The act required every militia member to provide himself with a musket or firelock, a bayonet and ammunition.[30]

The decades between the adoption of the Second Amendment and the Civil War brought little opportunity for federal court interpretation of the Constitutional provision. With the exception of statutes prohibiting the carrying of concealed weapons, there were few restrictions concerning either the keeping or the bearing of arms in antebellum America. Most laws restricting the possession of firearms were to be found in the slave states of the antebellum South. Generally, they prohibited the possession of firearms on the part of slaves and free blacks.

Outside of the slave states, the right to keep and bear arms was generally not impaired, not even for free Negroes. No federal legislation restricted firearms ownership and as it was generally held before the Civil War that the Bill of Rights only limited the power of the federal government, there was no occasion for the federal courts to pronounce upon the matter.

If the federal courts were largely silent on the subject of the Second Amendment, important steps towards development of a jurisprudence of the right to keep and bear arms were occurring in some state courts. By the early nineteenth century, most state constitutions recognized the principle of the people's right to bear arms, but state courts and legislatures realized that this principle alone did not settle every question that might arise with respect to the possession of weapons. In 1840 the Supreme Court of Tennessee heard the appeal of one William Aymette, who had been convicted under a state statute prohibiting the concealed carrying of bowie knives. The Tennessee Constitution had a provision declaring "that the free white men of this state have a right to keep and bear arms for their common defence." The court rejected Aymette's contention that the right to bear arms gave an unlimited right to carry any weapon and that it prevented all legislation on the subject. The Aymette Court held that the open carrying of weapons was protected by the right to bear arms and it made a distinction between arms useful for the common defense and those weapons that were essentially the tools of criminals.[31]

The two principal ideas that were developed in *Aymette,* the distinction between bearing arms openly and carrying concealed weapons and the notion that some weapons are suitable for the common defense, while others are not, what has become known as "the civilized-warfare test," would become enduring parts of the jurisprudence of the right to bear arms. These concepts were adopted in other state courts and to a limited extent by the federal courts in the twentieth century. The first concept, the distinction between concealed and openly carried weapons, seems unproblematic. Presumably, if weapons are carried openly, one can see at a distance whether or not an individual is armed and make the decision to avoid the individual if such action is warranted. The civilized-warfare test, or the notion that some weapons are inherently useful only for crime and not for legitimate purposes, including the common defense, seems somewhat more problematic. It is a line of thinking that seems common-sensical enough. And yet even in *Aymette* we can see the difficulties with this line of judicial thinking. Why were Bowie knives singled out by the legislature? They had, of course, a colorful and dangerous reputation on the old southwestern frontier, but they were in fact no more dangerous than many other knives and axes common at the time. The *Aymette* opinion helped launch a line of jurisprudence that recognized that some weapons were not protected under the notion of a right to bear arms, but that also often failed to develop well-reasoned guidelines as to why some weapons were protected while others were not.

Important though less far reaching, *Nunn v. Georgia* also involved the concealed carrying of a weapon, in this case a pistol. The important development in *Nunn* was Judge Joseph Henry Lumpkin's opinion that the Second Amendment to the federal Constitution was binding on the state of Georgia even though that ran counter to the Supreme Court's decision in *Barron v. Baltimore*[32] and to the generally held notions of constitutional jurisprudence at the time. Of perhaps especial significance was Nunn's view that the right extended beyond militia purposes:

". . . The right of the whole people, old and young, men, women and boys, and not militia only, to keep and bear arms of every description, and not such merely as are used by the militia, shall not be infringed, curtailed or broken in upon, in the smallest degree; and all this for the important end to be attained: the rearing up and qualifying a well-regulated militia, so vitally necessary to the security of a free state. Our opinion is, that any law, state or federal is repugnant to the Constitution, and void, which contravenes this right, originally belonging to our forefathers, trampled under foot by Charles I and his two wicked sons and successors, re-established by the revolution of 1688, . . ."[33]

Both *Aymette* and *Nunn* provide strong evidence of a common agreement among jurists in antebellum America concerning the purposes and importance of the right to bear arms. Both Judge Green of the Tennessee court and Judge Lumpkin of Georgia saw the right to bear arms as descending from the English experience of a need for an armed citizenry capable of resisting the excesses of the Crown. They saw the right as one that would enable the population to maintain freedom against potential governmental domination. Essentially their view was that it was one of the more important prerogatives of a free people.

Their views were echoed by other antebellum commentators. St. George Tucker contrasted the Second Amendment's robust guarantee with what he saw as the more restrictive English right. Supreme Court Justice Joseph Story also regarded the right as fundamental:

. . . The right of the citizens to keep, and bear arms has been justly considered, as the palladium of the liberties of a republic; since it offers a strong moral check against the usurpation and arbitrary power of rulers; and will generally, even if they are successful in the first instance, enable the people to resist, and triumph over them . . .[34]

The only antebellum pronouncement from the Supreme Court on the subject came in Chief Justice Taney's opinion in *Dred Scott v. Sanford*. Taney indicated that African Americans, slave or free, could be denied the right to possess arms the way they could also be denied freedom of speech, assembly and travel:

"It would give to persons of the negro race, who were recognized as citizens in any one State of the Union, the right to enter every other State whenever they pleased, . . . and it would give them the full liberty of speech in public and in private upon all subjects upon which its own citizens might speak, to hold public meetings upon political affairs, and *to keep and carry arms wherever they went.*[35]

The opinion invites interesting speculation concerning antebellum views on the scope of the Second Amendment. The only restrictions on the ownership or carrying of weapons by blacks were state statutes. There was no general federal prohibition and outside of the South most states permitted blacks to own and carry arms on the same basis as whites. Was Taney saying that the kind of restrictions enacted by southern states limiting the right of blacks to own arms would have been unconstitutional if applied to whites? Was Taney echoing Lumpkin's view that the Constitution limited the states' ability to restrict arms? Too much might be made of this, but Taney's opinion does invite such questions.[36]

It would take the turmoil of the Civil War and its aftermath, Reconstruction, to bring the Second Amendment squarely before the Supreme Court. The end of the War of the Rebellion brought about a new conflict over the status of former slaves and the power of the states. The defeated white South sought to preserve as much of the antebellum southern social order as could survive northern victory and national law. In the immediate aftermath of the war, southern states were not prepared to grant the newly emancipated black population the general liberties that white citizens enjoyed. Indeed southern states did not give the former slaves the rights that northern states had long given their free Negro populations. In 1865 and 1866 southern states passed a series of statutes known as the Black Codes. These statutes were designed, in part, to insure that traditional southern labor arrangements would be preserved. They often required blacks to sign labor contracts that bound black agricultural workers to their employers for a year. Blacks were forbidden from serving on juries and could not testify or act as parties against whites. Vagrancy laws were used to force blacks into labor contracts and to limit freedom of movement. And as further indication that the former slaves had not yet joined the ranks of free citizens, southern states passed legislation prohibiting blacks from carrying firearms without licenses, a requirement to which whites were not subjected. The Mississippi statute provides a typical example of restrictions of this kind:

"*Be it enacted,* . . . that no freedman, free Negro or mulatto, not in the military service of the United States government, and not licensed so to do by the board of police of his or her county, shall keep or carry firearms of any kind, or any ammunition, dirk or bowie knife, and on conviction thereof in the county court shall be punished by fine, not exceeding ten dollars, and pay the cost of such proceedings and all such arms or ammunition shall be forfeited to the informer; and it shall be the duty of every civil or military officer to arrest

any such freedman, free Negro or mulatto found with any such arms or
ammunition, and shall cause him or her to be committed to trial in default
of bail.[37]

Such measures caused strong concerns among northern Republicans. Many of
them charged that the South was trying to reinstitute slavery and deny former
slaves those rights long considered essential to a free people. The news that the
freedmen were being deprived of the right to keep and bear arms was of
particular concern to the champions of Negro citizenship and equality. For
them the right of the black population to possess weapons went beyond
symbolic importance. It was important both as a means of maintaining the
recently reunited union and as a means of insuring against the virtual reenslavement of those formerly in bondage. Faced with a hostile, often recalcitrant
South, determined, by legal and extra-legal means to preserve the antebellum
social order, northern Republicans were particularly alarmed at provisions that
in effect preserved the right to keep and bear arms for former Confederates
while disarming blacks, the one group in the South with clear unionist
sympathies. This helped feed the determination of many northern Republicans
to provide national enforcement for the Bill of Rights.[38]

The debates over the Fourteenth Amendment and the federal civil rights
legislation of the Reconstruction era reveal the determination of Congress to
protect the right to keep and bear arms, as well as other provisions of the Bill of
Rights against state infringement. Representative Jonathan Bingham of Ohio,
who authored the Fourteenth Amendment's privileges or immunities clause,
and other Republican supporters of the Fourteenth Amendment expressed the
view that the clause applied the Bill of Rights to the states. The southern efforts
to disarm the freedmen and to deny other basic rights to former slaves played an
important role in convincing the 39th Congress that traditional notions concerning
Federalism and individual rights needed to change.[39]

If the Black Codes persuaded the 39th Congress of the need to apply the Bill of
Rights to the states, the Supreme Court in its earliest decisions on the
Fourteenth Amendment moved to maintain much of the antebellum federal
structure. The Supreme Court's first pronouncements on the Second Amendment
came about after the enactment of the Fourteenth Amendment and concerned
the question of the extent to which the latter amendment extended the
protection of the right to keep and bear arms. Ironically, the first party to bring
a claim before the Court alleging a violation of Second Amendment rights was
the federal government. In *United States v. Cruikshank* federal authorities, using
civil rights legislation, brought charges against William Cruikshank and others
for violating the rights of two black men, Levi Nelson and Alexander Tillman.
Cruikshank was charged with violating the rights of the two men to peaceably
assemble and with interfering with their right to bear arms. The Court, in a

majority opinion authored by Chief Justice Morrison R. Waite, held that the federal government had no power to protect citizens against private action that deprived them of their constitutional rights. The opinion held that the First and Second Amendments were limitations on Congress, not on private individuals. It also declared that Congress could not protect individuals against actions by private parties that deprived them of civil rights; for such protection individuals would be forced to rely on state governments.[40]

The next case in which the Court examined the Second Amendment, *Presser v. Illinois*, more directly involved the question of whether or not the Fourteenth Amendment limited state action. That case involved a challenge to an Illinois statute which prohibited individuals who were not members of the organized militia from parading with arms. Although Justice William Woods, author of the majority opinion, noted that the statute did not infringe on the right to keep and bear arms, he nonetheless used the case to pronounce the view that the Second Amendment was a limitation on the federal and not the state governments. Although much of the Woods opinion can be viewed as *dicta* extraneous to the central issue in *Presser*, the precedent in that case has remained one of the major devices by which Second Amendment claims have been denied in recent times.[41]

In the postbellum era the Supreme Court contributed little toward the development of a jurisprudence of the Second Amendment, except to use Second Amendment claims as an occasion to limit the scope of federal authority under the Fourteenth Amendment. Nonetheless, state courts, interpreting state constitutional provisions, wrestled with the vexing problem of developing a body of legal doctrine that balanced the right to keep and bear arms with notions of public safety and state police power. One of the more significant of these cases, *Andrews v. the State*, was decided by the Tennessee Supreme Court in 1871. The decision in *Andrews* made several potential contributions to the as yet largely unattempted area of Second Amendment theory. The case's principal holding was that the right to keep arms and the right to bear arms are separate, that the former belongs to the individual in his private capacity while the latter is incidental to militia service. *Andrews* also analyzed the very modern issue of the importance and relevance of the right to keep and bear arms in the absence of a system of universal militia training. Judge Freeman's opinion reflects traditional thinking on the subject, namely that the right of the people to own military weapons helped insure that citizens summoned into militia service would be better able to perform such service because of their familiarity with military weapons and their ability to provide such weapons for the occasion. The need, of course, for a population that could be rapidly mobilized into impromptu militia or home guard forces with relatively little training was a matter of recent memory in Tennessee, a border state whose citizens had fought on both sides during the Civil War.[42]

If the question of the right to arms occupied state courts, it also attracted the
attention of constitutional commentators in the late nineteenth century. One of
the more prominent of these was conservative Michigan Supreme Court Justice
Thomas M. Cooley. Cooley viewed the right in traditional political terms as a
right that would enable the people to resist potential tyranny. His analysis also
anticipated and answered the modern view that the right only extended to
members of the militia:

> ". . . The Right is General. — It may be supposed from the phraseology of
> this provision that the right to keep and bear arms was only guaranteed to the
> militia; but this would be an interpretation not warranted by the intent. The
> militia, as has been elsewhere explained, consists of those persons who, under
> the law, are liable to the performance of military duty, and are officered and
> enrolled for service when called upon. But the law may make provision for
> the enrollment of all who are fit to perform military duty, or of a small
> number only, or it may wholly omit to make any provision at all; and if the
> right were limited to those enrolled, the purpose of this guaranty might be
> defeated altogether by the action or neglect to act of the government it was
> meant to hold in check. The meaning of the provision undoubtedly is, that
> the people, from whom the militia must be taken, shall have the right to keep
> and bear arms, and they need no permission or regulation of law for the
> purpose. But this enables the government to have a well regulated militia; for
> to bear arms implies something more than the mere keeping; it implies the
> learning to handle and use them in a way that makes those who keep them
> ready for their efficient use; in other words, it implies the right to meet for
> voluntary discipline in arms, observing in doing so the laws of public order.[43]

It is, I think, fair to say that the nineteenth century ended with large scale
agreement that the right to keep and bear arms was a fundamental right of
Americans. Although there was little in the way of federal court jurisprudence
concerning the Second Amendment, a number of state courts had begun the
difficult task of reconciling concerns for public safety with the unique risks
inherent in the right to bear arms. Federal courts remained largely silent on the
question in part because restrictions on firearms ownership and carrying were
relatively rare in nineteenth-century America, a reflection of the consensus that
firearms were something of a necessity in a frontier society. Also such restrictions
as did exist were the products of state and local legislation, and despite the
intentions of the 39th Congress, the Supreme Court would not begin the
process of applying the Bill of Rights to the states until well into the twentieth
century. Indeed for that reason, most provisions of the Bill of Rights would not
get rigorous Supreme Court scrutiny until the twentieth century. Widespread
firearms ownership and the virtual absence of stringent restrictions insured that
the Second Amendment, at least as far as the legal community was concerned,

would remain more the concern of the commentator and theoretician than the working jurist. It was also partly a reflection of the fact that nineteenth-century Americans largely saw the private ownership of arms as an essential liberty. It would take the social changes brought about by urbanization in twentieth-century America to bring about increased regulation and new attitudes concerning arms and the Second Amendment.

The general agreement concerning the importance of the right to bear arms was beginning to be tempered in turn-of-the-century America by the perception that new, dangerous classes of people were posing a threat to society. In the South, state governments, long freed from the federal scrutiny that existed in the Reconstruction era, attempted to use laws restricting the concealed carrying of pistols to accomplish what had been attempted through the Black Codes in the aftermath of the Civil War. Discriminatory enforcement of laws regulating the carrying of concealed weapons often left blacks disarmed in public places while whites remained free to carry firearms. This helped make possible the early twentieth-century terrorism in the South known as "Jim Crow."[44]

But the South was not the only region where social prejudice helped restrict the right of members of disfavored minority groups to possess firearms. If the white South saw armed blacks as a threat, politicians in other regions saw a similar threat arising from labor unrest and the large scale southern and eastern European immigration during the turn of the century. The new immigrants, like others before them, met with often hostile receptions. They were associated with crime and anarchy, stereotyped as lazy and mentally unfit. Many native-born Americans feared that they would bring anarchist-inspired crime from Europe, including political assassinations and politically motivated armed robberies.

These fears helped bring about the passage of New York's Sullivan Law in 1911. The statute, passed by the state's legislature, was aimed at New York City, where many feared that the large foreign-born population was peculiarly susceptible to crime and vice. The statute went far beyond typical gun-control measures of the day. It prohibited the unlicensed carrying of concealed weapons. The law required a permit not only for carrying but also for the ownership or purchase of pistols. Violation of the statute was a felony. The first person convicted under the statute was a member of one of the suspect classes, an Italian immigrant.[45]

It was in this early twentieth-century atmosphere that the collective rights view of the right to bear arms first began to attract the attention of the judiciary. In *Salina v. Blaksley*, one of the earliest cases to adopt this view, the Supreme Court of Kansas interpreted that state's constitution[46] to allow a statute prohibiting the carrying of deadly weapons, declaring that the right to bear arms was for militia and not individual purposes. The court, which admitted that it was relying more on its original interpretation of the Kansas provision than on previous cases from other jurisdictions, did not explicitly address the question, as the Tennessee Court had in *Andrews,* of whether a distinction should be made between keeping and bearing arms.[47]

Despite the holding in *Salina* and the passage of New York's Sullivan Law there was little occasion for serious thought concerning the Second Amendment and no real occasion for Supreme Court pronouncement before the First World War. The nation was still predominantly rural. Restrictions on firearms ownership were anomalies in early twentieth-century America. For most Americans, access to firearms was largely unimpaired at the beginning of the century, and there was little occasion for either the courts or constitutional commentators to spend much time on the subject of arms and rights.

This changed after the First World War. Prohibition brought about the rise of organized gangs engaged in the sale of bootlegged alcohol. Territorial rivalries among the gangs led to open warfare on the streets of the nation's major cities. That warfare was made even more terrifying by the introduction of a fearsome new weapon, the Thompson sub-machine gun. A fully automatic weapon, developed too late for general use in World War I, the "Tommy Gun" was one of the first sub-machine guns in widespread use. Used by violent criminals in their wars on each other, the Thompson also claimed the lives of a fair number of members of the general public as well.

The end of the twenties and the end of Prohibition did not bring a halt to notorious misuse of automatic weapons. In the thirties such twentieth-century desperadoes as John Dillinger, "Pretty Boy" Floyd, "Ma" Barker, George "Machine Gun" Kelly, and Bonnie Parker and Clyde Barrow became a part of American folklore. The exploits of such criminals were made more vivid and terrifying by the then new medium of talking motion pictures. The horrors of criminal misuse of automatic weapons and handguns were forcibly brought home to the public.

These events helped to bring about the first efforts toward national gun control. The Roosevelt Administration proposed the first federal gun-control legislation. The National Firearms Act of 1934 required registration, police permission and then a prohibitive tax for firearms that were deemed gangster weapons—automatic weapons, sawed-off rifles and shotguns and silencers. The legislation as originally proposed would have also required the registration of handguns with the non-prohibitive tax of $1.00, a recognition that pistols played a prominent role in firearms crime but that they were also used by large numbers of law-abiding citizens for self-defense. This provision was dropped after objections by a coalition that included the National Rifle Association, which at that point had relatively little in the way of political influence, the firearms industry and police chiefs in small towns and rural areas who still relied on the *posse comitatus* to fight crime, particularly bank robberies.

The 1934 act gave rise to the Supreme Court's last decision to date on the Second Amendment, *United States v. Miller*. Miller has left a curious legacy to the Second Amendment debate. Both sides claim that the *Miller* Court vindicated their position. *Miller* is made even more curious because it is the one case where the Supreme Court squarely addressed the issue of the Second Amendment, *Cruikshank* and *Presser* really had more to say about the Fourteenth Amendment than the Second Amendment, and it was the result of a case in which the Court only heard the argument of one side, the government.

The case arose in 1938 when Jack Miller and Frank Layton were indicted for transporting between Oklahoma and Arkansas an unregistered shotgun with a barrel length of less than 18 inches, the statutory limit under the 1934 Act. Paul Gutensohn, the attorney for Miller and Layton, filed a demurrer to the indictment contending that the National Firearms Act violated both the Second and Tenth Amendments.[48] Judge Heartsill Ragon of the United States District Court for the Western District of Arkansas sustained Gutensohn's demurrer, expressing the view that the relevant section of the 1934 statute violated the Second Amendment.[49]

The United States appealed the decision to the Supreme Court. Solicitor General Robert H. Jackson, the future associate justice of the Supreme Court, argued the case for the government. The government's brief offered several alternative theories as to why the the National Firearms Act did not violate the Second Amendment. First, the government asserted, echoing language in *Cruikshank* and *Presser,* that the Second Amendment did not create the right to bear arms; it merely recognized the pre-existing right that had existed at common law. Because the right at common law had always been subject to statutory restrictions in the interests of public safety, Congress was able to restrict the right to bear arms for similar reasons. Second, the Jackson brief argued that the right was a collective one that protected the people when carrying arms as members of the state militia. Finally, the government contended that even when granting an individual right to bear arms, it had a right to restrict those weapons that were peculiarly adaptable for criminal purposes and not suitable to the common defense or other legitimate purposes. The Jackson brief made much of this point, noting: ". . . But it is also indisputable that Congress was striking not at weapons intended for legitimate use but at weapons which form the arsenal of the gangster and desperado . . ."[50]

The Court's opinion, authored by Justice James C. McReynolds, focused on the third argument, the notion that certain weapons were not militia weapons.

> In the absence of any evidence tending to show that the possession of a [sawed-off shotgun] at this time has some reasonable relationship to the preservation or efficiency of a well regulated militia, we cannot say that the Second Amendment guarantees the right to keep and bear such an instrument.

Certainly it is not within judicial notice that this weapon is any part of the ordinary military equipment or that its use could contribute to the common defense.[51]

Advocates of the collective-rights view have emphasized the *Miller* Court's focus on the militia, claiming that it was an indication that the Court saw the Second Amendment as only being concerned with the preservation of state militia. But the *Miller* Court's discussion of the militia indicates that the Court saw a clear relationship between the individual right and the maintenance of the militia:

The signification attributed to the term Militia appears from the debates in the Convention, the history and legislation of Colonies and States, and the writings of approved commentators. These show plainly enough that the Militia comprises all males physically capable of acting in concert for the common defense." A body of citizens enrolled for military discipline." And further, that ordinarily when called for service these men were expected to appear bearing arms supplied by themselves and of the kind in common use at the time.[52]

Probably the most accurate way to view what the Court did in *Miller* was to see it as an updating of the nineteenth-century civilized-warfare doctrine. McReynolds' decision relied on the antebellum Tennessee case *Aymette v. State,* which allowed the state to restrict the carrying of weapons not suited for the common defense. The Supreme Court in *Miller* remanded the case to the lower courts to determine whether or not a sawed-off shotgun was a weapon appropriate for militia use. That determination was never made.[53]

One aspect of *Miller* deserves further discussion. At least one of the justices who voted for the unanimous[54] decision in *Miller,* Justice Hugo Black, had more to say on the Second Amendment later in his career. His statements on the subject can provide a further clue to the meaning of *Miller.* In his dissent in *Adamson v. California,*[55] he expressed the view that the entire Bill of Rights were applied to the states through the Fourteenth Amendment. The appendix to his dissent quoted Senator Jacob Howard's speech when he introduced the Fourteenth Amendment to the Senate:

"Such is the character of the privileges and immunities spoken of in the second section of the fourth article of the Constitution. To these privileges and immunities, whatever they may be — for they are not and cannot be fully defined in their entire extent and precise nature — to these should be added the personal rights guarantied and secured by the first eight amendments of the Constitution; such as freedom of speech and of the press; the right of the people peaceably to assemble and petition the government for a redress of greivances, a right appertaining to each and all the people; *the right to keep and the right to bear arms . . .* "[56]

Black's view that the entire Bill of Rights (throughout his dissent in *Adamson* he mentioned the first eight amendments) applied to the states serves as a strong indication that he saw the Second Amendment as protecting an individual right. It is difficult to reconcile the notions that the Second Amendment simply protects the state's right to maintain a militia against federal encroachment with Black's notion that the first eight amendments protect the individual against state action. Black would have still more to say on the subject. In his 1960 James Madison Lecture at the New York University School of Law entitled "The Bill of Rights," Black's discussion of the Second Amendment was brief but revealing:

> "Although the Supreme Court has held this Amendment (second amendment) to include only arms necessary to a well-regulated militia, as so construed, its prohibition is absolute." [57]

It is, of course, always somewhat problematic to interpret meaning based on an historical actor's subsequent statements; it is even more so when that actor was but one of several people who participated in a joint statement such as a judicial opinion. But certainly Justice Black's subsequent statements on the Second Amendment do not tend to support the view that he understood *Miller* as standing for the proposition that the amendment only protected a collective right.

Although *Miller* was the Court's most comprehensive exploration of the Second Amendment, it had little effect on either firearms regulation or the general public's view concerning the right to keep and bear arms. For nearly two decades after *Miller* little existed in the way of federal firearms regulation. State and local legislation, with a few exceptions, such as the New York Sullivan Law, usually provided traditional regulations governing the manner of carrying weapons, not outright prohibitions. There was little serious attempt to mount constitutional challenges to these restrictions. The Second Amendment was thus bypassed in the post-war Supreme Court's process of applying most of the provisions of the Bill of Rights to the states. It is probably accurate to say that at least until the 1960s most people, including attorneys and judges, accepted the view that the Second Amendment protected an individual right but otherwise thought very little about the matter because firearms restrictions, even on the state and local level were slight.

It would take the turmoil of the 1960s and the tragedy of three assassinations to bring about the birth of the modern gun-control movement and create the current debate over the meaning of the Second Amendment. The assassination of President John F. Kennedy in 1963 brought about calls for stricter national controls over the sale of firearms. Urban riots and the assassinations of Civil Rights leader Martin Luther King and Senator Robert F. Kennedy helped lead to the passage of the Gun Control Act of 1968, the first federal legislation that seriously affected the purchasing of firearms on the part of large numbers of Americans. The 1968 legislation limited the purchase of firearms through the mails and also restricted the importation of surplus military rifles. It also prohibited the purchase of firearms by those with felony convictions—though the legislation provided no means of checking a purchaser's record. Some of the provisions of the 1968 act would later be modified by legislation passed in the 1980s.

The 1968 legislation proved to be something of a watershed. Since then a national debate over gun control and the subsidiary debate over the meaning of the Second Amendment have become semi-permanent features of late twentieth-century American life, regularly and often passionately debated in the popular media and increasingly in academic journals. In the last two decades the debate has, of course, been made more vigorous by the development of organizations with strong institutional interests in arguing one side or the other of the debate. Thus, organizations advocating stricter gun controls frequently sponsor writings in the press or academic journals designed to persuade readers of the essential correctness of the collective-rights view. Similarly the gun-control movement has had the unintended consequence of transforming the National Rifle Association from what had been, before the 1960s, essentially a hobbyists' organization, into a political movement, one which has become quite adept at championing the individual-rights view of the Second Amendment in the popular and scholarly press. Since the 1960s a good deal of the writing on both sides of the Second Amendment issue has been done by people affiliated with groups either advocating or opposing stricter gun control measures.

If the popular and academic presses have shown considerable interest in the question of the right to bear arms in the last two decades, that interest has not been matched by the federal courts, particularly the United States Supreme Court. The high Court has not considered a case on the subject since *Miller* and indeed has generally denied *certiorari* petitions in cases involving Second Amendment claims. For the most part, not too much can be made of the modern federal court jurisprudence on the Second Amendment. Typically cases in which Second Amendment claims have been made have not involved general prohibitions against firearms ownership but instead have involved claims made by individuals involved in criminal activity who have raised Second Amendment claims as a defense against charges of illegal weapons possession. Lower federal courts have tended to dismiss these claims, either employing the collective-rights view of the Second Amendment, or on the grounds that the Second Amendment has not been applied against the states. The refusal of the Supreme Court to hear such cases cannot be taken as indicative of the Court's view of the Second Amendment.[58]

Despite this, there are strong indications that the Supreme Court in recent decades has had a somewhat ambivalent attitude towards the Second Amendment. If the Court's refusal to hear cases involving Second Amendment claims on the part of those involved in criminal activity has not provided a particularly good indicator of the Court's attitude concerning the Second Amendment, strong evidence exists that a number of recent justices have regarded stricter gun controls as good policy and that they would like to offer a narrow interpretation of the Second Amendment. In 1983 the Court denied *certiorari* in the case of *Quillici v. Morton Grove,* a case in which the Seventh Circuit Court of Appeals let stand an Illinois municipality's ban on the ownership of handguns by the general population. *Morton Grove* represented an opportunity to revisit *Presser* and the doctrine that the Second Amendment did not constrain action on the part of state and local governments. Additionally, a number of modern justices, including Burger, Douglas and Powell, have offered the opinion that the Second Amendment should be read narrowly in order not to interfere with what they have considered to be needed gun-control measures.[59]

But the story of the Second Amendment and the modern Supreme Court does not end with the Court's reluctance to hear direct Second Amendment claims and its willingness to let lower federal courts sustain gun-control measures against such claims. In recent decades, for at least the last thirty years, high Court opinions have curiously dragged out the Second Amendment in larger discussions of the Bill of Rights as a whole. In a way the Second Amendment has, for the Supreme Court, almost become like a somewhat disreputable member of a family. One does not want to spend too much time with this family member. One would not lend him money. But he is a member of the family and an effort is made to insure that he is present for the family portrait, however uncomfortable that event makes the more respectable family members. Thus the Second Amendment receives mention in the most unlikely of constitutional controversies. Justice Harlan's dissent in Poe v. Ullman, a case involving Connecticut's anti-contraception statute, has left behind language frequently invoked in cases involving the right to privacy:

> "The full scope of the liberty guaranteed by the Due Process Clause cannot be found in or limited by the precise terms of the specific guarantees elsewhere provided in the Constitution. This 'liberty' is not a series of isolated points priced out in terms of the taking of property; the freedom of speech, press and religion; the right to keep and bear arms; . . ."[60]

One recent case that many observers believe offers a clue to the attitude of some members of the Rehnquist Court towards the Second Amendment was the case of *United States v. Verdugo-Urquidez.* In his discussion of the scope of the term "the people," Chief Justice William Rehnquist gave a clue concerning his views on the scope of Second Amendment protection:

> . . . "the people" seems to have been a term of art employed in select parts of the Constitution. The preamble declares that the Constitution is ordained

and established by "The People of the United States" The Second Amendment protects "the right of the people to keep and bear Arms," and the Ninth and Tenth Amendments provide that certain rights and powers are reserved to "the people" . . . While this textual exegesis is by no means conclusive it suggests that "the people" protected by the Fourth Amendment and by the First and Second Amendments and to whom rights and powers are reserved in the Ninth and Tenth Amendments refers to a class of persons who are part of a national community or who have otherwise developed sufficient connections with this country to be considered part of that community.[61]

These hints notwithstanding, the modern Supreme Court has retained its institutional reluctance to examine gun-control measures in light of the Second Amendment and make a definitive modern ruling on the scope of the amendment. With the likely inclusion of a measure to ban so-called assault weapons in the 1994 federal crime bill, the Court may be forced to consider the issue. Whatever happens, the controversy over the right to keep and bear arms provides an important reminder that while the Supreme Court may have the last word in making constitutional determinations, it does not have a monopoly on such determinations, particularly where the Court has elected to remain silent. In the 1980s, Congress, which for political reasons has long been sympathetic to the individual-rights view of the Second Amendment, took two important if tentative steps toward potential Congressional enforcement of Second Amendment rights. In 1982, the Subcommittee on the Constitution of the Senate Judiciary Committee issued a report essentially agreeing with the individual-rights view of the Second Amendment. Four years later Congress passed the Firearms Owners Protection Act which, among other provisions, protected the right of individuals to travel interstate with their firearms, even if possession of those firearms might be illegal under the laws of the states through which they travelled.[62] Congress' Constitutional findings that prefaced the statute are of interest here:

"The Congress finds that:

1. the rights of citizens

    A. to keep and bear arms under the second amendment, to the United States Constitution (USCS Constitution, Amendment 2)

    B. to security against illegal and unreasonable search and seizures under the fourth amendment (USCS Constitution, Amendment 4)

    C. against uncompensated taking of property, double jeopardy and assurance of due process of law under the fifth amendment (USCS Constitution, Amendment 5) and

    D. against unconstitutional exercise of authority under the ninth and tenth amendments (USCS Constitution, Amendments 9 and 10);

requires additional legislation to correct existing firearms statutes and enforcement policies . . .[63]

The Congressional determinations in the 1980s raised an interesting if little
explored issue in the Second Amendment debate. While much of the debate
over the Second Amendment has centered on the extent to which that
provision might act to bar gun-control legislation, little attention has been paid
to the question of whether or not the Second Amendment might, perhaps in
conjunction with Section 5 of the Fourteenth Amendment[64], provide Congress with
the authority to protect Second Amendment rights against state deprivations.

Considerations of possible Congressional action notwithstanding, the concept
of a right to keep and bear arms raises fascinating jurisprudential questions. And
in this regard, interestingly enough, state courts interpreting state constitutional
provisions have grappled with many of the vexing problems raised by this
concept. The vast majority of states, some forty-three in all, have state
constitutional provisions that parallel the Second Amendment. Also, most gun
control legislation has been enacted at the state and local level. Consequently,
the state courts have produced a well-developed body of jurisprudence in this
area. It is likely that should the Supreme Court ever give serious consideration
to a Second Amendment claim, it might very well borrow constitutional
doctrine from state courts, as indeed it did previously in *Miller*. In one respect
champions of the right to bear arms were forced to discover and take seriously
state constitutional law long before the liberal rediscovery of state courts and
state constitutions that came about as the Supreme Court became more
conservative in the 1980s.[65]

In the twentieth century state Supreme Courts have dealt with a variety of issues
regarding the right to bear arms, including whether or not that right extended to
aliens, what kinds of weapons were protected under the right to bear arms,
whether or not the right extended to concealed weapons and whether or not
the right could be denied to those who had previously been convicted of
criminal activity. State courts have developed a variety of approaches to the
issue. At one end of the spectrum have been state courts that have construed the
right narrowly, such as Massachusetts and Illinois, the former interpreting its
constitutional provision as protecting only the right of the state to maintain a
militia, the latter holding that as long as a municipality permitted some arms
ownership it did not infringe the right to bear arms. At the other end of the
spectrum, the Supreme Court of Appeals of West Virginia struck down a statute
that prohibited the carrying of dangerous weapons on the grounds that the state
constitutional right to keep and bear arms included a right to carry arms for self-
defense. Another state whose high court has adopted a liberal construction of its
state's right to bear arms provision is Oregon. The Oregon Supreme Court has
held that its state provision protects small arms generally useful for personal self-
defense, law enforcement, sporting purposes and civilian participation in the

sedentary militia, an activity that the Oregon Court decided protected manually operated and semi-automatic but not fully automatic firearms, probably so as to avoid conflict between its interpretation of the Oregon Constitution and federal law.[66]

Whether it makes its appearance in judicial decisions, legislative enactments, academic journals, the popular press, or indeed the nation's quite voluminous gun press, the issue of the right to bear arms excites popular passion like few other constitutional issues in late twentieth-century America. Perhaps only the issue of abortion, another controversy where constitutional vision and cultural precept are often inextricably linked, excites greater intensity of feeling. Part of the reason for the instensity of the debate is cultural. It is, in part, a battle between those who see the easy availability of firearms as a remnant of an atavistic American past, complete with violence and vigilantism, lawlessness and lynchings, and others who see the gun as having played a positive role in the nation's history, providing protection and a measure of independence and self-reliance, whether from British forces in the eighteenth century, Indians and desperadoes in the nineteenth and even lynch mobs and predatory criminal gangs in the twentieth.[67]

If the debate over the Second Amendment is more than a conflict over constitutional and historical interpretation. It is also more than a clash of cultural visions. The debate is driven by our tragically high crime rate, the perception that it is getting worse and that public safety and the rule of law have all but ceased to exist in many parts of our increasingly dangerous inner cities. The high rate of inner-city violence, exacerbated by the increased drug trade of the last decade, has been accompanied by frightening increases in juvenile gang activity and juvenile homicide, leading simultaneously to calls for increased restrictions on firearms ownership and an increase in the public's purchase of guns for self-protection. Centuries of racial injustice coupled with decades of urban neglect and an American tradition of violence have combined to provide ammunition on both sides of the gun-control debate and to sharpen the debate over the meaning and extent of the right to keep and bear arms.[68]

A FEW THOUGHTS ON A MORE MULTI-DIMENSIONAL DEBATE

Let me suggest that in many ways we are having the wrong debate on the Second Amendment and make some brief suggestions on how that debate might be improved as a matter of bringing new intellectual perspectives to the debate and as a way of suggesting how an improved Second Amendment debate might serve as a guide toward public policy.

First we should move beyond the current debate over the collective-rights theory, at least in its most simplistic form. Little in the way of historical evidence or even the rulings of the Supreme Court supports the view that the framers of the Second Amendment simply meant to protect state militias without also securing the right of the people at large to have arms. Certainly an organization like the modern National Guard, whose members are recruited, trained, paid, armed and otherwise equipped and deployed around the world by the federal government, is not the militia-of-the-whole envisioned by Madison and Lee. It is instead a super-select militia. To claim, as some have, that the Second Amendment was meant to protect a body like the National Guard, is to severely misread the historical record in ways so fundamental as to warrant almost instant dismissal.

But there is a more sophisticated version of the collective-rights view that does merit closer attention and that can help to bring greater intellectual depth to the conversation on the Second Amendment. The more sophisticated collective-rights view recognizes that the Second Amendment was designed to protect individual ownership of arms but then goes on to argue that this individual guarantee was inextricably linked to the maintenance of the militia. In short, unlike the individual-rights theorists, the more sophisticated collective-rights adherents see the individual right as existing but also see the amendment's "well-regulated militia " clause as qualifying rather than amplifying. For many, then, the answer becomes simple: if the militia has essentially disappeared, the individual right also ceases to exist. The Second Amendment poses no impediment to gun-control measures, however restrictive.

The issue is not so simple. If the relationship between the armed citizen and the militia has become increasingly theoretical if not tenuous in late twentieth-century America, important questions nonetheless remain concerning arms and rights under the more sophisticated collective-rights view. Perhaps the most fundamental of these questions has to do with the militia itself. What, from the point of view of the framers of the Second Amendment, was the reason for attempting to guarantee a militia and an armed population to support it? One might view the sole purpose as military, to enable states and communities to meet their security needs by being able to draw upon the armed population when required. If so, then the argument, frequently advanced, that the pre-emption of national, state and community security by the police and armed forces has largely made the Second Amendment moot has considerable merit, even granting the claim that an armed population still has a residual security function. If the purpose of the Second Amendment was purely military, then the right of the government to dissolve the militia-of-the-whole and substitute more efficient police and military organizations is clear. The right protected is simply a right of the government to raise militias, posses or similar bodies. When the government no longer needs to do such, it may cease doing so and disarm the population. This purely military view of the Second Amendment in turn raises the question of why the amendment was ever needed. Governments that feel a need to raise emergency security forces on an ad hoc basis from the population at large can, of course, store weapons that would be distributed to the population during times of emergency. This can be, and often has been, done even by totalitarian states with no guarantee of a right to arms, or indeed much in the way of any other rights.

But there is considerable evidence that the armed population and the militia were intended to serve more than a simple military function. They were seen as fulfilling political and perhaps moral purposes as well. That complicates, or should complicate, for collective-rights theorists the question of the individual right to arms in light of the attenuated connection between the militia and the armed population. If the purposes of guaranteeing a right to arms and attempting to organize the population into a militia-at-large included allowing for the possibility of resistance to potential governmental tyranny and preventing the citizens from becoming overly dependent on government for survival, then the ability of the government to disarm the population in light of the dissolution of the militia becomes far more problematic. The right thus guaranteed is more than a right of the government to raise security forces. Can the government, in effect, extinquish the population's right to the means of potential resistance and self-reliance by making the reasonable determination that its right to raise police and military forces is best served by allocating resources to professional and semi-professional organizations rather than attempting to maintain the unwieldly and admittedly less effective militia-of-the-whole? This question is one of longstanding concern in the history of arms and rights. The seventeenth-century Stuart monarchs both established select militias and attempted to disarm large portions of the English population. In 1833 United States Supreme Court Justice Joseph Story expressed his fear that popular neglect of the militia, which even by that date had considerably less than universal participation, could weaken the arming of the population:

> . . . The militia is the natural defence of a free country against sudden foreign invasions, domestic insurrections, and domestic usurpations of power by rulers . . . The right of the citizens to keep, and bear arms has justly been considered, as the palladium of the liberties of a republic; since it offers a strong moral check against the usurpation and arbitrary power of rulers; and will generally, even if these are successful in the first instance, enable the people to resist, and triumph over them. And yet, though this truth would seem so clear, and the importance of a well regulated militia would seem so undeniable, it cannot be disguised, that among the American people there is a growing indifference to any system of militia discipline, and a strong disposition, from a sense of its burthens, to be rid of all regulations. How it is

practicable to keep the people duly armed without some organization, it is difficult to see. There is certainly no small danger, that indifference may lead to disgust, and disgust to contempt; and thus gradually undermine all the protection intended by this clause of our national bill of rights.[69]

Yet another issue that deserves exploration within the context of the collective-rights view is whether or not the Second Amendment should be discussed as an issue in federalism. If the Second Amendment should be viewed as protecting the right of states to maintain militias against potential federal encroachment, interesting questions arise concerning the federal government's assumption of virtual plenary authority over the National Guard in the twentieth century. Viewing the Second Amendment as an issue in federalism also leaves us with important questions concerning the federal government's ability to implement far-reaching gun-control measures. In both cases the central question is the ability of states to maintain the militia's institutional independence from the federal government, either through the organized militia or through being able to maintain the militia at large. Again the question arises whether the purpose of the Second Amendment is military or political, although in this case the question needs to be asked not from the perspective of the individual in relation to the government but instead from the perspective of the federal government in relation to the states. If the Second Amendment's purpose was simply to provide for state militias to augment federal forces, which again raises the question of why such an amendment was believed to be needed, then the federal government's assumption of control over the National Guard or any future disarming of the population is unproblematic. If the purposes were political or partially political, to allow the states the possibility of resisting potential excesses of the central government, then the issue is less clear. Should the states have broad power to determine militia membership and how the militia should be armed? This might include the ability to decide whether or not the citizenry at large should remain armed if individual states decided that this might be necessary to resist the federal government at some point in the future.

While a more sophisticated exploration of the collective-rights theory raises interesting questions, the individual-rights view provides even more challenging intellectual problems. Some of these are obvious at first blush. What sort of arms are protected? Can we continue to apply the traditional militia/civilized-warfare test in the modern age when the individual soldier is not only likely to be armed with a fully automatic weapon, but in all probability a grenade launcher, a flame-thrower, an antitank weapon or a hand-held antiaircraft missile as well? If we say that at some point a line has to be drawn between the weapons that are issued to military forces and the weapons permitted the civilian population, even conceding the population's residual militia status, how should that line be drawn?

The latter question becomes especially vexing if one treats seriously the issue of the armed population as a possible counterweight to potential tyranny and tries to balance that concern against the concern for public safety. That in turn of course raises, for individual-rights theorists, the issue of the continued viability of the Second Amendment's political dimension in late twentieth-century America. The framers of course lived in a world where the weapons of standing armies and armed civilians were not that dissimilar. And even though the armies of the day had cannons and other weapons less frequently found in private hands, battles were primarily fought with infantry and cavalry and the possibility of an ad hoc privately equipped militia vanquishing regular troops in pitched battle was not only conceivable, it was within the framers' experience.

Modern technology has of course changed this equation. The imbalance between military forces and the armed citizenry has increased and definitely to the advantage of the military forces. Certainly one of the issues that should be examined in our new, more sophisticated Second Amendment debate is whether or not modern weapons technology has made obsolete the idea of the armed citizenry resisting governmental tryanny. At one level, this issue might force many constitutional scholars into rather unfamiliar territory, considerations of weapons and tactics, vulnerabilities of conventional military and police forces, effectiveness of guerrilla formations and similarly strange ruminations. But I am not sure that the constitutional scholar need turn himself into a military analyst in order to begin approaching this question of technological change and the continued viability of popular resistance. Certain issues might be explored without getting too far into military minutae. One of these is the notion of deterrence. Even conceding that a government and its military and police forces would likely win an all out war with its armed citizens, would the fact that citizens were armed so raise the cost to a government and its agents that a government would be more likely to seek accomodation with its population and less likely to take measures likely to bring about armed resistance?

Another way to think of the problem of individual arms and resistance to tyranny that constitutional scholars might find useful is to think of the link between private terrorism, government inaction and the potential importance of a right to arms for those unable to rely on the state for protection. Here we need not invent some future apocalpypse and contemplate armed resistance to a hypothetical totalitarian government. Instead we might ask whether or not our definition of state tyranny should be expanded to include the systematic failure to protect unpopular minorities, whether those minorities be defined by race, ethnicity, lifestyle, politics, or religion. Certainly American history is not lacking in such examples of state tyranny, whether one considers violence visited against Mormons in the nineteenth-century Midwest, the lynchings of blacks in the twentieth-century Jim Crow South or the violent intimidation of civil rights workers in the South in the 1960s. A debate over the role of private arms in protecting unpopular groups that the government is reluctant to assist, juxtaposed against the dangers of vigilantism, particularly ethnically, religiously or politically rooted vigilantism with all the attendant social divisiveness that that implies, could greatly improve the debate over arms and resistance to tyranny.[70]

One could go on concerning the substantive issues that should be considered more carefully as part of a more sophisticated Second Amendment debate. Does the Second Amendment, perhaps in conjunction with the ninth amendment[71] imply an individual right to self-defense? Do public officials encourage an unhealthy dependency when they urge citizens not to defend themselves and not to arm for potential self-defense? Should we attempt to revitalize the militia-of-the-whole by encouraging or even requiring greater participation by citizens in armed auxiliary police forces and non-National Guard militia forces, both for whatever security benefits such participation might represent and to prevent the formation of separate police and military castes, distinct from and potentially hostile to the population at large? Is the military draft a Second Amendment issue, a modern way of insuring large scale popular participation in society's defense and also insuring that the kind of modern military skills that would be necessary to resist potential tyranny would be widespread in the population? Have we insured the kind of separation of protector and protected that many of the framers feared by abolishing conscription?[72]

But the debate over the Second Amendment should not end with a discussion of the various substantive issues raised by the right to arms. The Second Amendment raises important issues concerning constitutional process. It is clear that many regard the Second Amendment as an anachronism too dangerous to be applied in modern times. This view should be openly debated on two levels. First there should be a debate over whether the amendment should simply be repealed. A case could certainly be made for repeal. But there are political reasons, for people on both sides of the controversy, why repeal or even discussion of repeal is not a particularly attractive option. For opponents of stricter gun-control, repeal or even a debate over repeal would not be particularly attractive for obvious reasons. For those supporting such measures, repeal also has its drawbacks. First, an attempt at repeal would, at present, stand little likelihood of success. In a nation where politicians who support far reaching gun control measures feel compelled to proclaim their support for the right to keep and bear arms, the prospects for outright repeal of the Second Amendment seem slim indeed. But there may be another reason why little effort has been devoted to an attempt to repeal the Second Amendment. If, as common stereotypes suggest, supporters of stricter gun control are predominately liberal, that too might provide a reason for caution in amending the Constitution. Would a repeal of the Second Amendment, presumably brought about by our nation's concern over crime, lead to calls for repeal or modification of other provisions of the Bill of Rights? The Fourth Amendment's protection against unreasonable search and seizure and the Fifth Amendment's guarantee against self-incrimination, both of which have considerably less in the way of popular constituencies than the Second Amendment, immediately spring to mind.

As an issue involving constitutional process, the Second Amendment also provides new perspectives on some issues that have long interested constitutional scholars concerned with the courts and constitutional interpretation. The debate over the extent to which jurists, when interpreting the Constitution, should be bound by the intentions of the framers or should feel free to fashion constitutional doctrine based on the perceived needs of the day has been of particular concern to courts, scholars and indeed the general public. Since at least the days of the Warren Court, this debate has usually focused on the issue of expanding rights. Can the Fourteenth Amendment's equal-protection clause properly be used to prohibit segregated schools even though the framers probably did not intend that result? Can the principle of equal protection be extended to gender discrimination although it is clear that the framers of the Fourteenth Amendment were concerned with race? Should the Eighth Amendment's prohibition on cruel and unusual punishment be interpreted as outlawing or at least severely restricting the use of capital punishment, even though the framers seemed quite comfortable with the idea of the death penalty? Can we deduce a right to privacy in sexual matters from the Third, Fourth, Ninth or Fourteenth Amendments, even though it is unlikely that the framers of those constitutional provisions had any such right in mind?

The debate over the Second Amendment and the treatment of the Second Amendment in many federal courts since *Miller* reminds us that the notion of a living constitution can be a two-way street, a means of limiting as well as extending rights. This needs closer examination by constitutional scholars. Should courts be bound by the late eighteenth- or mid-nineteenth-century sensibilities that saw the right to keep and bear arms as critical to a free people or should they feel free to respond to late twentieth-century circumstances, including our high crime rate? Was the purpose of enacting a Bill of Rights to insure that the felt needs of the day would not be used as a pretext to do away with rights deemed fundamental and natural? Can the Second Amendment safely be deemed an eighteenth-century relic that twentieth-century courts can feel free to ignore when some forty-three states have enacted or reenacted similar provisions in their state constitutions, many in the twentieth century? If the Second Amendment can be essentially nullified to support modern policy objectives, can the same be done with other constitutional rights, as indeed has occurred in the past? Can the notion of a living constitution be handled in a principled manner or is it really just shorthand for the policy preferences of judges and legal commentators?

And what if the courts should seriously consider a Second Amendment claim? How should they decide to apply a right that admittedly has inherent dangers? How should the courts develop the kinds of balancing tests that they use with other rights to extend to a right to possess deadly weapons? What role should social science play in such an endeavor? Those who favor stricter gun controls make certain claims about the empirical universe: the average citizen is not likely to defend herself with a firearm and is indeed more likely to injure a friend or family member with a gun kept for protection; gun-control measures can reduce criminal and accidental misuse of firearms. Those skeptical of stricter controls make different empirical assumptions: that average people do effectively defend themselves with firearms and that gun violence, including accidents and crimes of passion, is largely the result of actions by aberrant individuals, people with long histories of criminal activity, mental instability and violence, who would secure guns regardless of the state of the law. Should the jurisprudence of the Second Amendment depend on which side wins this empirical battle?[73]

Finally there is an issue that all sides might want to consider. Has the effort to essentially nullify the Second Amendment had an unintended and perhaps counterproductive consequence, namely has it made the process of achieving effective gun control, as distinct from gun prohibition, politically difficult? Could the history of arms, rights and gun control have been different over the last thirty years or so? Had the Second Amendment been frankly acknowledged as what I believe the history indicates it was intended to be, a bar to government bans on firearms ownership, might we now have a more productive debate on gun control? What if the courts had unambiguously recognized the right to keep and bear arms and indicated that the right, like other rights, was subject to reasonable regulation? Would there be a large constituency fighting such measures as waiting periods, or truly fair licensing requirements if it were clear that the courts and indeed the civil liberties community would vigorously protect the underlying right to arms? There is no massive constituency protesting parade permits and other time, place and manner regulations of the First Amendment right of free speech precisely because everyone knows that the courts will prevent government officials from using such regulations to nullify basic First Amendment rights. Perhaps that too could have occurred with respect to gun regulation and the Second Amendment. Perhaps it may yet occur. This too should be part of the more multi-dimensional debate over arms and rights in America.

NOTES

1. I would like to acknowledge the contribution of Raymond T. Diamond, my collaborator, in a number of efforts concerning the Second Amendment and other areas. Although he did not formally participate in this project, his insight and scholarship have been helpful guides in putting together this collection and

have been of great value in composing this introduction. I would also like to acknowledge the helpful editorial guidance of Paul Finkelman and the splendid research assistance of Elaine Hahm.

2. U. S. Constitution, Amendment 2

3. Sanford Levinson, "The Embarrassing Second Amendment," *Yale Law Journal* vol. 99, pp 637–659 (1989); David C. Williams, "Civic Republicanism and the Citizen Militia: The Terrifying Second Amendment," *Yale Law Journal* 551–615 (1991); George Will, "Oh, that Annoying Second Amendment: It Shows No Signs of Going Away," *Philadelphia Inquirer*, March 22, 1991; Karen Foerstel, "New Members Respond to Recent Crime on Capital Hill with Flood of Bills; Stokes Urges New Panel," *Roll Call*, March 9, 1992; *MacNeil/Lehrer Newshour*, December 16, 1991, Monday Transcript # 4226; Harry Summers, "Gun Collecting and Lithuania," *Washington Times*, March 29, 1990 at F4

4. *United States v. Miller* 307 U. S. 174 (1939)

5. See Sanford Levinson, "The Embarrassing Second Amendment," *Yale Law Journal* vol. 99 pp 637–659, esp.pp 639–642 (1989). Levinson's article was particularly concerned with the failure of legal scholars and the elite law journals to treat the issue of the Second Amendment as a subject worthy of serious attention. Although Levinson's article, the heating up of the gun-control controversy, the bicentennial of the Bill of Rights and renewed interest in the question of the Fourteenth Amendment and the applicability of the Bill of Rights to the states have all helped to generate new examinations of the Second Amendment since the publication of Levinson's article, his basic contention that the Second Amendment is an area rarely considered, at least publicly, by most constitutional scholars remains valid.

6. James D. Wright, Peter H. Rossi, and Kathleen Daly, *Under the Gun: Weapons, Crime and Violence in America* (New York, 1983) at 103–122; Gary Kleck, *Point Blank: Guns and Violence in America* (New York, 1991) at xiii, 60–61

7. For two representative examples of these contrasting viewpoints see: Lawrence Delbert Cress, "An Armed Community: The Origins and Meanings of the Right to Bear Arms," *Journal of American History* vol. 71, pp 22–42 (1984); Don B. Kates, Jr., "Handgun Prohibition and the Original Meaning of the Second Amendment," *Michigan Law Review* vol. 82, pp 204–273 (1983)

8. *United States v. Miller* 307 U. S. 174 (1939)

9. Bernard Bailyn, *The Ideological Origins of the American Revolution* (1967)

10. See generally Joyce Lee Malcolm, "The Right to Keep and Bear Arms: The Common Law Tradition," vol. 10 *Hastings Constitutional Law Quarterly* 285 (1983); Joyce Lee Malcolm, *Disarmed: The Loss of the Right to bear Arms in Restoration England* (Pamphlet) (Cambridge, Ma. 1980); Article XLI of the Magna Carta seems to have indicated an early English distaste for at least foreign professional soldiers: "That the King shall remove all foreign knights, stipendiaries, crossbowmen, infringers, and servitors who come with horses and arms to the injury of the kingdom." See: Richard Thomson, *An Historical Essay on the Magna Carta of King John* (London, 1829) at 57

11. Malcolm, "The Right to Keep and Bear Arms: The Common Law Tradition," vol.10 *Hastings Constitutional Law Quarterly* 285-314 (1983)

12. ibid.; Joyce Lee Malcolm, "Book Review (Reviewing: Stephen P. Halbrook, *That Everyman Be Armed: The Evolution of A Constitutional Right)" George Washington University Law Review* vol. 54, pp 452–464 (1986)

13. 1 Wm and Mary Sess. 2 c.2 (1689)

14. William Blackstone, *Commentaries on the Laws of England: Of The Rights of Persons with an Introduction by Stanley Katz* vol. 1 (Chicago, 1979), at 139.

15. Robert J. Cottrol and Raymond T. Diamond, "The Second Amendment: Toward an Afro-Americanist Reconsideration," *The Georgetown Law Journal* vol. 80 (December, 1991) 309–361 Note 46, pp 322–323. Also reprinted in vol. 3

16. *Blackstone's Commentaries* vol. 2 at 398–402

17. See William Blackstone, *Commentaries on the Laws of England With an Introduction by A. W. Brian Simpson* vol. 2 (Chicago, 1979) at 411–412

18. St. George Tucker, ed., *Blackstone's Commentaries with Notes of Reference to the Constitution and Laws, of the Federal Government of the United States; and of the Commonwealth of Virginia in Five Volumes* (Philadelphia, 1803) Volume I note 41 at 143

19. ibid. note 40 at 143

20. Cottrol and Diamond, at 323–324

21. ibid.

22. ibid.

23. Robert E. Shalhope, "The Armed Citizen in the Early Republic," *Law and Contemporary Problems* vol. 49 (1986) pp 125–141

24. Cottrol and Diamond, at 323–330

25. C. M. Kenyon, ed. *The Anti-Federalists* (1966) at 228

26. "The Address and Reasons of Dissent of the Minority of the Convention of Pennsylvania to their Constituents," Herbert J. Storing, ed., *The Complete Anti-Federalist v. 2, Objections of Non-Signers of the Constitution and Major Series of Essays at the Outset* (Chicago, 1981) at 151 (Originally appeared *Pennsylvania Packet and Daily Advertiser* December 18, 1787)

27. *Letters From the Federal Farmer*, January 25, 1788, Storing, v. 2 at 341–342

28. *The Federalist No. 25* at 161 (Alexander Hamilton) (The Heritage Press 1945) — Hamilton called for the creation of a select militia because of its greater military efficiency. *The Federalist No. 29* at 183 (Alexander Hamilton) — Hamilton noted with respect to the militia of the whole "Little more can be reasonably aimed at, with respect to the people at large, than to have them properly armed and equipped; and in order to see that this not be neglected, it will be necessary to assemble them once or twice in the course of a year."

29. *The Federalist No. 46* (James Madison) (The Heritage Press 1945) at 319

30. 1 *Statutes at Large* 271 (May 1792)

31. *Aymette v. State* 21 Tenn. 154–162 (1840). Reprinted in volume 1

32. 32 U. S. (7 Pert.) 243 (1833)

33. 1 Georgia (Kelly) 243–251 (1846); For a discussion indicating that Lumpkin more generally rejected the reasoning in *Barron* see: Akhil Reed Amar, "The Bill of Rights and the Fourteenth Amendment," *Yale Law Journal* vol. 101 1193– , at 1210–1212

34. Joseph Story, *Commentaries on the Constitution of the United States* (1987) at 708

35. *Dred Scott v. Sanford*, 60 U. S. (19 How.) 393, 417 (1857) (emphasis added)

36. 60 US (19 How) 393 (1857) at 417; Paul Finkelman, "Prelude to the Fourteenth Amendment: Black Legal Rights in the Antebellum North," *Rutgers Law Journal* vol. 17 (Spring and Summer 1986) pp 415–482 at 476

37. W. L. Fleming, ed. *Documentary History of Reconstruction: Political, Military, Social, Religious, Educational and Industrial, 1865–1906* (1966) at 290

38. Cottrol and Diamond, at 342–346

39. For a good general discussion of the incorporation question see Michael Kent Curtis, *No State Shall Abridge: The Fourteenth Amendment and the Bill of Rights* (1986) For a good discussion of the 39th Congress' views concerning the Second Amendment and its applicability to the states through the Fourteenth Amendment see Stephen P. Halbrook, *That Every Man Be Armed: The Evolution of a Constitutional Right* (1984) at 107–123. It should be noted that many of the members of the 39th Congress who supported the Fourteenth Amendment believed that Congress would be the primary vehicle for enforcing the Bill of Rights against the states, indeed some believed that Section 2 of the Thirteenth Amendment already gave Congress that power. In 1866, the year the 39th Congress sent the Fourteenth Amendment to the states, Congress also passed the Civil Rights Act of 1866 and the Freedman's Bureau Act. Senators Lyman Trumbull and Willard Salsbury and Representative Henry Raymond expressed the view that the Civil Rights Act would protect the right to bear arms. The Freedman's Bureau Act explicitly mentioned its intention to protect "the constitutional right to bear arms." It was the view of Congressman Jonathan Bingham of Ohio that the Fourteenth Amendment was necessary to give Congress the power to enact such legislation. See Amar, p. 1245 note 228.

Akhil Amar makes the interesting and, I think, valid point that the Fourteenth Amendment did more than simply incorporate the Second Amendment; it transformed it as well. According to Amar, the original Second Amendment was a political right of white male citizens, similar to voting. They would participate in the militia and, together with state governments, would form a counter balance to federal power. The Fourteenth Amendment made it more of an individual right and one that the federal government, as it was originally envisioned, would guarantee against the states. Although I would disagree with

Amar's view that the original amendment was only meant to apply to white men, certainly white women and arguably free blacks were meant to be protected, nonetheless his point about the Fourteenth Amendment severing the link between the right to bear arms and the militia is an important one. This raises the question of whether faithful adherence to original intention would require a reinterpretation of the Second Amendment in light of the Fourteenth in much the same way the Supreme Court has imposed an equal protection requirement on the federal government through the Fifth Amendment see: *Bolling v. Sharp* 347 U. S. 497 (1954) See: Amar at 1260–1263

40. *US v. Cruikshank* 92 US (2 Otto) 542 (1876)

41. *Presser v. Illinois* 116 US 252 (1886)

42. *Andrews v. the State* 50 Tenn 165–201; 8 Am Rep. 8 (1871)

43. Thomas M. Cooley, *Principles of Constitutional Law* (Boston, 1898) at 298; See also Cooley's discussion in Thomas M. Cooley, *A Treatise on the Constitutional Limitations*, 7th Edition (Boston, 1903) at 498–499

44. Cottrol and Diamond, at 354–353

45. Don B. Kates, "Towards a History of Handgun Prohibition in the United States" in Don B. Kates, ed. *Restricting Handguns: The Liberal Skeptics Speak Out* (1979) at 7–30; Lee Kennett and James La Verne Anderson, *The Gun in America: The Origins of a National Dilemma* (1975) 174–180

46. The relevant provision declared:

"The people have the right to bear arms for their defense and security; but standing armies, in time of peace, are dangerous to liberty, and shall not be tolerated, and the military shall be in strict subordination to the civil power."

47. *City of Salina v. Blaksley* 72 Kansas 230–234 (1905)

48. U. S. Constitution, Amendment Ten. — The powers not delegated to the United States by the Constitution, nor prohibited by it to the States, are reserved to the States respectively, or to the people. The source that I have consulted in this area the Supreme Court Briefs in *Miller* (No. 696, *The United States of America, Appellant v. Jack Miller and Frank Layton, Appeal From the District Court of the United States for the Western District of Arkansas*, herinafter *Miller Briefs*) do not have Gutensohn specifically mentioning the Tenth Amendment; however, his contention that the 1934 Act usurped the police power of the states is a Tenth Amendment claim.

49. *United States v. Miller, et. al.* 26 F. Supp. 1002 (1939)

50. See generally, *Miller Briefs*

51. *United States v. Miller*, 307 US 174 at 178

52. ibid.

53. ibid.

54. Associate Justice William O. Douglas was on the Court at the time of the *Miller* decision but he took no part in the decision.

55. *Adamson v. California*, 332 U. S. 46 (1947); Justice Black dissenting 68–123

56. Justice Black's Dissent (*Adamson*) Appendix p. 105

57. Hugo Black, "The Bill of Rights," *New York University Law Review*, vol. 35, April, 1960 865–881

58. See, e. g. *United States v. Three Winchester 30–30 Caliber Lever Action Carbines* 504 F. 2d 1288 (7th Cir. 1974)

59. *Quilici v. Village of Morton Grove*, 695 F. 2d 261 (7th Cir. 1982), cert. denied, 464 U. S. 863 (1983)

60. *Poe v. Ullman* 367 U. S. 497 (1961) at 542. quoted in *Roe v. Wade* 410 U. S. 113 (1973); *Moore v. City of East Cleveland Ohio*, 431 U. S. 494 (1976); *Planned Parenthood of Southeastern Penn. v. Casey* 1992 U. S. Lexis 4751 (1992), among others

61. *United States v. Verdugo-Urquidez* 494 U.S. 259 (1989) at 264

62. *The Right to Keep and Bear Arms: Report of the Subcommitteeon the Constitution of the Committee on the Judiciary United States Senate, Ninety-Seventh Congress, Second Session* (1982); 18 U. S. C. S. at 921 (1992). It should be noted that the Firearms Owners' Protection Act of 1986 was not the first federal legislation designed to protect the right to keep and bear arms. The Freedman's Bureau Act of 1867 also contained a provision designed to protect the right of former slaves to keep and bear arms.

63. 18 USCS, section 921 (1992)

64. Section 5 of the Fourteenth Amendment reads: "The Congress shall have power to enforce, by appropriate legislation, the provisions of this article." Under this provision Congress is given broad powers to protect the civil rights of citizens against state deprivation of rights and potentially this could be used by Congress to enforce a more liberal view of the Second Amendment against relatively restrictive state legislation.

65. See former Associate Supreme Court Justice William Brennan's call for civil libertarians to pay more attention to state constitutional guarantees of individual rights in William J. Brennan, Jr., "The Bill of Rights and the States: The Revival of State Constitutions as Guardians of Individual Rights," *New York University Law Review*, vol. 61, pp. 535–553 (June, 1986).

66. For some of the state cases that have helped create a modern jurisprudence of the right to keep and bear arms see: *People v. Nakamura*, 99 Colo 262; 62 P2d 246 (1936); *State v. Amos* 343 So. 2d 166, 168 (1977); *State v. Kessler* 289 Ore 359; 614 P2d 94 (1980); *Kalodimos et. al. v. The Village of Morton Grove* 103 Ill 2d 483; 470 N. E. 2d 266 (1984); *State of West Virginia Ex Rel City of Princeton v. Harold L. Buckner, Magistrate of Mercer County* 1800 W. Va. 457 (1988). One important case decided in 1990 by the Indiana Supreme Court held that a government official infringing on a right to keep and bear arms guaranteed by the state constitution could be subject to civil damages under federal civil rights legislation, specifically 42 U. S. C. Sec 1983, see: *Kellogg et. al. v. City of Gary, Richard Hartcher* 562 N. E.

2d 685 (1990). The most comprehensive study of the right to keep and bear arms under state constitutions is: Halbrook, Stephen P., *A Right to Bear Arms: State and Federal Bills of Rights and Constitutional Guarantees* (Westport, 1989)

67. Barry Bruce-Briggs, "The Great American Gun War," *The Public Interest* vol. 45, pp. 37–62 (1976); Richard Maxwell Brown, "The American Vigilante Tradition," pp 144–218 in *Violence in America,* edited by Hugh Davis Graham and Ted Robert Gurr (New York, 1969); Carol Ruth Silver and Don B. Kates, Jr., "Self-Defense, Handgun Ownership and the Independence of Women in a Violent, Sexist Society," pp. 139–160 in *Restricting Handguns: The Liberal Skeptics Speak Out,* edited by Don B. Kates, Jr. (1979); John Salter and Don B. Kates, Jr., "The Necessity of Access to Firearms by Dissenters and Minorities Whom Government is Unwilling or Unable to Protect," pp 185–193

68. Homicide is the leading cause of death of black males between the ages of 15 and 34. See: Antonia C. Novello, John Shosky and Robert Froelke, "From the Surgeon General, US Public Health Service," *Journal of the American Medical Association (JAMA)* vol. 267 p. 3007 (June 10, 1992); Between 1979 and 1989 the firearm homicide rate for persons 15 through 19 increased 61% from 6.9 to 11.1 deaths per 100,000. See: Lois A. Fingerhut, Deborah D. Ingram, Jacob Feldman, "Firearm and Nonfirearm Homicide Among Persons 15 through 19 Years of Age; Difference by Level of Urbanization, United States, 1979 through 1989," *JAMA* vol. 267 3048–3053 (June, 1992)

69. Joseph Story, *Commentaries on the Constitution of the United States* with an Introduction by Ronald D. Rotunda and John E. Nowak (Durham NC, 1987) at 708–709

70. Sydney E. Ahlstrom, *A Religious History of the American People* (New Haven, 1972) at 501–509; For a discussion of the importance of private arms as a means of resisting private terror in the face of government inaction, see: Cottrol and Diamond, especially at 315 (note 22), 339–342, 349–358. There is a group of scholars and supporters of the individual-rights view of the Second Amendment whose perceptions on the issue were at least partially formed during their participation in the civil rights movement in the South in the 1960s. One of the more prominent and prolific of these is Don B. Kates, Jr. He noted:

"As a civil rights worker in a Southern state during the early 1960s, I found that the possession of firearms for self-defense was almost universally endorsed by the black community, for it could not depend on police protection from the KKK...

As a civil rights worker, I saw how possession of a firearm could shrink the threat of ultimate violence into just another more or less innocuous incident: When Klansmen catch you in some deserted area and open fire, you take cover and shoot back — if you have a gun. Then both sides depart with great speed, because no one wants to get shot. If you don't have a gun, however the Klansmen keep on shooting and moving closer, and your only hope is that their aim is poor and that you can outdistance their pursuit."

See: Salter and Kates at 186

The issue of whether or not arms might play an especially important role for minorities unable to rely on state protection is not exclusively an American concern. In the fall of 1992, with the rising tide of neo-Nazi violence against foreign residents and minorities in the now reunited Federal Republic of Germany, at least two prominent Germans, Ralph Giordano, a German Jewish writer, and Golo Mann, an historian and the son of German novelist Thomas Mann, have urged Jews and others to consider armed self-defense in light of the failure of Chancellor Kohl's government to protect members of minority groups against neo-Nazi violence. Press reports indicate that leaders of the German Jewish community have generally rejected this call to arms, although they have also been dissatisfied with the Kohl government's response to the violence.

See: Tyler Marshall, "Fearing Persecution, Jews Once Again Leaving Germany," *Los Angeles Times* Nov. 27, 1992, Friday, Home Edition, Part A, p 8, Col 1, Foreign Desk; "Nazi Survivor: German Jews Should Arm" *Chicago Tribune* Nov. 25, 1992, Wednesday, North Sports, Final Edition, p. 3, Zone:C; Robin Gedye, "Bonn Castigated over Right-Wing Violence," *The Daily Telegraph* Nov. 25, 1992, Wed, International, p. 11; Tom Heneghan, "German Jewish Writer Stirs Storm With Call to Arms," *Reuters* Nov. 24, 1992

71. U. S. Const. Amendment IX: "The enumeration in the Constitution, of certain rights, shall not be construed to deny or disparage others retained by the people."

72. Elaine Scarry has done some provocative writing concerning the Second Amendment and the distribution of war-making authority. See: Elaine Scarry, "War and the Social Contract: Nuclear Policy, Distribution and the Right to Bear Arms," *University of Pennsylvania Law Review* vol. 139 at 1257–1316 (May 1991)

73. For studies generally supporting the first set of empirical claims see: C.S. Hirsch, N.B. Rushford, A.B. Ford and L. Adelson, "Homicide and Suicide in a Metropolitan County: Long Term Trends," *Journal of the American Medical Association* vol. 223, pp. 900–905 (1973); Arthur L. Kellerman and Donald T. Reay, "Protection or Peril? An Analysis of Firearms-Related Deaths in the Home," *New England Journal of Medicine* vol. 314, pp. 1557–1560 (1986). For studies generally skeptical of these claims see James D. Wright, Peter H. Rossi and Kathleen Daly, *Under the Gun: Weapons, Crime and Violence in America* (New York, 1983); Gary Kleck, *Point Blank: Guns and Violence in America* (New York, 1991); David B. Kopel, *The Samurai, the Mountie and the Cowboy: Should America Adopt the Gun Controls of Other Democracies?* (Buffalo, 1992); Don B. Kates, Jr., "The Value of Civilian Handgun Possession as a Deterrent to Crime or a Defense Against Crime," *American Journal of Criminal Law* vol. 18, pp. 113–167 (1991)

Gun Control
and the Constitution

[Aymette *vs.* The State.]

AYMETTE *vs.* THE STATE.

1. The act of 1837–8, ch. 137, sec. 2, which prohibits any person from wearing any bowie knife, or Arkansas tooth-pick, or other knife or weapon in form, shape or size resembling a bowie knife or Arkansas tooth-pick under his clothes, or concealed about his person, does not conflict with the 26th section of the first article of the bill of rights, securing to the free white citizens the right to keep and bear arms for their common defence.

2. The arms, the right to keep and bear which is secured by the constitution, are such as are usually employed in civilized warfare, and constitute the ordinary military equipment; the legislature have the power to prohibit the keeping or wearing weapons dangerous to the peace and safety of the citizens, and which are not usual in civilized warfare.

3. The right to keep and bear arms for the common defence, is a great political right. It respects the citizens on the one hand, and the rulers on the other; and although this right must be inviolably preserved, it does not follow that the legislature is prohibited from passing laws regulating the manner in which these arms may be employed.

At the January term, 1840, of the circuit court of Giles county, Judge Dillahunty presiding, an indictment was filed against William Aymette. This indictment charged: 1st. That Aymette on the

26th day of June, 1839, in the county of Giles, "did wear a certain bowie knife under his clothes, and keep the same concealed about his person, contrary to the form of the statute," &c. 2d. "That on the same day, &c., the said Aymette did wear a certain other knife and weapon, in form, shape and size resembling a bowie knife, and under the clothes of him the said Aymette, and concealed about the person of him," &c.

The defendant pleaded not guilty, and the case was submitted to a jury at the October term, 1840, Judge Dillahunty presiding.

It appeared that Aymette, during the sitting of the circuit court in June, 1839, at Pulaski, Giles county, had fallen out with one Hamilton, and that about 10 o'clock, P.M. he went in search of him to a hotel, swearing he would have his heart's blood. He had a bowie knife concealed under his vest and suspended to the waistband of his breeches, which he took out occasionally and brandished in his hand. He was put out of the hotel and proceeded from place to place in search of Hamilton, and occasionally exhibited his knife.

The jury, under the charge of the court, returned a verdict of guilty.

The defendant moved the court in arrest of judgment, but the motion was overruled and the defendant sentenced to three months imprisonment in the common jail of Giles county, and to pay a fine of two hundred dollars to the State. From this judgment defendant appealed in error.

Washington and Ewing, for Aymette.

Attorney General, for the State.

Green, J. delivered the opinion of the court.

The plaintiff in error was convicted in the Giles circuit court, for wearing a bowie knife concealed under his clothes, under the act of 1837–S, ch. 137, sec. 2, which provides, "That if any person shall wear any bowie knife, or Arkansas tooth-pick, or other knife or weapon, that shall in form, shape or size resemble a bowie knife or Arkansas tooth-pick, under his clothes, or keep the same concealed about his person, such person shall be guilty of a misdemeanor, and upon conviction thereof, shall be fined in a sum not less than two hundred dollars, and shall be imprisoned in the county jail, not less than three months and not more than six months."

3

[Aymette *vs.* The State.]

It is now insisted that the above act of the legislature is unconstitutional, and therefore the judgment in this case should have been
arrested.

In the first article of the Constitution of this State, containing a
declaration of rights, sec. 26, it is declared, "That the free white
men of this State, have a right to keep and bear arms for their
common defence."

This declaration, it is insisted, gives to every man the right to arm
himself in any manner he may choose, however unusual or dangerous the weapons he may employ ; and thus armed, to appear
wherever he may think proper, without molestation or hindrance,
and that any law regulating his social conduct, by restraining the
use of any weapon or regulating the manner in which it shall be
carried, is beyond the legislative competency to enact, and is void.

In order to have a just and precise idea of the meaning of the
clause of the constitution under consideration, it will be useful to
look at the state of things in the history of our ancestors, and thus
comprehend the reason of its introduction into our constitution.

By the act of 22 and 23, Car. 2d, ch. 25, sec. 3, it is provided
that no person who has not lands of the yearly value of £100,
other than the son and heir apparent of an esquire, or other person of higher degree, &c., shall be allowed to keep a gun, &c. By
this act, persons of a certain condition in life were allowed to keep
arms, while a large proportion of the people were entirely disarmed. But King James the 2d, by his own arbitrary power, and contrary to law, disarmed the Protestant population, and quartered
his Catholic soldiers among the people. This, together with other
abuses, produced the revolution by which he was compelled to ab-
dicate the throne of England. William and Mary succeeded him,
and in the first year of their reign, Parliament passed an act recapitu-
lating the abuses which existed during the former reign, and declared the existence of certain rights which they insisted upon as
their undoubted privileges. Among these abuses, they say, in sec.
5, that he had kept a "standing army within the kingdom in time
of peace without consent of Parliament, and quartered soldiers contrary to law." Sec. 6. "By causing several good subjects, being
Protestants, to be disarmed, at the same time when Papists were
both armed and employed contrary to law."

In the declaration of rights that follows, sec. 7 declares, that
"the subjects which are Protestants may have arms for their de-

fence, suitable to their condition and as allowed by law." This declaration, although it asserts the right of the Protestants to have
arms, does not extend the privilege beyond the terms provided in
the act of Charles 2d, before referred to. "They may have arms,"
says the Parliament, "suitable to their condition, and as allowed by
law." The *law*, we have seen, only allowed persons of a certain
rank to have arms, and consequently this declaration of right had
reference to such only. It was in reference to these facts, and to
this state of the English law, that the second section of the amendments to the Constitution of the United States was incorporated
into that instrument. It declares that "a well regulated militia
being necessary to the security of a free State, the right of the people to keep and bear arms shall not be infringed."

In the same view, the section under consideration of our own
bill of rights was adopted.

The evil that was produced by disarming the people in the time
of James the second, was, that the King, by means of a standing
army, quartered among the people, was able to overawe them,
and compel them to submit to the most arbitrary, cruel and illegal
measures. Whereas, if the people had retained their arms, they
would have been able, by a just and proper resistance to those oppressive measures, either to have caused the King to respect their
rights, or surrender (as he was eventually compelled to do) the
government into other hands. No private defence was contemplated or would have availed any thing. If the subjects had been
armed, they could have resisted the payment of excessive fines, or
the infliction of illegal and cruel punishments. When, therefore,
Parliament says, that "subjects which are Protestants, may have
arms for their defence, suitable to their condition as allowed by
law," it does not mean for *private defence*, but being armed, they
may as a body, rise up to defend their just rights, and compel their
rulers to respect the laws. This declaration of right is made in
reference to the fact before complained of, that the people had
been disarmed, and soldiers had been quartered among them contrary to law. The complaint was against the *government*. The
grievances to which they were thus forced to submit, were for the
most part of a public character, and could have been redressed only
by the people rising up for their *common defence* to vindicate their
rights.

The section under consideration, in our bill of rights, was adopt-
20

5

ed in reference to these historical facts, and in this point of view its language is most appropriate and expressive. Its words are, "The free white men of this State have a right to keep and bear arms for their common defence." It, to be sure, asserts the right much more broadly than the statute of first William and Mary. For the right *there* asserted, is subject to the disabilities contained in the act of Charles the second. There lords and esquires, and their sons and persons, whose yearly income from land amounted to one hundred pounds, were of suitable condition to keep arms. But, with *us*, every free white man is of suitable condition; and, therefore, every free white man may *keep and bear arms*. But to keep and bear arms for what? If the history of the subject had left in doubt the object for which the right is secured, the *words* that are employed must completely remove that doubt. It is declared that they may keep and *bear* arms for their *common defence*. The word "*common*" here used, means according to Webster; 1. Belonging equally to more than one, or to many indefinitely. 2. Belonging to the public. 3. General. 4. Universal. 5. Public. The object then, for which the right of keeping and bearing arms is secured, is the defence of the *public*. The free white men may keep arms to protect the public liberty, to keep in awe those who are in power, and to maintain the supremacy of the laws and the constitution. The words "bear arms" too, have reference to their military use, and were not employed to mean wearing them about the person as part of the dress. As the object for which the right to keep and bear arms is secured, is of general and public nature, to be exercised by the people in a body, for their *common defence*, so the *arms*, the right to keep which is secured, are such as are usually employed in civilized warfare, and that constitute the ordinary military equipment. If the citizens have these arms in their hands, they are prepared in the best possible manner to repel any encroachments upon their rights by those in authority. They need not, for such a purpose, the use of those weapons which are usually employed in private broils, and which are efficient only in the hands of the robber and the assassin. These weapons would be useless in war. They could not be employed advantageously in the common defence of the citizens. The right to keep and bear them, is not, therefore, secured by the constitution.

A thousand inventions for inflicting death may be imagined, which might come under the appellation of an "arm" in the figurative use of that term, and which could by no possibility be rendered effectual in war, or in the least degree aid in the common defence. Would it not be absurd to contend that a constitutional provision, securing to the citizens the means of their common defence, should be construed to extend to *such* weapons, although they manifestly would not contribute to that end, merely because, in the hands of an *assassin*, they might take away life?

The legislature, therefore, have a right to prohibit the wearing, or keeping weapons dangerous to the peace and safety of the citizens, and which are *not* usual in civilized warfare, or would not contribute to the common defence. The right to keep and bear arms for the common defence is a great political right. It respects the citizens on the one hand and the rulers on the other. And although this right must be inviolably preserved, yet, it does not follow that the legislature is prohibited altogether from passing laws regulating the manner in which these arms may be employed.

To hold that the legislature could pass no law upon this subject, by which to preserve the public peace, and protect our citizens from the terror, which a wanton and unusual exhibition of arms might produce, or their lives from being endangered by desperadoes with concealed arms, would be to pervert a great political right to the worst of purposes, and to make it a social evil, of infinitely a greater extent to society, than would result from abandoning the right itself.

Suppose it were to suit the whim of a set of ruffians to enter the theatre in the midst of the performance, with drawn swords, guns and fixed bayonets, or to enter the church in the same manner, during service, to the terror of the audience ; and this were to become habitual; can it be, that it would be beyond the power of the legislature to pass laws to remedy such an evil? Surely not. If the use of arms in this way cannot be prohibited, it is in the power of fifty armed ruffians to break up the churches, and all other public assemblages, where they might lawfully come, and there would be no remedy. But we are perfectly satisfied that a remedy might be applied. The convention in securing the public political right in question, did not intend to take away from the legislature all power of regulating the social relations of the citizens upon this subject. It is true, it is somewhat difficult to draw the precise line where legislation must cease, and where the political right begins, but it is *not* difficult to state a case where the right of legislation would exist. The citizens have the unqualified right to *keep* the weapon, it being of the character before described, as being intended by this provision. But the right to *bear arms* is not of that unqualified character. The citizens may bear them for the *common defence;* but it does not follow, that they may be borne by an individual, merely to terrify the people, or for purposes of private assassination. And as the manner in which they are worn, and circumstances under which they are carried, indicate to every man, the purpose of the wearer, the legislature may prohibit such manner of wearing as would never be resorted to by persons engaged in the common defence.

We are aware that the court of appeals of Kentucky, in the case of *Bliss* vs. *The Commonwealth,* 2 Littel's Rep. 90, has decided that an act of their legislature, similar to the one now under consideration, is unconstitutional and void. We have great respect for the court by whom that decision was made, but we cannot concur in their reasoning.

We think the view of the subject which the opinion of the court in that case takes, is far too limited for a just construction of the meaning of the clause of the constitution they had under consideration. It is not precisely in the words of our constitution, nevertheless, it is of the same general import. The words are, that "the right of the citizens to bear arms in defence of themselves, and the State, shall not be questioned."

In the former part of this opinion, we have recurred to the circumstances under which a similar provision was adopted in England, and have thence deduced the reason of its adoption, and consequently have seen the object in view, when the right to keep and bear arms was secured. All these considerations are left out of view, in the case referred to, and the court confine themselves entirely to the consideration of the distinction between a law prohibiting the right, and a law merely regulating the manner in which arms may be worn. They say, there can be no difference between a law prohibiting the wearing concealed weapons, and one prohibiting the wearing them openly.

We think there is a *manifest* distinction. In the nature of things, if they were not allowed to bear arms openly, they could not bear them in their defence of the State at all. To bear arms in defence of the State, is to employ them in war, as arms are usually employed by civilized nations. The arms, consisting of swords, muskets, rifles, &c., must necessarily be borne openly; so that a prohibition to bear them openly, would be a denial of the right altogether. And as in their constitution, the right to bear arms in defence of themselves, is coupled with the right to bear them in defence of the State, we must understand the expressions as meaning the same thing, and as relating to public, and not private; to the common, and not the individual defence.

But a prohibition to wear a spear concealed in a cane, would in no degree circumscribe the right to bear arms in defence of the State; for this weapon could in no degree contribute to its defence, and would be worse than useless in an army. And, if, as is above suggested, the wearing arms in defence of the citizens, is taken to mean, the common defence, the same observations apply.

To make this view of the case still more clear, we may remark, that the phrase, *"bear arms,"* is used in the Kentucky constitution as well as in our own, and implies, as has already been suggested, their military use. The 28th section of our bill of rights provides, "that no citizen of this State shall be compelled to *bear arms,* provided he will pay an equivalent, to be ascertained by law." Here we know that the phrase has a military sense, and no other; and we must infer that it is used in the same sense in the 26th section, which secures to the citizen the *right to bear arms.* A man in the pursuit of deer, elk and buffaloes, might carry his rifle every day, for forty years, and, yet, it would never be said of him, that he had *borne arms,* much less could it be said, that a private citizen *bears arms,* because he has a dirk or pistol concealed under his clothes, or a spear in a cane. So that, with deference, we think the argument of the court in the case referred to, even upon the question it has debated, is defective and inconclusive.

In the case of *Simpson* vs. *The State,* 5th Yer. Rep. 356, Judge White, in delivering the opinion of the court, makes use of the general expression, that "by this clause in the constitution, an express power is given, and secured to all the free citizens in the State to keep and bear arms for their defence, without any qualification whatever, as to their kind and nature."

But in that case, no question as to the meaning of this provision in the constitution arose, or was decided by the court, and the expression is only an incidental remark of the judge who delivered the opinion, and, therefore, is entitled to no weight.

We think, therefore, that upon either of the grounds assumed in this opinion, the legislature had the right to pass the law under which the plaintiff in error was convicted. Let the judgment be affirmed.

———————

PRESSER *v.* ILLINOIS.

ERROR TO THE SUPREME COURT OF THE STATE OF ILLINOIS.

Argued November 23, 24, 1885.—Decided January 4, 1886.

The doctrine that statutes, constitutional in part only, will be upheld as to what is constitutional, if it can be separated from the unconstitutional provisions, reasserted.

A State statute providing that all able-bodied male citizens of the State between eighteen and forty-five, except those exempted, shall be subject to military duty, and shall be enrolled and designated as the State militia, and prohibiting all bodies of men other than the regularly organized volunteer militia of the State and the troops of the United States from associating together as military organizations, or drilling or parading with arms in any city of the State without license from the governor, as to these provisions is constitutional and does not infringe the laws of the United States: and it is sustained as to them, although the act contains other provisions, separable from the foregoing, which it was contended infringed upon the powers vested in the United States by the Constitution, or upon laws enacted by Congress in pursuance thereof.

The provision in the Second Amendment to the Constitution, that "the right of the people to keep and bear arms shall not be infringed," is a limitation only on the power of Congress and the national government, and not of the States. But in view of the fact that all citizens capable of bearing arms constitute the reserved military force of the national government as well as in view of its general powers, the States cannot prohibit the people from keeping and bearing arms, so as to deprive the United States of their rightful resource for maintaining the public security.

The provision in the Fourteenth Amendment to the Constitution that "no State shall make or enforce any law which shall abridge the privileges or immunities of citizens of the United States," does not prevent a State from passing such laws to regulate the privileges and and immunities of its own citizens as do not abridge their privileges and immunities as citizens of the United States.

Unless restrained by their own Constitutions, State legislatures may enact statutes to control and regulate all organizations, drilling, and parading of military bodies and associations, except those which are authorized by the militia laws of the United States.

Herman Presser, the plaintiff in error, was indicted on September 24, 1879, in the Criminal Court of Cook County, Illinois, for a violation of the following sections of Art. XI. of the Military Code of that State, Act of May 28, 1879, Laws of 1879, 192.

"§ 5. It shall not be lawful for any body of men whatever, other than the regular organized volunteer militia of this State, and the troops of the United States, to associate themselves together as a military company or organization, or to drill or parade with arms in any city, or town, of this State, without the license of the Governor thereof, which license may at any time be revoked: *And provided, further,* that students in educational institutions, where military science is a part of the course of instruction, may, with the consent of the Governor, drill and parade with arms in public, under the superintendence of their instructors, and may take part in any regimental or brigade encampment, under command of their military instructor; and while so encamped shall be governed by the provisions of this act. They shall be entitled only to transportation and subsistence, and shall report and be subject to the commandant of such encampment: *Provided*, that nothing herein contained shall be construed so as to prevent benevolent or social organizations from wearing swords.

"§ 6. Whoever offends against the provisions of the preceding section, or belongs to, or parades with, any such unauthorized body of men with arms shall be punished by a fine not exceeding the sum of ten dollars ($10), or by imprisonment in the common jail for a term not exceeding six months, or both."

The indictment charged in substance that Presser, on September 24, 1879, in the county of Cook, in the State of Illinois, "did unlawfully belong to, and did parade and drill in the city of Chicago with an unauthorized body of men with arms, who had associated themselves together as a military company and organization, without having a license from the Governor, and not being a part of, or belonging to, 'the regular organized volunteer militia' of the State of Illinois, or the troops of the United States."

A motion to quash the indictment was overruled. Presser then pleaded not guilty, and both parties having waived a jury the case was tried by the court, which found Presser guilty and sentenced him to pay a fine of $10.

The bill of exceptions taken upon the trial set out all the evidence, from which it appeared that Presser was thirty-one years old, a citizen of the United States and of the State of Illinois, and a voter; that he belonged to a society called the Lehr und Wehr Verein, a corporation organized April 16, 1875, in due form, under chapter 32, Revised Statutes of Illinois, called the General Incorporation Laws of Illinois, "for the purpose," as expressed by its certificate of association, "of improving the mental and bodily condition of its members, so as to qualify them for the duties of citizens of a republic. Its members shall therefore obtain, in the meetings of the association, a knowledge of our laws and political economy, and shall also be instructed in military and gymnastic exercises;" that Presser, in December, 1879, marched at the head of said company, about four hundred in number, in the streets of the city of Chicago, he riding on horseback and in command; that the company was armed with rifles and Presser with a cavalry sword; that the company had no license from the governor of Illinois to drill or parade as a part of the militia of the State, and was not a part of the regular organized militia of the State, nor a part of troops of the United States, and had no organization under the militia law of the United States. The evidence showed no other facts. Exceptions were reserved to the ruling of the court upon the motion to quash the indictment, to the finding of guilty, and to the judgment thereon. The case was taken to the Supreme Court of Illinois, where the judgment was affirmed. Thereupon Presser brought the present writ of error for a review of the judgment of affirmance.

Mr. Allan C. Story for plaintiff in error, argued the following Federal points.—I. The Illinois act is in conflict with Article I., section 8, subdivisions 12, 14, 15, 16 and 18 of the Constitution of the United States. *Houston* v. *Moore*, 5 Wheat. 1, 51, 68; *Gibbons* v. *Ogden*, 9 Wheat. 1, 209; *Passenger Cases*, 7 How. 283; *Railroad Co.* v. *Husen*, 95 U. S. 465; *McCulloch* v. *Maryland*, 4 Wheat. 315; *Sturges* v. *Crowninshield*, 4 Wheat. 122; *Opinions of Justices*, 14 Gray, 614; *United States* v. *Cruikshank*, 92 U. S. 542; *Martin* v. *Mott*, 12 Wheat. 19.—II. It is also in conflict with Article 1, section 18, subdivision 3, of the Constitution. *Luther* v. *Borden*, 7 How. 1; *Texas* v. *White*, 7 Wall. 700; *Green* v. *Biddle*, 8 Wheat. 1; *Poole* v. *Fleeder*, 11 Pet. 185; and cases cited above. —III. It is also in conflict with Article II. of the Amendments to the Constitution. See cases cited under Point I.— IV. It is also in conflict with Amendment XIV. to the Constitution. *Slaughter-House Cases*, 16 Wall. 36, 74; *Ward* v. *Maryland*, 12 Wall. 418, 430; *Crandall* v. *Nevada*, 6 Wall. 35, 49; *Dred Scott* v. *Sandford*, 19 How. 393, 580; *United States* v. *Cruikshank*, cited above.—V. It is also in conflict with Article I., section 9, subdivision 3 of the Constitution. *Fletcher* v. *Peck*, 6 Cranch, 87; *Cummings* v. *Missouri*, 4 Wall. 277; *Lapeyre* v. *United States*, 17 Wall. 191, 206; *Carpenter*

v. *Pennsylvania*, 17 How. 456; *Ex parte Garland*, 4 Wall. 333.

Mr. Lyman Trumbull also filed a supplemental brief for plaintiff in error, contending as follows :

I. The power of organizing, arming and disciplining the militia being confided by the Constitution to Congress, when Congress acts upon the subject and passes a law to carry into effect the constitutional provision, such action excludes the power of legislation by the State on the same subject. This is manifest, not only from the grant of power to Congress to organize, arm and discipline the militia, but from the restriction which the Constitution puts upon the States, limiting them simply to the appointment of the officers, and to the authority to train the militia as Congress shall prescribe. The power of each government in regard to the militia is distinctly stated in the Constitution itself. As well might the Federal government arrogate to itself the appointment of the officers of the militia as for the States to assume to organize and arm them in a different mode from that prescribed by Congress. Congress has exercised its functions, and covered, so far as it deemed expedient, the ground assigned to it by the Constitution, by providing for organizing, arming and disciplining the militia. See *Houston* v. *Moore*, 5 Wheat. 1, especially the language of the court on page 24. Counsel on the other side contend this case was overruled in *Sturges* v. *Crowninshield*, 4 Wheat. 122. That is a remarkable statement, as *Sturges* v. *Crowninshield*, was decided a year before *Houston* v. *Moore*. Moreover there is nothing in the former in conflict with the latter. The Military Code of Illinois differs from the act of Congress not only in details, but in its whole scope and object. Congress aims to arm, organize and discipline all able-bodied male citizens of the specified age. Illinois aims to prevent such arming, organizing and disciplining. Only 8000 are allowed to associate together and drill, and even those are not enrolled and organized as required by Congress.

II. The provisions for organizing, arming and disciplining the Illinois National Guard are in conflict with that clause of the Constitution which declares that no State shall, without the consent of Congress, keep troops in time of peace. Congress has never given its assent to that organization, and it is apparent that the guard are " troops " within the sense of the Constitution. The militia acts of Congress only excepted from their operation certain military organizations then existing, of which the Illinois National Guard was not one. It consists of 8000 men, raised for five years, formed into companies and regiments, with staff officers different in number and rank from those provided for by Congress; is divided into infantry, cavalry and artillery ; is required to drill often, to practise at target shooting and rifle practice, and is required to conform to the laws of the United States organizing the militia only in matters not provided for in the act. If these provisions do not constitute the Illinois National Guard "troops," the keeping of which in time of peace by the State is prohibited by the Constitution of the United States, I am at a loss to conceive what kind of troops it is that a State may not keep.

III. The provision of the State statute which prohibits other organizations than that of the " Illinois National Guard," from associating together as military companies, or to parade with arms, without the license of the governor, is in conflict with the act of Congress for the organization, &c., of the militia, and also violates Articles II. and XIV. of the Amendments to the Constitution. It may be admitted that Article II., securing to the people the right to keep and bear arms, by itself is a prohibition against the power of Congress, and not of the States, to interfere with that right, except when the keeping and bearing of arms is connected with some national purpose. When it is so connected, no State can pass any law abridging the right without a violation of the Second and Fourteenth Amendments.

The Fourteenth Amendment makes all persons born or naturalized in the United States, citizens of the United States, and of the State wherein they reside, and then declares that no State shall make any law which shall abridge the privileges and immunities of citizens of the United States. The citizen

VOL. CXVI—17

of the United States has secured to him the right to keep and bear arms as part of the militia which Congress has the right to organize, and arm, and to drill in companies. This is a national right which the national government has the power and which it is its duty to enforce.

This right of the people to keep and bear arms for the purpose of forming a well regulated militia, like "the right of the people peaceably to assemble for the purpose of petitioning Congress for a redress of grievances or for anything else connected with the powers or the duties of the national government, is an attribute of national citizenship, and as such, under the protection of, and guaranteed by the United States." *United States* v. *Cruikshank*, 92 U. S. 542, 552.

Whether a State may not prohibit its citizens from keeping or bearing arms for other than militia purposes is a question which need not be considered, as the Illinois statute is aimed against the organizing, arming and drilling of bodies of men as militia, except they belong to the Illinois National Guard of eight thousand.

It is contended that the Illinois act does not conflict with the act of Congress until the militia is actually mustered into the service of the United States. This is a mistaken view of the Constitution and of the object and intent of the law of 1792. The power of Congress to *organize* the militia is not limited to a period of war, or to such time as they may be employed in the service of the United States. It is only the power to *govern* them that is thus limited. The clause in the Constitution authorizing the President to call out the militia and put it into the service of the United States is separate and distinct from that which authorizes Congress to legislate for its organization, arming, and discipline. The manifest intent of the Constitution is to provide for an organized militia in time of peace, which may be called upon to execute the laws of the Union, and thus dispense with a standing army.

The acts of 1792 and 1795, authorizing the President to use military force to enforce the laws of the Union, suppress insurrections, and repel invasions, limited him to the use of the militia for such purposes. It was not until 1807 that he had authority to employ the land and naval forces of the United States therefor. Act of March 3, 1807, 2 Stat. 443.

The militia acts make definite provisions as to the persons to serve in the militia, the officers of that body, the times of parade and service, the returns to be made to the President, &c. It is absurd to suppose that these have no force till the militia is mustered into the service of the Union. State laws making other provisions are in conflict with it as much before as after such muster.

If it were admitted that State laws for organizing the militia are valid, except in so far as they conflict with the execution and operation of national laws on the same subject, the admission does not help the defendant in error, because it is insisted, and, as I think, shown, that the whole spirit, intent and effect of the Illinois statute is in conflict with the provisions of the act of Congress. If a State law is incompatible with the Constitution of the United States, or any law of Congress in pursuance thereof, it is invalid, whether the conflict arise in the execution and operation of the act of Congress, or in an attempt to put the State law in operation. It is enough if the State law, when sought to be put into execution and operation, conflicts with the national law on the same subject. It may be that a State law in partial execution of the military act of Congress, and conforming to its provisions, would be valid to that extent, upon the principle that power to organize all the militia implies the power to organize a part; but this principle can have no application to the Military Code of Illinois, for the reason that the organization of the Illinois National Guard, provided for by that code, does not, as has been already shown, conform to the act of Congress. It does not constitute any part of the militia upon which the President may call to enforce the laws of the United States, when resisted by combinations too powerful to be overcome by the ordinary course of judicial proceedings. Act of February 28, 1795, 1 Stat. 424; Rev. Stat. §§ 5298, 5299. It is purely a State force, sworn to serve the State in its military service, subject at all times to the orders of the governor, prohibited from leaving the State without his consent under a penalty, and so far from being part of

the militia organized in pursuance of the act of Congress, the
Illinois National Guard, in its organization, arming, and the
purpose for which it is organized, contravenes the spirit and
intent of the national act, and if permitted to stand, it prevents
the organizing, arming and disciplining all the male citizens
of the State, as Congress has prescribed.

Mr. George Hunt, Attorney-General of Illinois, for defendant in error.

MR. JUSTICE WOODS delivered the opinion of the court.
After stating the facts in the language above reported, he
continued:

The position of the plaintiff in error in this court was, that
the entire statute under which he was convicted was invalid
and void, because its enactment was the exercise of a power
by the legislature of Illinois forbidden to the States by the
Constitution of the United States.

The clauses of the Constitution of the United States referred
to in the assignments of error, were as follows:

Art. I., sec. 8. " The Congress shall have power . . . To
raise and support armies. . . . To provide for calling forth
the militia to execute the laws of the Union, suppress insurrections, and repel invasions. To provide for organizing, arming,
and disciplining the militia, and for governing such part of
them as may be employed in the service of the United States,
reserving to the States, respectively, the appointment of the
officers, and the authority of training the militia, according to
the discipline prescribed by Congress. . . . To make all
laws which shall be necessary and proper, for carrying into
execution the foregoing powers," &c.

Art. I., sec. 10. " No State shall, without the consent of Congress, keep troops . . . in time of peace."

Art. II. of Amendments. " A well regulated militia being
necessary to the security of a free State, the right of the people to keep and bear arms shall not be infringed."

The plaintiff in error also contended that the enactment of
the 5th and 6th sections of Article XI. of the Military Code

was forbidden by subdivision 3 of section 9, Art. I., which declares " No bill of attainder or *ex post facto* law shall be passed," and by Art. XIV. of Amendments, which provides that " No State shall make or enforce any law which shall abridge the privileges or immunities of citizens of the United States, nor shall any State deprive any person of life, liberty, or property without due process of law."

The first contention of counsel for plaintiff in error is that the Congress of the United States having, by virtue of the provisions of Article I., section 8, above quoted, passed the act of May 8, 1792, entitled " An Act more effectually to provide for the National Defence by establishing an Uniform Militia throughout the United States," 1 Stat. 271, the act of February 28, 1795, " to provide for calling forth the militia to execute the laws of the Union, suppress insurrections, and repel invasions," 1 Stat. 424, and the act of July 22, 1861, " to authorize the Employment of Volunteers to aid in enforcing the Laws and protecting Public Property," 12 Stat. 268, and other subsequent acts, now forming " Title XVI., The Militia," of the Revised Statutes of the United States, the legislature of Illinois had no power to pass the act approved May 28, 1879, " to provide for the organization of the State militia, entitled the Military Code of Illinois," under the provisions of which (sections 5 and 6 of Article XI.) the plaintiff in error was indicted.

The argument in support of this contention is, that the power of organizing, arming, and disciplining the militia being confided by the Constitution to Congress, when it acts upon the subject, and passes a law to carry into effect the constitutional provision, such action excludes the power of legislation by the State on the same subject.

It is further argued that the whole scope and object of the Military Code of Illinois is in conflict with that of the law of Congress. It is said that the object of the act of Congress is to provide for organizing, arming, and disciplining all the able-bodied male citizens of the States, respectively, between certain ages, that they may be ready at all times to respond to the call of the nation to enforce its laws, suppress insurrection, and repel invasion, and thereby avoid the necessity for maintaining a large standing army, with which liberty can never be safe, and that on the other hand, the effect if not object of the Illinois statute is to prevent such organizing, arming, and disciplining of the militia.

The plaintiff in error insists that the act of Congress requires absolutely all able-bodied citizens of the State between certain ages, to be enrolled in the militia; that the act of Illinois makes the enrolment dependent on the necessity for the use of troops to execute the laws and suppress insurrections, and then leaves it discretionary with the governor by proclamation to require such enrolment; that the act of Congress requires the entire enrolled militia of the State, with a few exemptions made by it and which may be made by State laws, to be formed into companies, battalions, regiments, brigades, and divisions, that every man shall be armed and supplied with ammunition, provides a system of discipline and field exercises for companies, regiments, &c., and subjects the entire militia of the State to the call of the President to enforce the laws, suppress insurrection, or repel invasion, and provides for the punishment of the militia officers and men who refuse obedience to his orders. On the other hand, it is said that the State law makes it unlawful for any of its able-bodied citizens, except eight thousand, called the Illinois National Guard, to associate themselves together as a military company, or to drill or parade with arms without the license of the governor, and declares that no military company shall leave the State with arms and equipments without his consent; that even the eight thousand men, styled the Illinois National Guard, are not enrolled or organized as required by the act of Congress, nor are they subject to the call of the President, but they constitute a military force sworn to serve in the military service of the State, to obey the orders of the governor, and not to leave the State without his consent; and that, if the State act is valid, the national act providing for organizing, arming, and disciplining the militia is of no force in the State of Illinois, for the Illinois act, so far from being in harmony with the act of Congress, is an insurmountable obstacle to its execution.

22

We have not found it necessary to consider or decide the question thus raised, as to the validity of the entire Military Code of Illinois, for, in our opinion, the sections under which the plaintiff in error was convicted may be valid, even if the other sections of the act were invalid. For it is a settled rule "that statutes that are constitutional in part only will be upheld so far as they are not in conflict with the Constitution, provided the allowed and prohibited parts are separable." *Packet Co.* v. *Keokuk,* 95 U. S. 80; *Penniman's Case,* 103 U. S. 714, 717; *Unity* v. *Burrage,* 103 U. S. 459. See also *Trade Mark Cases,* 100 U. S. 82.

We are of opinion that this rule is applicable in this case. The first two sections of Article I. of the Military Code provide that all able-bodied male citizens of the State between the ages of eighteen and forty-five years, except those exempted, shall be subject to military duty, and be designated the "Illinois State Militia," and declare how they shall be enrolled and under what circumstances. The residue of the Code, except the two sections on which the indictment against the plaintiff in error is based, provides for a volunteer active militia, to consist of not more than eight thousand officers and men, declares how it shall be enlisted and brigaded, and the term of service of its officers and men; provides for brigade generals and their staffs, for the organization of the requisite battalions and companies and the election of company officers; provides for inspections, parades, and encampments, arms and armories, rifle practice, and courts martial; provides for the pay of the officers and men, for medical service, regimental bands, books of instruction and maps; contains provisions for levying and collecting a military fund by taxation, and directs how it shall be expended; and appropriates $25,000 out of the treasury, in advance of the collection of the military fund, to be used for the purposes specified in the Military Code.

It is plain from this statement of the substance of the Military Code, that the two sections upon which the indictment against the plaintiff in error is based may be separated from the residue of the Code, and stand upon their own independent provisions. These sections might have been left out of the

Military Code and put in an act by themselves, and the act thus constituted, and the residue of the Military Code, would have been coherent and sensible acts. If it be conceded that the entire Military Code, except these sections, is unconstitutional and invalid, for the reasons stated by the plaintiff in error, these sections are separable, and, put in an act by themselves, could not be considered as forbidden by the clauses of the Constitution having reference to the militia, or to the clause forbidding the States, without the consent of Congress, to keep troops in time of peace. There is no such connection between the sections which prohibit any body of men, other than the organized militia of the State and the troops of the United States, from associating as a military company and drilling with arms in any city or town of the State, and the sections which provide for the enrolment and organization of the State militia, as makes it impossible to declare one, without declaring both, invalid

This view disposes of the objection to the judgment of the Supreme Court of Illinois, which judgment was in effect that the legislation on which the indictment is based is not invalid by reason of the provisions of the Constitution of the United States, which vest Congress with power to raise and support armies, and to provide for calling out, organizing, arming and disciplining the militia, and governing such part of them as may be employed in the service of the United States, and that provision which declares that "no State shall without the consent of Congress . . . keep troops . . . in time of peace."

We are next to inquire whether the 5th and 6th sections of article XI. of the Military Code are in violation of the other provisions of the Constitution of the United States relied on by the plaintiff in error. The first of these is the Second Amendment, which declares: "A well regulated militia being necessary to the security of a free State, the right of the people to keep and bear arms shall not be infringed."

We think it clear that the sections under consideration, which only forbid bodies of men to associate together as military organizations, or to drill or parade with arms in cities and towns unless authorized by law, do not infringe the right of the people to keep and bear arms. But a conclusive answer to the contention that this amendment prohibits the legislation in question lies in the fact that the amendment is a limitation only upon the power of Congress and the National government, and not upon that of the States. It was so held by this court in the case of *United States* v. *Cruikshank*, 92 U. S. 542, 553, in which the Chief Justice, in delivering the judgment of the court, said, that the right of the people to keep and bear arms " is not a right granted by the Constitution. Neither is it in any manner dependent upon that instrument for its existence. The Second Amendment declares that it shall not be infringed, but this, as has been seen, means no more than that it shall not be infringed by Congress. This is one of the amendments that has no other effect than to restrict the powers of the National government, leaving the people to look for their protection against any violation by their fellow-citizens of the rights it recognizes to what is called in *The City of New York* v. *Miln*, 11 Pet. [102] 139, the ' powers which relate to merely municipal legislation, or what was perhaps more properly called internal police,' ' not surrendered or restrained' by the Constitution of the United States." See also *Barron* v. *Baltimore*, 7 Pet. 243 ; *Fox* v. *The State of Ohio*, 5 How. 410 ; *Twitchell* v. *Commonwealth*, 7 Wall. 321, 327 ; *Jackson* v. *Wood*, 2 Cowen, 819 ; *Commonwealth* v. *Purchase*, 2 Pick. 521 ; *United States* v. *Cruikshank*, 1 Woods, 308 ; *North Carolina* v. *Newsom*, 5 Iredell, 250 ; *Andrews* v. *State*, 3 Heiskell, 165 ; *Fife* v. *State*, 31 Ark. 455.

It is undoubtedly true that all citizens capable of bearing arms constitute the reserved military force or reserve militia of the United States as well as of the States, and, in view of this prerogative of the general government, as well as of its general powers, the States cannot, even laying the constitutional provision in question out of view, prohibit the people from keeping and bearing arms, so as to deprive the United States of their rightful resource for maintaining the public security, and disable the people from performing their duty to the general government. But, as already stated, we think it clear that the sections under consideration do not have this effect.

The plaintiff in error next insists that the sections of the Military Code of Illinois, under which he was indicted, are an invasion of that clause of the first section of the Fourteenth Amendment to the Constitution of the United States which declares: " No State shall make or enforce any law which shall abridge the privileges or immunities of citizens of the United States."

It is only the privileges and immunities of citizens of the United States that the clause relied on was intended to protect. A State may pass laws to regulate the privileges and immunities of its own citizens, provided that in so doing it does not abridge their privileges and immunities as citizens of the United States. The inquiry is, therefore, pertinent, what privilege or immunity of a citizen of the United States is abridged by sections 5 and 6 of Article XI. of the Military Code of Illinois?

The plaintiff in error was not a member of the organized volunteer militia of the State of Illinois, nor did he belong to the troops of the United States or to any organization under the militia law of the United States. On the contrary, the fact that he did not belong to the organized militia or the troops of the United States was an ingredient in the offence for which he was convicted and sentenced. The question is, therefore, had he a right as a citizen of the United States, in disobedience of the State law, to associate with others as a military company, and to drill and parade with arms in the towns and cities of the State? If the plaintiff in error has any such privilege he must be able to point to the provision of the Constitution or statutes of the United States by which it is conferred. For, as was said by this court in *United States* v. *Cruikshank*, 92 U. S. 542, 560, 551, the government of the United States, although it is " within the scope of its powers supreme and above the States," " can neither grant nor secure to its citizens any right or privilege not expressly or by implication placed under its jurisdiction." " All that cannot be so granted or so secured are left to the exclusive protection of the State."

We have not been referred to any statute of the United States which confers upon the plaintiff in error the privilege which he asserts. The only clause in the Constitution which, upon any pretence, could be said to have any relation whatever to his right to associate with others as a military company is found in the First Amendment, which declares that "Congress shall make no law . . . abridging . . . the right of the people peaceably to assemble and to petition the government for a redress of grievances." This is a right which it was held in *United States* v. *Cruikshank,* above cited, was an attribute of national citizenship, and, as such, under the protection of, and guaranteed by, the United States. But it was held in the same case that the right peaceably to assemble was not protected by the clause referred to, unless the purpose of the assembly was to petition the government for a redress of grievances.

The right voluntarily to associate together as a military company or organization, or to drill or parade with arms, without, and independent of, an act of Congress or law of the State authorizing the same, is not an attribute of national citizenship. Military organization and military drill and parade under arms are subjects especially under the control of the government of every country. They cannot be claimed as a right independent of law. Under our political system they are subject to the regulation and control of the State and Federal governments, acting in due regard to their respective prerogatives and powers. The Constitution and laws of the United States will be searched in vain for any support to the view that these rights are privileges and immunities of citizens of the United States independent of some specific legislation on the subject.

It cannot be successfully questioned that the State governments, unless restrained by their own Constitutions, have the power to regulate or prohibit associations and meetings of the people, except in the case of peaceable assemblies to perform the duties or exercise the privileges of citizens of the United States; and have also the power to control and regulate the organization, drilling, and parading of military bodies and associations, except when such bodies or associations are authorized by the militia laws of the United States. The exercise of this power by the States is necessary to the public peace, safety and good order. To deny the power would be to deny the right of the State to disperse assemblages organized for sedition and treason, and the right to suppress armed mobs bent on riot and rapine.

In the case of *New York* v. *Miln*, 11 Pet. 102, 139, this court said: "We choose rather to plant ourselves on what we consider impregnable positions. They are these: that a State has the same undeniable and unlimited jurisdiction over all persons and things within its territorial limits as any foreign nation, where that jurisdiction is not surrendered or restrained by the Constitution of the United States; that by virtue of this, it is not only the right but the bounden and solemn duty of a State to advance the safety, happiness and prosperity of its people, and to provide for its general welfare by any and every act of legislation which it may deem to be conducive to these ends, where the power over the particular subject or the manner of its exercise is not surrendered or restrained in the manner just stated," namely, by the Constitution and laws of the United States. See also *Gibbons* v. *Ogden*, 9 Wheat. 1, 203; *Gilman* v. *Philadelphia*, 3 Wall. 713; *License Tax Cases*, 5 Wall. 462; *United States* v. *Dewitt*, 9 Wall. 41; *United States* v. *Cruikshank*, 92 U. S. 542. These considerations and authorities sustain the power exercised by the legislature of Illinois in the enactment of sections 5 and 6 of Art. XI. of the Military Code.

The argument of the plaintiff in error that the legislation mentioned deprives him of either life, liberty or property without due process of law, or that it is a bill of attainder or *ex post facto* law, is so clearly untenable as to require no discussion.

It is next contended by the plaintiff in error that sections 5 and 6 of Art. XI. of the Military Code, under which he was indicted, are in conflict with the acts of Congress for the organization of the militia. But this position is based on what seems to us to be an unwarranted construction of the sections referred to. It is clear that their object was to forbid voluntary military associations, unauthorized by law, from organizing or drilling and parading with arms in the cities or towns of the State, and not to interfere with the organization, arming and drilling of the militia under the authority of the acts of Congress. If the object and effect of the sections were in irreconcilable conflict with the acts of Congress they would of course be invalid. But it is a rule of construction that a statute must be interpreted so as, if possible, to make it consistent with the Constitution and the paramount law. *Parsons* v. *Bedford*, 3 Pet. 433 ; *Grenada County Supervisors* v. *Brogden*, 112 U. S. 261; *Marshall* v. *Grimes*, 41 Mississippi, 27. If we yielded to this contention of the plaintiff in error we should render the sections invalid by giving them a strained construction, which would make them antagonistic to the law of Congress. We cannot attribute to the legislature, unless compelled to do so by its plain words, a purpose to pass an act in conflict with an act of Congress on a subject over which Congress is given authority by the Constitution of the United States. We are therefore of opinion that fairly construed the sections of the Military Code referred to do not conflict with the laws of Congress on the subject of the militia.

The plaintiff in error further insists that the organization of the Lehr und Wehr Verein as a corporate body, under the general corporation law of the State of Illinois, was in effect a license from the governor, within the meaning of section 5 of Article XI. of the Military Code, and that such corporate body fell within the exception of the same section " of students in educational institutions where military science is a part of the course of instruction."

In respect to these points we have to say that they present no Federal question. It is not, therefore, our province to consider or decide them. *Murdock* v. *Memphis*, 20 Wall. 590.

All the Federal questions presented by the record were rightly decided by the Supreme Court of Illinois.

Judgment affirmed.

UNITED STATES *v.* MILLER ET AL.

APPEAL FROM THE DISTRICT COURT OF THE UNITED STATES
FOR THE WESTERN DISTRICT OF ARKANSAS.

No. 696. Argued March 30, 1939.—Decided May 15, 1939.

The National Firearms Act, as applied to one indicted for transporting in interstate commerce a 12-gauge shotgun with a barrel
less than 18 inches long, without having registered it and without
having in his possession a stamp-affixed written order for it, as
required by the Act, *held:*

   1. Not unconstitutional as an invasion of the reserved powers
of the States. Citing *Sonzinsky* v. *United States,* 300 U. S. 506,
and Narcotic Act cases. P. 177.

   2. Not violative of the Second Amendment of the Federal
Constitution. P. 178.

   The Court can not take judicial notice that a shotgun having
a barrel less than 18 inches long has today any reasonable relation to the preservation or efficiency of a well regulated militia;
and therefore can not say that the Second Amendment guarantees
to the citizen the right to keep and bear such a weapon.

26 F. Supp. 1002, reversed.

APPEAL under the Criminal Appeals Act from a judgment sustaining a demurrer to an indictment for violation of the National Firearms Act.

Mr. Gordon Dean argued the cause, and *Solicitor General Jackson, Assistant Attorney General McMahon,* and *Messrs. William W. Barron, Fred E. Strine, George F. Kneip, W. Marvin Smith,* and *Clinton R. Barry* were on a brief, for the United States.

No appearance for appellees.

MR. JUSTICE McREYNOLDS delivered the opinion of the Court.

An indictment in the District Court Western District Arkansas, charged that Jack Miller and Frank Layton

"did unlawfully, knowingly, wilfully, and feloniously transport in interstate commerce from the town of Claremore in the State of Oklahoma to the town of Siloam Springs in the State of Arkansas a certain firearm, to-wit, a double barrel 12-gauge Stevens shotgun having a barrel less than 18 inches in length, bearing identification number 76230, said defendants, at the time of so transporting said firearm in interstate commerce as aforesaid, not having registered said firearm as required by Section 1132d of Title 26, United States Code (Act of June 26, 1934, c. 737, Sec. 4 [§ 5], 48 Stat. 1237), and not having in their possession a stamp-affixed written order for said firearm as provided by Section 1132c, Title 26, United States Code (June 26, 1934, c. 737, Sec. 4, 48 Stat. 1237) and the regulations issued under authority of the said Act of Congress known as the 'National Firearms Act' approved June 26, 1934, contrary to the form of the statute in such case made and provided, and against the peace and dignity of the United States." [1]

---

[1] Act of June 26, 1934, c. 757, 48 Stat. 1236–1240, 26 U. S. C. § 1132.

That for the purposes of this Act—

"(a) The term 'firearm' means a shotgun or rifle having a barrel of less than eighteen inches in length, or any other weapon, except

A duly interposed demurrer alleged: The National Firearms Act is not a revenue measure but an attempt to usurp police power reserved to the States, and is therefore unconstitutional. Also, it offends the inhibition of the Second Amendment to the Constitution—"A well regulated Militia, being necessary to the security of a free State, the right of people to keep and bear Arms, shall not be infringed."

a pistol or revolver, from which a shot is discharged by an explosive if such weapon is capable of being concealed on the person, or a machine gun, and includes a muffler or silencer for any firearm whether or not such firearm is included within the foregoing definition, [The Act of April 10, 1936, c. 169, 49 Stat. 1192 added the words] but does not include any rifle which is within the foregoing provisions solely by reason of the length of its barrel if the caliber of such rifle is .22 or smaller and if its barrel is sixteen inches or more in length.

"Sec. 3. (a) There shall be levied, collected, and paid upon firearms transferred in the continental United States a tax at the rate of $200 for each firearm, such tax to be paid by the transferor, and to be represented by appropriate stamps to be provided by the Commissioner, with the approval of the Secretary; and the stamps herein provided shall be affixed to the order for such firearm, hereinafter provided for. The tax imposed by this section shall be in addition to any import duty imposed on such firearm.

"Sec. 4. (a) It shall be unlawful for any person to transfer a firearm except in pursuance of a written order from the person seeking to obtain such article, on an application form issued in blank in duplicate for that purpose by the Commissioner. Such order shall identify the applicant by such means of identification as may be prescribed by regulations under this Act: *Provided*, That, if the applicant is an individual, such identification shall include fingerprints and a photograph thereof.

"(c) Every person so transferring a firearm shall set forth in each copy of such order the manufacturer's number or other mark identifying such firearm, and shall forward a copy of such order to the Commissioner. The original thereof with stamps affixed, shall be returned to the applicant.

"(d) No person shall transfer a firearm which has previously been transferred on or after the effective date of this Act, unless such

The District Court held that section eleven of the Act violates the Second Amendment. It accordingly sustained the demurrer and quashed the indictment.

The cause is here by direct appeal.

Considering *Sonzinsky* v. *United States* (1937), 300 U. S. 506, 513, and what was ruled in sundry causes aris-

---

person, in addition to complying with subsection (c), transfers therewith the stamp-affixed order provided for in this section for each such prior transfer, in compliance with such regulations as may be prescribed under this Act for proof of payment of all taxes on such firearms.

"Sec. 5. (a) Within sixty days after the effective date of this Act every person possessing a firearm shall register, with the collector of the district in which he resides, the number or other mark identifying such firearm, together with his name, address, place where such firearm is usually kept, and place of business or employment, and, if such person is other than a natural person, the name and home address of an executive officer thereof: *Provided,* That no person shall be required to register under this section with respect to any firearm acquired after the effective date of, and in conformity with the provisions of, this Act.

"Sec. 6. It shall be unlawful for any person to receive or possess any firearm which has at any time been transferred in violation of section 3 or 4 of this Act.

"Sec. 11. It shall be unlawful for any person who is required to register as provided in section 5 hereof and who shall not have so registered, or any other person who has not in his possession a stamp-affixed order as provided in section 4 hereof, to ship, carry, or deliver any firearm in interstate commerce.

"Sec. 12. The Commissioner, with the approval of the Secretary, shall prescribe such rules and regulations as may be necessary for carrying the provisions of this Act into effect.

"Sec. 14. Any person who violates or fails to comply with any of the requirements of this Act shall, upon conviction, be fined not more than $2,000 or be imprisoned for not more than five years, or both, in the discretion of the court.

"Sec. 16. If any provision of this Act, or the application thereof to any person or circumstance, is held invalid, the remainder of the Act, and the application of such provision to other persons or circumstances, shall not be affected thereby.

"Sec. 18. This Act may be cited as the 'National Firearms Act.'"

161299°—39——12

ing under the Harrison Narcotic Act [2]—*United States* v.
Jin Fuey Moy (1916), 241 U. S. 394; *United States* v.
Doremus (1919), 249 U. S. 86, 94; *Linder* v. *United
States* (1925), 268 U. S. 5; *Alston* v. *United States*
(1927), 274 U. S. 289; *Nigro* v. *United States* (1928),
276 U. S. 332—the objection that the Act usurps police
power reserved to the States is plainly untenable.

In the absence of any evidence tending to show that
possession or use of a "shotgun having a barrel of less
than eighteen inches in length" at this time has some
reasonable relationship to the preservation or efficiency
of a well regulated militia, we cannot say that the Second
Amendment guarantees the right to keep and bear such
an instrument. Certainly it is not within judicial notice
that this weapon is any part of the ordinary military
equipment or that its use could contribute to the common defense. *Aymette* v. *State,* 2 Humphreys (Tenn.)
154, 158.

The Constitution as originally adopted granted to the
Congress power—"To provide for calling forth the Militia
to execute the Laws of the Union, suppress Insurrections and repel Invasions; To provide for organizing,
arming, and disciplining, the Militia, and for governing
such Part of them as may be employed in the Service of
the United States, reserving to the States respectively,
the Appointment of the Officers, and the Authority of
training the Militia according to the discipline prescribed
by Congress." With obvious purpose to assure the continuation and render possible the effectiveness of such
forces the declaration and guarantee of the Second
Amendment were made. It must be interpreted and
applied with that end in view.

The Militia which the States were expected to maintain and train is set in contrast with Troops which they

---

[2] Act December 17, 1914, c. 1, 38 Stat. 785; February 24, 1919, c.
18, 40 Stat. 1057.

were forbidden to keep without the consent of Congress. The sentiment of the time strongly disfavored standing armies; the common view was that adequate defense of country and laws could be secured through the Militia— civilians primarily, soldiers on occasion.

The signification attributed to the term Militia appears from the debates in the Convention, the history and legislation of Colonies and States, and the writings of approved commentators. These show plainly enough that the Militia comprised all males physically capable of acting in concert for the common defense. "A body of citizens enrolled for military discipline." And further, that ordinarily when called for service these men were expected to appear bearing arms supplied by themselves and of the kind in common use at the time.

Blackstone's Commentaries, Vol. 2, Ch. 13, p. 409 points out "that king Alfred first settled a national militia in this kingdom," and traces the subsequent development and use of such forces.

Adam Smith's Wealth of Nations, Book V, Ch. 1, contains an extended account of the Militia. It is there said: "Men of republican principles have been jealous of a standing army as dangerous to liberty." "In a militia, the character of the labourer, artificer, or tradesman, predominates over that of the soldier: in a standing army, that of the soldier predominates over every other character; and in this distinction seems to consist the essential difference between those two different species of military force."

"The American Colonies In The 17th Century," Osgood, Vol. 1, ch. XIII, affirms in reference to the early system of defense in New England—

"In all the colonies, as in England, the militia system was based on the principle of the assize of arms. This implied the general obligation of all adult male inhabitants to possess arms, and, with certain exceptions, to

cooperate in the work of defence." "The possession of
arms also implied the possession of ammunition, and the
authorities paid quite as much attention to the latter as
to the former." "A year later [1632] it was ordered that
any single man who had not furnished himself with arms
might be put out to service, and this became a permanent
part of the legislation of the colony [Massachusetts]."

Also "Clauses intended to insure the possession of arms
and ammunition by all who were subject to military service appear in all the important enactments concerning
military affairs. Fines were the penalty for delinquency,
whether of towns or individuals. According to the usage
of the times, the infantry of Massachusetts consisted of
pikemen and musketeers. The law, as enacted in 1649
and thereafter, provided that each of the former should
be armed with a pike, corselet, head-piece, sword, and
knapsack. The musketeer should carry a 'good fixed
musket,' not under bastard musket bore, not less than
three feet, nine inches, nor more than four feet three
inches in length, a priming wire, scourer, and mould, a
sword, rest, bandoleers, one pound of powder, twenty
bullets, and two fathoms of match. The law also required
that two-thirds of each company should be musketeers."

The General Court of Massachusetts, January Session
1784, provided for the organization and government of
the Militia. It directed that the Train Band should "contain all able bodied men, from sixteen to forty years of
age, and the Alarm List, all other men under sixty years
of age, . . ." Also, "That every non-commissioned officer
and private soldier of the said militia not under the con-
troul of parents, masters or guardians, and being of sufficient ability therefor in the judgment of the Selectmen
of the town in which he shall dwell, shall equip himself,
and be constantly provided with a good fire arm," &c.

By an Act passed April 4, 1786 the New York Legislature directed: "That every able-bodied Male Person, be-

ing a Citizen of this State, or of any of the United States, and residing in this State, (except such Persons as are hereinafter excepted) and who are of the Age of Sixteen, and under the Age of Forty-five Years, shall, by the Captain or commanding Officer of the Beat in which such Citizens shall reside, within four Months after the passing of this Act, be enrolled in the Company of such Beat. . . . That every Citizen so enrolled and notified, shall, within three Months thereafter, provide himself, at his own Expense, with a good Musket or Firelock, a sufficient Bayonet and Belt, a Pouch with a Box therein to contain not less than Twenty-four Cartridges suited to the Bore of his Musket or Firelock, each Cartridge containing a proper Quantity of Powder and Ball, two spare Flints, a Blanket and Knapsack; . . ."

The General Assembly of Virginia, October, 1785, (12 Hening's Statutes) declared, "The defense and safety of the commonwealth depend upon having its citizens properly armed and taught the knowledge of military duty."

It further provided for organization and control of the Militia and directed that "All free male persons between the ages of eighteen and fifty years," with certain exceptions, "shall be inrolled or formed into companies." "There shall be a private muster of every company once in two months."

Also that "Every officer and soldier shall appear at his respective muster-field on the day appointed, by eleven o'clock in the forenoon, armed, equipped, and accoutred, as follows: . . . every non-commissioned officer and private with a good, clean musket carrying an ounce ball, and three feet eight inches long in the barrel, with a good bayonet and iron ramrod well fitted thereto, a cartridge box properly made, to contain and secure twenty cartridges fitted to his musket, a good knapsack and canteen, and moreover, each non-commissioned officer and private shall have at every muster one pound of good powder, and four pounds of lead, including twenty blind cartridges; and each serjeant shall have a pair of moulds fit to cast balls for their respective companies, to be purchased by the commanding officer out of the monies arising on delinquencies. *Provided,* That the militia of the counties westward of the Blue Ridge, and the counties below adjoining thereto, shall not be obliged to be armed with muskets, but may have good rifles with proper accoutrements, in lieu thereof. And every of the said officers, non-commissioned officers, and privates, shall constantly keep the aforesaid arms, accoutrements, and ammunition, ready to be produced whenever called for by his commanding officer. If any private shall make it appear to the satisfaction of the court hereafter to be appointed for trying delinquencies under this act that he is so poor that he cannot purchase the arms herein required, such court shall cause them to be purchased out of the money arising from delinquents."

Most if not all of the States have adopted provisions touching the right to keep and bear arms. Differences in the language employed in these have naturally led to somewhat variant conclusions concerning the scope of the right guaranteed. But none of them seem to afford any material support for the challenged ruling of the court below.

In the margin some of the more important opinions and comments by writers are cited.[3]

---

[3] Concerning The Militia—*Presser* v. *Illinois,* 116 U. S. 252; *Robertson* v. *Baldwin,* 165 U. S. 275; *Fife* v. *State,* 31 Ark. 455; *Jeffers* v. *Fair,* 33 Ga. 347; *Salina* v. *Blaksley,* 72 Kan. 230; 83 P. 619; *People* v. *Brown,* 253 Mich. 537; 235 N. W. 245; *Aymette* v. *State,* 2 Humphr. (Tenn.) 154; *State* v. *Duke,* 42 Texas 455; *State* v. *Workman,* 35 W. Va. 367; 14 S. E. 9; Cooley's Constitutional Limitations, Vol. 1, p. 729; Story on The Constitution, 5th Ed., Vol. 2, p. 646; Encyclopaedia of the Social Sciences, Vol. X, p. 471, 474.

We are unable to accept the conclusion of the court below and the challenged judgment must be reversed. The cause will be remanded for further proceedings.

MR. JUSTICE DOUGLAS took no part in the consideration or decision of this cause.

FIREARMS OWNERS' PROTECTION ACT

*For Legislative History of Act see Report for P.L. 99–308
in Legislative History Section, post.*

An Act to amend chapter 44 (relating to firearms) of title 18, United States Code, and for other purposes.

*Be it enacted by the Senate and House of Representatives of the
United States of America in Congress assembled,*

SECTION 1. SHORT TITLE AND CONGRESSIONAL FINDINGS.

Firearms
Owners'
Protection Act.
18 USC 921 note.

(a) SHORT TITLE.—This Act may be cited as the "Firearms Owners'
Protection Act".

(b) CONGRESSIONAL FINDINGS.—The Congress finds that—
　(1) the rights of citizens—
　　(A) to keep and bear arms under the second amendment
to the United States Constitution;
　　(B) to security against illegal and unreasonable searches
and seizures under the fourth amendment;
　　(C) against uncompensated taking of property, double
jeopardy, and assurance of due process of law under the
fifth amendment; and
　　(D) against unconstitutional exercise of authority under
the ninth and tenth amendments;
require additional legislation to correct existing firearms statutes and enforcement policies; and
　(2) additional legislation is required to reaffirm the intent of
the Congress, as expressed in section 101 of the Gun Control Act
of 1968, that "it is not the purpose of this title to place any
undue or unnecessary Federal restrictions or burdens on law-
abiding citizens with respect to the acquisition, possession, or
use of firearms appropriate to the purpose of hunting, trap-
shooting, target shooting, personal protection, or any other
lawful activity, and that this title is not intended to discourage
or eliminate the private ownership or use of firearms by law-
abiding citizens for lawful purposes.".

18 USC 921 note.

SEC. 101. AMENDMENTS TO SECTION 921.

Section 921 of title 18, United States Code, is amended—
　(1) in subsection (a)(10), by striking out "manufacture of" and
inserting in lieu thereof "business of manufacturing";
　(2) in subsection (a)(11)(A), by striking out "or ammunition";
　(3) in subsection (a)(12), by striking out "or ammunition";
　(4) in subsection (a)(13), by striking out "or ammunition";
　(5) by amending paragraph (20) of subsection (a) to read as
follows:
"(20) The term 'crime punishable by imprisonment for a term
exceeding one year' does not include—

Crimes and
misdemeanors.

"(A) any Federal or State offenses pertaining to antitrust
violations, unfair trade practices, restraints of trade, or other
similar offenses relating to the regulation of business practices,
or

100 STAT. 449

41

"(B) any State offense classified by the laws of the State as a misdemeanor and punishable by a term of imprisonment of two years or less.

What constitutes a conviction of such a crime shall be determined in accordance with the law of the jurisdiction in which the proceedings were held. Any conviction which has been expunged, or set aside or for which a person has been pardoned or has had civil rights restored shall not be considered a conviction for purposes of this chapter, unless such pardon, expungement, or restoration of civil rights expressly provides that the person may not ship, transport, possess, or receive firearms."; and

Commerce and trade.

(6) in subsection (a), by inserting after paragraph (20) the following new paragraphs:

"(21) The term 'engaged in the business' means—

"(A) as applied to a manufacturer of firearms, a person who devotes time, attention, and labor to manufacturing firearms as a regular course of trade or business with the principal objective of livelihood and profit through the sale or distribution of the firearms manufactured;

"(B) as applied to a manufacturer of ammunition, a person who devotes time, attention, and labor to manufacturing ammunition as a regular course of trade or business with the principal objective of livelihood and profit through the sale or distribution of the ammunition manufactured;

18 USC 921.

"(C) as applied to a dealer in firearms, as defined in section 921(a)(11)(A), a person who devotes time, attention, and labor to dealing in firearms as a regular course of trade or business with the principal objective of livelihood and profit through the repetitive purchase and resale of firearms, but such term shall not include a person who makes occasional sales, exchanges, or purchases of firearms for the enhancement of a personal collection or for a hobby, or who sells all or part of his personal collection of firearms;

"(D) as applied to a dealer in firearms, as defined in section 921(a)(11)(B), a person who devotes time, attention, and labor to engaging in such activity as a regular course of trade or business with the principal objective of livelihood and profit, but such term shall not include a person who makes occasional repairs of firearms, or who occasionally fits special barrels, stocks, or trigger mechanisms to firearms;

Imports.

"(E) as applied to an importer of firearms, a person who devotes time, attention, and labor to importing firearms as a regular course of trade or business with the principal objective of livelihood and profit through the sale or distribution of the firearms imported; and

Imports.

"(F) as applied to an importer of ammunition, a person who devotes time, attention, and labor to importing ammunition as a regular course of trade or business with the principal objective of livelihood and profit through the sale or distribution of the ammunition imported.

"(22) The term 'with the principal objective of livelihood and profit' means that the intent underlying the sale or disposition of firearms is predominantly one of obtaining livelihood and pecuniary gain, as opposed to other intents, such as improving or liquidating a personal firearms collection.

"(23) The term 'machinegun' has the meaning given such term in section 5845(b) of the National Firearms Act (26 U.S.C. 5845(b)).

100 STAT. 450

"(24) The terms 'firearm silencer' and 'firearm muffler' mean any device for silencing, muffling, or diminishing the report of a portable firearm, including any combination of parts, designed or redesigned, and intended for use in assembling or fabricating a firearm silencer or firearm muffler, and any part intended only for use in such assembly or fabrication.".

SEC. 102. AMENDMENTS TO SECTION 922.

Section 922 of title 18, United States Code, is amended—

(1) so that paragraph (1) of subsection (a) reads as follows: "(1) for any person—

Crimes and misdemeanors. Commerce and trade.

"(A) except a licensed importer, licensed manufacturer, or licensed dealer, to engage in the business of importing, manufacturing, or dealing in firearms, or in the course of such business to ship, transport, or receive any firearm in interstate or foreign commerce; or

"(B) except a licensed importer or licensed manufacturer, to engage in the business of importing or manufacturing ammunition, or in the course of such business, to ship, transport, or receive any ammunition in interstate or foreign commerce;";

(2) in subsection (a)(2)—

(A) by striking out "or ammunition"; and

(B) by striking out "or licensed dealer for the sole purpose of repair or customizing;" and inserting in lieu thereof "licensed dealer, or licensed collector;";

(3) in subsection (a)(3), by striking out "(B)" and all that follows through "(b)(3) of this section," and inserting in lieu thereof the following: "(B) shall not apply to the transportation or receipt of a firearm obtained in conformity with subsection (b)(3) of this section,";

(4) in subsection (b)—

(A) in paragraph (2), by striking out "or ammunition" each place it appears;

(B) in paragraph (3), by striking out "(A)" and all that follows through "intrastate transactions other than at the licensee's business premises," and inserting in lieu thereof "(A) shall not apply to the sale or delivery of any rifle or shotgun to a resident of a State other than a State in which the licensee's place of business is located if the transferee meets in person with the transferor to accomplish the transfer, and the sale, delivery, and receipt fully comply with the legal conditions of sale in both such States (and any licensed manufacturer, importer or dealer shall be presumed, for purposes of this subparagraph, in the absence of evidence to the contrary, to have had actual knowledge of the State laws and published ordinances of both States),";

(C) in paragraph (3), by inserting "and" before "(B)";

(D) in paragraph (3), by striking out ", and (C)" and all that follows through the end of such paragraph and inserting in lieu thereof a semicolon; and

(E) in paragraph (5), by striking out "or ammunition except .22 caliber rimfire ammunition" and inserting "or armor-piercing ammunition" in lieu thereof;

(5) in subsection (d)—

100 STAT. 451

43

Drugs and drug
abuse.

Aliens.

Drugs and drug
abuse.

Aliens.

(A) by striking out "licensed importer, licensed manufacturer, licensed dealer, or licensed collector" the first place it appears and inserting in lieu thereof "person";

(B) by amending paragraph (3) to read as follows:

"(3) is an unlawful user of or addicted to any controlled substance (as defined in section 102 of the Controlled Substances Act (21 U.S.C. 802));";

(C) in paragraph (4), by striking out the period and inserting in lieu thereof a semicolon; and

(D) by inserting after paragraph (4) the following:

"(5) who, being an alien, is illegally or unlawfully in the United States;

"(6) who has been discharged from the Armed Forces under dishonorable conditions; or

"(7) who, having been a citizen of the United States, has renounced his citizenship.";

(6) in subsection (g)—

(A) in paragraph (1), by striking out "is under indictment for, or who";

(B) by amending paragraph (3) to read as follows:

"(3) is an unlawful user of or addicted to any controlled substance (as defined in section 102 of the Controlled Substances Act (21 U.S.C. 802));";

(C) by inserting after paragraph (4) the following new paragraphs:

"(5) who, being an alien, is illegally or unlawfully in the United States;

"(6) who has been discharged from the Armed Forces under dishonorable conditions; or

"(7) who, having been a citizen of the United States, has renounced his citizenship;"; and

(D) by striking out "to ship or transport any firearm or ammunition in interstate or foreign commerce." and inserting in lieu thereof "to ship or transport in interstate or foreign commerce, or possess in or affecting commerce, any firearm or ammunition; or to receive any firearm or ammunition which has been shipped or transported in interstate or foreign commerce.";

(7) so that subsection (h) reads as follows:

"(h) It shall be unlawful for any individual, who to that individual's knowledge and while being employed for any person described in any paragraph of subsection (g) of this section, in the course of such employment—

"(1) to receive, possess, or transport any firearm or ammunition in or affecting interstate or foreign commerce; or

"(2) to receive any firearm or ammunition which has been shipped or transported in interstate or foreign commerce.";

(8) by inserting after subsection (m) the following:

"(n) It shall be unlawful for any person who is under indictment for a crime punishable by imprisonment for a term exceeding one year to ship or transport in interstate or foreign commerce any firearm or ammunition or receive any firearm or ammunition which has been shipped or transported in interstate or foreign commerce."; and

(9) by inserting after the subsection added by paragraph (8) of this section the following:

100 STAT. 452

"(o)(1) Except as provided in paragraph (2), it shall be unlawful for any person to transfer or possess a machinegun.

"(2) This subsection does not apply with respect to—

"(A) a transfer to or by, or possession by or under the authority of, the United States or any department or agency thereof or a State, or a department, agency, or political subdivision thereof; or

"(B) any lawful transfer or lawful possession of a machinegun that was lawfully possessed before the date this subsection takes effect."

SEC. 103. AMENDMENTS TO SECTION 923.

Section 923 of title 18, United States Code, is amended—

(1) in subsection (a)—

Imports.

(A) by striking out the first sentence and inserting in lieu thereof "No person shall engage in the business of importing, manufacturing, or dealing in firearms, or importing or manufacturing ammunition, until he has filed an application with and received a license to do so from the Secretary."; and

(B) by striking out "and contain such information", and inserting in lieu thereof "and contain only that information necessary to determine eligibility for licensing.";

(2) in subsection (a)(3)(B), by striking out "or ammunition for firearms other than destructive devices,";

(3) in subsection (b), by striking out "and contain such information" and inserting in lieu thereof "and contain only that information necessary to determine eligibility";

(4) in subsection (c), by adding at the end "Nothing in this chapter shall be construed to prohibit a licensed manufacturer, importer, or dealer from maintaining and disposing of a personal collection of firearms, subject only to such restrictions as apply in this chapter to dispositions by a person other than a licensed manufacturer, importer, or dealer. If any firearm is so disposed of by a licensee within one year after its transfer from his business inventory into such licensee's personal collection or if such disposition or any other acquisition is made for the purpose of willfully evading the restrictions placed upon licensees by this chapter, then such firearm shall be deemed part of such licensee's business inventory.";

(5) in subsection (e), by inserting "willfully" before "violated";

(6) in subsection (f)—

(A) in paragraph (3)—

(i) by inserting "de novo" before "judicial"; and

(ii) by inserting "whether or not such evidence was considered at the hearing held under paragraph (2)." after "to the proceeding"; and

(B) by adding at the end the following new paragraph:

Law enforcement.

"(4) If criminal proceedings are instituted against a licensee alleging any violation of this chapter or of rules or regulations prescribed under this chapter, and the licensee is acquitted of such charges, or such proceedings are terminated, other than upon motion of the Government before trial upon such charges, the Secretary shall be absolutely barred from denying or revoking any license granted under this chapter where such denial or revocation is based in whole or in part on the facts which form the basis of such criminal charges. No proceedings for the revocation of a license shall be

100 STAT. 453

LAWS OF 99th CONG.—2nd SESS.   May 19

Records.

instituted by the Secretary more than one year after the filing of the indictment or information.";

(7) so that subsection (g) reads as follows:

"(g)(1)(A) Each licensed importer, licensed manufacturer, and licensed dealer shall maintain such records of importation, production, shipment, receipt, sale, or other disposition of firearms at his place of business for such period, and in such form, as the Secretary may by regulations prescribe. Such importers, manufacturers, and dealers shall not be required to submit to the Secretary reports and information with respect to such records and the contents thereof, except as expressly required by this section. The Secretary, when he has reasonable cause to believe a violation of this chapter has occurred and that evidence thereof may be found on such premises, may, upon demonstrating such cause before a Federal magistrate and securing from such magistrate a warrant authorizing entry, enter during business hours the premises (including places of storage) of any licensed firearms importer, licensed manufacturer, licensed dealer, licensed collector, or any licensed importer or manufacturer of ammunition, for the purpose of inspecting or examining—

"(i) any records or documents required to be kept by such licensed importer, licensed manufacturer, licensed dealer, or licensed collector under this chapter or rules or regulations under this chapter, and

"(ii) any firearms or ammunition kept or stored by such licensed importer, licensed manufacturer, licensed dealer, or licensed collector, at such premises.

"(B) The Secretary may inspect or examine the inventory and records of a licensed importer, licensed manufacturer, or licensed dealer without such reasonable cause or warrant—

"(i) in the course of a reasonable inquiry during the course of a criminal investigation of a person or persons other than the licensee;

"(ii) for ensuring compliance with the record keeping requirements of this chapter not more than once during any twelve-month period; or

"(iii) when such inspection or examination may be required for determining the disposition of one or more particular firearms in the course of a bona fide criminal investigation.

"(C) The Secretary may inspect the inventory and records of a licensed collector without such reasonable cause or warrant—

"(i) for ensuring compliance with the record keeping requirements of this chapter not more than once during any twelve-month period; or

"(ii) when such inspection or examination may be required for determining the disposition of one or more particular firearms in the course of a bona fide criminal investigation.

"(D) At the election of a licensed collector, the annual inspection of records and inventory permitted under this paragraph shall be performed at the office of the Secretary designated for such inspections which is located in closest proximity to the premises where the inventory and records of such licensed collector are maintained. The inspection and examination authorized by this paragraph shall not be construed as authorizing the Secretary to seize any records or other documents other than those records or documents constituting material evidence of a violation of law. If the Secretary seizes such records or documents, copies shall be provided the licensee within a

100 STAT. 454

reasonable time. The Secretary may make available to any Federal, State, or local law enforcement agency any information which he may obtain by reason of this chapter with respect to the identification of persons prohibited from purchasing or receiving firearms or ammunition who have purchased or received firearms or ammunition, together with a description of such firearms or ammunition, and he may provide information to the extent such information may be contained in the records required to be maintained by this chapter, when so requested by any Federal, State, or local law enforcement agency.

State and local governments.

"(2) Each licensed collector shall maintain in a bound volume the nature of which the Secretary may by regulations prescribe, records of the receipt, sale, or other disposition of firearms. Such records shall include the name and address of any person to whom the collector sells or otherwise disposes of a firearm. Such collector shall not be required to submit to the Secretary reports and information with respect to such records and the contents thereof, except as expressly required by this section.

"(3) Each licensee shall prepare a report of multiple sales or other dispositions whenever the licensee sells or otherwise disposes of, at one time or during any five consecutive business days, two or more pistols, or revolvers, or any combination of pistols and revolvers totalling two or more, to an unlicensed person. The report shall be prepared on a form specified by the Secretary and forwarded to the office specified thereon not later than the close of business on the day that the multiple sale or other disposition occurs.

Report.

"(4) Where a firearms or ammunition business is discontinued and succeeded by a new licensee, the records required to be kept by this chapter shall appropriately reflect such facts and shall be delivered to the successor. Where discontinuance of the business is absolute, such records shall be delivered within thirty days after the business discontinuance to the Secretary. However, where State law or local ordinance requires the delivery of records to other responsible authority, the Secretary may arrange for the delivery of such records to such other responsible authority.

"(5)(A) Each licensee shall, when required by letter issued by the Secretary, and until notified to the contrary in writing by the Secretary, submit on a form specified by the Secretary, for periods and at the times specified in such letter, all record information required to be kept by this chapter or such lesser record information as the Secretary in such letter may specify.

"(B) The Secretary may authorize such record information to be submitted in a manner other than that prescribed in subparagraph (A) of this paragraph when it is shown by a licensee that an alternate method of reporting is reasonably necessary and will not unduly hinder the effective administration of this chapter. A licensee may use an alternate method of reporting if the licensee describes the proposed alternate method of reporting and the need therefor in a letter application submitted to the Secretary, and the Secretary approves such alternate method of reporting."; and

(8) so that subsection (j) reads as follows:

"(j) A licensed importer, licensed manufacturer, or licensed dealer may, under rules or regulations prescribed by the Secretary, conduct business temporarily at a location other than the location specified on the license if such temporary location is the location for a gun show or event sponsored by any national, State, or local organization, or any affiliate of any such organization devoted to the collec-

Commerce and trade.

100 STAT. 455

47

Records.

tion, competitive use, or other sporting use of firearms in the community, and such location is in the State which is specified on the license. Records of receipt and disposition of firearms transactions conducted at such temporary location shall include the location of the sale or other disposition and shall be entered in the permanent records of the licensee and retained on the location specified on the license. Nothing in this subsection shall authorize any licensee to conduct business in or from any motorized or towed vehicle. Notwithstanding the provisions of subsection (a) of this section, a separate fee shall not be required of a licensee with respect to business conducted under this subsection. Any inspection or examination of inventory or records under this chapter by the Secretary at such temporary location shall be limited to inventory consisting of, or records relating to, firearms held or disposed at such temporary location. Nothing in this subsection shall be construed to authorize the Secretary to inspect or examine the inventory or records of a licensed importer, licensed manufacturer, or licensed dealer at any location other than the location specified on the license. Nothing in this subsection shall be construed to diminish in any manner any right to display, sell, or otherwise dispose of firearms or ammunition, which is in effect before the date of the enactment of the Firearms Owners' Protection Act.".

Crimes and misdemeanors. Law enforcement.

SEC. 104. AMENDMENTS TO SECTION 924.

(a) IN GENERAL.—Section 924 of title 18, United States Code, is amended—

(1) so that subsection (a) reads as follows:

18 USC 929.

"(a)(1) Except as otherwise provided in paragraph (2) of this subsection, subsection (b) or (c) of this section, or in section 929, whoever—

"(A) knowingly makes any false statement or representation with respect to the information required by this chapter to be kept in the records of a person licensed under this chapter or in applying for any license or exemption or relief from disability under the provisions of this chapter;

18 USC 922.

"(B) knowingly violates subsection (a)(4), (a)(6), (f), (g), (i), (j), or (k) of section 922;

"(C) knowingly imports or brings into the United States or any possession thereof any firearm or ammunition in violation of section 922(l); or

"(D) willfully violates any other provision of this chapter, shall be fined not more than $5,000, imprisoned not more than five years, or both, and shall become eligible for parole as the Parole Commission shall determine.

"(2) Any licensed dealer, licensed importer, licensed manufacturer, or licensed collector who knowingly—

"(A) makes any false statement or representation with respect to the information required by the provisions of this chapter to be kept in the records of a person licensed under this chapter, or

"(B) violates subsection (m) of section 922,

shall be fined not more than $1,000, imprisoned not more than one year, or both, and shall become eligible for parole as the Parole Commission shall determine.";

(2) in subsection (c)—

(A) by inserting "(1)" before "Whoever,";

100 STAT. 456

(B) by striking out "violence" each place it appears and inserting in lieu thereof "violence or drug trafficking crime,";

(C) by inserting "or drug trafficking crime" before "in which the firearm was used or carried.";

(D) in the first sentence, by striking out the period at the end and inserting in lieu thereof ", and if the firearm is a machinegun, or is equipped with a firearm silencer or firearm muffler, to imprisonment for ten years.";

(E) in the second sentence, by striking out the period at the end and inserting in lieu thereof ", and if the firearm is a machinegun, or is equipped with a firearm silencer or firearm muffler, to. imprisonment for twenty years."; and

(F) by adding at the end the following:

"(2) For purposes of this subsection, the term 'drug trafficking crime' means any felony violation of Federal law involving the distribution, manufacture, or importation of any controlled substance (as defined in section 102 of the Controlled Substances Act (21 U.S.C. 802)).

"(3) For purposes of this subsection the term 'crime of violence' means an offense that is a felony and—

"(A) has as an element the use, attempted use, or threatened use of physical force against the person or property of another, or

"(B) that by its nature, involves a substantial risk that physical force against the person or property of another may be used in the course of committing the offense.";

(3) by amending subsection (d) to read as follows:

"(d)(1) Any firearm or ammunition involved in or used in any knowing violation of subsection (a)(4), (a)(6), (f), (g), (h), (i), (j), or (k) of section 922, or knowing importation or bringing into the United States or any possession thereof any firearm or ammunition in violation of section 922(l), or knowing violation of section 924, or willful violation of any other provision of this chapter or any rule or regulation promulgated thereunder, or any violation of any other criminal law of the United States, or any firearm or ammunition intended to be used in any offense referred to in paragraph (3) of this subsection, where such intent is demonstrated by clear and convincing evidence, shall be subject to seizure and forfeiture, and all provisions of the Internal Revenue Code of 1954 relating to the seizure, forfeiture, and disposition of firearms, as defined in section 5845(a) of that Code, shall, so far as applicable, extend to seizures and forfeitures under the provisions of this chapter: *Provided,* That upon acquittal of the owner or possessor, or dismissal of the charges against him other than upon motion of the Government prior to trial, the seized firearms or ammunition shall be returned forthwith to the owner or possessor or to a person delegated by the owner or possessor unless the return of the firearms or ammunition would place the owner or possessor or his delegate in violation of law. Any action or proceeding for the forfeiture of firearms or ammunition shall be commenced within one hundred and twenty days of such seizure.

"(2)(A) In any action or proceeding for the return of firearms or ammunition seized under the provisions of this chapter, the court shall allow the prevailing party, other than the United States, a reasonable attorney's fee, and the United States shall be liable therefor.

Imports.

18 USC 922.

26 USC 1 *et seq.*

26 USC 5845.

100 STAT. 457

49

"(B) In any other action or proceeding under the provisions of this chapter, the court, when it finds that such action was without foundation, or was initiated vexatiously, frivolously, or in bad faith, shall allow the prevailing party, other than the United States, a reasonable attorney's fee, and the United States shall be liable therefor.

"(C) Only those firearms or quantities of ammunition particularly named and individually identified as involved in or used in any violation of the provisions of this chapter or any rule or regulation issued thereunder, or any other criminal law of the United States or as intended to be used in any offense referred to in paragraph (3) of this subsection, where such intent is demonstrated by clear and convincing evidence, shall be subject to seizure, forfeiture, and disposition.

"(D) The United States shall be liable for attorneys' fees under this paragraph only to the extent provided in advance by appropriation Acts.

"(3) The offenses referred to in paragraphs (1) and (2)(C) of this subsection are—

18 USC 924.

"(A) any crime of violence, as that term is defined in section 924(c)(3) of this title;

"(B) any offense punishable under the Controlled Substances Act (21 U.S.C. 801 et seq.) or the Controlled Substances Import and Export Act (21 U.S.C. 951 et seq.);

18 USC 922.

"(C) any offense described in section 922(a)(1), 922(a)(3), 922(a)(5), or 922(b)(3) of this title, where the firearm or ammunition intended to be used in any such offense is involved in a pattern of activities which includes a violation of any offense described in section 922(a)(1), 922(a)(3), 922(a)(5), or 922(b)(3) of this title;

"(D) any offense described in section 922(d) of this title where the firearm or ammunition is intended to be used in such offense by the transferor of such firearm or ammunition;

"(E) any offense described in section 922(i), 922(j), 922(l), 922(n), or 924(b) of this title; and

"(F) any offense which may be prosecuted in a court of the United States which involves the exportation of firearms or ammunition."; and

(4) by adding at the end the following new subsection:

"(e)(1) In the case of a person who violates section 922(g) of this title and has three previous convictions by any court referred to in section 922(g)(1) of this title for robbery or burglary, or both, such person shall be fined not more than $25,000 and imprisoned not less than fifteen years, and, notwithstanding any other provision of law, the court shall not suspend the sentence of, or grant a probationary sentence to, such person with respect to the conviction under section 922(g), and such person shall not be eligible for parole with respect to the sentence imposed under this subsection.

"(2) As used in this subsection—

"(A) the term 'robbery' means any crime punishable by a term of imprisonment exceeding one year and consisting of the taking of the property of another from the person or presence of another by force or violence, or by threatening or placing another person in fear that any person will imminently be subjected to bodily harm; and

"(B) the term 'burglary' means any crime punishable by a term of imprisonment exceeding one year and consisting of

100 STAT. 458

entering or remaining surreptitiously within a building that is the property of another with intent to engage in conduct constituting a Federal or State offense.".

(b) CONFORMING REPEAL.—Title VII of the Omnibus Crime Control and Safe Streets Act of 1968 (18 U.S.C. App. 1201 et seq.) is repealed.

SEC. 105. AMENDMENTS TO SECTION 925.

Section 925 of title 18, United States Code, is amended—

(1) in subsection (c)—

(A) by striking out "has been convicted of a crime punishable by imprisonment for a term exceeding one year (other than a crime involving the use of a firearm or other weapon or a violation of this chapter or of the National Firearms Act)" and inserting in lieu thereof "is prohibited from possessing, shipping, transporting, or receiving firearms or ammunition"; 26 USC 5801.

(B) by inserting "transportation," after "shipment,";

(C) by striking out "and incurred by reason of such conviction"; and

(D) by inserting "Any person whose application for relief from disabilities is denied by the Secretary may file a petition with the United States district court for the district in which he resides for a judicial review of such denial. The court may in its discretion admit additional evidence where failure to do so would result in a miscarriage of justice." after "the public interest."; and

(2) in subsection (d)—

(A) by striking out "may authorize" and inserting in lieu thereof "shall authorize";

(B) by striking out "the person importing or bringing in the firearm or ammunition establishes to the satisfaction of the Secretary that";

(C) in paragraph (3), by inserting before the semicolon ", except in any case where the Secretary has not authorized the importation of the firearm pursuant to this paragraph, it shall be unlawful to import any frame, receiver, or barrel of such firearm which would be prohibited if assembled"; and

(D) by striking out "may permit" and inserting in lieu thereof "shall permit".

SEC. 106. AMENDMENTS TO SECTION 926.

Section 926 of title 18 of the United States Code is amended—

(1) by inserting "(a)" before "The Secretary" the first place it occurs;

(2) by inserting "only" after "prescribe";

(3) by striking out "as he deems reasonably" and inserting in lieu thereof "as are";

(4) by striking out the last sentence and inserting in lieu thereof "No such rule or regulation prescribed after the date of the enactment of the Firearms Owners' Protection Act may require that records required to be maintained under this chapter or any portion of the contents of such records, be recorded at or transferred to a facility owned, managed, or controlled by the United States or any State or any political subdivision thereof, nor that any system of registration of firearms, firearms owners, or firearms transactions or dispositions be established.

100 STAT. 459

Nothing in this section expands or restricts the Secretary's authority to inquire into the disposition of any firearm in the course of a criminal investigation."; and

(5) by adding at the end the following:

"(b) The Secretary shall give not less than ninety days public notice, and shall afford interested parties opportunity for hearing, before prescribing such rules and regulations.

18 USC 845.

"(c) The Secretary shall not prescribe rules or regulations that require purchasers of black powder under the exemption provided in section 845(a)(5) of this title to complete affidavits or forms attesting to that exemption.".

SEC. 107. TRANSPORTATION OF FIREARMS.

(a) IN GENERAL.—Chapter 44 of title 18, United States Code, is amended by inserting between section 926 and section 927 the following new section:

18 USC 926A.

"§ 926A. Interstate transportation of firearms

"Any person not prohibited by this chapter from transporting, shipping, or receiving a firearm shall be entitled to transport an unloaded, not readily accessible firearm in interstate commerce notwithstanding any provision of any legislation enacted, or any rule or regulation prescribed by any State or political subdivision thereof.".

(b) CLERICAL AMENDMENT.—The table of sections for chapter 44 of title 18, United States Code, is amended by inserting between the item relating to section 926 and the item relating to section 927 the following new item:

"926A. Interstate transportation of firearms.".

SEC. 108. AMENDMENTS TO SECTION 929.

Section 929(a) of title 18, United States Code, is amended—

(1) by inserting "(1)" before "Whoever,";

(2) by striking out "violence" each place it appears and inserting in lieu thereof "violence or drug trafficking crime,"; and

(3) by adding at the end the following:

"(2) For purposes of this subsection, the term 'drug trafficking crime' means any felony violation of Federal law involving the distribution, manufacture, or importation of any controlled substance (as defined in section 102 of the Controlled Substances Act (21 U.S.C. 802)).".

SEC. 109. AMENDMENT OF NATIONAL FIREARMS ACT.

(a) Section 5845(b) of the National Firearms Act (26 U.S.C. 5845(b)) is amended by striking out "any combination of parts designed and intended for use in converting a weapon into a machinegun," and inserting in lieu thereof "any part designed and intended solely and exclusively, or combination of parts designed and intended, for use in converting a weapon into a machinegun,".

(b) CONFORMING AMENDMENT.—Section 5845(a)(7) of the National Firearms Act (26 U.S.C. 5845(a)(7)) is amended to read "(7) any silencer (as defined in section 921 of title 18, United States Code);".

18 USC 921 note.

SEC. 110. EFFECTIVE DATE.

(a) IN GENERAL.—The amendments made by this Act shall become effective one hundred and eighty days after the date of the enactment of this Act. Upon their becoming effective, the Secretary shall

100 STAT. 460

publish and provide to all licensees a compilation of the State laws and published ordinances of which licensees are presumed to have knowledge pursuant to chapter 44 of title 18, United States Code, as amended by this Act. All amendments to such State laws and published ordinances as contained in the aforementioned compilation shall be published in the Federal Register, revised annually, and furnished to each person licensed under chapter 44 of title 18, United States Code, as amended by this Act.

18 USC 921 *et seq.*

Federal Register, publication.

(b) PENDING ACTIONS, PETITIONS, AND APPELLATE PROCEEDINGS.— The amendments made by sections 103(6)(B), 105, and 107 of this Act shall be applicable to any action, petition, or appellate proceeding pending on the date of the enactment of this Act.

(c) MACHINEGUN PROHIBITION.—Section 102(9) shall take effect on the date of the enactment of this Act.

Approved May 19, 1986.

LEGISLATIVE HISTORY—S. 49 (H.R. 4332):

HOUSE REPORT No. 99–495 accompanying H.R. 4332 (Comm. on the Judiciary).
CONGRESSIONAL RECORD:
    Vol. 131 (1985): June 24, July 9, considered and passed Senate.
    Vol. 132 (1986): Apr. 9, 10, H.R. 4332 considered and passed House; S. 49,
        amended, passed in lieu.
    May 6, Senate concurred in House amendments.

Public Law 103-159
103rd Congress
H.R. 1025

An Act

To provide for a waiting period before the purchase of a handgun, and for the establishment of a national instant criminal background check system to be contacted by firearms dealers before the transfer of any firearm.

Be it enacted by the Senate and House of Representatives of the United States of America in Congress assembled,

TITLE I—BRADY HANDGUN CONTROL

SEC. 101. SHORT TITLE.

This title may be cited as the "Brady Handgun Violence Prevention Act".

SEC. 102. FEDERAL FIREARMS LICENSEE REQUIRED TO CONDUCT CRIMINAL BACKGROUND CHECK BEFORE TRANSFER OF FIREARM TO NON-LICENSEE.

(a) INTERIM PROVISION.—

(1) IN GENERAL.—Section 922 of title 18, United States Code, is amended by adding at the end the following:

"(s)(1) Beginning on the date that is 90 days after the date of enactment of this subsection and ending on the day before the date that is 60 months after such date of enactment, it shall be unlawful for any licensed importer, licensed manufacturer, or licensed dealer to sell, deliver, or transfer a handgun to an individual who is not licensed under section 923, unless—

"(A) after the most recent proposal of such transfer by the transferee—

"(i) the transferor has—

"(I) received from the transferee a statement of the transferee containing the information described in paragraph (3);

"(II) verified the identity of the transferee by examining the identification document presented;

"(III) within 1 day after the transferee furnishes the statement, provided notice of the contents of the statement to the chief law enforcement officer of the place of residence of the transferee; and

"(IV) within 1 day after the transferee furnishes the statement, transmitted a copy of the statement

4814   *54*

to the chief law enforcement officer of the place of residence of the transferee; and

"(ii)(I) 5 business days (meaning days on which State offices are open) have elapsed from the date the transferor furnished notice of the contents of the statement to the chief law enforcement officer, during which period the transferor has not received information from the chief law enforcement officer that receipt or possession of the handgun by the transferee would be in violation of Federal, State, or local law; or

"(II) the transferor has received notice from the chief law enforcement officer that the officer has no information indicating that receipt or possession of the handgun by the transferee would violate Federal, State, or local law;

"(B) the transferee has presented to the transferor a written statement, issued by the chief law enforcement officer of the place of residence of the transferee during the 10-day period ending on the date of the most recent proposal of such transfer by the transferee, stating that the transferee requires access to a handgun because of a threat to the life of the transferee or of any member of the household of the transferee;

"(C)(i) the transferee has presented to the transferor a permit that—

"(I) allows the transferee to possess or acquire a handgun; and

"(II) was issued not more than 5 years earlier by the State in which the transfer is to take place; and

"(ii) the law of the State provides that such a permit is to be issued only after an authorized government official has verified that the information available to such official does not indicate that possession of a handgun by the transferee would be in violation of the law;

"(D) the law of the State requires that, before any licensed importer, licensed manufacturer, or licensed dealer completes the transfer of a handgun to an individual who is not licensed under section 923, an authorized government official verify that the information available to such official does not indicate that possession of a handgun by the transferee would be in violation of law;

"(E) the Secretary has approved the transfer under section 5812 of the Internal Revenue Code of 1986; or

"(F) on application of the transferor, the Secretary has certified that compliance with subparagraph (A)(i)(III) is impracticable because—

"(i) the ratio of the number of law enforcement officers of the State in which the transfer is to occur to the number of square miles of land area of the State does not exceed 0.0025;

"(ii) the business premises of the transferor at which the transfer is to occur are extremely remote in relation to the chief law enforcement officer; and

"(iii) there is an absence of telecommunications facilities in the geographical area in which the business premises are located.

"(2) A chief law enforcement officer to whom a transferor has provided notice pursuant to paragraph (1)(A)(i)(III) shall make a reasonable effort to ascertain within 5 business days whether receipt or possession would be in violation of the law, including research in whatever State and local recordkeeping systems are available and in a national system designated by the Attorney General.

"(3) The statement referred to in paragraph (1)(A)(i)(I) shall contain only—

"(A) the name, address, and date of birth appearing on a valid identification document (as defined in section 1028(d)(1)) of the transferee containing a photograph of the transferee and a description of the identification used;

"(B) a statement that the transferee—

"(i) is not under indictment for, and has not been convicted in any court of, a crime punishable by imprisonment for a term exceeding 1 year;

"(ii) is not a fugitive from justice;

"(iii) is not an unlawful user of or addicted to any controlled substance (as defined in section 102 of the Controlled Substances Act);

"(iv) has not been adjudicated as a mental defective or been committed to a mental institution;

"(v) is not an alien who is illegally or unlawfully in the United States;

"(vi) has not been discharged from the Armed Forces under dishonorable conditions; and

"(vii) is not a person who, having been a citizen of the United States, has renounced such citizenship;

"(C) the date the statement is made; and

"(D) notice that the transferee intends to obtain a handgun from the transferor.

"(4) Any transferor of a handgun who, after such transfer, receives a report from a chief law enforcement officer containing information that receipt or possession of the handgun by the transferee violates Federal, State, or local law shall, within 1 business day after receipt of such request, communicate any information related to the transfer that the transferor has about the transfer and the transferee to—

"(A) the chief law enforcement officer of the place of business of the transferor; and

"(B) the chief law enforcement officer of the place of residence of the transferee.

"(5) Any transferor who receives information, not otherwise available to the public, in a report under this subsection shall not disclose such information except to the transferee, to law enforcement authorities, or pursuant to the direction of a court of law.

"(6)(A) Any transferor who sells, delivers, or otherwise transfers a handgun to a transferee shall retain the copy of the statement of the transferee with respect to the handgun transaction, and shall retain evidence that the transferor has complied with subclauses (III) and (IV) of paragraph (1)(A)(i) with respect to the statement.

"(B) Unless the chief law enforcement officer to whom a statement is transmitted under paragraph (1)(A)(i)(IV) determines that a transaction would violate Federal, State, or local law—

"(i) the officer shall, within 20 business days after the date the transferee made the statement on the basis of which the notice was provided, destroy the statement, any record

containing information derived from the statement, and any
record created as a result of the notice required by paragraph
(1)(A)(i)(III);

"(ii) the information contained in the statement shall not
be conveyed to any person except a person who has a need
to know in order to carry out this subsection; and

"(iii) the information contained in the statement shall not
be used for any purpose other than to carry out this subsection.

"(C) If a chief law enforcement officer determines that an
individual is ineligible to receive a handgun and the individual
requests the officer to provide the reason for such determination,
the officer shall provide such reasons to the individual in writing
within 20 business days after receipt of the request.

"(7) A chief law enforcement officer or other person responsible
for providing criminal history background information pursuant
to this subsection shall not be liable in an action at law for
damages—

"(A) for failure to prevent the sale or transfer of a handgun
to a person whose receipt or possession of the handgun is
unlawful under this section; or

"(B) for preventing such a sale or transfer to a person
who may lawfully receive or possess a handgun.

"(8) For purposes of this subsection, the term 'chief law enforcement officer' means the chief of police, the sheriff, or an equivalent
officer or the designee of any such individual.

"(9) The Secretary shall take necessary actions to ensure that
the provisions of this subsection are published and disseminated
to licensed dealers, law enforcement officials, and the public.".

(2) HANDGUN DEFINED.—Section 921(a) of title 18, United
States Code, is amended by adding at the end the following:
"(29) The term 'handgun' means—

"(A) a firearm which has a short stock and is designed
to be held and fired by the use of a single hand; and

"(B) any combination of parts from which a firearm
described in subparagraph (A) can be assembled.".

(b) PERMANENT PROVISION.—Section 922 of title 18, United
States Code, as amended by subsection (a)(1), is amended by adding
at the end the following:

"(t)(1) Beginning on the date that is 30 days after the Attorney
General notifies licensees under section 103(d) of the Brady Handgun Violence Prevention Act that the national instant criminal
background check system is established, a licensed importer,
licensed manufacturer, or licensed dealer shall not transfer a firearm to any other person who is not licensed under this chapter,
unless—

"(A) before the completion of the transfer, the licensee
contacts the national instant criminal background check system
established under section 103 of that Act;

"(B)(i) the system provides the licensee with a unique
identification number; or

"(ii) 3 business days (meaning a day on which State offices
are open) have elapsed since the licensee contacted the system,
and the system has not notified the licensee that the receipt
of a firearm by such other person would violate subsection
(g) or (n) of this section; and

"(C) the transferor has verified the identity of the transferee
by examining a valid identification document (as defined in

section 1028(d)(1) of this title) of the transferee containing a photograph of the transferee.

"(2) If receipt of a firearm would not violate section 922 (g) or (n) or State law, the system shall—

"(A) assign a unique identification number to the transfer;

"(B) provide the licensee with the number; and

"(C) destroy all records of the system with respect to the call (other than the identifying number and the date the number was assigned) and all records of the system relating to the person or the transfer.

"(3) Paragraph (1) shall not apply to a firearm transfer between a licensee and another person if—

"(A)(i) such other person has presented to the licensee a permit that—

"(I) allows such other person to possess or acquire a firearm; and

"(II) was issued not more than 5 years earlier by the State in which the transfer is to take place; and

"(ii) the law of the State provides that such a permit is to be issued only after an authorized government official has verified that the information available to such official does not indicate that possession of a firearm by such other person would be in violation of law;

"(B) the Secretary has approved the transfer under section 5812 of the Internal Revenue Code of 1986; or

"(C) on application of the transferor, the Secretary has certified that compliance with paragraph (1)(A) is impracticable because—

"(i) the ratio of the number of law enforcement officers of the State in which the transfer is to occur to the number of square miles of land area of the State does not exceed 0.0025;

"(ii) the business premises of the licensee at which the transfer is to occur are extremely remote in relation to the chief law enforcement officer (as defined in subsection (s)(8)); and

"(iii) there is an absence of telecommunications facilities in the geographical area in which the business premises are located.

"(4) If the national instant criminal background check system notifies the licensee that the information available to the system does not demonstrate that the receipt of a firearm by such other person would violate subsection (g) or (n) or State law, and the licensee transfers a firearm to such other person, the licensee shall include in the record of the transfer the unique identification number provided by the system with respect to the transfer.

"(5) If the licensee knowingly transfers a firearm to such other person and knowingly fails to comply with paragraph (1) of this subsection with respect to the transfer and, at the time such other person most recently proposed the transfer, the national instant criminal background check system was operating and information was available to the system demonstrating that receipt of a firearm by such other person would violate subsection (g) or (n) of this section or State law, the Secretary may, after notice and opportunity for a hearing, suspend for not more than 6 months or revoke any license issued to the licensee under section 923, and may impose on the licensee a civil fine of not more than $5,000.

"(6) Neither a local government nor an employee of the Federal Government or of any State or local government, responsible for providing information to the national instant criminal background check system shall be liable in an action at law for damages—

"(A) for failure to prevent the sale or transfer of a firearm to a person whose receipt or possession of the firearm is unlawful under this section; or

"(B) for preventing such a sale or transfer to a person who may lawfully receive or possess a firearm.".

(c) PENALTY.—Section 924(a) of title 18, United States Code, is amended—

(1) in paragraph (1), by striking "paragraph (2) or (3) of"; and

(2) by adding at the end the following:

"(5) Whoever knowingly violates subsection (s) or (t) of section 922 shall be fined not more than $1,000, imprisoned for not more than 1 year, or both.".

SEC. 103. NATIONAL INSTANT CRIMINAL BACKGROUND CHECK SYSTEM.

(a) DETERMINATION OF TIMETABLES.—Not later than 6 months after the date of enactment of this Act, the Attorney General shall—

(1) determine the type of computer hardware and software that will be used to operate the national instant criminal background check system and the means by which State criminal records systems and the telephone or electronic device of licensees will communicate with the national system;

(2) investigate the criminal records system of each State and determine for each State a timetable by which the State should be able to provide criminal records on an on-line capacity basis to the national system; and

(3) notify each State of the determinations made pursuant to paragraphs (1) and (2).

(b) ESTABLISHMENT OF SYSTEM.—Not later than 60 months after the date of the enactment of this Act, the Attorney General shall establish a national instant criminal background check system that any licensee may contact, by telephone or by other electronic means in addition to the telephone, for information, to be supplied immediately, on whether receipt of a firearm by a prospective transferee would violate section 922 of title 18, United States Code, or State law.

(c) EXPEDITED ACTION BY THE ATTORNEY GENERAL.—The Attorney General shall expedite—

(1) the upgrading and indexing of State criminal history records in the Federal criminal records system maintained by the Federal Bureau of Investigation;

(2) the development of hardware and software systems to link State criminal history check systems into the national instant criminal background check system established by the Attorney General pursuant to this section; and

(3) the current revitalization initiatives by the Federal Bureau of Investigation for technologically advanced fingerprint and criminal records identification.

(d) NOTIFICATION OF LICENSEES.—On establishment of the system under this section, the Attorney General shall notify each licensee and the chief law enforcement officer of each State of the existence and purpose of the system and the means to be used to contact the system.

(e) ADMINISTRATIVE PROVISIONS.—

(1) AUTHORITY TO OBTAIN OFFICIAL INFORMATION.—Notwithstanding any other law, the Attorney General may secure directly from any department or agency of the United States such information on persons for whom receipt of a firearm would violate subsection (g) or (n) of section 922 of title 18, United States Code or State law, as is necessary to enable the system to operate in accordance with this section. On request of the Attorney General, the head of such department or agency shall furnish such information to the system.

(2) OTHER AUTHORITY.—The Attorney General shall develop such computer software, design and obtain such telecommunications and computer hardware, and employ such personnel, as are necessary to establish and operate the system in accordance with this section.

(f) WRITTEN REASONS PROVIDED ON REQUEST.—If the national instant criminal background check system determines that an individual is ineligible to receive a firearm and the individual requests the system to provide the reasons for the determination, the system shall provide such reasons to the individual, in writing, within 5 business days after the date of the request.

(g) CORRECTION OF ERRONEOUS SYSTEM INFORMATION.—If the system established under this section informs an individual contacting the system that receipt of a firearm by a prospective transferee would violate subsection (g) or (n) of section 922 of title 18, United States Code or State law, the prospective transferee may request the Attorney General to provide the prospective transferee with the reasons therefor. Upon receipt of such a request, the Attorney General shall immediately comply with the request. The prospective transferee may submit to the Attorney General information to correct, clarify, or supplement records of the system with respect to the prospective transferee. After receipt of such information, the Attorney General shall immediately consider the information, investigate the matter further, and correct all erroneous Federal records relating to the prospective transferee and give notice of the error to any Federal department or agency or any State that was the source of such erroneous records.

(h) REGULATIONS.—After 90 days' notice to the public and an opportunity for hearing by interested parties, the Attorney General shall prescribe regulations to ensure the privacy and security of the information of the system established under this section.

(i) PROHIBITION RELATING TO ESTABLISHMENT OF REGISTRATION SYSTEMS WITH RESPECT TO FIREARMS.—No department, agency, officer, or employee of the United States may—

(1) require that any record or portion thereof generated by the system established under this section be recorded at or transferred to a facility owned, managed, or controlled by the United States or any State or political subdivision thereof; or

(2) use the system established under this section to establish any system for the registration of firearms, firearm owners, or firearm transactions or dispositions, except with respect to persons, prohibited by section 922 (g) or (n) of title 18, United States Code or State law, from receiving a firearm.

(j) DEFINITIONS.—As used in this section:

(1) LICENSEE.—The term "licensee" means a licensed importer (as defined in section 921(a)(9) of title 18, United States Code), a licensed manufacturer (as defined in section 921(a)(10) of that title), or a licensed dealer (as defined in section 921(a)(11) of that title).

(2) OTHER TERMS.—The terms "firearm", "handgun", "licensed importer", "licensed manufacturer", and "licensed dealer" have the meanings stated in section 921(a) of title 18, United States Code, as amended by subsection (a)(2).

(k) AUTHORIZATION OF APPROPRIATIONS.—There are authorized to be appropriated, which may be appropriated from the Violent Crime Reduction Trust Fund established by section 1115 of title 31, United States Code, such sums as are necessary to enable the Attorney General to carry out this section.

SEC. 104. REMEDY FOR ERRONEOUS DENIAL OF FIREARM.

(a) IN GENERAL.—Chapter 44 of title 18, United States Code, is amended by inserting after section 925 the following new section:

"§ 925A. Remedy for erroneous denial of firearm

"Any person denied a firearm pursuant to subsection (s) or (t) of section 922—

"(1) due to the provision of erroneous information relating to the person by any State or political subdivision thereof, or by the national instant criminal background check system established under section 103 of the Brady Handgun Violence Prevention Act; or

"(2) who was not prohibited from receipt of a firearm pursuant to subsection (g) or (n) of section 922,

may bring an action against the State or political subdivision responsible for providing the erroneous information, or responsible for denying the transfer, or against the United States, as the case may be, for an order directing that the erroneous information be corrected or that the transfer be approved, as the case may be. In any action under this section, the court, in its discretion, may allow the prevailing party a reasonable attorney's fee as part of the costs.".

(b) TECHNICAL AMENDMENT.—The chapter analysis for chapter 44 of title 18, United States Code, is amended by inserting after the item relating to section 925 the following new item:

"925A. Remedy for erroneous denial of firearm.".

SEC. 105. RULE OF CONSTRUCTION.

This Act and the amendments made by this Act shall not be construed to alter or impair any right or remedy under section 552a of title 5, United States Code.

SEC. 106. FUNDING FOR IMPROVEMENT OF CRIMINAL RECORDS.

(a) USE OF FORMULA GRANTS.—Section 509(b) of title I of the Omnibus Crime Control and Safe Streets Act of 1968 (42 U.S.C. 3759(b)) is amended—

(1) in paragraph (2) by striking "and" after the semicolon;

(2) in paragraph (3) by striking the period and inserting "; and"; and

(3) by adding at the end the following new paragraph:

"(4) the improvement of State record systems and the sharing with the Attorney General of all of the records described in paragraphs (1), (2), and (3) of this subsection and the records

4821

required by the Attorney General under section 103 of the Brady Handgun Violence Prevention Act, for the purpose of implementing that Act.".

(b) ADDITIONAL FUNDING.—

(1) GRANTS FOR THE IMPROVEMENT OF CRIMINAL RECORDS.— The Attorney General, through the Bureau of Justice Statistics, shall, subject to appropriations and with preference to States that as of the date of enactment of this Act have the lowest percent currency of case dispositions in computerized criminal history files, make a grant to each State to be used—

(A) for the creation of a computerized criminal history record system or improvement of an existing system;

(B) to improve accessibility to the national instant criminal background system; and

(C) upon establishment of the national system, to assist the State in the transmittal of criminal records to the national system.

(2) AUTHORIZATION OF APPROPRIATIONS.—There are authorized to be appropriated for grants under paragraph (1), which may be appropriated from the Violent Crime Reduction Trust Fund established by section 1115 of title 31, United States Code, a total of $200,000,000 for fiscal year 1994 and all fiscal years thereafter.

TITLE II—MULTIPLE FIREARM PURCHASES TO STATE AND LOCAL POLICE

SEC. 201. REPORTING REQUIREMENT.

Section 923(g)(3) of title 18, United States Code, is amended—

(1) in the second sentence by inserting after "thereon," the following: "and to the department of State police or State law enforcement agency of the State or local law enforcement agency of the local jurisdiction in which the sale or other disposition took place,";

(2) by inserting "(A)" after "(3)"; and

(3) by adding at the end thereof the following:

"(B) Except in the case of forms and contents thereof regarding a purchaser who is prohibited by subsection (g) or (n) of section 922 of this title from receipt of a firearm, the department of State police or State law enforcement agency or local law enforcement agency of the local jurisdiction shall not disclose any such form or the contents thereof to any person or entity, and shall destroy each such form and any record of the contents thereof no more than 20 days from the date such form is received. No later than the date that is 6 months after the effective date of this subparagraph, and at the end of each 6-month period thereafter, the department of State police or State law enforcement agency or local law enforcement agency of the local jurisdiction shall certify to the Attorney General of the United States that no disclosure contrary to this subparagraph has been made and that all forms and any record of the contents thereof have been destroyed as provided in this subparagraph.".

TITLE III—FEDERAL FIREARMS LICENSE REFORM

SEC. 301. SHORT TITLE.

This title may be cited as the "Federal Firearms License Reform Act of 1993".

SEC. 302. PREVENTION OF THEFT OF FIREARMS.

(a) COMMON CARRIERS.—Section 922(e) of title 18, United States Code, is amended by adding at the end the following: "No common or contract carrier shall require or cause any label, tag, or other written notice to be placed on the outside of any package, luggage, or other container that such package, luggage, or other container contains a firearm.".

(b) RECEIPT REQUIREMENT.—Section 922(f) of title 18, United States Code, is amended—

(1) by inserting "(1)" after "(f)"; and

(2) by adding at the end the following new paragraph:

"(2) It shall be unlawful for any common or contract carrier to deliver in interstate or foreign commerce any firearm without obtaining written acknowledgement of receipt from the recipient of the package or other container in which there is a firearm.".

(c) UNLAWFUL ACTS.—Section 922 of title 18, United States Code, as amended by section 102, is amended by adding at the end the following new subsection:

"(u) It shall be unlawful for a person to steal or unlawfully take or carry away from the person or the premises of a person who is licensed to engage in the business of importing, manufacturing, or dealing in firearms, any firearm in the licensee's business inventory that has been shipped or transported in interstate or foreign commerce.".

(d) PENALTIES.—Section 924 of title 18, United States Code, is amended by adding at the end the following new subsection:

"(i)(1) A person who knowingly violates section 922(u) shall be fined not more than $10,000, imprisoned not more than 10 years, or both.

"(2) Nothing contained in this subsection shall be construed as indicating an intent on the part of Congress to occupy the field in which provisions of this subsection operate to the exclusion of State laws on the same subject matter, nor shall any provision of this subsection be construed as invalidating any provision of State law unless such provision is inconsistent with any of the purposes of this subsection.".

SEC. 303. LICENSE APPLICATION FEES FOR DEALERS IN FIREARMS.

Section 923(a)(3) of title 18, United States Code, is amended—

(1) in subparagraph (A), by adding "or" at the end;

(2) in subparagraph (B) by striking "a pawnbroker dealing in firearms other than" and inserting "not a dealer in";

(3) in subparagraph (B) by striking "$25 per year; or" and inserting "$200 for 3 years, except that the fee for renewal of a valid license shall be $90 for 3 years."; and

(4) by striking subparagraph (C).

HANDGUN PROHIBITION AND THE ORIGINAL MEANING OF THE SECOND AMENDMENT

Don B. Kates, Jr. *

INTRODUCTION

Federal or state handgun prohibition legislation[1] is often suggested as one way to reduce the incidence of homicide and other violent crime in the United States.[2] Whatever the criminological merits of this suggestion,[3] constitutionally speaking it raises a diverse set of issues. Among those which this Article will not cover in any depth are:

---

* LL.B. 1966, Yale Law School. Member of the California, District of Columbia, Missouri and United States Supreme Court Bars. Partner, Benenson, Kates and Hardy (San Francisco office). Of counsel, O'Brien & Hallisey, San Francisco, California. Mr. Kates authored one of the petitions for certiorari in *Quilici v. City of Morton Grove*. — Ed.

The author wishes to thank the following for their assistance: Professors William Van Alstyne (Law, Duke University Law School), Roy Wortman (History, Kenyon College), and Stephen Halbrook (Philosophy, George Mason University); Dr. Joyce Malcolm (Law Fellow, Harvard Law School), Dr. David I. Caplan, Mr. Willis Hannawalt (Pillsbury, Madison and Sutro, San Francisco), and Mr. David Hardy (Office of the Solicitor, U.S. Interior Department, Washington, D.C.). Of course, the responsibility for any errors of fact or interpretation is the author's alone.

1. Such legislation could, for example, take the form of a restrictive permit requirement designed and administered to exclude more than 99% of the civilian population from handgun ownership. On the constitutionality of restrictive permit systems, see notes 253-54 *infra* and accompanying text.

2. *See* J. ALVIANI & W. DRAKE, HANDGUN CONTROL: ISSUES AND ALTERNATIVES 48-54 (U.S. Conference of Mayors, 1975) (quoting resolutions to that effect from: The Board of Church and Society, United Methodist Church, Common Cause, National Alliance for Safer Cities, Union of America Hebrew Congregations and Unitarian Universalist Association).

3. The criminological literature is as bitterly divided as anything else in this emotion-laden area. Studies that minimize the extent or importance of firearms crime receive severe censure in Zimring, *Games with Guns and Statistics*, 1968 WIS. L. REV. 1113. On the other hand, various statistical arguments purporting to show that widespread gun ownership causes violence or that severe anti-gun laws reduce it are convincingly mauled in Benenson, *A Controlled Look at Gun Controls*, 14 N.Y.L.F. 718 (1968), and in Hardy & Stompoly, *Of Arms and the Law*, 51 CHI.-KENT L. REV. 62, 79-114 (1974).

The most complete and authoritative study to date, done by Professors J. Wright and P. Rossi of the Social and Demographic Research Institute of the University of Massachusetts under a three-year grant from the U.S. Dept. of Justice, involved a comprehensive review and analysis of all the various studies and relevant criminological data developed as of 1980. NATIONAL INSTITUTE OF JUSTICE, U.S. DEPARTMENT OF JUSTICE, WEAPONS, CRIME AND VIOLENCE IN AMERICA (1981) [hereinafter cited as WEAPONS, CRIME AND VIOLENCE IN AMERICA]. Scrupulously neutral despite its authors' admitted anti-gun sentiments, this study evenhandedly rebukes champions of both sides for having been so result-oriented that most of the pre-1975 work in the area is simply not credible. Its abstract provides the following "bottom-line" conclusions:

(1) whether Congress has jurisdiction under the commerce clause or otherwise to enact a federal handgun prohibition;[4]
(2) whether such a prohibition would violate the "castle doctrine" embodied in the third and fourth amendments;[5]
(3) whether the constitutional privacy protections of the fourth and fifth amendments would inhibit enforcement of such a ban;[6] and
(4) whether handgun confiscation would trigger the fifth amendment's just compensation requirement.[7]

The constitutional issue that comes most immediately to mind in

---

There appear to be no strong causal connections between private gun ownership and the crime rate. . . . There is no compelling evidence that private weaponry is an important cause of, or a deterrent to, violent criminality.

. . . .

It is commonly hypothesized that much criminal violence, especially homicide, occurs simply because the means of lethal violence (firearms) are readily at hand, and thus, that much homicide would not occur were firearms generally less available. There is no persuasive evidence that supports this view.

Id. at 1-2.

4. Clearly, the commerce power provides Congress jurisdiction to prohibit the continued importation of firearms, their domestic manufacture for interstate sale or their sale after travel in interstate commerce. In theory, the extension of commerce clause jurisdiction to the confiscation of handguns which might have been purchased by the present owner or his family 25 or more years ago would be questionable. *But see* Scarborough v. United States, 431 U.S. 563 (1977) (indicating that the commerce power extends to prohibiting possession of any firearm which has at any time traveled in interstate or foreign commerce). Since a substantial minority of firearms are foreign imports, and the rest are manufactured by a few firms located in the New England states, most, if not all, firearms would have the required "minimal nexus" of having crossed a state or federal border at some time. Moreover, existing precedents at least arguably extend the commerce power to confiscation of even those firearms which have never crossed a state or federal border on the ground that the metals and other materials out of which they are fabricated have so moved. *See, e.g.,* Katzenbach v. McClung, 379 U.S. 294 (1964).

5. In Stanley v. Georgia, 394 U.S. 557 (1969), the Supreme Court barred legislation prohibiting the home possession of pornography. The implications of that holding have become increasingly ambiguous, as it has been honored more in the breach than in the observance. *Cf.* Leary v. United States, 544 F.2d 1266, 1270 (5th Cir. 1977) (no federal right of privacy preempts legislative prohibition of home possession of marijuana). *Stanley* has been described as no more than "a reaffirmation that 'a man's home is his castle.' " Paris Adult Theatre I v. Slaton, 413 U.S. 49, 66 (1973). Yet if *Stanley* has any vitality at all it surely encompasses the right to equip one's "castle" with firearms, locks, metal grilles and other devices specifically designed to protect its privacy. However the *Stanley* castle doctrine may be narrowed, it would be difficult logically to exclude from it the home possession of firearms since the doctrine that "a man's home is his castle" originated in cases upholding the right to possess and use arms for home defense. Semayne's Case, 5 Co. Rep. 91a, 91b, 77 Eng. Rep. 194, 195 (K.B. 1603) (quoted with approval in Payton v. New York, 445 U.S. 573, 596 n.44 (1980)); Dhutti's Case, Northumberland Assize Rolls (1255) (88 Publications of Surtees Society 94 (1891)) (household servant privileged to kill nocturnal intruder); Rex v. Compton, 22 *Liber Assisarum* pl. 55 (1347) (homicide of burglar is no less justifiable than that of criminal who resists arrest under warrant); Anonymous 1353, 26 *Liber Assisarum* (Edw. III), pl. 23 (householder privileged to kill arsonist).

6. *See* Hardy & Chotiner, *The Potentiality for Civil Liberties Violations in the Enforcement of Handgun Prohibition*, in RESTRICTING HANDGUNS: THE LIBERAL SKEPTICS SPEAK OUT (D. Kates ed. 1979) [hereinafter cited as RESTRICTING HANDGUNS]; Kessler, *Enforcement Problems of Gun Control: A Victimless Crimes Analysis*, 16 CRIM. L. BULL. 131 (1980).

7. *See* Chicago B. & Q. R.R. v. Chicago, 166 U.S. 226 (1897). *But cf.* Miller v. Schoene, 276 U.S. 272 (1928) (no duty to compensate if one class of property is destroyed rather than taken for public use).

connection with handgun prohibition-confiscation, however, is the
second amendment's injunction:

> A well regulated Militia, being necessary to the security of a free State,
> the right of the people to keep and bear Arms, shall not be infringed.[8]

The meaning of this language has been extensively debated in light
of what has aptly been termed "The Great American Gun War."[9]
Predictably, but unfortunately, the discussion has mirrored the
terms, conditions and bitterness of that "war." Debate has been
sharply polarized between those who claim that the amendment
guarantees nothing to individuals, protects only the state's right to
maintain organized military units, and thus poses no obstacle to gun
control (the "exclusively state's right" view), and those who claim
that the amendment guarantees some sort of individual right to arms
(the "individual right" view).

The individual right view is endorsed by only a minority of legal
scholars,[10] but accepted by a majority of the general populace who,
though supporting the idea of controlling guns, increasingly oppose
their prohibition, believing that law-abiding citizens may properly
have them for self-defense.[11] Though the individual right view reigns

---

8. U.S. CONST. amend. II.

9. *See* Bruce-Briggs' article with that title in PUBLIC INTEREST 37 (1976).

10. *See, e.g.,* Caplan, *Restoring the Balance: The Second Amendment Revisited,* 5 FORD-
HAM URB. L. J. 31 (1976); Dowlut, *The Right to Arms: Does the Constitution or the Predilection
of Judges Reign?,* 36 OKLA. L. REV. 65 (1983); Gardiner, *To Preserve Liberty — A Look at the
Right to Keep and Bear Arms,* 10 N. KY. L. REV. 63 (1982); Hardy & Stompoly, *supra* note 3;
Hays, *The Right to Bear Arms, A Study in Judicial Misinterpretation,* 2 WM. & MARY L. REV.
381 (1960); Sprecher, *The Lost Amendment,* 51 A.B.A. J. 554 (1965). Based upon special research by its staff in the archives of the Library of Congress, the Subcommittee on the Constitution of the U.S. Senate Judiciary Committee has also endorsed the individual right view.
SENATE SUBCOMM. ON THE CONSTITUTION OF THE COMM. ON THE JUDICIARY, 97TH CONG.,
2D SESS., THE RIGHT TO KEEP AND BEAR ARMS (Comm. Print 1982) [hereinafter cited as
REPORT OF THE SUBCOMMITTEE ON THE CONSTITUTION]. Dr. Joyce Malcolm, an historian
whose study in England of the antecedent English legal principles was funded by the American Bar Foundation, Harvard Law School and the National Endowment for the Humanities,
has also accepted the individual right view. Malcolm, *The Right of the People to Keep and Bear
Arms: The Common Law Tradition,* 10 HASTINGS CONST. L. Q. 285 (1983) (in press), *reprinted
in* FIREARMS & VIOLENCE: ISSUES OF PUBLIC POLICY (D. Kates ed., forthcoming 1984) [here-
inafter cited as FIREARMS & VIOLENCE]

Though not necessarily agreeing with all of their conclusions, this Article relies heavily
upon the research and insights that appear in Malcolm, Caplan and the REPORT OF THE
SUBCOMMITTEE ON THE CONSTITUTION, *supra,* and Halbrook, *The Second Amendment as a
Phenomenon of Classical Political Philosophy,* in FIREARMS & VIOLENCE, *supra.* The following
unpublished materials have also been extremely useful: C. Asbury, The Right to Keep and
Bear Arms in America: The Origins and Application of the Second Amendment to the Consti-
tution (1974) (unpublished doctoral thesis in history, U. of Michigan) (available at U. of Mich-
igan Graduate Library); A. Lugo Janer, The System of Defense in the Massachusetts Bay
Colonies from 1630 to 1650 (1982) (graduate paper, U. of Pa. Law School); A. Lugo Janer, A
Thesis on the Second Amendment (1982) (masters thesis, U. of Pa. Law School); J. Smith, The
Constitutional Right to Keep and Bear Arms (1959) (thesis, Harvard Law School).

11. In answer to a 1975 national poll asking whether the second amendment "applies to
each individual citizen or only to the National Guard," 70% of the respondents endorsed the

among nonlegal scholars,[12] the exclusively state's right position is dominant among lawyers and law professors[13] and enjoys the support of the American Bar Association.[14] That bastion of individual rights, the American Civil Liberties Union — a member organization of the National Coalition to Ban Handguns — emphatically denies that the second amendment has anything to do with individuals.[15]

---

individual right alternative, with another 3% saying it applied to both. 121 Cong. Rec. 42, 112 (1975). A 1978 national poll which asked, "Do you believe the Constitution of the United States gives you the right to keep and bear arms?" received an 87% affirmative response. Decision Making Information, Attitudes of the American Electorate Toward Gun Control (1978) (Mimeo).

At the same time, national polls generally show widespread public support for the concept of "gun control." But since there are presently more than 20,000 federal, state and local "gun control" laws, the relevant inquiry is: What specific kinds of present or proposed "gun controls" does the public endorse? Polls seeking opinion on specific proposals suggest that the public approves replacement of the present hodgepodge of diverse federal, state and local controls by a national system. This system would be at once substantially less onerous than those presently in effect in the most restrictive jurisdictions and yet substantially more onerous than those of the least restrictive jurisdictions. Registration would be required for all guns (not just handguns) and lawful ownership would be dependent upon qualification for a permit. On the other hand, permits would be automatically available as a matter of right to every responsible law-abiding adult. *See* Bordua, *Gun Control and Opinion Measurement: Adversary Polling and the Construction of Social Meaning*, in FIREARMS & VIOLENCE, *supra* note 10; Kates, *Toward a History of Handgun Prohibition in the United States*, in RESTRICTING HANDGUNS, *supra* note 6, at 27-30; Tonso, *Social Problems and Sagecraft in the Debate over Gun Control*, 5 LAW & POLY. Q. 325 (1983); Wright, *Public Opinion and Gun Control: A Comparison of Results From Two Recent National Surveys*, 455 ANNALS 24 (1981); *cf.* Part IV-C *infra* (on the constitutionality of such a system).

12. *See, e.g.*, REPORT OF THE SUBCOMMITTEE ON THE CONSTITUTION, *supra* note 10; J. MALCOLM, DISARMED: THE LOSS OF THE RIGHT TO BEAR ARMS IN RESTORATION ENGLAND (1980); Halbrook, *supra* note 10; Marina, *Weapons, Technology and Legitimacy: The Second Amendment in Global Perspective*, in FIREARMS & VIOLENCE, *supra* note 10; Shalhope, *The Ideological Origins of the Second Amendment*, 69 J. AM. HIST 599 (1982); Whisker, *Historical Development and Subsequent Erosion of the Right to Keep and Bear Arms*, 78 W. VA. L. REV. 171 (1975); C. Asbury, *supra* note 10. *But see* Shalhope, *supra*, at 599-600 (citations to several historians who embrace the exclusively state's right view).

13. "For some years, the second amendment has been regarded by the great majority of constitutional scholars as irrelevant to the issue of gun control." Kaplan, *Foreword*, in FIREARMS & VIOLENCE, *supra* note 10; *see, e.g.*, G. NEWTON & F. ZIMRING, FIREARMS AND VIOLENCE IN AMERICAN LIFE 113 (1970) [hereinafter cited as G. NEWTON & F. ZIMRING]; Feller & Gotting, *The Second Amendment, A Second Look*, 61 NW. U. L. REV. 46 (1966); Jackson, *Handgun Control: Constitutional and Critically Needed*, 8 N.C. CENTRAL L.J. 867 (1977); Levin, *The Right to Bear Arms: The Development of the American Experience*, 48 CHI.-KENT L. REV. 148 (1971); Rohner, *The Right to Bear Arms*, 16 CATH. U. L. REV. 53 (1966); Weatherup, *Standing Armies and Armed Citizens: An Historical Analysis of the Second Amendment*, 2 HASTINGS CONST. L.Q. 961 (1972); Note, *Right to Keep and Bear Arms*, 26 DRAKE L. REV. 423 (1977).

L. TRIBE, AMERICAN CONSTITUTIONAL LAW 266 n.6 (1978), considers these views so clearly established that he echoes them without admitting even the possiblity of any alternative interpretation.

14. AMERICAN BAR ASSOCIATION, POLICY BOOK (August 1975).

15. The ACLU's Summary of its national board's action at the June 14-15, 1980 meeting sets out the following policy declaration:

The setting in which the Second Amendment was proposed and adopted demonstrates

Indeed, "The Great American Gun War" bristles with ironies that turn our stereotypes of liberalism and conservatism topsy-turvy: While the *New York Times* editorializes that "[t]he urban handgun offers no benefits,"[16] its publisher is among the few privileged to possess a New York City permit to carry one at all times.[17] Arch-conservatives who passionately denounce marijuana and homosexuality wax eloquent against the "victimless criminalization" of gun own-

---

that the right to bear arms is a collective one existing only in the collective population of each state for the purpose of maintaining an effective state militia.

The ACLU agrees with the Supreme Court's long-standing interpretation of the Second Amendment that the individual's right to bear arms applies only to the preservation of efficiency of a well regulated militia. Except for lawful police and military purposes, the possession of weapons by individuals is not constitutionally protected. Therefore there is no constitutional impediment to the regulation of firearms.

Nor does the ACLU believe that there is a significant civil liberties value, apart from the Second Amendment, in an individual right to own or use firearms. Interests of privacy and self expression may be involved in any individual's choice of activities or possessions, but these interests are attenuated when the activity, or the object sought to be possessed, is inherently dangerous to others. With respect to firearms, the ACLU believes that this quality of dangerousness justifies legal regulation which substantially restricts the individual's interest in freedom of choice.

At the same meeting the board approved the following clarification: "It is the sense of this body that the word 'justifies' in the policy means we will affirmatively support gun control legislation."

16. *The Real Politics of Guns*, N.Y. Times, May 6, 1983, at A30, col. 1; *see also Taming the White Panthers*, N.Y. Times, Feb. 16, 1983, at A30, col. 1 (in response to the assertion that handgun prohibition would discriminate against the poor who have less access to police protection, the editorial claims that "most civilians, *whatever their income level*, are likely to lack the training and alertness" required to "us[e] a gun to stop an armed criminal") (emphasis added); *see* n.17 *infra* and accompanying text.

17. Although such permits are officially available only on a showing of "unique need" to carry a defensive weapon, the list of permit holders is composed of people noted more for their political influence, wealth and social prominence than for their residence in high-crime areas. Along with Arthur Ochs Sulzberger, the list has included such other well-known gun prohibition advocates as Nelson Rockefeller and John Lindsay. Psychologist Joyce Brothers, whose public position is that men possess handguns in order to compensate for sexual dysfunction, was not on the list. Her husband was. Kates, Some Comparisons Between The Prohibition of Alcohol and the Banning of Handguns, at n.21 & accompanying text (paper delivered to the 1981 annual meeting of the American Society of Criminology), revised & *reprinted as Handgun Banning in Light of the Prohibition Experience*, in FIREARMS & VIOLENCE, *supra* note 10.

Of course, contrary to the suggestions of the gun organizations which ferreted it out, this information does not *per se* demonstrate the invalidity of handgun prohibition-confiscation legislation — any more than the fact that the children of the influencial parents often manage to avoid the consequences of their peccadilloes demonstrates the undesirability of having criminal laws, or the fact that the rich are best able to take advantage of tax breaks demonstrates the invalidity thereof. If we were to repeal every law or governmental program — however beneficial to society generally — from which the rich and the influential are in a position to obtain special benefits, or to avoid the most onerous effects, there would be neither government nor laws.

But such anomalies are particularly detrimental to the *enforceability* of handgun prohibition-confiscation. How can the resident of a high-crime area be convinced to give up what he believes to be his family's only real security when people who live and work in high-security buildings in the best-policed areas of the city are privileged not to do so? How can he be dissuaded from thinking that guns give security when many of those who have so derisively assailed that idea turn out to mean only that handguns are useless to those who lack the special influence necessary to secure a permit?

ers.[18] The National Rifle Association (NRA) has its own gun control program, involving mandatory minimum prison sentences for the use of a gun in the commission of a crime — a scheme which the NRA's opponents decry.[19] But these same opponents endorse mandatory minimum prison sentences for people who (without misuse) simply carry a handgun illegally — people who turn out overwhelmingly to be not criminals but frightened shopkeepers, secretaries and the elderly — respectable citizens who must live or work in high-crime areas but lack the political influence necessary to get a permit.[20] Normally antipathetic political extremists of virtually every persuasion join with apolitical gun collectors in paranoid visions of gun bans as persecutions directed especially against them.[21] Usually liberal jurists and newspaper columnists frankly call for abrogation of the fourth amendment insofar as it would hinder police confiscation of guns — "unlimited search and seizure" against anyone suspected of being a handgun owner.[22]

Equally ironic, the legal community's endorsement of the exclusively state's right interpretation has actually aided the gun organizations in one way. By concentrating attention on the state's right position, the gun-owner organizations have been able to avoid the details of their own individual right position, which seems inconsistent with the kinds of gun controls the organizations have themselves endorsed.[23] In almost every state, the basic handgun legislation, in-

---

18. Examples could be multiplied almost endlessly, but among the more prominent are Rep. John Ashbrook (R-Ohio), who was, until his death in 1982, a member of the NRA national board, and California State Sen. H.L. Richardson, who is both an NRA board member and the founder and head of Gun Owners of America.

19. *See, e.g.,* M. YEAGER, DO MANDATORY PRISON SENTENCES FOR HANDGUN OFFENDERS CURB VIOLENT CRIME (U.S. Conference of Mayors, 1976). Criticism of this NRA gun control alternative is not, however, limited to professional anti-gun analysts. *See* Kates, *Why Gun Control Won't Work*, COMMONWEAL, Mar. 13, 1981, at 136; Loftin & McDowall, *One with a Gun Gets You Two*, 455 ANNALS 150 (1981).

20. *See* Kates, *supra* note 19, at 136; *see also* Kates, *supra* note 17, at n.16 & accompanying text (unpaginated manuscript).

21. *See, e.g.,* G. NEWTON & F. ZIMRING, *supra* note 13, at 195 app. F (statements of various extremist political groups); Marwick, *What Gun Collectors and Political Activists Have in Common*, FIRST PRINCIPLES, June 1979. For historical examples of the use of gun confiscations to persecute political enemies, see notes 136-40 *infra* and accompanying text. Others are collected in Kessler, *Gun Control and Political Power*, 5 LAW & POLY. Q. 381 (1983).

22. *See* Wilkey, Wall St. J., Oct. 7, 1977, at 12, col. 4; Keegan, *U.S.A., "Nation of Hypocrites" on Enforcement of Gun Laws*, Chicago Tribune, Apr. 1, 1981, at 1, col. 2. *See generally* Hardy & Chotiner, *supra* note 6.

23. Notwithstanding their portrayal in the news media (and indeed, their own self-portraits), gun-owner organizations are not necessarily against gun *control*, as opposed to gun prohibition-confiscation. While they frequently cite the failure of our present 20,000 gun control measures as evidence of the uselessness of a gun ban, they fail to point out that they and their predecessors are responsible for many of those controls. In addition to the controls derived from the Uniform Revolver Act, *see* notes 24-26 *infra* and accompanying text, the NRA

cluding both the prohibition on the carrying of concealed weapons and the restrictions on gun ownership by felons, minors, and incompetents,[24] stems from the Uniform Revolver Act,[25] drafted and promoted by the NRA and the now defunct United States Revolver Association in the first three decades of this century.[26] However socially desirable these and other controls may be, they raise problems for the individual right interpretation which its proponents have rarely, if ever, attempted to address. For example:

(1) Since the amendment contains no express limitation on the kind of "arms" guaranteed, why does it only protect possession of ordinary small arms (rifles, shotguns, handguns)? Why not of artillery, flamethrowers, machine guns, and so on, to the prohibition of which gunowner groups have readily acceded?

(2) Likewise, since the amendment's guarantee does not explicitly limit gun ownership to responsible adults, why does it not proscribe the laws restricting handgun ownership by lunatics, criminals and juveniles?

(3) Since the amendment guarantees an (apparently unqualified) right to "bear" as well as to "keep" arms, how can individual right proponents endorse concealed-carry proscriptions?

(4) Conversely, if all these controls are consistent with the gun-owner groups' position, how can they contend that registration and licensing requirements are not?[27]

In short, even if the historical evidence does establish an individual right to arms, it remains to define its parameters, particularly with regard to gun control rather than gun prohibition-confiscation.[28] One of the purposes of this Article will be to sketch out at

---

also cooperated in enacting the Federal Firearms Act of 1938, Act of June 30, 1938, ch. 850, 52 Stat. 1250 (1938) (repealed 1968). L. KENNETT & J. ANDERSON, THE GUN IN AMERICA 211 (1975). Although the NRA did not affirmatively support the Gun Control Act of 1968, 18 U.S.C. §§ 921-28 (1976), the American firearms industry supported it for economic reasons. Kates, *Towards a History of Handgun Prohibition in the United States*, in RESTRICTING HANDGUNS, *supra* note 6, at 25. Nevertheless, the NRA has sought only certain civil liberty modifications to the Act. For example, the Firearm Owners Protection Act, S. 1914, 98th Cong., 1st Sess., 129 CONG. REC. 3872-74 (1983), introduced by Senator McClure (R-Idaho), seeks to amend the Act by prohibiting warrantless searches and other alleged abuses without repealing the provisions designed to forbid firearms to violent felons, juveniles and the mentally unstable.

24. *See* note 265 & 268 *infra* and accompanying text.

25. *A Bill To Provide For Uniform Regulation of Revolver Sales* (The United States Revolver Association), *reprinted in* HANDBOOK OF THE NATIONAL CONFERENCE OF COMMISSIONERS ON UNIFORM STATE LAWS AND PROCEEDINGS OF THE THIRTY-FOURTH ANNUAL MEETING 728 (1924) [hereinafter cited as HANDBOOK].

26. *See* L. KENNETT & J. ANDERSON, *supra* note 23, at ch. 8; United States Revolver Association, *The Argument for a Uniform Revolver Act*, in HANDBOOK, *supra* note 25, at 716; *Report of the Committee on a Uniform Act to Regulate the Sale and Possession of Firearms*, in HANDBOOK, *supra* note 25, at 711.

27. These and other issues relating to the constitutionality of specific gun control options are treated in detail in Part IV. *See* notes 235-71 *infra* and accompanying text.

28. This Article does not purport to resolve, or even to address, the current debate among

least some of the very substantial limitations on the right of individuals to keep and bear arms suggested by the historical evidence.[29] First, however, the controversy between the individual right and the exclusively state's right views must be resolved. The evidence to be examined must include: the literal language of the second amendment; the history of its proposal and ratification; the philosophical and historical background that gave rise to the Founders' belief in "the necessity of an armed populace to effect popular sovereignty";[30] and the contemporary understanding of the second amendment. This Article will then consider the amendment's subsequent judicial interpretation, and the question of its incorporation against the states, before returning to constitutional limitations on the right to keep and bear arms.

I. The Original Understanding of the Second Amendment

The two opposing camps naturally rely on different interpretations of the origins of the second amendment. Proponents of the exclusively state's right view[31] see the amendment as responding to

---

constitutional scholars over the proper role of original intent in constitutional adjudication. As to that debate, see, *e.g.*, J. Ely, Democracy and Distrust (1980) (evaluating interpretive and fundamental value approaches and arguing for his own form of "ultimate interpretivism"; Bork, *Neutral Principles and Some First Amendment Problems*, 47 Ind. L.J. 1 (1971) (arguing that neutral derivation of principle requires adherence to original intent); Brest, *The Misconceived Quest for the Original Understanding*, 60 B.U. L. Rev. 204 (1980) (arguing that interpretivism is impossible and does not serve the ends of constitutionalism); Monaghan, *Our Perfect Constitution*, 56 N.Y.U. L. Rev. 353 (1981) (original intent is proper interpretive mode for ascertaining constitutional meaning). For the purposes of this Article, it is sufficient to note that courts and commentators continue to refer to the text and the intent behind it, taking as their guides the writings of Madison, Jefferson and the other Framers, and the historical background in colonial and English law of the provision under consideration. *See, e.g.*, Powell v. McCormack, 395 U.S. 486, 547 (1969); Everson v. Board of Educ., 330 U.S. 1 (1947). Even Thomas Grey, who would read the Constitution in light of modern values, justifies his interpretation on the ground that this was the Framers' intent. Grey, *Do We Have an Unwritten Constitution?*, 27 Stan. L. Rev. 703, 715-17 (1975).

29. *See* notes 235-71 *infra* and accompanying text.

30. Halbrook, *supra* note 10, at n. 79 & accompanying text (unpaginated manuscript).

31. What is here denominated the "exclusively state's right" position is sometimes also described as the "collective right" theory. That phrase is not used here because of the potential for confusion with a related, but occasionally discretely stated, "collective right" theory. This second "collective right" theory was first enunciated by the Kansas Supreme Court in a decision which eviscerated the right to arms provision of that state's constitution. Salina v. Blaksely, 72 Kan. 230, 83 P. 61 (1905). Under this theory constitutional right to arms guarantees, whether federal or state, involve only a "collective right" of the entire people, by which is apparently meant a right that cannot be invoked by anyone either in his own behalf or on behalf of the people as a whole.

It will be unnecessary to consider at length this discrete "collective right" theory because it is patently wrong. If the amendment was intended to guarantee a right to the people (and not the states), it is self-contradictory to say that because that right was conferred on everyone, no single person may assert it, or indeed, to describe something that guarantees nothing to any

article I, section 8, clauses 15 and 16, of the original Constitution. Those clauses give Congress the power to call out the militia and "to provide for organizing, arming and disciplining" it. According to the state's right interpretation, the amendment was motivated by fear that Congress might order the states' organized militias disarmed, thereby leaving the states powerless against federal tyranny. Thus, this view sees the amendment as a response to concerns that time and the course of American history have rendered anachronistic. During the Revolution, and the subsequent period of the Articles of Confederation, the states loomed larger than the federal government and jealously guarded their prerogatives against it. While the Constitution itself heralded a decisive (though limited) repudiation of those attitudes, they remained strong enough to assure two precatory admonitions a place in the Bill of Rights. These became the second and tenth amendments. The purpose of the second amendment was simply to place the states' organized military forces beyond the federal government's power to disarm, guaranteeing that the states would always have sufficient force at their command to nullify federal impositions on their rights and to resist by arms if necessary.[32] State's right proponents also link the amendment to the traditional Whig fear of standing armies. Though the federal government could not be denied authority to maintain a small army, the basic military defense of the country would rest in the states' reserved power to maintain their own organized military forces. These could be joined together to resist foreign invasion in time of need. Thus, the philosophy underlying the second amendment not only guaranteed the states' right to keep armed forces, but obviated any need for a massive federal military which might defeat them if they found it necessary to revolt.[33]

This state's right analysis renders the amendment little more than a holdover from an era of constitutional philosophy that received its death knell in the decision rendered at Appomattox Courthouse. Though it yet lingers in the Constitution, it does not (for it was never

---

specific person or entity as a "right" at all. Thus, the discrete "collective right" theory fails to meet Chief Justice Marshall's elementary test for constitutional construction: "It cannot be presumed that any clause in the Constitution is intended to be without effect . . . ." *Marbury v. Madison*, 5 U.S. (1 Cranch) 137 (1803); *cf.* Hardy & Stompoly, *supra* note 3, at 74-75 (state provisions meaningless if right to keep and bear arms refers only to right of state to form a militia); REPORT OF THE SUBCOMMITTEE ON THE CONSTITUTION, *supra* note 10, at 11 (individual rights interpretation gives full meaning to the words chosen by the First Congress to reflect the right to keep and bear arms).

32. *See generally* the sources cited at notes 13-15 *supra*. The historical accuracy of this view of the amendment is analyzed at notes 86-89 *infra* and accompanying text.

33. *See* notes 86-89 & 113 *infra* and accompanying text.

so intended) guarantee the right of any *individual* against confiscation of arms. Rather, it guarantees an exclusive right of the states, which only the states have standing to invoke. This they need not do today when any value the amendment might presently have for them is satisfied by their federally-provided National Guard structure.

Advocates of the individual right position, on the other hand, rely on the fact that the natural reading of the amendment's phrase "right of the people" is that it creates not a state right, but one which individuals can assert. This is how the identically phrased[34] first and fourth amendments are interpreted.[35] Furthermore, the individual right advocate may accept the state's right theory and simply assert that, even though one of the amendment's purposes may have been to protect the states' militias,[36] another was to protect the individual right to arms. Indeed, the evidence suggests it was precisely by protecting the individual that the Framers intended to protect the militia.[37] In thus yielding to the primary strength of the opposing argument, individual right advocates define the burden that the exclusively state's right theorist must bear. To demonstrate that no individual right was intended, he must show not just that there was a desire to protect the states, but that there was *no desire* to protect individuals — despite the most natural reading of the amendment's phraseology. As we shall see, this is a particularly difficult burden to bear. Such debate as the amendment received is sparse and inconclusive, while other legislative history strongly supports the proposition that protection of an individual right was at least one of the amendment's purposes.[38]

---

34. U.S. CONST. amend. I ("Congress shall make no law . . . abridging . . . the right of the people peaceably to assemble . . . ."); U.S. CONST. amend. IV ("The right of the people to be secure in their persons, houses, papers and effects . . . .").

35. *See, e.g.,* Richmond Newspapers, Inc., v. Virginia, 488 U.S. 555, 577-78 (1980) (right to assemble peacefully is as fundamental as free press and speech and exists as an independent right as well as a catalyst for the exercise of other first amendment rights); United States v. Salvucci, 448 U.S. 83, 85 (1980) (defendants charged with crimes of possession may claim benefits of the exclusionary rule to vindicate their fourth amendment rights).

36. For the specialized 18th century usage of "militia" to encompass the entire military-age male population, see notes 39-55 *infra* and accompanying text.

37. *See* notes 53-55 and accompanying text.

38. The recorded debate, which centered on a tangential issue, is discussed at note 90 *infra*. Other direct legislative history is set out at notes 75-89 *infra* and accompanying text. The philosophical underpinning of the amendment is set out at notes 90-134 *infra* and accompanying text. Much of this material derives from unpublished background studies by Professor Halbrook which, along with some additional material, are embodied in his article *To Keep and Bear Their Private Arms: The Adoption of the Second Amendment, 1787-1797,* 10 N. KY. L. REV. 13 (1982).

A. *Parsing the Language of the Second Amendment and the Bill of Rights*

In general, the text of the second amendment, and of the Bill of Rights as a whole, provides a series of insuperable obstacles to an exclusively state's right interpretation. State's right analyses have tended not to come to grips with these obstacles; if they focus on the amendment's wording at all, it is only on the word "militia," assuming that the Framers meant "militia" to refer to "a particular military force," *i.e.*, the states' home reserve, now federalized as the National Guard.[39] In fact, though not unknown in the 18th Century,[40] that usage was wholly secondary to the one Webster classifies as now least used. "The whole body of able-bodied male citizens declared by law as being subject to call to military service."[41] As the paragraphs below demonstrate, the Framers' understanding of the meaning of "militia" and the other phrases of the second amendment seriously embarrasses the state's right argument.

1. *The Militia*

Throughout their existence, the American colonies had endured the constant threat of sudden attack by Indians or any of Britain's Dutch, French and Spanish colonial rivals.[42] Even if they had wanted a standing army, the colonists were unable either to afford the cost or to free up the necessary manpower. Instead, they adopted the ancient practice that was still in vogue in England, the militia system. The "militia" was the entire adult male citizenry, who were not simply *allowed* to keep their own arms, but affirmatively *required* to do so. In the pre-colonial English tradition there had been no police and no standing army in peacetime.[43] From time immemorial every free Englishman had been both permitted and required to keep such arms as a person of his class could afford both for law enforcement and for military service.[44] With arms readily available

---

39. *See, e.g.*, sources cited in note 13 *supra*.

40. WEBSTER'S THIRD NEW INTERNATIONAL DICTIONARY (1971).

41. *Id.*

42. *See* Dowlut, *supra* note 10, at 69. (Dowlut also mentions that the colonists were exposed to general crime against which they both armed themselves individually and acted jointly in the *posse comitatus*.).

43. When a large scale threat, such as invasion, presented itself, the civilian militia was mobilized for military duty. In addition, civilian subjects participated in ordinary police work, both individually and as members of posses. *Id.* at 93.

44. C. GREENWOOD, FIREARMS CONTROL: A STUDY OF ARMED CRIME AND FIREARMS CONTROL IN ENGLAND AND WALES 7 (1972); C. HOLLISTER, ANGLO-SAXON MILITARY INSTITUTIONS ch. 2 (1962). As weapons improved or new technologies, including firearms, took their place, successive monarchs and parliaments constantly found it necessary to redefine and

in their homes, Englishmen were theoretically prepared at all times to chase down felons in response to the hue and cry, or to assemble together as an impromptu army in case of foreign invasion of their shire.[45]

When the American colonies were founded the militia system was in full flower in England. It was adopted perforce in the colonies, which were thousands of miles by sail from any succor the Mother Country might provide. With slight variations, the different colonies imposed a duty to keep arms and to muster occasionally for drill upon virtually every able-bodied white man between the age of majority and a designated cut-off age. Moreover, the duty to keep arms applied to *every* household, not just to those containing persons subject to militia service.[46] Thus, the over-aged and seamen, who were exempt from militia service, were required to keep arms for law enforcement and for the defense of their homes from criminals or foreign enemies.[47] In at least one colony a 1770 law actually required

---

reemphasize citizens' continuing obligation to arm themselves with the most effectual weapons they could afford. For the legislation of Mary Tudor and Elizabeth I, see A. Lugo Janer, *supra* note 10, at 6-13. Legislation enacted by their father, Henry VIII, is discussed at note 235 *infra* and accompanying text. For the tergiversatous course followed by their Stuart successors, see notes 136-39 *infra* and accompanying text.

45. F. MAITLAND, THE CONSTITUTIONAL HISTORY OF ENGLAND 276 (Fisher ed. 1961), particularly stresses the joinder of military and law enforcement purposes served by the requirement that every free man possess weapons. *See also* Malcolm, *supra* note 10; J. Smith, *supra* note 10, at 6; note 44 *supra*.

46. From the earliest times the duty to possess arms was imposed on the entire colonial populace, with actual militia service contemplated for every male of 15, 16, or 18 through 45, 50, or 60 (depending on the colony). As noted in the REPORT OF THE SUBCOMMITTEE ON THE CONSTITUTION, *supra* note 10, at 3 (footnotes omitted):

In the colonies, availability of hunting and need for defense led to armament statutes comparable to those of the early Saxon times. In 1623, Virginia forbade its colonists to travel unless they were "well armed"; in 1631 it required colonists to engage in target practice on Sunday and to "bring their peeces [*sic*] to Church." In 1658 it required every householder to have a functioning firearm within his house and in 1673 its laws provided that a citizen who claimed he was too poor to purchase a firearm would have one purchased for him by the government, which would then require him to pay a reasonable price when able to do so. In Massachusetts, the first session of the legislature ordered that not only free men, but also indentured servants own firearms and in 1644 it imposed a stern 6 shilling fine upon any citizen who was not armed.

For examples of subsequent legislation to the same effect, see An Act for Regulating the Militia, 1741, *reprinted in* 8 COLONIAL RECORDS OF CONNECTICUT 379 (1874); Act for Regulating the Militia, 1693-1694, 1st sess., ch. 3, *reprinted in* 1 ACTS AND RESOLVES OF THE PROVINCE OF MASSACHUSETTS BAY 128 (1869); An Act for Settling the Militia, 1691, 1st sess., ch.5, *reprinted in* 1 THE COLONIAL LAWS OF NEW YORK FROM THE YEAR 1664 TO THE REVOLUTION 231 (1894). Colonial practice is extensively summarized in United States v. Miller, 307 U.S. 174, 179 (1939) ("[T]he term Militia [in the amendment] . . . comprised all males physically capable of acting in concert for the common defense . . . [who] were expected to appear bearing arms supplied by themselves . . . .").

47. *See, e.g.,* THE LAWS AND LIBERTIES OF MASSACHUSETTS 42 (M. Farrard ed. 1929, reprinted from the 1648 ed.) ("But all persons exempted whatsoever as foresaid, except Magistrates and Teaching Elders shall be provided of Arms and Ammunition, as other men are."); *see also* Dowlut, *supra* note 10, at 74 n.37 (quoting similar provisions of various New York

men to carry a rifle or pistol every time they attended church; church officials were empowered to search each parishioner no less than fourteen times per year to assure compliance.[48] In 1792 Congress, meeting immediately after the enactment of the second amendment, defined the militia to include the entire able-bodied military-age male citizenry of the United States and required each of them to own his own firearm.[49]

What does this suggest about the word "militia" as used in the amendment? The American Civil Liberties Union's argument against an individual right interpretation states that the amendment uses "militia" in the sense of a formal military force separate from the people.[50] But this is plainly wrong. The Founders stated what they meant by "militia" on various occasions. Invariably they defined it in some phrase like "the whole body of the people,"[51] while their references to the organized-military-unit usage of militia, which they called a "select militia," were strongly pejorative.[52]

---

and Virginia statutes). As in England, the requirement of keeping arms was as much directed toward prevention of crime and apprehension of criminals as the repelling of foreign enemies. Militiamen (apparently selected by rotation) staffed the night watch which both patrolled the city and watched out over it from stationary positions to raise the hue and cry in case of felony and the alarm in case of foreign attack. A. Lugo Janer, *supra* note 10, at 33-34.

48. An Act for the Better Security of the Inhabitants by Obliging the Male White Persons to Carry Fire Arms to Places of Public Worship, 1770, *reprinted in* 1775-1770 GEORGIA COLONIAL LAWS 471 (1932).

49. First Militia Act, 1 Stat. 271 (1792). Legislation by Congress immediately following adoption of an amendment is entitled to great weight in the construction thereof. *See, e.g.,* Hampton & Co. v. U.S., 276 U.S. 394, 412 (1928), and cases cited therein.

50. Over and above the historical inaccuracy of the ACLU's interpretation is that, so interpreted, the amendment conflicts with Art. I § 10, cl. 3 which forbids the states to raise "troops" (i.e. formal military units) without the consent of Congress. There is not one iota of historical evidence suggesting that Madison and his Federalist colleagues who dominated the first Congress intended the amendment to undercut either the military-militia clauses of the original Constitution in general or Art. I § 10, cl. 3 in particular. See notes 86-9 & 113 infra and accompanying discussion.

51. *See, e.g.,* VA. CONST. art. I, §13 (1776) ("[A] well-regulated militia, composed of the body of the people . . . ."); DEBATES IN THE CONVENTION OF THE COMMONWEALTH OF VIRGINIA, *reprinted in* 3 J. ELLIOT, DEBATES IN THE SEVERAL STATE CONVENTIONS 425 (3d ed. 1937) (statement of George Mason, June 14, 1788) ("Who are the Militia? They consist now of the whole people. . . ."); LETTERS FROM THE FEDERAL FARMER TO THE REPUBLICAN 123 (W. Bennett ed. 1978) (ascribed to Richard Henry Lee) [hereinafter cited as LETTERS FROM THE FEDERAL FARMER] ("[a] militia, when properly formed, are in fact the people themselves. . . ."); Letter from Tench Coxe to the Pennsylvania Gazette (Feb. 20, 1778), *reprinted in* THE DOCUMENTARY HISTORY OF THE RATIFICATION OF THE CONSTITUTION (Mfm. Supp.) 1779 (M. Jensen ed. 1976) ("Who are these militia? *are [sic] they not ourselves.*") (emphasis in original); *see also* R. TRENCH, DICTIONARY OF OBSOLETE ENGLISH 159 (1958); Sprecher *supra* note 10, at 556 n.29 (citing several other state constitutions).

52. Typical expressions of hostility are cited by Halbrook, *supra* note 38, at 18-19, 23-25, and REPORT OF THE SUBCOMMITTEE ON THE CONSTITUTION, *supra* note 10, at 4-5. These expressions reflect a traditional Whig attitude, dating back to the reign of Charles II, who was thought to have used the "select militia" to disarm and tyrannize the people. Malcolm, *supra* note 10.

In short, one purpose of the Founders having been to guarantee the arms of the militia, they accomplished that purpose by guaranteeing the arms of the individuals who made up the militia. In this respect it would never have occurred to the Founders to differentiate between the arms of the two groups in the context of the amendment's language.[53] The personally owned arms of the individual were the arms of the militia.[54] Thus, the amendment's wording, so opaque to us, made perfect sense to the Framers: believing that a militia (composed of the entire people possessed of their individually owned arms) was necessary for the protection of a free state, they

---

53. This is not to say that the amendment's only purpose was to guarantee the arms of the militia. The philosophical tradition underlying the amendment involved three separate purposes. Certain of the early English commentators on the right to bear arms:

> subtly blended several distinct, yet related, ideas: opposition to standing armies, dependence upon militias, and support of the armed citizen. Thus, while the concept of the armed citizen was sometimes linked with that of the militia, libertarians just as often stressed this idea as an independent theme or joined it to other issues.

. . . .

> The observations of Madison, Washington, Dwight, and Story reveal an interesting relationship between the armed citizen and the militia. These men firmly believed that the character and spirit of the republic rested on the freeman's possession of arms as well as his ability and willingness to defend himself and his society. This was the bedrock, the "palladium," of republican liberty. The militia was equally important in their minds. Militia laws insured that freemen would remain armed, and thus vigorous republican citizens.

Shalhope, *supra* note 12, at 604, 612. Thus, by guaranteeing individuals the right to arms the amendment killed three birds with one stone. First, the independence and self reliance necessary to the citizen of a republic was protected by assuring to each individual the right to possess the arms necessary to defending, and securing food for himself and his family. On the possession of arms as a vital component in the theory of virtuous republican citizenship, see notes 117-18 *infra* and accompanying text. Second and third, by guaranteeing the arms of the individual, the amendment was simultaneously guaranteeing arms to the militia and the *posse comitatus* for military and law enforcement purposes. In this connection it is important to remember that, although these can be stated as three separate functions — and it seems natural to the modern mind to so conceptualize them — it would not have seemed so to the Founders. *See* note 93 *infra* and accompanying text.

54. That one result of guaranteeing the people's privately owned arms was to guarantee the militia's arms should not, however, be understood as suggesting that the only arms protected were those belonging to militiamen. Among other things, the amendment surely was intended at least to protect those non-militia members who were obligated to possess arms, such as the over-aged and seamen, *see* note 47 *supra* and accompanying text. More important, a "right" to possess arms is obviously broader than an obligation to do so. The amendment's use of "right" without further definition suggests that its purpose was to constitutionalize the right to arms which the Founders knew from the common law. This unquestionably included not only militiamen and others obligated to possess arms, but also women, the clergy and those public officials who were exempt from militia service. On the other hand, it is necessary to distinguish those whose right the amendment was intended to protect although they were *exempt* from militia service, from those who were *excluded* because of perceived unfitness, untrustworthiness or alienage. The Founders would not have understood the amendment as extending to felons, children or those so physically or mentally impaired as to preclude militia service. *See* notes 72, 267 and 258 *infra*. The original intention would unquestionably also have been to exclude Indians and blacks on the ground of alienage or untrustworthiness. For evidence that one purpose of the fourteenth amendment was to guarantee blacks the right to arms, see notes 221-30 *infra* and accompanying text.

guaranteed the people's right to possess those arms.[55] At the very least, the Framers' understanding of "militia" casts doubt on an interpretation that would guarantee only the state's right to arm organized military units.[56]

2. *A "Right of the People"*

The second amendment's literal language creates another, even more embarrassing problem for the exclusively state's right interpretation. To accept such an interpretation requires the anomalous assumption that the Framers ill-advisedly used the phrase "right of the people" to describe what was being guaranteed when what they actually meant was "right of the states."[57] In turn, that assumption leads to a host of further anomalies. The phrase "the people" appears in four other provisions of the Bill of Rights, always denoting rights pertaining to individuals. Thus, to justify an exclusively state's right view, the following set of propositions must be accepted: (1) when the first Congress drafted the Bill of Rights it used "right of the people" in the first amendment to denote a right of individuals (assembly); (2) then, some sixteen words later, it used the same phrase in the second amendment to denote a right belonging exclusively to the states; (3) but then, forty-six words later, the fourth amendment's "right of the people" had reverted to its normal individual right meaning; (4) "right of the people" was again used in the natural sense in the ninth amendment; and (5) finally, in the tenth amendment the first Congress specifically distinguished "the states" from "the people," although it had failed to do so in the second amendment. Any one of these textual incongruities demanded by an exclusively state's right position dooms it. Cumulatively they present a truly grotesque reading of the Bill of Rights.

---

55. Smith "translates" the amendment's language into modern terms as follows:
Because a free state cannot be secure from either internal or external enemies unless every able-bodied [adult] in the state is trained to use weapons; the right of each individual person, in any of the 50 states, to keep in his house weapons sufficient for his own use, and to use them in such military training as is directed by his state government, shall not be interferred with by the United States Government.
J. Smith, *supra* note 10, at 72. Note that Smith's formulation here reflects usage in colonial statutes and related documents which he concludes indicates an intention to broadly guarantee individuals the right to "keep" arms in their homes, but to "bear" them outside the home only in the course of actual militia service. *See* notes 59-61, 271 *infra* and accompanying text.

56. As we shall see, the joint-purpose interpretation of the second amendment inherent in the Framers' conception of an armed citizenry — that is, self-defense, law enforcement, and defense against invasion — implies certain limitations on any individual right that amendment may guarantee. *See* notes 233-71 *infra* and accompanying text.

57. In constitutional or statutory construction, language should always be accorded its plain meaning. *See, e.g.,* Martin v. Hunter's Lessee, 14 U.S. (1 Wheat.) 304, 326 (1816).

3. *Keeping and Bearing Arms*

The casual attention state's right proponents pay to the text is exemplified by a third problem inherent in the amendment's literal language. Professor Levin argues that the amendment's use of the term "to bear" arms supports an exclusively state's right view: contemporary statutory usage shows eighteenth-century writers using "bear" in reference to militiamen carrying their arms when mustered to duty; whereas Blackstone uses the phrase to "have" arms in referring to individual possession of them by right.[58] Remarkably, Professor Levin seems to have overlooked the fact that the word that the amendment uses to guarantee a right to *possess* arms is "keep," "bear" being used only to denote carrying them outside the home. Obviously, even if a negative pregnant as to possession could have been inferred had the amendment used "bear arms" alone, that inference disappears completely when "to keep" is added.

Had Professor Levin explored colonial statutory usage of "to keep," as well as "to bear," he would have found his "to bear" argument confirmed, but only in a way which decisively refutes his exclusively state's right interpretation. Smith's extensive statutory review confirms that "bear" did generally refer to the carrying of arms by militiamen.[59] Since statutes referring to the transportation of arms by individuals outside the militia context *(e.g.,* statutes forbidding blacks and Indians to transport them) invariably used the word "carry" instead of "bear," he concludes that the amendment's use of "bear" is designed to protect the carrying of arms outside the home only in the course of militia service.[60] In contrast, Smith finds that "keep" was commonly used in colonial and early state statutes to describe arms possession by individuals in all contexts, not just in relation to militia service. Colonial statutes did require militiamen to "keep" arms in their homes, but they also required the over-aged, seamen and others exempt from militia service to "keep" arms in their homes. Moreover, what blacks and Indians (who were excluded from the militia) were forbidden to do was "keep" guns in their homes. The one context in which "keep" was *not* used was as a description of arms possession by public agencies (as opposed to individuals): "only occasionally, and then only in the 17th Century, are towns and colony governments said to 'keep' the public arms."[61]

---

58. Levin, *supra* note 13, at 148.

59. *See* J. Smith, *supra* note 10, at 42-55.

60. *Id.* at 42-47. The implications of this conclusion for some types of gun controls are discussed in the text following note 271 *infra*.

61. *Id.* at 49; *see also id.* at 47-55. In contrast to the "keeping" by individuals of their

Based on colonial statutory usage then, the amendment's phrase "right of the people to keep" imports not a right of the states or one limited to military service, but a personal right to possess arms in the home for any lawful purpose.

Additional textual evidence of the unsoundness of the exclusively state's right position is that it renders the phrase "to keep" in "to keep and bear" superfluous — as Professor Levin's obliviousness to it unconsciously dramatizes. If the Framers' only concern had been to protect the militia's right to have arms when actually mustered, "to bear" would have sufficed. The words "to keep" take on meaning only if what is being protected is the individual's own arms, rather than those arms of the state that would be dispensed to him from an armory whenever the militia was mustered.[62]

Finally, the organizational structure of the Bill of Rights cuts against the exclusively state's right position. The rights specifically guaranteed to the people are contained in the first nine amendments, with the rights reserved to the states being relegated to the tenth. If the Framers had viewed the second amendment as a right of the states, they would have moved it back to the ninth or tenth amendment instead of placing it second.[63]

B. *The Proposal and Ratification of the Second Amendment*

As we have seen, the language of the second amendment supports the individual interpretation of the right to keep and bear arms. The nature of the controversy over ratification of the Constitution and the various proposals for and debate over the Bill of Rights also buttress the individual right view, for the one thing all

---

private arms in their own homes, the statutes described publicly owned arms as being "lodged" in armories at such times as they were not actually being borne.

62. By the same token, however, the phrase "keep and bear" implies at least one important limitation. Because what is being guaranteed is an individual right to keep *and* bear arms, the arms could only be such if the ordinary individual could conveniently lift and transport them about with his body. For the gun control implications of this observation see text at note 241 *infra*.

63. *See* note 77 and accompanying text. Gardiner has suggested that the organization of the Constitution and Bill of Rights was deliberately modeled after Blackstone's organization of the five legal precepts he considered fundamental to the maintenance of English liberty. *See* Gardiner, *supra* note 10, at 65 n.8. The correspondence can be established as follows: parliamentary powers and privileges are comprehended in art. I; the limitations on the powers of the monarch (executive branch) are comprehended in art. II; the institution and powers of the courts of justice are comprehended in art. III; the right to apply to Parliament for redress of grievances is comprehended in the first amendment; and the right to possess arms is covered in the second amendment. If meritorious, this analysis further buttresses the individual right position since Blackstone included the right to arms among the "absolute rights of individuals." *See* note 153 *infra*.

the Framers agreed on was the desirability of allowing citizens to arm themselves.

1. *The Debate Over the Constitution*

The Founding Fathers were necessarily influenced by the fact that the entire corpus of republican philosophy known to them took English and classical history as a lesson that popular possession of arms was vital to the preservation of liberty and a republican form of government.[64] The proponents and the opponents of ratification of the Constitution equally buttressed their conflicting arguments on the universal belief in an armed citizenry.[65] The proponents denied that the newly strengthened federal government could ever be strong enough to destroy the liberties of an armed populace: "While the people have property, arms in their hands and only a spark of noble spirit, the most corrupt congress must be mad to form any project of tyranny."[66] As Noah Webster put it in a pamphlet urging ratification: "Before a standing army can rule, the people must be disarmed; as they are in almost every kingdom in Europe."[67]

But this line of argument opened the Federalists up to a telling riposte: Since the Constitution contained no guarantee of the citizenry's right to arms, the new federal government could outlaw and confiscate them, thereby destroying the supposed barrier to federal despotism. George Mason recalled to the Virginia delegates the colonies' experience with Britain, in which the monarch's goal had been "to disarm the people; that . . . was the best and most effectual way to enslave them."[68] Together Mason and Richard Henry Lee are generally given preponderant credit for the compromise under which the Constitution was ratified subject to the understanding that it would immediately be augmented by a Bill of Rights. Lee's influential writing on the ratification question extolled the importance of the individual right to arms, opining that "to preserve liberty, it is

64. The influence of such philosophers as Harrington, Nedham and Machiavelli is documented at notes 114-27 *infra* and accompanying text. *See also* Granter, *The Machiavellianism of George Mason*, 17 W. & M. QUARTERLY 239 (2d ser. 1937). *See generally* Halbrook, *supra* note 10; Shalhope, *supra* note 12. For the historical origins of this philosophy, see notes 114-28 *infra*.

65. *See* Part I-C *infra*.

66. REPORT OF THE SUBCOMMITTEE ON THE CONSTITUTION, *supra* note 10, at 4-5; Halbrook, *supra* note 10, at 17 (quoting a newspaper columnist); *see also id.* at 24, 37.

67. REPORT OF THE SUBCOMMITTEE ON THE CONSTITUTION, *supra* note 10, at 5. For Madison's similar expressions from *The Federalist*, see note 100 *infra* and accompanying text. For similar expressions pro and con, see the quotations collected by Halbrook, *supra* note 10.

68. 3 J. ELLIOT, DEBATES IN THE SEVERAL STATE CONVENTIONS 380 (2d ed. 1836). *See generally* Shalhope, *supra* note 12, at 606-13 (on the Federalist and Anti-Federalist arguments based on the individual right to arms).

essential that the whole body of the people always possess arms and be taught alike, especially when young, how to use them."[69]

In line with these sentiments, New Hampshire, the first state to ratify the Constitution, officially recommended that it include a bill of rights providing "Congress shall never disarm any citizen, unless such as are or have been in actual rebellion."[70] New York and Rhode Island also recommended constitutionalizing the right to arms.[71] Although a majority of the Pennsylvania convention ratified the Constitution unconditionally, rejecting suggestions that a bill of rights be recommended or required, a substantial portion of the Pennsylvania delegates broke away on this issue. As a rump they formulated and published a series of proposals, including freedom of speech, press, due process of law and the right to keep and bear arms, which proved particularly influential in spurring the adoption of similar recommendations in the subsequent state conventions. The individual right nature of the Pennsylvania right to arms proposal is unmistakable:

> That the people have a right to bear arms for the defense of themselves and their own State or the United States, or for the purpose of killing game; and no law shall be passed for *disarming the people or any of them* unless for crimes committed, or real danger of public injury from individuals . . . .[72]

Similarly, Samuel Adams proposed to the Massachusetts ratification convention an amendment guaranteeing the right to bear arms.[73]

The strength and universality of contemporary sentiment on the issue of the individual's right to arms may be gauged with reference to the number of amendatory proposals which included it. Amending the constitution to assure the right to arms was endorsed by five state ratifying conventions. By comparison, only four states suggested that the rights to assemble, to due process, and against cruel and unusual punishment be guaranteed; only three states suggested that freedom of speech be guaranteed or that the accused be entitled to know the crime for which he would be tried, to confront his accuser, to present and cross-examine witnesses, to be represented by counsel, and to not be forced to incriminate himself; only two states proposed that double jeopardy be barred.[74] Such unanimity helps

---

69. LETTERS FROM THE FEDERAL FARMER, *supra* note 51, at 124; *see also id.* at 21-22.

70. 1 J. ELLIOT, *supra* note 68, at 326.

71. *See id.* at 328, 335.

72. 2 B. SCHWARTZ, THE BILL OF RIGHTS: A DOCUMENTARY HISTORY 665 (1971)(emphasis added).

73. *Id.* at 675; *see also* note 83 *infra*.

74. *Id.* at 1167.

demonstrate that both Federalists and Anti-Federalists accepted an individual right to arms; the only debate was over how best to guarantee it.

2. *The Proposal and Ratification of the Second Amendment*

To secure ratification of the Constitution, the Federalists had committed themselves to the addition of "further guards *for private rights.*"[75] To this end, the Federalists put forward Madison, the leading and most ardent supporter of the original Constitution in Congress, to draft the proposed amendments. Madison's own notes on his proposal reflect the ultimate organization of the Bill of Rights;[76] his notes on the amendments, in which the right to arms appears very early, state that the amendments "relate first to private rights."[77] Equally corrosive of the exclusively state's right view is the original organizational scheme revealed by Madison's notes. Not conceiving the idea of simply appending the whole set of amendments to the Constitution as a discrete document (today's "Bill of Rights"), Madison intended to attach them to, or after, each section of the original Constitution to which they related. Had he viewed the right to arms as merely a limitation on article I, section 8's provisions concerning congressional control over the militia, he would have inserted it in section 8 immediately after clauses 15 and 16. Instead, he planned to insert it with freedom of religion, of the press and various other personal rights in section 9, immediately following clause 3, which establishes the rights against bills of attainder and ex post facto laws.[78]

Certainly the amendment was understood by Madison's congressional colleagues as guaranteeing an individual right. For instance, in private correspondence Congressman Fisher Ames noted of Madison's proposals that "the rights of conscience, of bearing arms, [*etc.*] . . ., are declared to be inherent in the people."[79] In addition, two written interpretations on the proposed amendments were avail-

---

75. 11 PAPERS OF JAMES MADISON 307 (R. Rutland & C. Hobson ed. 1977) (letter of Oct. 20, 1788, from Madison to Edmund Pendelton) (emphasis added). The Anti-Federalists' objections to the Constitution had not been limited to the lack of individual rights guarantees. For discussion of their objections to art. I, sec. I, see notes 86-89 *infra* and accompanying text.

76. *See* text at note 63 *supra*.

77. *See, e.g.,* 12 PAPERS OF JAMES MADISON, *supra* note 75, at 193-94.

78. *Id.*

79. 1 WORKS OF FISHER AMES 52-53 (1854) (letter of June 11, 1789 to Thomas Dwight). The next day U.S. Senator William Gray wrote Patrick Henry that Madison had introduced a "string of amendments" which "respected personal liberty." 3 PATRICK HENRY 391 (1951); *see also* Senator Gallatin's letter of Oct. 7, 1789 ("essential and sacred rights" which "each individual reserves to himself"), *quoted in* Halbrook, *supra* note 38, at 36 n.90.

able to the members of the first Congress.[80] The first, and more authoritative — by virtue of having received Madison's imprimatur — was a widely reprinted article by his ally and correspondent Tench Coxe.[81] Having discussed the first amendment, Coxe moved on to describe the second in unmistakably individual right terms:

> As civil rulers, not having their duty to the people duly before them, may attempt to tyrannize, and as the military forces which must be occasionally raised to defend our country, might pervert their power to the injury of their fellow citizens, the people are confirmed by the next article in their right to keep and bear *their private arms*.[82]

A similar interpretation appears from Anti-Federalist editorials. Samuel Adams, who had taken the modified Anti-Federalist position of conditioning ratification upon the addition of a guarantee of personal rights, had proposed in the Massachusetts Convention that "the said constitution be never construed . . . to prevent the people of the United States who are peaceable citizens, from keeping their own arms."[83] Anti-Federalist editorials triumphantly quoted this and Adams' other proposals as Madison's Bill of Rights was wending its way through the House of Representatives. The editorials crowed that the Anti-Federalist champion, Adams, had been vindicated because "every one of" his proposals (except the prohibition against a standing army) had been adopted in Madison's bill and "most probably will be adopted by the federal legislature."[84] Calling upon the public to compare Madison's bill to Adams' previous proposals, the editorials demanded that the Federalists "in justice therefor for that long tried republican" formally acknowledge Samuel Adams as the real father of Madison's bill.[85]

The significance of the bipartisan interpretation so partisanly reflected in these editorials and the Tench Coxe article is incontrovertible. The arch-Federalist Coxe described the amendment as guaranteeing to the people "their private arms." The Anti-Federalist editorials agreed totally, seeing the amendment's language as identi-

---

80. Madison, apparently considering the amendment's language and purposes too clear to require comment, did not bother to discuss it in his introductory and subsequent remarks.

81. Originally published under the pseudonym "A Pennsylvanian," these "*Remarks on the First Part of the Amendments to the Federal Constitution*" first appeared in the Philadelphia Federal Gazette, June 18, 1789, at 2, col. 1. They were reprinted by the New York Packet, June 23, 1789, at 2, cols. 1-2, and by the Boston Centenniel, July 4, 1789, at 1, col. 2.

Coxe sent a copy to Madison who replied commending its "explanatory strictures" of his proposal. 12 PAPERS OF JAMES MADISON, *surpa* note 75, at 257 (letter of June 24, 1789, to Tench Coxe).

82. Coxe, *supra* note 81, at 2 (emphasis added).

83. B. SCHWARTZ, *supra* note 72, at 675.

84. Editorial in the Boston Independent Chronicle, Aug. 20, 1789, at 2, col. 2.

85. *Id.*

cal to Adams' previous clearly individual right formulation. If any member of the first Congress had any difficulty in understanding that the amendment's intention was to protect the individual possession of private arms by the general citizenry, these newspaper articles would surely have stilled it. Nor is there reason to imagine that they experienced any such difficulty. Absent some substantial reason particular to the context, the phrase "right of the people" clearly indicates that an individual right was intended. The context here — its use throughout the Bill of Rights — consistently supports an individual right intent.

The second amendment, then, was a response to the perceived lack of individual rights guarantees, not, as state's right proponents contend,[86] a reaction to the standing army and militia control provisions of article I, section 8. The latter source of Anti-Federalist wrath was simply not addressed by the second amendment.[87] Nothing on the face of the amendment deals with the article I, section 8, concerns; certainly Madison did not see it as changing those portions of the Constitution.[88] The Anti-Federalists themselves were not placated by the amendment: when the proposed Bill of Rights reached the Senate, they unsuccessfully attempted to amend or repeal the offending clauses.[89] Thus, the second amendment cannot be read as a response to the Anti-Federalist objections to article I, section 8. Rather, the fear of federal government encroachment on the states was allayed by guaranteeing the individual right to arms, and thereby, the arms of the militia.

C. *The Philosophical and Historical Origins of the Second Amendment*

The unanimity with which Federalists and Anti-Federalists sup-

---

86. *See* sources cited in notes 13-15 *supra*. The comments of Patrick Henry and George Mason typify those cited by the state's right advocates. *See* 3 J. ELLIOT, *supra* note 68, at 43-47, 379-81.

87. The Anti-Federalists objected to the militia and standing army provisions on the ground that the federal government might so abuse its control of the militia — either by making militia service intolerable or by failing to organize the militia at all — that a standing army would be necessary. Standing armies were considered a threat to the development of the virtuous, self-reliant citizen on whom the vitality of the republic rested. *See* Shalhope, *supra* note 12, at 604-07; notes 117-18 *infra* and accompanying text. The unwillingness of Madison and the other Federalists who dominated the first Congress to deprive the federal government of the military and militia powers conferred by the original Constitution will be discussed in detail by Dr. Joyce Malcolm (to whom I am indebted on this point) in her forthcoming book.

88. *See* text at notes 76-78 *supra*. Madison modeled his draft of the amendments on the recommendations made by the state ratifying conventions, but deleted any language dealing with the art. I, sec. 8 concerns. *See generally* B. SCHWARTZ, *supra* note 72.

89. *See generally* B. SCHWARTZ, *supra* note 72.

ported an individual right to arms is a reflection of their shared philosophical and historical heritage.[90] Examination of contemporary materials reveals that the Founders ardently endorsed firearms possession as a personal right[91] and that the concept of an exclusively state's right was wholly unknown to them. The most that such an examination does to dispel the amendment's individual right phraseology is to suggest that the amendment had multiple purposes: the people were guaranteed "arms for their own personal defense, for the defense of their states and their nation, and for the purpose of keeping their rulers sensitive to the right of the people."[92] In short, detailed exploration of the Founding Fathers' attitudes as expressed in their utterances powerfully supports an individual right interpretation, though one which recognizes that the right was viewed as beneficial to society as a whole.[93]

Though such attitudes are apparent in the Founders' utterances, such contemporary materials have been so completely ignored in

---

90. The unanimity in the contemporary understanding of the second amendment helps explain the relative absence of recorded debate over it. What little debate there is appears at 1 ANNALS OF CONG. 778-80 (J. Gales ed. 1834) and relates to Madison's proposal that the amendment provide that "no person religiously scrupulous shall be compelled to bear arms." Elbridge Gerry assailed this provision, expressing the peculiar fear that it would give "an opportunity to the people in power to . . . declare who are those religiously scrupulous and prevent them from bearing arms." Gerry apparently feared that a particular faction in control of the federal government could mendaciously classify its opponents as conscientious objectors "and prevent them from bearing arms" in the militia. Moreover, the government might exclude so vast a portion of the populace from service as to turn the militia into a "select militia" of their own faction, *see* note 52 *supra* and accompanying text, or as to require raising a standing army because of the militia's insufficiency.

Gerry's statement remains both ambiguous and tangential to the modern debate. The most that can be said is that his usage is consistent with Levin's and Smith's view that "bear arms" is used purely in the sense of carrying them in the course of militia service. But this only emphasizes the irrelevance of Gerry's remarks to the amendment's guarantee that arms might be kept.

91. James Monroe included "the right to keep and bear arms" in a list of basic "human rights" that he would propose be amended into the Constitution. *See* James Monroe Papers, N.Y. Public Library (miscellaneous papers in his own handwriting). *See also* 3 J. ELLIOT, *supra* note 68, at 386 (quoting Patrick Henry) ("The great object is, that every man be armed . . . . Everyone who is able may have a gun."); *see also* notes 79-81 *supra* and accompanying text.

92. Shalhope, *supra* note 12, at 614.

93. There is, of course, nothing untoward in the idea of a constitutional right bestowed upon private individuals for purposes that are largely (or even exclusively) public in nature. That is, after all, the earliest and best established explanation of freedom of expression. *See, e.g.,* De Jonge v. Oregon, 299 U.S. 353, 364-65 (1937) (freedom of expression promotes peaceful change in government pursuant to the public will, thereby obviating any need for violent change); Whitney v. California, 274 U.S. 357, 375-76 (1927) (Holmes and Brandeis, JJ., concurring) (first amendment expresses Founders' faith that free competition in the marketplace of ideas is the only sure means of consistently achieving public policies best suited to the public welfare); Abrams v. United States, 250 U.S. 616, 630 (1919) (Holmes and Brandeis, JJ., dissenting) (same); Meiklejohn, *What Does the First Amendment Mean?*, 20 U. CHI. L. REV. 461 (1953) (freedom of expression is necessary to the American political process).

much of the modern legal literature on the amendment that they require extended consideration here.[94] Perhaps the difficulty experienced by many modern scholars in dealing with the Framers' positive attitudes toward gun ownership can be explained in terms of Bruce-Briggs' "culture conflict" theory of the gun control controversy:

> But underlying the gun control struggle is a fundamental division in our nation. The intensity of passion on this issue suggests to me that we are experiencing a sort of low-grade war going on between two alternative views of what America is and ought to be. On the one side are those who take bourgeois Europe as a model of a civilized society: a society just, equitable, and democratic; but well ordered, with the lines of responsibility and authority clearly drawn, and with decisions made rationally and correctly by intelligent men for the entire nation. To such people, hunting is atavistic, personal violence is shameful, and uncontrolled gun ownership is a blot upon civilization.
>
> On the other side is a group of people who do not tend to be especially articulate or literate, and whose world view is rarely expressed in print. Their model is that of the independent frontiersman who takes care of himself and his family with no interference from the state. They are "conservative" in the sense that they cling to America's unique pre-modern tradition — a non-feudal society with a sort of medieval liberty at large for everyman. To these people, "sociological" is an epithet. Life is tough and competitive. Manhood means responsibility and caring for your own.[95]

If we assume that most modern scholars fall into the first of the modern value categories described, it becomes understandable why they might find the views of the Founders so foreign, indeed repugnant, as to eschew exploring them — instead reflexively projecting their own values onto the amendment. For the second of the value categories described accords perfectly with the views of the Founders, except that, as intellectuals themselves, its aura of anti-intellectualism would have struck no responsive chord in them.

---

94. Whatever the explanation for it, the fact that proponents of the exclusively state's right view have shunned exploration of the Founding Fathers' attitudes toward firearms cannot be gainsaid. None of the quotations referenced at notes 66-69 *supra* and 96-107 *infra* are mentioned (much less discussed) in any of the state's right interpretation articles listed at note 13 *supra*. The sole exception is Levin, who quotes Sam Adams' clearly individual right proposal, characterizing it as *atypical*. Levin, *supra* note 13, at 159. As will become evident, that characterization is made viable only by a failure to discuss, or even acknowledge, the copious expressions of similar sentiment set out in this Article.

95. Bruce-Briggs, *supra* note 9, at 61. Various implications of this cultural conflict explanation are explored in detail in W. R. TONSO, GUN AND SOCIETY: THE SOCIAL AND EXISTENTIAL ROOTS OF THE AMERICAN ATTACHMENT TO FIREARMS, chs. 1, 2, 8 & 9 (1982) and in Tonso, *supra* note 11, at 330ff. *See also* Kessler, Gun Control: A Symbolic Crusade? (Mimeo, Rockhurst Coll., 1981).

1. *Personal Attitudes of the Founders*

"One loves to possess arms," Thomas Jefferson, the doyen of American intellectuals, wrote to George Washington on June 19, 1796.[96] We may presume that Washington agreed, for his collection contained fifty guns, and his own writings are full of laudatory references to various firearms he owned or examined.[97] John Adams also agreed. In a book on American constitutional principles he suggested that "arms in the hands of citizens" might appropriately be used in "private self-defense" or "under partial order of towns."[98] Likewise, writing after the ratification of the Constitution, but before the election of the First Congress, James Monroe included "the right to keep and bear arms" in a list of basic "human rights" that he would propose be added to the Constitution.[99]

While Monroe and Adams both supported ratification of the Constitution, its most influential advocate was James Madison. In *The Federalist No. 46* he confidently contrasted the federal government it would create to the European despotisms he contemptuously described as "afraid to trust the people with arms." He assured his fellow countrymen that they need never fear their government because of "the advantage of being armed, which the Americans possess over the people of almost every other nation . . . ."[100] Madison, who had, during the Revolution, exulted at his own and his militia comrades' ability to hit a target the size of a man's head at one hundred paces, many years later restated the sentiments of *The Federalist No. 46* thusly:

> A government resting on a minority is an aristocracy, not a Republic, and could not be safe with a numerical and physical force against it, without a standing army, an enslaved press, and a disarmed populace.[101]

On the other side of the ratification debate, Anti-Federalist Patrick Henry left no doubt as to his feelings regarding the right to possess arms. During the Virginia ratification convention he objected equally to the Constitution's inclusion of clauses specifically author-

---

96. 9 WRITINGS OF THOMAS JEFFERSON 341 (A.A. Lipscomb ed. 1903).

97. Halsey, *George Washington's Favorite Guns*, AM. RIFLEMAN, Feb. 1968, at 23. In urging Congress to pass an act enrolling the entire adult male citizenry in a general militia, President Washington opined that "a free people ought not only to be armed but disciplined. . . ." 1 PAPERS OF THE PRESIDENT 65 (Richardson ed.) Congress responded with the First Militia Act. *See* note 49 *supra*.

98. 3 J. ADAMS, A DEFENSE OF THE CONSTITUTIONS OF THE GOVERNMENT OF UNITED STATES OF AMERICA 475 (1787-88).

99. James Monroe Papers, *supra* note 91.

100. THE FEDERALIST No. 46, at 371 (J. Madison) (J.C. Hamilton ed. 1864).

101. R. KETCHAM, JAMES MADISON: A BIOGRAPHY, 64, 640 (1971).

izing a standing army and giving the federal government control of the militia, and to its omission of a clause forbidding disarmament of the individual citizen: "The great object is that every man be armed. . . . Everyone who is able may have a gun."[102] The Virginia delegates, remembering that the Revolutionary War had been sparked by the British attempt to confiscate the patriots' privately owned arms at Lexington and Concord, apparently agreed. Henry was appointed co-chairman of a committee to draft a Bill of Rights to be added to the Constitution.[103] The other co-chairman was George Mason, whose warning against a federal constitution that failed to guarantee a right to arms has already been quoted.[104]

Thomas Jefferson played little part in this debate from the remote vantage of his position as ambassador to France, but his views on arms possession as a right may be deduced from the model state constitution he wrote for Virginia in 1776. That document included the explicit guarantee that "[n]o free man shall be debarred the use of arms in his own lands."[105] All the evidence suggests that Jefferson was strongly in favor of gun ownership. A talented inventor and amateur gunsmith himself, Jefferson maintained a substantial armory of pistols and long guns at Monticello and introduced the concept of interchangeable parts into American firearms manufacture.[106] In a letter to a nephew (then fifteen) Jefferson offered the following advice:

> A strong body makes the mind strong. As to the species of exercises, I advise the gun. While this gives a moderate exercise to the Body, it gives boldness, enterprise and independence to the mind. Games played with the ball, and others of that nature, are too violent for the body and stamp no character on the mind. Let your gun therefore be the constant companion of your walks.[107]

One intellectual historian has summarized the utterances of the Founding Fathers as expressing "an almost religious quality about the relationship between men and arms."[108] When viewed in the light of this attitude and their English militia tradition, as buttressed

---

102. 3 J. ELLIOT, *supra* note 68, at 45.

103. Note, *supra* note 13, at 43.

104. *See* note 68 *supra* and accompanying text.

105. THE JEFFERSON CYCLOPEDIA 51 (Foley ed., reissued 1967).

106. Tarassuk & Wilson, *Gun Collecting's Stately Pedigree*, AM. RIFLEMAN, July 1981, at 24.

107. THE JEFFERSON CYCLOPEDIA, *supra* note 105, at 318. Another nephew tells us that Jefferson believed every boy should be given a gun at the age of ten, as Jefferson himself had been. T. JEFFERSON RANDOLPH, NOTES ON THE LIFE OF THOMAS JEFFERSON (Edgehill Randolph Collection) (1879).

108. C. Asbury, *supra* note 10, at 88.

by the republican philosophical school with which the Founders were familiar, the language of the second amendment becomes perfectly intelligible: believing self-defense an inalienable natural right,[109] and deriving from it the right to resist tyranny,[110] they guaranteed the right (derived from the foregoing) of individuals to possess arms.[111] Further, this also protected the possession of privately owned arms of the militia (which they understood to include most of the adult male population),[112] an institution they regarded as "necessary to the security of a free state."[113]

2. *The Philosophical Environment of the Founding Fathers*

Fully as great an obstacle to modern understanding as Bruce-

---

109. *See, e.g.,* 3 W. BLACKSTONE, COMMENTARIES *4 ("Self-Defense, therefore, as it is justly called the primary law of nature, so it is not, neither can it be, in fact, taken away by the law of society."); T. HOBBES, LEVIATHAN 88, 95 (1964) ("a covenant not to defend myselfe from force by force is always voyd"); Halbrook, *supra* note 10, discussion at text accompanying notes 56-78 *supra* (unpaginated manuscript) (analyzing views of Sidney and Locke). English and American divines went further still, declaring self-defense not simply a right but an obligation as well:

> He that suffers his life to be taken from him by one that hath no authority for that purpose, when he might preserve it by defense, incurs the Guilt of self murder since God hath enjoined him to seek the continuance of his life, and Nature itself teaches every creature to defend himself . . . .

C. Asbury, *supra* note 10, at 39-40 (quoting a 1747 Philadelphia sermon); *see also id.* at 28 (English writers making the same point at the time of the Glorious Revolution).

110. Eighteenth-century liberals derived the right to revolution against tyrants from Sidney and Locke, who believed that all persons possessed a universally acknowledged personal right to defend themselves against robbery or enslavement. Throughout the writings of the Founders, and particularly in the debates over the Constitution, the equation between personal self-protection and resistance to tyranny occurs again and again:

> If the representatives of the people betray their constituents, there is then no recourse left but in the exertion of that original right of self defense, which is paramount to all positive forms of government . . . ."

THE FEDERALIST NO. 28, at 227 (J. Hamilton ed. 1864); *see also* Halbrook, *supra* note 38, at 22-24 (similar statements from lesser known figures).

111. For instance, Blackstone's classification of "arms for their defense" as being among the absolute rights of individuals was derived from "the natural right of resistance and self-preservation when the sanctions of society and law are found insufficient to restrain the violence of oppression." 1 W. BLACKSTONE, COMMENTARIES *121, *143-44.

112. *See* notes 46-49 *supra* and accompanying text.

113. The Federalists viewed a small standing army as a necessity for dealing with the Indian threat and as a first line of defense against any foreign invasion. To them the militia and the armed citizenry from which it was raised were the ultimate defense in a military emergency too great to be dealt with by the standing army. The militia and armed citizenry were also the counter-poise to any danger posed by the standing army to personal liberty or the republican form of government. "Before a standing army can rule, the people must be disarmed" argued the Federalists; the inherent danger of a standing army was ameliorated in the American situation where "the whole body of the people are armed and constitute a force superior to any band of regular troops that can be, on any pretense, raised . . . ." REPORT OF THE SUBCOMMITTEE ON THE CONSTITUTION, *supra* note 10, at 4-6 (quoting Noah Webster and various other contemporary arguments in favor of ratification). The conventional pro-militia sentiment expressed in the amendment's language was as far as the Federalists would go to appease the Anti-Federalists. *Id.*

Briggs' culture conflict is the inattention of modern political philosophy to "the dynamic relationship" that the Founders' philosophy saw "between arms, the individual, and society."[114] Our world is the product of its history: our view of that world is the product of the lessons drawn from that history by the thinkers our society embraces. A conscious effort of will and imagination is necessary to assume the mind-set of eighteenth-century men whose education began with the classics, particularly the works of Plato, Aristotle and Cicero, and ended with the works of Sidney, Rousseau and Montesquieu. Thus were the Framers steeped in an understanding of liberty grounded in the role of arms in society. Thus,

> the very character of the people — the cornerstone and strength of a republican society — was related to the individual's ability and desire to arm himself against threats to his person, his property and his state.[115]

This viewpoint devolved upon eighteenth-century liberals through historical exegesis which was then viewed as the key to philosophical truth. To them classical Greece and Rome represented the highest point that civilization had yet achieved — followed by a long dark age of brutal authoritarianism from which humanity in their time was still recovering. The history of the Greek city-states and "the Roman Republic provided at once an ideal and a condign warning of the frailty of republican institutions."[116] Both that ideal and that warning were inextricably connected in the Founders' minds with the individual possession of arms. English and classical law recognized in arms possession the hallmark of citizenship and personal freedom. Thus the Greeks and Romans distinguished the mere *helot* or *metic* who was deemed to have no right to arms from the free citizen whose privilege and obligation it was to keep arms in his home so as always to be ready to defend his own rights and to rush to defend the walls when the tocsin warned of approaching enemies.[117] The philosophical tradition embraced by the Founders regarded the survival of popular government and republican institutions as wholly dependent upon the existence of a citizenry that was "virtuous" in upholding that ancient privilege and obliga-

---

114. Shalhope, *supra* note 12, at 601.

115. *Id.* at 604.

116. Halbrook, *supra* note 10, at text accompanying n.31 (unpaginated manuscript); *see also* J. MALCOLM, *supra* note 12 (on the Framer's philisophical tradition); C. Asbury, *supra* note 10.

117. *See* notes 43-44 & 54 *supra* and accompanying text. James Burgh, the late-18th-century English libertarian writer "most attractive to Americans," proclaimed that "the possession of arms is the distinction between a freeman and a slave," it being the ultimate means by which freedom was to be preserved. *See* Shalhope, *supra* note 12, at 604 (quoting Burgh).

tion. In this philosophy, the ideal of republican virtue was the armed freeholder, upstanding, scrupulously honest, self-reliant and independent — defender of his family, home and property, and joined with his fellow citizens in the militia for the defense of their polity.[118] The congruence between this ideal of republican virtue and the second of the modern value attitudes described by Bruce-Briggs is evident.

The same thought that held arms ownership vital to republican citizenship also warned the Framers that to be disarmed by government was tantamount to being enslaved by it; the possession of arms was the vital prerequisite to the right to resist tyranny.[119] The Founders learned from Aristotle that a basic characteristic of tyrants was "mistrust of the people; hence they deprive them of arms."[120] Aristotle showed that confiscation of the Athenians' personal arms had been instrumental to the tyrannies of the Peisistratus and the Thirty.[121] Machiavelli taught the Founders that Augustus and Tiberius had similarly destroyed the Roman republic.[122] Only so long as Greek and Roman citizens retained their personal arms did they retain their personal liberties and their republican form of government. That lesson was brought home to the Founders by the entire corpus of political philosophy and historical exegesis they knew: "Among Renaissance theorists as dissimilar as Nicholas Machiavelli and Sir Thomas More, Thomas Hobbes and James Harrington, there was a concensus that only men willing and able to defend themselves could possibly preserve their liberties."[123] The theme of personal

---

118. In the line of republican political philosophers beginning with Machiavelli and extending through Harrington, Nedham, Sidney, Trenchard, Gordon and Rousseau, "[c]ivic virtue came to be defined as the freeholder bearing arms in defense of his property and his state." Shalhope, *supra* note 12, at 603. For a discussion of classical republican theory, see J. POCOCK, THE POLITICAL WORKS OF JAMES HARRINGTON 54 (1977), which states:

> The rigorous equation of arms-bearing with civic capacity is one of the Machiavelli's most enduring legacies to later political thinkers. . . . Classical [republican political] theory, especially in its Machiavellian form, had emphasized the notion that the bearing and possession of arms was the individual's passsport to citizenship. . . .
>
> [T]he concept of the people active in politics because disciplined arms was a vital component in republican and Machiavellian theory. . . . [Subsequent philosophers elaborated on it] in the rapturous oratory of . . . King People [based] not merely on rotatory balloting but on the union of "arms and counsel", bullets and ballots, in a setting in which the citizens appeared in arms to manifest their citizenship, casting their votes even as they advanced and retired in the evolutions of military exercise.

119. *See* notes 109-11 *supra* and accompanying text.

120. ARISTOTLE, POLITICS 218 (J. Sinclair trans. 1962).

121. ARISTOTLE, THE ATHENIAN CONSTITUTION 47, 105 (H. Rackham trans. 1935); *see generally* Halbrook *supra* note 10.

122. MACHIAVELLI, THE ART OF WAR 20 (E. Farnsworth trans. 1965). *See generally* J. POCOCK, THE MACHIAVELLIAN MOMENT (1975).

123. J. MALCOLM, *supra* note 12, at 1. These elements in the thought of Machiavelli and

arms possession as both the hallmark and the ultimate guarantee of personal liberty appears equally in the writings of Cicero, Sidney, Locke, Trenchard, Rousseau,[124] Sir Walter Raleigh,[125] Blackstone[126] and Nedham.[127] That lesson must have been even more firmly cemented in the Founders' minds by the fact that authoritarian philosophers made the same observation in reverse, recommending arms prohibitions as the surest security for absolutism.[128]

Moreover, although the Founders' antipathy to gun bans arose out of political philosophy, it should not be supposed that eighteenth-century liberals were unaware of the crime control rationale for such legislation and had no answer to it. In the French despotism they abhorred, the single most important duty of the police, "protecting" the public security, was effected through enforcing arms prohibitions.[129] Although actually aimed at continuing the subordination of the peasantry, the ostensible reason for the French arms prohibition was to reduce homicide and other violent crime, and so was it rationalized by the French monarchs and their apologists.[130] The Founders gave such arguments short shrift, believing that if a population were actually unfit to possess arms, it was only because of the degradation induced by subjection to the oppression and exploitation of aristocratic and monarchical authoritarianism.[131] For a

---

Hobbes were relayed to the Founding Fathers through Sidney, Locke and Rousseau. *See* Halbrook, *supra* note 10.

The works of Harrington provided an equally important conduit for bringing these views to the Founders. "[I]t was [Harrington] who had first stated in English terms, the theses that only the armed freeholder was capable of independence and virtue . . . ." J. POCOCK, *supra* note 118, at 145. "As [the 17th Century] went on its way, Harringtonian and neo-Harringtonian ideas were absorbed into the opposition tradition of Whig political culture, a powerful current of thought whose effects can be traced in Europe and America, as well as in England and Scotland." *Id.* at 143.

124. *See* Halbrook, *supra* note 10; *see also* Shalhope, *supra* note 12, at 603 (quoting Trenchard and Moyle to the effect that classical republics and commonwealths had maintained popular liberty by "a general Exercise of the best of their People in the use of Arms, . . . the People being secured thereby as well against the Domestick Affronts of any of their own Citizens, as against the Foreign Invasions of ambitious and unruly Neighbors.")

125. *See* Shalhope, *supra* note 12, at 602.

126. *See* 1 W. BLACKSTONE, COMMENTARIES *143-44; 2 W. BLACKSTONE, COMMENTARIES *411-12 (citation of classical examples).

127. *See, e.g.,* NEDHAM, THE RIGHT CONSTITUTION OF A COMMONWEALTH (1656) *quoted in* J. ADAMS, *supra* note 98, at 471-72.

128. *See* Halbrook, *supra* note 10, discussion at notes 3-16 and 48-51 *supra* (discussing Plato and Jean Bodin).

129. I. CAMERON, CRIME AND REPRESSION IN THE AUVERGNE AND THE GUYENNEA 1720-1790, at 7-8 (1982).

130. *See* L. KENNETT & J. ANDERSON, *supra* note 23, at 8-16; *see also* Halbrook, *supra* note 10, discussion at notes 48-51 *supra* (discussing Jean Bodin).

131. If pressed, Madison might have admitted that the European despotisms he contemptuously dismissed as "afraid to trust the people with arms," *see* note 100 *supra* and accompanying text, were nevertheless justified in denying arms to populations so brutalized and

free and virtuous people, eighteenth-century liberalism's response, as formulated by Montesquieu and Beccaria, to the crime control argument was simply an expansive rhetorical rendition of today's slogan "when guns are outlawed, only outlaws will have guns."

> False is the idea of utility that sacrifices a thousand real advantages for one imaginary or trifling inconvenience; that would take fire from men because it burns, and water because one may drown in it; that has no remedy for evils, except destruction. The laws that forbid the carrying of arms are laws of such a nature. They disarm those only who are neither inclined nor determined to commit crimes. Can it be supposed that those who have the courage to violate the most sacred laws of humanity, the most important of the code, will respect the less important and arbitrary ones, which can be violated with ease and impunity, and which, if strictly obeyed, would put an end to personal liberty — so dear to men, so dear to the enlightened legislator — and subject innocent persons to all the vexations that the guilty alone ought to suffer? Such laws make things worse for the assaulted and better for the assailants; they serve rather to encourage than to prevent homicides, for an unarmed man may be attacked with greater confidence than an armed man. They ought to be designated as laws not preventive but fearful of crimes, produced by the tumultuous impression of a few isolated facts, and not by thoughtful consideration of the inconveniences and advantages of a universal decree.[132]

---

demoralized by generations of subjection to the *ancien regime* as to be unfit to possess them. By contrast, the proud, gun-loving Americans were upstanding, responsible, strong, independent, self-reliant — the epitome of virtuous republican citizenship. Expressing this self-satisfied attitude, Joel Barlow wrote of Americans, "[i]t is because the [Americans] are civilized," *i.e.*, not demoralized by oppression or luxury, "that they are with safety armed":

> The danger (where there is any) from armed citizens, is only to the *government*, not to the *society*; and as long as they have nothing to revenge in the government (which they cannot have while it is in their own hands) there are many advantages in their being accustomed to the use of arms, and no possible disadvantage.

Shalhope, *supra* note 12, at 607 (quoting Barlow in *Advice to the Privileged Orders in the Several States of Europe: Resulting From the Necessity and Propriety of a General Revolution in the Principle of Government*) (emphasis in original). Similarly, Timothy Dwight stated,

> [I]f proper attention be paid to the education of children in knowledge and religion, few men will be disposed to use arms, unless for their amusement, and for the defense of themselves and their country.

Shalhope, *supra* note 12, at 607 (quoting Timothy Dwight in *Travels in New England and New York*). Nevertheless, the Founders were not so Panglossian about the American character as to blind themselves to the fact that even among the virtuous there would always be a tiny fraction of evilly-disposed people whom it would be desirable to disarm selectively. *See* notes 258 & 267 *infra* and accompanying text.

    132. C. BECCARIA, ON CRIMES AND PUNISHMENTS 145 (1819). Originally published in 1764, this work was sufficiently familiar to the colonists ten years later for John Adams to have opened the Boston Massacre trial by quoting from it. *See* 3 LEGAL PAPERS OF JOHN ADAMS 28 (1965). Montesquieu's pejorative remarks on gun prohibitions (which may well have influenced Beccaria's) appear at 2 Montesquieu, SPIRIT OF LAWS 79-80 (Nugent trans., Colonial Press 1900).

    The English libertarian/republican philosophers were, if anything, even more solicitous than Beccaria and Montesquieu (who lived on the relatively peaceful Continent) of the right to possess arms for the defense of family, home and self from criminal attack as well as the oppression of government. As Shalhope noted, amidst the endemic criminal violence of 16th-

The influence of the republican philosophical tradition of the armed people upon the Founding Fathers is obvious from their own statements.[133] Likewise, the writings of lesser known figures and newspaper editorials of the period abound with favorable references to the citizenry's widespread possession of personal arms as characteristic of the "diffusion of power" necessary to preserve liberty. These writings also express fears that the new federal government might disarm the populace, leading to a "monopoly of power [which] is the most dangerous of all monopolies."[134] In short, the accepted philosophy of the times treated the right to arms as among the most vital of personal rights.

3. *English Gun Prohibition and the English Bill of Rights*

Further evidence of the link between republican government and the possession of arms was given the Founders by their view of the mother country's history. Despite England's lack of a police force, legislation prohibiting possession of firearms by others than the high nobility had been instituted under the aegis of the hated Game Acts.[135] Though the ostensible purpose was to protect England's dwindling game resources, the Acts' covert purpose was confirmed by Blackstone: "prevention of popular insurrections and resistance to the government, by disarming the bulk of the people . . . is a reason oftener meant than avowed . . . ."[136] Particularly indicative of the nefarious intent of the 1671 Game Act (at least to the minds of the Founders) was that it was evidently modeled on the French example,[137] and had appeared in the reign of Charles II. Living as we do several centuries removed, in an age in which religious tolerance is so much the norm as to be taken for granted, it is difficult for us to understand the almost hysterical execration the Founders felt for the restored Stuarts. The dissolute and debauched Charles II had martyred Algernon Sidney, the Founders' beloved philosopher of the armed people. Charles and his upright but intolerantly Catholic

---

18th century England, "[t]he individual's need to protect himself from vicious fellow citizens and corrupt authorities — both banes of any republican society — also became clear." Shalhope, *supra* note 12, at 603; *see also* note 140 *infra* and accompanying text.

133. *See* notes 96-113 *supra* and accompanying text.

134. Halbrook, *supra* note 38, at 33 (quoting *Political Maxims*, New York Daily Advertiser, Aug. 15, 1789, at 2, col. 1).

135. The Game Act of 1671, 22 Cor. II, c. 25 § 3.

136. 2 W. BLACKSTONE, COMMENTARIES *412.

137. The Game Act of 1671 followed the French pattern in limiting firearms possession to the nobility. The French legislation went even further in that it prohibited commoners from possessing swords as well as guns. *See* M. JOSSERANT & J. STEVENSON, PISTOLS, REVOLVERS AND AMMUNITION 271-72 (1972); L. KENNETT & J. ANDERSON, *supra* note 23.

brother James II were viewed as traitors who had plotted to place
England under the yoke of their Catholic ally Louis XIV of France;
through the mechanisms of a standing army and the importation of
French troops, the free English population was to be disarmed and
reduced to the condition of the French peasantry, and the Protestant
religion was to be extirpated with fire and sword in England as Louis
had done in France.[138]

Arms confiscation was a basic technique of the absolutism that
the Stuarts, at least in the Framers' eyes, had determined to impose
on England after their return from exile in France. To that end both
Charles and James seized upon a series of new and old confiscatory
devices, not the least of which was the 1671 Game Act.[139] Conscious
of the disaffection of many of his subjects, and of the precariousness
of his hold on the rest, the wily Charles never went beyond sporadic
and highly selective arms confiscations. But enforcement under the
Game Act and other legislation was enormously (though still selectively) increased during James' short reign. In addition to disarming
the actively rebellious, this policy deterred the expression of any
kind of dissent or opposition. In an age as subject to apolitical crime
and violence as seventeenth- to eighteenth-century England, few
people were courageous or foolhardy enough to want to live without
weapons to defend themselves and their families.[140]

Having rid itself of James through the "Glorious Revolution,"
Parliament composed a list of grievances against him, turning it into
a Bill of Rights to which royal assent was required as part of the
compact under which William and Mary were allowed to ascend the
English throne. Seventh among the grievances was that James had
caused his Protestant subjects "to be disarmed at a time when Papists
were both armed and imployed [*sic*] contrary to law."[141] It was concomitantly guaranteed "that the subjects which are Protestant may
have arms for their defense suitable to their conditions and as allowed by law." The significance of the phrase "as allowed by law" is

---

138. M. DAVIDSON, THE HORIZON CONCISE HISTORY OF FRANCE 96 (1971); J. GARRITY &
P. GAY, THE COLUMBIA HISTORY OF THE WORLD 738 (1972).

139. These devices and the uses made of them are detailed in J. MALCOLM, *supra* note 12,
at chs. 2-4; Malcolm, *supra* note 10, and the REPORT OF THE SUBCOMMITTEE ON THE CONSTI-
TUTION, *supra* note 10, at 2-3, from which this narrative follows. *See also* notes 148-50 *infra*
and accompanying text.

140. Throughout the colonial and pre-colonial period, England suffered a remarkable degree of violence surprising in light of its relative peacefulness today. *See, e.g.*, J. OSBORNE,
THE SILENT REVOLUTION 9 (1970) ("[T]he English were noted throughout Europe for their
turbulence and proclivity to violence."); Gurr, *Historical Trends in Violent Crime: A Critical
Review of Evidence*, 3 ANNUAL REVIEW OF CRIME AND JUSTICE (1981).

141. W. & M. Sess. 2, ch. 2 (1689).

unclear. It could have been meant to specify that the right to arms which Protestants (who then composed about ninety-eight percent of the English population)[142] were receiving was no greater than that which had pre-existed at common law. To avoid a lengthy debate which might delay the Bill's enactment, Parliament had strictly agreed that "no new principle of law" was to be included; the Bill was to be "a mere recital of those existing rights of Parliament and of the subject, which James had outraged, and which William must promise to observe."[143]

More likely, Parliament meant the phrase "as allowed by law" to preserve its own power to disarm the subjects, simply clarifying that only the king was prevented from doing so. If this is what the phrase stood for, the qualification it adds to the English Bill of Rights is manifestly unimportant in interpreting the second amendment, which was expressly intended to restrict the legislative as well as the executive branch.[144] Partisans of the exclusively state's right theory have seemed to invest the question of Parliament's power with some significance, commenting that twentieth-century England has adopted one of the world's most stringent anti-gun policies, notwithstanding the 1689 Bill of Rights.[145] If this is intended to suggest that Congress is free to do likewise, it completely misses the distinction between the American system of constitutional rights and the non-constitutional English system in which even the most sacrosanct

---

142. *Cf.* J. JONES, THE REVOLUTION OF 1688 IN ENGLAND 77 n. 2 (1972) (Catholics comprised 2% of the population of England during the 17th century). As Smith points out, Catholicism was illegal and Catholics were banned from public office in England through the mid-19th century. J. Smith, *supra* note 10, at 24.

143. G. TREVELYAN, THE ENGLISH REVOLUTION, 1688-1689, at 150-51 (1954).

144. Madison's notes in formulating the Bill of Rights expressly reflect his dissatisfaction with the English Bill of Rights because it applied only to Protestants and because, being no more than an act of one Parliament, it was subject to repeal by a later one. 12 PAPERS OF JAMES MADISON, *supra* note 75, at 193-94. Indeed, the Founders apparently believed that contemporary English arms policies were highly restrictive and assigned the blame for this to the defective and equivocal language of the English Bill of Rights. Provincial Americans like Madison, who had never been abroad, gained their knowledge of current English institutions and character from the hyperbolic philipics of the alienated English republican/libertarian philosophers. Thus the Continental Congress compared our robust men, "trained to arms from their infancy and animated by the love of liberty," to the "debauched" British population, so corrupted by "luxury and dissipation" that they had allowed themselves to be disarmed and made utterly dependent on a standing army. Shalhope, *supra* note 12, at 606. Similarly, St. George Tucker, a distinguished American jurist and member of Madison's Virginia circle, contemptuously compared the second amendment's unqualified guarantee to the English Bill of Rights, which he believed to be so rotten with exceptions "that not one man in five hundred can keep a gun in house without being subject to a penalty." 1 ST. G. TUCKER, BLACKSTONE'S COMMENTARIES WITH NOTES OF REFERENCE TO THE CONSTITUTION AND LAW OF THE FEDERAL GOVERNMENT 143 n.40 (1803).

145. *See, e.g.,* Feller & Gotting, *supra* note 13, at 49 n.10; G. NEWTON & F. ZINRING, *supra* note 13, at 225.

rights guaranteed by one Parliament may be abrogated by its successors. Parliament's power to disarm no more proves that Congress can violate the second amendment than the fact that twentieth-century Parliaments have abolished various traditional rights of the criminally accused in Northern Ireland[146] proves that Congress is free to legislate in derogation of the fourth, fifth and sixth amendments.

What is significant about the English Bill of Rights is the undeniable support that it provides for the individual right position. There were no states in England to be protected against disarmament. So what Parliament was complaining of could only have been the seizure of arms from *individual* citizens in violation of their common-law rights. Because the Founders knew that the English forerunner to their own Bill of Rights contained an individual right to arms, and because the Founders themselves emphatically endorsed such a right, it seems unlikely that the right to arms which they wrote into their own Constitution was not intended, at least partly, to protect such an individual right.

To avoid the highly adverse implications of the English Bill of Rights, some state's right exponents have resorted to what can only be described as fudging the facts. They deny that James II was actually confiscating any arms from his Protestant subjects. They assert, instead, that Parliament used the word "disarmed" merely figuratively, referring to the fact that James had replaced various Protestant officials with Catholics, particularly in the English military.[147] This interpretation is demonstrably untrue. Space does not permit full detailing of the later Stuarts' arms confiscation efforts.[148] Sufficient for present purposes are the details noted in the *Report of the Subcommittee on the Constitution*:

> In 1662, the Militia Act was enacted empowering officials "to search for and seize all arms in the custody or possession of any person or persons whom the said lieutenants or any two or more of their deputies shall judge dangerous to the peace of the kingdom." Gunsmiths were ordered to deliver to the government lists of all purchasers.

---

146. *See generally* Bishop, *Law in the Control of Terrorism and Insurrection: The British Laboratory Experience*, 42 LAW & CONTEMP. PROB. 140 (1978).

147. *See, e.g.,* Note, *supra* note 13, at 426:

As one commentator has pointed out, these grievances were not intended to assert that James II disarmed Protestants in any literal sense, but instead referred to his practice of replacing Protestants with Catholics at important military posts . . . .

The commentator referred to is Weatherup, *supra* note 13, at 973.

148. These efforts are the subject of a forthcoming book by Dr. Joyce Malcolm. The results of her exhaustive original research in English records (many of which are available only in that country) are summarized in J.MALCOLM, *supra* note 12; Malcolm, *supra* note 10.

These confiscations were continued under James II, who directed them particularly against the [Protestant] Irish population: "Although the country was infested by predatory bands, a Protestant gentleman could scarcely obtain permission to keep a brace of pistols." [Quoting Macauley's History of England; footnotes deleted.]

In 1688, the government of James was overturned in a peaceful uprising which came to be known as "The Glorious Revolution." Parliament resolved that James had abdicated and promulgated a Declaration of Rights, later enacted as the Bill of Rights. Before coronation, his successor William of Orange, was required to swear to respect these rights. The debates in the House of Commons over this Declaration of Rights focused largely upon disarmament under the 1662 Militia Act. One member complained that "an act of Parliament was made to disarm all Englishmen, who the lieutenant should suspect, by day or night, by force or otherwise — this was done in Ireland for the sake of putting arms into Irish [Catholic] hands." The speech of another is summarized as "militia bill — power to disarm all England — now done in Ireland." A third complained of "Arbitrary power exercised by the ministry . . . Militia — imprisoning without reason; disarming — *himself disarmed*." Yet another summarized his complaints "Militia Act — an abominable thing to disarm the nation . . . ."[149]

These and various other examples establish beyond peradventure that James II aggressively enforced the largely dormant arms proscriptions he had inherited so as to affect not only the common people but some of their elected representatives,[150] that this policy was diametrically contrary to the principles of the common law as they were then understood, and that one purpose of the English Bill of Rights was to place the possession of arms beyond monarchical interference — at least as far as the Protestant ninety-eight percent of the population was concerned.[151]

---

149. REPORT OF THE SUBCOMMITTEE ON THE CONSTITUTION, *supra* note 10, at 2-3.

150. One of the Members of Parliament was Sir John Knight, former Mayor of Bristol (then England's second city), and the defendant in Rex v. Knight, 87 Eng. Rep. 73 (K.B. 1686). This case's rejection of James II's attempt to prosecute so prominent a Protestant under the arms laws was a *cause célèbre* and one of the events leading to the Glorious Revolution. Personal communication from Dr. Malcolm.

151. Having nullified the 1671 Game Act's gun prohibition by the 1689 Bill of Rights, Parliament went on to delete the prohibition in subsequent Game Acts. *See, e.g.,* 4 & 5 W. & M. 23 (1692); 6 Anne 16 (1706); *see also* Rex v. Gardner, 7 Mod. 279, 280, 87 Eng. Rep. 1240, 1241 (K.B. 1739) (holding that these Game Acts do "not extend to prohibit a man from keeping a gun for his necessary defense"); Mallock v. Eastly, 7 Mod. 482, 87 Eng. Rep. 1370 (K.B. 1744) ("the mere having a gun was no offense within the game laws, for a man may keep a gun for the defense of his house and family"). Writing in 1793, Edward Christian, the English editor of Blackstone's 12th edition, annotated Blackstone's strictures against the gun confiscation provisions of the Game Acts with the comment that these had long since been repealed so that "every one is at liberty to keep or carry a gun, if he does not use it for the destruction of game." 2 W. BLACKSTONE, COMMENTARIES 411 (12th ed. London 1793-95). Even Catholics, though forbidden to stockpile arms, were acknowledged the right to retain such as were necessary to defend their homes by the 1689 "Act for better securing the Government by disarming Papists and reputed Papists." 1 W. & M. sess. 1, ch. 15 (1689).

D. *Eighteenth- and Nineteenth-Century Interpretation of the Second Amendment*

The final proof that an individual right was guaranteed by the second amendment lies in Madison's formulation of the amendment in terms that he must have known his contemporaries would interpret as protecting an individual right. As we shall see, that is how his contemporaries did read the amendment. Fundamental to understanding the original intention behind the Constitution is the observation that the Founders

> were born and brought up in the atmosphere of the common law, and *thought and spoke in its vocabulary.* . . . [W]hen they came to put their conclusions into the form of fundamental law in a compact draft, they expressed them in terms of the common law, *confident that they would be shortly and easily understood.* [For that reason,] the language of the Constitution cannot be interpreted safely except by reference to the common law and to British institutions as they were when the instrument was framed and adopted.[152]

Reference to the great common law commentators known to the Founders shows Hawkins, Bracton and Coke all affirming the existence of a common law right to possess arms for home defense, while Blackstone included that right among those he classified as the five "absolute rights of individuals" at common law.[153]

Not only the great common law commentators, but also the English courts affirmed the individual right to arms. When Parliament overthrew the Stuarts, it wrote the common law liberty to possess arms into the English Bill of Rights. Thereafter English court decisions, reports of which were available to the Founders, had recognized that "a man may keep a gun for the defense of his house and family," denying that the Game Acts then current "prohibit a man from keeping a gun for his necessary defense. . . ."[154] Moreover, the English Game Acts that prohibited firearms had never been a part of the colonial law,[155] which the Founders knew from their own

---

152. *Ex parte* Grossman, 267 U.S. 87, 108-09 (1925) (emphasis added).

153. 1 W. BLACKSTONE, COMMENTARIES *144; *see also* 3 E. COKE, INSTITUTES 161-62 (5th ed. 1671); III HENRICI DE BRACTON, DE LEGIBUS ET CONSUETUDINIBUS ANGLIAE 20-25 (Twiss ed. 1880); 1 W. HAWKINS, PLEAS OF THE CROWN 135-36 (5th ed. 1771).

154. Mallock v. Eastly, 7 Mod. 482, 489, 87 Eng. Rep. 1370, 1374 (K.B. 1744); Rex v. Gardner, 7 Mod. 279, 280, 87 Eng. Rep. 1240, 1241 (K.B. 1739); *see* note 151 *supra*. These cases were printed in English law reports that were available both in the personal collections of American lawyers and in American law libraries by the mid-18th century. In addition, the *Gardner* opinion is reported almost in full in a volume referred to by Blackstone. R. BURNS, THE JUSTICE OF THE PEACE AND PARISH OFFICER, *Game* § 8, at 442 (1755); *see* 4 W. BLACK-STONE, COMMENTARIES * 175, n."j". This legal commentary was available in the colonies. The Adams family donated John Adams' personal copy to the Boston Public Library, which still owns it. *See* J. Smith, *supra* note 10, at 63.

155. Although colonial law was generally derived from English common law, any common

experience and to which they presumably referred in determining what the pre-existing "rights" were that the amendment guaranteed. Not only did colonial law allow every trustworthy adult to possess arms, but it deemed this right so vital that every colony or state had exempted firearms from distraint for execution because of debt.[156] Given this background, it is inconceivable that Madison and his colleagues in the first Congress would have chosen the language they did for the amendment unless they intended a personal right. They must necessarily have known that their undefined phrase "right of the people to keep and bear arms" would be understood by their contemporaries in light of to common law formulations like Blackstone's "absolute rights of individuals."

That indeed is precisely how their contemporaries did interpret it. The second amendment was analyzed in at least four legal commentaries, authored by men who were closely acquainted with Madison or other members of the first Congress. The earliest of these commentaries, written by Madison's ally Tench Coxe, has already been quoted.[157] Next came St. George Tucker's 1803 edition of Blackstone's Commentaries, annotated to explain parallel developments in American law.[158] We may assume that Tucker was learned in American law since he was a justice of the most distinguished court of his day, the Virginia Supreme Court. His familiarity with the thought underlying the Bill of Rights may also be assumed. Not only was he an important member of the generation that produced it, but the Virginia circles in which he moved included both Madison and Jefferson.[159] Tucker annotated Blackstone's inclusion

---

law or statutory principle inapplicable to the situation or conditions prevailing in the colonies was excluded. *See* W. LaFave & A. Scott, Criminal Law § 9, at 60 (1972); Smith, *The English Criminal Law in Early America* in J. Smith & T. Barnes, The English Legal System: Carry Over To The Colonies 14-17 (1975). Parliamentary acts designed to provide the nobility a monopoly both of arms and of the shrinking English game resources were plainly inapplicable to the colonies, where there was no nobility and the supply of game seemed inexhaustible. It bears emphasis in this connection that the import of English common law precedent in interpreting the American Bill of Rights "is subject to the qualification that the common law rule invoked shall not be one rejected by our ancestors as unsuited to their civil or political condition." Grosjean v. American Press, 297 U.S. 233, 249 (1936); *see also* note 234 *infra*.

156. *See* J. Smith, *supra* note 10, at 34. In general, the colonies and early states knew only four kinds of gun laws: (a) those which required/allowed every trustworthy citizen to possess arms, both for militia service and otherwise; (b) those prohibiting gun ownership or carrying for Indians and blacks; (c) those which prohibited hunting or shooting in or near urban areas; and (d) those which prohibited the carrying or brandishing of arms in such a manner as to cause fear.

157. *See* notes 81-82 *supra* and accompanying text.

158. St. George Tucker, *supra* note 144.

159. "The Jefferson Papers in the Library of Congress show that both Tucker and Rawle were friends of, and corresponded with, Thomas Jefferson." Report of the Subcommittee

of the right to possess firearms as among the "absolute rights of individuals" in England, with the observation that in America this right had been constitutionalized by the enactment of the second amendment.[160] William Rawle, whose general commentary on the Constitution appeared in 1825, seems also to have never considered any but an individual right interpretation of the second amendment. Rawle was both influential and well-known enough to have been offered the attorney generalship several times by Washington.[161] So far was Rawle from the state's right concept that he flatly declared that the second amendment prohibited state, as well as federal, laws disarming individuals.[162] More enduring in its fame than Rawle's work, though not necessarily more influential in its time, is the *Commentaries on the Constitution* of Mr. Justice Story, a younger contemporary of the Founders and a Jefferson appointee to the United States Supreme Court. He, too, eulogized "[t]he right *of the citizens* to keep and bear arms" as "the palladium of the liberties of a republic."[163]

One further point about the contemporaneity of these commentaries suggests itself: as we have seen, Coxe's article received Madison's approval even before the Amendment's enactment.[164] Published almost fifteen years thereafter, St. George Tucker's American edition of Blackstone became a standard reference work on Anglo-American common law for early nineteenth-century Americans. Literally hundreds of those who had served in Congress or state legislatures during the enactment of the Bill of Rights were still alive at that time. Many of them, including Madison himself, were still liv-

---

ON THE CONSTITUTION, *supra* note 10, at 7. The Jefferson papers archived at the Library of Congress contain 22 letters between Jefferson and Tucker spanning the period 1775 to 1809. LIBRARY OF CONGRESS, INDEX TO THOMAS JEFFERSON'S PAPERS 139 (Wash. D.C., Govt. Printing Off. 1976). Their actual correspondence probably exceeded this, since much of Jefferson's pre-1780 correspondence was lost when the British occupied Richmond in that year. *Id.* at viii. Tucker's association with Madison began at least as early as the Annapolis Convention of 1786 to which they were both delegates. *See* M. COLEMAN, ST. GEORGE TUCKER, CITIZEN OF NO MEAN CITY 87, 124, 182. In addition, both Tucker's brother and his best friend were members of the first Congress. *Id.* at 35, 61, 113-14.

160. 1 ST. G. TUCKER, *supra* note 144, at 143 n.40, 300.

161. D. BROWN, EULOGIUM UPON WILLIAM RAWLE 15 (1837). As to Rawle's correspondence and friendship with Jefferson, see note 159 *supra*. The Jefferson papers include five letters between them in the 1792-1793 period. LIBRARY OF CONGRESS, *supra* note 159, at 118.

162. W. RAWLE, A VIEW OF THE CONSTITUTION 125-26 (2d ed. 1829). Rawle shared this view with Hamilton, who saw the people's possession of arms as guaranteeing freedom from state as well as from federal tyranny. The armed populace, "by throwing themselves into either scale, will infallibly make it preponderate" against either a federal or a state invasion of popular rights. THE FEDERALIST No. 28, at 228 (A. Hamilton) (J.C. Hamilton ed. 1864).

163. 3 J. STORY, COMMENTARIES ON THE CONSTITUTION 746 (1833) (emphasis added).

164. *See* note 81 *supra*.

ing twenty-five years later when Rawle's and Story's commentaries were published.[165] Those commentaries remained the standard nineteenth-century reference works on the Constitution at least until Cooley appeared.[166] If these commentaries were erroneously presenting as an individual right of the people what was intended to be only a collective right of the states, surely one or more former legislators would have remonstrated the authors or publishers and, if correction was not forthcoming, publicly clarified the record.

To reiterate, the amendment was written in language which its authors would have adopted only if they intended to secure an individual right, because they knew that that was how their audience would inevitably understand it. Equally dispositive, that audience, composed of people like Coxe, Tucker, Rawle, and Story of the Framers' own generation, and of judges and commentators from the succeeding generations closest in time to the Framers, uniformly did so understand the amendment.[167] The general rule in constitutional construction is one of deference to contemporary interpretations with the greatest weight being accorded those interpretations closest in time to the enactment of the constitutional provision in question.[168] The tone and unanimity of contemporary interpretation of the second amendment discloses what was apparently a perfectly clear understanding to those generations closest in time to the amendment's formulation. Thus, an exclusively state's right theory cannot survive the observation that it is so much a product of the twentieth century that neither the Framers nor any eighteenth- or nineteenth-century commentator or court breathed even the slightest intimation of it.

---

165. Madison lived until 1836, reiterating to the last his belief in an individually armed citizenry. *See* notes 96-113 *supra* and accompanying text. John Adams and Thomas Jefferson both died on July 4, 1826. Without attempting to document the longevity of each legislator who passed on the amendment, thumbing through D. MORRIS & I. MORRIS, WHO WAS WHO IN AMERICAN POLITICS (1974), yields the following dates of death: U.S. Senator Albert Gallatin, 1849; U.S. Representative Jeremiah Smith, 1842; U.S. Senator Paine Wingate, 1838; U.S. Senator Aaron Burr, 1836.

166. The individual right interpretation seems to have been as self evident to Cooley as it was to his predecessors Rawle and Story. *See, e.g.,* T. COOLEY, THE GENERAL PRINCIPLES OF CONSTITUTIONAL LAW IN THE UNITED STATES OF AMERICA 298-99 (3d ed. 1898); *cf.* T. COOLEY, A TREATISE ON THE CONSTITUTIONAL LIMITATIONS WHICH REST UPON THE LEGISLATIVE POWER OF THE STATES OF THE AMERICAN UNION 498-99 (7th ed. 1903) (federal and state constitutions protect the right to bear arms).

167. For 19th-century judicial interpretation, see notes 169-84 *infra* and accompanying text.

168. *See, e.g.,* Powell v. McCormack, 395 U.S. 486, 547 (1969).

II. Subsequent Interpretation of the Right to Arms

In attempting to identify a pre-twentieth century origin for the exclusively state's right position, several of its proponents have noted that one pre-1789 state constitutional guarantee of a right to arms, and several early post-1789 ones specified a "common defense" purpose, without mentioning any individual self-defense purpose.[169] If such provisions had been interpreted as not guaranteeing an individual right to provide for common defense, they would be persuasive evidence that such a position was known to the Framers. Instead, every one of the twenty-two pre-1906 state cases construing a state constitutional right to arms provision, including some provisions that referred only to a common defense purpose, recognized an individual right to possess at least militia-type arms.[170] A nonindividual right interpretation first appeared in a 1906 Kansas decision which is plainly wrong even as a construction of the Kansas constitution.[171]

---

169. *See, e.g.,* MASS. CONST. of 1780, 1st Part, art. XVII ("The people have a right to keep and to bear arms for the common defence."). Other pre-20th-century state constitutional provisions with a right to arms "for the [or their] common defence" include ARK. CONST. of 1836, art. II, § 21; FLA. CONST. of 1838, art. I, § 21; ME. CONST. of 1819, art. 1, § 16; S.C. CONST. of 1868, art. I, § 28; TENN. CONST. of 1796, art. XI, § 26; *see also* GA. CONST. of 1865, art. I, § 4 ("A well-regulated militia, being necessary to the security of a free state, the right of the people to keep and bear arms shall not be infringed."); LA. CONST. of 1879, art. III (same as Georgia, plus: "This shall not prevent the passage of laws to punish those who carry weapons concealed."); N.C. CONST. of 1776, Declaration of Rights, art. XVII ("for the defence of the state").

But see, e.g., PA. CONST. of 1776, Declaration of Rights, art. XIII ("The people have a right to bear arms *for the defence of themselves* and the state.") (emphasis added). Other early state constitutional provisions providing for a right to arms "for the defence of themselves [or himself] and the state" include the following: ALA. CONST. of 1819, art. I, § 23; CONN. CONST. of 1818, art. I, § 17; IND. CONST. of 1816, art. I, § 20; KY. CONST. of 1792, art. XII, § 23; MICH. CONST. of 1835, art. I, § 13; MISS. CONST. of 1817, art. I, § 23; MO. CONST. of 1820, art. XIII, § 3; OHIO CONST. of 1802, art. VIII, § 20; PA. CONST. of 1790, art. IX, § 21; VT. CONST. of 1777, ch. I, § 15.

170. Wilson v. State, 33 Ark. 557, 34 Am. Rep. 52 (1878); Nunn v. State, 1 Ga. 243 (1846); *In re* Brickey, 8 Idaho 597, 70 P. 609 (1902); Bliss v. Commonwealth, 12 Ky. 90, 2 Litt. 80 (1822); Andrews v. State, 50 Tenn. (3 Heisk.) 165 (1871); Smith v. Ishenhour, 43 Tenn. (3 Cold.) 214 (1866); State v. Rosenthal, 75 Vt. 295, 55 A. 610 (1903); *see* State v. Reid, 1 Ala. 612, 619 (1840); Fife v. State, 31 Ark. 455, 459-62 (1876); State v. Buzzard, 4 Ark. 18, 27, 32 (1842); Hill v. State, 53 Ga. 472, 474-75 (1874); State v. Chandler, 5 La. Ann. 489 (1850); Aymette v. State, 21 Tenn. 154, 2 Hum. 119 (1840); Simpson v. State, 13 Tenn. 356, 5 Yer. 292 (1833); Cockrum v. State, 24 Tex. 394, 402 (1859); *cf.* State v. Mitchell, 3 Blackf. 229 (Ind. 1833) (statute prohibiting wearing or carrying concealed weapons is constitutional); State v. Jumel, 13 La. Ann. 399 (1858) (same); State v. Newsom, 27 N.C. 250, 5 Ired.. 181 (1844) (same); State v. Duke, 42 Tex. 455 (1875) (similar statute); English v. State, 35 Tex. 473 (1872) (statute prohibiting certain unusual weapons is constitutional); State v. Workman, 35 W. Va. 367, 373, 14 S.E. 9 (1891) (concealed weapon statute).

171. *See* Salina v. Blaksley, 72 Kan. 230, 83 P. 619 (1905); note 31 *supra*. This case, which presents a "collective right" theory, is sometimes viewed as an early example of the exclusively state's right approach. It is difficult to believe, however, that the Kansas Supreme Court meant to suggest that its constitution's right to arms guarantee was intended to protect the state's own right to possess arms. Such an interpretation reduces the state constitutional guarantee to nonsense, construing it as if it read: "the state shall not infringe the state's right to keep arms or

Implicit in some of these nineteenth-century individual right cases is the proposition that even if a militia or "common defense" motive is specified for guaranteeing a right, that right is measured by the language of the guarantee given, and is not qualified or limited in the absence of some specific qualifying language.[172] As we shall see, other courts and commentators have construed the statement of a militia or "common defense" purpose as limiting the kinds of arms guaranteed individuals to those commonly used by soldiers.[173] Even where the right specified is to have a gun for one purpose, however, one who lawfully has it for that purpose may properly use it for such other purposes as hunting or the defense of his life or another's.

Some of these nineteenth-century state cases were based upon the second amendment in addition to the state constitutional provision.[174] Many of them upheld specific and limited arms controls on the ground that, while the right was individual in nature, it included only militia-type arms and extended only to carrying them openly, not concealed.[175] The only flat prohibitions of gun ownership that were upheld were laws from the slave states that prohibited guns to slaves or free blacks. The reasoning of these cases makes them the proverbial exception that proves the rule. Beginning from the universally accepted individual right premise, these courts reasoned that

---

have its militia bear them." The REPORT OF THE SUBCOMMITTEE ON THE CONSTITUTION, *supra* note 10, at 11, argues that while it is possible to argue that a right to arms provision in the *federal* constitution was intended to protect the states, it is conceptually absurd to suggest that such a provision inserted into a *state* constitution was intended to protect the state rather than individuals. "State bills of rights necessarily protect only against action by the state, and by definition a state cannot infringe its own rights; to attempt to protect a right belonging to the state by inserting it in a limitation of the state's own powers would create an absurdity."

172. Hardy & Stompoly, *supra* note 3, at 76-77, make this argument explicit in regard to the second amendment, analogizing to the first amendment's guarantee of a right to assembly. Although the motive of allowing the people to petition for redress of grievances is specified in the first amendment, the right of assembly has not been construed as strictly limited by that statement of motivation. Indeed, it has been extrapolated into a right of association for innumerable purposes, of which petitioning for redress of grievances is but an infrequently encountered one. *See also* Gardiner, *supra* note 10, at 83.

173. *See, e.g.,* English v. State, 35 Tex. 473, 475 (1872) (quoting 2 J. BISHOP, THE CRIMINAL LAW § 124 (3d ed. 1865)):

As to its interpretation, if we look to this question in the light of judicial reason, without the aid of specific authority, we shall be led to the conclusion that the provision protects only the right to "keep" such "arms" as are used for purposes of war, in distinction from those which are employed in quarrels and broils, and fights between maddened individuals, since such only are adapted to promote "the security of a free state." In like manner the right to "bear" arms refers merely to the military way of using them, not to their use in bravado and affray.

See also notes 193-94 *infra* and accompanying text.

174. *E.g.,* State v. Buzzard, 4 Ark. 18 (1842); Nunn v. State, 1 Ga. 243 (1846); State v. Chandler, 5 La. Ann. 489 (1850); Cockrum v. State, 24 Tex. 394 (1859).

175. *E.g.,* State v. Buzzard, 4 Ark. 18 (1842); Nunn v. State, 1 Ga. 243 (1846); Aymette v. State, 21 Tenn. 154, 2 Hum. 119 (1840).

blacks could be denied the right to arms because they were excluded by race from *all* privileges of citizenship.[176] Adopting that conclusion in *Dred Scott*,[177] Mr. Chief Justice Taney offered an *argumentum ad horribilis* that exemplified the individual right interpretation expounded by all the courts and commentators relatively close in time to the amendment. Obviously blacks could not be recognized as citizens, Taney declared, because then the (to him) salutary Southern laws requiring their disarmament could not stand in the face of constitutional guarantees of the right to arms.[178]

Dred Scott was apparently the only ante-bellum Supreme Court reference to right-to-arms guarantees. Several years after the Civil War the Court voided a federal prosecution of private persons for attempting to deprive blacks of their newly recognized rights as freedmen to assemble and to bear arms.[179] Pointing out that only private action had been alleged, the Court denied federal jurisdiction on the ground that freedom of assembly and the right to arms are guaranteed only against congressional infringement. But it obviously viewed the right to arms as an individual one, stating that the amendment leaves "the people to look [to state law] for their protection against any violation by their fellow citizens" of that right.[180]

Next came *Presser v. Illinois*,[181] in which the petitioner claimed that the amendment invalidated laws which prohibited the unlicensed organization, training and marching of para-military groups. The *Presser* Court responded by stressing the obvious: the subject matter of the second amendment is only the right of *individuals* to possess arms; constitutional provisions relating to *group* arm-bearing appear only in article I, sections 8 and 10. Moreover, those provisions refer only to the militia and formal state or federal military forces, not to private armies. Thus, the challenged state legislation simply did not fall within the amendment's subject matter. The Court also noted that, even if the right to arms had been implicated, the amendment guarantees it against only the federal government, not the states. This was standard nineteenth-century doctrine, based on prior holdings that the provisions of the Bill of Rights, standing alone, did not apply against the states themselves and were not made

---

176. *E.g.*, State v. Newsom, 27 N.C. 250, 5 Ired. 181 (1844); *cf.* Cooper v. Mayor of Savannah, 4 Ga. 68 (1848) (blacks were not citizens).

177. Scott v. Sanford, 60 U.S. (19 How.) 690 (1856).

178. *See* 60 U.S. (19 How.) at 416-17.

179. United States v. Cruikshank, 92 U.S. 542 (1875).

180. 92 U.S. at 553.

181. 116 U.S. 252 (1886).

applicable by the privileges and immunities clause of the fourteenth amendment.[182] That the Court rejected a first amendment claim on the same nonincorporation grounds emphasizes its implicit individual right view of the second amendment. Second and fourth amendment challenges were also rejected on that rationale as an additional ground in *Miller v. Texas*.[183] In both cases the Court treated the second amendment right similarly to first and fourth amendment rights, subjecting all three to the contemporary doctrine that individual rights were protected only against the federal government and not against the states. Likewise, in *Robertson v. Baldwin* the amendment was grouped with the Bill of Rights as a whole in illustrating the generalization that rights guaranteed to individuals are nevertheless subject to qualifications.[184]

United States v. Miller,[185] a 1939 case, is the Supreme Court's only extended analysis of the second amendment. *Miller* arose out of a challenge to an early federal gun law. During the decade of Prohibition, with its gang wars, and the subsequent depression years of John Dillinger and Bonnie and Clyde, sawed-off shotguns and submachine guns had become widely identified in the public mind as "gangster weapons."[186] The National Firearms Act of 1934[187] contained various provisions against such weapons, including a prohibition, which Miller and a confederate were accused of violating, against the possession of a sawed-off shotgun that had been transported in interstate commerce. The defendants successfully moved the trial court to void their indictment on the ground that this prohibition violated the second amendment. On the Government's ap-

---

182. *See* Slaughter-House Cases, 83 U.S. (16 Wall.) 36 (1872) (denying that the Bill of Rights had been made applicable to the states by virtue of the privileges and immunities clause of the 14th amendment); Barron v. Mayor of Baltimore, 32 U.S. (7 Pet.) 243 (1833) (holding that the fifth amendment applies only against the federal government, not against the states).

183. 153 U.S. 535 (1894). Although this case and its predecessors represent a doctrine which has long been superseded by the concept of selective incorporation, *see, e.g.,* Duncan v. Louisiana, 391 U.S. 145 (1968) (sixth amendment right to jury trial), extended analysis of these cases is required if only to correct the extraordinary way in which they have sometimes been read in relation to the second amendment. For instance, J. ALVIANI & W. DRAKE, *supra* note 2, at 9, cite the *Miller v. Texas* line of cases as evidence that "the Second Amendment does not guarantee a personal right to own firearms. . . . Personal self protection was never an issue in the adoption of the Second Amendment." In fact, nothing to support that interpretation will be found anywhere in those cases. Nor does it at all follow from their doctrine that the Bill of Rights applies only against the federal government. On the incorporation issue, see notes 206-32 *infra* and accompanying text.

184. 165 U.S. 275, 281-82 (1897).

185. 307 U.S. 174 (1939).

186. *See* L. KENNETT & J. ANDERSON, *supra* note 23, at 202-03.

187. National Firearms Act, ch. 757, 48 Stat. 1236 (1934). L. KENNETT & J. ANDERSON, *supra* note 23, at 204-12, extensively discuss the history of the Act's provisions.

peal, the Supreme Court reversed, emphasizing that the defendants had merely attacked the indictment (and, therefore, the statute) on its face, without any attempt at a factual demonstration that sawed-off shotguns were the kind of weapons contemplated by the amendment. The Court followed the reasoning of those nineteenth- century courts and commentators who construed the right to arms as individual but applicable only to those weapons commonly used for militia purposes:

> In the absence of any evidence tending to show that possession or use of any "shotgun having a barrel of less than eighteen inches in length" at this time has some reasonable relationship to the preservation or efficiency of a well regulated militia, we cannot say that the Second Amendment guarantees the right to keep and bear such an instrument. Certainly it is not within judicial notice that this weapon is any part of the ordinary military equipment or that its use could contribute to the common defense. *Aymette v. State*, 2 Humphreys (Tenn.) 154, 158.[188]

This holding has been widely misunderstood, most surpisingly by proponents of the individual right position. They have even gone so far as to denigrate its authority by pointing out that it was rendered on the basis of only the Government's one-sided briefing.[189] Additionally, critics have attacked what they suppose to be the opinion's factual basis, pointing out that shotguns were used by regular troops in World War I and Vietnam, and by guerrillas, commandos, and so on in World War II and other twentieth-century conflicts.[190]

Equally surprising, state's right proponents have acclaimed the opinion. Ignoring the fact that its holding focuses entirely on the weapon, they have emphasized its language linking the amendment's purpose to the "militia": "With obvious purpose to assure the continuation and render possible the effectiveness of [militia] forces the declaration and guarantee of the Second Amendment were made. It must be interpreted and applied with that end in view."[191] But this statement, which appears at approximately the median point of the opinion, in fact repudiates the state's right argument when read in the context of what the Court indicated "the militia" to be. The ensuing half of the opinion is given over to exhaustive citations of original and secondary sources that demonstrated to the Court that:

> The signification attributed to the term Militia appears from the de-

---

188. 307 U.S. at 178; *see also* note 173 *supra*.

189. *See, e.g.,* Caplan, *supra* note 10, at 44-48; Gardiner, *supra* note 10, at 88. Having been released by the trial court, the defendants filed no brief on appeal, but simply disappeared into the criminal milieu from which they had involuntarily surfaced.

190. *See* Cases v. United States, 131 F.2d 916, 922 (1st Cir. 1942); Black, *From Trenches to Squad Cars*, AM. RIFLEMAN, June 1982, at 30, 72-73.

191. 307 U.S. at 178.

bates in the [Constitutional] Convention, the history and legislation of Colonies and States, and the writings of approved commentators. These show plainly enough that the Militia comprised *all males physically capable of acting in concert for the common defense* . . . [a]nd further, that ordinarily when called for service these men were expected to appear bearing *arms supplied by themselves* and of the kind in common use at the time.[192]

Perhaps *Miller* has been so misunderstood by zealous partisans because it steers an almost perfect middle course between today's contending extremes — those who claim that the amendment guarantees nothing to individuals versus those who claim that its guarantee is unlimited. Far from upholding the state's right position, the Court clearly recognized that the defendants could claim the amendment's protection as individuals, and that, in doing so, they need not prove themselves members of some formal military unit like the National Guard.[193] At the same time the Court's focus on the weapon

---

192. 307 U.S. at 179 (emphasis added). The real difficulty with *Miller*'s flawed militia-centric interpretation is not that it diminishes the individual right approach, but that it tends to exaggerate to absurdity the extent of the right afforded. *Miller*'s concentration on militia-type weaponry has sometimes been taken as suggesting the unwelcome conclusion that private citizens have a guaranteed right to own all the mass destructive weaponry of sophisticated modern warfare, from tanks and rocket launchers to ICBMs and nuclear devices. When the amendment's other two purposes of personal self-defense and law enforcement are recognized, however, it becomes possible to conclude that the guarantee applies only to such military-type small arms as can reasonably be used also in law enforcement and civilian self defense. *See* notes 238-41 *infra* and accompanying text.

193. Although the opinion contains no such language, its flawed militia-centric rationale plausibly leads to the conclusion that the amendment right is limited to the military-aged male population, which makes up the constitutional militia. Such a limitation ill accords with the amendment's intention and text, however. *See* notes 53-54 *supra*. Nor does it follow *Miller*'s axis of limitation, which revolves around the question of what kind of arms are by right protected, rather than what individuals enjoy that right. The court probably eschewed any discussion of the latter question as unnecessary because the defendants, being adult male citizens, were presumptively members of the constitutional militia.

If *Miller* is confined strictly to its facts, it goes no further than implicitly recognizing that the home possession of firearms by one who is presumptively a member of the constitutional militia preserves the efficiency thereof under modern conditions. Such a view follows from current military thinking that considers militiamen as a resource only for times of dire necessity, *e.g.*, keeping order when both the Army and the federalized National Guard have been committed overseas and/or in the aftermath of an atomic attack. Given that the very circumstances which require the calling up of militiamen today may also preclude their drawing arms from centralized armories, their home possession of arms facilitates militia service today no less than in the 18th century. Moreover, the home possession of firearms by potential militia members would presumably facilitate familiarity with at least those weapons. To be able to call upon a cadre of people already familiar with weapons (particularly those weapons they would actually be using) would seem particulary important for the militia today, in the absence of a compulsory training requirement like those that existed in the 18th century. *See* text at note 49 *supra*.

Significantly, home and/or individual possession of firearms is the rule today in nations like Israel and Switzerland, which continue to rely substantially upon the militia concept. In Switzerland, every man of military age is required to keep a fully automatic assault rifle (or, if an officer, a pistol) in his home, along with ammunition; and the shooting sports are strongly encouraged for the entire population. C. GREENWOOD, *supra* note 44, at 4; J. STEINBERG, WHY SWITZERLAND? ch. 6 (1976). In Israel, voluntary ownership of firearms is encouraged for

suggests rational limitations on the kinds of arms that the amendment guarantees to individuals. Such arms must be both of the kind in "common use" at the present time and provably "part of the ordinary military equipment."[194] Those who have accused the Court of factual inaccuracy have simply misunderstood its legal conclusion as a finding of fact. *Miller* does not characterize shotguns (or even sawed-off shotguns) as outside the amendment's protection *per se.* *Miller* rests on the obvious proposition that it is not judicially noticeable, in the absence of factual proof, that sawed-off shotguns are "in common use" and form "part of the ordinary military equipment."[195] The *Miller* Court therefore returned the case to the trial court, where the defendants could have attempted the unenviable feat of demonstrating that sawed-off shotguns fell within the limiting criteria that *Miller* enunciated as defining the weaponry protected by the amendment.[196]

Miller is the Supreme Court's first and last extended treatment of the second amendment. This may seem surprising in light of the amount of legislation which the previous twenty-five years had seen on this controversial subject. But federal law has never gone beyond denying firearms to criminals, the mentally unstable and juveniles. Nor, until recently, has any state or local jurisdiction attempted to deny responsible adults the possession of firearms for lawful purposes. So the cases have involved only various provisions of the federal Gun Control Act of 1968. Challenges to these under the amendment have been summarily rejected by lower federal courts. Typical, and often repeated, are observations to the effect that "there is no showing that prohibiting possession of firearms by felons," the mentally unsound, children, or narcotics addicts "obstructs the maintenance of a 'well regulated militia.' "[197]

In 1981, Morton Grove, Illinois, banned the civilian possession of

---

the entire population, while the government has donated firearms to kibbutzim and other farming villages in areas likely to be subject to terrorist or military attack. Reservists are encouraged to carry their submachine guns or assault rifles with them at all times, particularly when traveling on the public streets. *See* Bruce-Briggs, *supra* note 9, at 56-57; *Order by Israel Puts Even More Guns on Street,* L.A. Times, July 5, 1978, at 1, col. 3.

194. On the limitations of the individual right, see notes 235-71 *infra* and accompanying text.

195. *See* text accompanying note 188 *supra.* As to standards for judicial notice, *see generally* C. McCORMICK, HANDBOOK OF THE LAW OF EVIDENCE 687; 9 J. WIGMORE, EVIDENCE §§ 2565-83 (1940).

196. On the applicability of these criteria to handguns, see notes 239-40 *infra* and accompanying text.

197. United States v. Synnes, 438 F.2d 764, 772 (8th Cir. 1971), *vacated on other grounds,* 404 U.S. 1009 (1972); *see also* United States v. Warin, 530 F.2d 103, 106 (6th Cir.), *cert. denied,* 426 U.S. 948 (1976).

handguns,[198] thus becoming the only American jurisdiction to have attempted the confiscation of a common form of civilian armament since the Civil War.[199] The district court rejected a second amendment challenge to that ordinance without endorsing or accepting either the state's right or the individual right interpretation.[200] It felt bound by *Presser* and other nineteenth-century holdings that the amendment was inapplicable against the states. Many state courts have also endorsed this proposition in rejecting second amendment challenges.[201]

A few state or federal cases have gone beyond upholding gun laws on these limited grounds, or those suggested in *Miller*, to embrace the exclusively state's right viewpoint.[202] At least one of these cases, holding that the amendment provides for no individual right, expressly divorces itself from *Miller*.[203] But a number of other such cases actually cite *Miller* as their authority.[204] This is startling in light of the inconsistency between their usage of "militia" as a particular military force and *Miller's* exhaustive exposition of the eighteenth-century definition of "militia" as comprising "all [militarily capable] males . . . bearing arms supplied by themselves."[205]

---

198. Morton Grove ordinance 81-11. In 1982 the cities of San Francisco and Berkeley, California, followed suit, but their ordinances were quickly invalidated on state statutory grounds. Doe v. City and County of San Francisco, 136 Ca. App. 3d 509, 186 Cal. Rptr. 380 (1982).

199. In 1861 the secessionist legislature of Tennessee ordered the confiscation of all firearms. This was intended both to disarm the state's substantial Unionist minority and to gather arms for the Confederates. *See* Moon, *A Brief Historical Note on Gun Control in Tennessee*, 82 CASE & COM. 38 (1977). The enactment was declared unconstitutional shortly after the war's end. Smith v. Ishenhour, 43 Tenn. (3 Cold.) 214 (1866). Detailed discussions of the history of American firearms legislation, both state and federal, appear in L. KENNETT & J. ANDERSON, *supra* note 23, ch. 8, and Kates, *Toward a History of Handgun Prohibition in the United States*, in RESTRICTING HANDGUNS, *supra* note 6.

200. *See* Quilici v. Morton Grove, 532 F. Supp. 1169 (N.D. Ill. 1981), *aff'd.*, 695 F.2d 261 (7th Cir. 1982), *cert. denied*, 52 U.S.L.W. 3266 (U.S. Oct. 3, 1983) (No. 82-1822).

201. *E.g.*, Galvan v. Superior Court, 70 Cal. 2d 851, 452 P.2d 930, 76 Cal. Rptr. 642 (1969); State v. Amos, 343 So. 2d 166 (La. 1977); Hardison v. State, 84 Nev. 125, 437 P.2d 868 (1968); Harris v. State, 83 Nev. 404, 432 P.2d 929 (1967); Burton v. Sills, 53 N.J. 86, 248 A.2d 426 (1967), *appeal dismissed*, 394 U.S. 812 (1969).

202. *E.g.*, United States v. Oakes, 564 F.2d 384, 387 (10th Cir. 1977); Stevens v. United States, 440 F.2d 144, 149 (6th Cir. 1971), Cases v. United States, 131 F.2d 916 (1st Cir. 1942); United States v. Tot, 131 F.2d 261, 266 (3d Cir. 1942), *rev'd on other grounds*, 319 U.S. 463 (1943).

203. Cases v. United States, 131 F.2d 916, 922 (1st Cir. 1942).

204. *See* Quilici v. Morton Grove, 695 F.2d 261, 270 (7th Cir. 1982), *cert. denied*, 52 U.S.L.W. 3266 (U.S. Oct. 3, 1983) (No. 82-1822); United States v. Oakes, 564 F.2d 384, 387 (10th Cir. 1977); Stevens v. United States, 440 F.2d 144, 149 (6th Cir. 1971).

205. 307 U.S. at 179; *see* text accompanying notes 35-56 & 191-93 *supra*.

III. ON THE QUESTION OF INCORPORATION AGAINST THE STATES

The discussion thus far has focused almost entirely upon the second amendment as a restraint upon federal governmental activity. The cases just mentioned suggest that state or municipal regulation is not within the scope of the amendment. As a practical matter, however, although the kind of prohibitionary-confiscatory legislation that the amendment forbids,[206] has been proposed at the federal level, it has never come close to enactment there. Nor does this seem likely in the foreseeable future.[207] From time to time, a few states have enacted legislation which could conceivably be subject to second amendment objection,[208] but in recent years legislative activity raising questions central to the second amendment has been limited to the municipal level. The most drastic example is the complete prohibition on home possession of handguns recently enacted by Morton Grove, Illinois.[209] This legislation clearly raises the question of whether the amendment should be considered incorporated against state and local governments through the due process clause of the fourteenth amendment.

The numerous cases citing *Presser v. Illinois* and *Miller v. Texas* for the proposition that the amendment is not incorporated[210] cannot survive rigorous analysis. The *Presser/Miller* view derives from a concept of federalism (*i.e.*, that civil liberties are guaranteed only against the federal government and that their infringement by the states is not the business of the federal judiciary) that has long been

---

206. *See* notes 235-41 *infra* and accompanying text.

207. H.R. 40, 97th Cong., 1st Sess., 127 CONG. REC. H32 (daily ed. Jan. 5, 1981), introduced by Representatives Bingham and Yates, would have completely prohibited the home possession of handguns by civilians. It was apparently never introduced into the Senate and was not expected to pass out of committee even in the House of Representatives. Back in 1972 a more modest bill, which would have prohibited new sales of nonsporting handguns (but not confiscated those already in circulation), passed the Senate, but failed to pass the House. This bill represents the high water mark for prohibitionist legislation.

208. *Compare* 1886-1887 Ala. Acts No. 4 § 17; 1881 Ark. Acts ch. 96 § 3; 1901 S.C. Acts No. 435; 1879 Tenn. Pub. Acts ch. 96 (banning the sale of "Saturday night special"-type pistols), *with* 1923 Ark. Acts No. 430, § 1; 1933-34 Hawaii Sess. Laws ch. 26, § 3; 1925 Mich. Pub. Acts No. 313; 1921 Mo. Laws ¶ 69,691 § 3; 1911 N.Y. Laws ch. 195; 1919 N.C. Sess. Laws ch. 197, § 1; 1913 Or. Laws ch. 256, § 1 (requiring permits for the sale and/or ownership of pistols). Most of these laws appear to have been at least partially motivated by desire to deny access to firearms to racial or ethnic minorities and political dissenters. Whether in repudiation of these purposes or for other reasons, the Oregon, Arkansas, Tennessee and Alabama laws have been repealed. *See* Kates, *supra* note 11, at 14-22. Minnesota and Illinois have recently passed laws aimed at prohibiting the sale of "Saturday Night specials" variously defined. *See* ILL. ANN. STAT. ch. 38, § 24-3(g) (Smith-Hurd 1977); MINN. STAT. ANN. § 624-716 (West Supp. 1983). For a discussion of this legislation and its validity within the second amendment, see note 240 *infra* and accompanying text.

209. *See* note 198 *supra*.

210. *See* note 201 *supra*.

discredited.[211] Moreover, strictly speaking, the suggestion that *Presser v. Illinois* and *Miller v. Texas* reject *due process* incorporation misreads the actual holdings in those cases. What they literally held was only that the Bill of Rights did not apply against the states *ab initio* and was not incorporated against them by the *privileges and immunities* clause of the fourteenth amendment. Presumably the attitude toward federalism which led the nineteenth-century Court to reject privileges and immunities incorporation would equally have led it to reject due process incorporation, if anyone had then imagined it.[212] But to apply the *Presser/Miller* reasoning to negate due process incorporation of the second amendment today is to extend those cases beyond their holdings. However logical that extension might have seemed in 1886, it is absurd today when the result would be to contradict the entire doctrinal basis of modern incorporation of the Bill of Rights against state and local government.[213]

Absent the misleading spectre of *Presser* and *Miller*, the weakness of the argument against application of the second amendment

---

211. *Compare* Miller v. Texas, 153 U.S. 535, 538 (1894) ("[I]t is well-settled that the restrictions of the [second and fourth] amendments operate only on the Federal power and have no reference whatever to proceedings in state courts."); Presser v. Illinois, 116 U.S. 252, 265 (1886) ("[T]he [second] amendment is a limitation only upon. . .the National government, and not upon. . .the States."), *with* Duncan v. Louisiana, 391 U.S. 145, 147-50 (1968) ("[M]any of the rights guaranteed by the first eight amendments . . . have been held to be protected against state action by the Due Process Clause of the Fourteenth Amendment."); Mapp v. Ohio 367 U.S. 643, 650-55 (1961) (holding the fourth amendment search and seizure protections applicable to the states through the fourteenth amendment); Gitlow v. New York, 268 U.S. 652, 666 (1925) (holding the first amendment freedom of speech binding on the state through the fourteenth amendment); Twining v. New Jersey, 211 U.S. 78, 99 (1908) ("it is possible that some of the personal rights safeguarded by the first eight Amendments against the National action may also be safeguarded against state action").

212. Due process incorporation's first appearance in a Supreme Court case appears to be as a dictum in Twining v. New Jersey, 211 U.S. 78, 99 (1908). *See* note 211 *supra*.

213. *Presser* does, however, contain a far-reaching, but little noted, dictum suggesting that U.S. CONST. art. I, § 8, cl. 15 and 16 proscribes state or local wholesale arms prohibitions or confiscation. In the *Presser* court's view, cl. 15 envisions an armed citizenry which Congress is empowered to call forth whenever necessary to execute the laws, suppress rebellions or repel invasion. A state would directly infringe that congressional prerogative if it prohibits firearms possession by the constitutional militia, *i.e.*, the military-age male populace. As the court stated:

> It is undoubtedly true that all citizens capable of bearing arms constitute the reserved military force or reserve militia of the United States as well of the States, and, in view of this prerogative of the general government, as well as of its general powers, the States cannot, even laying the [second amendment] out of view, prohibit the people from keeping and bearing arms, so as to deprive the United States of their rightful resource for maintaining the public security and disable the people from performing their duty to the general government.

116 U.S. at 265. Authorities indicating the continued importance of an armed citizenry for militia duty are reviewed at notes 283-84 *infra*. Militia considerations might not, however, preclude legislation against the possession, ownership, sale or manufacture of "Saturday Night Special"-type firearms that are unfit for military or police duty. *See* note 240 *infra* and accompanying text.

to the states is evident. In deciding whether a provision of the Bill of Rights is so fundamental as to justify incorporation, the Supreme Court has traditionally employed two criteria: The extent to which the right is rooted in our Anglo-American common law heritage, as well as its Greek and Roman antecedents;[214] and how highly the Founders themselves valued the right.[215] The great esteem in which the Founders held the right to arms has already been exhaustively detailed. Familiar to them in their own colonial law,[216] derived from the earliest known English legal codes,[217] the right to arms was in their day hailed as not only fundamental to their English legal and political heritage, but implicit in the (to them) premier and seminal natural law right of self-defense.[218] Likewise the right to keep personal arms was so fundamental a part of Graeco-Roman law that every commentator known to the Founders proclaimed it the basis of republican institutions and popular liberty.[219]

Above and beyond the general criteria which normally govern incorporation is the question of specific legislative intent. There is ample evidence that the authors of the fourteenth amendment actually intended to protect the right to arms from state or local interference. The quantum of that evidence considerably exceeds the evidence that they intended to protect any of the rights which have heretofore received incorporation. The fourteenth amendment was enacted at a time when the Republicans were still utterly dominant in Congress by reason of their continuing exclusion of the delegations of the southern states. Section 1 goes virtually unmentioned in the debate on the fourteenth amendment — beyond the statement of Representative Thaddeus Stevens that it was intended to constitutionalize the underlying principles of the immediately preceding 1866 Civil Rights Act,[220] thereby placing them beyond repeal upon

---

214. *See, e.g.,* Benton v. Maryland, 395 U.S. 784, 795 (1969) (protection of double jeopardy held fundamental), Duncan v. Louisiana, 391 U.S. 145, 151-54 (1968) (right to jury trial fundamental); Klopfer v. North Carolina, 386 U.S. 213, 225-26 (1967) (right to speedy trial fundamental); Gideon v. Wainwright, 372 U.S. 335, 344 (1963) (right to counsel fundamental).

215. *See, e.g.* Duncan v. Louisiana, 391 U.S. 145, 152-53 (1968); Klopfer v. North Carolina, 386 U.S. 213, 225 (1967).

216. *See* notes 46-48, 156 *supra* and accompanying text.

217. Professor Whisker finds references to, or recognition of, the right in pre-Norman law, back to the period before the reign of Alfred the Great (871-899) when England was divided into various kingdoms. *See* J. WHISKER, OUR VANISHING FREEDOM: THE RIGHT TO KEEP AND BEAR ARMS 3 (1973) (citing the 602 Code of Ethelbert of Kent and a circa 650 law of Edric of Kent). The Laws of Canute (reigned 1016-1035) imposed a fine on anyone who illegally disarmed a subject.

218. *See* notes 109, 111 & 153 *supra* and accompanying text.

219. *See* text at notes 114-28 *supra*.

220. Act of Apr. 9, 1866, ch. 31, 14 Stat. 27.

the southern delegations' return.[221] It is therefore to the 1866 Act that we must turn to understand the purposes of section one of the fourteenth amendment.

The principle underlying the 1866 Civil Rights Act was nothing less than the repudiation of the whole juridical basis of southern slavery. Under the legal theory of slavery, blacks were not human beings, but intelligent livestock, incapable of possessing property or of having a right to defend it or themselves.[222] Pursuant to this theory, *Dred Scott* and various preceding southern court decisions had declared blacks incapable of citizenship and upheld legislation against their possessing arms.[223] The 1866 Act in effect overruled

---

221. CONG. GLOBE, 39th Cong., 1st Sess., 2459 (1866). *See generally* Frank & Munro, *The Original Understanding of Equal Protection of the Laws*, 50 COLUM. L. REV. 131, 141 (1950). Although the drafting of the amendment was a joint effort by a number of Republicans, of whom Stevens was the most prominent, the assignment of its introduction to Rep. Bingham, (R-Ohio) further demonstrates its relationship to the 1866 Civil Rights Act, which had passed a few weeks earlier. Bingham had opposed that Act, not out of any fundamental disagreement with its provisions, but because he believed them to exceed federal constitutional authority under the thirteenth amendment. By constitutionalizing the basic principles of the 1866 Act, the fourteenth amendment removed the danger, of which the Republicans were highly cognizant after Dred Scott v. Sanford, 60 U.S. (19 How.) 690 (1856), that the Act might be overturned by the Supreme Court. Fairman, *Does the Fourteenth Amendment Incorporate the Bill of Rights?*, 2 STAN. L. REV. 5 (1949). Indeed, in advocating the fourteenth amendment's enactment, one prominent Republican complained that southern courts were declaring the 1866 Act unconstitutional — and enforcing laws banning guns for freedmen. CONG. GLOBE, 39th Cong., 1st Sess. 3210 (1866) (statement of George W. Julian).

222. Kates, *Abolition, Deportation, Integration: Attitudes Toward Slavery in the Early Republic*, 53 J. NEGRO HIST. 33, 37 & n.25 (1968):

> The majesty and consistency of [ante-bellum] American law uniformly regarded slaves as property, incapable of possessing a cognizable interest in personal security. Within this theory the rape or murder of a slave was no more than a crime against property—and no crime at all if committed by the master.
>
> . . . .
>
> By constitutional, statutory, decisional, administrative and customary law the position of the slave was fixed. He could not possess arms or liquor, make contracts, own land or personalty, travel freely, give testimony or serve as a juror or in any other public office, learn to read or write, act independently as a religious leader, intermarry with whites, compete in the free labor market—above all, he had no political rights. The prohibitions of arms, liquor and travel were enforced by a more or less well organized system of special and general searches and night patrols of the *posse comitatus.* Justice to the slave was, within the law or within its enforcement, summarily meted out by masters, possemen and judicial officials alike. As Mr. Chief Justice Taney succinctly expressed it: "[the Negro slave had] no rights which the white man was bound to respect." Scott v. Sanford, 60 U.S. (19 How.) 690, 701 (1856) (footnote omitted).

223. *See* notes 176-78 *supra* and accompanying text. Conversely, abolitionist legal treatises had offered as plain evidence of the unconstitutionality of slavery the fact that its legal theory abridged the second amendment right of blacks to keep arms. *See, e.g.,* L. SPOONER, THE UNCONSTITUTIONALITY OF SLAVERY 98 (1860); J. TIFFANY, TREATISE ON THE UNCONSTITUTIONALITY OF SLAVERY 117-18 (1849) (reprinted 1969). Since these commentaries provided the legal underpinnings for the constitutional thought of the Radical (and moderate) Republicans of 1866, they are of particular significance for understanding the scope of the fourteenth amendment. *See* J. TEN BROEK, EQUAL UNDER LAW 125 (1965) (originally published as THE ANTISLAVERY ORIGINS OF THE FOURTEENTH AMENDMENT); Graham, *The Early Antislavery Background of the Fourteenth Amendment*, 1950 WIS. L. REV. 479.

Dred Scott[224] as an adjunct to its general purpose of immutably conferring upon blacks legal standing as free citizens.[225] In so doing it implicity conferred upon them the right of arms under the second amendment. As we have seen, central to the idea of freedom and citizenship in Anglo-American law and philosophy were the rights to personal security and property, to self defense — and to the possession of arms for those purposes.[226]

Moreover, it appears that proscribing anti-gun laws was expressly contemplated by the authors of the 1866 Act and fourteenth amendment. The *betes noir* of the Congress of 1866 were the Black Codes that had immediately spewed from the all-white southern legislatures after Appomattox. These Codes sought to reduce the new freedman to peonage, perpetuating against him all the legal disabilities which had previously characterized his status as a slave. As the *Special Report of the Anti-Slavery Conference of 1867* noted, among the most obnoxious provisions of these Codes were those by which blacks were "forbidden to own or bear firearms," as they had been under slavery, "and thus were rendered defenseless against assaults" by their former masters or other whites.[227] Congressman after congressman, including the Senate sponsors of both the 1866 Act and the fourteenth amendment, expressed their outrage at the denial of the freedman's right to arms.[228] In summarizing what the 1866 Act would accomplish, its House and Senate sponsors cited Blackstone's classification of the "absolute rights of individuals", stating that these were the essential human rights being conveyed.[229] Finally, myriad statements and an official committee report in relation to the anti-KKK legislation enacted in 1871[230] shows an unchallenged as-

---

224. *Dred Scott* is overruled by § 1 of the 1866 Act, *supra* note 220, which declares "that all persons born in the United States and not subject to any foreign power, excluding Indians not taxed, are . . . citizens of the Unites States." This clause was adopted later as the first sentence of the fourteenth amendment.

225. Stating that its purpose was to guarantee the former slaves the rights inherent in their new status, both the House and the Senate sponsors of the 1866 Act quoted Chancellor Kent's listing of the rights of a free person: " 'the right of personal security, the right of personal liberty and the right to acquire and enjoy property.' " CONG. GLOBE, 39th Cong., 1st Sess. 1118 & 1757 (1866) (statements of Rep. Wilson and Sen. Trumbull) (quoting 2 J. KENT, COMMENTARIES 1 (New York 1827)).

226. *See* notes 109-11 & 117-18 *supra* and accompanying text.

227. *Reprinted* in H. HYMAN, THE RADICAL REPUBLICANS AND RECONSTRUCTION 217 (1967). *See generally* E. COULTER, THE SOUTH DURING RECONSTRUCTION 1865-1877, at 40 n.43 (1947); W. DU BOIS, BLACK RECONSTRUCTION IN AMERICA 167, 172, 223 (1962).

228. *See* Halbrook, *The Jurisprudence of the Second and Fourteenth Amendments*, 4 GEO. MASON U. L. REV. 1, 21-25 (1981).

229. *See* CONG. GLOBE, *supra* note 225, at 1115-18; text accompanying note 153 *supra*.

230. Legislation designed to enforce the fourteenth amendment, and in particular to suppress the KKK was introduced in 1871. CONGRESSIONAL GLOBLE, 42d Cong., 1st Sess. 174

sumption by a Congress largely identical in personnel to that of 1866 that the fourteenth amendment they had enacted five years earlier encompassed second amendment rights.[231]

In sum, the only viable justification for denying incorporation of the second amendment against the states today is the exclusively state's right view that the amendment does not confer an individual right. If the amendment only guaranteed a right of the states it would be self contradictory to incorporate it into the fourteenth amendment.[232] But as this state's right interpretation of the amendment is itself not viable historically, it therefore follows that the second amendment should be held applicable to the states through the due process clause of the fourteenth.

IV. TOWARD A DEFINITION OF SECOND AMENDMENT RIGHTS AND THE PROPER SCOPE OF GUN CONTROL

Recognizing that the amendment guarantees an individual right applicable against both federal and state governments by no means forecloses all gun control options. Gun control advocates must, however, come to grips with the limitations imposed by the amendment — just as advocates of increasing police powers to deal with crime must come to grips with the limitations imposed by the fourth, fifth and sixth amendments. As with those amendments, determining what limitations the second imposes will require detailed examination of its colonial and common law antecedents.[233] The phrase "the right of the people to keep and bear arms," so opaque to us, was apparently self-defining to the Founders, who used it baldly and

---

(1871) (Introduced as "an act to protect loyal and peaceable citizens in the South. . . .", H.R. No. 189). Passed as the Enforcement Act, 17 Stat. 13 (1871). Section 1 of the legislation survives as 42 U.S.C. § 1983 (1976). *See* Halbrook, *supra* note 228, at 25 n.141, 27 n.146 and accompanying text.

231. *See* Halbrook, *supra* note 228, at 25-28. For the relationship between the two Acts and the personnel of the two Congresses which enacted them, see Kates, *Immunity of State Judges Under the Federal Civil Rights Acts: Pierson v. Ray Reconsidered*, 65 Nw. U. L. REV. 615, 621-23 (1970).

232. *See, e.g.,* J. NOWAK, R. ROTUNDA & J. YOUNG, CONSTITUTIONAL LAW 455 (2d ed. 1983); *see also* note 171 *supra*.

233. *Cf.* Payton v. New York, 445 U.S. 573, 593-96 (1980) (interpreting fourth amendment by reference to a combination of materials including Coke's *Institutes*, pre-colonial case law, and American colonial commentary and practice); Benton v. Maryland, 395 U.S. 784, 795 (1969) (guarantee against double jeopardy construed by reference to Blackstone both as an authority on pre-colonial English practice and as the guide followed by the colonists in establishing American legal principles); Duncan v. Louisiana, 391 U.S. 145, 151-52 (1968) (right to jury trial defined by reference to Blackstone, as well as to independent evidence of American colonial and preceding English legal practice); Klopfer v. North Carolina, 386 U.S. 213, 223-25 (1967) (right to speedy trial defined by reference to Coke and English legal practice back to the Magna Carta).

without any attempt to define it. Presumably they felt that clarification was unnecessary because they were constitutionalizing a pre-existing right to arms whose parameters they knew under their colonial law and practice as it had developed out of the early English common law.[234]

The remainder of this Article is devoted to sketching out some of the amendment's implications in relation to a few of the more commonly encountered "gun control" proposals. The intention is not to resolve definitively the constitutionality of any of these, much less of the entire gamut of possible control options, but only to outline some relevant lines of inquiry.

A. *Limitations on the Right of the General Citizenry To "Keep" Weapons*

The preceding sections of this Article demonstrate that, in general, the second amendment guarantees individuals a right to "keep" weapons in the home for self defense.[235] Several limitations on this

---

234. This is not to suggest that the meaning will be as readily understandable to us or as easily applied, particularly as to control proposals or options that bear little resemblance to those with which the Founders were familiar. Indeed, it will not be easy to determine even what control options were familiar to them outside of those commonly embraced by colonial law, *see* note 156 *supra*, the early common law principles set out by English commentators, *see* note 153 *supra*, and the absolute prohibition of the 1671 Game Act and the other Stuart arms confiscation devices, *see* notes 135-39 *supra* and accompanying text. It is difficult if not impossible to determine precisely what knowledge the Founders had of English arms controls contemporary to their own time. In general, Americans seem to have believed the contemporary English law (or practice) far more restrictive than their colonial law or the original common law and Madison and Tucker found the exception-riddled English Bill of Rights guarantee insufficient. *See* notes 144 & 155 *supra*. In view of these real or perceived differences, the amendment cannot be slavishly construed with reference to contemporary English law. As with any constitutional guarantee whose "historic roots are in English history," it nevertheless "must be interpreted in light of the American experience, and in the context of the American constitutional scheme of government rather than the English . . . ." United States v. Brewster, 408 U.S. 501, 508 (1972). On the debate over the relevance of original intent in determining constitutional rights, see note 28 *supra*.

235. *See* notes 53-64 & 192-95 *supra* and accompanying text. G. NEWTON & F. ZIMRING, *supra* note 13, at 255, suggests that the 1671 Game Act's prohibition of firearms ownership to all but the high nobility demonstrates that the common law right to *arms* did not apply to *firearms*. By the same token, reference might be made to a series of statutes of Henry VIII which prohibited both gun and crossbow ownership by commoners. *See* REPORT OF THE SUB-COMMITTEE ON THE CONSTITUTION, *supra* note 10, at 12 nn.9-12. Incredible as it may seem, the primary rationale for these Henrician prohibitions (explicitly avowed in all five statutes) was that crossbow and gun possession was distracting Englishmen from their legally required ownership of, and arduous regular practice with, the long bow, which was still thought of as vitally necessary to English military defense. A secondary purpose (several times avowed) was that the "king's dere" were being "distroyd" by crossbow or gun-armed poachers. A tertiary concern (mentioned in only one of the five enactments) was to prevent the misuse of these weapons in crime. *Id.* at 1-2.

It is difficult to see any of this Henrician legislation playing an affirmative part in the colonial right-to-arms tradition upon which the amendment is based. In all probability the Founders were entirely ignorant that the Henrician legislation had ever existed. The anachronism of its principal purpose having become evident by the latter part of Henry's reign, he

right have already been suggested, however. First and foremost are those implicit in *United States v. Miller*, suggesting that the amendment protects only such arms as are (1) "of the kind in common use" among law-abiding people and (2) provably "part of the ordinary military equipment" today.[236] The analysis presented throughout this Article indicates that the "ordinary military equipment" criterion is infected by *Miller*'s conceptually flawed concentration on the amendment's militia purpose, to the exclusion of its other objectives. Decisions recognizing that concerns for individual self-protection and for law enforcement also underlie right to arms guarantees involve at once greater historical fidelity and more rigorous limitation upon the kinds of arms protected. These decisions suggest that only such arms as have utility for *all three* purposes and are lineally descended from the kinds of arms the Founders knew fall within the amendment's guarantee.[237] Reformulating *Miller*'s dual test in this way produces a triple test that anyone claiming the amendment's protection must satisfy as to the particular weapon he owns. That weapon must provably be (1) "of the kind in common use" among law-abiding people today; (2) useful and appropriate not just for military purposes, but also for law enforcement and individual self-defense, and (3) lineally descended from the kinds of weaponry known to the Founders.

This triple test resolves the *ad absurdum* and *ad horribilus* results (to which *Miller*'s sketchy and flawed militia-centric discussion greatly contributed) sometimes viewed as flowing from an individual right interpretation of the amendment.[238] Handguns, for example,

---

repealed the legislation by proclamation — more than 65 years before the settlement of the American colonies and over 200 before Madison's birth. *Id.* Doubtless the Founders were familiar with the 1671 Act since its repudiation had been one of the purposes of the arms guarantee in the English Bill of Rights. But the only relevance that execrated Act had to the Founders' thought was as a model of what the second amendment was intended to foreclose. *See* notes 137-51 *supra* and accompanying text. Moreover, legally speaking, neither the Henrician legislation nor the 1671 Game Act could have formed any part of the colonial law on arms. They were excluded by the inapplicability principle as they were clearly not suited to colonial conditions. *See* note 155 *supra*. Such legislation was wholly inconsistent with the arms policy upon which both Britain and the Colonies had operated from the colonies' inception. This policy, *see* notes 46-48 *supra* and accompanying text, called for the colonists to arm themselves for self defense rather than burdening or depending upon the remote military resources of the mother country. The weapons with which they were to be armed expressly included "pistols." Yet these would plainly have been forbidden had the Henrician legislation been considered applicable. *See* the colonial statutes cited at notes 46-48 *supra*.

236. *See* notes 188, 192-96 *supra* and accompanying text.

237. *See* People v. Brown, 253 Mich. 537, 541, 235 N.W. 245, 246-47 (1931); *see also* State v. Kessler, 289 Or. 359, 364-66, 614 P.2d 94, 98-100 (1980); State v. Duke, 42 Tex. 455, 458 (1875) (construing state constitutions).

238. *See, e.g.,* Cases v. United States, 131 F.2d 916, 922 (1st Cir. 1942) (arguing that, since any and all weapons have proved useful in modern (particularly guerrilla) warfare, *Miller*'s

clearly fall within the amendment's protection. That handguns are *per se* "in common use" among law-abiding people and combine utility for civilian, police and military activities is not only provable but judicially noticeable.[239] On the other hand, such a factual demonstration would be difficult as to at least some of the weapons commonly denominated "Saturday Night Specials."[240] Legislation selectively prohibiting them might, therefore, be consistent with the amendment. Gangster weapons like brass knuckles, blackjacks, sandbags, switchblade knives and sawed-off shotguns unquestionably can be prohibited since they fail to meet both the "common use" and tripartite appropriateness branches of the test. The possession of

militia-centric rationale provides no viable limit on the kinds of arms guaranteed by the amendment); Royko, *Machine Guns Don't Kill, People Kill*, Chi. Sun Times, Dec. 19, 1981, at 2, col. 1; *cf.* United States v. Warin, 530 F.2d 103 (6th Cir.) (reasoning that the amendment does not guarantee an individual right to possess machine guns because, if it did, there would be no limit to the kinds of weaponry embraced in the right), *cert. denied,* 426 U.S. 948 (1976); J. WHISKER, *supra* note 217, at 112-13 (arguing that since bazookas, cannon, and the like have never been used by criminals or terrorists in this country, and since such weapons are generally too heavy, bulky and expensive to operate for criminals or terrorists, government should not deny the law-abiding citizen's "right" to own, for instance, "a 20 mm. recoilless rifle simply for his own pleasure and perhaps to shoot ten times a year in a deserted part of the country").

239. As to the commonality of the handgun, exclusive of militarily-owned weapons, the American gun stock was estimated in 1981 as including not less than 54 million handguns. Kates, *supra* note 17, at n.2 and accompanying text (unpaginated manuscript). In general, a broad range of large-caliber, high-quality handguns combine suitability for military, law enforcement and civilian self-defense uses. Indeed, the vast majority of such weapons commonly sold to civilians in the United States for self-defense were specifically developed for the military and/or police market (or are the lineal descendants of models that were so developed). *See, e.g.,* A. BRISTOW, THE SEARCH FOR AN EFFECTIVE POLICE HANDGUN (1971); M. JOSSERAND & J. STEVENSON, PISTOLS, REVOLVERS AND AMMUNITION, ch. 7 (1967); W. SMITH, SMALL ARMS OF THE WORLD, chs. 10-12 (J. Smith 9th ed. 1960). The military/police origin of these weapons is often evidenced by their current designations: Smith and Wesson model 10 ("Military and Police"), and models 36, 37 and 60 ("Chiefs Special" — regular, airweight and stainless); Colt "Government Model" (.45 ACP), "Lawman," and "Trooper" (.357 magnum), "Official Police," "Police Positive," "Detective Special," and "Agent" (.38 special). The origins and designations of imported handguns are similar: Walther PP and PPK (the initials stand for German police organizations), the standard weapon of the German Luftwaffe during World War II; Star "Guardia Civil"; and Webley R.I.C. ("Royal Irish Constabulary"). Even those handguns which are not specifically designed with military and/or police use in mind are designed, manufactured and operate in manners closely analogous, or identical, to those used by the police or military forces of various nations. *See, e.g., id.* at 58-93, 159-92. Indeed, a substantial proportion of the civilian gun stock consists of former military weapons, captured in warfare or kept by veterans as souvenirs. The Comptroller General has estimated that 8.8 million "war trophies" returned from World War II alone. GOVERNMENT ACCOUNTING OFFICE, HANDGUN CONTROL: EFFECTIVENESS AND COST 17-18 (1978).

240. "Saturday Night Special" is the derisive name for a more or less distinct subspecies of handgun, identified primarily by inexpensiveness, small size and low quality of manufacture and metallurgy. *See* McClain, *"Saturday Night Special" Gun Regulation: A Feasible Policy Option?*, in FIREARMS & VIOLENCE, *supra* note 10. Twentieth-century countries have rarely if ever adopted as standard handguns for military and/or police purposes those of less than .32 caliber; the weapons they standardize tend to be relatively large and heavy and very well made. *See* A. BRISTOW, *supra* note 239; I. HOGG & J. WEEKS, MILITARY SMALL ARMS OF THE 20TH CENTURY (4th ed. 1981); J. OWEN, BRASSEY'S INFANTRY WEAPONS OF THE WORLD, 1950-1975; W. SMITH, *supra* note 239.

billy clubs is clearly protected, but mace or similar chemical spray weapons would not be unless they can be shown to be lineally descended from some form of weapon known to the Founders. Likewise, the amendment does not protect the possession of fully automatic weapons, grenades, rocket launchers, flame throwers, artillery pieces, tanks, nuclear devices, and so on. Although such sophisticated devices of modern warfare do have military utility, they are not also useful for law enforcement or for self-protection, nor are they commonly possessed by law-abiding individuals. Moreover, many of them may not be lineally descended from the kinds of weapons known to the Founders.

In addition to the tripartite test, two further limiting principles would tend to exclude the sophisticated military technology of mass destruction — or, indeed, anything beyond ordinary small arms — from the amendment's protection. First, since the text refers to arms that the individual can "keep *and* bear," weapons too heavy or bulky for the ordinary person to carry are apparently not contemplated. Second, according to Blackstone and Hawkins, the common-law right did not extend to "dangerous or unusual weapons" whose mere possession or exhibition "are apt to terrify the people."[241] Naturally, it would terrify the citizenry for unauthorized individuals to possess weapons that could not realistically be used even in self-defense without endangering innocent people in adjacent areas or buildings.

B. *Laws Prohibiting the Urban Possession of Rifles, Shotguns and Highly Penetrative Handgun Bullets*

This last limiting principle might also allow legislation against keeping rifles and shotguns loaded for defense, at least in urban areas. Although it appears that most people who keep firearms for self-defense today depend upon handguns, it is unfortunately the case that some urbanites continue to rely on long guns.[242] While a rifle or shotgun is clearly more effective than a handgun if the sole consideration is instantly killing a burglar,[243] the various potential

---

241. 4 W. BLACKSTONE, COMMENTARIES *149; 1 W. HAWKINS, *supra* note 153, at 136. Blackstone was discussing a statute that properly made the carrying of such weapons a criminal breach of the peace. Similarly, Hawkins approved the criminalization of "affray," an offense that included the display of terrifying weapons.

242. *See* McClain, *Firearms Ownership, Gun Control Attitudes and Neighborhood Environment*, 5 LAW & POLICY Q. 299, 305-07 (1983).

243. The superior deadliness of long guns is touted by the field director of the National Coalition to Ban Handguns among others. Deriding the message behind NRA publicity of instances in which handgun-armed householders routed burglars, he recommends "a twelve gauge shotgun," for it will not only protect the householder better, but serve society as well by "permanently ending the intruder's crime career," — that is, a shotgun blast will kill him

side effects of firing such a weapon in an urban environment make it unacceptable.

Consider penetration: even the .44 magnum, the most powerful of all handguns, penetrates no more than thirteen inches in wood, while revolvers in the far more commonly owned .32 to .38 calibers range from two to seven inches in penetration.[244] In contrast, the relatively underpowered military surplus carbine with which President Kennedy was killed penetrates forty-seven inches.[245] So a householder or shopkeeper who uses a rifle against a robber is imposing on others a very considerable risk that the bullet will penetrate all the way through the intended target and successive wood or stucco walls, entering the street or a neighboring building with enough remaining velocity to kill an innocent third party. While a shotgun's discharge does not have equivalent penetration because its velocity is far less, that velocity still substantially exceeds all but the most powerful handguns.[246] Moreover, a householder or shopkeeper who elects to defend his premises with a riot gun's promiscuous spray may end up hitting one or more of his own innocent children or customers, along with the robber. In contrast, a handgun fires one bullet at a time which, if accurately aimed, is unlikely to pass through the robber, or, if it does so, will bury itself harmlessly in the wall.

By the same token, accidental discharges with long guns (particularly rifles, which can penetrate horizontally through successive houses on a city block or vertically through the floors and ceilings of successive apartments in a high rise) are much more dangerous than with handguns. This danger is multiplied by the fact that a rifle or shotgun kept loaded for home or store defense is much more likely to suffer accidental discharge than is a handgun. A rifle or shotgun

---

instead of inflicting a nonfatal wound such as a handgun would be likely to do. Fields, *Handgun Prohibition and Social Necessity*, 23 ST. LOUIS U. L.J. 35, 41 (1979). A handgun wound will result in death 5-10% of the time, while a comparable 12-gauge shotgun wound will result in death 80% or more of the time. *See* Kleck, *Handgun-Only Gun Control: A Policy Disaster in the Making*, in FIREARMS & VIOLENCE, *supra* note 10.

244. D. GRENNELL & M. WILLIAMS, LAW ENFORCEMENT HANDGUN DIGEST 194-95 (1972); Steindler, *Warning: Your Walls Are Not Bullet Proof* in GUNS FOR HOME DEFENSE (G. James ed. 1975).

245. Lattimer & Lattimer, *The Kennedy-Connally Single Bullet Theory*, 50 INTL. SURGERY 524, 529 (1968).

246. The more powerful military-caliber rifles which Americans generally favor exhibit muzzle velocities in the range of 2500-3500 feet per second. A shotgun expels its projectiles at 1300-1350 feet per second, a velocity level reached only by handguns in the .44 magnum and .357 magnum calibers. Most handguns generate velocities of less than 1000 feet per second. *See* D. GRENNELL & M. WILLIAMS, *supra* note 244, at 188; GUN DIGEST 257-68 (K. Warner ed. 1982).

kept ready to fire can discharge simply through impact if dropped on a floor; a modern revolver will not. A long gun is also much more difficult than a handgun to lock or hide away from inquisitive children. Finally, if an inquisitive three-year-old does locate a loaded rifle or shotgun, pushing the safety to "off" and pulling the trigger is literally "child's play"; he would not be strong enough to operate the trigger on a revolver or the slide on an automatic pistol.[247]

These technical factors are reflected in the concrete form of firearms accident statistics. Fifty years ago, long guns outnumbered handguns seven-to-one and were the principal weapons kept loaded in the home — handguns being possessed by less than one in thirteen Americans. In contrast, handguns today represent one-third of the total gunstock and one in every four American households contains them.[248] Even though the handgun stock has grown to the point of displacing long guns in the home defense role, however, Americans continue to buy many more long guns (apparently for sport) each year than they do handguns.[249] Yet this enormous increase in all kinds of firearms has been accompanied by the decline of per capita accidental firearms fatalities to the lowest point since the compilation of such statistics began.[250] It is difficult not to attribute this decline to the general change-over to handguns for home defense. Indicative of the dangers presented by the practice of keeping loaded long guns is the fact that, although handguns undoubtedly represent 90% or more of the weapons kept loaded at any one time today, only 15.5% of accidental firearms deaths appear to involve handguns.[251]

Based on these statistics, an urban community (or a state legislature) might arguably rely on the "dangerous or unusual" weapon exclusion to prohibit the keeping of loaded long guns within densely populated municipal areas. By parity of reasoning, cognate restric-

247. The author has confirmed this by actual experiment with children of this age.

248. *Compare* Benenson, *supra* note 3, at 720 (quoting 1937 estimate by U.S. Attorney General Homer Cummings), *with* Kates, *supra* note 17, at n.2 (unpaginated manuscript), *and* WEAPONS, CRIME AND VIOLENCE IN AMERICA, *supra* note 3, at ch. 2.

249. The controversy surrounding the quadrupling of handgun sales over the past 20 years has tended to obscure the fact that long gun production has always exceeded that of handguns in the United States. For the seven years preceding 1980, for instance, long gun production outstripped handguns by 75%. Indicative of the phenomenal increase in long gun ownership is the fact that in that seven-year period more than one-third as many long guns were manufactured as in the entire preceding 70-year period. *Compare* G. NEWTON & F. ZIMRING, *supra* note 13, at 172 (giving 1899-1968 statistics), *with Production Figures of the American Firearms Industry 1973-1979*, AM. FIREARMS INDUS. MAG., Dec. 1980, at 32.

250. NATIONAL SAFETY COUNCIL, 1982 ACCIDENT FACTS 15 (indicating a 68% decline in the per capita rate of accidental firearms fatalities from 1913-1932, when it was 2.5 per hundred thousand population, to 1978-81, when it was 0.8 per hundred thousand population).

251. Private communication from National Safety Council (Mar. 28, 1983). This estimate is based on 1979 figures only, as no others are available.

tions might be placed on the kind of handguns which could be kept for self-defense or at least on kinds of ammunition. Such legislation might prohibit special high-penetration ammunition like the controversial KTW bullet, magnum ammunition for magnum revolvers, or full metal-jacketed ammunition for high-powered automatic pistols. Alternatively or cumulatively, the legislature might affirmatively limit those possessing high-velocity handguns to ammunition specially designed for low penetration, such as hollow point and semi-wadcutter.

C. *Licensing and Registration Requirements for Gun Ownership*

The terms gun "licensing" and "registration" are susceptible to multiple interpretations, although most people, including nonlegal scholars and opinion poll formulators, seem lamentably ignorant of this fact.[252] Under the form known as discretionary or "restrictive" licensing, the applicant has no right to have a gun or to be issued a permit by the police *even if* he meets all statutorily prescribed criteria. His application may be denied simply because enough permits have already been issued to others, or because his reason for desiring a firearm is not deemed important or compelling enough.[253] Such a discretionary or restrictive licensing system, which is the form advocated by proponents of eliminating or radically reducing civilian gun ownership,[254] is clearly inconsistent with the second amendment's guarantee of a personal right to possess arms.

In sharp contrast to restrictive licensing are both "permissive" licensing and registration. Under a permissive licensing system the applicant is entitled to licensure as of right unless he falls into certain proscribed categories — *e.g.,* juveniles, convicted felons and the

252. *See* Kates, *Toward a History of Handgun Prohibition in the United States*, in RE-STRICTING HANDGUNS, *supra* note 6, at 27-28.

253. *See* Kates, *supra* note 17, at n.1 and accompanying text (unpaginated manuscript). In one jurisdiction, informally established administrative criteria automatically deny handgun-purchase permits to homosexuals, nonvoters, women who lack their husband's permission, and anyone whom the sheriff personally dislikes. New York City permits have been denied on such bases as: post-nasal drip that caused the applicant to repeatedly clear his throat during the application interview demonstrated that he was "too nervous" to be trusted with a hand-gun; a son who "had been in trouble with the police," although the applicant himself had "a spotless record." Hardy & Chotiner, *supra* note 6, at 205, 209-11. In 1957, the New York City Police Department announced that henceforth applications would be entertained only from those desiring handguns to defend property. Reasons like target shooting or gun collecting, which did not contemplate the use of the gun against another human being, were not deemed important or compelling enough to warrant receiving an application form. Kates, *supra* note 17, at n.1 and accompanying text (unpaginated manuscript).

254. *See, e.g.,* G. NEWTON & F. ZIMRING, *supra* note 13, at 83 (coining the terms "restrictive" and "permissive" licensing, and favoring the former).

mentally unbalanced.[255] Registration, though often confused with licensing, literally means only that owners must identify themselves and their firearms to the police or some other designated authority.[256] Registration is generally tied to an overall control system, however, which, like permissive licensing, proscribes handgun ownership by classes of persons, such as felons and juveniles, with a high potential for misuse.[257] Neither registration nor permissive licensing are *per se* violative of the amendment since they operate only to exclude gun ownership by those upon whom the amendment confers no right.[258]

Nevertheless, it has been argued that registration and permissive licensing cannot sustain scrutiny under the amendment, in that they undercut one of its most important purposes: deterring potential despots by the prospect that, in a country with perhaps 160 million civilian firearms, even an initially successful coup would result in internecine civil or guerilla warfare.[259] By destroying the anonymity of gun ownership, licensing or registration laws would make it possible for a despot to follow up his coup by confiscating all firearms.

Whatever the abstract cogency of this argument, the concept of anonymity or privacy in gun ownership profoundly departs from the conditions under which the Founders envisioned the amendment operating. Under the militia laws (first colonial, then state and eventually federal), every household, and/or male reaching the age of majority, was required to maintain at least one firearm in good condition. To prove compliance these firearms had to be submitted for inspection periodically.[260] While the firearms-maintenance provisions of state law and the First Militia Act have long since been repealed, federal law continues to classify the entire able-bodied male citizenry aged seventeen to forty-five as "the militia of the United States."[261] This being the country's ultimate military resource, men

255. *See, e.g.,* CONN. GEN. STAT. §§ 29-33 (1983) (handgun may be purchased only upon application, which is deemed granted unless within two weeks licensing authority rejects, based on finding of felony conviction); MASS. ANN. LAWS, ch. 140, § 129B (Michie/Law. Co-op. 1981) (every applicant "shall be entitled to" issuance of a firearms identification card allowing purchase or possession of firearms unless he has been convicted of a felony within the last five years, is under treatment for drug addiction, or habitual drunkenness, has been an inmate of a psychiatric institution, or penetitiary, etc.).

256. *See* Bruce-Briggs, *supra* note 9, at 42; Kaplan, *supra* note 13, at 17-18.

257. *See, e.g.,* CAL. PENAL CODE §§ 12072, 12073 (Deering 1980).

258. As to felons, see text accompanying notes 266-67 *infra*. As to juveniles, suffice it to say that the militia laws specifically excluded those below the age of majority. *See* notes 46-48, 54 *supra*.

259. *See* Caplan, *supra* note 10, at 51; notes 281-82 *infra* and accompanying text.

260. *See* notes 46, 48-49 *supra* and accompanying text.

261. 10 U.S.C. § 311 (1982).

in this group remain liable for muster in dire military emergencies, *e.g.,* when necessary to keep order in the aftermath of an atomic attack or when both the Army and the National Guard have been deployed overseas.[262] Since one can scarcely argue that the First Militia Act violated the amendment,[263] it is difficult to see that it would be unconstitutional for Congress even today to require every member of the present militia to possess a firearm and regularly present it for inspection to assure that it is being maintained in good working order. Alternatively, and fully consistent with these purposes, a national gun registration scheme could allow federal authorities to mobilize selectively those members of the unorganized militia who are already armed and presumably familiar with the handling of weapons.[264] In sum, the historical background of the second amendment seems inconsistent with any notion of anonymity or privacy insofar as the mere fact of one's possessing a firearm is concerned.

D. *Laws Prohibiting Firearms to Felons*

Current federal, and many state, laws prohibit the possession of firearms by anyone who has been convicted of a felony.[265] Since a substantial majority of murderers appear to have prior felony records, it has recently been suggested that strong enforcement of such laws could effectively reduce homicidal violence.[266] The constitutionality of such legislation cannot seriously be questioned on a theory that felons are included within "the people" whose right to arms is guaranteed by the second amendment. Felons simply did not fall within the benefits of the common law right to possess arms. That law punished felons with automatic forfeiture of all goods, usually accompanied by death. We may presume that persons confined in gaols awaiting trial on criminal charges were also debarred from the possession of arms. Nor does it seem that the Founders considered felons within the common law right to arms or intended to confer any such right upon them. All the ratifying convention proposals which most explicitly detailed the recommended right-to-arms amendment excluded criminals and the violent.[267]

---

262. *See* Sprecher, *supra* note 10, at 667.

263. *See* note 49 *supra* and accompanying text.

264. *See* note 193 *supra* and accompanying text as to the militia value of allowing individual ownership and home possession of firearms.

265. *See, e.g.,* 18 U.S.C. § 922(g), (h) (1982) (all firearms); CAL. PENAL CODE § 12021 (Deering 1980 & Supp. 1983) (handguns).

266. Kleck & Bordua, *The Factual Foundation for Certain Key Assumptions of Gun Control*, 5 LAW & POLY. Q. 271, 291-94 (1983).

267. *See* notes 70, 72 & 83 *supra* and accompanying text.

E.   *Laws Restricting the Right To Carry Arms Outside of the Owner's Own Premises*

Largely as a result of gun-owner organizations' own legislative proposals, the laws of every state but Vermont prohibit at least the carrying of a concealed handgun off one's own premises.[268] A common proposal, already the law in many jurisdictions, is to prohibit even the open carrying of handguns (or all firearms), with limited exceptions for target shooting and the like, without a permit.[269] A further proposal would impose a mandatory minimum jail sentence for the unauthorized carrying of a handgun (or any firearm) off the owner's premises.[270]

The constitutionality of such legislation under the amendment can be established on the same basis as the unconstitutionality of a ban on possession. Smith's research in seventeenth and eighteenth-century colonial statutes indicates that, while the statutes used "keep" to refer to a person's having a gun in his home, they used "bear" only to refer to the bearing of arms while engaged in militia activities.[271] Thus the amendment's language was apparently intended to protect the possession of firearms for all legitimate purposes, but to guarantee the right to carry them outside the home only in the course of militia service. Outside that context the only carrying of firearms which the amendment appears to protect is such transportation as is implicit in the concept of a right to possess — *e.g.,* transporting them between the purchaser or owner's premises and a shooting range, or a gun store or gunsmith and so on.

CONCLUSION

The second amendment's language and historical and philosophical background demonstrate that it was designed to guarantee indi-

---

268. *See* VT. STAT. ANN. tit. 13, § 4003 (1974) (prohibition limited to carrying with intent to commit crime, or within a state institution or upon its grounds). As to the NRA's sponsorship of the Uniform Revolver Act, from which such legislation largely derives, see note 23 *supra*.

269. *See, e.g.,* TEX. PENAL CODE ANN. § 46.02(a) (Vernon 1974).

270. Scholars continue to debate whether this legislation has any significant impact on the crime rate. *Compare* Deutsch & Alt, *The Effect of Massachusetts' Gun Control Law on Gun-Related Crimes in the City of Boston*, 1 EVALUATION Q. 543 (1977), *with* Hay & McCleary, *Box-Tiao Time Series Models for Impact Assessment: A Comment on the Recent Work of Deutsch and Alt*, 3 EVALUATION Q. 277 (1979). For a general discussion of the strengths and weaknesses of the studies, see WEAPONS, CRIME AND VIOLENCE IN AMERICA, *supra* note 3, at 9-20. The latest and most negative assessment of the mandatory penalty device, a study done for the U.S. Department of Justice, is K. CARLSON, MANDATORY SENTENCING: THE EXPERIENCE OF TWO STATES (1982).

271. *See* notes 58-62 *supra* and accompanying text.

viduals the possession of certain kinds of arms for three purposes: (1) crime prevention, or what we would today describe as individual self-defense; (2) national defense; and (3) preservation of individual liberty and popular institutions against domestic despotism. It is often suggested that each of these purposes is obsolete and, therefore, that the amendment itself is obsolete. The national defense is fully provided for by our Armed Forces, supplemented by the National Guard, and a citizenry possessing only small arms could neither deter nor overthrow a domestic military despotism possessing tanks, aircraft and the other paraphernalia of modern war.[272] Likewise the possession of arms for self defense "is becoming anachronistic. As the policing of society becomes more efficient, the need for arms for personal self-defense becomes more irrelevant . . . ."[273]

Yet evidence can be offered to dispute each of these claims of obsolesence. As to the necessity of personal self-defense it is regrettably the case that enormous increases in police budgets and personnel have not prevented, for instance, the per capita incidence of reported robbery, rape and aggravated assault from increasing by 300%, 400% and 300% respectively since 1960.[274] Increasingly police are concluding, and even publicly proclaiming, that they cannot protect the law-abiding citizen, and that it is not only rational for him to choose to protect himself with firearms,[275] but a socially beneficial deterrent to violent crime.[276] This is, of course, a highly controver-

---

272. *See* Clark, *Reducing Firearms Availability: Constitutional Impediments to Effective Legislation and an Agenda for Research*, in FIREARMS & VIOLENCE, *supra* note 10.

273. Levin, *supra* note 13, at 166-67.

274. *Compare* FEDERAL BUREAU OF INVESTIGATION, U.S. DEPT. OF JUSTICE, CRIME IN THE UNITED STATES - 1960, at 33, *with* FEDERAL BUREAU OF INVESTIGATION, U.S. DEPT. OF JUSTICE, CRIME IN THE UNITED STATES - 1980. *See generally* WEAPONS, CRIME AND VIOLENCE IN AMERICA, *supra* note 3.

275. *See, e.g., Urban Merchants Find Guns Vital, And Most Police Units Now Agree,* N.Y. Times, July 20, 1974, § 1, at 39, col. 1; Kates, *supra* note 17, at n.14 and accompanying text (unpaginated manuscript) (collecting similar evidence):

Of over 5,000 officers who responded to a 1977 poll, 64% felt that an armed citizenry deters crime, and 86% stated that, if they were private citizens, they would keep a firearm for self defense. . . . These results may be subject to question since the poll was done for an organization which lobbies against handgun prohibition legislation. But in 1976 police chiefs and high ranking administrators were polled nationwide by the Research Division of the Boston Police Department which was then headed by Robert DiGrazia, an outspoken proponent of handgun prohibition. [The departmental survey reported]: "A substantial majority of the respondents looked favorably upon the general possession of handguns by the citizenry (excludes those with criminal records and a history of mental instability). Strong approval was also elicited from the police administrators concerning possession of handguns in the home or place of business." Indeed, by a bare majority, the respondents endorsed the idea that private citizens should be allowed to actually carry firearms with them at all times for self-protection. In answer to another question, the respondents opined that officers lower ranking than themselves would be even less favorably disposed toward "gun control."

276. Fundamental to systematic discussion of these issues is the distinction between any

sial matter,[277] though the more recent scholarship has tended to vindicate the police point of view.[278] For present purposes it is unnecessary to resolve this controversy. The mere fact of its exist-

---

self-defense value gun ownership may have and any potential crime deterrence value. For instance, G. NEWTON & F. ZIMRING, *supra* note 13, at 62-68, are unassailably correct in asserting that a gun owner rarely has the opportunity to *defend* his home or business against burglars because they generally take pains to strike only at unoccupied premises. But this fails to address two important issues of *deterrence*. First, Kleck and Bordua calculate that a burglar's small chance of being confronted by a gun-armed defender probably exceeds that of his being apprehended, tried, convicted and actually serving any time. One would then ask which is a greater deterrent: a slim chance of being punished or a slim chance of being shot? *See* Kleck & Bordua, *supra* note 266, at 282. Second, and even more important, fear of meeting a gun-armed defender may be one factor in the care most burglars take to strike at only unoccupied premises. In this connection, remember that it is precisely because burglary is generally a non-confrontation crime that victim injury or death is so very rarely associated with it — in contrast to robbery, where victim death is an all too frequent occurrence. If the deterrent effect of victim gun possession reduces victim death or injury by helping make burglary an overwhelmingly nonconfrontation crime, that *deterrent* benefits burglary victims and society in general, even though the *defense* value to the gun owners themselves is negligible.

Polls of convicted felons suggest that the average criminal has no more desire to meet an armed citizen than the average citizen has to meet an armed criminal:

> Surveys among prison populations uniformly find felons stating that, whenever possible, they avoid victims who are thought to be armed, and that they know of planned crimes that were abandoned when it was discovered that the prospective victim was armed. Indeed, in these surveys prison denizens expressed support for handgun prohibition on [the grounds] . . . that it would make life safer and easier for the criminal by disarming his victims without affecting his own ability to attack them. Typical of prisoner comments, according to criminologist Ernest van den Haag of New York University, was: "Ban guns; I'd love it. I'm an armed robber."

Silver & Kates, *Self-Defense, Handgun Ownership, and the Independence of Women in a Violent, Sexist Society*, in RESTRICTING HANDGUNS, *supra* note 6, at 139, 151 (footnote omitted). These conclusions are confirmed by the largest such survey yet conducted. The as-yet-unpublished results of this study in ten major prisons across the nation by the Social and Demographic Institute of the University of Massachusetts, are set out in its director's letter of May 10, 1983, to the author [hereinafter cited as Prison Survey].

277. *See, e.g.,* G. NEWTON & F. ZIMRING, *supra* note 13, at 61-68; M. YEAGER, J. ALVIANI & N. LOVING, HOW WELL DOES THE HANDGUN PROTECT YOU AND YOUR FAMILY? (1976); Rushforth, Hirsch, Ford & Adelson, *Accidental Firearm Fatalities in a Metropolitan County (1958-1973)*, 100 AM. J. EPIDEMIOLOGY 499 (1975). The Rushforth study is the source of the well-known statistic that a handgun held by a homeowner is six times more likely accidentally to kill a relative or acquaintance of the homeowner than to kill a burglar. It and the Yeager study are assailed as partisan and unreliable by Wright, who concludes that the six-to-one figure is arrived at through statistical legerdemain. Wright, *The Ownership of Firearms for Reasons of Self-Defense*, (paper delivered to the 1981 annual meeting of the American Society of Criminology), *reprinted in* FIREARMS & VIOLENCE, *supra* note 10; *see also* Kleck & Bordua, *supra* note 266, at 281 (criticizes the Yeager study); Silver & Kates, *supra* note 276, at 152-56 (discusses the efficacy of citizens keeping guns for self-defense purposes).

278. G. NEWTON & F. ZIMRING, *supra* note 13, at 61-68, conclude from the fact that householders in Detroit and Los Angeles killed few burglars in the mid-1960's, that gun owners rarely have the opportunity to foil criminal misconduct. The opposite is suggested by later figures from broader geographic areas and encompassing a fuller range of violent and confrontational felonies. Nationwide, 1981 FBI statistics show that citizens justifiably kill 30% more criminals than do police. In California, 1981 statistics show citizens justifiably killing twice as many felons as do the police; in Chicago and Cleveland it is three times as many. *See* Kleck & Bordua, *supra* note 266, at 290; Rushforth, Ford, Hirsch, Rushforth & Adelson, *Violent Deaths in a Metropolitan County — Changing Patterns in Homicide (1958-1974)*, 297 NEW ENG. J. MED. 531 (1977); Silver & Kates, *supra* note 276, at 156; Kates, *Can We Deny Citizens Both Guns and Protection?*, Wall St. J., Aug. 17, 1983, at 22, col. 6. Similar statistics for Hous-

ence demonstrates that the asserted irrelevancy of self-defense today has not been so clearly proved as to justify the abandonment of an expressly guaranteed constitutional right.

The argument that an armed citizenry cannot hope to overthrow a modern military machine flies directly in the face of the history of partisan guerilla and civil wars in the twentieth century. To make this argument (which is invariably supported, if at all, by reference only to the *American* military experience in *non*-revolutionary struggles like the two World Wars[279]), one must indulge in the assumption that a handgun-armed citizenry will eschew guerrilla tactics in favor of throwing themselves headlong under the tracks of advancing tanks. Far from proving invincible, in the vast majority of cases in this century in which they have confronted popular insurgencies, modern armies have been unable to suppress the insurgents. This is why the British no longer rule in Israel and Ireland, the French in Indo-China, Algeria and Madagascar, the Portugese in Angola, the whites in Rhodesia, or General Somoza, General Battista, or the Shah in Nicaragua, Cuba and Iran respectively — not to mention the examples of the United States in Vietnam and the Soviet Union in Afghanistan.[280] It is, of course, quite irrelevant for present purposes whether each of the struggles just mentioned is or was justified or whether the people benefited therefrom. However one may appraise those victories, the fact remains that they were achieved against regimes equipped with all the military technology which, it is asserted, inevitably dooms popular revolt.

Perhaps more important, in a free country like our own, the issue is not really *overthrowing* a tyranny but *deterring* its institution in the first place. To persuade his officers and men to support a coup, a potential military despot must convince them that his rule will suc-

---

ton-Dallas are reported in *Citizens' Gun Use on Rise in Houston*, N.Y. Times, Nov. 21, 1982, § 1, at 27, col. 1.

Moreover, justifiable homicide statistics provide an inherently distorted, under-representative picture of the value of civilian gun ownership. By analogy, the value of the police is not measured simply by how many criminals they kill, but rather by the entire universe of criminal activity deterred, as well as those criminals they wound, apprehend or scare off. Considering evidence on the entire universe of defensive handgun uses, Wright concludes that they are used at least as frequently in defense against criminals as they are by criminals in attacking citizens. *See* Wright, *supra* note 277. This conclusion is buttressed in Prison Survey, *supra* note 276, which reports that about 50% of the felons questioned (and a much higher proportion of the violent felons) stated that they had been interrupted, wounded, arrested or scared off by an armed citizen.

279. *See, e.g.*, DeZee, *National Rifle Association and Gun Control*, in Business Lobbying and Social Goals 212 (1979).

280. *See* Marina, *Weapons, Technology and Legitimacy: The Second Amendment in Global Perspective*, in Firearms & Violence, *supra* note 10; Kessler, *Gun Control and Political Power*, 5 Law & Poly. Q. 381 (1983).

ceed where our current civilian leadership and policies are failing. In a country whose widely divergent citizenry possesses upwards of 160 million firearms, however, the most likely outcome of usurpation (no matter how initially successful) is not benevolent dictatorship, but prolonged, internecine civil war:

> A general may have pipe dreams of a sudden and peaceful take-over and a nation moving confidently forward, united under his direction. But the realistic general will remember the actual fruits of civil war — shattered cities like Hue, Beirut, and Belfast, devastated countrysides like the Mekong Delta, Cyprus, and southern Lebanon.[281]

Even if the general's ambition does not recoil from the prospect of victory at such cost, will his officers and men accept it? Additionally, he and they must evaluate the effect of civil war in leaving the country vulnerable to the very foreign enemies their coup is designed to unite it against:

> Because it leads any prospective dictator to think through such questions, the individual, anonymous ownership of firearms is still a deterrent today to the despotism it was originally intended to obviate.
>
> Implicit in the Bill of Rights, as in the entire structure of our Constitution, are the twin hallmarks of traditional liberal thought: trust in the people, and distrust in government, particularly the military and the police. We are apt to forget these constant principles in light of our government's generally quite good record of exerting power without abusing it. But the deterrent effect of an armed citizenry is one little-recognized factor that may have contributed to this. In the words of the late Senator Hubert Humphrey, "[t]he right of citizens to bear arms is just one more guarantee against arbitrary government, one more safeguard against the tyranny which now appears remote in America, but which historically has proved to be always possible."[282]

Moving to the argument that a militia is not necessary to the national defense, for constitutional purposes the issue appears to have been resolved by Congress. For Congress has determined that it remains necessary to classify the entire able-bodied male population aged seventeen to forty-five as the militia of the United States, subject to a potential call to arms in the case of dire military emergency.[283] Moreover, the recent military history of the United States

---

281. Hardy, *The Second Amendment as a Restraint on State and Federal Firearm Restrictions*, in RESTRICTING HANDGUNS, *supra* note 6, at 171, 184.

282. *Id.* at 184-85.

283. 10 U.S.C. § 311 (1982). Sprecher, *supra* note 10, at 667, notes that the unorganized militia constitutes the only available substitute for national defense purposes in circumstances, like those of World War II, in which both the Army and the federalized National Guard have been deployed overseas. Recognizing that the unorganized militia can "not prevent an atomic attack," its mobilization may nevertheless be necessary to "preserve internal order after one." "Thus militias (by whatever name) are as important as ever, and perhaps more so in the atom-and-missile age . . . ."

shows that such militia units are still being called upon in time of military emergency.[284]

Finally, arguments as to whether the amendment is obsolete are of at most tangential import to its proper interpretation by the courts. After all, the second amendment is not the only provision of the Bill of Rights which is assertedly obsolete (or with the idea of which some Americans may today just happen to disagree). For instance, a judge may be absolutely convinced by scientific argument that the premise of free will which underlies freedom of religion has been invalidated by the modern psychological concept of brainwashing. He may believe a mother's anguished claims that only by such insidious techniques could her son have been induced by a "cult" to drop out of college and abandon the beliefs and lifestyle to which she raised him. Nevertheless, so long as the first amendment stands, no judge is free to disregard as obsolete the rights it confers on that young man and commit him to the custody of a "deprogrammer."[285] The seventh amendment, to take another example, clearly is obsolete, at least insofar as it requires jury trials in civil cases exceeding twenty dollars in controversy. Nevertheless, the courts continue faithfully to apply that amendment's dictate in all cases fairly covered by its literal wording and original spirit.[286] Though courts sometimes give constitutional rights *additional* scope in order to effectuate what is deemed to be their original intent, courts have no authority to reduce or eliminate the plain terms of a constitutional guarantee because they disagree with that intent or view it as obsolete.[287] The duty of the courts is to enforce the Constitution, not to

---

284. As late as Pearl Harbor, a military emergency was deemed to require mustering individually armed citizens. Because available military personnel were insufficient to repel the Japanese invasion that seemed imminent, the Governor of Hawaii called upon citizens to use their personal arms in manning checkpoints and remote beach areas. (Ironically, many of those who responded were Japanese-Americans whose colleagues in California were soon to be imprisoned without benefit of trial or habeas corpus.) Across the country the unorganized militia proved a successful substitute for the National Guard, which was federalized and activated for overseas duty. OFFICE OF THE ASSISTANT SECRETARY OF DEFENSE, U.S. DEPT. OF DEFENSE, U.S. HOME DEFENSE FORCES STUDY, 32, 34 (1981). Members of the unorganized militia, many of whom belonged to gun clubs and whose ages ranged from 16 to 65, served without pay and provided their own arms. *Id* at 58, 62-63. The U.S. government, however, not only could not supply sufficient arms to the militia but "turned out to be an Indian giver" by recalling rifles. M. SCHLEGEL, VIRGINIA ON GUARD 131 (1949).

285. *See, e.g.,* Rankin v. Howard, 633 F.2d 844 (9th Cir. 1980), *cert. denied,* 451 U.S. 939 (1981).

286. *See, e.g.,* Curtis v. Loether, 415 U.S. 189 (1974) (applying seventh amendment to damage actions for housing discrimination under the 1968 Civil Rights Act); Pernell v. Southall Realty, 416 U.S. 363 (1974) (applying seventh amendment to actions under special District of Columbia statute).

287. *See, e.g.,* State v. Kessler, 289 Or. 359, 360, 614 P.2d 94, 95 (1980):
We are not unmindful that there is current controversy over the wisdom of a right to bear

arrogate to themselves the power to delete its provisions.[288] Generally speaking, the power to withdraw a right explicitly guaranteed to the people is reserved exclusively to their state and federal legislatures in a process which is ornately hedged with safeguards, not the least of which is its protracted length.[289] As Mr. Justice Frankfurter noted in reference to criticism of the privilege against self-incrimination as an obstacle to the needs of law enforcement in an era of rampant crime: "If it be thought that the privilege is outmoded in the conditions of this modern age, then the thing to do is to take it out of the Constitution, not to whittle it down by the subtle encroachments of judicial opinion."[290]

Unmistakably the Founders intended the second amendment to guarantee an individual right to possess certain kinds of weapons in the home certain kinds of circumstances. The precise details and parameters of that guarantee remain significantly unclear. In part this is because neither federal, state nor local governments have generally moved beyond gun control to the extreme of confiscation. In even larger part the delay in defining its parameters is attributable to the diversion and monopolization of legal analysis by the false dichotomy between the exclusively state's right and the unrestricted individual right interpretations. In fact, the arms of the state's militias were and are the personally owned arms of the general citizenry, so that the amendment's dual intention to protect both was achieved by guaranteeing to the citizenry a right to possess arms individually. Having dispelled the ahistorical exclusively state's right notion, it will become possible to move forward to analyzing how rational, effectual gun control strategies can be reconciled with the constitutional scheme.

---

arms, and that the original motivations for such a provision might not seem compelling if debated as a new issue. Our task, however, in construing a constitutional provision is to respect the principles given the status of constitutional guarantees and limitations by the drafters; it is not to abandon these principles when this fits the needs of the moment. *Cf.* note 28 *supra* (discussing the proper role of original intent in constitutional adjudication).

288. Hamilton's explanation of the judicial function in THE FEDERALIST No. 78 remains as true today as it was when he penned it:

[T]he right of the courts to pronounce legislative acts void . . . [does not] by any means suppose a superiority of the judicial to the legislative power. It only supposes that the power of the people is superior to both; and that where the will of the legislature declared in its statutes, stands in opposition to that of the people declared in the constitution, the judges ought to be governed by the latter, rather than the former.

THE FEDERALIST No. 78, at 577-78 (A. Hamilton) (J. Hamilton ed. 1864).

289. We are reminded by Mr. Justice Douglas of Mr. Chief Justice Marshall's dictum that "it would be dangerous in the extreme to infer from extrinsic circumstances, that a case for which the words of [the Constitution] expressly provide, shall be exempted from its operation." Richfield Oil Corp. v. State Bd. of Equalization, 329 U.S. 69, 77 (1946).

290. Ullmann v. United States, 350 U.S. 422, 427-28 (1956) (quoting Maffie v. United States, 209 F.2d 225, 227 (1st Cir. 1954)).

Comments

The Embarrassing Second Amendment

Sanford Levinson†

One of the best known pieces of American popular art in this century is the *New Yorker* cover by Saul Steinberg presenting a map of the United States as seen by a New Yorker. As most readers can no doubt recall, Manhattan dominates the map; everything west of the Hudson is more or less collapsed together and minimally displayed to the viewer. Steinberg's great cover depends for its force on the reality of what social psychologists call "cognitive maps." If one asks inhabitants ostensibly of the same cities to draw maps of that city, one will quickly discover that the images carried around in people's minds will vary by race, social class, and the like. What is true of maps of places—that they differ according to the perspectives of the mapmakers—is certainly true of all conceptual maps.

To continue the map analogy, consider in this context the Bill of Rights: Is there an agreed upon "projection" of the concept? Is there even a canonical text of the Bill of Rights? Does it include the first eight, nine,

---

† Charles Tilford McCormick Professor of Law, University of Texas Law School. This essay was initially prepared for delivery at a symposium on Interpretation and the Bill of Rights at Williams College on November 4, 1988. I am grateful for the thought and effort put into that conference by its organizer, Professor Mark Taylor. It was he who arranged for Wendy Brown, then a member of the Williams Department of Political Science, to deliver the excellent response that can be found following this article. A timely letter from Linda Kerber contributed to the reorganization of this article. Two long-distance friends and colleagues, Akhil Reed Amar and Stephen Siegel, contributed special and deeply appreciated insights and encouragement. Finally, as always, I took full advantage of several of my University of Texas Law School colleagues, including Jack Balkin, Douglas Laycock, and Lucas Powe.

I should note that I wrote (and titled) this article before reading Nelson Lund's *The Second Amendment, Political Liberty, and the Right to Self-Preservation*, 39 ALA. L. REV. 103 (1987), which begins, "The Second Amendment to the United States Constitution has become the most embarrassing provision of the Bill of Rights." I did hear Lund deliver a talk on the Second Amendment at the University of Texas Law School during the winter of 1987, which may have penetrated my consciousness more than I realized while drafting the article.

or ten Amendments to the Constitution?[1] Imagine two individuals who
are asked to draw a "map" of the Bill of Rights. One is a (stereo-) typical
member of the American Civil Liberties Union (of which I am a card-
carrying member); the other is an equally (stereo-) typical member of the
"New Right." The first, I suggest, would feature the First Amendment[2]
as Main Street, dominating the map, though more, one suspects, in its
role as protector of speech and prohibitor of established religion than as
guardian of the rights of religious believers. The other principal avenues
would be the criminal procedure aspects of the Constitution drawn from
the Fourth,[3] Fifth,[4] Sixth,[5] and Eighth[6] Amendments. Also depicted
prominently would be the Ninth Amendment,[7] although perhaps as in the
process of construction. I am confident that the ACLU map would exclude any display of the just compensation clause of the Fifth Amendment[8] or of the Tenth Amendment.[9]

The second map, drawn by the New Rightist, would highlight the free

---

1. It is not irrelevant that the Bill of Rights submitted to the states in 1789 included not only
what are now the first ten Amendments, but also two others. Indeed, what we call the First Amendment was only the third one of the list submitted to the states. The initial "first amendment" in fact
concerned the future size of the House of Representatives, a topic of no small importance to the Anti-
Federalists, who were appalled by the smallness of the House seemingly envisioned by the Philadelphia framers. The second prohibited any pay raise voted by members of Congress to themselves from
taking effect until an election "shall have intervened." *See* J. GOEBEL, 1 THE OLIVER WENDELL
HOLMES DEVISE HISTORY OF THE SUPREME COURT OF THE UNITED STATES: ANTECEDENTS AND
BEGINNINGS TO 1801, at 442 n.162 (1971). Had all of the initial twelve proposals been ratified, we
would, it is possible, have a dramatically different cognitive map of the Bill of Rights. At the very
least, one would neither hear defenses of the "preferred" status of freedom of speech framed in terms
of the "firstness" of (what we know as) the First Amendment, nor the wholly invalid inference drawn
from that "firstness" of some special intention of the Framers to safeguard the particular rights laid
out there.
2. "Congress shall make no law respecting an establishment of religion . . . or abridging the
freedom of speech, or of the press; or the right of the people peaceably to assemble, and to petition the
Government for a redress of grievances." U.S. CONST. amend. I.
3. "The right of the people to be secure in their persons, houses, papers, and effects, against
unreasonable searches and seizures, shall not be violated; and no Warrants shall issue but upon probable cause, supported by Oath or affirmation, and particularly describing the place to be searched,
and the persons or things to be seized." U.S. CONST. amend. IV.
4. "No person shall be held to answer for a capital, or otherwise infamous crime, unless on a
presentment or indictment of a Grand Jury, except in cases arising in the land or naval forces, or in
the Militia, when in actual service in time of War or public danger; nor shall any person be subject
for the same offence to be twice put in jeopardy of life or limb; nor shall be compelled in any criminal
case to be a witness against himself, nor be deprived of life, liberty, or property, without due process
of law . . . ." U.S. CONST. amend. V.
5. "In all criminal prosecutions, the accused shall enjoy the right to a speedy and public trial, by
an impartial jury of the State and district wherein the crime shall have been committed, which district
shall have been previously ascertained by law, and to be informed of the nature and cause of the
accusation; to be confronted with the witnesses against him; to have compulsory process for obtaining
witnesses in his favor, and to have the Assistance of Counsel for his defense." U.S. CONST. amend VI.
6. "Excessive bail shall not be required, nor excessive fines imposed, nor cruel and unusual punishments inflicted." U.S. CONST. amend. VIII.
7. "The enumeration in the Constitution, of certain rights, shall not be construed to deny or
disparage others retained by the people." U.S. CONST. amend. IX.
8. "[N]or shall private property be taken for public use, without just compensation." U.S. CONST.
amend. IV.
9. "The powers not delegated to the United States by the Constitution, nor prohibited by it to the
States, are reserved to the States respectively, or to the people." U.S. CONST. amend. X.

exercise clause of the First Amendment,[10] the just compensation clause of the Fifth Amendment,[11] and the Tenth Amendment.[12] Perhaps the most notable difference between the two maps, though, would be in regard to the Second Amendment: "A well regulated Militia being necessary to the security of a free State, the right of the people to keep and bear Arms shall not be infringed." What would be at most only a blind alley for the ACLU mapmaker would, I am confident, be a major boulevard in the map drawn by the New Right adherent. It is this last anomaly that I want to explore in this essay.

I. The Politics of Interpreting the Second Amendment

To put it mildly, the Second Amendment is not at the forefront of constitutional discussion, at least as registered in what the academy regards as the venues for such discussion—law reviews,[13] casebooks,[14] and other

---

10. "Congress shall make no law . . . prohibiting the free exercise thereof [religion]. . . ." U.S. Const. amend I.

11. See supra note 8.

12. See supra note 9.

13. There are several law review articles discussing the Amendment. See, e.g., Lund, supra note †, and the articles cited in Dowlut & Knoop, State Constitutions and the Right to Keep and Bear Arms, 7 Okla. City U.L. Rev. 177, 178 n.3 (1982). See also the valuable symposium on Gun Control, edited by Don Kates, in 49 Law & Contemp. Probs. 1-267 (1986), including articles by Shalhope, The Armed Citizen in the Early Republic, at 125; Kates, The Second Amendment: A Dialogue, at 143; Halbrook, What the Framers Intended: A Linguistic Analysis of the Right to "Bear Arms," at 151. The symposium also includes a valuable bibliography of published materials on gun control, including Second Amendment considerations, at 251-67. The most important single article is almost undoubtedly Kates, Handgun Prohibition and the Original Meaning of the Second Amendment, 82 Mich. L. Rev. 204 (1983). Not the least significant aspect of Kates' article is that it is basically the only one to have appeared in an "elite" law review. However, like many of the authors of other Second Amendment pieces, Kates is a practicing lawyer rather than a legal academic. I think it is accurate to say that no one recognized by the legal academy as a "major" writer on constitutional law has deigned to turn his or her talents to a full consideration of the Amendment. But see LaRue, Constitutional Law and Constitutional History, 36 Buffalo L. Rev. 373, 375-78 (1988) (briefly discussing Second Amendment). Akhil Reed Amar's reconsideration of the foundations of the Constitution also promises to delve more deeply into the implications of the Amendment. See Amar, Of Sovereignty and Federalism, 96 Yale L.J. 1425, 1495-1500 (1987). Finally, there is one book that provides more in-depth treatment of the Second Amendment: S. Halbrook, That Every Man Be Armed, the Evolution of a Constitutional Right (1984).

George Fletcher, in his study of the Berhard Goetz case, also suggests that Second Amendment analysis is not frivolous, though he does not elaborate the point. G. Fletcher, A Crime of Self-Defense 156-58, 210-11 (1988).

One might well find this overt reference to "elite" law reviews and "major" writers objectionable, but it is foolish to believe that these distinctions do not exist within the academy or, more importantly, that we cannot learn about the sociology of academic discourse through taking them into account. No one can plausibly believe that the debates that define particular periods of academic discourse are a simple reflection of "natural" interest in the topic. Nothing helps an issue so much as its being taken up as an obsession by a distinguished professor from, say, Harvard or Yale.

14. One will search the "leading" casebooks in vain for any mention of the Second Amendment. Other than its being included in the text of the Constitution that all of the casebooks reprint, a reader would have no reason to believe that the Amendment exists or could possibly be of interest to the constitutional analyst. I must include, alas, P. Brest & S. Levinson, Processes of Constitutional Decisionmaking (2d ed. 1983), within this critique, though I have every reason to believe that this will not be true of the forthcoming third edition.

scholarly legal publications. As Professor LaRue has recently written, "the second amendment is not taken seriously by most scholars."[15]

Both Laurence Tribe[16] and the Illinois team of Nowak, Rotunda, and Young[17] at least acknowledge the existence of the Second Amendment in their respective treatises on constitutional law, perhaps because the treatise genre demands more encyclopedic coverage than does the casebook. Neither, however, pays it the compliment of extended analysis. Both marginalize the Amendment by relegating it to footnotes; it becomes what a deconstructionist might call a "supplement" to the ostensibly "real" Constitution that is privileged by discussion in the text.[18] Professor Tribe's footnote appears as part of a general discussion of congressional power. He asserts that the history of the Amendment "indicate[s] that the central concern of [its] framers was to prevent such federal interferences with the state militia as would permit the establishment of a standing national army and the consequent destruction of local autonomy."[19] He does note, however, that "the debates surrounding congressional approval of the second amendment do contain references to individual self-protection as well as to states' rights," but he argues that the presence of the preamble to the Amendment, as well as the qualifying phrase " 'well regulated' makes any invocation of the amendment as a restriction on state or local gun control measures extremely problematic."[20] Nowak, Rotunda, and Young mention the Amendment in the context of the incorporation controversy, though they discuss its meaning at slightly greater length.[21] They state that "[t]he Supreme Court has not determined, at least not with any clarity, whether the amendment protects only a right of state governments against federal interference with state militia and police forces . . . or a right of individuals against the federal and state government[s]."[22]

Clearly the Second Amendment is not the only ignored patch of text in our constitutional conversations. One will find extraordinarily little discussion about another one of the initial Bill of Rights, the Third Amendment: "No Soldier shall, in time of peace be quartered in any house, with-

---

15. LaRue, *supra* note 13, at 375.

16. L. TRIBE, AMERICAN CONSTITUTIONAL LAW (2d ed. 1988).

17. J. NOWAK, R. ROTUNDA & J. YOUNG, CONSTITUTIONAL LAW (3d ed. 1986).

18. For a brilliant and playful meditation on the way the legal world treats footnotes and other marginal phenomena, see Balkin, *The Footnote*, 83 Nw. U.L. REV. 275, 276-81 (1989).

19. TRIBE, *supra* note 16, at 299 n.6.

20. *Id.; see also* J. ELY, DEMOCRACY AND DISTRUST 95 (1980) ("[T]he framers and ratifiers . . . opted against leaving to the future the attribution of [other] purposes, choosing instead explicitly to legislate the goal in terms of which the provision was to be interpreted."). As shall be seen below, *see infra* text accompanying note 38, the preamble may be less plain in its meaning than Tribe's (and Ely's) confident argument suggests.

21. J. NOWAK, R. ROTUNDA & J. YOUNG, *supra* note 17, at 316 n.4. They do go on to cite a spate of articles by scholars who have debated the issue.

22. *Id.* at 316 n.4.

out the consent of the Owner, nor in time of war, but in a manner to be prescribed by law." Nor does one hear much about letters of marque and reprisal[23] or the granting of titles of nobility.[24] There are, however, some differences that are worth noting.

The Third Amendment, to take the easiest case, is ignored because it is in fact of no current importance whatsoever (although it did, for obvious reasons, have importance at the time of the founding). It has never, for a single instant, been viewed by any body of modern lawyers or groups of laity as highly relevant to their legal or political concerns. For this reason, there is almost no caselaw on the Amendment.[25] I suspect that few among even the highly sophisticated readers of this Journal can summon up the Amendment without the aid of the text.

The Second Amendment, though, is radically different from these other pieces of constitutional text just mentioned, which all share the attribute of being basically irrelevant to any ongoing political struggles. To grasp the difference, one might simply begin by noting that it is not at all unusual for the Second Amendment to show up in letters to the editors of newspapers and magazines.[26] That judges and academic lawyers, including the ones who write casebooks, ignore it is most certainly not evidence for the proposition that no one cares about it. The National Rifle Association, to name the most obvious example, cares deeply about the Amendment, and an apparently serious Senator of the United States averred that the right to keep and bear arms is the "right most valued by free men."[27] Campaigns for Congress in both political parties, and even presidential

---

23. U.S. CONST. art. I, § 10.

24. U.S. CONST. art. I, § 9, cl. 8.

25. See, e.g., LEGISLATIVE REFERENCE SERV., LIBRARY OF CONGRESS, THE CONSTITUTION OF THE UNITED STATES OF AMERICA: ANALYSIS AND INTERPRETATION 923 (1964), which quotes the Amendment and then a comment from MILLER, THE CONSTITUTION 646 (1893): "This amendment seems to have been thought necessary. It does not appear to have been the subject of judicial exposition; and it is so thoroughly in accord with our ideas, that further comment is unnecessary." Cf. Engblom v. Carey, 724 F.2d 28 (2d Cir. 1983), aff'g 572 F. Supp. 44 (S.D.N.Y. 1983). Engblom grew out of a "statewide strike of correction officers, when they were evicted from their facility-residences . . . and members of the National Guard were housed in their residences without their consent." The district court had initially granted summary judgment for the defendants in a suit brought by the officers claiming a deprivation of their rights under the Third Amendment. The Second Circuit, however, reversed on the ground that it could not "say that as a matter of law appellants were not entitled to the protection of the Third Amendment." Engblom v. Carey, 677 F.2d 957, 964 (2d Cir. 1982). The District Court on remand held that, as the Third Amendment rights had not been clearly established at the time of the strike, the defendants were protected by a qualified immunity, and it is this opinion that was upheld by the Second Circuit. I am grateful to Mark Tushnet for bringing this case to my attention.

26. See, e.g., The Firearms the Second Amendment Protects, N.Y. Times, June 9, 1988, at A22, col. 2 (three letters); Second Amendment and Gun Control, L.A. Times, March 11, 1989, Part II, at 9 col. 1 (nine letters); What 'Right to Bear Arms'?, N.Y. Times, July 20, 1989, at A23, col. 1 (national ed.) (op. ed. essay by Daniel Abrams); see also We Rebelled To Protect Our Gun Rights, Washington Times, July 20, 1989, at F2, col. 4.

27. See SUBCOMMITTEE ON THE CONSTITUTION OF THE COMM. ON THE JUDICIARY, THE RIGHT TO KEEP AND BEAR ARMS, 97th Cong., 2d Sess. viii (1982) (preface by Senator Orrin Hatch) [hereinafter THE RIGHT TO KEEP AND BEAR ARMS].

campaigns, may turn on the apparent commitment of the candidates to a
particular view of the Second Amendment. This reality of the political
process reflects the fact that millions of Americans, even if (or perhaps
especially if) they are not academics, can quote the Amendment and
would disdain any presentation of the Bill of Rights that did not give it a
place of pride.

I cannot help but suspect that the best explanation for the absence of
the Second Amendment from the legal consciousness of the elite bar, including that component found in the legal academy,[28] is derived from a
mixture of sheer opposition to the idea of private ownership of guns and
the perhaps subconscious fear that altogether plausible, perhaps even
"winning," interpretations of the Second Amendment would present real
hurdles to those of us supporting prohibitory regulation. Thus the title of
this essay—*The Embarrassing Second Amendment*—for I want to suggest
that the Amendment may be profoundly embarrassing to many who both
support such regulation and view themselves as committed to zealous adherence to the Bill of Rights (such as most members of the ACLU). Indeed, one sometimes discovers members of the NRA who are equally committed members of the ACLU, differing with the latter only on the issue
of the Second Amendment but otherwise genuinely sharing the libertarian
viewpoint of the ACLU.

It is not my style to offer "correct" or "incorrect" interpretations of the
Constitution.[29] My major interest is in delineating the rhetorical structures of American constitutional argument and elaborating what is sometimes called the "politics of interpretation," that is, the factors that explain why one or another approach will appeal to certain analysts at
certain times, while other analysts, or times, will favor quite different approaches. Thus my general tendency to regard as wholly untenable any
approach to the Constitution that describes itself as obviously correct and
condemns its opposition as simply wrong holds for the Second Amendment as well. In some contexts, this would lead me to label as tendentious
the certainty of NRA advocates that the Amendment means precisely
what they assert it does. In this particular context—i.e., the pages of a
journal whose audience is much more likely to be drawn from an elite,
liberal portion of the public—I will instead be suggesting that the skepticism should run in the other direction. That is, we might consider the
possibility that "our" views of the Amendment, perhaps best reflected in
Professor Tribe's offhand treatment of it, might themselves be equally deserving of the "tendentious" label.

28. *See supra* notes 13-14.
29. *See* Levinson, *Constitutional Rhetoric and the Ninth Amendment*, 64 Chi.-Kent L. Rev.
131 (1988).

II. THE RHETORICAL STRUCTURES OF THE RIGHT TO BEAR ARMS

My colleague Philip Bobbitt has, in his book *Constitutional Fate*,[30] spelled out six approaches—or "modalities," as he terms them—of constitutional argument. These approaches, he argues, comprise what might be termed our legal grammar. They are the rhetorical structures within which "law-talk" as a recognizable form of conversation is carried on. The six are as follows:

1) textual argument—appeals to the unadorned language of the text;[31]

2) historical argument—appeals to the historical background of the provision being considered, whether the history considered be general, such as background but clearly crucial events (such as the American Revolution), or specific appeals to the so-called intentions of the framers;[32]

3) structural argument—analyses inferred from the particular structures established by the Constitution, including the tripartite division of the national government; the separate existence of both state and nation as political entities; and the structured role of citizens within the political order;[33]

4) doctrinal argument—emphasis on the implications of prior cases decided by the Supreme Court;[34]

5) prudential argument—emphasis on the consequences of adopting a proferred decision in any given case;[35] and, finally,

6) ethical argument—reliance on the overall "ethos" of limited government as centrally constituting American political culture.[36]

I want to frame my consideration of the Second Amendment within the first five of Bobbitt's categories; they are all richly present in consideration of what the Amendment might mean. The sixth, which emphasizes the ethos of limited government, does not play a significant role in the debate of the Second Amendment.[37]

A. Text

I begin with the appeal to text. Recall the Second Amendment: "A well regulated Militia, being necessary to the security of a free State, the right of the people to keep and bear Arms, shall not be infringed." No one has

---

30. P. BOBBITT, CONSTITUTIONAL FATE (1982).

31. *Id.* at 25-38.

32. *Id.* at 9-24.

33. *Id.* at 74-92.

34. *Id.* at 39-58.

35. *Id.* at 59-73.

36. *Id.* at 93-119.

37. For the record, I should note that Bobbitt disagrees with this statement, making an eloquent appeal (in conversation) on behalf of the classic American value of self-reliance for the defense of oneself and, perhaps more importantly, one's family. I certainly do not doubt the possibility of constructing an "ethical" rationale for limiting the state's power to prohibit private gun ownership. Nonetheless, I would claim that no one unpersuaded by any of the arguments derived from the first five modes would suddenly change his or her mind upon being presented with an "ethical" argument.

ever described the Constitution as a marvel of clarity, and the Second Amendment is perhaps one of the worst drafted of all its provisions. What is special about the Amendment is the inclusion of an opening clause—a preamble, if you will—that seems to set out its purpose. No similar clause is a part of any other Amendment,[38] though that does not, of course, mean that we do not ascribe purposes to them. It would be impossible to make sense of the Constitution if we did not engage in the ascription of purpose. Indeed, the major debates about the First Amendment arise precisely when one tries to discern a purpose, given that "literalism" is a hopelessly failing approach to interpreting it. We usually do not even recognize punishment of fraud—a classic speech act—as a free speech problem because we so sensibly assume that the purpose of the First Amendment could not have been, for example, to protect the circulation of patently deceptive information to potential investors in commercial enterprises. The sharp differences that distinguish those who would limit the reach of the First Amendment to "political" speech from those who would extend it much further, encompassing non-deceptive commercial speech, are all derived from different readings of the purpose that underlies the raw text.[39]

A standard move of those legal analysts who wish to limit the Second Amendment's force is to focus on its "preamble" as setting out a restrictive purpose. Recall Laurence Tribe's assertion that that purpose was to allow the states to keep their militias and to protect them against the possibility that the new national government will use its power to establish a powerful standing army and eliminate the state militias. This purposive reading quickly disposes of any notion that there is an "individual" right to keep and bear arms. The right, if such it be, is only a state's right. The consequence of this reading is obvious: the national government has the power to regulate—to the point of prohibition—private ownership of guns, since that has, by stipulation, nothing to do with preserving state militias. This is, indeed, the position of the ACLU, which reads the Amendment as protecting only the right of "maintaining an effective state militia. . . . [T]he individual's right to bear arms applies only to the preservation or efficiency of a well-regulated [state] militia. Except for lawful police and military purposes, the possession of weapons by individuals is not constitutionally protected."[40]

This is not a wholly implausible reading, but one might ask why the

---

38. *Cf., e.g.,* the patents and copyrights clause, which sets out the power of Congress "[t]o promote the Progress of Science and useful Arts, by securing for limited Times to Authors and Inventors the exclusive Right to their respective Writings and Discoveries." U.S. CONST. art. I., § 8.

39. For examples of this, see F. SCHAUER, FREEDOM OF SPEECH: A PHILOSOPHICAL ENQUIRY (1982); Levinson, *First Amendment, Freedom of Speech, Freedom of Expression: Does It Matter What We Call It?* 80 Nw. U.L. REV. 767 (1985) (reviewing M. REDISH, FREEDOM OF EXPRESSION: A CRITICAL ANALYSIS (1984)).

40. ACLU Policy #47. I am grateful to Joan Mahoney, a member of the national board of the ACLU, for providing me with a text of the ACLU's current policy on gun control.

Framers did not simply say something like "Congress shall have no power to prohibit state-organized and directed militias." Perhaps they in fact meant to do something else. Moreover, we might ask if ordinary readers of late 18th Century legal prose would have interpreted it as meaning something else. The text at best provides only a starting point for a conversation. In this specific instance, it does not come close to resolving the questions posed by federal regulation of arms. Even if we accept the preamble as significant, we must still try to figure out what might be suggested by guaranteeing to "the people the right to keep and bear arms;" moreover, as we shall see presently, even the preamble presents unexpected difficulties in interpretation.

B. *History*

One might argue (and some have) that the substantive right is one pertaining to a collective body—"the people"—rather than to individuals. Professor Cress, for example, argues that state constitutions regularly used the words "man" or "person" in regard to "individual rights such as freedom of conscience," whereas the use in those constitutions of the term "the people" in regard to a right to bear arms is intended to refer to the "sovereign citizenry" collectively organized.[41] Such an argument founders, however, upon examination of the text of the federal Bill of Rights itself and the usage there of the term "the people" in the First, Fourth, Ninth, and Tenth Amendments.

Consider that the Fourth Amendment protects "[t]he right of the people to be secure in their persons," or that the First Amendment refers to the "right of the people peaceably to assemble, and to petition the Government for a redress of grievances." It is difficult to know how one might plausibly read the Fourth Amendment as other than a protection of individual rights, and it would approach the frivolous to read the assembly and petition clause as referring only to the right of state legislatures to meet and pass a remonstrance directed to Congress or the President against some governmental act. The Tenth Amendment is trickier, though it does explicitly differentiate between "states" and "the people" in terms of retained rights.[42] Concededly, it would be possible to read the Tenth Amendment as suggesting only an ultimate right of revolution by the collective people should the "states" stray too far from their designated role of protecting the rights of the people. This reading follows directly from the social contract theory of the state. (But, of course, many of these rights are held by individuals.)

Although the record is suitably complicated, it seems tendentious to re-

---

41. Cress, *An Armed Community: The Origins and Meaning of the Right to Bear Arms*, 71 J. AM. HIST. 22, 31 (1984).
42. *See* U.S. CONST. amend. X.

ject out of hand the argument that one purpose of the Amendment was to recognize an individual's right to engage in armed self-defense against criminal conduct.[43] Historian Robert E. Shalhope supports this view, arguing in his article *The Ideological Origins of the Second Amendment*[44] that the Amendment guarantees individuals the right "to possess arms for their own personal defense."[45] It would be especially unsurprising if this were the case, given the fact that the development of a professional police force (even within large American cities) was still at least a half century away at the end of the colonial period.[46] I shall return later in this essay to this individualist notion of the Amendment, particularly in regard to the argument that "changing circumstances," including the development of a professional police force, have deprived it of any continuing plausibility. But I want now to explore a second possible purpose of the Amendment, which as a sometime political theorist I find considerably more interesting.

Assume, as Professor Cress has argued, that the Second Amendment refers to a communitarian, rather than an individual, right.[47] We are still left the task of defining the relationship between the community and the state apparatus. It is this fascinating problem to which I now turn.

Consider once more the preamble and its reference to the importance of a well-regulated militia. Is the meaning of the term obvious? Perhaps we should make some effort to find out what the term "militia" meant to 18th century readers and writers, rather than assume that it refers only to Dan Quayle's Indiana National Guard and the like. By no means am I arguing that the discovery of that meaning is dispositive as to the general meaning of the Constitution for us today. But it seems foolhardy to be entirely uninterested in the historical philology behind the Second Amendment.

I, for one, have been persuaded that the term "militia" did not have the limited reference that Professor Cress and many modern legal analysts assign to it. There is strong evidence that "militia" refers to all of the

---

43.   For a full articulation of the the individualist view of the Second Amendment, see Kates, *Handgun Prohibition and the Original Meaning of the Second Amendment*, 82 MICH. L. REV. 204 (1983). One can also find an efficient presentation of this view in Lund, *supra* note †, at 117.

44.   Shalhope, *The Ideological Origins of the Second Amendment*, 69 J. AM. HIST. 599 (1982).

45.   *Id.* at 614.

46.   See Daniel Boorstin's laconic comment that "the requirements for self-defense and food-gathering had put firearms in the hands of nearly everyone" in colonial America. D. BOORSTIN, THE AMERICANS—THE COLONIAL EXPERIENCE 353 (1958). The beginnings of a professional police force in Boston are traced in R. LANE, POLICING THE CITY: BOSTON 1822-1855 (1967). Lane argues that as of the earlier of his two dates, "all the major eastern cities . . . had several kinds of officials serving various police functions, all of them haphazardly inherited from the British and colonial past. These agents were gradually drawn into better defined and more coherent organizations." *Id.* at 1. However, as Oscar Handlin points out in his introduction to the book, "to bring into being a professional police force was to create precisely the kind of hireling body considered dangerous by conventional political theory." *Id.* at vii.

47.   *See* Cress, *supra* note 41.

people, or at least all of those treated as full citizens of the community. Consider, for example, the question asked by George Mason, one of the Virginians who refused to sign the Constitution because of its lack of a Bill of Rights: "Who are the Militia? They consist now of the whole people."[48] Similarly, the *Federal Farmer*, one of the most important Anti-Federalist opponents of the Constitution, referred to a "militia, when properly formed, [as] in fact the people themselves."[49] We have, of course, moved now from text to history. And this history is most interesting, especially when we look at the development of notions of popular sovereignty. It has become almost a cliche of contemporary American historiography to link the development of American political thought, including its constitutional aspects, to republican thought in England, the "country" critique of the powerful "court" centered in London.

One of this school's important writers, of course, was James Harrington, who not only was influential at the time but also has recently been given a certain pride of place by one of the most prominent of contemporary "neo-republicans," Professor Frank Michelman.[50] One historian describes Harrington as having made "the most significant contribution to English libertarian attitudes toward arms, the individual, and society."[51] He was a central figure in the development of the ideas of popular sovereignty and republicanism.[52] For Harrington, preservation of republican liberty requires independence, which rests primarily on possession of adequate property to make men free from coercion by employers or landlords. But widespread ownership of land is not sufficient. These independent yeoman should also bear arms. As Professor Morgan puts it, "[T]hese independent yeomen, armed and embodied in a militia, are also a popular government's best protection against its enemies, whether they be aggressive foreign monarchs or scheming demagogues within the nation itself."[53]

A central fear of Harrington and of all future republicans was a standing army, composed of professional soldiers. Harrington and his fellow republicans viewed a standing army as a threat to freedom, to be avoided at almost all costs. Thus, says Morgan, "A militia is the only safe form of military power that a popular government can employ; and because it is

---

48. 3 J. ELLIOT, DEBATES IN THE GENERAL STATE CONVENTIONS 425 (3d ed. 1937) (statement of George Mason, June 14, 1788), *reprinted in* Kates, *supra* note 13, at 216 n.51.

49. LETTERS FROM THE FEDERAL FARMER TO THE REPUBLICAN 123 (W. Bennett ed. 1978) (ascribed to Richard Henry Lee), *reprinted in* Kates, *supra* note 13, at 216 n.51.

50. Michelman, *The Supreme Court 1985 Term—Foreword: Traces of Self-Government*, 100 HARV. L. REV. 4, 39 (1986) (Harrington is "pivotal figure in the history of the 'Atlantic' branch of republicanism that would find its way to America").

51. Shalhope, *supra* note 44, at 602.

52. Edmund Morgan discusses Harrington in his recent book, INVENTING THE PEOPLE 85-87 (1988) (analyzing notion of popular sovereignty in American thought).

53. *Id.* at 156.

composed of the armed yeomanry, it will prevail over the mercenary professionals who man the armies of neighboring monarchs."[54]

Scholars of the First Amendment have made us aware of the importance of John Trenchard and Thomas Gordon, whose *Cato's Letter's* were central to the formation of the American notion of freedom of the press. That notion includes what Vincent Blasi would come to call the "checking value" of a free press, which stands as a sturdy exposer of governmental misdeeds.[55] Consider the possibility, though, that the ultimate "checking value" in a republican polity is the ability of an armed populace, presumptively motivated by a shared commitment to the common good, to resist governmental tyranny.[56] Indeed, one of Cato's letters refers to "the Exercise of despotick Power [as] the unrelenting War of an armed Tyrant upon his unarmed Subjects. . . ."[57]

Cress persuasively shows that no one defended universal possession of arms. New Hampshire had no objection to disarming those who "are or have been in actual rebellion," just as Samuel Adams stressed that only "peaceable citizens" should be protected in their right of "keeping their own arms."[58] All these points can be conceded, however, without conceding as well that Congress—or, for that matter, the States—had the power to disarm these "peaceable citizens."

Surely one of the foundations of American political thought of the period was the well-justified concern about political corruption and consequent governmental tyranny. Even the Federalists, fending off their opponents who accused them of foisting an oppressive new scheme upon the American people, were careful to acknowledge the risks of tyranny. James Madison, for example, speaks in *Federalist* Number Forty-Six of "the advantage of being armed, which the Americans possess over the people of

---

54. *Id.* at 157. Morgan argues, incidentally, that the armed yeomanry was neither effective as a fighting force nor particularly protective of popular liberty, but that is another matter. For our purposes, the ideological perceptions are surely more important than the "reality" accompanying them. *Id.* at 160-65.

55. Blasi, *The Checking Value in First Amendment Theory*, 1977 AM. B. FOUND. RES. J. 521.

56. *See* Lund, *supra* note †, at 111-16.

57. Shalhope, *supra* note 44, at 603 (quoting 1755 edition of *Cato's Letters*).

Shalhope also quotes from James Burgh, another English writer well known to American revolutionaries:

> The possession of arms is the distinction between a freeman and a slave. He, who has nothing, and who himself belongs to another, must be defended by him, whose property he is, and needs no arms. But he, who thinks he is his own master, and has what he can call his own, ought to have arms to defend himself, and what he possesses; else he lives precariously, and at discretion.

Id. at 604. To be sure, Burgh also wrote that only men of property should in fact comprise the militia: "A militia consisting of any others than the men of *property* in a country, is no militia; but a mungrel army." Cress, *supra* note 41, at 27 (emphasis in original) (quoting J. BURGH, 2 POLITICAL DISQUISITIONS: OR, AN ENQUIRY INTO PUBLIC ERRORS, DEFECTS, AND ABUSES (1774-75). Presumably, though, the widespread distribution of property would bring with it equally widespread access to arms and membership in the militia.

58. *See* Cress, *supra* note 41, at 34.

almost every other nation."[59] The advantage in question was not merely the defense of American borders; a standing army might well accomplish that. Rather, an armed public was advantageous in protecting political liberty. It is therefore no surprise that the Federal Farmer, the nom de plume of an anti-federalist critic of the new Constitution and its absence of a Bill of Rights, could write that "to preserve liberty, it is essential that the whole body of the people always possess arms, and be taught alike, especially when young, how to use them. . . ."[60] On this matter, at least, there was no cleavage between the pro-ratification Madison and his opponent.

In his influential *Commentaries on the Constitution*, Joseph Story, certainly no friend of Anti-Federalism, emphasized the "importance" of the Second Amendment.[61] He went on to describe the militia as "the natural defence of a free country" not only "against sudden foreign invasions" and "domestic insurrections," with which one might well expect a Federalist to be concerned, but also against "domestic usurpations of power by rulers."[62] "The right of the citizens to keep and bear arms has justly been considered," Story wrote, "as the palladium of the liberties of a republic; since it offers a strong moral check against the usurpation and arbitrary power of rulers; and will generally, even if these are successful in the first instance, enable the people to resist and triumph over them."[63]

We also see this blending of individualist and collective accounts of the right to bear arms in remarks by Judge Thomas Cooley, one of the most influential 19th century constitutional commentators. Noting that the state might call into its official militia only "a small number" of the eligible citizenry, Cooley wrote that "if the right [to keep and bear arms] were limited to those enrolled, the purpose of this guaranty might be defeated altogether by the action or neglect to act of the government it was meant to hold in check."[64] Finally, it is worth noting the remarks of Theodore

---

59. THE FEDERALIST No. 46, at 299 (J. Madsion) (C. Rossiter ed. 1961).
60. LETTERS FROM THE FEDERAL FARMER TO THE REPUBLICAN 124 (W. Bennett ed. 1978).
61. 3 J. STORY, COMMENTARIES § 1890 (1833), *quoted in* 5 THE FOUNDERS' CONSTITUTION 214 (P. Kurland & R. Lerner eds. 1987).
62. *Id.*
63. *Id.* Lawrence Cress, despite his forceful critique of Shalhope's individualist rendering of the Second Amendment, nonetheless himself notes that "[t]he danger posed by manipulating demagogues, *ambitious rulers*, and foreign invaders to free institutions required the vigilance of citizen-soldiers cognizant of the common good." Cress, *supra* note 41, at 41 (emphasis added).
64. T. COOLEY, THE GENERAL PRINCIPLES OF CONSTITUTIONAL LAW IN THE UNITED STATES OF AMERICA 298 (3d ed. 1898):
   The right of the people to bear arms in their own defence, and to form and drill military organizations in defence of the State, may not be very important in this country, but it is significant as having been reserved by the people as a possible and necessary resort for the protection of self-government against usurpation, and against any attempt on the part of those who may for the time be in possession of State authority or resources to set aside the constitution and substitute their own rule for that of the people. Should the contingency ever arise when it would be necessary for the people to make use of the arms in their hands for the protection of constitutional liberty, the proceeding, so far from being revolutionary, would be in strict accord with popular right and duty.

Schroeder, one of the most important developers of the theory of freedom of speech early in this century.[65] "[T]he obvious import [of the constitutional guarantee to carry arms]," he argues, "is to promote a state of preparedness for self-defense even against the invasions of government, because only governments have ever disarmed any considerable class of people as a means toward their enslavement."[66]

Such analyses provide the basis for Edward Abbey's revision of a common bumper sticker, "If guns are outlawed, only the government will have guns."[67] One of the things this slogan has helped me to understand is the political tilt contained within the Weberian definition of the state—i.e., the repository of a monopoly of the legitimate means of violence[68]—that is so commonly used by political scientists. It is a profoundly statist definition, the product of a specifically German tradition of the (strong) state rather than of a strikingly different American political tradition that is fundamentally mistrustful of state power and vigilant about maintaining ultimate power, including the power of arms, in the populace.

We thus see what I think is one of the most interesting points in regard to the new historiography of the Second Amendment—its linkage to conceptions of republican political order. Contemporary admirers of republican theory use it as a source both of critiques of more individualist liberal theory and of positive insight into the way we today might reorder our political lives.[69] One point of emphasis for neo-republicans is the value of participation in government, as contrasted to mere representation by a distant leadership, even if formally elected. But the implications of republicanism might push us in unexpected, even embarrassing, directions: just as ordinary citizens should participate actively in governmental decision-making through offering their own deliberative insights, rather than be confined to casting ballots once every two or four years for those very few individuals who will actually make decisions, so should ordinary citizens participate in the process of law enforcement and defense of liberty rather

---

Cooley advanced this same idea in *The Abnegation of Self-Government*, 12 PRINCETON REV. 213-14 (1883).

65. *See* Rabban, *The First Amendment in Its Forgotten Years*, 90 YALE L.J. 514, 560 (1981) ("[P]rodigious theoretical writings of Theodore Schroeder . . . were the most extensive and libertarian treatments of freedom of speech in the prewar period"); *see also* GRABER, TRANSFORMING FREE SPEECH (forthcoming 1990) (manuscript at 4-12; on file with author).

66. T. SCHROEDER, FREE SPEECH FOR RADICALS 104 (reprint ed. 1969).

67. Shalhope, *supra* note 44, at 45.

68. See M. WEBER, THE THEORY OF SOCIAL AND ECONOMIC ORGANIZATION 156 (T. Parsons ed. 1947), where he lists among "[t]he primary formal characteristics of the modern state" the fact that:

to-day, the use of force is regarded as legitimate only so far as it is either permitted by the state or prescribed by it . . . . The claim of the modern state to monopolize the use of force is as essential to it as its character of compulsory jurisdiction and of continuous organization.

69. *See, e.g., Symposium: The Republican Civil Tradition*, 97 YALE L.J. 1493-1723 (1988).

than rely on professionalized peacekeepers, whether we call them standing armies or police.

C. Structure

We have also passed imperceptibly into a form of structural argument, for we see that one aspect of the structure of checks and balances within the purview of 18th century thought was the armed citizen. That is, those who would limit the meaning of the Second Amendment to the constitutional protection of state-controlled militias agree that such protection rests on the perception that militarily competent states were viewed as a potential protection against a tyrannical national government. Indeed, in 1801 several governors threatened to call out state militias if the Federalists in Congress refused to elect Thomas Jefferson president.[70] But this argument assumes that there are only two basic components in the vertical structure of the American polity—the national government and the states. It ignores the implication that might be drawn from the Second, Ninth, and Tenth Amendments: the citizenry itself can be viewed as an important third component of republican governance insofar as it stands ready to defend republican liberty against the depredations of the other two structures, however futile that might appear as a practical matter.

One implication of this republican rationale for the Second Amendment is that it calls into question the ability of a state to disarm its citizenry. That is, the strongest version of the republican argument would hold it to be a "privilege and immunity of United States citizenship"—of membership in a liberty-enhancing political order—to keep arms that could be taken up against tyranny wherever found, including, obviously, state government. Ironically, the principal citation supporting this argument is to Chief Justice Taney's egregious opinion in *Dred Scott*,[71] where he suggested that an uncontroversial attribute of citizenship, in addition to the right to migrate from one state to another, was the right to possess arms. The logic of Taney's argument at this point seems to be that, because it was inconceivable that the Framers could have genuinely imagined blacks having the right to possess arms, it follows that they could not have envisioned them as being citizens, since citizenship entailed that right. Taney's seeming recognition of a right to arms is much relied on by opponents of gun control.[72] Indeed, recall Madison's critique, in *Federalist* Numbers Ten and Fourteen, of republicanism's traditional emphasis on the desira-

---

70. *See* D. MALONE, 4 JEFFERSON AND HIS TIMES: JEFFERSON THE PRESIDENT: FIRST TERM, 1801-1805, at 7-11 (1970) (republican leaders ready to use state militias to resist should lame duck Congress attempt to violate clear dictates of Article II by designating someone other than Thomas Jefferson as President in 1801).

71. Scott v. Sanford, 60 U.S. (19 How.) 393, 417 (1857).

72. *See, e.g.*, Featherstone, Gardiner & Dowlut, *The Second Amendment to the United States Constitution Guarantees an Individual Right to Keep and Bear Arms*, in THE RIGHT TO KEEP AND BEAR ARMS, *supra* note 27, at 100.

bility of small states as preservers of republican liberty. He transformed
this debate by arguing that the states would be less likely to preserve liberty because they could so easily fall under the sway of a local dominant
faction, whereas an extended republic would guard against this danger.
Anyone who accepts the Madisonian argument could scarcely be happy
enhancing the powers of the states over their own citizens; indeed, this has
been one of the great themes of American constitutional history, as the
nationalization of the Bill of Rights has been deemed necessary in order to
protect popular liberty against state depredation.

D. Doctrine

Inevitably one must at least mention, even though there is not space to
discuss fully, the so-called incorporation controversy regarding the application of the Bill of Rights to the states through the Fourteenth Amendment. It should be no surprise that the opponents of gun control appear to
take a "full incorporationist" view of that Amendment.[73] They view the
privileges and immunities clause, which was eviscerated in the *Slaughter-
house Cases*,[74] as designed to require the states to honor the rights that
had been held, by Justice Marshall in *Barron v. Baltimore* in 1833,[75] to
restrict only the national government. In 1875 the Court stated, in *United
States v. Cruikshank*,[76] that the Second Amendment, insofar as it grants
any right at all, "means no more than that it shall not be infringed by
Congress. This is one of the amendments that has no other effect than to
restrict the powers of the national government. . ." Lest there be any remaining doubt on this point, the Court specifically cited the *Cruikshank*
language eleven years later in *Presser v. Illinois*,[77] in rejecting the claim
that the Second Amendment served to invalidate an Illinois statute that
prohibited "any body of men whatever, other than the regular organized
volunteer militia of this State, and the troops of the United States. . .to
drill or parade with arms in any city, or town, of this State, without the
license of the Governor thereof. . . ."[78]

---

73. *See, e.g.*, Halbrook, *The Fourteenth Amendment and the Right to Keep and Bear Arms: The
Intent of the Framers*, in THE RIGHT TO KEEP AND BEAR ARMS, *supra* note 27, at 79. Not the least
of the ironies observed in the debate about the Second Amendment is that N.R.A.-oriented conservatives like Senator Hatch could scarcely have been happy with the wholesale attack leveled by former
Attorney General Meese on the incorporation doctrine, for here is one area where some "conservatives" may in fact be more zealous adherents of that doctrine than are most liberals, who, at least
where the Second Amendment is concerned, have a considerably more selective view of incorporation.
74. 83 U.S. 36 (1873).
75. 32 U.S. (7 Pet.) 243 (1833).
76. 92 U.S. 542, 553 (1875).
77. 116 U.S. 252, 267 (1886). For a fascinating discussion of *Presser*, see Larue, *supra* note 13,
at 386-90.
78. 116 U.S. at 253. There is good reason to believe this statute, passed by the Illinois legislature
in 1879, was part of an effort to control (and, indeed, suppress) widespread labor unrest linked to the
economic troubles of the time. For the background of the Illinois statute, see P, AVRICH, THE
HAYMARKET TRAGEDY 45 (1984):

The first "incorporation decision," *Chicago, B. & Q. R. Co. v. Chicago,*[79] was not delivered until eleven years after *Presser*; one therefore cannot know if the judges in *Cruikshank* and *Presser* were willing to concede that *any* of the amendments comprising the Bill of Rights were anything more than limitations on congressional or other national power. The obvious question, given the modern legal reality of the incorporation of almost all of the rights protected by the First, Fourth, Fifth, Sixth, and Eighth Amendments, is what exactly justifies treating the Second Amendment as the great exception. Why, that is, should *Cruikshank* and *Presser* be regarded as binding precedent any more than any of the other "preincorporation" decisions refusing to apply given aspects of the Bill of Rights against the states?

If one agrees with Professor Tribe that the Amendment is simply a federalist protection of state rights, then presumably there is nothing to incorporate.[80] If, however, one accepts the Amendment as a serious substantive limitation on the ability of the national government to regulate the private possession of arms based on either the "individualist" or "neorepublican" theories sketched above, then why not follow the "incorporationist" logic applied to other amendments and limit the states as well in their powers to regulate (and especially to prohibit) such possession? The

---

As early as 1875, a small group of Chicago socialists, most of them German immigrants, had formed an armed club to protect the workers against police and military assaults, as well as against physical intimidation at the polls. In the eyes of its supporters . . . the need for such a group was amply demonstrated by the behavior of the police and [state-controlled] militia during the Great Strike of 1877, a national protest by labor triggered by a ten percent cut in wages by the Baltimore and Ohio Railroad, which included the breaking up of workers' meetings, the arrest of socialist leaders, [and] the use of club, pistol, and bayonet against strikers and their supporters . . . . Workers . . . were resolved never again to be shot and beaten without resistance. Nor would they stand idly by while their meeting places were invaded or their wives and children assaulted. They were determined, as Albert Parsons [a leader of the anarchist movement in Chicago] expressed it, to defend both "their persons and their rights."

79. 166 U.S. 226 (1897) (protecting rights of property owners by requiring compensation for takings of property).

80. My colleague Douglas Laycock has reminded me that a similar argument was made by some conservatives in regard to the establishment clause of the First Amendment. Thus, Justice Brennan noted that "[i]t has been suggested, with some support in history, that absorption of the First Amendment's ban against congressional legislation 'respecting an establishment of religion' is conceptually impossible because the Framers meant the Establishment Clause also to foreclose any attempt by Congress to *disestablish* the existing official state churches." Abington School Dist. v. Schempp, 374 U.S. 203, 254 (1963) (Brennan, J., concurring) (emphasis added). According to this reading, it would be illogical to apply the establishment clause against the states "because that clause is not one of the provisions of the Bill of Rights which in terms protects a 'freedom' of the individual," *id.* at 256, inasmuch as it is only a federalist protection of states against a national establishment (or disestablishment). "The fallacy in this contention," responds Brennan, "is that it underestimates the role of the Establishment Clause as a co-guarantor, with the Free Exercise Clause, of religious liberty." *Id.* Whatever the sometimes bitter debates about the precise meaning of "establishment," it is surely the case that Justice Brennan, even as he almost cheerfully concedes that at one point in our history the "states-right" reading of the establishment clause would have been thoroughly plausible, expresses what has become the generally accepted view as to the establishment clause being some kind of limitation on the state as well as on the national government. One may wonder whether the interpretive history of the establishment clause might have any lessons for the interpretation of the Second Amendment.

Supreme Court has almost shamelessly refused to discuss the issue,[81] but that need not stop the rest of us.

Returning, though, to the question of Congress' power to regulate the keeping and bearing of arms, one notes that there is, basically, only one modern case that discusses the issue, *United States v. Miller*,[82] decided in 1939. Jack Miller was charged with moving a sawed-off shotgun in interstate commerce in violation of the National Firearms Act of 1934. Among other things, Miller and a compatriot had not registered the firearm, as required by the Act. The court below had dismissed the charge, accepting Miller's argument that the Act violated the Second Amendment.

The Supreme Court reversed unanimously, with the arch-conservative Justice McReynolds writing the opinion.[83] Interestingly enough, he emphasized that there was no evidence showing that a sawed-off shotgun "at this time has some reasonable relationship to the preservation or efficiency of a well regulated militia."[84] And "[c]ertainly it is not within judicial notice that this weapon is any part of the ordinary military equipment or that its use could contribute to the common defense."[85] *Miller* might have had a tenable argument had he been able to show that he was keeping or bearing a weapon that clearly had a potential military use.[86]

Justice McReynolds went on to describe the purpose of the Second Amendment as "assur[ing] the continuation and render[ing] possible the effectiveness of [the Militia]."[87] He contrasted the Militia with troops of a standing army, which the Constitution indeed forbade the states to keep without the explicit consent of Congress. "The sentiment of the time strongly disfavored standing armies; the common view was that adequate defense of country and laws could be secured through the Militia—civilians primarily, soldiers on occasion."[88] McReynolds noted further that "the debates in the Convention, the history and legislation of Colonies and States, and the writings of approved commentators [all] [s]how plainly enough that the Militia comprised all males physically capable of acting in concert for the common defense."[89]

It is difficult to read *Miller* as rendering the Second Amendment meaningless as a control on Congress. Ironically, *Miller* can be read to support

---

81. It refused, for example, to review the most important modern gun control case, Quilici v. Village of Morton Grove, 695 F.2d 261 (7th Cir. 1982), *cert. denied*, 464 U.S. 863 (1983), where the Seventh Circuit Court of Appeals upheld a local ordinance in Morton Grove, Illinois, prohibiting the possession of handguns within its borders.

82. 307 U.S. 174 (1939).

83. Justice Douglas, however, did not participate in the case.

84. *Miller*, 307 U.S. at 178.

85. *Id.* at 178 (citation omitted).

86. Lund notes that "commentators have since demonstrated that sawed-off or short-barreled shotguns are commonly used as military weapons." Lund, *supra* note †, at 109.

87. 307 U.S. at 178.

88. *Id.* at 179.

89. *Id.*

some of the most extreme anti-gun control arguments, e.g., that the individual citizen has a right to keep and bear bazookas, rocket launchers, and other armaments that are clearly relevant to modern warfare, including, of course, assault weapons. Arguments about the constitutional legitimacy of a prohibition by Congress of private ownership of handguns or, what is much more likely, assault rifles, might turn on the usefulness of such guns in military settings.

E. *Prudentialism*

We have looked at four of Bobbitt's categories—text, history, structure, and caselaw doctrine—and have seen, at the very least, that the arguments on behalf of a "strong" Second Amendment are stronger than many of us might wish were the case. This, then, brings us to the fifth category, prudentialism, or an attentiveness to practical consequences, which is clearly of great importance in any debates about gun control. The standard argument in favor of strict control and, ultimately, prohibition of private ownership focuses on the extensive social costs of widespread distribution of firearms. Consider, for example, a recent speech given by former Justice Lewis Powell to the American Bar Association. He noted that over 40,000 murders were committed in the United States in 1986 and 1987, and that fully sixty percent of them were committed with firearms. England and Wales, however, saw only 662 homicides in 1986, less than eight percent of which were committed with firearms.[90] Justice Powell indicated that, "[w]ith respect to handguns," in contrast "to sporting rifles and shotguns[,] it is not easy to understand why the Second Amendment, or the notion of liberty, should be viewed as creating a right to own and carry a weapon that contributes so directly to the shocking number of murders in our society."[91]

It is hard to disagree with Justice Powell; it appears almost crazy to protect as a constitutional right something that so clearly results in extraordinary social costs with little, if any, compensating social advantage. Indeed, since Justice Powell's talk, the subject of assault rifles has become a staple of national discussion, and the opponents of regulation of such weapons have deservedly drawn the censure even of conservative leaders like William Bennett. It is almost impossible to imagine that the judiciary would strike down a determination by Congress that the possession of assault weapons should be denied to private citizens.

Even if one accepts the historical plausibility of the arguments advanced above, the overriding temptation is to say that times and circumstances have changed and that there is simply no reason to continue enforcing an

---

90. L. Powell, Capital Punishment, Remarks Delivered to the Criminal Justice Section, ABA 10 (Aug. 7, 1988).

91. *Id.* at 11.

outmoded, and indeed dangerous, understanding of private rights against public order. This criticism is clearest in regard to the so-called individualist argument, for one can argue that the rise of a professional police force to enforce the law has made irrelevant, and perhaps even counterproductive, the continuation of a strong notion of self-help as the remedy for crime.[92]

I am not unsympathetic to such arguments. It is no purpose of this essay to solicit membership for the National Rifle Association or to express any sympathy for what even Don Kates, a strong critic of the conventional dismissal of the Second Amendment, describes as "the gun lobby's obnoxious habit of assailing all forms of regulation on 2nd Amendment grounds."[93] And yet . . . .

Circumstances may well have changed in regard to individual defense, although we ignore at our political peril the good-faith belief of many Americans that they cannot rely on the police for protection against a variety of criminals. Still, let us assume that the individualist reading of the Amendment has been vitiated by changing circumstances. Are we quite so confident that circumstances are equally different in regard to the republican rationale outlined earlier?

One would, of course, like to believe that the state, whether at the local or national level, presents no threat to important political values, including liberty. But our propensity to believe that this is the case may be little more than a sign of how truly different we are from our radical forbearers. I do not want to argue that the state is necessarily tyrannical; I am not an anarchist. But it seems foolhardy to assume that the armed state will necessarily be benevolent. The American political tradition is, for good or ill, based in large measure on a healthy mistrust of the state. The development of widespread suffrage and greater majoritarianism in our polity is itself no sure protection, at least within republican theory. The republican theory is predicated on the stark contrast between mere democracy, where people are motivated by selfish personal interest, and a republic, where civic virtue, both in citizens and leadership, tames selfishness on behalf of the common good. In any event, it is hard for me to see how one can argue that circumstances have so changed as to make mass disarmament constitutionally unproblematic.[94]

Indeed, only in recent months have we seen the brutal suppression of the Chinese student demonstrations in Tiananmen Square. It should not surprise us that some N.R.A. sympathizers have presented that situation as an object lesson to those who unthinkingly support the prohibition of

92. This point is presumably demonstrated by the increasing public opposition of police officials to private possession of handguns (not to mention assault rifles).
93. D. Kates, Minimalist Interpretation of the Second Amendment 2 (draft Sept. 29, 1986) (unpublished manuscript available from author).
94. See Lund, supra note †, at 116.

private gun ownership. "[I]f all Chinese citizens kept arms, their rulers would hardly have dared to massacre the demonstrators . . . . The private keeping of hand-held personal firearms is within the constitutional design for a counter to government run amok . . . . As the Tianamen Square tragedy showed so graphically, AK-47s fall into that category of weapons, and that is why they are protected by the Second Amendment."[95] It is simply silly to respond that small arms are irrelevant against nuclear-armed states: Witness contemporary Northern Ireland and the territories occupied by Israel, where the sophisticated weaponry of Great Britain and Israel have proved almost totally beside the point. The fact that these may not be pleasant examples does not affect the principal point, that a state facing a totally disarmed population is in a far better position, for good or for ill, to suppress popular demonstrations and uprisings than one that must calculate the possibilities of its soldiers and officials being injured or killed.[96]

III. TAKING THE SECOND AMENDMENT SERIOUSLY

There is one further problem of no small import: If one does accept the plausibility of any of the arguments on behalf of a strong reading of the Second Amendment, but, nevertheless, rejects them in the name of social prudence and the present-day consequences produced by finicky adherence to earlier understandings, why do we not apply such consequentialist criteria to each and every part of the Bill of Rights?[97] As Ronald Dworkin

---

95. Wimmershoff-Caplan, *The Founders and the AK-47*, Washington Post, July 6, 1989, at A18, col. 4, *reprinted as Price of Gun Deaths Small Compared to Price of Liberty*, Austin American-Statesman, July 11, 1989, at A11. Ms. Wimmershoff-Caplan is identified as a "lawyer in New York" who is "a member of the National Board of the National Rifle Association." *Id.* One of the first such arguments in regard to the events at Tianamen Square was made by William A. Black in a letter, *Citizens Without Guns*, N.Y. Times, June 18, 1989 at D26, col. 6. Though describing himself as "find[ing] no glory in guns [and] a very profound anti-hunter," he nonetheless "stand[s] with those who would protect our right to keep and bear arms" and cited for support the fact that "none [of the Chinese soldiers] feared bullets: the citizens of China were long ago disarmed by the Communists." "Who knows," he asks, "what the leaders and the military and the police of our America will be up to at some point in the future? We need an armed citizenry to protect our liberty."
As one might expect, such arguments draw heated responses. *See* Rudlin, *The Founders and the AK-47 (Cont'd)*, Washington Post, July 20, 1989, at A22, col. 3. Jonathan Rudlin accused Ms. Wimmershoff-Caplan of engaging in Swiftian satire, as no one could "take such brilliant burlesque seriously." Neal Knox, however, endorsed her essay in full, adding the Holocaust to the list of examples: "Could the Holocaust have occurred if Europe's Jews had owned thousands of then-modern military Mauser bolt action rifles?" *See also* Washington Post, July 12, 1989, at A22, for other letters.
96. *See* Lund, *supra* note †, at 115:
The decision to use military force is not determined solely by whether the contemplated benefits can be successfully obtained through the use of available forces, but rather is determined by the *ratio* of those benefits to the expected costs. It follows that any factor increasing the anticipated cost of a military operation makes the conduct of that operation incrementally more unlikely. This explains why a relatively poorly armed nation with a small population recently prevailed in a war against the United States, and it explains why governments bent on the oppression of their people almost always disarm the civilian population before undertaking more drastically oppressive measures.
97. *See* D. Kates, *supra* note 93, at 24-25 n.13, for a discussion of this point.

has argued, what it means to take rights seriously is that one will honor them even when there is significant social cost in doing so. If protecting freedom of speech, the rights of criminal defendants, or any other part of the Bill of Rights were always (or even most of the time) clearly costless to the society as a whole, it would truly be impossible to understand why they would be as controversial as they are. The very fact that there are often significant costs—criminals going free, oppressed groups having to hear viciously racist speech and so on—helps to account for the observed fact that those who view themselves as defenders of the Bill of Rights are generally antagonistic to prudential arguments. Most often, one finds them embracing versions of textual, historical, or doctrinal argument that dismiss as almost crass and vulgar any insistence that times might have changed and made too "expensive" the continued adherence to a given view. "Cost-benefit" analysis, rightly or wrongly, has come to be viewed as a "conservative" weapon to attack liberal rights.[98] Yet one finds that the tables are strikingly turned when the Second Amendment comes into play. Here it is "conservatives" who argue in effect that social costs are irrelevant and "liberals" who argue for a notion of the "living Constitution" and "changed circumstances" that would have the practical consequence of removing any real bite from the Second Amendment.

As Fred Donaldson of Austin, Texas wrote, commenting on those who defended the Supreme Court's decision upholding flag-burning as compelled by a proper (and decidedly non-prudential) understanding of the First Amendment, "[I]t seems inconsistent for [defenders of the decision] to scream so loudly" at the prospect of limiting the protection given expression "while you smile complacently at the Second torn and bleeding. If the Second Amendment is not worth the paper it is written on, what price the First?"[99] The fact that Mr. Donaldson is an ordinary citizen rather than an eminent law professor does not make his question any less pointed or its answer less difficult.

For too long, most members of the legal academy have treated the Second Amendment as the equivalent of an embarrassing relative, whose mention brings a quick change of subject to other, more respectable, family members. That will no longer do. It is time for the Second Amendment to enter full scale into the consciousness of the legal academy. Those of us who agree with Martha Minow's emphasis on the desirability of encour-

---

98. See, e.g., Justice Marshall's dissent, joined by Justice Brennan, in Skinner v. Railway Labor Executive Ass'n, 109 S. Ct. 1402 (1989), upholding the government's right to require drug tests of railroad employees following accidents. It begins with his chastising the majority for "ignor[ing] the text and doctrinal history of the Fourth Amendment, which require that highly intrusive searches of this type be based on probable cause, not on the evanescent cost-benefit calculations of agencies or judges," id. at 1423, and continues by arguing that "[t]he majority's concern with the railroad safety problems caused by drug and alcohol abuse is laudable; its cavalier disregard for the Constitution is not. There is no drug exception to the Constitution, any more than there is a communism exception or an exception for other real or imagined sources of domestic unrest." Id. at 1426.
99. Donaldson, Letter to the Editor, Austin American-Statesman, July 8, 1989, at A19, col. 4.

aging different "voices" in the legal conversation[100] should be especially aware of the importance of recognizing the attempts of Mr. Donaldson and his millions of colleagues to join the conversation. To be sure, it is unlikely that Professor Minow had those too often peremptorily dismissed as "gun nuts" in mind as possible providers of "insight and growth," but surely the call for sensitivity to different or excluded voices cannot extend only to those groups "we" already, perhaps "complacent[ly]," believe have a lot to tell "us."[101] I am not so naive as to believe that conversation will overcome the chasm that now separates the sensibility of, say, Senator Hatch and myself as to what constitutes the "right[s] most valued by free men [and women]."[102] It is important to remember that one will still need to join up sides and engage in vigorous political struggle. But it might at least help to make the political sides appear more human to one another. Perhaps "we" might be led to stop referring casually to "gun nuts" just as, maybe, members of the NRA could be brought to understand the real fear that the currently almost uncontrolled system of gun ownership sparks in the minds of many whom they casually dismiss as "bleeding-heart liberals." Is not, after all, the possibility of serious, engaged discussion about political issues at the heart of what is most attractive in both liberal *and* republican versions of politics?

---

100. *See* Minow, *The Supreme Court 1986 Term—Foreword: Justice Engendered*, 101 Harv. L. Rev. 10, 74-90 (1987). "We need settings in which to engage in the clash of realities that breaks us out of settled and complacent meanings and creates opportunities for insight and growth." *Id.* at 95; *see also* Getman, *Voices*, 66 Tex. L. Rev. 577 (1988).

101. And, perhaps more to the point, "you" who insufficiently listen to "us" and to "our" favored groups.

102. *See supra* note 27 and accompanying text.

ARMS, ANARCHY AND THE SECOND AMENDMENT[*]

DENNIS A. HENIGAN[**]

I. INTRODUCTION

An enduring feature of the contemporary debate over gun control is the effort to give the debate a constitutional dimension. Opponents of strict government regulation of private firearms invariably claim that regulation cannot be reconciled with the Second Amendment: "A well regulated Militia, being necessary to the security of a free State, the right of the people to keep and bear Arms, shall not be infringed."[1] This constitutional argument has been a recurring theme of those in Congress opposed to a national waiting period for handgun sales[2] and of those opposed to restraints on private ownership of military-style assault weapons.[3]

While the Second Amendment has acquired significance as a source of political rhetoric opposing gun control, it has been devoid of importance as a constitutional barrier to gun control laws. Federal and state courts in this century have reached a consensus interpretation of the Amendment that permits government at all levels broad power to limit private access to firearms. The nation's strictest gun control laws have been upheld against Second Amendment challenge,[4] including a local ban on private possession of handguns.[5]

---

[*] © 1991, Center To Prevent Handgun Violence. All Rights reserved.

[**] Dennis Henigan is Director of the Legal Action Project at the Center To Prevent Handgun Violence in Washington, D.C. The Legal Action Project has appeared as *amicus curiae* in constitutional litigation involving gun control laws, including Farmer v. Higgins and Fresno Rifle & Pistol Club v. Van de Kamp, discussed in the text. The author gratefully acknowledges the suggestions of Robert Vanderet of O'Melveny & Myers, and Judith Bonderman of the Legal Action Project staff, as well as the editorial assistance of Jacqueline Sternberg of the Project's staff. The responsibility for any errors or omissions is the author's alone.

1. U.S. CONST. amend. II.

2. *See, e.g.*, 137 CONG. REC. H2823 (daily ed. May 8, 1991) (statements of Reps. Unsoeld and Quillen).

3. *See, e.g.*, 136 CONG. REC. S6743 (daily ed. May 22, 1990) (statement of Sen. Hatch); 136 CONG. REC. S6748-49 (daily ed. May 22, 1990) (statement of Sen. Heflin).

4. *See, e.g.*, Sandidge v. United States, 520 A.2d 1057 (D.C. 1987), *cert. denied*, 484 U.S. 868 (1987); Burton v. Sills, 248 A.2d 521 (N.J. 1968), *appeal dismissed*, 394 U.S. 812 (1969).

5. Quilici v. Village of Morton Grove, 695 F.2d 261 (7th Cir. 1982), *cert. denied*, 464 U.S. 863 (1983). The Morton Grove ban included several exemptions, including police, the military, licensed gun collectors and licensed gun clubs. 695 F.2d at 263-64, n.1.

According to the judicial consensus, the scope of the people's right to keep and bear arms is limited by the introductory phrase of the Amendment about the necessity of a "well regulated Militia" to the "security of a free State." Over fifty years ago, the Supreme Court held in *United States v. Miller*,[6] that the "obvious purpose" of the Amendment was "to assure the continuation and render possible the effectiveness of . . ." the state militias and cautioned that the Amendment "must be interpreted and applied with that end in view."[7] The militia, composed of ordinary citizens, was seen by the Framers as a check on the power of the federal standing army, composed of professional soldiers. As the Court wrote in *Miller*, "[t]he sentiment of the time strongly disfavored standing armies; the common view was that adequate defense of country and laws could be secured through the Militia -- civilians primarily, soldiers on occasion."[8]

Following the Court's guidance, lower federal courts and state courts since *Miller* have unanimously held that regulation of the private ownership of firearms offends the Second Amendment only if it interferes with the arming of the state militia.[9] Since the Supreme Court also has held that the modern

---

6. 307 U.S. 174 (1939).

7. *Id.* at 178.

8. *Id.* at 179.

9. As the U.S. Court of Appeals for the Eighth Circuit wrote in United States v. Nelsen, 859 F.2d 1318, 1320 (8th Cir. 1988), courts "have analyzed the Second Amendment purely in terms of protecting state militias, rather than individual rights." The lower court decisions endorsing the militia interpretation include Quilici v. Village of Morton Grove, 695 F.2d 261, 270 (7th Cir. 1982), *cert. denied*, 464 U.S. 863 (1983); United States v. Oakes, 564 F.2d 384, 387 (10th Cir. 1977), *cert. denied*, 435 U.S. 926 (1978); United States v. Graves, 554 F.2d 65, 66-67, n.2 (3d Cir. 1977); United States v. Warin, 530 F.2d 103, 106 (6th Cir. 1976), *cert. denied*, 426 U.S. 948 (1976); United States v. Johnson, 497 F.2d 548, 550 (4th Cir. 1974); United States v. Day, 476 F.2d 562, 568 (6th Cir. 1973); Cody v. United States, 460 F.2d 34, 36-37 (8th Cir. 1972), *cert. denied*, 409 U.S. 1010 (1972); Stevens v. United States, 440 F.2d 144, 149 (6th Cir. 1971); United States v. McCutcheon, 446 F.2d 133, 135-36 (7th Cir. 1971); United States v. Johnson, 441 F.2d 1134, 1136 (5th Cir. 1971); United States v. Tot, 131 F.2d 261, 266 (3d Cir. 1942), *rev'd on other grounds*, 319 U.S. 463 (1943); Cases v. United States, 131 F.2d 916, 922-23 (1st Cir. 1942), *cert. denied sub nom* Velazquez v. United States, 319 U.S. 770 (1943); Vietnamese Fishermen's Ass'n v. Knights of the Ku Klux Klan, 543 F. Supp. 198, 210 (S.D. Tex. 1982); Thompson v. Dereta, 549 F. Supp. 297, 299 (D. Utah 1982); Sandidge v. United States, 520 A.2d 1057 (D.C. 1987), *cert. denied*, 484 U.S. 868 (1987); Kalodimos v. Village of Morton Grove, 470 N.E.2d 266 (Ill. 1984); Commonwealth v. Davis, 343 N.E.2d 847, 850 (Mass. 1976); *In re* Atkinson, 291 N.W.2d 396, 398, n.1 (Minn. 1980); State v. Fennell, 382 S.E.2d 231, 232 (N.C. Ct. App. 1989); Harris v. State, 432 P.2d 929, 930 (Nev. 1967); Burton v. Sills, 248 A.2d 521, 525-29 (N.J. 1968), *appeal dismissed*, 394 U.S. 812 (1969); City of East Cleveland v. Scales, 460 N.E.2d 1126, 1130 (Ohio App. 1983); Masters v. State, 653 S.W.2d 944 (Tex. Ct. App. 1983); State v. Vlacil, 645 P.2d 677, 679 (Utah 1982).

embodiment of the "well regulated militia" is the National Guard,[10] which does not use privately owned guns at all, gun control laws are regularly upheld.

In recent years, various articles have appeared in academic journals which offer an interpretation of the Amendment quite at odds with the consensus judicial view.[11] These writers contend that the right to keep and bear arms can be a broad personal right of all citizens *even if* it is tied to the necessity for a militia.[12] This claim rests upon two distinct, but related, theses: (1) that the constitutionally protected "militia" is not an organized military force of the

---

10. *See* Maryland v. United States, 381 U.S. 41, 46 (1965) ("The National Guard is the modern Militia . . . ."); Perpich v. Department of Defense, 110 S. Ct. 2418, 2426 (1990). ("Notwithstanding the brief periods of federal service, the members of the state Guard unit continue to satisfy [the] description of a militia.") In *Perpich*, the Court held that Congress may authorize the President to order members of the state National Guard to engage in training exercises outside the United States without the governor's consent or a declaration of a national emergency. Such power, the Court determined, "is not inconsistent with the Militia Clauses . . ." of the Constitution, which divide authority over the militia between the state and federal government. 110 S. Ct. at 2430. *See* discussion *infra* at 8-9. That the Court analyzed the issue before it under the Militia Clauses itself establishes that it regards the National Guard as the modern militia. *Perpich* is especially interesting because the Court had before it an *amicus* brief filed by the "Firearms Civil Rights Legal Defense Fund," an arm of the National Rifle Association, urging it to find that the National Guard is not the militia, but rather is a component of the U.S. Army. Brief of *Amicus Curiae* Firearms Civil Rights Legal Defense Fund in Support of Appellees, *Perpich* (No. 89-542) (on file with author).

11. *See e.g.*, Sanford Levinson, *The Embarrassing Second Amendment*, 99 YALE L.J. 637 (1989) [hereinafter Levinson]; Nelson Lund, *The Second Amendment, Political Liberty, and the Right to Self-Preservation*, 39 ALA. L. REV. 103 (1987); David T. Hardy, *Armed Citizens, Citizen Armies: Toward a Jurisprudence of the Second Amendment*, 9 HARV. J.L. & PUB. POL'Y, 559 (1986) [hereinafter Hardy]; Don B. Kates, Jr., *Handgun Prohibition and the Original Meaning of the Second Amendment*, 82 MICH. L. REV. 204 (1983) [hereinafter Kates]; Stephen P. Halbrook, *To Keep and Bear Their Private Arms: The Adoption of the Second Amendment, 1787-1791*, 10 N. KY. L. REV. 13 (1982) [hereinafter Halbrook].

12. These articles also typically contend that the right to keep and bear arms is not qualified or limited by the reference to the militia, and thereby assert a right to be armed for other purposes, such as personal self-defense. This claim is flatly contradicted by the Supreme Court's opinion in United States v. Miller, 307 U.S. 174 (1939). The issue in *Miller* was whether the Second Amendment barred the prosecution of two individuals for transporting in interstate commerce a sawed-off shotgun without first registering the weapon as required by the National Firearms Act of 1934. The Court refused to hold that the Second Amendment guarantees the right to keep and bear the gun because no showing had been made that it "has some reasonable relationship to the preservation or efficiency of a well regulated militia." *Id.* at 178. The Court declined to take judicial notice that "this weapon is any part of the ordinary military equipment or that its use could contribute to the common defense." *Id.* Thus, the Court saw the issue as turning entirely on the connection between possession of the weapon and the viability of the militia. At no point did the Court even raise the question whether a sawed-off shotgun could have a legitimate non-military use, such as self-defense. For a historical defense of the view that the concern of the Second Amendment is solely the distribution of military power between the states and the federal government, see Keith A. Ehrman and Dennis A. Henigan, *The Second Amendment in the Twentieth Century: Have You Seen Your Militia Lately?*, 15 U. DAYTON L. REV. 5 (1989) [hereinafter Ehrman and Henigan].

states, but is rather the armed citizenry at large; and (2) that the right of the people to keep and bear arms was intended by the Framers as a fundamental check on the power of both state and federal government, by ensuring the means for armed resistance to tyranny.

In defense of the consensus judicial interpretation, this essay contends that the alternative view of the Second Amendment is contradicted by the text of the Constitution itself, as well as by key historical materials bearing on the original intent of the Framers. In addition, this discussion will expose the implications of the alternative view for the fundamental relationship between citizens and their government. As explained below, the alternative view amounts to the startling assertion of a generalized constitutional right of all citizens to engage in armed insurrection against their government. This "insurrectionist theory" of the Second Amendment, in the judgment of this writer, represents a profoundly dangerous doctrine of unrestrained individual rights which, if adopted by the courts, would threaten the rule of law itself.

II. THE INSURRECTIONIST THEORY OF THE SECOND AMENDMENT

Professor Sanford Levinson's article *The Embarrassing Second Amendment*[13] will be used here as representative of the articles advancing one form or another of the insurrectionist theory. Levinson's essay has been chosen both because its arguments (and supporting material) are typical of the genre and because it has received far more attention than other similar articles, particularly from the popular press.[14]

The selection of Levinson's piece as a foil should acknowledge his own disclaimer that it is not his "style to offer 'correct' or 'incorrect' interpretations of the Constitution."[15] Nevertheless, it clearly is his purpose to convince those inclined to give a broad reading to other guarantees in the Bill of Rights to seriously consider a similarly broad view of the right to keep and bear arms.[16]

---

13. *See* Levinson, *supra* note 11.

14. Richard Bernstein, *The Right to Bear Arms: A Working Definition*, N.Y. TIMES, Jan. 28, 1990, at 6E; Michael Kinsley, *Second Thoughts*, THE NEW REPUBLIC, Feb. 26, 1990, at 4; George F. Will, *America's Crisis of Gunfire*, THE WASHINGTON POST, March 21, 1991, at A21.

15. Levinson, *supra* note 11, at 642. In light of this statement, Levinson may be surprised to learn of the use of his article by anti-gun control partisans. His article, along with others advocating the insurrectionist theory, is cited by the National Rifle Association (NRA) in proclaiming "Victory in the Law Journals" for the NRA's view that the Second Amendment guarantees a broad, individual right to own guns. *See* 5 NRA ACTION No. 10, at 7 (Oct. 19, 1991).

16. The title of Levinson's piece expresses his view that the Second Amendment "may be profoundly embarrassing to many who both support [prohibitory] regulation [of firearms] and view themselves as committed to zealous adherence to the Bill of Rights . . . ." Levinson, *supra* note 11, at 642.

In this writer's view, Levinson pursues this purpose by manipulating his supporting material so as to exclude that which would cast doubt on the existence of a broad, individual right.[17] As a result, the Levinson essay is certainly fair game for criticism, in spite of its effort to avoid the appearance of dogma.

The two central theses of the insurrectionist theory are stated throughout the Levinson piece. About the meaning of the "militia," Levinson recommends that "we should make some effort to find out what the term 'militia' meant to eighteenth century readers and writers, rather than assume that it refers only to Dan Quayle's Indiana National Guard and the like."[18] He then concludes that "[t]here is strong evidence that 'militia' refers to all of the people, or at least all of those treated as full citizens of the community."[19] As to the ultimate constitutional importance of the armed citizenry, Levinson relies on the theory of checks and balances:

> [O]ne aspect of the structure of checks and balances within the purview of 18th century thought was the armed citizen. That is, those who would limit the meaning of the Second Amendment to the constitutional protection of state-controlled militias agree that such protection rests on the perception that militarily competent states were viewed as potential protection against a tyrannical national government . . . . But this argument assumes that there are only two basic components in the vertical structure of the American polity -- the national government and the states. It ignores the implication that might be drawn from the Second, Ninth and Tenth Amendments: that the citizenry itself can be viewed as an important third component of republican governance insofar as it stands ready to defend republican liberty against the depredations of the other two structures, however futile that might appear as a practical matter.[20]

---

17. One conspicuous example of Levinson's manipulation is his discussion of the existing law review literature on the Second Amendment. Levinson, *supra* note 11, at 639, n.13. He cites several law review articles, all of which are critical of the consensus judicial interpretation, but omits mention of the following articles which support it: Peter Feller and Karl Gotting, *The Second Amendment, A Second Look*, 61 NW. U. L. REV. 46 (1966); John Levin, *The Right to Bear Arms: The Development of the American Experience*, 48 CHI.-KENT L. REV. (1971); Ralph Rohner, *The Right to Bear Arms*, 16 CATH. U. L. REV. 53 (1966); Roy Weatherup, *Standing Armies and Armed Citizens: An Historical Analysis of the Second Amendment*, 2 HASTINGS CONST. L.Q. 961 (1972). Levinson complains that most of the articles on the Second Amendment have been written by lawyers, not academics, and yet two of the articles he omitted (John Levin and Ralph Rohner) were written by law professors.

18. Levinson, *supra* note 11, at 646.

19. *Id.* at 646-47.

20. *Id.* at 651.

Thus, in Levinson's words, it may be "a privilege and immunity of United States citizenship' -- of membership in a liberty-enhancing political order -- to keep arms that could be taken up against tyranny wherever found, including, obviously, state government."[21]   In Levinson's theory, therefore, the constitutional militia -- properly understood as the collection of armed citizens -- is not an instrument of state government authority. The militia is rather a potential revolutionary force poised to use violence against the excesses of government at all levels.

Of course, the right to keep arms for that purpose would hardly be an effective check on tyranny if the right did not also extend to the *use* of those arms against a tyrannical government. To Levinson, an armed population is constitutionally important because it creates the potential for armed uprising: "[A] state facing a totally disarmed population is in a far better position, for good or for ill, to suppress popular demonstrations and uprisings than is one that must calculate the possibilities of its soldiers and officials being injured or killed."[22]   What is really being asserted by Professor Levinson is a constitutional right to engage in armed insurrection against tyrannical governmental authority, whether state or federal.

III. The Insurrectionist Theory and the Language of the Constitution

The most obvious problem with Levinson's theory is reconciling it with the language of the Second Amendment itself. By its words, the constitutional value protected by the Amendment is "the security of a free State." Presumably, the term "free State" is a reference to the states as entities of governmental authority. Moreover, the reference to the "security" of a free State must have something to do with the need to defend the state as an entity of government. How, then, can the Amendment that purports to express distrust of state governmental power, and to create a right to be armed against abuses of that power, also elevate the defense of state government to a constitutionally protected value?[23]   The inclusion of this phrase in the Second Amendment

---

21. *Id.*

22. Levinson, *supra* note 11, at 657.

23. The Second Amendment is, of course, the only provision in the Bill of Rights proclaiming "the security of a free State" as its object. This is surely relevant to the issue whether the Second Amendment should be regarded as "incorporated" through the Fourteenth Amendment as a limitation on the states. Levinson, *supra* note 11, at 652-53, correctly notes that although the nineteenth century Supreme Court decisions on the Second Amendment, United States v. Cruikshank, 92 U.S. 542, 553 (1875) and Presser v. Illinois, 116 U.S. 252 (1886), found the Amendment to be a limit on only the federal government, these cases were decided during an era when the entire Bill of Rights was held inapplicable to the states. *See* Barron v. Baltimore, 32 U.S. (7 Pet.) 243 (1833). Levinson argues that these decisions should be reconsidered in light of the modern "selective

makes Levinson's theory immediately implausible. Nowhere in Levinson's analysis does he offer an explanation of its meaning that is consistent with the insurrectionist theory.

The words of the Amendment also pose a problem for Levinson's view that the term "militia" as used in the Amendment refers simply to the collection of citizens who are armed. The insurrectionist theory has difficulty accounting for the modifier "well regulated" which precedes "militia." In what sense is the "militia," as defined by Levinson, "well regulated"? The use of "well regulated" in the Amendment certainly implies that the militia is subject to a set of legal rules and obligations, which suggests that the militia is an organized military force, not an ad hoc group of armed individuals.

The meaning of "well regulated" is illuminated by examining the nature of the militia as it existed in colonial times. It is true that the *membership* of the militia of the several states was broad-based; it generally consisted of white males between the ages of eighteen to forty-five or sixty years.[24] However,

---

incorporation" doctrine, but never addresses the unique implications of the Second Amendment's language. If the security of state government is the object of the people's right to be armed, would it not be paradoxical to apply the Amendment to limit the power of state government? At the very least, it is illogical to argue that the Second Amendment should be applied to the states *by the same reasoning* that has led the Supreme Court to incorporate other provisions of the Bill of Rights that do not expressly protect the security of the states. It remains the law of the land that the Second Amendment does not apply to the states, Malloy v. Hogan, 378 U.S. 1, 4 n.2 (1964), and therefore is no restraint on state regulation of firearms. *See, e.g.*, Justice v. Elrod, 832 F.2d 1048, 1051 (7th Cir. 1987); Quilici v. Village of Morton Grove, 695 F.2d 261, 270 (7th Cir. 1982), *cert. denied*, 464 U.S. 863 (1983); Cases v. United States, 131 F.2d 916, 921-22 (1st Cir. 1942), *cert. denied sub nom.* Velazquez v. United States, 319 U.S. 770 (1943); Fresno Rifle & Pistol Club, Inc. v. Van de Kamp, 746 F. Supp. 1415, 1419 (E.D. Cal. 1990), *appeal docketed*, No. 91-15466 (9th Cir.); Krisko v. Oswald, 655 F. Supp. 147, 149 (E.D. Pa. 1987); Engblom v. Carey, 522 F. Supp. 57, 71 (S.D.N.Y. 1981), *aff'd in part and rev'd in part and remanded in part*, 677 F.2d 957 (2d Cir. 1982); Eckert v. City of Philadelphia, 329 F. Supp. 845, 846 (E.D. Pa. 1971), *aff'd*, 477 F.2d 610 (3d Cir.), *cert. denied*, 414 U.S. 839 (1973); Kellogg v. City of Gary, 562 N.E.2d 685, 692 (Ind. 1990); State v. Swanton, 629 P.2d 98, 99 (Ariz. App. 1981); State v. Amos, 343 So. 2d 166, 168 (La. 1977); Commonwealth v. Davis, 343 N.E.2d 847, 850 (Mass. 1976); Application of Atkinson, 291 N.W.2d 396, 398 n.1 (Minn. 1980); Harris v. State, 432 P.2d 929, 930 (Nev. 1967); State v. Sanne, 364 A.2d 630 (N.H. 1976); State v. Goodno, 511 A.2d 456, 457 (Me. 1986); Masters v. State, 685 S.W.2d 654, 655 (Tex. Ct. App. 1985), *cert. denied*, 474 U.S. 853 (1985).

24. WILLIAM RIKER, SOLDIERS OF THE STATES: THE ROLE OF THE NATIONAL GUARD IN AMERICAN DEMOCRACY 12 (1957) [hereinafter RIKER]. Levinson's claim that "militia" refers to "all of the people, or at least all of those treated as full citizens of the community" (Levinson, *supra* note 11, at 646-47) does not appear to be historically accurate. Older white males were certainly considered citizens and yet were exempt from militia service. The restriction of membership to a defined age group supports the idea of the militia as a *military* force; membership was restricted to those perceived by the colonial governments to be best able to engage in military activity. As the Supreme Court noted in United States v. Miller, 307 U.S. 174, 179, (1939), "the Militia comprised all males physically capable of acting in concert for the common defense . . . ."

it is also true that, by virtue of their membership in the colonial militia, persons were subject to various legal requirements imposed by the colonial governments. Colonial legislatures early on had enacted general draft laws modelled after the English militia system.[25] Militiamen "were required to muster for training, usually four to eight days per year, two to four days in the spring (usually a company parade), and two to four days in the autumn (usually a battalion parade)."[26] They also were required to furnish their own equipment, including muskets, powder and shot for the infantry, and horses for the cavalry.[27] Fines were levied and collected for failure to attend musters and adequately maintain equipment.[28] Militia service away from one's home community also was required, although it generally was limited in time.[29] Although some classes of persons were exempt from militia requirements (usually ministers and teachers),[30] the existence of these specified exemptions itself underscores the nature of the colonial militia as an organized military force subject to rules and regulations imposed by colonial governments. As the Supreme Court wrote in *United States v. Miller*, the militia was a "body of citizens enrolled for military discipline."[31]

A fundamental flaw in the insurrectionist theory is its confusion of the *membership* of the colonial militia with the *definition* of the colonial militia. Simply because the militia was composed of all white males of a certain age group does not mean that the term "militia" as used by the Framers *means* all white males of a certain age group. Rather, the colonial militia was an organized military force governed by rules and regulations. It was, in short, a form of compulsory military service imposed on much of the male population. "White males between the ages of 18 and 45" does not *define* the colonial militia any more than "nations of the world" *defines* the United Nations.[32]

The Second Amendment, however, is not the only provision of the Constitution that addresses the militia. The nature of the militia, as understood by the Framers, also is revealed by two clauses of Article I -- Clauses 15 and

---

25. RIKER, *supra* note 24, at 11.

26. *Id*.

27. *Id*.

28. LAWRENCE CRESS, CITIZENS IN ARMS: THE ARMY AND THE MILITIA IN AMERICAN SOCIETY TO THE WAR OF 1812, at 4 (1982).

29. *Id*.

30. RIKER, *supra* note 24, at 12.

31. United States v. Miller, 307 U.S. 174, 179 (1939).

32. Although the Militia Act of 1792 required every male citizen between the ages of eighteen and forty-five to be enrolled in the militia and equip himself with specific military weaponry, 1 Stat. 271, this broad-based citizen militia proved over time to be unworkable. The evolution of the early militia to the National Guard of today is briefly described in Perpich v. Department of Defense, 110 S. Ct. 2418, 2423 (1990). *See also* Ehrman and Henigan, *supra* note 12, at 34-39.

16 of Section 8 -- commonly known as the "Militia Clauses":

The Congress shall have Power...

To provide for calling forth the Militia to execute the Laws of the Union, suppress Insurrections and repel Invasions;

To provide for organizing, arming, and disciplining, the Militia, and for governing such Part of them as may be employed in the Service of the United States, reserving to the States respectively, the Appointment of the Officers, and the Authority of training the Militia according to the discipline prescribed by Congress.[33]

It is transparent from these provisions that the Framers understood the militia to be *an instrument of governmental authority*. Clause 15 gives Congress the power to call out the militia for various purposes. Clause 16 divides authority over the militia between the federal government and the states, giving Congress the power to organize, arm and discipline the militia while reserving to the states the power to appoint its officers and to train it "according to the discipline prescribed by Congress." Levinson's theory, however, is that the militia is to function as a *check* on the power of government, both federal and state, which must mean that the militia must exist *apart from* government. This idea simply cannot be reconciled with the Militia Clauses, which are ignored in Levinson's essay.

The insurrectionist theory also has difficulty explaining the function of the militia as set forth in the Militia Clauses. How can the militia be a collection of citizens with the constitutionally guaranteed right to engage in armed resistance against their government if the Constitution itself grants Congress the power to call out the militia "to execute the Laws of the Union [and] suppress Insurrections. . . ."? The Constitution cannot view the militia *both* as a means by which government can suppress insurrection *and* as an instrument for insurrection against the government. It must be one or the other. The Militia Clauses make clear which one it is.

Before leaving the text of the Constitution, one additional point is worth noting. Given the self-evident importance to our constitutional scheme of an individual right to engage in armed revolution, is it not curious that this right is not more explicitly stated in the text? Whatever else may be said in defense of the insurrectionist theory, surely it must be admitted that the Second Amendment is hardly a model of clarity as a declaration of the right to overthrow the

---

33. U.S. CONST. art. I, § 8, cls. 15, 16.

government.   Yet other parts of the Constitutional text affirm, without ambiguity, the power of the government to preserve itself against insurrection. This is true not only in the Militia Clauses, but throughout the document. For example, the crime of treason receives special treatment in the Constitution. The entirety of Article III, Section 3, is devoted to defining the crime, specifying the proof sufficient for a conviction and giving Congress the power to declare its punishment.[34]   Treason also is, of course, listed as an impeachable offense for federal officers.[35] In addition, Article IV, Section 4, requires the federal government, on request of a state, to defend the state "against domestic Violence."[36]

According to the insurrectionist theory, the "right to keep and bear Arms" is to be taken to create an individual right to engage in armed insurrection, even though the Framers left intact various provisions which strongly affirm the power of government to punish conduct disloyal to government and to preserve order. Acceptance of the insurrectionist theory leaves us with a Constitution very much at war with itself, a conclusion that suggests a profound weakness in the theory itself.

Of course, it must be acknowledged that the Second Amendment did effect some change in the Constitutional scheme; presumably the Framers did not adopt the Bill of Rights in 1791 with the intent to leave things as they were in 1787. What, then, was the nature of the change brought about by the Second Amendment? The answer is contained in various key historical materials, which are themselves inconsistent with the insurrectionist theory.

IV. THE INSURRECTIONIST THEORY AND THE HISTORY OF THE SECOND
AMENDMENT

Following the conclusion of the Constitutional Convention in 1787, the states began to debate the issue of ratification.   A battle of pamphlets and newspaper articles commenced between the Antifederalists, who opposed ratification, and the Federalists, who supported it.[37] The Bill of Rights was the outgrowth of the Antifederalist critique.

One consistent Antifederalist theme was that the Constitution had created an excessively powerful central authority, which would lead to the destruction of the states. For example, the Antifederalists feared that the Militia Clauses of

---

34. U.S. CONST. art. III, § 3.
35. U.S. CONST. art. II, § 4.
36. U.S. CONST. art. IV, § 4.
37. *See* 1 BERNARD SCHWARTZ, THE BILL OF RIGHTS: A DOCUMENTARY HISTORY 468-69 (1971) [hereinafter B. SCHWARTZ].

the Constitution had given the central government excessive control over the state militia, which was regarded as the guardian of the states' integrity. Luther Martin stated the argument before the Maryland legislature:

> [Through] this extraordinary provision, by which the militia, the only defence and protection which the State can have for the security of their rights against arbitrary encroachments of the general government, is taken entirely out of the power of the respective States, and placed under the power of Congress . . . . It was urged [at the Constitutional convention] that, if after having retained to the general government the great powers already granted, and among those, that of raising and keeping up regular troops, without limitations, the power over the Militia should be taken away from the States, and also given to the general government, it ought to be considered as the last coup de grace to the State governments; that it must be the most convincing proof, the advocates of this system design the destruction of the State governments, and that no professions to the contrary ought to be trusted; and that every State in the Union ought to reject such a system with indignation, since, if the general government should attempt to oppress and enslave them, they could not have any possible means of self-defense . . . and, by placing the militia under [Congress'] power, enable it to leave the militia totally unorganized, undisciplined, and even to disarm them . . . .[38]

Implicit in this argument is the idea that the militia was an instrument of state government. Martin's argument was not that the Constitution deprived the people of a right to be armed against the power of state and federal government, but rather that it gave the federal government excessive power over the military force which state governments relied upon for their security.

Of particular interest on this issue are the debates in the Virginia ratification convention, both because this was the convention in which the militia issue was most extensively discussed and because it no doubt had a profound influence on the Virginian James Madison, who authored the Second Amendment. The Virginia debate is replete with expressions of fear that federal control over the militias would destroy them.

George Mason argued that the power given Congress to "organize, arm and discipline" the militia would allow Congress to destroy the militia by "rendering them useless -- by disarming them . . . Congress may neglect to provide for arming and disciplining the militia; and the state governments cannot do it, for

---

38. 3 RECORDS OF THE FEDERAL CONVENTION 208-09 (Max Farrand ed., 1974).

Congress has an exclusive right to arm them. . . ."[39] Patrick Henry also was concerned about the arming of the state militia. He stated that "necessary as it is to have arms, and though our Assembly has, by a succession of laws for many years, endeavored to have the militia completely armed, it is still far from being the case. When this power is given up to Congress . . . how will your militia be armed?"[40]   Mason and Henry proposed that, "if Congress should refuse to find arms for [the militia], this country may lay out their own money to purchase them."[41]   Federalist James Madison countered this argument by maintaining that the Congressional power to arm the militia was not exclusive, and thus Congress lacked the power to paralyze the state militia.[42] Similarly, John Marshall asked: "If Congress neglect our militia, we can arm them ourselves. Cannot Virginia import arms? Cannot she put them into the hands of her militia-men?"[43] Significantly, there is not a word in the Virginia debates about the need to ensure that the people are armed to ensure the potential for revolution against state or federal governmental excesses.

These speakers took it for granted that the arming of the militia was a governmental function; the issue being debated is the need to affirm the states' concurrent power with the federal government to furnish arms to the militia.[44] It is difficult for the insurrectionist theory to account for this debate at all. If the militia is simply the collection of citizens with their own arms, why all the concern about whether the central government's power to arm the militia is exclusive, or rather concurrent with the states' power? More fundamentally, if the function of the militia is to check the excesses of state and federal government by ensuring the potential for armed revolt by the people, how could the militia also be dependent on those same governments for its arms?

The Virginia debates, ignored in Levinson's account, make it clear that the

---

39. 3 JONATHAN ELLIOT, THE DEBATES IN THE SEVERAL STATE CONVENTIONS OF THE ADOPTION OF THE FEDERAL CONSTITUTION, AS RECOMMENDED BY THE GENERAL CONVENTION AT PHILADELPHIA IN 1787, at 379 (1836) [hereinafter J. ELLIOT].

40. *Id.* at 386.

41. 2 B. SCHWARTZ, *supra* note 37, at 831.

42. 3 J. ELLIOT, *supra* note 39, at 382-83.

43. *Id.* at 421.

44. Even though colonial militiamen were generally expected to supply their own arms for militia service, there is little doubt that these privately-owned weapons were supplemented by state-provided arms. The Articles of Confederation had provided that "every State shall always keep a well-regulated and disciplined militia, sufficiently armed and accoutered, and shall provide and have constantly ready for use, *in public stores*, a due number of field pieces and tents, and a proper quantity of arms, ammunition and camp equipage." (*Quoted in* John K. Mahon, THE AMERICAN MILITIA, DECADE OF DECISION, 1789-1800, at 4 (U. Fla. Monographs, Spring 1960) (emphasis added)). This provision suggests that some militia arms were regarded as public property. It also underscores the colonial understanding of the militia as a military force maintained by the states, a concept totally alien to the insurrectionist view of the militia.

Second Amendment arose from a concern by the Antifederalists that the Constitution had made the existence of an armed militia a matter of federal preference, rather than a right of the people of the several states. The purpose of the Amendment was to affirm the people's right to keep and bear arms *as a state militia*, against the possibility of the federal government's hostility, or apathy, toward the militia.

Levinson's review of the historical material places heavy reliance on quotations by certain historical figures and early Constitutional commentators extolling the importance of the armed individual to the defense of liberty. However, scrutinizing the most dramatic of these quotations reveals that Levinson is able to use them to support his argument only by stripping away their context. Once the context is restored, they turn out not to support the insurrectionist theory, but to defeat it.

One example is Levinson's use of Justice Joseph Story's *Commentaries on the Constitution of the United States.*[45] Levinson lifts the following quotation from Story:

> The right of the citizens to keep and bear arms has justly been considered as the palladium of the liberties of a republic; since it offers a strong moral check against the usurpation and arbitrary power of rulers; and will generally, even if these are successful in the first instance, enable the people to resist and triumph over them.[46]

Levinson omits the sentences which immediately follow:

> And yet, though this truth would seem so clear, and the importance of a well regulated militia would seem so undeniable, it cannot be disguised that, among the American people, there is a growing indifference to any system of militia discipline, and a strong disposition, from a sense of its burdens, to be rid of all regulations. How it is practicable to keep the people duly armed, without some organization, it is difficult to see. There is certainly no small danger that indifference may lead to disgust, and disgust to contempt; and thus gradually undermine all the protection intended by this clause of

---

45. JOSEPH STORY, COMMENTARIES ON THE CONSTITUTION OF THE UNITED STATES (1833) [hereinafter STORY].

46. *Id.* at 677. This quotation is relied upon by other insurrectionist theorists, *see* Kates, *supra* note 11, at 242 and Hardy, *supra* note 11, at 614, and is prominently featured in the literature of the National Rifle Association. *See, e.g.*, NRA INSTITUTE FOR LEGISLATIVE ACTION, *The Right to Keep and Bear Arms...An Analysis of the Second Amendment* 9 (1985).

our national bill of rights.[47]

What was the protection intended by the Second Amendment? Levinson also omits the footnote to the above quoted passage, which contains the following passage from Tacitus: "Is there any escape from a large standing army, but in a well-disciplined militia?"[48]

Story believed the armed citizenry to be essential to liberty only insofar as it was subject to "a system of militia discipline." To the extent that the people were armed "without some organization" or "rid of all regulations," he saw the Second Amendment as unable to accomplish its purpose to protect liberty against the power of the standing army. Presumably, the regulations he was referring to were those imposed on the early militia by state governmental authority.

Story's discussion therefore is consistent with the theory that the Second Amendment guarantees a right of the people to be armed only in service to an organized militia. If he saw the armed citizenry per se as the protector of liberty (the foundation of the insurrectionist theory), why would he express such dismay at the people's lack of enthusiasm for militia discipline? Moreover, Levinson himself quotes Story's reference to the militia as the natural defense "against . . . domestic insurrections," which is itself inconsistent with the notion that the militia is the armed citizenry poised to engage in domestic insurrection.

An even more telling instance of Levinson's omission of context is his use of James Madison's *Federalist No. 46*, which speaks of "the advantage of being armed, which the Americans possess over the people of almost every other nation."[49] This statement appears in the following passage concerning the dangers of a standing army, which must be quoted at length to understand Madison's meaning:

> Let a regular army, fully equal to the resources of the country, be formed; and let it be entirely at the devotion of the federal government: still it would not be going too far to say that *the State governments with the people on their side would be able to repel the danger.* The highest number to which, according to the best computation, a standing army can be carried in any country does not exceed one hundredth part of the whole number of souls; or one twenty-fifth part of the number able to bear arms. This proportion would not yield, in the United States, any army of more than twenty-five or thirty thousand men. To these would be opposed a militia

---

47. STORY, *supra* note 45, at 678.
48. *Id.* at 678, n.2 (quoting TACITUS, HISTORIES IV, ch. 74).
49. THE FEDERALIST NO. 46, at 299 (James Madison) (Clinton Rossiter ed., 1961).

amounting to near half a million of citizens with arms in their hands, *officered by men chosen from among themselves,* fighting for their common liberties and united and *conducted by governments possessing their affections and confidence.* It may well be doubted whether a militia thus circumstanced could ever be conquered by such a proportion of regular troops. Those who are best acquainted with the late successful resistance of this country against the British arms will be most inclined to deny the possibility of it. Besides the advantage[1] of being armed, which the Americans possess over the people of almost every other nation, *the existence of subordinate governments, to which the people are attached and by which the militia officers are appointed,* forms a barrier against the enterprises of ambition, more insurmountable than any which a simple government of any form can admit of.[50]

The Federalist Madison is here arguing that the Constitution does not strip the states of their militia, while conceding that a strong, armed militia is necessary as a military counterpoint to the power of the regular standing army. However, as the underscored language indicates, Madison saw the militia as the military instrument of state government, not simply as a collection of unorganized, privately armed citizens. Madison saw the armed citizen as important to liberty to the extent that the citizen was part of a military force organized by state governments, which possesses the people's "confidence and affections" and "to which the people are attached."[51] This is hardly an argument for the right of people to be armed against government per se.[52]

This is not to deny that there may well have been some colonial thinkers who believed in the right of individuals to be armed regardless of their connection to an organized militia. There were, indeed, proposals for constitutional language that would have guaranteed a broader right. For instance, Levinson points to the amendment proposed by the New Hampshire ratification convention: "Congress shall never disarm any citizen unless such

---

50. *Id.* (emphasis added).

51. Alexander Hamilton also saw the militia as a means by which state government preserved itself against popular insurrection. If the revolt be "a slight commotion in a small part of a State, the militia of the residue would be adequate to its suppression; and the natural presumption is that they would be ready to do their duty. An insurrection, whatever may be its immediate cause, eventually endangers all government." THE FEDERALIST NO. 28, at 178 (Alexander Hamilton) (Clinton Rossiter ed., 1961).

52. The misuse of FEDERALIST NO. 46 is typical of the other insurrectionist theorists. *See, e.g.,* Kates, *supra* note 11, at 228; Halbrook, *supra* note 11, at 16; Hardy, *supra* note 11, at 601-02.

as are or have been in Actual Rebellion."[53] It is surely significant that, even though this formulation of the right was available to those who sought a Bill of Rights, it did not find its way into the Constitution. Levinson also points to the proposal of Sam Adams, guaranteeing to "peaceable citizens" the right of "keeping their own arms."[54] This proposal, however, was defeated by the Massachusetts convention.[55]

Finally, Levinson relies upon the text of 19th century constitutional commentator Thomas Cooley.[56] Levinson quotes from the Third Edition of Cooley's treatise *The General Principles of Constitutional Law in the United States of America*, in which Cooley expressly objects to the idea that the Second Amendment protects only the arms of those actually enrolled in the militia and suggests a general right to form private armies; that is, to "meet for voluntary discipline in arms . . ." for which the people "need no permission or regulation of law for the purpose."[57] Levinson, however, would have been well-advised to read the Fourth Edition of Cooley's text. Although Cooley retains his view on the scope of the right to keep and bear arms, he endorses the proposition that the Second Amendment "is a limitation upon Congress and not upon the legislatures of the several States."[58] This addition was no doubt prompted by the Supreme Court's ruling in *Presser v. Illinois*.[59] *Presser* was cited in Cooley's Fourth Edition, but omitted in the Third, even though it was decided several years before the publication of the Third Edition. Indeed, Cooley's later edition concludes that "the State could prohibit altogether the carrying or selling of arms by private citizens."[60] This view, of course, is utterly inconsistent with Levinson's suggestion that each individual may be guaranteed a right to be armed against the excesses of state, as well as federal, government.

V. THE IMPLICATIONS OF THE INSURRECTIONIST THEORY

As noted, Levinson suggests the possibility that the Second Amendment

---

53. *Quoted in* EDWARD DUMBAULD, THE BILL OF RIGHTS AND WHAT IT MEANS TODAY 182 (1957) and cited by Levinson, *supra* note 11, at 648. It should be noted that even this broad formulation denied any right to use arms in rebellion against the government.

54. *Quoted in* Levinson, *supra* note 11, at 648.

55. BRANDFORD PIERCE AND CHARLES HALE, DEBATES AND PROCEEDINGS IN THE CONVENTION OF THE COMMONWEALTH OF MASSACHUSETTS 86-87 (1856), *cited in*, Martin C. Ashman, *Handgun Control by Local Government*, 10 N. KY. L. REV. 97, 108 (1982).

56. Levinson, *supra* note 11, at 649.

57. THOMAS M. COOLEY, THE GENERAL PRINCIPLES OF CONSTITUTIONAL LAW IN THE UNITED STATES OF AMERICA 298 (3d ed. 1898). This quotation also is relied upon by Hardy, *supra* note 11, at 64.

58. THOMAS M. COOLEY, THE GENERAL PRINCIPLES OF CONSTITUTIONAL LAW IN THE UNITED STATES OF AMERICA 341 (4th ed. 1931) [hereinafter COOLEY].

59. 116 U.S. 252 (1886).

60. COOLEY, supra note 58, at 341.

may guarantee a right "to keep arms that could be taken up against tyranny wherever found . . . ." Since Levinson is making assertions about constitutional rights which presumably are to be enforced by courts, it is curious that he does not ask the obvious threshold question about the insurrectionist theory. By what standards are the courts to determine whether the government has become sufficiently "tyrannical" so that armed insurrection becomes constitutionally protected? If the right guaranteed by the Second Amendment is an "individual" right, must not the courts defer to the judgment of the individual asserting the right on the question of whether the government has become a tyranny? Surely the right would be an empty one if it permitted governmental authority, in the form of the courts, to substitute its judgment for that of the individual citizen on the issue of whether the government had abused its power.

The logical extension of Levinson's position is that courts are powerless to punish armed insurrection against the government as long as the revolutionaries believe in good faith that the government had become a tyranny. Presumably, this would mean that the government could not constitutionally prosecute persons for shooting public officials, as long as the shooting was motivated by the belief that the official was abusing his/her power. No one could deny that such a doctrine would be a prescription for anarchy. Levinson must have sensed how close he was coming to this view, for he takes pains to state: "I do not want to argue that the state is necessarily tyrannical; I am not an anarchist."[61] He may not regard himself as an anarchist, but if his constitutional theory guarantees to each citizen the right to take up arms against the government if his/her conscience so directs, anarchy appears to be a highly appropriate label for such a state of affairs. Although the proper limit of government power to suppress dissent in our society has always been a matter of robust debate in the courts, the government's constitutional authority to preserve itself against violence has remained unquestioned. As the Supreme Court wrote in *Dennis v. United States*:[62] "We reject any principle of governmental helplessness in the face of preparation for revolution, which principle, carried to its logical conclusion, must lead to anarchy."[63]

Were the insurrectionist theory of the Second Amendment to be adopted by the courts, surely much of our accepted First Amendment jurisprudence about the limits of dissent would need radical revision. In *Brandenburg v. Ohio*,[64] the Supreme Court ruled that "the constitutional guarantees of free speech and free press do not permit a State to forbid or prescribe advocacy of the use of force or of law violation except where such advocacy is directed to inciting or

---

61. Levinson, *supra* note 11, at 656.
62. 341 U.S. 494 (1951).
63. *Id.* at 501.
64. 395 U.S. 444 (1969).

producing imminent lawless action and is likely to incite or produce such action."[65] While broadly protecting freedom of expression, *Brandenburg* recognized that First Amendment freedoms do not extend to speech intended to produce, and likely to produce, violent revolution. How can this continue to be a valid limit on First Amendment freedom, if the Second Amendment guarantees each individual the right to engage in armed revolution?[66]

Moreover, if the people are to be an effective armed force against tyranny, then the Second Amendment also must guarantee their right to join together in resisting the government. The insurrectionist theory therefore leads inexorably to the assertion of a constitutional right to form private military forces. To get some sense of the frightening consequences of such a right, the case of *Vietnamese Fishermen's Ass'n v. Knights of the Ku Klux Klan*,[67] is instructive.

The case arose from the Ku Klux Klan's systematic and violent harassment of Vietnamese fishermen along the Gulf Coast of Texas. The plaintiff organization sought to enjoin the activities of the Klan's Texas Emergency Reserve (TER), the military arm of the Klan which operated training camps in the State of Texas. The Court found that the Klan used the Reserve to train individuals to intimidate the Vietnamese, who the Klan felt were unfairly competing commercially with white fishermen.[68]

The Klan alleged that any injunction against its military activities would violate the Second Amendment. It further argued that the Amendment rendered unconstitutional the Texas statute providing that "no body of men, other than the regularly organized state military forces of this State and the troops of the United States, shall associate themselves together as a military company or organization . . . ."[69]

The Court rejected the Klan's argument, finding that "the Second Amendment does not imply any general constitutional right for individuals to bear arms and form private armies."[70] It upheld the state law against private armies by adopting the view that the Second Amendment protects only the keeping and

---

65. *Id.* at 447.

66. Indeed, if the insurrectionist theory is accepted, the entire First Amendment debate about the limits of dissent becomes rather quaint. How can we seriously debate the right of an individual to burn the American flag in protest over governmental policies, *see* United States v. Eichman, 110 S. Ct. 2404 (1990), when the Second Amendment gives that individual the right to bear arms against the government?

67. 543 F. Supp. 198 (S.D. Tex. 1982).

68. *Id.* at 206-07.

69. TEX. REV. CIV. STAT. ANN. art. 5780 § 6 (West Supp. 1982), *quoted in* Vietnamese Fishermen's Ass'n v. Knights of the Ku Klux Klan, 543 F. Supp. 198, 211 (S.D. Tex. 1982).

70. *Vietnamese Fisherman's Ass'n*, 543 F. Supp. at 210.

bearing of arms that have some relationship to a government-sponsored militia, finding that:

> [D]efendants' military operations obviously have absolutely no relationship whatsoever to any state or federal militia. In fact, defendants pride themselves on the fact that the TER is an alternative to Texas' state militia.[71]

The *Vietnamese Fishermen* case poses a difficult question for Levinson: If the Court had been guided by the insurrectionist theory, how could it have enjoined the military activities of the Klan? The definition of the constitutionally-protected "militia" asserted by the Klan is identical to the insurrectionist concept: a group of individuals bearing their private arms. Perhaps Professor Levinson would argue that the Klan's intimidation of the Vietnamese was not resistance against the government, and therefore not entitled to Constitutional protection under his theory. But what if the Klan's military camps were training individuals to threaten government officials charged with implementing school desegregation, a policy which the Klan sincerely believed to be the essence of tyranny? Surely the tolerance of private armies sponsored by extremist groups cannot turn on whether the groups are prepared to use force against government officials, as opposed to private individuals. The *Vietnamese Fishermen* case illustrates the fundamental, real-world problem with the insurrectionist theory. How does the theory permit the government to prevent the formation and use of private armies by extremist groups, whether of the right or of the left?

In rejecting the constitutional right to raise private armies, the opinion in *Vietnamese Fishermen* relied on the Supreme Court's ruling in *Presser v. Illinois*.[72] Although Levinson notes *Presser*'s holding that the Second Amendment does not apply to the states, he does not seem to recognize that the Court's opinion is wholly inconsistent with the insurrectionist theory. In *Presser* the Court upheld, against Second Amendment challenge, an Illinois statute barring the formation of private armies, which was similar to the Texas law upheld in *Vietnamese Fishermen*. The Supreme Court wrote:

> Military organization and military drill and parade under arms are subjects especially under the control of the government of every country . . . Under our political system they are subject to the regulation and control of the State and Federal governments, acting in due regard to their respective prerogatives and powers.[73]

---

71. *Id.* at 216.
72. 116 U.S. 252 (1886).
73. *Id.* at 267.

The Supreme Court's denunciation of private armies was echoed years later by a New York court in *Application of Cassidy*:[74]

> There can be no justification for the organization of such an armed force. Its existence would be incompatible with the fundamental concept of our form of government. The inherent potential danger of any organized private militia, even if never used or even if ultimately placed at the disposal of the government, is obvious. Its existence would be sufficient, without more, to prevent a democratic form of government, such as ours, from functioning freely, without coercion, and in accordance with the constitutional mandate.[75]

The seemingly uncontroversial principle of government control of military forces is impossible to reconcile with the insurrectionist theory.

In addition, if the armed population is to be an effective check on the power of government in this age of weapons of mass destruction, how can there be limits on the kind of arms the people have the constitutional right to keep and bear? If the Second Amendment guarantees the right to form effective private military forces, it should also guarantee that individuals have the right to be armed with weaponry that matches the destructive potential of the government's arms. Indeed, the insurrectionist theory would dictate that the greater the military utility of a weapon, the greater its constitutional protection. The government would have more power to regulate single-shot rifles than to regulate machine guns and bazookas.

One of the most peculiar aspects of Professor Levinson's argument is that he does not appear at all repelled by such a conclusion. In his discussion of the Supreme Court's refusal in *United States v. Miller* to accord constitutional protection to a sawed-off shotgun, he places great emphasis on the Court's finding that "it is not within judicial notice that this weapon is any part of the ordinary military equipment or that its use could contribute to the common defense."[76] Levinson reads this to mean that if a showing had been made of the military utility of the shotgun, the Court might have accorded it constitutional protection.[77] Levinson concludes:

> Ironically, *Miller* can be read to support some of the most extreme anti-gun control arguments, e.g., that the individual citizen has a right to keep and bear bazookas, rocket launchers, and other armaments that

---

74. 51 N.Y.S.2d 202 (N.Y. App. Div. 1944).
75. *Id.* at 205.
76. United States v. Miller, 307 U.S. 174, 178. *Quoted in* Levinson, *supra* note 11, at 654.
77. Levinson, *supra* note 11, at 654.

are clearly relevant to modern warfare, including, of course, assault weapons.   Arguments about the constitutional legitimacy of a prohibition by Congress of private ownership of handguns or, what is much more likely, assault rifles, might turn on the usefulness of such guns in military settings.[78]

Thus, instead of concluding that a right to keep and bear bazookas is the *reductio ad absurdum* of the insurrectionist interpretation of *Miller*, Levinson appears to be comfortable with the possibility that this is exactly what the Court meant.[79]   If such a bizarre view of the Second Amendment seems divorced from real courts and real cases, consider the fact that the National Rifle Association and its lawyers have made the identical argument, invoking *Miller*, to urge courts to strike down the 1986 federal machine gun ban,[80] and the California law banning possession and sale of semi-automatic military assault weapons.[81]

If it is extremist and dangerous to admit to a generalized right to bear arms

---

78. *Id.*

79. There is no basis for reading *Miller* to grant constitutional protection to any weapon with a military use. The issue in *Miller* turned on whether a sawed-off shotgun could be shown to have "some reasonable relationship to the preservation or efficiency of a well regulated militia." *Miller*, 307 U.S. at 178. Simply because the Court held that the absence of evidence suggesting a military utility for the gun precluded constitutional protection does not mean that such evidence would have been sufficient to confer constitutional protection. Because the Court was able to decide the case before it based on the nature of the weapon alone, it did not need to reach the further question whether the circumstances of the weapon's possession by the particular defendant may preclude a finding of its relationship to the well regulated militia. Nothing in *Miller* suggests that the Court would confer constitutional protection on weapons of obvious military utility -- such as machine guns -- insofar as they are possessed for reasons unconnected to service in an organized state militia.

80. In Farmer v. Higgins, 907 F.2d 1041 (11th Cir. 1990), *cert. denied*, 111 S. Ct. 753 (1991), lawyers for the NRA's "Firearms Civil Rights Legal Defense Fund" represented a machine gun manufacturer seeking to overturn the 1986 federal law banning possession and sale of new machine guns. The Circuit Court rejected, without comment, the plaintiff's Second Amendment challenge to the law. Plaintiff's unsuccessful petition for certiorari to the Supreme Court argued that *Miller* grants constitutional protection to machine guns because of their military utility. *Farmer*, 907 F.2d 1041 (11th Cir. 1990), *petition for cert.* (No. 90-600) (Copy on file with author).

81. In Fresno Rifle & Pistol Club v. Van de Kamp, 746 F. Supp. 1415 (E.D. Cal. 1990), *appeal docketed*, No. 91-15466 (9th Cir. 1991), the NRA joined a suit charging that California's Roberti-Roos Assault Weapon Control Act violates the Second Amendment. The district court upheld the law. Plaintiffs' brief to the U.S. Court of Appeals for the Ninth Circuit relies on *Miller* for the proposition that all weapons with a conceivably military use are constitutionally protected. Brief for Appellants, *Fresno Rifle & Pistol Club*, (No. 91-15466) (Copy of brief on file with author). Levinson says that "[i]t is almost impossible to imagine that the judiciary would strike down a determination by Congress that the possession of assault weapons should be denied to private citizens." Levinson, *supra* note 11, at 655. Such a prospect would seem impossible only if the courts are unwilling to take seriously the very theory which Levinson believes to deserve consideration.

against the government, is it not equally troubling to deny any right on the part of the general population to rise up against tyranny? Are we really prepared to deny the individual the right to engage in armed resistance against an authoritarian government? Would we have denied the Jews in Nazi Germany the right to resist their government by force of arms? Levinson himself invokes the brutal suppression of Chinese students in Tianamen Square.[82] Regardless of whether access to assault rifles would have made a practical difference in the outcome of that confrontation, were we ready to deny such freedom-fighters the right to organize themselves as an armed force against the Chinese government?

Regardless of how we answer these questions, we must first understand that they are not questions of constitutional law. Indeed, the questions themselves presuppose the end of constitutional government. Whether the Chinese students had a right to bear arms against their government is not a question about what rights are granted by the United States Constitution. If there is a right to resist totalitarianism through violent resistance, its origin is *extra*-constitutional, whether it be some notion of "natural law" or "moral rights."

Nowhere is the natural right of all persons to resist tyranny more eloquently defended than in Jefferson's Declaration of Independence. To secure the right to "life, liberty and the pursuit of happiness," Jefferson wrote, "governments are instituted among men, deriving their just powers from the consent of the governed" and "whenever any form of government becomes destructive of these ends, it is the right of the people to alter or to abolish it . . . ."

Jefferson, however, was not interpreting the Constitution; he was appealing to the natural right of persons to establish constitutional government. It is surely significant that his immortal call to revolution is not duplicated in the text of the Constitution. The constitutional authors realized that were this natural right to become a *constitutional* right, the constitutional system itself would be threatened. A constitutional right in our system is, by definition, a limitation on the power of the democratically elected majority. To the extent that the right to be armed against the government is a constitutional right, it must operate to restrain the power of that majority to prevent armed insurrection. Once democratic government is stripped of that power, it is stripped of the power to protect all of our other liberties. It is as true as it is ironic that, although a natural right to revolution may have been necessary to achieve constitutional government, it cannot be a principle of constitutional government.

In short, the existence of a constitutional right to use arms against tyranny would, itself, create the conditions for tyranny. As Dean Roscoe Pound wrote,

---

82. Levinson, *supra* note 11, at 656.

"In the urban industrial society of today a general right to bear efficient arms so as to be enabled to resist oppression by the government would mean that gangs could exercise an extra-legal rule which would defeat the whole Bill of Rights."[83] This is the insurrectionist vision of America.

VI. FINAL THOUGHTS

Unlike the Declaration of Independence, our Constitution is not a charter for revolution; it is a charter for government. The Constitution establishes a system of democratic institutions and instructs us that, if the system is carefully protected, liberty will be ensured. It does not address the question of the individual's rights against tyranny because its only subject matter is the creation of democratic institutions to ensure against tyranny. One can believe in a natural right to resist tyranny by force of arms without conceding that a democratic government is powerless to prevent insurrection or to regulate privately-owned firearms.

As important as the gun control controversy is, there is far more at stake in the Second Amendment debate than whether a waiting period for handguns or a prohibition of assault weapons is constitutional. The insurrectionist theorists like Levinson have upped the ante. They are posing one of the fundamental questions of American government: What is the origin of our liberty under the Constitution? If the courts are prepared to follow the insurrectionists to the conclusion that constitutional liberty ultimately comes from the barrel of a gun, the Second Amendment may prove to be a weapon of destruction aimed at the rest of the Bill of Rights.

---

83. ROSCOE POUND, THE DEVELOPMENT OF CONSTITUTIONAL GUARANTEES OF LIBERTY 91 (1957).

Standing Armies And Armed Citizens: An Historical Analysis of The Second Amendment

By Roy G. Weatherup[*]

I. Introduction: Guns and the Constitution

As a result of a steadily rising crime rate in recent years, a sharp public debate over the merits of federal firearms regulation has developed. "Crime in the streets" has become a national preoccupation; politicians cry out for "law and order"; and the handgun has become a a target of attention. The number of robberies jumped from 138,000 in 1965 to 376,000 in 1972, while murders committed by guns shot up from 5,015 to 10,379 in the same period, and the proportion of cases in which the murder weapon was a firearm rose from 57.2 percent to 65.6 percent.[1] The recent attempt on the life of President Ford in Sacramento by an erstwhile member of the "Manson Gang" serves to heighten the terror of a nation already stunned by the assassinations of John F. Kennedy, Martin Luther King and Robert F. Kennedy, and the maiming of George Wallace. Many people assert that these tragedies could have been prevented by keeping the murder weapons out of the hands that used them. Others vehemently dispute this claim.

The free flow of firearms across state lines has undermined the traditional view of crime and gun control as local problems. In New York City, long noted for strict regulation of all types of weapons, only 19 percent of the 390 homicides of 1960 involved pistols, by 1972, this proportion had jumped to 49 percent of 1,691. In 1973, there were only 28,000 lawfully possessed handguns in the nation's largest city, but police estimated that there were as many as *1.3 million* illegal handguns, mostly imported from southern states with lax laws.[2] These statistics give credence to the arguments of proponents of gun control that federal action is needed, if only to make local laws enforcible.

The great majority of the American people now support registration of both handguns and rifles. When the Gallup Poll asked the

---

[*]   J.D., 1972 Stanford University; Member of the California Bar.

1.   U.S. Bureau of the Census, Statistical Abstract of the United States: 1974, at 147-51. (95th ed. 1974).

2.   N.Y. Times, Dec. 2, 1973, § 1, at 1, col. 5 (city ed.).

question: "Do you favor or oppose registration of all firearms?" in a recent survey, more than two-thirds (67 percent) favored the concept, while 27 percent opposed it, and 6 percent had no opinion. Even gun-owners endorsed registration by a margin of 55 percent to 39 percent with 6 percent undecided.[3] Yet, although the intensity of belief is undoubtedly far stronger in the minority than in the majority Congress has remained dormant.[4] The zeal of those individuals dedicated to the preservation of the "right to keep and bear arms" in its present form cannot be doubted.

American history has often seen social and political problems transformed into constitutional issues.[5] The gun control issue is no exception to this phenomenon, and particular attention has been focused on the Second Amendment to the United States Constitution, which provides: "A well regulated Militia, being necessary to the security of a free State, the right of the people to keep and bear Arms, shall not be infringed."

Proponents of gun control seize the phrase "a well regulated Militia" and find in it the sole purpose of the constitutional guarantee. They therefore assert that "the right of the people to keep and bear Arms" is a collective right which protects only members of the organized militia, e.g., the National Guard, and only in the performance of their duties. It is their belief that no one else can claim a personal right

3. L.A. Times, June 5, 1975, § 1, at 29, col. 1.
4. Congressional lethargy cannot be attributed to a lack of proposed legislation. At every session of the Congress, a number of bills for the control of handguns and other weaponry are introduced, only to be shunted to committee and never heard from again. For example, the following is only a partial listing of proffered statutes for the First Session of the 94th Congress: S. 750 was introduced by Senator Hart (Mich.) to prohibit the importation, manufacture, sale, purchase, transfer, receipt, possession or transportation of handguns unless authorized by federal or state authorities. S. 1477, introduced by Senator Kennedy (Mass.) and known as the Federal Handgun Control Act of 1975 is basically a registration and licensing statute. It would prohibit the private sale or manufacture of handguns under six inches in length. (Both bills are currently pending in the Senate Judiciary Subcommittee on Juvenile Delinquency.)

S. 1880, authored by Senator Bayh (Ind.) was passed by the Senate by a vote of 68 to 25, only to die on the floor of the House of Representatives. Entitled the Violent Crime and Repeat Offender Act of 1975, it would have provided additional penalties for felonies committed with firearms, and required the prompt reporting of theft of firearms by licensees.

In addition, there is a major bill pending in the House of Representative which is not duplicated in the Senate. H.R. 2381 would prohibit the importation and manufacture of hollow-point bullets. This bill is now pending in the House Ways and Means Committee as well as in the House Interstate and Foreign Commerce Committee.

5. See, e.g., Roe v. Wade, 410 U.S. 113 (1973) (the question of abortion); Schechter Corp. v. United States, 295 U.S. 495 (1935) (the New Deal's National Recovery Administration); Dred Scott v. Sanford, 60 U.S. (19 How.) 393 (1857) (the spread of slavery controversy).

to keep and bear arms for any purpose whatsoever, criminal or otherwise.

Opponents maintain that having guns is a constitutionally protected individual right, similar to other guarantees of the Bill of Rights. Some hold this right to be absolute, while others would allow reasonable restrictions, perhaps even licensing and registration. Still others would limit the protection of the Second Amendment to individuals capable of military service and to weapons useful for military purposes. The essential characteristic of the "individualist" interpretation, as opposed to the "collectivist" view, is that the Second Amendment precludes, to some extent at least, congressional interference in the private use of firearms for lawful purposes such as target shooting, hunting and self-defense.

It is one of the ironies of contemporary politics that the many of the most vocal supporters of "law and order" are persistent critics of federal firearms regulation. "Guns don't kill people; people kill people" is their philosophy. Firearms in private hands are viewed as a means of protecting an individual's life and property, as well as a factor in helping to preserve the Republic against foreign and domestic enemies. Whereas strict constructionism is often the preferred doctrine in interpreting the constitutional rights of criminals, such a narrow view of the Second Amendment is unacceptable. Far from being narrowly construed, the Second Amendment is held out to be a bulwark of human freedom and dignity as well as a means of safeguarding the rights of the individual against encroachment by the federal government. It thus becomes a weapon in the arsenal of argument against gun control, and each new proposal is said to infringe upon the rights of the people to keep and bear arms.

The clash between "collectivist" and "individualist" interpretations of the Second Amendment has not been definitely resolved. Even members of Congress believe that their power to regulate firearms is limited by the existence of an individual right to have, to hold, and to use them. Senator Hugh Scott, Republican of Pennsylvania, writes in *Guns & Ammo* magazine: "As my record shows, I have always defended the right-to-bear-arms provision of the Second Amendment. I have a gun in my own home and I certainly intend to keep it."[6]

There has been very little case law construing the Second Amendment, perhaps because there has been very little federal legislation on the subject of firearms. This may change, and it may become necessary for the Supreme Court to rule upon constitutional challenges to federal statutes based on the Second Amendment. Even before this

---

6. Scott, *Leading Senator Admits Gun Law Mistake!*, Mar. 1970 GUNS & AMMO., 46, 47.

occurs, it would be helpful to dispel the uncertainties that exist in Congress about the extent of federal legislative power.

In order to determine accurately the intended meaning of the Second Amendment, it is necessary to delve into history. It is necessary to consider the very nature of a constitutional guarantee—whether it is an inherent, fundamental right, derived from abstract human nature and natural law or, alternatively, a restriction on governmental power imposed after experience with abuse of power.

Historically, the right to keep and bear arms has been closely intertwined with questions of political sovereignty, the right of revolution, civil and military power, military organization, crime and personal security. The Second Amendment was written neither by accident nor without purpose; it was the product of centuries of Anglo-American legal and political experience. This development will be examined in order to determine whether the "collectivist" or "individualist" construction of the Second Amendment is correct.[7]

II. The Evolution of British Military Power

Victorious at the Battle of Hastings in 1066, William the Conqueror was able to assert personal ownership over all the land of England and sovereignty over its people. All power emanated from the King, and all persons held their property and privileges at his sufferance.

Feudal society was organized along military lines in 1181. King Henry II, great grandson of the Conqueror, issued the Assize of Arms, which formalized the military duties of subjects. The first three articles of the decree specify what armament each level of society is to maintain—ranging from the holder of a knight's fee, who must equip himself with a hauberk, a helmet, a shield and a lance, down to the poorest freeman armed only with an iron headpiece and a lance. The philosophy of the law is expressed in the fourth article, which is as follows:

> Moreover, let each and every one of them swear that before the feast of St. Hilary he will possess these arms and will bear allegiance to the lord king, Henry, namely the son of the Empress Maud, and that he will bear these arms in his service according to his order and in allegiance to the lord king and his realm. And let none of those who hold these arms sell them or pledge them or offer them, or in any other way alienate them; neither let a lord

---

7. For an earlier article which discusses the "collectivist" versus the "individualist" approach to the Second Amendment, see Feller & Gotting, *The Second Amendment: A Second Look*, 61 Nw. U.L. REV. 46 (1966-67). The authors conclude: "[T]he 'right of the people' refers to the collective right of the body politic of each state to be under the protection of an independent, effective state militia . *Id.* at 69. (citation omitted). But see Hays, *The Right to Bear Arms, a Study in Judicial Misinterpretation*, 2 WM. & MARY L. REV. 381 (1960). Hays contends that the right to bear arms is an individual one.

in any way deprive his men of them either by forfeiture or gift, or as surety or in any other manner.[8]

The remainder of the statute prescribes rules and procedures governing its administration. The Assize of Arms marked the beginning of the militia system; its clear purpose was to strengthen and maintain the King's authority.

In 1215, the rebellious Norman barons forced King John to sign the Magna Carta, a document justly regarded as the foundation of Anglo-American freedom. The Great Charter consists of sixty-three articles which set forth in great detail certain restrictions on the King's prerogative. Its introductory article concludes, "Ye have also granted to all the free men of Our kingdom, for Us and Our heirs forever, all the liberties underwritten, to have and to hold to them and their heirs of Us and Our heirs."[9] Implicit in this statement is the fact that sovereignty is deemed to be vested in the office of kingship, and that the King is restricting his powers in favor of his subjects. Roscoe Pound makes this comment on the Magna Carta:

> The ground plan to which the common-law polity has built ever since was given by the Great Charter. It was not merely the first attempt to put in legal terms what became the leading ideas of constitutional government. It put them in the form of limitations on the exercise of authority, not of concessions to free human action from authority. It put them as legal propositions, so that they could and did come to be a part of the ordinary law of the land invoked like any other legal precepts in the ordinary course of orderly litigation. Moreover, it did not put them abstractly. In characteristic English fashion it put them concretely in the form of a body of specific provisions for present ills, not a body of general declarations in universal terms. Herein, perhaps, is the secret of its enduring vitality.[10]

Centuries were to pass before an English sovereign would again proclaim the doctrine of unrestricted royal power which William the Conqueror had established by force of arms, and which King John had lost in the same manner.

Even though medieval England had not yet developed firearms, the government found it necessary to severely restrict such weapons as did exist. In 1328 Parliament passed the celebrated Statute of Northhampton, which made it an offense to ride armed at night, or by day in fairs, markets, or in the presence of king's ministers.[11]

---

8. The Assize of Arms, ¶ 4 (1181), in 2 English Historical Documents 416 (D. Douglas & G. Greenaway ed. 1953).

9. Magna Carta: Text and Commentary 34 (A.E.D. Howard ed. 1964).

10. R. Pound, The Development of Constitutional Guarantees of Liberty 18-19 (1957).

11. Statute of Northhampton, 2 Edw. 3, c.3 (1328).

The fifteenth century dynastic struggle known as the War of Roses virtually destroyed the feudal system, and prepared the way for a new consolidation of royal power beginning with the coronation of Henry Tudor as King Henry VII in 1485. The Tudors maintained a large degree of national unity. Their task was made easier by practical applications of gunpowder. The royal cannon made resistance by the nobility futile.

Perhaps because of the weakness of their hereditary claims, the Tudor monarchs attempted to control and manipulate Parliament, rather than assert the royal prerogative in defiance of Parliament. It was even admitted that Parliament could regulate the succession to the throne, acting in conjunction with the reigning monarch, of course. In the reign of Elizabeth, it was declared to be high treason to deny that Parliament and the Queen could "make laws and statutes of sufficient force and validity to limit and bind the crown of this realm, and the descent, limitation, inheritance, and government thereof."[12]

The long war with the Hapsburg Empire that began at the time of the Spanish Armada contributed to an upsurge of national sentiment. Faith in the English militia was vindicated as free men had held their own against the massive, professional standing armies of the Spanish King. Englishmen came to believe the militia was the best security for their country and their liberties.

At the death of Elizabeth I in 1603, King James VI of Scotland ascended the English throne as James I. The advent of the House of Stuart marked the beginning of a century of religious and political struggle between Crown and Parliament. Out of this struggle, what we know as the English Constitution emerged. The monarchy was finally and firmly restricted, but preserved, the supremacy of Parliament was established, the common law became a strong, independent force, and the liberties of the people were encased in a Bill of Rights.

Although a model constitutional monarch in some respects, in the realm of political theory, James I challenged the sensibilities of the nation. He boldly proclaimed the divine right theory of government—that kings hold their thrones by the will of God alone, and not by the will of peoples or parliaments. Typical of his sentiment are these excerpts from his speech to Parliament on March 21, 1610:

> The State of MONARCHIE is the spremest thing upon earth: For Kings are not onely GODS Lieutenants upon earth, and sit upon GODS throne, but even by GOD himselfe they are called Gods. . . . In the Scriptures Kings are called Gods, and so their power after a certaine relation compared to the Divine Power.

The King concluded that "to dispute what GOD may doe, is blas-

---

12. Treasons Act, 13 Eliz. 1, c. 1 (1571).

phemie," and thus it is "sedition in Subjects, to dispute what a King may do in the height of his power."[13]   Here was a King not restricted by any human law.

Neither the legal profession nor Parliament was willing to accept such a boundless royal prerogative.   Having grown up in the civil law tradition of Scotland, James I was indifferent to the common law, but the English lawyers argued that, while the King had many privileges at common law, he was limited by and subordinate to it.   When James I asserted that Parliament existed only by "the grace and permission of our ancestors and us,"[14] the House of Commons passed the famous Protestation of December 18, 1621, which asserted:

> That the Liberties, Franchises, Privileges and Jurisdictions of Parliament, are the ancient and undoubted birthright and inheritance of the subjects of England; and that the arduous and urgent affairs concerning the King, State and defence of the realm, and of the Church of England, and the making and maintenance of laws, and redress of michiefs and grievances, which daily happen within this realm, are proper subjects and matter of counsel and debate in Parliament: and that in the handling and proceeding of those businesses every member of the House hath, and of right ought to have, Freedom of Speech, to propound, treat, reason and bring to conclusion the same. . . .[15]

The King's response was to walk into the House of Commons and to tear from the Journal the page containing these words.

The leading legal theorist of the time was Sir Edward Coke, whose writings and leadership were to enhance the prestige of the common law, and bring it into alliance with Parliament against the monarchy. In response to an inquiry from James I, Coke and his colleagues declared:

> That the King by his proclamation cannot create any offence which was not an offence before, for then he may alter the law of the land by his proclamation in a high point; for if he may create an offence where none is, upon that ensues fine and imprisonment . . .; That the King hath no prerogative, but that which the law of the land allows him. . . .[16]

The common law courts asserted jurisdiction to inquire into the legality of acts of servants of the Crown, and thus began the doctrine of the rule of law.

In response to the wars waged by James I's improvident heir, Charles I, Parliament enacted the Petition of Right in 1628, inspired

---

13. KING JAMES I, THE WORKES OF THE MOST HIGH AND MIGHTIE PRINCE JAMES 529, 531 (1616).

14. 1 PARL. HIST. ENG. 1351 (1621).

15. *Id.* at 1361.

16. 7 THE REPORTS OF SIR EDWARD COKE, KNT 76 (G. Wilson trans. 1777).

and drafted largely by Coke. The petition was an assertion of the power of Parliament and the common law, and contained a long list of grievances. The abuses of the King's military power—billeting, martial law, imprisonment without trial, and forced loans—were particularly resented. Charles I had no choice but to sign the petition, since he needed revenues from Parliament, but he secretly consulted his judges who assured him that his signature would not be binding. Soon afterward, in 1629, the King dissolved Parliament and began the long period of personal rule which was to end in the Great Rebellion.

Charles I was short of money, and revived an ancient tax; his judges upheld the legality of this action in the famous Ship Money case of 1635. The King also wished to strengthen the Church of England, the mainstay of the monarchy. The ecclesiastical canons of 1640 emphatically affirmed the theory of Divine Right of Kings and, in addition, promulgated the doctrine of nonresistançe:

> For subjects to bear arms against their kings, offensive or defensive, upon any pretence whatsoever, is at least to resist the powers which are ordained of God; and though they do not invade but only resist, St. Paul tells them plainly they shall receive to themselves damnation.[17]

This doctrine of "nonresistance" was to have an important role in religion and politics in both England and America, for the next century and a half.

Faced with a Scottish rebellion, Charles I was forced to summon the English Parliament in 1640 in order to obtain the resources necessary to put down the insurrection. After eleven years of personal royal government, Parliament trusted neither the King nor his leading minister, the Earl of Strafford. Parliament demanded a wide array of religious and political concessions, including the removal of Strafford as governor of Ireland and the disbanding of the strong army he had created there. When the King acceded to these demands, Ireland rebelled.

Charles I was now desperate. Scotland and Ireland were in open rebellion, and the Parliament of England was dominated by the King's enemies. The King had made numerous concessions, but to no avail. Strafford wanted to bring John Pym, the parliamentary leader, to trial for treasonable dealings with the Scottish army invading England, but Pym struck first with a bill of attainder against Strafford. The main charge was the creation of a powerful army in Ireland for the purpose of crushing opposition in England. The bill of attainder passed, and the King was forced to send his ablest servant to the scaffold in 1641

---

17. Constitutions and Cannons Ecclesiastical, Treated Upon by the Archbishops of Canterbury and York (1640), in 1 SYNODALIA 390-91 (E. Cardwell ed. 1842).

Still unsatisfied, Parliament presented its Nineteen Propositions as
an ultimatum to the King in 1642. The Propositions, if acceded to,
would have established a very limited monarchy with the King
surrendering the power of the sword and Parliament obtaining complete control over the militia. Instead, the King raised the royal standard at Nottingham and proclaimed Parliament to be in rebellion. Thus
began the Civil Wars, which resulted in the decapitation of Charles I
and the proclamation of a republic in 1649.

Oliver Cromwell and the Puritans came to power by force of arms
and the creation of a disciplined standing army. Cromwell soon quarreled with Parliament and assumed the role of a military dictator. The
soldiers supported their leader because Parliament proposed to disband
much of the army thus depriving them of their livelihood, and also because they feared that Parliament might once again come under the
control of the Anglicans, who would revive persecution of the Puritan
sects.

It was soon proposed that Cromwell be made king, but only
because that office would have definite constitutional restrictions.
Finally Cromwell assumed the title of Lord Protector in 1653, under
a written constitution that gave him virtually royal power. Although
Cromwell's government brought domestic peace and ruled efficiently,
it did not gain in popularity. The Lord Protector's government was
created and maintained by bayonets, and the people came to hate it.
The end of the Protectorate and its legacy have been described by historian Eric Sheppard as follows:

> The great soldier's death in 1658, while the army he had made was
> still fighting victoriously in Flanders, marked the beginning of the
> end of that army's rule; its leaders soon had no choice but to accept
> the inevitable, and in May 1660 the red coats of the New Model
> were arrayed on Blackheath to do honor to the monarch whom nine
> years before it had hunted into exile. A few months later, setting
> an example which has since been followed by all the great armies
> of England, it . . . laid down its arms and passed silently and
> peacefully into the pursuits of peace, leaving behind it, in the minds
> of the governing class and the people, besides a deservedly high
> military reputation, a legacy of hatred and distrust of all standing
> armies which has endured to our own day.[18]

The mood of England at the restoration of Charles II, son
of the martyred Charles I, was one of relief and enthusiasm. An act
was swiftly passed which recited that "the people of this kingdom lie
under a great burden and charge in the maintenance and payment of
the present army," and provided that it should be disbanded with "all
convenient speed."[19]

---

18. E. Sheppard, A Short History of the British Army (4th ed. 1959).
19. Disbanding Act, 12 Car. 2, c. 15 (1660).

Once again reliance for the country's security was placed in the militia system, which had fallen into disuse after two decades of professional armies, civil wars and military government. Statutes were passed in 1661 and 1662 declaring that the King had the sole right of command and disposition of the militia, and providing for its organization.[20] Winston Churchill makes this comment on the Cavalier Parliament, which had restored the monarchy:

> It rendered all honour to the King. It had no intention of being governed by him. The many landed gentry who had been impoverished in the royal cause were not blind monarchists. They did not mean to part with any of the Parliamentary rights which had been gained in the struggle. They were ready to make provision for the defence of the country by means of militia; but the militia must be controlled by the Lord-Lieutenants of the counties. They vehemently asserted the supremacy of the Crown over the armed forces; but they took care that the only troops in the country should be under the local control of their own class. Thus not only the King but Parliament was without an army. The repository of force had now become the county families and gentry.[21]

The revival of the militia did not mean that the King was forbidden to raise and maintain armies. He had no means of doing so, however, because Parliament held the purse strings, and the quartering of soldiers had been condemned since the days of the Petition of Right.

Foreign wars made the development of a standing army inevitable, and it reached 16,000 men by the end of the reign of Charles II. It was done with the consent of Parliament, and English country gentlemen were secure in their control of the domestic armed power—the militia. In addition, guns were taken out of the hands of the common people. Among the conditions of a 1670 statute was one that no person, other than heirs of the nobility, could have a gun unless he owned land with a yearly value of L100.[22] The protection of the people's liberties was thus committed entirely to Parliament and other legal institutions. The possibility of a citizen army, such as that created by Oliver Cromwell, was precluded.

In the reign of Charles II, religious controversy dominated politics. The Cavalier Parliament wished to maintain the established Anglican Church and persecute dissenters, Catholic and Puritan alike. Parliament was also alarmed by the prospect that the King's Catholic brother, the Duke of York, would succeed to the throne. A parliamentary attempt to exclude the Duke failed, but in 1673 and 1678, two Test Acts

---

20. First Militia Act, 13 Car. 2, Stat. I, c. 6 (1661); Second Militia Act, 14 Car. 2, c. 3 (1662).

21. 2 W. CHURCHILL, A HISTORY OF THE ENGLISH-SPEAKING PEOPLES 336 (1956).

22. Game Preservation Act, 22 Car. 2, c. 25, § 3 (1670).

were passed, which barred Catholics from all civil and military offices and from both Houses of Parliament.[23]

In 1685, the Catholic Duke of York ascended to the throne of James II. The new King quieted the fears of his subjects by proclaiming his intention to maintain church and state as they were by law established. The people were also comforted by the fact that the heirs to the throne were his Protestant daughters, Mary and Anne, and his Protestant nephew, William of Orange, stadholder of the Dutch Republic and Mary's husband. Because of the Test Acts, James II inherited an entirely Protestant government.

At the same time a rebellion, led by the Duke of Monmouth, broke out in the western counties. The King successfully crushed the uprising, but in the process succeeded in doubling his standing army to 30,000 men, granting commissions to catholic officers, and bringing in recruits from Catholic Ireland. In addition he quartered his new army in private homes. These arbitrary actions were in direct violation of previous parliamentary proclamations.

James II then asked Parliament to repeal the Test Acts and the Habeas Corpus Act, which Parliament refused to do. The King also asked the representatives of the nation to abandon their reliance on the militia, in favor of standing armies:

> My Lords and Gentlemen,
>
>   After the storm that seemed to be coming upon us when we parted last, I am glad to meet you all again in so great Peace and Quietness. God Almighty be praised, by those Blessing that Rebellion was suppressed: But when we reflect, what an inconsiderable Number of Men began it, and how long they carried [it] on without any Opposition, I hope every-body will be convinced, that the Militia, which hath hitherto been so much depended on, is not sufficient for such Occasions; and that there is nothing but a good Force of well disciplined Troops in constant Pay, that can defend us from such, as, either at Home or Abroad, are disposed to disturb us . . .[24]

John Dryden, the poet, shared the King's attitude toward the militia when he wrote these timeless words:

> The country rings around with loud alarms,
> And raw in fields the rude militia swarms;
> Mouths without hands; maintained at vast expense,
> In peace a charge, in war a weak defence;
> Stout once a month they march, a blustering band,
> And ever, but in times of need, at hand.

---

23. Test Act. 25 Car. 2, c. 2. (1673); Parliamentary Test Act, 30 Car. 2, Stat. 2, c. 1 (1678) (an exemption allowed the Duke of York to retain his seat in the House of Lords).

24. 9 H.C. Jour. 756 (1685).

This was the morn when, issuing on the guard,
Drawn up in rank and file they stood prepared
Of seeming arms to make a short essay,
Then hasten to be drunk, the business of the day.[25]

Parliament adjourned in 1686 without resolving any of the basic issues. The King kept his army and pursued his policies through extra-parliamentary means.

To get rid of the Test Act, and to revive the royal prerogative at the same time, the King arranged a collusive lawsuit. A coachman in the service of a Roman Catholic officer brought suit under the Test Act to recover the statutory reward for discovering violators, and the officer pleaded a royal dispensation in defense. The King's judges in *Godden v. Hales*[26] upheld the validity of the dispensation and gave judgment for the defendant. Lord Chief Justice Herbert stated:

> We are satisfied in our judgments before, and having the concurrence of eleven out of twelve, we think we may very well declare an opinion of the court to be, that the King may dispense in this case: and the judges go upon these grounds;
> 1. That the kings of England are sovereign princes.
> 2. That the laws of England are the king's laws.
> 3. That therefore 'tis an inseparable prerogative in the kings of England, to dispense with penal laws in particular cases and upon particular necessary reasons.
> 4. That of those reasons and those necessities the king himself is sole judge: And then, which is consequent upon all,
> 5. That this is not a trust invested in or granted to the king by the people, but the ancient remains of the sovereign power and prerogative of the kings of England; which never yet has taken from them, nor can be.[27]

Thus armed with the law, the King proceeded to dispense with statutes as he saw fit. He replaced Protestants and Catholics at high posts in government, particularly at important military garrisons. The army was further enlarged and 13,000 men were stationed at Hounslow Heath, just outside London, in order to hold the city in subjection if necessary. How far James II planned to carry his religious and political program is unknown, but his powerful standing army made many Protestants fearful and uneasy about the future.

With the birth of a son, who would take precedence over the King's Protestant daughters in the succession, fear led to revolution.

---

25. J. DRYDEN, CYMON AND IPHIGENIA, IN THE POETICAL WORKS OF JOHN DRYDEN 641 (W. Christie ed. 1893).
26. Godden v. Hales, 89 Eng. Rep. 1050 (Ex. 1686), *as reported in,* 11 STATE TRIALS 66 (T. Howell comp. 1811).
27. *Id.* at 1199.

Leading subjects sent a secret invitation to William of Orange to come to England in defense of the liberties of the people and his wife's right to the Crown. When William landed with a large Dutch army, the English army and government deserted James II who fled to France. Thus the Glorious Revolution of 1688 was accomplished. James II had believed that his enemies were paralyzed by the Anglican doctrine of nonresistance, but he had so alienated his subjects that he was deposed without being able to put up any resistance himself.

William and Mary were offered the Crown jointly after they accepted the Declaration of Rights on February 13, 1689. The Declaration was later enacted in the form of a statute, known as the Bill of Rights.[28] The document is divided into two main parts: 1) a list of allegedly illegal actions of James II, and 2) a declaration of the "ancient rights and liberties" of the realm.

The sections of the first part of the statute that are relevant to the right to bear arms are the allegations that James II

did endeavor to subvert and extirpate the Protestant Religion and the Laws and Liberties of this Kingdom . . .

5. By raising and keeping a Standing army within this Kingdom in Time of Peace without Consent of Parliament and quartering Soldiers contrary to Law.

6. By causing several good Subjects, being Protestants, to be disarmed at the same Time when Papists were both armed and employed contrary to Law.[29]

It should be pointed out that the King did not disarm Protestants in any literal sense; the reference is to his desire to abandon the militia in favor of a standing army and his replacement of Protestants by Catholics at important military posts.

The parallel sections of the declaration of rights part of the statute are:

5. That the raising or keeping a Standing Army within the Kingdom in Time of Peace unless it be with the Consent of Parliament is against Law.

6. That the Subjects which are Protestants may have Arms for their Defence suitable to their Conditions, and as allowed by Law.[30]

The purpose, and meaning of, the right to have arms recognized by these provisions is clear from their historical context. Protestant members of the militia might keep and bear arms in accordance with

28. Bill of Rights, 1 W. & M., sess. 2, c. 2 (1689).
29. *Id.*
30. *Id.* Securing the Peace in Scotland Act.

their militia duties for the defense of the realm. The right was recognized as a restriction on any future monarch who might wish to emulate James II and abandon the militia system in favor of a standing army without the consent of Parliament. There was obviously no recognition of any personal right to bear arms on the part of subjects generally, since existing law forbade ownership of firearms by anyone except heirs of the nobility and prosperous landowners.

In summary, the English Bill of Rights represents the culmination of the centuries old problem of the relationship of sovereignty and armed force. The king could have an army, but only with the express consent of Parliament. The king could not, however, dismantle and disarm the militia. There was no individual right to bear arms; the rights of subjects could be protected only by the political process and the fundamental laws of the land.

III.   England and Her Colonies

The revolutionary settlement that followed the accession of William and Mary gave the English people permanent security. England, however, had become the center of an Empire, and the relationship between England and the outlying territories raised legal and political problems.

When William and Mary, and, later, Queen Anne, all died without heirs, the Crown passed to the distantly-related House of Hanover in Germany. Uprisings led by the son and grandson of James II were suppressed in 1715 and in 1745, and Parliament felt it necessary to deprive the people entirely of the right to bear arms in large parts of Scotland.[31]

The history of the English colonies in America was closely intertwined with that of the Mother Country. The New England colonies had been settled by Puritan refugees from the early Stuart kings. When Cromwell and the Puritans came to power in England, thousands of royalists fled to the southern colonies, swelling their populations.

The foundation of government in the colonies was the charter granted by the king. An important feature of a charter was the provision securing for the inhabitants of the colony the rights of Englishmen. For example, the 1606 Charter of Virginia contains this passage:

> Also we do . . . DECLARE . . . that all and every the Persons being our Subjects, which shall dwell and inhabit within every or any of the said several Colonies and Plantations, and every of their children, which shall happen to be born within any of the

---

31. 1 Geo. 1, Stat. 2, c. 54 (1715).

Limits and Precincts of the said several Colonies and Plantations, shall HAVE and enjoy all Liberties, Franchises, and Immunities, within any of our other Dominions, to all Intents and Purposes, as if they had been abiding and born, within this our Realm of *England*, or any other of our said Dominions.[32]

During the seventeenth century and the first half of the eighteenth century, the North American colonies were essentially self-governing republics following the political and legal model of England. In 1720, Richard West, counsel to the Board of Trade, gave this description of the state of law in the colonies:

The Common Law of England is the Common Law of the Plantations, and all statutes in affirmance of the Common Law, passed in England antecedent to the settlement of a colony, are in force in that colony, unless there is some private Act to the contrary; though no statutes, made since those settlements, are there in force unless the colonies are particularly mentioned. Let an Englishman go where he will, he carries as much of law and liberty with him, as the nature of things will bear.[33]

The legal relationship of Britain and the colonies became more than an academic problem after the end of the Seven Years' War in 1763. That war, known in America as the French and Indian War, brought large British armies to colonies which had hitherto known no armed force but the colonial militia. The cost of the war was enormous, and the British government decided that the colonies should share it.

In his efforts to tax and govern the colonies, George III acted in two capacities: as King, armed with the prerogatives of his office, and as the agent of the British Parliament which at that time was under his personal control. The colonists acknowledged the authority of the King, but only in accordance with their charters and with the same restrictions that limited his power in Britain. Many of the colonists denied the authority of the British Parliament to regulate their internal affairs in any way.

Colonial resistance forced the British government to abandon the Stamp Tax, but Parliament passed the Declaratory Act in 1766 entitled "An Act for the better securing the Dependency of his majesty's dominions in *America* upon the Crown and parliament of *Great Britain*."

Whereas several of the Houses of Representatives in his Majesty's Colonies and Plantations in *America*, have of late, against Law,

---

32. VA. CHARTER (1606), in 7 THE FEDERAL AND STATE CONSTITUTIONS, COLONIAL CHARTERS, AND OTHER ORGANIC LAWS OF THE STATES, TERRITORIES, AND COLONIES 3788 (F. Thorpe ed. 1909) [hereinafter cited as CONSTITUTIONS].

33. 1 G. CHALMERS, OPINIONS OF EMINENT LAWYERS ON VARIOUS POINTS OF ENGLISH JURISPRUDENCE 194, 195 (1814).

claimed to themselves or to the General Assemblies of the same, the sole and exclusive Right of imposing Duties and Taxes upon his Majesty's Subjects in the said Colonies and Plantations; and have, in pursuance of such Claim, passed certain Votes, Resolutions and Orders, derogatory to the Legislative Authority of Parliament, and inconsistent with the Dependency of the said Colonies and Plantations upon the Crown of *Great Britain* be it declared . . . That the said Colonies and Plantations in *America* have been, are, and of Right ought to be, subordinate unto, and dependent upon, the Imperial Crown and Parliament of *Great Britain*; and that the King's Majesty, by and with the Advice and Consent of the Lords Spiritual and Temporal, and Commons of *Great Britain* in Parliament assembled, had, hath, and of Right ought to have, full Power and Authority to make Laws and Statutes of sufficient Force and Validity to bind the Colonies and People of *America,* Subjects of the Crown of *Great Britain,* in all Cases whatsoever.[34]

The colonists were free-born Englishmen and they were not willing to accept inferior status. They could not admit the authority of Crown and Parliament to bind them "in all cases whatsoever." They fell back on the doctrine of fundamental law as expressed in 1764 by James Otis:

'Tis hoped it will not be considered as a new doctrine, that even the authority of the Parliament of *Great-Britain* is circumscribed by certain bounds, which if exceeded their acts become those of meer *power* without *right,* and consequently void. The judges of England have declared in favour of these sentiments, when they expressly declare; that *acts of Parliament against natural equity are void.* That *acts against the fundamental principles of the British constitution are void.* This doctrine is agreeable to the law of nature and nations, and to the divine dictates of natural and revealed religion.[35]

The concept of fundamental law was developed and grounded squarely on the English legal tradition. In 1772, Samuel Adams wrote in response to another writer in the *Gazette*:

Chromus talks of *Magna Charta* as though it were of no greater consequence that an act of Parliament for the establishment of a corporation of button-makers. Whatever low ideas he may entertain of the *Great Charter* . . . it is affirm'd by Lord Coke, to be declaratory of the principal grounds of the fundamental laws and liberties of England. "It is called *Charta Libertatum Regni, the Charter of the Liberties of the kingdom,* upon great reason . . . because *liberos facit, it makes and preserves the people free."* . . . But if it be declaratory of the principal grounds of the fundamental laws and liberties of England, it cannot be altered in any of its essential parts, without altering the constitution. . . . Vatel tells us plainly and without hesitation, that "the supreme legislative can-

---

34. Declaratory Act, 6 Geo. 3, c. 12 (1766).
35. J. OTIS, THE RIGHTS OF THE BRITISH COLONIES ASSERTED AND PROVED 72-73 (1764).

not change the constitution." . . . If then according to Lord Coke, *Magna Charta* is declatory of the principal grounds of the *fundamental* laws and liberties of the people, and Vatel is right in his opinion, that the supreme legislative cannot change the constitution, I think it follows, whether Lord Coke has expressly asserted it or not, that an act of parliament made against Magna Charta in violation of its essential parts, is void.[36]

This statement of fundamental law later influenced the intellectual foundation of judicial review in the United States.

In order to sustain his claim of full and unrestricted sovereignty, George III sent large standing armies to the colonies. America was outraged. The colonists drew their arguments from Whig political theorists on both sides of the Atlantic who maintained that standing armies in time of peace were tools of oppression, and that the security of a free people was best preserved by a militia.

The American colonists, who had always relied on their own militia, hated and feared standing armies even more than their English brethren. In quartering his redcoats in private homes, suspending charters and laws, and eventually imposing martial law, George III was doing in America what he could not do in England. The royal prerogative had virtually ended in England with the Revolution of 1688, but the King was reviving it in America.

The Fairfax County Resolutions, drawn up under the leadership of George Washington and passed on July 18, 1774, reflect the colonial attitude in the year prior to the outbreak of war. Of particular interest is the following paragraph:

> *Resolved*, That it is our greatest wish and inclination, as well as interest, to continue our connection with, and dependence upon, the *British* Government; but though we are its subjects, we will use every means which Heaven hath given us to prevent our becoming its slaves.[37]

In October of the same year, the First Continental Congress assembled and stated the position of the colonies in these resolutions:

> *Resolved*, . . . 1. That they are entitled to life, liberty, & property, and they have never ceded to any sovereign power whatever, a right to dispose of either without their consent.
>
> *Resolved*, . . . 2. That our ancestors, who first settled these colonies, were at the time of their emigration from the mother country, entitled to all the rights, liberties, and immunities of free and natural-born subjects, within the realm of England.

---

36. S. ADAMS, *Candidus Letters* (1772), in 2 THE WRITINGS OF SAMUEL ADAMS 324-26 (H. Cushing ed. 1906).

37. Fairfax Co. Resolutions, (1774) in A. E. D. Howard, THE ROAD FROM RUNNYMEDE: MAGNA CARTA AND CONSTITUTIONALISM IN AMERICA 435 (1968).

> *Resolved*, . . .3.   That by such emigration they by no means forfeited, surrendered, or lost any of those rights, but that they were, and their decendants now are, entitled to the exercise and enjoyment of all such of them, as their local and other circumstances enable them to exercise and enjoy.
>
> *Resolved*, . . . 4.   That the foundation of English liberty, and of all free government, is a right in the people to participate in their legislative council: and as the English colonists are not represented, and from their local and other circumstances, cannot properly be represented in the British parliament, they are entitled to a free and exclusive power of legislation in their several provincial legislatures, where their right of representation can alone be preserved, in all cases of taxation and internal polity, subject only to the negative of their sovereign, in such manner as has been heretofore used and accustomed. . . .[38]

After stating these general principles, the Congress listed specific rights that had been violated by George III, including the following:

> *Resolved*, . . . 9.   That the keeping a Standing army in these colonies, in times of peace, without the consent of the legislature of that colony, in which such army is kept, is against law.[39]

The colonists were asserting, in effect, that the restrictions on royal power that had been won by Parliament in its long struggle against the Stuart kings were binding against the sovereign, in favor of the colonial legislatures as well as Parliament.   In order to make that claim good, the colonists were forced to take up arms.

IV.   Popular Sovereignty and the New Nation

America's long war in defense of the rights of Englishmen began in 1775.   Although many colonists still hoped for a reconciliation with the mother country, it was necessary to set up state governments in the interim.   In Connecticut and Rhode Island, all that was necessary was to strike the King's name from the colonial charters, which continued to serve for many years as state constitutions.

In other states, written constitutions were drawn up.   They generally had these features: 1) an assertion that political power derives from the people; 2) provision for the organization of the government with a three-fold separation of powers; 3) a powerful legislature with authority to pass all laws not forbidden by the Constitution; and 4) a specific bill of rights restricting governmental power in the same way that the English Bill of Rights restricted the King.   It is important to emphasize that the concept of enumerated powers had not yet been

---

38.   1 Journals of the Continental Congress 1774-1789, 67-68 (Oct. 14, 1774) (W. C. Ford ed. 1904-1907).

39.   *Id.* at 70.

developed, and that rights were, as always before, conceived to be in the nature of restrictions on power, not as individual freedoms.[40]

The Declaration of Independence substituted the sovereignty of the people for that of the King, and appealed to the "Laws of Nature and of Nature's God," but it did not proclaim a social or legal revolution. It listed the colonists' grievances, including the presence of standing armies, subordination of civil to military power, use of foreign mercenary soldiers, quartering of troops, and the use of the royal prerogative to suspend laws and charters. All of these legal actions resulted from reliance on standing armies in place of the militia.

Although America repudiated the British King, it did not repudiate British law. The Constitution of Maryland, for example, declared:

> That the inhabitants of Maryland are entitled to the common law of England, and the trial by jury according to the course of that law, and to the benefit of such of the English statutes as existed on the fourth day of July, seventeen hundred and seventy six, and which, by experience, have been found applicable to their local and other circumstances, and have been introduced, used and practiced by the courts of law or equity, . . .[41]

The War for Independence was fought by fourteen different military organization—the Continental Army under Washington, and the thirteen colonial militias. The debate over the relative merits of standing armies and the militia continued even during the fighting. A defender of standing armies, Washington wrote to the Continental Congress in September of 1776 as follows:

> To place any dependence upon Militia, is, assuredly, resting upon a broken staff. Men just dragged from the tender Scenes of domestick life; unaccustomed to the din of Arms; totally unac-

---

40. For example, the Virginia Bill of Rights, adopted June 12, 1776, declared: "That a well-regulated militia, composed of the body of the people, trained to arms, is the proper, natural, and safe defence of a free State; that standing armies, in time of peace, should be avoided, as dangerous to liberty; and that in all cases the military should be under strict subordination to, and governed by the civil power." VA. CONST., Bill of Rights, § 13 (1776) in 7 CONSTITUTIONS 3814.

The comparable provision in Massachusetts was as follows: "The people have a right to keep and to bear arms for the common defence. And as, in time of peace, armies are dangerous to liberty, they ought not to be maintained without the consent of the legislature; and the military power shall always be held in an exact subordination to the civil authority, and be governed by it." MASS. CONST., Declaration of Rights, art. 17 (1780) in 3 CONSTITUTIONS 1892. (Considered in its context, the meaning of the "right to keep and bear arms" is clear. The words "for the common defence" makes it obvious that a collective right is intended. The people of Massachusetts did not want to risk a second British occupation.)

41. MD. CONST., Declaration of Rights, art. 3 (1851), in 3 CONSTITUTIONS 1713.

quainted with every kind of military skill, which being followed by a want of confidence in themselves, when opposed to Troops regularly train'd, disciplined, and appointed, superior in knowledge and superior in Arms, makes them timid, and ready to fly from their own shadows. . . .

The Jealousies of a standing Army, and the Evils to be apprehended from one, are remote; and, in my judgment, situated and circumstanced as we are, not at all to be dreaded; but the consequence of wanting one, according to my Ideas, formed from the present view of things, is certain, and inevitable Ruin; for if I was called upon to declare upon Oath, whether the Militia have been most serviceable or hurtful upon the whole; I should subscribe to the latter.[42]

To maintain the supremacy of civil power over that of the military Article II of the Articles of Confederation provided that each state would retain "its sovereignty, freedom, and independence."[43] A provision that "every state shall always keep up a well regulated and disciplined militia, sufficiently armed and accoutred" was included in Article VI.[44] In contrast, the military powers of the United States rested in Congress were strictly limited; Congress could not maintain standing armies without the consent of nine of the thirteen states.

The government of the United States under the Articles of Confederation was weak. Experience was to show that it needed to be strengthened in its military powers.

V. Forging a More Perfect Union

When the War for Independence ended, the government of the Confederation was faced with one gigantic, insoluble problem—money. As troublesome as foreign and domestic bondholders were, there was one stronger pressure group that simply could not be ignored: the former soldiers who had been promised back pay and large pensions. Organized under the name of the Society of Cincinnati, these veterans were viewed with suspicion by many Americans, who nurtured fears of standing armies.

The danger to civil authority from the military was not entirely imaginary. In the summer of 1783 there was a direct attempt to coerce the Confederation into paying what had been promised to the army. Originally intended as a peaceful protest march on the capitol in Philadelphia, the ex-soldiers were soon "mediating more violent measures,"

---

42. Letter from George Washington to the President of Congress, Sept. 24, 1776, in 6 THE WRITINGS OF GEORGE WASHINGTON 110, 112 (J. Fitzpatrick ed. 1931-1944).

43. *See generally* M. JENSEN, THE NEW NATION: A HISTORY OF THE UNITED STATES DURING THE CONFEDERATION, 1781-1789 (1950).

including "seizure of the members of Congress."[44]   Alarmed, Congress adjourned and fled to Trenton, New Jersey.   The soldiers eventually gave up, and the officers who led them escaped.

Following the abortive demonstrations in Philadelphia in the summer of 1783, Madison and other leaders felt the need to reorder the nation's military structure.

The other important military event that precipitated demands for a stronger national government was Shays' Rebellion in Massachusetts in 1786.   Oppressed by debt, farmers in the western part of the state seized military posts and supplies and defied the state government. Although the insurrection was suppressed fairly easily and Shays himself pardoned, exaggerated reports of the uprising circulated among the states, and conservatives were aghast.   Madison, in writing the introduction to his notes on the Federal Convention, lists Shays' Rebellion as one of the "ripening incidents" that led to the Convention.[45]

Thomas Jefferson, in contrast, was not alarmed by the apparent dangers of anarchy, and he criticized the clamor of the Federalists. Just after receiving a copy of the proposed Constitution, he wrote from Paris:

> . . . We have had 13 states independent 11 years.   There has been one rebellion.   That comes to one rebellion in a century & a half for each state.   What country before ever existed a century & a half without rebellion?   & what country can preserve its liberties if their rulers are not warned from time to time that their people preserve the spirit of resistance?   Let them take arms.   The remedy is set them right as to facts, pardon & pacify them. What signify a few lives lost in a century or two?   The tree of liberty must be refreshed from time to time with the blood of patriots & tyrants. It is natural manure. Our Convention has been too much impressed by the insurrection of Massachusetts: and in the spur of the moment they are setting up a kite to keep the henyard in order.[46]

Whatever the merits of Jefferson's beliefs, they were not shared by the majority of the Convention, which wished to prevent insurrections by strengthening the military powers of the general government.

---

44. Debates of the Congress of the Confederation (June 2, 1783), in 5 THE DEBATES IN THE SEVERAL STATE CONVENTIONS ON THE ADOPTION OF THE FEDERAL CONSTITUTION 93 (J. Elliot ed. 1836-1845) [hereinafter cited as STATE DEBATES].

45. DRAFTING THE FEDERAL CONSTITUTION: A REARRANGEMENT OF MADISON'S NOTES GIVING CONSECUTIVE DEVELOPMENTS OF PROVISIONS IN THE CONSTITUTION OF THE UNITED STATES 10 (A. Prescott ed. 1941) [hereinafter cited as MADISON REARRANGED].

46. Letter from Thomas Jefferson to William Stephen Smith, Nov. 13, 1787, in 4 THE WORKS OF THOMAS JEFFERSON 362 (P. Ford ed. 1892-1899).

The new military powers of Congress were listed in Article I, Section 8 of the proposed constitution, and include the following authority:

> To raise and support Armies, but no Appropriation of Money to that Use shall be for a longer Term than two Years;
>
> To provide and maintain a Navy;
>
> To make Rules for the Government and Regulation of the land and naval Forces;
>
> To provide for calling forth the Militia to execute the Laws of the Union, suppress Insurrections and repel Invasions;
>
> To provide for organizing, arming, and disciplining, the Militia, and for governing such Part of them as may be employed in the Service of the United States, reserving to the States respectively, the Appointment of the Officers, and the Authority of training the Militia according to the discipline prescribed by Congress;

The spirited debate over these provisions in the Federal Convention reflects the purposes and fears of the framers of the Constitution.

There was universal distrust of standing armies. For example, in June of 1787, Madison stated:

> . . . A standing military force, with an overgrown Executive will not long be safe companions to liberty. The means of defence agst. foreign danger, have been always the instruments of tyranny at home. Among the Romans it was a standing maxim to excite a war, whenever a revolt was apprehended. Throughout all Europe, the armies kept up under the pretext of defending, have enslaved the people. It is perhaps questionable, whether the best concerted system of absolute power in Europe cd. maintain itself, in a situation, where no alarms of external danger c. tame the people to the domestic yoke. The insular situation of G. Britain was the principal cause of her being an exception to the general fate of Europe. It has rendered less defence necessary, and admitted a kind of defence wch. c. not be used for the purpose of oppression.[47]

The defense "which could not be used for the purpose of oppression" was the militia, which was still revered on both sides of the Atlantic, even with its shortcomings.

Yet, despite the preference for the militia, it was generally agreed that Congress must have authority to raise and support standing armies in order to protect frontier settlements, the national government, and the nation when threatened by foreign powers. However, a few members were still fearful. Elbridge Gerry and Luther Martin, both of whom later opposed the Constitution, moved that a definite limit—two or three thousand men—be placed on the size of the national standing army. Voting by states, as always, the Convention unani-

---

47. 1 THE RECORDS OF THE FEDERAL CONVENTION OF 1787, at 465 (M. Farrand ed. 1911).

mously rejected the motion. The judgment of Congress and the two year appropriation limitation were thought to be sufficient safeguards.[48]

The proper extent of federal authority over the militia was much more heatedly debated. The subject was introduced by George Mason, author of the Virginia Bill of Rights, who later opposed the Constitution, but who now maintained that uniformity of organization, training and weaponry was essential to make the state militias effective. His hope was that the need for a standing army would be minimized; perhaps only a few garrisons would be required. Mason's opinions were shared by Madison, who gave this analysis:

> The primary object is to secure an effectual discipline of the Militia. This will no more be done if left to the states separately than the requisitions have been hitherto paid by them. The states neglect their militia now, and the more they are consolidated into one nation, the less each will rely on its own interior provisions for its safety, and the less prepare its militia for that purpose; in like manner as the militia of a state would have been still more neglected than it has been, if each county had been independently charged with the care of its militia. The discipline of the militia is evidently a *national* concern, and ought to be provided for in the *national* Constitution.[49]

Despite such explanations, there were still opponents to the militia clauses. Gerry, for example, declared:

> This power in the United States, as explained, is making the states drill sergeants. He had as lief-let the citizens of Massachusetts be disarmed as to take the command from the states and subject them to the general legislature. It would be regarded as a system of despotism.[50]

Later, as the Convention moved toward resolution of the issue, Gerry marshalled his final arguments. One can sense his feeling of outrage, as he solemnly warned of the dangers of centralized military power: "Let us at once destroy the state governments, have an executive for life or hereditary, and a proper Senate; and then there would be some consistency in giving full powers to the general government. . . ."[51] But as the states are not to be abolished, he wondered at the attempts that were made to give powers inconsistent with their existence. He warned the Convention against pushing the experiment too far. Some people will support a plan of vigorous government at every risk. Others, of a more democratic cast, will oppose it with equal determination; and a civil war may be produced by the conflict.

---

48. Madison Rearranged 513-26.
49. *Id.* at 522.
50. *Id.* at 521.
51. *Id.* at 523-24.

Madison rose immediately and answered Gerry in these words:

> As the greatest danger is that of disunion of the states, it is necessary to guard against it by sufficient powers to the common government; and as the greatest danger to liberty is from large standing armies, it is best to prevent them by an effectual provision for a good militia.[52]

The last discussion of the militia clauses took place on September 14, 1787, just before the Convention finished its work. Mason moved to add a preface to the clause that allowed federal regulation of the militia, in order to define its purpose. His proposed addition was "that the liberties of the people may be better secured against the danger of standing armies in time of peace." The motion was opposed as "setting a dishonourable mark of distinction on the military class of citizens," and was rejected.[53]

Thus ended the Convention's debate over the relative merits and difficulties of standing armies and the militia. The debate was soon to be revived, however, as the new nation prepared to consider the proposed new form of government.

VI.   The Ratification Controversy and the Bill of Rights

The new Constitution was signed on September 17, 1787 and the contest over its ratification soon began. The controversy was carried on mainly through the printed media. It was an unequal contest because the proponents of the new government, who now called themselves Federalists, controlled most of the newspapers. The Antifederalists resorted mainly to pamphlets and handbills.

Because the Antifederalist effort was decentralized and local in nature, it is difficult to generalize about the arguments used against the Constitution. The unifying theme, to the extent there was one, was that the new government would overreach its powers, destroy the states, deprive the people of their liberty, and create an aristrocratic or monarchical tyranny. In finding evidence of such dangers, the Antifederalists often made inconsistent interpretations of what the Constitution provided. In the case of the militia powers, for example, it was said that Congress would disarm the militia in order to remove opposition to its standing army; at the same time it was argued that Congress would ruthlessly discipline the militia and convert it into a tool of oppression.

---

52. *Id.* at 524.
53. *Id.* at 525.

Bearing in mind the inconsistency of the Antifederalist position, some of the pamphlets and articles will be examined in order to show how the fears of military power existed. One of the most scurrilous critics of the Constitution was "Philadelphiensis." His identity is uncertain, but he is believed to have been Benjamin Workman, a radical Irishman and a tutor at the University of Pennsylvania. His comments include the following:

> Who can deny but the *president general* will be a *king* to all intents and purposes, and one of the most dangerous kinds too; a king elected to command a standing army? Thus our laws are to be administered by this *tyrant*; for the whole, or at least the most important part of the executive department is put in his hands.
>
> The thoughts of a military officer possessing such powers, as the proposed constitution vests in the president general, are sufficient to excite in the mind of a freeman the most alarming apprehensions; and ought to rouse him to oppose it at *all events.* Every freeman of America ought to hold up this idea to himself, *that he has no superior but God and the laws.* But this tyrant will be so much his superior, that he can at any time he thinks proper, order him out in the militia to exercise, and to march when and where he pleases. His officers can wantonly inflict the most disgraceful punishment on a peaceable citizen, under pretense of disobedience, or the smallest neglect of militia duty.[54]

Another anonymous writer, Brutus, appealed to history as proof that standing armies in peacetime lead to tyranny:

> The same army, that in Britain, vindicated the liberties of that people from the encroachments and despotism of a tyrant king, assisted Cromwell, their General, in wresting from the people that liberty they had so dearly earned. . . .
>
> I firmly believe, no country in the world had ever a more patriotic army, than the one which so ably served this country in the late war. But had the General who commanded them been possessed of the spirit of a Julius Caesar or a Cromwell, the liberties of this country . . . [might have] in all probability terminated with the war.[55]

Still another unknown, styling himself "A Democratic Federalist," asserted that the Revolution had proved the superiority of the militia over standing armies:

> Had we a standing army when the British invaded our peaceful shores? Was it a standing army that gained the battles of Lexington and Bunker Hill, and took the ill-fated Burgoyne? Is not a well-regulated militia sufficient for every purpose of internal defense? And which of you, my fellow citizens, is afraid of any

---

54. 'Philadelphiensis' *Letter*, Independent Gazetteer (Phila.), Feb. 7, 1788.
55. 'Brutus' *Letter*, N. Y. Journal, Jan. 24, 1788.

invasion from foreign powers that our brave militia would not be able immediately to repel?[56]

Some writers, such as "Centinel," feared that national control over the militia would transform that bulwark of democracy into a tool of oppression:

> This section will subject the citizens of these states to the most arbitrary military discipline: even death may be inflicted on the disobedient; in the character of militia, you may be dragged from your families and homes to any part of the continent and for any length of time, at the discretion of the future Congress; and as militia you may be made the unwilling instruments of oppression, under the direction of government; there is no exemption upon account of conscientious scruples of bearing arms, no equivalent to be received in lieu of personal services. The militia of Pennsylvania may be marched to Georgia or New Hampshire, however incompatible with their interests or consciences; in short, they may be made as mere machines as Prussian soldiers.[57]

Other Antifederalist propagandists believed that the true motive for assertion of national control over the militia was not to use it, but to destroy it, and thus eliminate any opposition to the new standing army. The Bostonian who used the pseudonym "John De Witt" asked these questions about the militia clauses:

> Let us inquire why they have assumed this great power. Was it to strengthen the power which is now lodged in your hands, and relying upon you and *you solely* for aid and support to the civil power in the execution of all the laws of the new Congress? Is this probable? Does the complexion of this new plan countenance such a supposition? When they unprecedently claim the power of raising and supporting armies, do they tell you for what purposes they are to be raised? How they are to be employed? How many they are to consist of, and where stationed? Is this power fettered with any one of those restrictions, which will show they depend upon the militia, and not upon this infernal engine of oppression to execute their civil laws? The nature of the demand in itself contradicts such a supposition, and forces you to believe that it is for none of these causes—but rather for the purpose of consolidating and finally destroying your strength, as your respective governments are to be destroyed. They well know the impolicy of putting or keeping arms in the hands of a nervous people, at a distance from the seat of a government, upon whom they mean to exercise the powers granted in that government. . . .
>
> It is asserted by the most respectable writers upon government, that a well regulated militia, composed of the yeomanry of the country, have ever been considered as the bulwark of a free people. Tyrants have never placed any confidence on a militia composed of freemen.[58]

---

56. 'A Democratic Federalist' *Letter*, Pa. Packet (Phila.), Oct. 23, 1787.
57. 'Centinel' *Letter*, Independent Gazetteer (Phila.), Nov. 8, 1787.
58. 'John De Witt' *Letter*, Am. Herald (Boston), De. 3, 1787.

Anonymous pamphleteers and propagandists were not the only persons concerned about standing armies and the militia. Richard Henry Lee, in a letter that was widely circulated in Virginia, combined the contradictory arguments that the militia would be abandoned in favor of a standing army, and that the militia would be strengthened and forged into an instrument of tyranny. He foresaw that a small proportion of the total militia would be made into a select unit, much like a standing army, while the rest of the militia would be disarmed:

> Should one fifth, or one eighth part of the men capable of bearing arms, be made a select militia, as has been proposed, and those the young and ardent part of the community, possessed of but little or no property, and all the others put upon a plan that will render them of no importance, the former will answer all the purposes of any army, while the latter will be defenceless.[59]

A necessary premise underlying Antifederalist attack on the militia clauses of the Constitution was that these clauses operated to place exclusive jurisdiction over the militia in the hands of the general government. Though the Federalists denied this premise, it was affirmed even by Luther Martin and Elbridge Gerry, who had been members of the Federal Convention, but who now opposed the Constitution. Martin is particularly interesting because he advanced all of the contradictory arguments used by the antifederalists. Speaking on November 29, 1787 to the Maryland legislature, he said:

> . . . Engines of power are supplied by the standing Army— unlimited as to number or its duration, in addition to this Government has the entire Command of the Militia, and may call the whole Militia of any State into Action, a power, which it was vainly urged ought never to exceed a certain proportion. By organizing the Militia Congress have taken the whole power from the State Governments; and by neglecting to do it and encreasing the Standing Army, their power will increase by those very means that will be adopted and urged as an ease to the People.[60]

Martin later invoked the opposite approach, that the milita would be subject to ruthless discipline and martial law, and would be marched to the ends of the continent in the service of tyranny. In a letter published on January 18, 1788, Martin wrote that the new system for governing the militia was "giving the states the last coup de grace by taking from them the only means of self preservation."[61]

Elbridge Gerry, like many of the pamphleteers, viewed centralized military power as inseparable from monarchy:

---

59. R. H. LEE, OBSERVATIONS LEADING TO A FAIR EXAMINATION OF THE SYSTEM OF GOVERNMENT PROPOSED BY THE LATE CONVENTION 24-25 (1787).

60. 3 THE RECORDS OF THE FEDERAL CONVENTION OF 1787, at 157 (M. Farrand ed. 1911).

61. Martin, *Letter*, Md. Journal, Jan. 18, 1788.

By the edicts of authority vested in the sovereign power by the proposed constitution, the militia of the country, the bulwark of defence, and the security of national liberty is no longer under the control of civil authority; but at the rescript of the Monarch, or the aristocracy, they may either be employed to extort the enormous sums that will be necessary to support the civil list—to maintain the regalia of power—and the splendour of the most useless part of the community, or they may be sent into foreign countries for the fulfilment of treaties, stipulated by the President and two thirds of the Senate.[62]

The supporters of the proposed constitution were well-prepared to meet these and similar arguments. They had the support of America's two national heroes, George Washington and Benjamin Franklin, and this helped make the Constitution respectable, as well as alleviating fears. Articles favoring the Constitution, such as the *Federalist Papers*, were often reprinted in distant states. Intelligent and well-educated, the proponents of the new government carefully and consistently answered the arguments of their rivals.

To the general argument that there were not sufficient restrictions on the power of the proposed general government, the federalists replied that no bill of rights was necessary. This was because the Constitution would establish a novel type of government, one of enumerated powers; restrictions were necessary only where full sovereignty was conferred. In Federalist Number 84, Alexander Hamilton made the argument in these words:

It has been several times truly remarked that bills of rights are, in their origin, stipulations between kings and their subjects, abridgements of prerogative in favor of privilege, reservations of rights not surrendered to the prince Such was MAGNA CHARTA, obtained by the barons, sword in hand from King John. Such were the subsequent confirmations of that charter by succeeding princes. Such was the Petition of Right assented to by Charles I, in the beginning of his reign. Such, also, was the Declaration of Right presented by the Lords and Commons to the Prince of Orange in 1688, and afterwards thrown into the form of an act of parliament called the Bill of Rights. It is evident, therefore, that, according to their primitive signification, they have no application to constitutions professedly founded upon the power of the people, and executed by their immediate representatives and servants.[63]

To particular criticism of the military clauses of the proposed Constitution, both Hamilton and Madison replied in detail in the Federalist Papers.

---

62. E. GERRY, OBSERVATIONS ON THE NEW CONSTITUTION AND ON THE FEDERAL AND STATE CONVENTIONS 10 (1788).

63. THE FEDERALIST No. 84, at 536 (H. Lodge ed. 1888) (A. Hamilton).

Hamilton denied that a standing army was unnecessary, citing recent experience:

> Here I expect we shall be told that the militia of the country is its natural bulwark, and would be at all times equal to the national defence. This doctrine, in substance, had like to have lost us our independence. It cost millions to the United States that might have been saved. . . .
>
> The American militia, in the course of the late war, have, by their valor on numerous occasions, erected eternal monuments to their fame; but the bravest of them feel and know that the liberty of their country could not have been established by their efforts alone, however great and valuable they were. War, like most other things, is a science to be acquired and perfected by diligence, by perseverance, by time, and by practice.[64]

Hamilton did not, however, go so far as to say that standing armies were a good thing. Instead, he argued that a strong militia would minimize the need for them.[65]

Madison also addressed himself to the fear that the new national government would disarm the militia and destroy state government. He first argued that the states would still have concurrent power over the militia, thus denying that the proposed Constitution gave exclusive jurisdiction over the militia to the general government. He also pointed out that the militia, comprised of half a million men, was a force that could not be overcome by any tyrant.[66]

The arguments of the federalists appear to have quieted the fears of their countrymen, since the early state conventions were all easy victories for the new Constitution. Between December 7, 1787 and January 9, 1788, Delaware, Pennsylvania, New Jersey, Georgia and Connecticut all ratified unconditionally and overwhelmingly; the vote was unanimous in three of these states. In Massachusetts, the contest was close. On February 6, 1787, the state convention ratified the new Constitution by a narrow margin.

---

64. *Id.* No. 25 at 150 (A. Hamilton).

65. Hamilton explained: "If a well-regulated militia be the most natural defence of a free country, it ought certainly to be under the regulation and at the disposal of that body which is constituted the guardian of the national security. If standing armies are dangerous to liberty, an efficacious power over the militia, in the body to whose care the protection of the state is committed ought, as far as possible, to take away the inducement and the pretext to such unfriendly institutions. If the federal government can command the aid of the militia in those emergencies which call for the military arm in support of the civil magistrate, it can the better dispense with the employment of a different kind of force. If it cannot avail itself of the former, it will be obliged to recur to the latter. To render an army unnecessary will be a more certain method of preventing its existence than a thousand prohibitions upon paper." *Id.* No. 29, at 169 (A. Hamilton).

66. *Id.* No. 46, at 297-99 (J. Madison).

On the other hand, Maryland overwhelmingly approved the Constitution on April 28, 1787. South Carolina was next, on May 23, 1787. Eight states had now ratified the document and only one more was needed. All of the ratifications, except Massachusetts, had been by majorities of two-thirds or more. The remaining states were to see close contests, and all of them would suggest that a Bill of Rights be added to the Constitution.

New Hampshire, on June 21, 1787, became the ninth state to approve the new form of government, thus assuring that the proposed Constitution would go into effect. The New Hampshire convention proposed some amendments in its ratifying resolution. Among the proposals were a three-fourths vote requirement for keeping standing armies, a flat prohibition on quartering troops, and a prohibition against Congressional disarmament of the militia. Although no records were kept of the debates, it seems likely that the delegates feared that New England's experiences with General Gage's redcoats would be repeated.

As yet undecided, Virginia was vital to the Union as the largest, richest, and most populous state. The Virginia convention was also important because it was the only one in which the military clauses of the Constitution were extensively discussed.

The main protagonist of the Virginia debates was Patrick Henry, backwoods lawyer, ardent republican, and incomparable orator. By means of the rhetorical question, Henry was able to capture the fears and emotions which led to the adoption of the Second Amendment:

> A standing army we shall have, also, to execute the execrable commands of tyranny; and how are you to punish them? Will you order them to be punished? Who shall obey these orders? Will your mace-bearer be a match for a disciplined regiment? In what situation are we to be? . . .
>
> Your militia is given up to Congress, also, in another part of this plan: they will therefore act as they think proper: all power will be in their own possession. You cannot force them to receive their punishment: of what service would militia be to you when, most probably, you will not have a single musket in the state? for, as arms are to be provided by Congress, they may or may not furnish them. . . .
>
> By this, sir, you see that their control over our last and best defence is unlimited. If they neglect or refuse to discipline or arm our militia, they will be useless: the states can do neither—this power being exclusively given to Congress. . . .
>
> . . . If we make a king, we may prescribe the rules by which he shall rule his people, and interpose such checks as shall prevent him from infringing them; but the President, in the field, at the head of his army, can prescribe the terms on which he shall reign master,

so far that it will puzzle any American ever to get his neck from under the galling yoke. . . .[67]

While other critics lacked Henry's oratorical talents, they also feared disarmament of the militia by the new national government. George Mason, for example, spoke as follows:

> . . . There are various ways of destroying the militia. A standing army may be perpetually established in their stead. I abominate and detest the idea of government, where there is a standing army. The militia may be here destroyed by that method which has been practised in other parts of the world before; that is, by rendering them useless—by disarming them. Under various pretences, Congress may neglect to provide for arming and disciplining the militia; and the state governments cannot do it, for Congress has an exclusive right to arm them . . .[68]

Mason then went on to cite the case of a former British governor of Pennsylvania who had allegedly advised disarmament of the militia as part of the British government's scheme for "enslaving America." The suggested method was not to act openly, but "totally disusing and neglecting the militia."[69] Mason said:

> . . . This was a most iniquitous project. Why should we not provide against the danger of having our militia, our real and natural strength, destroyed? The general government ought, at the same time, to have some such power. But we need not give them power to abolish our militia . . .[70]

In these words lie the origin of the Second Amendment. The new government should be allowed to keep its broad general military powers, but it should be forbidden to disarm the militia.

Madison, leader of the Federalist forces, still argued that the militia clauses were adequate as written. He said the states and national government would have concurrent power over the militia. In response to a question, he explained why the general government was to have power to call out the militia in order to execute the laws of the union:

> . . . If resistance should be made to the execution of the laws, he said, it ought to be overcome. This could be done only in two ways—either by regular forces or by the people. If insurrections should arise, or invasions should take place, the people ought unquestionably to be employed, to suppress and repel them, rather than a standing army. The best way to do these things was to put the militia on a good and sure footing, and enable the government to make use of their services when necessary.[71]

---

67. Spoken at the Virginia Convention 3 STATE DEBATES 51-59.
68. *Id.* at 379.
69. *Id.* at 380.
70. *Id.*
71. *Id.* at 378.

It is interesting to note that Madison uses the words "people" and "militia" as synonymous, as does the Second Amendment, which he was later to draft.

The Federalists still maintained that a bill of rights was unnecessary where there was a government of enumerated powers. Governor Randolph, who had attended the Philadelphia Convention and had refused to sign the Constitution, but who was now supporting its adoption, spoke as follows:

> On the subject of a bill of rights, the want of which has been complained of, I will observe that it has been sanctified by such reverend authority, that I feel some difficulty in going against it. I shall not, however, be deterred from giving my opinion on this occasion, let the consequence be what it, may. At the beginning of the war, he had no certain bill of rights; for our charter cannot be considered as a bill of rights; it is nothing more than an investiture, in the hands of the Virginia citizens, of those rights which belonged to British subjects. When the British thought proper to infringe our rights, was it not necessary to mention, in our Constitution, those rights which ought to be paramount to the power of the legislature? Why is the bill of rights distinct from the Constitution? I consider bills of rights in this view—that the government should use them, where there is a departure from its fundamental principles, in order to restore them.[72]

This statement is very important, because it clearly explains how men in the eighteenth century conceived of a right. A right was a restriction on governmental power, necessitated by a particular abuse of that power.

The Virginia convention, however, decided that it would be wise to impose restrictions on the power of the general government before abuses occurred. So the delegates appended to their ratification resolution a long document recommended to the consideration of the Congress. This document is divided into two distinct parts: a declaration of principles and specified suggested amendments to the Constitution designed to secure these principles.

The declaration of principles tells much about the social and political philosophy of eighteenth century Americans. The theory of government as a social compact is affirmed. There are five provisions that relate directly to the background of the Second Amendment.

The third principle condemns the Anglican doctrine of nonresistance as "absurd, slavish, and destructive of the good and happiness of mankind."[73] This is not surprising, since Virginia had recently dis-

---

72. *Id.* at 466.

73. J. MADISON, THE DEBATES IN THE FEDERAL CONVENTION OF 1787 660 (G. Hunt & J.B. Scott ed. 1920).

established the Anglican Church, and had taken up arms to resist the authority of the head of that church.

The seventh principle is "that all power of suspending laws or the execution of laws by any authority, without the consent of the representatives of the people in the legislature is injurious to their rights, and ought not to be exercised."[74] The attempt to assert such power had cost James II his throne and George III his American colonies, even though both Kings had been backed by powerful standing armies.

The seventeenth, eighteenth and nineteenth principles are as follows:

> Seventeenth, That the people have a right to keep and bear arms; that a well regulated Militia composed of the body of the people trained to arms is the proper, natural and safe defence of a free State. That standing armies in time of peace are dangerous to liberty, and therefore ought to be avoided, as far as the circumstances and protection of the Community will admit; and that in all cases the military should be under strict subordination to and governed by the Civil power.
>
> Eighteenth, That no Soldier in time of peace ought to be quartered in any house without the consent of the owner, and in the time of war in such manner only as the laws direct.
>
> Nineteenth, That any person religiously scrupulous of bearing arms ought to be exempted upon payment of an equivalent to employ another to bear arms in his stead.[75]

These words encapsulate the Whig point of view in the long debate over the relative merits of standing armies and the militia. The specific amendments that were proposed to protect these principles were:

> Ninth, That no standing army or regular troops shall be raised or kept up in time of peace, without the consent of two thirds of the members present in both houses.
>
> Tenth, That no soldier shall be inlisted for any longer term than four years, except in time of war, and then for no longer term than the continuance of the war.
>
> Eleventh, That each State respectively shall have the power to provide for organizing, arming and disciplining it's own Militia, whensoever Congress shall omit or neglect to provide for the same. That the Militia shall not be subject to Martial law, except when in actual service in time of war, invasion, or rebellion; and when not in the actual service of the United States, shall be subject only to such fines, penalties and punishments as shall be directed or inflicted by the laws of its own State.[76]

It is important for our purposes to note that there is no mention here of any individual right.

---

74. *Id.* at 661.
75. *Id.* at 662.
76. *Id.* at 663.

The Purpose of the Second Amendment

There might never have been a federal Bill of Rights had it not been for one alarming event that is almost forgotten today. As part of the price of ratification in New York, it was agreed unanimously that a second federal convention should be called by the states, in accordance with Article V of the Constitution, to revise the document. Governor Clinton wrote a circular letter making this proposal to the governors of all the states.

Madison feared that a new convention would reconsider the whole structure of government and undo what had been achieved. Professor Merrill Jensen, in *The Making of the American Constitution*, analyzes the situation as follows:

> The Bill of Rights was thus born of Madison's concern to prevent a second convention which might undo the work of the Philadelphia Convention, and also of his concern to save his political future in Virginia. On the other side such men as Patrick Henry understood perfectly the political motives involved. He looked upon the passage of the Bill of Rights as a political defeat which would make it impossible to block the centralization of all power in the national government.[77]

Madison had outmanuevered the antifederalists by drafting the Bill of Rights very soon after the First Congress met.

Madison's original draft of the provision that eventually became the Second Amendment read:

> The right of the people to keep and bear arms shall not be infringed; a well armed but well regulated militia being the best security of a free country; but no person religiously scrupulous of bearing arms shall be compelled to render military service in person.[78]

There was debate in Congress over the religious exemption, and it was removed. Otherwise, there was general discussion of standing armies and the militia, and widespread support for the proposal. It became part of the Constitution with the rest of the Bill of Rights on December 15, 1791.

Considering the immediate political context of the Second Amendment, as well as its long historical background, there can be no doubt about its intended meaning. There had been a long standing fear of military power in the hands of the executive, and, rightly or wrongly, many people believed that the militia was an effective military force which minimized the need for such executive military power. The pro-

---

77. M. JENSEN, THE MAKING OF THE AMERICAN CONSTITUTION 149 (1964).
78. 1 ANNALS OF CONG. 434 (1789).

posed Constitution authorized standing armies, and granted sweeping Congressional power over the militia. Some even feared disarmament of the militia. The Second Amendment was clearly and simply an effort to relieve that fear.

Neither in the Philadelphia Convention, in the writings of the pamphleteers, in the newspapers, in the convention debates, nor in Congress was there any reference to hunting, target shooting, duelling, personal self-defense, or any other subject that would indicate an individual right to have guns. Every reference to the right to bear arms was in connection with military service.

Thus the inevitable conclusion is that the "collectivist" view of the Second Amendment rather than the "individualist" interpretation is supported by history. It thus becomes necessary to examine the decisions of the Supreme Court in order to determine whether that body has expanded the right to bear arms beyond what was intended in 1789.

VII. Supreme Court Interpretation of the Second Amendment

The Second Amendment has been directly considered by the Supreme Court in only four cases: *United States v. Cruikshank*,[79] *Presser v. Illinois*,[80] *Miller v. Texas*[81] and *United States v. Miller*.[82]

In *Cruikshank*, the defendants had been convicted of conspiracy to deprive negro citizens of the rights and privileges secured to them by the Constitution and laws of the United States, in violation of the criminal provisions of the Civil Rights Act of 1870. Among the rights violated were the right to peaceably assemble and the right to keep and bear arms for a lawful purpose.

Chief Justice Waite, speaking for the majority, held that the rights violated by the defendants were not secured by the Constitution or laws of the United States, and thus the judgment of conviction was affirmed. The chief justice began with a long discussion of the nature of the federal system in general, and the attributes of state and national citizenship in particular. The only rights protected by the national government were those necessary for participation in that government. The right to petition Congress would be such a right, but a person must look

79. 92 U.S. 542 (1875).
80. 116 U.S. 252 (1886).
81. 153 U.S. 535 (1894).
82. 307 U.S. 174 (1939).

to his state government for protection of similar rights in other situations.

In particular reference to the Second Amendment, the opinion states:

> The second and tenth counts are equally defective. The right there specified is that of "bearing arms for a lawful purpose." This is not a right granted by the Constitution. Neither is it in any manner dependent upon that instrument for its existence. The second amendment declares that it shall not be infringed; but this, as has been seen, means no more than that it shall not be infringed by Congress. This is one of the amendments that has no other effect than to restrict the powers of the national government, leaving the people to look for their protection against any violation by their fellow-citizens of the rights it recognizes, to what is called, in *The City of New York v. Miln*, 11 Pet. 139, the "powers which relate to merely municipal legislation, or what was, perhaps, more properly called internal police," "not surrendered or restrained" by the Constitution of the United States.[83]

The only dissenter in *Cruikshank* was Justice Clifford, who found the indictment vague on its face. He thus concurred in the result reached by the majority without discussing any constitutional issues.

The next, and undoubtedly the most important Second Amendment case was *Presser v. Illinois*[84] decided in 1886. Herman Presser, a German-American, was the leader of *Lehr und Wehr Verein*, a fraternal, athletic and paramilitary association incorporated under Illinois law. He was convicted for parading and drilling with men under arms, in violation of an Illinois statute, and was fined ten dollars.

On appeal to the United States Supreme Court, it was contended that the Illinois statute conflicted with the military powers given to Congress by the Constitution, with federal statutes passed in pursuance of those powers, and with various other parts of the Constitution, including the Second Amendment. The Supreme Court unanimously rejected all of these claims and affirmed the conviction.

It should be emphasized that *Presser* was argued and decided as a case presenting broad issues of the relationship of state and federal military power, and that the Second Amendment was only one aspect of that question. In reference to the Illinois statute, the Court observed:

> We think it clear that the sections under consideration, which only forbid bodies of men to associate together as military organizations, or to drill or parade with arms in cities and towns unless authorized by law, do not infringe the right of the people to keep

---

83. 92 U.S. at 553 (1875).
84. 116 U.S. 252 (1886).

and bear arms. But a conclusive answer to the contention that this amendment prohibits the legislation in question lies in the fact that the amendment is a limitation only upon the power of Congress and the National government, and not upon that of the States.[85]

The Court cited *Cruikshank* in support of this proposition. The inapplicability of the Second Amendment to the states was a sufficient ground for rejecting Presser's Second Amendment contentions, but the Court did not stop there. It preferred to discuss the problem further and make clear the nature of the right protected by the Second Amendment.

> It is undoubtedly true that all citizens capable of bearing arms constitute the reserved military force or reserve militia of the United States as well as of the States, and, in view of this prerogative of the general government, as well as of its general powers, the States cannot, even laying the constitutional provision in question out of view, prohibit the people from keeping and bearing arms, so as to deprive the United States of their rightful resource for maintaining the public security, and disable the people from performing their duty to the general government.[86]

One view of the Second Amendment suggests that this dicta constitutes the first step toward incorporating the right to bear arms into the Fourteenth Amendment,[87] apparently forgetting that the Court was laying the Second Amendment "out of view." The Court had stated that the Illinois law does not have the effect of depriving the federal government of its military capacity.

To further clarify its view that the Second Amendment is concerned only with military matters, the opinion focuses on *Presser*:

> The plaintiff in error was not a member of the organized volunteer militia of the State of Illinois, nor did he belong to the troops of the United States or to any organization under the militia law of the United States. On the contrary, the fact that he did not belong to the organized militia or the troops of the United States was an ingredient in the offence for which he was convicted and sentenced. The question is, therefore, had he a right as a citizen of the United States, in disobedience of the State law, to associate with others as a military company, and to drill and parade with arms in the towns and cities of the State? If the plaintiff in error has any such privilege he must be able to point to the provision of the Constitution or statutes of the United States by which it is conferred.[88]

The obvious implication here is that any right to bear arms by virtue of the Second Amendment, even if asserted against the national gov-

---

85. *Id.* at 264-65.
86. *Id.* at 265.
87. *See generally* H. Black, *The Bill of Rights,* 35 N.Y.U.L. Rev. 865 (1960).
88. *Id.* at 266.

ernment, is contingent upon military service in accordance with statutory law. This implication is confirmed later in the opinion, as the
Court declared:

> The right to voluntarily associate together as a military com-
> pany or organization, or to drill or parade with arms, without, and
> independent of, an act of Congress or law of the State authorizing
> the same, is not an attribute of national citizenship. Military
> organization and military drill and parade under arms are subjects
> especially under the control of the government of every country.
> They cannot be claimed as a right independent of law.[89]

Thus the *Presser* case clearly affirms the meaning of the Second
Amendment that was intended by its framers. It protects only members of a state militia, and it protects them only against being disarmed
by the federal government. There is no individual right that can be
claimed independent of state militia law. Furthermore, the dicta
relating to preservation of the nation's military capacity could not be
used as the basis for questioning any regulation of private firearms,
unless such a regulation violated an act of Congress; Congress is
obviously the best judge of the proper means of preserving the nation's
military capacity.

The third, and least important, of the Second Amendment cases
was *Miller v. Texas*.[90] A convicted murderer asserted that the state
had violated his Second and Fourth Amendment rights. The Supreme
Court unanimously dismissed the claim in one sentence, relying on the
inapplicability of these provisions to the states, and citing *Cruikshank*
and other cases.

The fourth and last time that the Supreme Court considered the
Second Amendment was in *United States v. Miller*.[91] The result
reached by Justice McReynolds for a unanimous Court was obviously
correct, but the opinion is so brief and sketchy that it has undoubtedly
caused much of the uncertainty that exists today about the meaning of
the Second Amendment.

Defendants Miller and Layton were indicted for violation of the
National Firearms Act of 1934,[92] which was designed to help control
gangsters, and which infringed the right to keep and bear sawed off
shotguns, among other arms. The District Court of the United States
for the Western District of Arkansas sustained a demurrer and quashed
the indictment, holding the 1934 Act unconstitutional on Second

89. *Id.* at 267.
90. 153 U.S. 535 (1894).
91. 307 U.S. 174 (1939).
92. National Firearms Act *as amended* 26 U.S.C. §§ 5801-5872 (1972).

Amendment grounds. The government appealed to the Supreme Court, which reversed and remanded.

When *Miller* was argued before the High Court, there was no appearance for the defendants. With only one side presenting a case, it is easy to understand why the Court viewed the issues as rather simple, and not needing very much analysis.

The Court began by observing that the National Firearms Act was a valid revenue measure, and not a usurpation of the police powers of the states. The opinion then addresses itself to the Second Amendment issue:

> In the absence of any evidence tending to show that possession or use of a "shotgun having a barrel of less than eighteen inches in length" at this time has some reasonable relationship to the preservation or efficiency of a well regulated militia, we cannot say that the Second Amendment guarantees the right to keep and bear such an instrument. Certainly it is not within judicial notice that this weapon is any part of the ordinary military equipment or that its use could contribute to the common defense.[93]

It is this paragraph that is the source of the uncertainty and confusion arising from the *Miller* case. The Court was merely correcting the error of the district judge, but it made the mistake of looking at the weapon, rather than the person, in determining that the Second Amendment is not applicable.

Fortunately, however, Justice McReynolds went on and partially clarified the ambiguity in the above paragraph. He cited the militia clauses of the Constitution and said:

> With obvious purpose to assure the continuation and render possible the effectiveness of such forces the declaration and guarantee of the Second Amendment were made. It must be interpreted and applied with that end in view.[94]

These words alone undercut any individual right interpretation of the Second Amendment.

Justice McReynolds then proceeded to give a brief history of the militia, stressing its function as a military force. He then considered the relevance of state interpretations of the right to bear arms, and noted:

> Most if not all of the States have adopted provisions touching the right to keep and bear arms. Differences in the language employed in these have naturally led to somewhat variant conclusions concerning the scope of the right guaranteed.[95]

---

93. 307 U.S. at 178.
94. *Id.*
95. *Id.* at 182.

He concluded that such decisions did not support the trial judge's ruling. He then referred the reader to "some of the more important opinions" concerning the militia. First among these opinions was *Presser v. Illinois*.[96]

Thus, in spite of some ambiguity in the Court's opinion in *Miller*, there is no reason to suppose that there was any change in the established view that the Second Amendment defines and protects a collective right that is vested only in the members of the state militia.

VIII. Conclusion

In the last angry decades of the twentieth century, members of rifle clubs, paramilitary groups and other misguided patriots continue to oppose legislative control of handguns and rifles. These ideological heirs of the vigilantes of the bygone western frontier era still maintain that the Second Amendment guarantees them a personal right to "keep and bear arms."[97] But the annals of the Second Amendment attest to the fact that its adoption was the result of a political struggle to restrict the power of the national government and to prevent the disarmament of state militias.[98] Not unlike their English forbears, the American revolutionaries had a deep fear of centralized executive power, particularly when standing armies were at its disposal. The Second Amendment was adopted to prevent the arbitrary use of force by the national government against the states and the individual.

Delegates to the Constitutional Convention had no intention of establishing any personal right to keep and bear arms. Therefore the "individualist" view of the Second Amendment must be rejected in favor of the "collectivist" interpretation, which is supported by history and a handful of Supreme Court decisions on the issue.

As pointed out previously, the nature of the Second Amendment does not provide a right that could be interpreted as being incorporated into the Fourteenth Amendment. It was designed solely to protect the states against the general government, not to create a personal right which either state or federal authorities are bound to respect.

---

96. 116 U.S. 252 (1886).

97. A recent call to action was made by an organization which calls itself the *Sheriff's Posse Comitatus*. This group, dismayed over claimed violations of the Second Amendment promises to "come together and do something about it." Its propaganda concludes rather ominously, "The PEOPLE are the rightful masters to both congress and courts, not to over throw (sic) the Constitution, but to over throw (sic) the men who pervert the Constitution." *Flyer, Sheriff's Posse Comitatus*, Petaluma, California, 1975.

98. See notes 60-66 and accompanying text.

The contemporary meaning of the Second Amendment is the same as it was at the time of its adoption. The federal government may regulate the National Guard, but may not disarm it against the will of state legislatures. Nothing in the Second Amendment, however, precludes Congress or the states from requiring licensing and registration of firearms; in fact, there is nothing to stop an outright congressional ban on private ownership of all handguns and all rifles.

The Right of the People to Keep and Bear Arms: The Common Law Tradition

By Joyce Lee Malcolm*

Introduction**

Every generation suffers to some degree from historic amnesia. However, when the history of a major political tradition, along with the assumptions and passions that forged it, are forgotten, it becomes extraordinarily difficult to understand or evaluate its legacy. This is particularly unfortunate when that legacy has been written into the enduring fabric of government. The Second Amendment to the United States Constitution is such a relic, a fossil of a lost tradition. Even a century ago its purpose would have been clearly appreciated. To nineteenth century exponents of limited government, the checks and balances that preserved individual liberty were ultimately guaranteed by the right of the people to be armed. The preeminent Whig historian, Thomas Macaulay, labelled this "the security without which every other is insufficient,"[1] and a century earlier the great jurist, William Blackstone, regarded private arms as the means by which a people might vindicate their other rights if these were suppressed.[2] Earlier generations of political philosophers clearly had less confidence in written constitutions, no matter how wisely drafted. J.L. De Lolme, an eighteenth century author much read at the time of the American Revolution[3] pointed out:

* Visiting Scholar, Harvard Law School; B.A., 1963, Barnard College; Ph.D., 1977, Brandeis University.
** This article is part of a larger project on the history of the right to bear arms, the research for which has been made possible from the following generous awards: a Research Fellowship from the National Endowment for the Humanities, a Fellowship in Legal History from the American Bar Foundation, a Summer Fellowship from the Liberty Fund, and a Mark DeWolfe Howe research grant from Harvard Law School.
1. 1 T. Macaulay, Critical and Historical Essays, Contributed to the Edinburgh Review 154, 162 (Leipzig 1850).
2. *See* 1 W. Blackstone, Commentaries *139-40 (1st ed. Oxford 1765).
3. De Lolme's book, The Constitution of England, was first published in 1771 and quickly went through an impressive number of editions. D'Israeli later referred to De

But all those privileges of the People, considered in themselves, are but feeble defences against the real strength of those who govern. All those provisions, all those reciprocal Rights, necessarily suppose that things remain in their legal and settled course: what would then be the recourse of the People, if ever the Prince, suddenly freeing himself from all restraint, and throwing himself as it were out of the Constitution, should no longer respect either the person, or the property of the subject, and either should make no account of his conversation with the Parliament, or attempt to force it implicitly to submit to his will?—It would be resistance . . . the question has been decided in favour of this doctrine by the Laws of England, and that resistance is looked upon by them as the ultimate and lawful resource against the violences of Power.[4]

This belief in the virtues of an armed citizenry had a profound influence upon the development of the English, and in consequence the American, system of government. However, the many years in which both the British and American governments have remained "in their legal and settled course[s]," have helped bring us to the point where the history of the individual's right to keep and bear arms is now obscure. British historians, no longer interested in the issue, have tended to ignore it, while American legal and constitutional scholars, ill-equipped to investigate the English origins of this troublesome liberty, have made a few cursory and imperfect attempts to research the subject.[5] As a result, Englishmen are uncertain of the circumstances surrounding the establishment of a right to bear arms and the Second Amendment to the Constitution remains this country's most hotly debated but least understood liberty.

In a report on the legal basis for firearms controls, a committee of the American Bar Association observed:

There is probably less agreement, more misinformation, and less understanding of the right of citizens to keep and bear arms than on any other current controversial constitutional issue. The crux of the controversy is the construction of the Second Amendment to the Constitution, which reads: "A well-regulated militia, being

---

Lolme as "the English Montesquieu." *See* OXFORD UNIVERSITY PRESS, 1 THE CONCISE DICTIONARY OF NATIONAL BIOGRAPHY 332 (2d ed. 1903); 7 ENCYCLOPAEDIA BRITANNICA 970 (11th ed. 1910).

4. J. DE LOLME, THE CONSTITUTION OF ENGLAND 227 (New York 1793).

5. *See, e.g.,* L. KENNET & J. ANDERSON, THE GUN IN AMERICA 25-27 (1975); G. Newton & F. Zimring, Firearms & Violence in American Life; A Staff Report Submitted to the National Commission on the Causes & Prevention of Violence 255 (1968); Levin, *The Right to Bear Arms: The Development of the American Experience* 48 CHI-KENT L. REV. 148 (1971); Weatherup, *Standing Armies and Armed Citizens: An Historical Analysis of the Second Amendment,* 2 HASTINGS CONST. L.Q. 961 (1975).

necessary to the security of a free State, the right of the people to keep and bear arms, shall not be infringed."[6]
Few would disagree that the crux of this controversy is the construction of the Second Amendment, but, as those writing on the subject have demonstrated, that single sentence is capable of an extraordinary number of interpretations.[7] The main source of confusion has been the meaning and purpose of the initial clause. Was it a qualifying or an amplifying clause? That is, was the right to arms guaranteed only to members of "a well-regulated militia" or was the militia merely the most pressing reason for maintenance of an armed community? The meaning of "militia" itself is by no means clear. It has been argued that only a small, highly trained citizen army was intended,[8] and, alternatively, that all able-bodied men constituted the militia.[9] Finally, emphasis on the militia has been proffered as evidence that the right to arms was only a "collective right" to defend the state, not an individual right to defend oneself.[10] Our pressing need to understand the Second Amendment has served to define areas of disagreement but has brought us no closer to a consensus on its original meaning.

The fault lies not with the legal, but with the scholarly, community. For if the crux of the controversy is the construction of the Second Amendment, the key to that construction is the English tradition the colonists inherited, and the English Bill of Rights from which much of the American Bill of Rights was drawn. Experts in English constitutional and legal history have neglected this subject, however, with the result that no full-scale study of the evolution of the right to keep and bear arms has yet been published. Consequently, there is doubt about such elementary facts as the legality and availability of arms in seventeenth and eighteenth century England, and uncertainty about whether the English right to have arms extended to the entire Protestant population or only to the aristocracy. Experts in American constitutional theory have nevertheless endeavored to define the common law tradition behind the Second Amendment without the benefit of research into these basic questions. These experts' findings are contradictory, often involve serious mistakes of fact, and muddle, rather than clarify, mat-

---

6. Miller, Sec. III *The Legal Basis for Firearms Controls*, in REPORT TO THE AMERICAN BAR ASSOCIATION 22 (1975).

7. *See, e.g.*, Caplan, *Handgun Control: Constitutional or Unconstitutional? A Reply to Mayor Jackson*, 10 N.C. CENT. L.J. 53, 54 (1978); Weatherup, *supra* note 5, at 973-74; Whisker, *Historical Development and Subsequent Erosion of the Right to Keep and Bear Arms*, 78 W. VA. L. REV. 171, 176-78 (1975).

8. *See* Miller, *supra* note 6, at 25-28.

9. *See* Caplan, *supra* note 7, at 54-55.

10. *See, e.g.*, Levin, *supra* note 5, at 154, 159; Weatherup, *supra* note 5, at 973-74.

ters. For example, in their report to the National Commission on the Causes and Prevention of Violence, George Newton and Franklin Zimring insist that any traditional right of Englishmen to own weapons was "more nominal than real,"[11] while the authors of *The Gun in America* conclude that few Englishmen ever owned firearms because prior to the adoption of the English Bill of Rights in 1689, firearms were expensive and inefficient, and thereafter guns were not considered "suitable to the condition" of the average citizen.[12] Neither set of authors provides more than cursory evidence.[13] On the other hand, one British author found that until modern times his countrymen's right to keep arms was "unimpaired as it was then [in 1689] deliberately settled"[14] and a second noted that with only "minor exceptions" the Englishman's "right to keep arms seems not to have been questioned."[15]

The continuing confusion is apparent in the articles that have appeared on this subject in American law journals. David Caplan, writing in the *North Carolina Central Law Journal*, finds that "the private keeping of arms was completely guaranteed by the common law as an 'absolute right of individuals,' "[16] while James Whisker argues in the *West Virginia Law Review* that long before the American Revolution "Englishmen came to view the retention of arms by individuals or by private groups as productive only of rebellion or insurrection."[17] There is a temptation to superimpose the debate over the Second Amendment's militia clause back onto the English guarantee of the right to have arms, although the English guarantee contained no such clause. Roy Weatherup, for example, interprets the clear English guarantee that "Protestant subjects may have arms for their defence" to mean "Protestant members of the militia might keep and bear arms in ac-

11. G. NEWTON & F. ZIMRING, *supra* note 5, at 255.

12. L. KENNET & J. ANDERSON, *supra* note 5, at 25-27.

13. For example, Newton and Zimring, fail to cite a single seventeenth or eighteenth century source for the critical assertion that the English Convention Parliament of 1688 intended to guarantee only a general, not an individual, right to have arms. *See* G. NEWTON & F. ZIMRING, *supra* note 5, at 254-55, n.12. Kennet and Anderson conclude that in the seventeenth century firearms "were not generally held . . . because of their inefficiency, costliness, and general scarcity," but provide no evidence of their efficiency, cost, or availability in that period. *See* L. KENNET & J. ANDERSON, *supra* note 5, at 27.

14. 1 J. PATERSON, COMMENTARIES ON THE LIBERTY OF THE SUBJECT AND THE LAWS OF ENGLAND RELATING TO THE SECURITY OF THE PERSON 442 (London 1877).

15. C. GREENWOOD, FIREARMS CONTROL: A STUDY OF ARMED CRIME AND FIREARMS CONTROL IN ENGLAND AND WALES 10 (1972).

16. Caplan, *supra* note 7, at 54.

17. Whisker, *supra* note 7, at 176.

cordance with their militia duties for the defense of the realm."[18] Despite the fact that the Convention Parliament which drafted the English Bill of Rights purposely adopted the phrase "their defence" in preference to "their common defence"[19] he could find "no recognition of any personal right to bear arms."[20] In short, there is disagreement over who could, or did, own firearms both before and after passage of the English Bill of Rights.

Nearly all writers agree, however, that an accurate reading of the Second Amendment is indispensable to resolving current debates over gun ownership, and that a clarification of the common law tradition is necessary to that reading.[21] There are compelling reasons for this consensus. To begin with, the royal charters that created the new colonies assured potential emigrants that they and their children would "have and enjoye all Liberties and Immunities of free and naturall Subjects . . . as if they and every of them were borne within the Realme of England."[22] Furthermore, the entire body of common law, with the exception of those portions inappropriate to their new situation, crossed the Atlantic with the colonists.[23] The perilous circumstances of the infant colonies made the common law tradition of an armed citizenry both appropriate and crucial to the survival of the plantations.[24] Indeed, the colonies began very early requiring residents to keep firearms and establishing militias.[25]

---

18. Weatherup, *supra* note 5, at 973-74. For the precise English guarantee of the rights of the subject to have arms, see The Bill of Rights, I W. & M., Sess. 2, ch. 2 (1689).

19. 10 H.C. JOUR., 1688-93, 21-22; 1 W. & M., Sess. 2, ch. 2 (1689).

20. Weatherup, *supra* note 5, at 974.

21. *See, e.g.*, Caplan, *supra* note 7, at 53-54; Emery, *The Constitutional Right to Keep and Bear Arms*, 28 HARV. L. REV. 473-75 (1915); Hays, *The Right to Bear Arms, A Study in Judicial Misinterpretation*, 2 WM. & MARY L. REV. 383 (1960); Levin, *supra* note 5, at 148; Weatherup, *supra* note 5, at 964; Whisker, *supra* note 7, at 175-76.

22. Charter of Connecticut, Charles II, 1 THE PUBLIC RECORDS OF THE COLONY OF CONNECTICUT 7 (Hartford 1850) [hereinafter cited as RECORDS OF CONNECTICUT]. *See also* Charter of the Province of Massachusetts-Bay, William and Mary, 1 ACTS AND RESOLVES OF THE PROVINCE OF MASSACHUSETTS BAY 14 (Boston 1869).

23. *See* T. BARNES, THE ENGLISH LEGAL SYSTEM: CARRYOVER TO THE COLONIES 16 (1975).

24. *See, e.g.*, RECORDS OF CONNECTICUT, *supra* note 22, at 285-86; 19 THE COLONIAL RECORDS OF THE STATE OF GEORGIA 137 *passim* (Atlanta 1911); THE BOOK OF THE GENERAL LAWES AND LIBERTYES CONCERNING THE INHABITANTS OF THE MASSACHUSETTS 39-41 (Hunt. Lib. reprint 1975) (1st ed. Boston 1648); 1 RECORDS OF THE COLONY OF RHODE ISLAND AND PROVIDENCE PLANTATIONS IN NEW ENGLAND 77, 94 (Providence 1856); W. BILLINGS, THE OLD DOMINION IN THE SEVENTEENTH CENTURY 172 (1975).

25. *See, e.g.*, ACTS OF THE GRAND ASSEMBLY OF VIRGINIA 1623-24, Nos. 24 & 25; ACTS OF THE GRAND ASSEMBLY OF VIRGINIA 1673, Act 2; THE COMPACT WITH THE CHARTER AND GENERAL LAWS OF THE COLONY OF NEW PLYMOUTH 44-45 (1836); 8 RECORDS OF

There is a further reason for examining the Second Amendment in the light of English legal traditions. Not only did colonists arrive in the new land equipped with an elaborate legal framework, they were for the most part imbued with that attitude of antiauthoritarianism that had fueled the traumatic upheavals of the seventeenth century: the English Civil War of 1642, and the Glorious Revolution of 1688. This general distrust of central power resulted in the English Bill of Rights in 1689 and was to produce the American Bill of Rights a century later. Bernard Bailyn, in *The Ideological Origins of the American Revolution*, is emphatic about there being a connection between English opposition philosophy and American political thought:

> To say simply that this tradition of opposition thought was quickly transmitted to America and widely appreciated there is to understate the fact. Opposition thought, in the form it acquired at the turn of the seventeenth century and in the early eighteenth century, was devoured by the colonists. . . . There seems never to have been a time after the Hanoverian succession when these writings were not central to American political expression or absent from polemical politics.[26]

When they had won their battle to retain the rights of Englishmen, and came to write the federal and state constitutions and draw up the federal Bill of Rights, American statesmen borrowed heavily from English models.[27] Since the federal Bill of Rights, including the Second Amendment, is to a very great extent an example of such borrowing, it behooves us to take a closer look at their English models.

I.   The Traditional Obligation to be Armed[28]

During most of England's history, maintenance of an armed citizenry was neither merely permissive nor cosmetic but essential. Until late in the seventeenth century England had no standing army, and until the nineteenth century no regular police force. The maintenance of order was everyone's business and an armed and active citizenry was

---

CONNECTICUT, *supra* note 22, at 380; 1 COLONIAL LAWS OF NEW YORK 161 (1894); South Carolina Stat. No. 206 (1703).

26. B. BAILYN, THE IDEOLOGICAL ORIGINS OF THE AMERICAN REVOLUTION 43 (1967).

27. *See, e.g.,* 2 THE RECORDS OF THE FEDERAL CONVENTION OF 1787, 509, 617 (M. Ferrand ed. 1911); DEBATES AND PROCEEDINGS IN THE CONVENTION OF THE COMMONWEALTH OF MASSACHUSETTS, HELD IN THE YEAR 1788, 198-99 (Boston 1856); DEBATES AND OTHER PROCEEDINGS OF THE CONVENTION OF VIRGINIA, 1788, 271 (2d ed. Richmond 1805); THE FEDERALIST Nos. 26, 84 (Hamilton).

28. Earlier versions of sections I, II, & III of this article appear in Malcolm, *Disarmed: The Loss of the Right to Bear Arms in Restoration England* (Bunting Inst., Radcliffe College 1980).

written into the system. All able-bodied men between the ages of sixteen and sixty were liable to be summoned to serve on the sheriff's
posse to pursue malefactors or to suppress local disorders.[29] For larger
scale emergencies, such as invasion or insurrection, a civilian militia
was intermittently mustered for military duty.[30] While all able-bodied
males were liable for this service, the practice during the late sixteenth
and seventeenth centuries had been to select a group of men within
each county to be intensively trained.[31] Whenever possible, members
of these trained bands were supposed to be prosperous farmers and
townsmen, but in practice, the rank-and-file were usually men of modest means—small freeholders, craftsmen, or tenant-farmers.[32] They
were, however, invariably led by prestigious members of their community, and commanded by lords lieutenant, who were peers appointed
by, and directly responsible to, the Crown.[33] The effectiveness of the
militia varied with the need for their services, the interest of particular
monarchs, and even with the enthusiasm of individual muster masters
and captains.[34] During some reigns, the trained bands were scarcely
mustered from one year to the next; in others they were drilled with
regularity. In the 1630's, a major effort was made to re-equip these
citizen-soldiers and have them instructed in the latest European military tactics.[35]

The militia and the posse were summoned only occasionally, but
English subjects were frequently involved in everyday police work.
The old common law custom persisted that when a crime occurred citizens were to raise a "hue and cry" to alert their neighbors, and were
expected to pursue the criminals "from town to town, and from county
to county."[36] Villagers who preferred not to get involved were subject
to fine and imprisonment.[37] As an additional incentive to aid in crime

---

29. See R. BURN, 2 THE JUSTICE OF THE PEACE AND PARISH OFFICER 16-20 (London
1755); F. MAITLAND, THE CONSTITUTIONAL HISTORY OF ENGLAND 276-77 (1968) (1st ed.
Cambridge 1908).

30. See ASSIZES OF ARMS, Hen. 2 (1181); STATUTE OF WINCHESTER, Edw. (1285); 4 & 5
Phil. and M., ch. 3 (1557).

31. See C. CRUICKSHANK, ELIZABETH'S ARMY 24-25 (2d ed. 1966).

32. Manuscripts of the sixteenth and seventeenth centuries contain repeated complaints
to this effect. For printed comment, see, e.g., J. MORRILL, CHESHIRE, 1630-1660, 26 (1974);
G. TREVELYAN, ENGLAND UNDER THE STUARTS 187-88 (1928).

33. See C. CRUICKSHANK, supra note 31, at 19-20; H. HALLAM, THE CONSTITUTIONAL
HISTORY OF ENGLAND 386 (London 1870).

34. See, e.g., R. ASHTON, THE ENGLISH CIVIL WAR 55-59, 66 (1978); L. BOYNTON, THE
ELIZABETHAN MILITIA 212 passim, 264-65 (1967); C. CRUICKSHANK, supra note 31, at 5-11.

35. See L. BOYNTON, supra note 34, at 245-54.

36. See R. BURN, supra note 29, at 17-20.

37. See id.

prevention, local residents were expected to make good half the loss caused by robbers or rioters.[38]

The most frequent police duty was the keeping of watch and ward. Town gates were closed from sundown until sunrise and all householders, "sufficiently weaponed" according to the requirement, took turns standing watch at night or ward during that day.[39] Widows, disabled men, and other townsmen unable to carry out the task had to hire substitutes to serve in their stead.[40]

Citizens were not only expected to have suitable weapons at the ready for these duties, but, since passage of the Statute of Winchester in 1285, were assessed according to their wealth for a contribution of arms for the militia.[41] When not in use for musters or emergencies, nearly all of this equipment remained in private hands. A series of later statutes spelled out in detail the arms each household was required to own and the frequency of practice sessions.[42] During the reign of Queen Elizabeth, for example, every family was commanded to provide a bow and two shafts for each son between the ages of seven and seventeen and to train them in their use or be subject to a fine.[43] To promote proficiency in arms, Henry VIII and his successors ordered every village to maintain targets on its green at which local men were to practice shooting "in holy days and other times convenient."[44]

The obligation to own and be skilled in the use of weapons does not, of course, imply that there were no restrictions upon the type of weapon owned or the manner of its use. A statute passed in 1541, for instance, cited the problem of "evil-disposed" persons who daily rode the King's highway armed with crossbows and handguns—weapons easily concealed beneath a cloak—and preyed upon Henry VIII's good subjects. The new law limited ownership of such questionable weapons to persons with incomes over one hundred pounds a year—citizens presumably more trustworthy—whereas those with less income were not to carry a crossbow bent, or a gun charged "except it be in time and

---

38. *See id.*

39. *See id.* at 512.

40. *See id.*

41. *See* STATUTE OF WINCHESTER, Edw. (1285).

42. *See, e.g.*, 2 ACTS & ORDS. INTERREGNUM 397-402 (London 1911); AN ACT FOR SETLING THE MILITIA OF THE COMMONWEALTH OF ENGLAND (London 1650); 4 & 5 Phil. & M., ch. 3 (1557); AN ACT DECLARING THE SOLE RIGHT OF THE MILITIA TO BE IN THE KING, 14 Car. 2, ch. 3 (1662).

43. *See* G. SHARP, TRACTS, CONCERNING THE ANTIENT AND ONLY TRUE LEGAL MEANS OF NATIONAL DEFENCE, BY A FREE MILITIA 12 (London 1782).

44. *Id.* at 13.

service of war."[45] This law, often misinterpreted as restricting all ownership of firearms to the upper classes, merely limited the use of those weapons most common in crime. Indeed, the statute specifically states that it is permissible not only for gentlemen, but for yeomen, servingmen, the inhabitants of cities, boroughs, market towns, and those living outside of towns "to have and keep in every of their houses any such hand-gun or hand-guns, of the length of one whole yard."[46] The use of shot was forbidden, as was the brandishing of a firearm so as to terrify others, and the use of guns in hunting by unqualified persons.[47] It is notable that in cases in which crossbows, handguns, or other weapons were confiscated because of improper use, the courts were at pains to specify that the weapon in question was "noe muskett or such as is used for defence of the realm."[48]

The kingdom's Catholics formed an important exception to the tolerant attitude toward individual ownership of weapons. After the English Reformation they were regarded as potential subversives, and as such were liable to have their arms impounded. They were still assessed for a contribution of weapons for the militia, but were not permitted to keep these in their homes or to serve in the trained bands.[49] They were allowed to keep personal weapons for their defense, although in times of extreme religious tension their homes might be searched and all weapons removed.[50] The various restrictions on Catholic subjects are significant for demonstrating that a particular group could be singled out for special arms controls, but they did not advantage a substantial proportion of the community, for, by the second half of the seventeenth century, Catholics seem to have comprised not more than one in fifty of the English population.[51]

For the great majority of Englishmen there was a natural tendency during tranquil years or in periods of government indifference to become blasé about military duties; complaints of widespread negligence echo through the years. In 1569, a jury presented a grievance "that

---

45. 33 Hen. 8, ch. 6 (1541).

46. *Id.*

47. 2 & 3 Edw. 6, ch. 14 (1549); STATUTE OF NORTHAMPTON, 2 Edw. 3, ch. 3 (1328).

48. W. FISHER, THE FOREST OF ESSEX 214-15 (1887).

49. *See* C. CRUICKSHANK, *supra* note 31, at 24.

50. This occurred, for example, just prior to the outbreak of the English Civil War in 1642. *See* Manning, *The Outbreak of the English Civil War,* in THE ENGLISH CIVIL WAR AND AFTER, 1642-1658, 16 (R. Perry ed. 1970). Charles I empowered Catholics who had been disarmed to rearm in 1642. *See A Discourse of the Warr in Lancashire,* 62 CHETHAM SOC. 12-14 (1864); *Tracts Relating to Military Proceedings in Lancashire during the Great Civil War* 2 CHETHAM SOC. 38-40 (1844).

51. *See* J. JONES, THE REVOLUTION OF 1688 IN ENGLAND 77 n.2 (1972).

there is to much bowling and to little shoting,"[52] and fifty years later, in the 1620's, Charles I had to resort to the closure of alehouses on Sundays to keep men at their shooting practice.[53] In 1621 Sir James Parrett complained of the lamentable decline in the numbers of armed retainers maintained by the wealthy. "Those gentlemen whose grandfathers kept 15 or 17 lusty serveing men and but one or 2 good silver boules to drinke in," he noted, had been succeeded by "grand-children fallen from Charity to impiety [who] keepe scarce 6 men and greate Cubards of plate to noe purpose." Worse still, Parrett reported that public complacency had reached the stage where "in two shyres [there was] not a barrell of Gunn-powder to bee seene."[54]

During the 1620's and 1630's there was a serious effort to modernize the militia, but the increased expenses and requirement of additonal participation aroused popular resistance. Robert Ward, author of a military manual published just prior to the Civil War, was distressed at the failure of many bandsmen to appreciate

how deeply every man is interested in it, for if they did, our yeomandrie would not be so proud and base to refuse to be taught, and to thinke it a shame to serve in their own armes, and to understand the use of them; were they but sensible, that there is not the worth of the peny in a kingdome well secured without the due use of Armes.[55]

Two years later, with the commencement of frantic preparations for civil war and party struggles over public arsenals, the public's attitude had completely altered. Wails of despair were heard from city after city as the royal army confiscated public magazines and disarmed local residents. "The best of it is," a disarmed and distraught townsman of Nantwich wrote, "if we stay at home, we are now their slaves. Being naked they will have of us what they list, and do with us what they list."[56] Forewarned was forearmed, and from 1642 Englishmen learned to hide their firearms and to stockpile weapons.

Nearly twenty years later, this proliferation of privately owned weapons would be regarded by the restored monarch and his supporters as a menace. It was their efforts to control weapons that convinced

52. *See* G. ROBERTS, THE SOCIAL HISTORY OF THE PEOPLE OF THE SOUTHERN COUNTIES OF ENGLAND IN PAST CENTURIES viii-ix (London 1856).
53. *Id.*
54. 6 COMMONS DEBATES 1621, at 318 (1935).
55. R. WARD, ANIMADVERSIONS OF WARRE, OR A MILITAIRE MAGAZINE OF THE TRUEST RULES AND ABLEST INSTRUCTION FOR THE MANAGING OF WARRE 150 (London 1639).
56. *The Latest Remarkable Truths from Worcester, Chester, Salop* in TRACTS RELATING TO THE CIVIL WAR IN CHESHIRE, 1641-1659, *reprinted in* 65 CHETHAM SOC. (n.s.) 238 app. B (1909).

Englishmen that the duty to keep arms must be recognized as a right. The events of the Restoration period, therefore, are of crucial importance.

II. Royal Efforts to Control Arms

To grasp the magnitude of the problem that awaited Charles II upon his return in 1660 it is useful to get some idea of the numbers of firearms kept in private homes. In ordinary times each household was expected to possess arms suitable to its defense, but what was considered suitable? It is possible to obtain an indication of what was regarded as a minimal arsenal by examining the responses of those charged by Charles II's government with stockpiling weapons. For example, in 1660, in reply to allegations that he had concealed weapons, one Robert Hope pleaded that in the past he had, indeed, kept guns for neighbors, but at present he had only "one light rapire and a small birdinge gunne."[57] Hope obviously considered this small stock beyond exception. In 1667, a Catholic subject informed an official that he was "not so well furnished with arms" as formerly, having only two fowling pieces and two swords.[58] Those not suspected of disaffection had, or at least admitted to having, comparatively more weapons. A Buckinghamshire squire kept for private use a pair of pocket pistols, another pair of "screwed" pistols, a suit of light armour, a sword, and a carbine.[59] A country curate in the early eighteenth century, unqualified to hunt and certainly no soldier, nonetheless owned two guns and a blunderbuss.[60] While wealthier citizens usually owned more weapons, firearms seem to have been well distributed throughout the community.[61] Quarter Session records reveal that men charged with illegal use of a gun for hunting were most often poor laborers, small farmers, or

---

57. William Cavendish, Earl of Devonshire, *Correspondence as Lord Lieutenant of Derbyshire from 1660 to 1666*, Additional MS. 34, 306, fol. 12, British Library, London.

58. LeFleming MS, HISTORICAL MANUSCRIPTS COMMISSION, 12TH REPORT, Pt. 7, at 44 (1890).

59. *See* 4 MEMOIRS OF THE VERNEY FAMILY 167 (1899).

60. *See* E. THOMPSON, WHIGS AND HUNTERS 71 (1975).

61. Much evidence of the widespread ownership of firearms is scattered throughout the personal and public documents of this period. The most accessible proof is found in the county quarter session records, some of which are in print, which cite English men and women from all walks of life for misuse of firearms. *See, e.g., Minutes of the Proceedings in Quarter Sessions Held for the Parts of Kesteven in the County of Lincoln, 1674-1695, reprinted in* LINCOLN RECORD SOC. 25, 26 (1931); *Quarter Session Records for the County of Somerset, 1607-77, reprinted in* SOMERSET REC. SOC. 23-24, 28, 34 (1907-19); *Warwick County Records: Quarter Session Order Books, 1625-90, reprinted in* WARWICK COUNTY COUNCIL 6,7 (1935-53); *Worcestershire County Records Division 1: Documents Relating to Quarter Sessions, in* WORCESTERSHIRE HIST. SOC. *passim* (1899-1900).

craftsmen.[62] This is not surprising, since guns abounded during and after the Civil War[63] and seem not to have been beyond the means of the poorer members of the community. In 1664 a musket could be purchased for ten shillings, a sum that would take only a little over a week for a foot soldier in a militia band to accumulate from his wages, and a little more than two weeks for a citizen to afford with the modest wages paid for standing night watch.[64] Used weapons could probably be bought even more cheaply.

The anxious period between Cromwell's death and the arrival of Charles II was no ordinary time, and many citizens began to assemble caches of weapons, some of which turned up years later in homes, churches, and guildhalls throughout the realm.[65] In 1660 a Bristol prebendary notified authorities that the stables of his predecessor's house were full of cannon balls and, even twenty years later, a Shropshire man and his son were found with a cache of some thirty muskets and other guns and admitted to having owned and burned fifty pikes.[66] City officials stockpiled weapons as well, and Northampton and Exeter were among those communities later embarrassed by the disclosure of stocks of arms hidden in public buildings. In 1661 the city of Exeter surrendered 937 musket barrels only to have another hoard of weapons discovered shortly afterwards in the guildhall.[67]

As his subjects and the republican army of some 60,000 men waited, "armed to the teeth," to greet their new monarch, Charles II found himself virtually unarmed. In the months before his arrival public arsenals had suffered such extensive embezzlements that the King's men were unable to find in them "firearms enough . . . to arm three thousand men."[68] The King was careful to conceal the fact "that it might not be known abroad or at home, in how ill a posture he was to defend himself against an enemy."[69]

It is scarcely surprising, therefore, that the wild rejoicing that

---

62. See sources cited supra note 61.

63. See, e.g., E. THOMPSON, supra note 60, at 71; J. WESTERN, THE ENGLISH MILITIA IN THE EIGHTEENTH CENTURY 4, 5 (1965); 4 MEMOIRS OF THE VERNEY FAMILY 167 (1899); Letter from West to Fleming, Jan. 27, 1667, LeFleming MS, supra note 58, at 44.

64. See 92 Clarendon MS 143, Bodleian Library, Oxford.

65. See J. WESTERN, supra note 63, at 4-5.

66. See id.

67. See id. at 4; Privy Council Registers, P.C. 2, vol. 55, fol. 520 (Jan. 22, 1661), Public Record Office, London.

68. E. HYDE, 2 THE LIFE OF EDWARD EARL OF CLARENDON 117 (Oxford 1827).

69. Id.

greeted Charles II upon his return to London in May, 1660[70] failed to disguise from the King the precariousness of his position. He was painfully aware that many of these same citizens had gathered for his father's execution eleven years earlier and that despite its obedient professions, Parliament had never been at "so high a pitch," for "the power which brought in may cast out, if the power and interest be not removed."[71] A study sent to his Court recommended the removal of that power. The anonymous author argued that no prince could be safe "where Lords and Commons are capable of revolt," hence it was essential to disarm the populace and establish a professional army. "It is not the splendor of precious stones and gold, that makes Ennemies submit," he observed, "but the force of armes. The strength of title, and the bare interest of possession will not now defend, the stres will not lye there, the sword is the thing."[72]

Charles agreed completely. But to achieve a shift in the balance of armed might from the general populace to reliable supporters, he needed an obedient police establishment and a series of legal or quasi-legal enactments that would permit the disarmament of his opponents, among whom he counted members of the republican army.[73] In this latter task he had help from Parliament, whose members had learned a lasting distrust of all armies at the hands of Cromwell's soldiers. Parliament speedily devised a scheme to pay off regiments by lot, taking care to secure their weapons "for his Majesty's service."[74] While Charles was relieved to have this particular army disbanded, he was anxious to launch a permanent establishment of his own, and shortly after his return to England secretly began to plan for a force of eight thousand men. A loophole in the disbandment bill permitted the King to maintain as many soldiers as he liked, provided he paid for their upkeep.[75]

The militia was a knottier problem. Both King and Parliament were eager to reestablish the old trained band system, but Parliament was reluctant to confront the numerous difficulties any militia act would have to resolve. A bill submitted at the time of the Restoration had been rejected because many representatives believed its provision

---

70. *See* 3 MEMOIRS ILLUSTRATIVE OF THE LIFE AND WRITINGS OF JOHN EVELYN 246 (deBeer ed. 1955).

71. *Two Treatises Addressed to the Duke of Buckingham*, Lansdowne MS 805, fol. 79 British Library, London.

72. *Id.*

73. *See* 8 H. C. JOUR. 5-6; E. HYDE, *supra* note 68, vol. 1 at 335.

74. *See* 8 H. C. JOUR. 142-43, 161, 163, 167.

75. *See id.* at 167.

for martial law might make Englishmen "wards of an army."[76] The struggle over control of the militia had driven the realm to war in 1642;[77] the issue of royal command would have to be clarified and a militia assessment set, which would involve an evaluation of every subject's property. Despite vigorous pressure from the Court, members of Parliament refused to approve even a temporary militia bill for more than a year.[78] The King, however, was unwilling to wait even a few days before establishing a militia, and was reported within ten days of his return to London to be "settling the militia in all counties by Lords Lieutenants."[79] His right to do so, even in the absence of a valid militia act, does not seem to have been questioned. All candidates for the post of lord lieutenant were carefully screened, and officers were instructed to select bandsmen of unblemished royalist complexion.[80] The resulting force should in no way be seen as representative of the people.

In conjunction with this purged and loyal militia, Charles created a new military body as large again as the militia for which there was far less precedent. It was composed of regiments of volunteers who met at their own, rather than the county's, expense and drilled alongside the regular militia.[81] Both the size of this private army and its longevity were impressive. It continued as an organized force well after the Militia Act of 1662 took effect, and at least through 1667, when the entire militia fell into decline.[82] Although the official task of the volunteers was "to assist on occasion," occasion occurred with great frequency, particularly when such controversial and unpopular duties as the disarmament of fellow subjects were involved.[83]

---

76. 4 PARL. HIST. ENG., 145 (London 1808-20).

77. *See* J. KENYON, THE STUART CONSTITUTION 196 (1966); J. MALCOLM, CAESAR'S DUE: LOYALTY AND KING CHARLES 1642-1646, at 17-21 (1983).

78. A militia act was not passed until the spring of 1662, although a temporary measure was passed a year earlier. *See* 13 Car. 2, ch. 6 (1661); 13 & 14 Car. 2, ch. 3 (1662).

79. HISTORICAL MANUSCRIPTS COMMISSION, 5TH REPORT 153 (1876).

80. *See id.*; *State Papers Domestic, Charles II*, S.P. 29, vol. 11, fols. 146-74 (Aug. 26, 1660), Public Record Office, London; *Instructions to Lords Lieutenants, Whitehall, 1660*, Egerton MS 2542, fol. 512, British Library, London.

81. *See* sources quoted in Malcolm, *supra* note 28, at 8-9.

82. *See, e.g., Letter Book of Thomas Belasyse, Viscount Fauconberg Lord Lieutenant of the North Riding of Yorkshire, 1665-84*, Additional MS 41,254, fols. 20-22, British Library, London, which reported that the militia had not been ordered to muster for several years. *See also* J. WESTERN, *supra* note 63, at 48.

83. *See, e.g., Norfolk Lieutenancy Journal, 1661-1674*, Additional MS 11,601, fol. 29, British Library, London; *Earl of Westmorland Letter Book, 1660-1665, Northamptonshire Militia*, Additional MS 34,222, fols. 25-26, 32, British Library, London; Westmorland to Vane, July 21, 1662, *Clarendon State Papers*, vol. 77, fol. 66a, Bodleian Library, Oxford.

Charles II employed his militia and volunteer regiments differently from the manner in which militia had been used before the Civil War. In place of the occasional muster in time of peace and mobilization during an invasion or rebellion, his men were to be ready for action at an hour's warning.[84] Their main task was to police possible opponents of the regime. Their first order was to monitor the "motions" of persons of "suspected or knowne disaffection" and prevent their meeting or stockpiling weapons.[85] All arms and munitions in the possession of such suspects beyond what they might require for personal defense were to be confiscated.[86]

With this police apparatus in place, the King turned to the royal proclamation, a device of uncertain legal status, to tighten arms control. In September, 1660, he issued a proclamation forbidding footmen to wear swords or to carry other weapons in London.[87] In December another proclamation expressed alarm that many "formerly cashiered Officers and Soldiers, and other dissolute and disaffected persons do daily resort to this City."[88] All such soldiers and others "that cannot give a good Account for their being here" were to leave London within two days and remain at least twenty miles away indefinitely.[89] At the same time the royal government launched a campaign to control firearms at the source. Gunsmiths were ordered to produce a record of all weapons they had manufactured over the past six months together with a list of their purchasers.[90] In future they were commanded to report every Saturday night to the ordnance office the number of guns made and sold that week.[91] Carriers throughout the kingdom were required

---

84. Additional MS 34,306, *supra* note 57, at fol. 14. The King went still further and, for a time, required militia commanders to keep a portion of their men on duty at all times. This scheme proved unworkable. *See* Additional MS 34,222, *supra* note 83, at fol. 43; Additional MS 34,304, fol. 44; D. OGG, ENGLAND IN THE REIGN OF CHARLES II 253 (1967).

85. *Instructions to Lords Lieutenants, Whitehall, 1660*, Egerton MS 2542, *supra* note 80, at fol. 512.

86. *See id.*

87. "*A Proclamation For Suppressing of disorderly and unseasonable Meetings, in Taverns and Tipling Houses, And also forbidding Footmen to wear Swords, or other Weapons, within London, Westminster, and their Liberties*", Sept. 29, 1660, B.M. 669, fol. 26 (13), British Library, London. This and subsequent proclamations cited in this article are calendared in R. STEELE, TUDOR AND STUART PROCLAMATIONS (1910). Originals can be found at the British Library and the citations will be to these.

88. "*A Proclamation commanding all cashiered Soldiers and other Persons that cannot give a good account of their being here to depart out of the Cities of London and Westminster*", Dec. 17, 1660, B.M. 669, fol. 26 (37), British Library, London.

89. *Id.*

90. *See* Privy Council Registers, P.C. 2, vol. 55, fol. 71 (Dec. 1660), Public Record Office, London.

91. *See id.*

to obtain a license if they wished to transport guns, and all importation of firearms was banned.[92]

Events then played into Charles's hands, for on January 6, 1661, an uprising by a handful of religious zealots provided the perfect excuse to crack down on all suspicious persons and to recruit his own standing army. Thomas Venner, a cooper, had led his small band of Fifth Monarchists into the streets of London to launch the prophesied fifth universal monarchy of the world. Although the group was soon subdued,[93] the Court administration blatantly exaggerated the threat they had posed. Speaking to Parliament six months later, the Lord Chancellor characterized the pitiful uprising as the "most desperate and prodigious Rebellion . . . that hath been heard of in any Age" and insisted the plot had "reached very far," and that "there hath not been a Week since that Time in which there hath not been Combinations and Conspiracies formed."[94]

The timing of the Fifth Monarchist uprising was especially opportune, for it occurred the very day the last regiments of the Commonwealth army were due to be disbanded. In response to this visible danger, these regiments were retained and twelve more companies were recruited to form the nucleus of a royalist army.[95] The militia and volunteers throughout the realm were ordered to carry out a general disarmament of everyone of doubtful loyalty.[96] By January 8, 1661, two days after the Venner uprising, Northamptonshire lieutenants reported that all men of known "evill Principles" had been disarmed and secured "so as we have not left them in any ways of power to attempt a breach of the peace."[97]

By the autumn of 1661, with his enemies in prison or at least disarmed and under surveillance, with strict monitoring of both production and distribution of weapons, and with a small standing army and a large police establishment, Charles was ready to disarm the most dan-

---

92. See Privy Council Register, P.C. 2, vol. 55, fol. 187 (Sept. 4, 1661), fol. 189 (Mar. 29, 1661), Public Record Office, London.

93. See Burrage, The Fifth Monarchy Insurrections, 25 THE ENGLISH HIST. REV. 722-47 (1910).

94. 11 H.L. JOUR. 243.

95. See 1 J. CLARKE, THE LIFE OF JAMES THE SECOND, KING OF ENGLAND, ETC. COLLECTED OUT OF MEMOIRS WRIT OF HIS OWN HAND 390-91 (London 1816).

96. See Additional MS. 34,222, supra note 83, at fol. 15.

97. Id. at fol. 17. The seizure of arms and persons was so zealously carried out—a Derbyshire man claimed his house had been searched nine times in one week—that in mid-January the King had to issue a proclamation to reassure outraged Londoners that the customary restrictions against unwarranted search and seizure were still in effect. See B.M. 669, fol. 26 (49), British Library, London.

gerous element of the population—the thousands of disbanded soldiers of the republican army. Acting by proclamation on November 28, he ordered all veterans of that army and all those who had ever fought against the Stuarts to depart from the capital within the week and to remain at least twenty miles away until June 24, 1662.[98] During their six months of banishment the veterans were warned not to "weare, use, or carry or ryde with any sword, pistoll or other armes or weapons."[99] Two days before this proclamation was due to expire, another appeared which extended the ban and the prohibition against carrying arms for an additional six months.[100] The scope of these bans was so broad it is doubtful whether the militia and volunteers were capable of enforcing them. Nevertheless, the proclamations had the practical effect of depriving a large portion of the male population of its legal right to carry firearms.

Endless alarms of plots provided an excuse to keep the militia on full alert, to impose restrictions on the production, importation, and movement of arms, and to create a standing royal army. Parliament cooperated in this policy by passing militia acts in 1661 and 1662 which reaffirmed the King's control of that force and specifically authorized bandsmen to continue the seizure of arms that Charles's militia had been undertaking on the King's orders alone.[101] Any two deputy lieutenants could initiate a search for, and seizure of, arms in the possession of any person whom they judged "dangerous to the Peace of the Kingdom."[102] This definition of those who could be disarmed was less precise than that of any former militia act, and permitted lower ranking officers great latitude in disarming their neighbors.

Charles II's program to police his realm and control its arms demonstrated skill, timing, and resourcefulness. Arriving unarmed in 1660 to confront an armed nation and a veteran republican army, he succeeded within two years in molding the militia and volunteers into a police force of unprecedented size and effectiveness. All possible adversaries were watched, harassed, disarmed, and in many instances imprisoned. And the men of Oliver Cromwell's army, once the pride of England and terror of Europe, were flattened, disbanded, psychologically disarmed, and then actually deprived of their right to carry weap-

---

98. *See* B.M. 1851, ch. 8 (133), (134), (135), British Library, London.

99. *Id.*

100. This proclamation was issued on June 22, 1662. There is no record of a proclamation for 1663, but on November 18, 1664, June 28, 1665, and June 10, 1670, the proclamation was reissued. *See* R. STEELE, *supra* note 87.

101. 13 Car. 2, ch. 6 (1661); 14 Car. 2, ch. 3 (1662).

102. *Id.*

ons. Many members of Parliament were skeptical about the need for such broad powers or the actual danger of rebellion[103] but were content to give the King what he wished as long as their own interests were protected.

III. Parliament's Campaign to Regulate Arms

The royalist aristocrats who flocked to welcome Charles II on his return had every reason to rejoice, for his restoration was theirs as well. After twenty years during which their prestige, pocketbooks, and property had been ravaged by war, revolution, and a republican government, they had an opportunity to restore, and even enhance, their former position. The royalists were to be so successful in this aim that their position by 1688 was described as like that of the barons of Henry III.[104] In order to restore order they were prepared to concede much to the Crown, but jealously guarded the power of the sword and mastery of the localities. They administered local justice, staffed the militia, served in the royal volunteers, and sat in Parliament.[105] The King was dependent upon them to carry out his policies and shore up his regime.[106] For the sake of maintaining their political dominance they acquiesced in the King's program of arms control and, in the Militia Act of 1662, extended the power of militia officers to disarm suspects.[107] But the aristocracy went beyond approving the royal controls. On its own initiative, Parliament passed a game act in 1671 that, for the first time, deprived the vast majority of Englishmen of their legal right to keep weapons.[108]

Game acts had been passed from time to time and were ostensibly designed to protect wild game and to reserve the privilege of hunting for the wealthy. But disarming the rural population was sometimes an

---

103. Sir John Dalrymple observed that in government rhetoric, "mobs were swelled into insurrections, and insurrections into concerted rebellion." J. DALRYMPLE, 1 MEMOIRS OF GREAT BRITAIN AND IRELAND 26 (2d ed. London 1771-73).

104. *See* J. PLUMB, THE GROWTH OF POLITICAL STABILITY ENGLAND, 1675-1725, at 21-22 (1967).

105. *See id.* at 20-21. *See also* C. HILL, REFORMATION TO INDUSTRIAL REVOLUTION 110-11 (1967).

106. The English monarch had only a small bureaucracy and was dependent upon the nobility and, in particular, the gentry throughout the realm to carry out numerous functions of government as unpaid volunteers. In reference to the militia itself, *see* J. WESTERN, *supra* note 63, at 16-17, 63.

107. *See* 13 & 14 Car. 2, ch. 3 (1662-63).

108. *See* 22 & 23 Car. 2, ch. 25 (1671).

underlying motive for their passage.[109] Game acts of the sixteenth and early seventeenth centuries had made possession of certain breeds of dog and possession of equipment specifically designed for hunting illegal for all those not qualified by income to hunt.[110] However, since guns were acknowledged to have legitimate purposes, they were confiscated only if used illegally.[111]

The Game Act passed in 1671 differed from its predecessors in several important respects. To begin with, it raised the property qualification necessary to hunt from forty pounds to one hundred pounds annual income from land, a figure so high that only the nobility, gentry, and a very few yeomen could qualify, whereas all those whose wealth came from a source other than land—such as lawyers and merchants—were forbidden to hunt.[112] This extraordinarily high qualification divided the rural population into two very unequal groups and placed the aristocracy at odds with everyone else. Many critics would later express astonishment that "the legislature of a mighty empire should require one hundred [pounds] a year to shoot a poor partridge, and only forty shillings to vote for a senator!"[113] The qualification to hunt was fifty times that required to vote.

Of more importance, this game law stated that all persons unqualified to hunt, at least ninety-five percent of the population, were not qualified to keep or bear arms. In the language of the statute: "[A]ll and every person and persons, not having Lands and Tenements of the clear yearly value of One hundred pounds . . . are . . . not allowed to have or keep for themselves, or any other person or persons, any Guns,

---

109. The very first game act to set a property qualification on the right to hunt appeared in 1389, eight years after that century's devastating peasant rebellion. The preamble to 13 Ric. 2, ch. 13, "None shall hunt but they which have a sufficient living" read: "Item, for as much as divers artificers, labourers, and servants, and grooms, keep greyhounds and other dogs, and on the holy days, when good christian people be at church, hearing divine service, they go hunting in parks, warrens, and connigries of lords and others, to the very great destruction of the same, and sometimes under such colour they make their assemblies, conferences, and conspiracies for to rise and disobey their allegiance." *See* J. CHITTY, A TREATISE ON THE GAME LAWS, AND ON FISHERIES 368 (2d ed. London 1826); W. HOLDSWORTH, 4 A HISTORY OF ENGLISH LAW 505 (1924).

110. *See* 19 Hen. 7, ch. 11 (1495); 5 Eliz., ch. 21 (1562); 3 Jac. ch. 13 (1605); 7 Jac. ch. 13 (1609); 13 Car. 2, ch. 10 (1663).

111. *See* sources cited *supra* note 110.

112. The Game Act of 1609, in effect until the act of 1671, provided that those who had personal property of £400 were entitled to hunt. This permitted merchants and professionals whose wealth was not based on land to hunt. The Act of 1671, however, abolished this category. *Compare* 7 Jac., ch. 13 (1609) *with* 22 & 23 Car. 2, ch. 25 (1671).

113. J. CHITTY, OBSERVATIONS OF THE GAME LAWS, WITH PROPOSED ALTERATIONS FOR THE PROTECTION AND INCREASE OF GAME, AND THE DECREASE OF CRIME 180 (London 1816).

Bowes, . . . or other Engines."[114] It was no longer necessary to prove illegal use or intent; the mere possession of a firearm was illegal. The new act also empowered owners of forests and parks to appoint game-keepers who, by warrant, could search the homes of persons suspected of harboring weapons, and confiscate any arms they found.[115]

There can be little doubt that it was the intention of the promoters of the Game Act to give themselves the power to disarm their tenants and neighbors and to bolster the position of their class with respect to that of the King and of the wealthy members of the middle class. They had begun to be suspicious of Charles II by 1671, and frightened by a spate of rural violence.[116] Hence, the provision of the Game Act that enabled country squires to set up their own gamekeeper-police and to confiscate the weapons of unqualified persons at their discretion must have seemed most desirable. As James II was to demonstrate, however, it was a statute with great potential for the Crown.

There appears to have been no overt protest or widespread alarm over the royalist program of arms control. While this may have been due to the conviction that such controls were necessary, it seems more likely that the real reason was that the program was not rigidly enforced during the reign of Charles II. It would have been difficult to carry out the proclamations against the carriage of arms by parliamentary veterans, and the militia's disarmament of suspicious persons was always selective.[117] The prosecution of the Game Act of 1671 was left to the gentry and from the scant evidence available appears to have been sporadic.

---

114. 22 & 23 Car. 2, ch. 25 (1671).

115. *Id.*

116. From at least 1665 there was growing distrust of the regime of Charles II. At the beginning of 1667, Samuel Pepys, a civil servant, found the royal court "[a] sad, vicious, negligent Court, and all sober men there fearful of the ruin of the whole kingdom this next year; from which good God, deliver us!" *Cited by* D. WITCOMBE, CHARLES II AND THE CAVALIER HOUSE OF COMMONS, 1663-1674, at 55 (1966); *see* D. OGG, *supra* note 84, at 313; 22 & 23 Car. 2, ch. 7 (1671).

117. Persons judged to be suspicious by the royal administration were those active in the parliamentary party during the Civil War and its aftermath, and those who belonged to the Protestant sects that refused to remain within the Church of England. The Quakers were prominent sufferers. *See, e.g.*, fol. 18, Additional MS 34,306, British Library, London, *and* 13 Car. 2, ch. 6 (1661), a militia act which noted that since June 24, 1660, less than a month after Charles II's return, "divers persons suspected to be fanaticks, sectaries or disturbers of the peace have been assaulted, arrested, detained or imprisoned, [by the militia] and divers arms have been seized and houses searched for arms." The militia had specifically been ordered to disarm all persons "notoriously knowne to be of ill principles or [who] have lately . . . by words or actions shewn any disaffection to his Majestie or his Government, or in any kind disturbed the publique peace." Additional MS 34,222, *supra* note 83, at 15.

After 1680, however, Charles II began to use the Militia Act to disarm his Whig opponents, and in 1686, James II made use of both the Militia Act and the Game Act to disarm his Protestant subjects.[118] Englishmen were outraged and alarmed, and finally convinced of the need to guarantee their right to own weapons. After James II had fled from the kingdom, members of the Convention Parliament convened by William of Orange[119] felt it incumbent upon them to shore up the rights of English subjects before a new monarch ascended the throne. During their discussions, the need for Protestant subjects to have arms came up repeatedly.[120] When the many rights considered most in need of reaffirmation had been pared to thirteen, and a Declaration of Rights presented to William and Mary, the seventh among the "true, ancient, and indubitable" rights proclaimed was the right of all Protestants "to have Arms for their Defence suitable to their Conditions and as allowed by Law."[121]

IV. The English Bill of Rights and the Present Controversy

As an article of the English Bill of Rights, the right to have arms was part and parcel of that bundle of rights and privileges that English-

---

118. *See* J. WESTERN, *supra* note 63, at 48-51; CALENDAR OF STATE PAPERS DOMESTIC, 1686-87, at 314 (1964).

119. James II decided to abandon his kingdom in the face of a growing army of his subjects led by William of Orange and the desertion of his own army. The realm was thrown into a constitutional crisis, as no Parliament was in session and only the king could legally summon a parliament. William consulted with the nobility and former members of the Commons and on their advice summoned a convention parliament to meet to resolve the kingdom's succession. He promised to abide by its decision. A convention parliament had been called in 1659 by George Monck, again in the absence of a reigning monarch, and it was this body that invited Charles II to return as king. Unlike its predecessor, however, the Convention Parliament of 1688 was determined to ensure the rights of subjects and to prevent any infringement by future monarchs. *See infra* sources cited at note 120.

120. We have only sketchy records remaining of the debates of the Convention Parliament. The best of these in print are the notes made by John Somers, chairman of the committee that drafted the English Bill of Rights *reprinted in* 2 MISCELLANEOUS STATE PAPERS FROM 1501 TO 1726 *passim* & esp. 407-18 (London 1778). Somers's notes are punctuated with the angry comments of members at the use of the Militia Act in particular to disarm law-abiding citizens. Sir John Maynard was furious that "an Act of Parliament was made to disarm all Englishmen, whom the lieutenant should suspect, by day or night, by force or otherwise" and branded it "an abominable thing to disarm a nation, to set up a standing army." *Id.* at 407. Another member argued that there was "no safety but the consent of the nation—the constitution being limited, there is a good foundation for defensive arms—It has given us right to demand full and ample security." *Id.* at 410. *See also* L. SCHWOERER, THE DECLARATION OF RIGHTS, 1689 (1981) (a recent study of the Convention Parliament).

121. 1 W. & M., Sess. 2, ch. 2 (1689). The English Declaration of Rights drawn up by the Convention Parliament was approved by the first parliament summoned by William and Mary and incorporated with the legislation recognizing them as king and queen. It was thereafter known as the English Bill of Rights.

men carried with them to America and which they later fought to preserve. Much of the present confusion over the Second Amendment to the United States Constitution stems from the failure to understand the meaning or to determine the effect of the English right—problems that can both be finally solved by a careful reading of the historic record.

Roy Weatherup is one of several authors who fail in the attempt to fix the meaning of the English right by slipping into the common trap of imposing a modern controversy upon past events.[122] Weatherup is so caught up in the debate over the reference to the militia in the Second Amendment and the attendant quarrel over whether that amendment conveys a collective or an individual right[123] that he totally ignores the fact that the English right to arms makes no mention whatsoever of the militia. Undeterred, Weatherup insists that the English right conveyed "no recognition of any personal right to bear arms on the part of subjects generally" but merely granted members of the militia the right to "keep and bear arms in accordance with their militia duties."[124] Such an interpretation ignores the clear language of the English right and disregards the accompanying historic record. The militia was certainly of grave concern to members of the Convention Parliament, but this was not because members of the militia had been disarmed. Quite the contrary. The militia was a problem because the Militia Act of 1662 had permitted its officers wide latitude to disarm *law-abiding citizens*. The correction of this abuse and many others that preoccupied the members required new legislation which, they reluctantly admitted, in the present emergency they did not have the leisure to draft.[125] Instead, they decided to concentrate their energies upon reaffirming those ancient rights most recently imperiled through a declaration of rights they hoped would be "like a new magna charta."[126] Legislative reform was meant to follow when time allowed.

Weatherup is somewhat nearer the mark in his assertion that a collective right was intended.[127] A collective right to arms was discussed by the Convention, but it was rejected in favor of an individual

---

122. *See* Weatherup, *supra* note 5.

123. *See id.* at 962-64.

124. *Id.* at 973-74.

125. *Anonymous Account of the Convention Proceeding, 1688*, Rawlinson MS D1079, fol. 10, Bodleian Library, Oxford. The committee was instructed "to distinguish such of the . . . heads [of grievances] as are introductory of new laws, from those that are declaratory of ancient rights." The revised version of their report can be found in 10 H.C. JOUR. 1688-93, at 21-22.

126. *See* G. BURNET, 2 BISHOP BURNET'S HISTORY OF HIS OWN TIME 534 (London 1840).

127. *See* Weatherup, *supra* note 5, at 974.

right alone. The Whig members of the Convention had pressed hard for a collective as well as an individual right[128] and the first version of the arms article adhered to their view that the public should be armed to protect their rights:

> It is necessary for the publick Safety, that the Subjects which are Protestants, should provide and keep Arms for their common Defence. And that the Arms which have been seized, and taken from them, be restored.[129]

The second version of this article retreated somewhat from this stance. It stated:

> That the Subjects, which are Protestants, may provide and keep Arms, for their common Defence.[130]

All mention of arms being "necessary for the publick Safety" was omitted although this version still asserts that arms could be kept for "common" defense; instead of the exhortation that citizens "should" provide and keep arms, the permissive "may" is used.

It was the third, and final version, however, that constituted a complete retreat from any collective right to have arms. It read:

> That the Subjects which are Protestants may have Arms for their Defence suitable to their Conditions, and as allowed by Law.[131]

The reference to a need for arms for "their common Defence" was replaced by the right to keep arms for "their Defence," and two modifying clauses were added at the last moment at the instigation of the cautious House of Lords.

In the opinion of a modern British scholar, the retreat from a collective to an exclusively individual right to have arms "emasculated" the article: "The original wording implied that everyone had a duty to be ready to appear in arms whenever the state was threatened. The revised wording suggested only that it was lawful to keep a blunderbuss to repel burglars."[132] The Whigs continued to press for the notion that it was necessary for the safety of the constitution that subjects be armed and, in the course of the eighteenth century, Blackstone among others

---

128. The Whigs had sizable majorities on the committes which drafted the Declaration of Rights, and those most outspoken in favor of a general possession of arms for the purpose of resisting tyranny were Whigs. See L. SCHWOERER, supra note 120, at 152; and members quoted in J. SOMERS, supra note 120, at 107-18, with their affiliation as described by Schwoerer. See also D. LACEY, DISSENT AND PARLIAMENTARY POLITICS IN ENGLAND, 1661-1689, at 382-83, 422-23 (1969).

129. Rawlinson MS D1079, supra note 125, at fol. 8.

130. 10 H.C. JOUR., 1688-93, at 21-22.

131. 1 W. & M., Sess. 2, ch. 2 (1689).

132. J. WESTERN, MONARCHY AND REVOLUTION: THE ENGLISH STATE IN THE 1680's, 339 (1972).

reinterpreted the English right to arms to include that position.[133] At the time it was drafted, however, the English right to have arms was solely an individual right. By the outbreak of the American Revolution, it had been transformed into both an individual and a collective right.

The actual impact of the English right as stated in the new Bill of Rights is far more difficult to determine than its meaning. Modern critics have argued that the limitation to Protestants of the right to have arms and the qualifying clauses further restricting lawful possession by Protestants to those weapons "suitable to their conditions" and "as allowed by Law" made this right so exclusive and uncertain as to be "more nominal than real."[134] But if, at first glance, the article's exclusiveness appears striking, much hinges on how these clauses, added at the last moment, were in fact interpreted. There is no doubt that "as allowed by law" included those sixteenth century laws which placed certain restrictions on the type of arms subjects could own, but did not deprive Protestant subjects of their right to have firearms.[135] However, the Game Act of 1671 was in direct conflict with that right. Since the Convention Parliament had agreed to restate rights but leave legislative reform for the future,[136] it is not surprising that the right to have arms contradicted laws still on the statute books. The best means of determining the extent to which the qualifying clauses limited ownership of firearms is to examine subsequent legislation and those legal cases that decided permissible use.

Early in the reign of William and Mary, Parliament approved two acts affecting arms ownership: "An Act for the better securing the Government by disarming Papists and reputed Papists" in 1689,[137] and, in 1692, "An Act for the more easie Discovery and Conviction of such as shall Destroy the Game of this Kingdom."[138] A militia act was also

---

133. For examples of Whig efforts to incorporate into legislation their view that the citizenry must be armed to prevent tyranny, see 10 H.C. JOUR. 621; 5 PARL. HIST. ENG., *supra* note 76, at 344; N. LUTTRELL, THE PARLIAMENTARY DIARY OF NARCISSUS LUTTRELL, 1691-1693, at 444 (H. Horwitz ed. 1972). *See also* 2 W. BLACKSTONE, COMMENTARIES 441 (E. Christian ed. London 1793-95) (editor's comment); and 1 W. BLACKSTONE, *surpa* note 2, at * 140-41.

134. G. NEWTON & F. ZIMRING, *supra* note 5, at 255 (quoting from 2 J. STORY, COMMENTARIES ON THE CONSTITUTION 678 (3d ed. 1858)).

135. These acts were: 33 Henry 8, ch. 6 (1541) and 2 & 3 Edw. 6, ch. 14 (1549). For evidence of their continued enforcement, see sources cited *supra* note 61 (relating to quarter session records); G. SHARP, *supra* note 43, at 17-18; Rex v. Alsop, 4 Mod. Rep. 51 (K.B. 1691).

136. *See supra* notes 125-26 and accompanying text.

137. 1 W. & M., ch. 15 (1689).

138. 4 & 5 W. & M., ch. 23 (1692).

approved by the House of Commons in July 1689, but failed to pass the House of Lords.[139] The first of these acts, the act for disarming Catholics, was meant to secure the realm against a rising on behalf of the deposed Catholic king, James II. It prohibited Catholics from keeping all "Arms, Weapons, Gunpowder, or Ammunition," but did permit a Catholic to retain those weapons that local justices at Quarter Sessions thought necessary "for the Defence of his House or Person."[140] This exception is especially significant, as it demonstrates that even when there were fears of religious war, Catholic Englishmen were permitted the means to defend themselves and their households; they were merely forbidden to stockpile arms. The need for individual self-defense was conceded to have precedence over other considerations. Furthermore, while the Bill of Rights excluded Catholics from any absolute right to have arms, members of that faith were, in practice, accorded the privilege of retaining some weapons.

In 1692, Parliament passed a game statute designed to supercede all previous game acts.[141] This act incorporated many articles of the Game Act of 1671, but altered that act's ban on ownership of firearms by persons unqualified to hunt by omitting all mention of guns from the list of forbidden devices. Whereas the Game Act of 1671 stated that persons not qualified to hunt were "not allowed to have or keep for themselves, or any other person or persons, any Guns, Bowes, Greyhounds . . . or other Engines,"[142] the new act prohibited such persons from keeping and using "any bows, greyhounds . . . or any other instruments for destruction of . . . game."[143] According to the rule of law of that era, a later statute expressed in terms contrary to those of a former statute takes away the force of the first statute even without express negative words.[144] Of course, it was possible that guns could be included among "other instruments for destruction of . . . game." All evidence, however, points to the intentional exclusion of firearms from the terms of the statute.

---

139. In July, 1689, members of the House of Commons passed a measure "for ordering the Forces in the several Counties of this Kingdom," which was designed to make the militia more efficient, to strengthen local control over it, and to eliminate its powers to search for and seize weapons of so-called suspects. The measure ran into opposition in the House of Lords and was lost when the King dissolved Parliament. *See* J. WESTERN, *supra* note 132, at 340 n.1, 343; J. WESTERN, *supra* note 63, at 85-89; 5 PARL. HIST. ENG., *supra* note 76, at 344.

140. 1 W. & M. ch. 15 (1689).

141. 4 & 5 W. & M., ch. 23 (1692).

142. 22 Car. 2, ch. 25 (1671).

143. 4 & 5 W. & M., *supra* note 141.

144. H. ROLLE, REPORTS 91 (London 1675).

The House of Commons journals reveal the sensitivity of members to the new act's potential for disarming Englishmen. At the time of the bill's third reading, an engrossed clause, offered as a rider, stated that "any Protestant may keep a Musquet in his House, notwithstanding this or any other Act."[145] This was a very sweeping proposal, as it made no allowance for factors such as the sanity or previous criminality of the gun owner, and would, moreover, have purportedly bound future parliaments—something no session was really at liberty to do.[146] On the question of whether this rider should have a second reading, there was sufficient controversy to compel a division. The proposal lost by sixty-five votes to one hundred sixty-nine.[147] Despite its failure to become part of the new game act, it is of interest for two reasons: first, because it indicated the awareness of members that a game act could jeopardize the right of Protestants to have arms; second, because although it was an extreme proposal, it was not dismissed out of hand but occasioned a rare division in the House of Commons.

There is a frustrating lack of commentary or cases bearing on the issue of whether the omission of guns from the list of proscribed devices in the Game Act of 1692 should be regarded as legalizing their ownership, or whether firearms ought to be included under "any other engine." But the fact that there is no recorded instance of anyone charged under the new act for mere possession of a firearm, coupled with decisions from cases under a later law with similar language,[148] lends weight to the conclusion that guns were meant to be excluded from the terms of the statute.

In reference to the successor to the Game Act of 1692, "An act for the better preservation of the game," passed in 1706,[149] Joseph Chitty, an expert on game law, notes: "We find that guns which were expressly mentioned in the former acts were purposely omitted in this because it

---

145. 10 H.C. JOUR. 824.
146. A future parliament was always at liberty to amend a statute or to repeal it. During the debate on this rider an opponent of the measure argued that it "savours of the politics to arm the mob, which I think is not very safe for any government." See N. LUTTRELL, supra note 133, at 444. The Whig view expressed later by Blackstone did not yet prevail.
147. 10 H.C. JOUR. 824.
148. See 5 Ann, ch. 14 (1706). This statute levied a fine against any person or persons "not qualified by the laws of this realm so to do" who "shall keep or use any greyhounds, setting dogs . . . or any other engines to kill and destroy the game." Id.
The Devonshire Quarter Sessions clearly regarded the possession of firearms as legal after passage of the 1692 Game Act, for in 1704 it explained that while the houses of unqualified persons could be searched for dogs, nets and other "engines," no Protestant was to be deprived of his gun. See A.H.A. HAMILTON, QUARTER SESSIONS FROM QUEEN ELIZABETH TO QUEEN ANN 289 (1878).
149. 5 Ann, ch. 14 (1706).

might be attended with great inconvenience to render the mere possession of a gun *prima facie* evidence of its being kept for an unlawful
purpose."[150] Two cases brought under that game act dealt specifically
with the question of the inclusion of firearms under prohibited devices.
Perhaps the most important of these was *Rex v. Gardner*,[151] in which
the defendant had been convicted by a justice of the peace for keeping
a gun in alleged violation of the Game Act. There was no evidence
that the gun in question had been wrongfully used. But it was argued
that a gun was mentioned in the 1671 Game Act[152] and considered
there as an engine, and that the use of the general words "other engines" in the 1706 Act should be taken to include a gun.[153] It was objected "that a gun is not mentioned in the statute [of 1706], and though
there may be many things for the bare keeping of which a man may be
convicted, yet they are only such as can only be used for destruction of
the game, whereas a gun is necessary for defence of a house, or for a
farmer to shoot crows."[154]

The court concluded that "a gun differs from nets and dogs, which
can only be kept for an ill purpose, and therefore this conviction must
be quashed."[155] The justices reasoned:

> [I]f the statute is to be construed so largely, as to extend to the
> bare having of any instrument, that may possibly be used in de-
> stroying game, it will be attended with very great inconvenience;
> there being scarce any, tho' ever so useful, but what may be ap-
> plied to that purpose. And tho' a gun may be used in destroying
> game, and when it is so, doth then fall within the words of the
> act; yet as it is an instrument proper, and frequently necessary to
> be kept and used for other purposes, as the killing of noxious
> vermin, and the like, it is not the having a gun, without applying
> it in the destruction of game, that is prohibited by the act.[156]

Indeed, Lord Macclesfield commented in this regard that he himself
was in the House of Commons when that game act was drafted and
personally objected to the insertion of the word gun therein "because it
might be attended with great inconvenience."[157]

---

150. J. CHITTY, *supra* note 109, at 83 & note c.

151. Rex v. Gardner, Strange, 2 Reports 1098, 93 Eng. Rep. 1056 (K.B. 1739); 1 R.
BURN, *supra* note 29, at 442-43.

152. *See supra* text accompanying note 114.

153. Rex v. Gardner, 93 Eng. Rep. at 1056.

154. *Id*.

155. *Id*.

156. *Id*.

157. 1 R. BURN, *supra* note 29, at 443. Lord Macclesfield sat on an earlier case, King v.
King, 3 Geo. 2, in which the question of whether guns were intentionally omitted from the

In *Wingfield v. Stratford & Osman*,[158] appellant challenged his conviction under the Game Act and the confiscation of his gun and dog, the dog being a setting dog, the gun allegedly "an engine" for killing of game. The prosecution's plea was held faulty because it amounted to a general issue,[159] but the court pointed out that it would have held for appellant in any case as the prosecution had not alleged that the gun had been used for killing game:

> It is not to be imagined, that it was the Intention of the Legislature, in making the 5 Ann.c.14 to disarm all the People of England. As Greyhounds, Setting Dogs . . . are expressly mentioned in that Statute, it is never necessary to alledge, that any of these have been used for killing or destroying the Game; and the rather, as they can scarcely be kept for any other Purpose than to kill or destroy the Game. But as Guns are not expressly mentioned in that Statute, and as a Gun may be kept for the Defence of a Man's House, and for divers other lawful Purposes, it was necessary to alledge, in order to its being comprehended within the Meaning of the Words "any other Engines to kill the Game", that the Gun had been used for killing the Game.[160]

By the middle of the eighteenth century, therefore, English courts could not "imagine" that Parliament intended to disarm the people of England.

In 1775, the American colonists fought for what they regarded as the rights of Englishmen.[161] Fortunately, there is ample contemporary evidence defining exactly what the rights of Englishmen were at that time in respect to the keeping and bearing of arms. In 1782, Granville Sharp, an English supporter of the American cause, wrote that no Englishman "can be truly Loyal" who opposed the principles of English law whereby the people are required to have "arms of defence and peace, for mutual as well as private defence."[162] He argued that the laws of England "always required the people to be armed, and not only

---

statute was raised but never determined. This is noted in the *Gardner* decision, along with his comments. *See* 93 Eng. Rep. at 1056.

158. Wingfield v. Stratford & Osman, Sayer, Reports 15-17, 96 Eng. Rep. 787 (K.B. 1752).

159. *Id.* at 16, 96 Eng. Rep. at 787.

160. *Id.* (Lee, C.J., concurring).

161. For extensive treatment of this subject *see* B. BAILYN, *supra* note 26. Bailyn writes, for example: "For the primary goal of the American Revolution, which transformed American life and introduced a new era in human history, was not the overthrow or even the alteration of the existing social order but the preservation of political liberty threatened by the apparent corruption of the [English] constitution, and the establishment in principle of the existing conditions of liberty." *Id.* at 19.

162. G. SHARP, *supra* note 43, at 18, 27.

to be *armed*, but to be *expert in arms*."[163] Edward Christian noted in his edition of Blackstone's *Commentaries*, published in 1793, that "ever since the modern practice of killing game with a gun had prevailed, everyone is at liberty to keep or carry a gun, if he does not use it for the destruction of game."[164] But the most definitive opinion on the rights of Englishmen "to bear arms, and to instruct themselves in the use of them" came from the Recorder of London, the chief legal adviser to the mayor and council, in 1780. He stated:

> The right of his majesty's Protestant subjects, to have arms for their own defence, and to use them for lawful purposes, is most clear and undeniable. It seems, indeed, to be considered, by the ancient laws of this kindom, not only as a *right*, but as a *duty*; for all the subjects of the realm, who are able to bear arms, are bound to be ready, at all times, to assist the sheriff, and other civil magistrates, in the execution of the laws and the preservation of the public peace. And that right, which every Protestant most unquestionably possesses, *individually*, *may*, and in many cases *must*, be exercised collectively, is likewise a point which I conceive to be most clearly established by the authority of judicial decisions and ancient acts of parliament, as well as by reason and common sense.[165]

V. Conclusion

Prior to the Restoration, Englishmen had the obligation to be armed for the public defense and the privilege of keeping arms for their personal defense. During the reigns of Charles II and James II, from 1660 to 1688, the Court and Parliament passed laws and issued proclamations that severely restricted the rights of the people to possess firearms, and followed a policy designed to control production and distribution of weapons. The English Bill of Rights of 1689, however, not only reasserted, but guaranteed, the right of Protestant subjects to be armed. The qualifying clauses of the Bill that appear to limit arms ownership were, in fact, interpreted in a way that permitted Catholics to have personal weapons and allowed Protestants, regardless of their social and economic station, to own firearms. The ancillary clause "as allowed by Law" merely limited the type of weapon that could be legally owned to a full-length firearm, enforced the ban on shot, and permitted legal definition of appropriate use. The right of Englishmen to have arms was a very real and an individual right. For all able-bodied

---

163. *Id.* at 18.
164. 2 W. BLACKSTONE, COMMENTARIES 411 (E. Christian ed. 1793-95).
165. W. BLIZARD, DESULTORY REFLECTIONS ON POLICE 59-60 (London 1785) (emphasis in original).

men there was also the civic duty to bear arms in the militia. The twin concepts of a people armed and a people trained to arms were linked, but not inseparably.

If one applies English rights and practice to the construction of the Second Amendment to the United States Constitution, it is clear that the Amendment's first clause is an amplifying rather than a qualifying clause, and that a general rather than a select militia was intended. In fact, every American colony formed a militia that, like its English model, comprised all able-bodied male citizens.[166] This continued to be the practice when the young republic passed its first uniform militia act under its new constitution in 1792.[167] Such a militia implied a people armed and trained to arms.

The Second Amendment should properly be read to extend to every citizen the right to have arms for personal defense. This right was a legacy of the English, whose right to have arms was, at base, as much a personal right as a collective duty. It is significant that the American right to keep arms was unfettered, unlike the English right, which was limited in various ways throughout its development.

Thus, in guaranteeing the individual right to keep and bear arms, and the collective right to maintain a general militia, the Second Amendment amplified the tradition of the English Bill of Rights for the purpose of preserving and protecting government by and for the people.

---

166. *See supra* notes 24-25 and accompanying text.

167. That act stipulated that "each and every free able-bodied white male citizen . . . between the ages of 18 and 45 . . . shall severally and respectively be enrolled in the militia." Act of May 8, 1792, 2d Cong., 1st Sess., ch. 33.

The Ideological Origins of the Second Amendment

Robert E. Shalhope

> A well regulated Militia, being necessary to the
> security of a free State, the right of the people to
> keep and bear Arms, shall not be infringed.

Since its ratification in 1791 the Second Amendment has remained in relative obscurity. Virtually ignored by the Supreme Court, the amendment has been termed "obsolete," "defunct," and an "unused provision" with no meaning for the twentieth century by scholars dealing with the Bill of Rights.[1] And yet, many Americans consider this amendment as vital to their liberties today as did the founders nearly two hundred years ago. Their sense of urgency arises from the current debate over gun control.

Disagreements over gun legislation reveal disparate perceptions of American society that rest upon, or inspire, dissimilar interpretations of the Second Amendment. Opponents of restrictive measures emphasize the free individual's rights and privileges and adamantly contend that the "right to bear arms" phrase constitutes the essence of the amendment. Their bumper stickers—modern day cockades—declare: "When guns are outlawed only outlaws will have guns," or "Hitler got his start registering guns." These simplistic ideas, symbolic of much deeper and more complex ideological beliefs, gain sustenance from a wide variety of popular sources. It is the National Rifle Association (NRA), however, that transforms this popular impulse into one of the most powerful and active lobbies in Washington. Its magazine, *The American Rifleman*, clearly states the issue: "The NRA, the foremost guardian of the traditional American right to 'keep and bear arms,' believes that every law-abiding citizen is entitled to the ownership and legal use of firearms."[2]

For their part, advocates of restrictive gun legislation emphasize collective rights and communal responsibilities. In order to protect society from the violence they associate with armed individuals, these people stress the "well reg-

---

Robert E. Shalhope is professor of history at the University of Oklahoma.

[1] Edward Dumbauld, *The Bill of Rights: And What It Means Today* (Norman, Okla., 1957), 60, 62; Robert Allen Rutland, *The Birth of the Bill of Rights, 1776-1791* (Chapel Hill, 1955), 229.

[2] This message appears on the title page of each issue of the magazine.

ulated Militia" phrase within the Second Amendment. Irving Brant's *The Bill of Rights* typifies their position. Claiming that the Second Amendment, "popularly misread, comes to life chiefly on the parade floats of rifle associations," Brant contends that the amendment's true purpose was "to forbid Congress to prohibit the maintenance of a state militia." Therefore, by its very nature, "that amendment cannot be transformed into a personal right to bear arms, enforceable by federal compulsion upon the states."[3] The President's Commission on Law Enforcement and Administration of Justice (1967) reiterated this belief even more forcefully: "The U.S. Supreme Court and lower Federal courts have consistently interpreted this Amendment only as a prohibition against Federal interference with State militia and not as a guarantee of an individual's right to keep or carry firearms." Therefore, the commission concluded: "The argument that the Second Amendment prohibits State or Federal regulation of citizen ownership of firearms has no validity whatsoever."[4]

This bifurcation of the Second Amendment into its two separate phrases invariably rests upon appeals to history. Advocates of both sides draw upon the same historical data but interpret them differently in light of their present-day beliefs.[5] Opponents of gun control keep emphasizing the individualistic character of the founders whereas supporters of restrictive legislation keep insisting that these men were far more concerned with the collective behavior of Americans. Given this impasse, an attempt to understand the origins of the amendment within the perspective of the late eighteenth, rather than that of the late twentieth, century should provide useful insights into both the beliefs of the founders and the intent of the amendment.

[3] Irving Brant, *The Bill of Rights: Its Origin and Meaning* (Indianapolis, 1965), 486–87.

[4] *The Challenge of Crime in a Free Society: A Report by the President's Commission on Law Enforcement and Administration of Justice* (Washington, 1967), 242. Sen. Edward Kennedy, too, claims that the "Supreme Court has repeatedly said that this amendment has nothing to do with the right to personal ownership of guns but only with the right of a state to establish a militia." Edward M. Kennedy, "The Need for Gun Control Legislation," *Current History*, 71 (July/Aug. 1976), 27. These observations state the case more definitively than the evidence warrants. The Supreme Court has touched upon the Second Amendment in four cases: *United States* v. *Cruikshank* (1876); *Presser* v. *Illinois* (1886); *Miller* v. *Texas* (1894); and *United States* v. *Miller* (1939). In only one of these cases, *United States* v. *Miller*, did the court relate gun ownership to the militia. Lower federal court and state court decisions regarding the Second Amendment are simply a labyrinth of judicial interpretation. For detailed analyses of these cases, see Robert A. Sprecher, "The Lost Amendment," *American Bar Association Journal*, 51 (June 1965), 554–57; *ibid.* (July, 1965), 665–69; Stuart R. Hays, "The Right to Bear Arms, a Study in Judicial Misinterpretation," *William and Mary Law Review*, 2 (no. 2, 1960), 381–406; Ronald B. Levine and David B. Saxe, "The Second Amendment: The Right to Bear Arms," *Houston Law Review*, 7 (Sept. 1969), 1–19; and Ralph J. Rohner, "The Right to Bear Arms: A Phenomenon of Constitutional History," *Catholic University of America Law Review*, 16 (Sept. 1966), 53–84.

[5] The following essays deal with identical material (English Bill of Rights, Sir William Blackstone, colonial declarations, and state bills of rights) and yet reach diametrically opposed conclusions. Peter Buck Feller and Karl L. Gotting, "The Second Amendment: A Second Look," *Northwestern University Law Review*, 61 (March-April 1966), 46–70; Lucilius A. Emery, "The Constitutional Right to Keep and Bear Arms," *Harvard Law Review*, 28 (March 1915), 473–77; and Rohner, "Right to Bear Arms," argue that the amendment supports the collective right of state militias to bear arms. However, Sprecher, "Lost Amendment"; Hays, "Right to Bear Arms"; Levine and Saxe, "Second Amendment"; and Nicholas Olds, "The Second Amendment and the Right to Keep and Bear Arms," *Michigan State Bar Journal*, 46 (Oct. 1967), 15–25, contend that it protects individual rights to keep arms.

During the last several decades many scholars dealing with the Revolution have labored to reconstruct the participants' view of their era as a primary means of understanding the period.[6] As a result we now recognize the importance of "republicanism," a distinctive universe of ideas and beliefs, in shaping contemporary perceptions of late-eighteenth-century American society. Within such a political culture thoughts regarding government were integrated into a much larger configuration of beliefs about human behavior and the social process. Drawing heavily upon the libertarian thought of the English commonwealthmen, colonial Americans believed that a republic's very existence depended upon the character and spirit of its citizens. A people noted for their frugality, industry, independence, and courage were good republican stock. Those intent upon luxury lost first their desire and then their ability to protect and maintain a republican society. Republics survived only through the constant protection of the realm of Liberty from the ceaselessly aggressive forces of Power. America would remain a bastion of Liberty, in stark contrast to the decadent and corrupt societies of Europe, only so long as its people retained their virility and their virtue.

The historical literature devoted to explicating American republicanism has grown immense. Among the strands of thought most commonly discussed as central to this persuasion two are immediately relevant to understanding the Second Amendment. These are the fear of standing armies and the exaltation of militias composed of ordinary citizens. There is, however, an equally vital theme contained in libertarian literature which, except in the work of J. G. A. Pocock, has been largely ignored in the recent literature dealing with republicanism. This is the dynamic relationship that libertarian writers believed existed between arms, the individual, and society. To gain a fuller comprehension of the origins of the Second Amendment it is essential therefore to understand the place of the armed citizen in libertarian thought and the manner in which this theme became an integral part of American republicanism.

In order to delineate libertarian beliefs regarding the relationship between arms and society it is necessary to start with the Florentine tradition upon which republican thought drew so heavily.[7] This tradition, articulated most clearly by Niccolò Machiavelli, idealized the citizen-warrior as the staunchest bulwark of a republic. For Machiavelli the most dependable protection against corruption was the economic independence of the citizen and his ability and willingness to become a warrior. From this developed a sociology of liberty that rested upon the role of arms in society: political conditions must allow the arming of all citizens; moral conditions must be such that all citizens would willingly fight for the republic; and economic conditions must provide the citizen-soldier a home and occupation outside the army. This theme,

[6] This literature is reviewed in Robert E. Shalhope, "Toward a Republican Synthesis: The Emergence of an Understanding of Republicanism in American Historiography," *William and Mary Quarterly*, 29 (Jan. 1972), 49-80, and Robert E. Shalhope, "Republicanism and Early American Historiography," *ibid.*, 39 (April 1982), 334-56.

[7] The following discussion of Niccolò Machiavelli is drawn from J. G. A. Pocock, *The Machiavellian Moment: Florentine Political Thought and the Atlantic Republican Tradition* (Princeton, 1975), esp. 199-213, 290-92.

relating arms and civic virtue, runs throughout Machiavelli, and from it emerged the belief that arms and a full array of civic rights were inseparable. To deny arms to some men while allowing them to others was an intolerable denial of freedom. Machiavelli's belief that arms were essential to liberty—in order for the individual citizen to protect himself, to hunt, to defend his state against foreign invasion, to keep his rulers honest, and to maintain his republican character—provided an important foundation upon which subsequent republican writers could build.

With the passage of time the essential character of Florentine thought, which emphasized a connection between the distribution of arms within a society and the prevalence of aristocracy or republicanism, liberty or corruption, remained vital to many writers. Both Sir Walter Raleigh and Jean Bodin stressed the relationship between arms and the form of government and society that emerged within a nation. Indeed Raleigh enunciated several "sophisms" of the tyrant. Among these were: "To unarm his people of weapons, money, and all means whereby they may resist his power." The more subtle tyrant followed this rule: "To unarm his people, and store up their weapons, under pretence of keeping them safe, and having them ready when service requireth, and then to arm them with such, and as many as he shall think meet, and to commit them to such as are sure men."[8] For his part, Bodin, philosopher of the French monarchy, emphasized the essential difference between democratic societies and monarchies regarding arms. He believed that monarchs courted disaster by arming the common people for "it is to be feared they will attempt to change the state, to have a part in the government." In a monarchy "the most usuall way to prevent sedition, is to take away the subjects armes." Where democracy was the rule the general populace could be and should be armed.[9]

The English libertarian writers in the latter half of the seventeenth century amplified and shaped the Florentine tradition in response to changing circumstances. Marchamont Nedham declared that a republican society and government rested upon the popular possession of arms as well as on the regular election of magistrates and representatives. Convinced that free states could survive and remain virtuous only if their citizens were familiar with the use of arms, Nedham claimed that arms should not, however, be "in the hands of any, but such as had an Interest in the Publick."[10] The idea that only freemen—responsible citizens—should bear arms soon became a standard theme among libertarians.

Of all the commonwealthmen James Harrington made the most significant contribution to English libertarian attitudes toward arms, the individual, and society.[11] Harrington offered a crucial innovation to Machiavellian theory

[8] *The Works of Sir Walter Ralegh, Kt., Now First Collected: To Which Are Prefixed the Lives of the Author, by Oldys and Birch* [8 vols., Oxford, Eng., 1829], VIII, 22, 25.

[9] Jean Bodin, *The Six Bookes of a Commonwealth*, ed. Kenneth Douglas McRae [Cambridge, Mass., 1962], 605, 542, 599–614.

[10] *Mercurius Politicus*, 103 [May 20 to May 27, 1652], 1609–13.

[11] The following discussion of James Harrington draws upon Pocock, *Machiavellian Moment*, 383–400.

(perhaps *the* crucial innovation in light of later American attitudes). Accepting entirely the Machiavellian theory of the possession of arms as necessary to political personality, he grounded this basic idea upon the ownership of land. Like Machiavelli, Harrington considered the bearing of arms to be the primary means by which individuals affirmed their social power and political participation as responsible moral agents. But now landownership became the essential basis for the bearing of arms. Civic virtue came to be defined as the freeholder bearing arms in defense of his property and of his state.

Harrington's work provided an intellectual foundation for subsequent writers who linked the subject of arms to the basic themes of power and oppression which permeated libertarian thought. Andrew Fletcher's warning, "he that is armed, is always master of the purse of him that is unarmed," blended nicely with the libertarian's deep suspicion of authority.[12] The individual's need to protect himself from vicious fellow citizens and corrupt authorities—both banes of any republican society—also became clear. To accomplish this the responsible citizen must be armed.

John Trenchard and Thomas Gordon also integrated the idea of the armed citizen with the constant struggle libertarians perceived between Power and Liberty. Their *Cato's Letters* exclaimed: "The Exercise of despotick Power is the unrelenting War of an armed Tyrant upon his unarmed Subjects: It is a War of one Side, and in it there is neither Peace nor Truce." Rulers must always be restrained. An unarmed populace merely encouraged their natural tendency toward oppression: "Men that are above all Fear, soon grow above all Shame."[13]

Trenchard also collaborated with Walter Moyle in an attack upon standing armies which elaborated on the theme that citizens must jealously guard their liberties. Nations that remained free, warned Trenchard and Moyle, never maintained "any Souldiers in constant Pay within their Cities, or ever suffered any of their Subjects to make War their Profession." Those nations knew "that the Sword and Sovareignty always march hand in hand, and therefore they trained their own Citizens and the Territories about them perpetually in Arms, and their whole Commonwealths by this means became so many several formed Militias." Further, "a general Exercise of the best of their People in the use of Arms, was the only Bulwark of their Liberties; this was reckon'd the surest way to preserve them both at home and abroad, the People being secured thereby as well against the Domestick Affronts of any of their own Citizens, as against the Foreign Invasions of ambitious and unruly Neighbours." Arms were, however, "never lodg'd in the hands of any who had not an Interest in preserving the publick Peace. . . . In those days there was no difference between the Citizen, the Souldier, and the Husbandman."[14]

Throughout their essay Trenchard and Moyle reiterated the idea that citizens must be able to defend themselves against their rulers or they would

[12] Andrew Fletcher, *The Political Works of Andrew Fletcher, Esq.* (London, 1737), 9.

[13] [John Trenchard and Thomas Gordon], *Cato's Letters: Or, Essays on Liberty, Civil and Religious, and Other Important Subjects* (4 vols., London, 1755), I, 189, 255.

[14] [John Trenchard and Walter Moyle], *An Argument Shewing, That a Standing Army Is Inconsistent with a Free Government, and Absolutely Destructive to the Constitution of the English Monarchy* (London, 1697), 7.

lose their liberties and live in tyranny. "It's the misfortune of all Countries, that they sometimes lie under a unhappy necessity to defend themselves by Arms against the Ambition of their Governours, and to fight for what's their own." If those in government were heedless of reason, the people "must patiently submit to [their] Bondage, or stand upon [their] own Defence; which if [they] are enabled to do, [they] shall never be put upon it, but [their] Swords may grow rusty in [their] hands; for that Nation is surest to live in Peace, that is most capable of making War; and a Man that hath a Sword by his side, shall have least occasion to make use of it."[15]

The essays of Trenchard, Gordon, and Moyle subtly blended several distinct, yet related, ideas: opposition to standing armies, dependence upon militias, and support of the armed citizen. Thus, while the concept of the armed citizen was sometimes linked with that of the militia, libertarians just as often stressed this idea as an independent theme or joined it to other issues.

This latter tendency is evident in the writing of James Burgh, the libertarian most attractive to Americans. His *Political Disquisitions* provided a grab bag of ideas which Americans integrated into their vision of republicanism. Stressing the relationship between arms and power in a society, Burgh declared: "Those, who have the command of the arms in a country, says *Aristotle*, are masters of the state, and have it in their power to make what revolutions they please." Thus, "there is no end to observations on the difference between the measures likely to be pursued by a minister backed by a standing *army*, and those of a court awed by the fear of an *armed people*." For Burgh the very nature of society was related to whether or not its citizens had arms and were vigorous in their use. "No kingdom can be secured otherwise than by arming the people. The possession of arms is the distinction between a freeman and a slave. He, who has nothing, and who himself belongs to another, must be defended by him, whose property he is, and needs no arms. But he, who thinks he is his own master, and has what he can call his own, ought to have arms to defend himself, and what he possesses; else he lives precariously, and at discretion."[16]

A number of significant ideas came together in Burgh's *Disquisitions*. Like all libertarians he opposed a standing army and praised the militia as the bulwark of liberty. Then, going beyond these stock ideas, he clearly articulated the idea that the very character of the people—the cornerstone and strength of a republican society—was related to the individual's ability and desire to arm and defend himself against threats to his person, his property, and his state. An integral relationship existed between the possession of arms and the spirit and character of the people. For this reason Burgh lamented the state to which English society had fallen. Having become a people interested only in luxury and commerce, Englishmen had surrendered their arms. Lauding the Scots ("bred up in hardy, active, and abstemious courses of life, they were always

[15] *Ibid.*, 12.
[16] [James Burgh], *Political Disquisitions: Or, an Enquiry into Public Errors, Defects, and Abuses* (3 vols., London, 1774–1775), II, 345, 476, 390.

prepared to march"| Burgh lamented that "the common people of *England*, on the other hand, having been long used to pay an army for fighting for them, had at this time forgot all the military virtues of their ancestors."[17]

Burgh's distress over the loss of virility and virtue in English society echoed that of his fellow libertarians since Harrington. These men related the downfall of English society to an increasingly luxury-loving people who freely chose to yield their military responsibilities to a professional army. Once armies were paid for by taxes, taxes were collected by armies, and the liberties of the English were at an end. True virtue sprang from the agrarian world of self-sufficient warriors. This was gone from England and with it all opportunity for a virtuous republic. There was, however, still some hope in the libertarians' minds: America was an agrarian society of self-sufficient husbandmen trained in arms. There the lamp of liberty might still burn brightly.

Richard Price drew the clearest contrast between the perceived decadence of England and the virtuous strength of America in his *Observations on the Importance of the American Revolution*. In that pamphlet he extolled the virtues of republican America, including the prevalence of the armed citizen, which he considered an integral part of America's strength. "Free States ought to be bodies of armed *citizens*, well regulated, and well disciplined, and always ready to turn out, when properly called upon, to execute the laws, to quell riots, and to keep the peace. Such, if I am rightly informed, are the citizens of America." In his view, "The happiest state of man is the middle state between the *savage* and the *refined*, or between the wild and the luxurious state. Such is the state of society in CONNECTICUT, and in some others of the *American* provinces; where the inhabitants consist, if I am rightly informed, of an independent and hardy YEOMANRY, all nearly on a level—trained to arms,—instructed in their rights—cloathed in home-spun—of simple manners— strangers to luxury—drawing plenty from the ground—and that plenty, gathered easily by the hand of industry." By contrast, "Britain, indeed, consisting as it does of *unarmed* inhabitants, and threatened as it is by ambitious and powerful neigh[b]ours, cannot hope to maintain its existence long after becoming open to invasion by losing its naval superiority."[18]

The conviction that Americans were a virtuous republican people—particularly when contrasted with decadent European populations—became a common theme in pamphlet literature on both sides of the Atlantic. George Mason boasted that "North America is the only great nursery of freemen now left upon the face of the earth." Matthew Robinson-Morris Rokeby, too, contended that while the flame of liberty in England was little more than "the last snuff of an expiring lamp," Americans were a "new and uncorrupted people." In addition, however, Rokeby linked the libertarian belief in a dynamic relationship between arms and a free society to his observations. Arguing that monarchs purposely kept their people unarmed, Rokeby exclaimed that the American

---

[17] *Ibid.*, 415.

[18] Richard Price, *Observations on the Importance of the American Revolution, and the Means of Making It a Benefit to the World* (London, 1784), 16, 69, 76.

colonies were "all democratical governments, where the power is in the hands of the people and where there is not the least difficulty or jealousy about putting arms into the hands of every man in the country." Europeans should be aware of the consequences of this and not "be ignorant of the strength and the force of such a form of government and how strenuously and almost wonderfully people living under one have sometimes exerted themselves in defence of their rights and liberties and how fatally it has ended with many a man and many a state who have entered into quarrels, war and contests with them."[19]

The vision of their nation as a virile and uncorrupted society permeated the writings of Americans during and after the Revolution. And, like Machiavelli and Harrington before them, these American writers perceived a vital relationship between vigorous republican husbandmen and the possession of arms. Under the pseudonym "A British Bostonian," the Baptist preacher John Allen warned the British what would happen if they attempted "to make the Americans subject to their *slavery*." "This bloody scene can never be executed but at the expence of the destruction of England, and you will find, my Lord, that the Americans will not submit *to be* SLAVES, they know the use of the gun, and the military art, as well as any of his Majesty's troops at St. James's, and where his Majesty has one soldier, who art in general the refuse of the earth, America can produce fifty, free men, and all volunteers, and raise a more potent army of men in three weeks, than England can in three years."[20] Even Charles Lee, a British military man, observed in a widely circulated pamphlet that "the Yeomanry of America . . . are accustomed from their infancy to fire arms; they are expert in the use of them:—Whereas the lower and middle people of England are, by the tyranny of certain laws almost as ignorant in the use of a musket, as they are of the ancient Catepulta."[21] The Continental Congress echoed this theme in its declaration of July 1775. "On the sword, therefore, we are compelled to rely for protection. Should victory declare in your favour, yet men trained to arms from their infancy, and animated by the love of liberty, will afford neither a cheap or easy conquest." Further, "in Britain, where the maxims of freedom were still known, but where luxury and dissipation had diminished the wonted reverence for them, the attack [of tyranny] has been carried on in a more secret and indirect manner: Corruption has been employed to undermine them. The Americans are not enervated by effeminacy, like the inhabitants of India; nor debauched by luxury, like those of Great-Britain."[22] In writing the *Federalist Papers* James Madison drew a similar contrast. Noting "the advantage of being armed, which the Americans possess over the people

[19] George Mason, "Remarks on Annual Elections for the Fairfax Independent Company," in *The Papers of George Mason, 1725–1792*, ed. Robert A. Rutland (3 vols., Chapel Hill, 1970), I, 231; Matthew Robinson-Morris Rokeby, *Considerations on the Measures Carrying on with Respect to the British Colonies in North America* (London, 1774), 133–35, 57.

[20] [John Allen], *An Oration, upon the Beauties of Liberty, or the Essential Rights of the Americans* (Boston, 1773), xiii–xiv.

[21] [Charles Lee], *Strictures on a Pamphlet Entitled, a "Friendly Address to All Reasonable Americans, on the Subject of Our Political Confusions." Addressed to the People of America* (Philadelphia, 1774), 12.

[22] *Journals of Congress* (13 vols., Philadelphia, 1800–1801), I, 148, 163.

of almost every other nation," he observed that in Europe "the governments are afraid to trust the people with arms."[23] Years later Timothy Dwight testified to the strength and durability of this belief when he wrote that "to trust arms in the hands of the people at large has, in Europe, been believed . . . to be an experiment fraught only with danger. Here by a long trial it has been proved to be perfectly harmless. . . . If the government be equitable; if it be reasonable in its exactions; if proper attention be paid to the education of children in knowledge and religion, few men will be disposed to use arms, unless for their amusement, and for the defence of themselves and their country."[24]

It was Joel Barlow, however, who most eloquently articulated the vital role of arms in American republican thought. Barlow firmly believed that one of America's greatest strengths rested in "making every citizen a soldier, and every soldier a citizen; not only *permitting* every man to arm, but *obliging* him to arm." Whereas in Europe this "would have gained little credit; or at least it would have been regarded as a mark of an uncivilized people, extremely dangerous to a well ordered society," Barlow insisted that in America "it is *because the people are civilized, that they are with safety armed.*" He exulted that it was because of "their conscious dignity, as citizens enjoying equal rights, that they wish not to invade the rights of others. The danger (where there is any) from armed citizens, is only to the *government*, not to the *society*; and as long as they have nothing to revenge in the government (which they cannot have while it is in their own hands) there are many advantages in their being accustomed to the use of arms, and no possible disadvantage." In contrast, Barlow continued, European societies employed professional soldiers "who know no other God but their king; who lose all ideas of themselves, in contemplating their officers; and who forget the duties of a man, to practise those of a soldier,—this is but half the operation: an essential part of the military system is to disarm the people, to hold all the functions of war, as well the arm that executes, as the will that declares it, equally above their reach." Then, by integrating libertarian orthodoxy with Adam Smith's more recent observation that a people who lost their martial spirit suffered "that sort of mental mutilation, deformity and wretchedness which cowardice necessarily involves in it," Barlow revealed the essence of the role of arms in American republican thought: Any government that disarmed its people "palsies the hand and brutalizes the mind: an habitual disuse of physical forces totally destroys the moral; and men lose at once the power of protecting themselves, and of discerning the cause of their oppression." A man capable of defending himself with arms if necessary was prerequisite for maintaining the moral character to be a good republican. Barlow then deduced that in a democratic society with equal representation "the people will be universally armed: they will assume those weapons for security, which the art of war has

<hr/>

[23] James Madison, "The Federalist No. 46 [45]," in *The Federalist*, ed. Jacob E. Cooke (Middletown, Conn., 1961), 321–22. This essay, originally published as number 45, appears as number 46 in the Cooke edition. For an explanation, see *ibid.*, xviii–xix.

[24] Timothy Dwight, *Travels in New-England and New-York* (4 vols., London, 1823), I, xiv.

invented for destruction." Only tyrannical governments disarmed their people. A republican society needed armed citizens and might remain vigorous and uncorrupted only so long as it had them.[25]

When Madison wrote the amendments to the Constitution that formed the basis of the Bill of Rights, he did not do so within a vacuum. Instead, he composed them in an environment permeated by the emergent republican ideology and with the aid of innumerable suggestions from his countrymen. These came most commonly from the state bills of rights and the hundreds of amendments suggested by the state conventions that ratified the Constitution. These sources continually reiterated four beliefs relative to the issues eventually incorporated into the Second Amendment: the right of the individual to possess arms, the fear of a professional army, the reliance on militias controlled by the individual states, and the subordination of the military to civilian control.

The various state bills of rights dealt with these four issues in different ways. Some considered them as separate rights, others combined them. New Hampshire, for example, included four distinct articles to deal with the militia, standing armies, military subordination, and individual bearing of arms. For its part, Pennsylvania offered a single inclusive article: "That the people have a right to bear arms for the defence of themselves and the state; and as standing armies in the time of peace are dangerous to liberty, they ought not to be kept up; And that the military should be kept under strict subordination to, and governed by, the civil power." Virginia, too, presented an inclusive statement: "That a well-regulated militia, composed of the body of the people, trained to arms, is the proper, natural, and safe defence of a free State; that standing armies, in time of peace, should be avoided, as dangerous to liberty; and that in all cases the military should be under strict subordination to, and governed by, the civil power."[26]

The amendments suggested by the various state ratifying conventions were of a similar nature.[27] Examples include New Hampshire, which did not mention the militia but did state "that no standing Army shall be Kept up in time of Peace unless with the consent of three fourths of the Members of each branch of Congress, nor shall Soldiers in Time of Peace be quartered upon private Houses without the consent of the Owners." Then in a separate amendment: "Congress shall never disarm any Citizen unless such as are or have been in Actual Rebellion."[28] Maryland's convention offered five separate amendments dealing with these issues while Virginia's integrated them by

[25] Joel Barlow, *Advice to the Privileged Orders in the Several States of Europe: Resulting from the Necessity and Propriety of a General Revolution in the Principle of Government* (Ithaca, N.Y., 1956) 16–17, 45–46; Adam Smith, *An Inquiry into the Nature and Causes of the Wealth of Nations* (2 vols., London, 1776), II, 373. For an excellent discussion of Adam Smith's attitudes toward the relationship between martial spirit and the public character, see Donald Winch, *Adam Smith's Politics: An Essay in Historiographic Revision* (Cambridge, Eng., 1978), esp. 103–20.
[26] Francis Newton Thorpe, ed., *The Federal and State Constitutions, Colonial Charters, and Other Organic Laws of the States, Territories and Colonies Now or Heretofore Forming the United States of America* (7 vols., Washington, 1909), IV, 2455–56, V, 3083, VII, 3814. All of the state bills of rights appear in this collection.
[27] These amendments are conveniently grouped together in Dumbauld, *Bill of Rights*, 173–205.
[28] *Ibid.*, 182.

stating: "That the people have a right to keep and bear arms; that a well regulated Militia composed of the body of the people trained to arms is the proper, natural and safe defence of a free State. That standing armies in time of peace are dangerous to liberty, and therefore ought to be avoided, as far as the circumstances and protection of the Community will admit; and that in all cases the military should be under strict subordination to and governed by the Civil power."[29] The New York convention, which offered over fifty amendments, observed: "That the People have a right to keep and bear Arms; that a well regulated Militia, including the body of the People *capable of bearing Arms*, is the proper, natural and safe defence of a free state."[30] The minority report of the Pennsylvania convention, which became a widely publicized Antifederalist tract, was the most specific: "That the people have a right to bear arms for the defence of themselves and their own State, or the United States, or for the purpose of killing game; and no law shall be passed for disarming the people or any of them, unless for crimes committed, or real danger of public injury from individuals; and as standing armies in the time of peace are dangerous to liberty, they ought not to be kept up; and that the military shall be kept under strict subordination to and be governed by the civil power."[31]

On the specific right of individuals to keep arms, Madison could also draw upon the observations of Samuel Adams, then governor of Massachusetts, and his close friend and confidant Thomas Jefferson. For his part, Adams offered an amendment in the Massachusetts convention that read: "And that the said Constitution be never construed to authorize Congress to infringe the just liberty of the press or the rights of conscience; or to prevent the people of the United States who are peaceable citizens from keeping their own arms; or to raise standing armies, unless when necessary for the defence of the United States, or of some one or more of them."[32] In his initial draft of a proposed constitution for the state of Virginia Jefferson did not mention a militia but did state that no standing army should exist except in time of actual war. Then, in a separate phrase, he wrote: "No freeman shall ever be debarred the use of arms." He amended this statement in his next two drafts to read: "No freeman shall be debarred the use of arms within his own lands or tenements."[33]

Madison and his colleagues on the select committee charged with creating a bill of rights were anxious to capture the essence of the rights demanded by so many Americans in so many different forms. To do this they eliminated many suggestions, reworded others, and consolidated as many as possible in order to

[29] *Ibid.*, 178–79, 185. The Maryland amendments include minority proposals.

[30] *Ibid.*, 189. New York's was the only state amendment to distinguish between *keeping* and *bearing* arms. It allowed all citizens to possess arms, but only those with the capability to bear them were asked to do so.

[31] *Ibid.*, 174. For an excellent analysis of this report, see Merrill Jensen, ed., *The Documentary History of the Ratification of the Constitution* (3 vols., Madison, 1976–1978), II, 617–40.

[32] William V. Wells, *Life and Public Services of Samuel Adams, Being a Narrative of His Acts and Opinions, and of His Agency in Producing and Forwarding the American Revolution* (3 vols., Boston, 1865), III, 267.

[33] *The Papers of Thomas Jefferson*, ed. Julian P. Boyd et al. (19 vols., Princeton, 1950–1974), I, 344, 353, 363.

come up with a reasonable number of amendments.[34] What became the Second Amendment resulted from this last process. The committee took the two distinct, yet related rights—the individual possession of arms and the need for a militia made up of ordinary citizens—and merged them into a single amendment. As with other amendments that combined various essential rights, it was the intent of the committee neither to subordinate one right to the other nor to have one clause serve as subordinate to the other.[35] This became obvious in the discussion of the amendment that took place on the floor of Congress.

Although brief, the discussion occasioned by the Second Amendment is instructive for its indication of congressional intent to protect two separate rights: the individual's right to possess arms and the right of the states to form their own militia. Elbridge Gerry made this clear when he attacked the phrase dealing with conscientious objectors, those "scrupulous of bearing arms," that appeared in the original amendment. Manifesting the standard libertarian distrust of government, Gerry claimed that the amendment under discussion "was intended to secure the people against the mal-administration of the Government; if we could suppose that, in all cases, the rights of the people would be attended to, the occasion for guards of this kind would be removed." However, Gerry was suspicious that the federal government might employ this phrase "to destroy the constitution itself. They can declare who are those religiously scrupulous, and prevent them from bearing arms."[36] This would be a return to European-style governments in which those in authority systematically disarmed the populace. Thomas Scott of Pennsylvania also objected to this phrase for fear that it "would lead to the violation of another article in the constitution, which secures to the people the right of keeping arms."[37] The entire thrust of this discussion, as well as one related to a militia bill also under consideration, was that congressmen distinguished not only between the militia and the right of the individual to possess arms but between the individual's *possession* of arms and his *bearing* of them. That is, they believed that all should have the right to possess arms but that all should not necessarily be responsible for bearing them in defense of the state. In the discussion over the militia bill, for example, one representative declared: "As far as the whole body of the people are necessary to the general defence, they ought to be armed; but the law ought not to require more than is necessary; for that would be a just cause of complaint." Another believed that "the people of America

[34] For an excellent analysis of this process, see Bernard Schwartz, *The Great Rights of Mankind: A History of the American Bill of Rights* (New York, 1977), 160–91.

[35] In their interpretations of the Second Amendment various authors have stressed the wording of the amendment. (See note 5 above.) It is clear, however, that James Madison and the committee worked toward succinctness. Indeed, Madison's original suggestion read: "The right of the people to keep and bear arms shall not be infringed; a well armed and well regulated militia being the best security of a free country: but no person religiously scrupulous of bearing arms shall be compelled to render military service in person." Dumbauld, *Bill of Rights*, 207.

[36] *Ibid.; Annals of the Congress*, 1 Cong., 1 sess., Aug. 17, 1789, p. 778.

[37] *Annals of the Congress*, 1 Cong., 1 sess., Aug. 20, 1789, p. 796.

would never consent to be deprived of the privilege of carrying arms." Others even argued that those Americans who did not possess arms should have them supplied by the states.[38] This discussion clearly indicated that the problem perceived by the representatives was how to get arms into the hands of all American males between the ages of eighteen and forty-five, not how to restrict such possession to those in militia service.[39]

It is apparent from such discussions that Americans of the Revolutionary generation distinguished between the individual's right to *keep* arms and the need for a militia in which to *bear* them. Yet it is equally clear that more often than not they considered these rights inseparable. This raises the question of why so many Americans so often fused these rights as to make it logical to combine them in the Second Amendment. Here comments by Madison, George Washington, Dwight, and Joseph Story provide excellent insight.

In his forty-fifth number of the *Federalist Papers* Madison drew the usual contrast between the American states, where citizens were armed, and European nations, where governments feared to trust their citizens with arms. Then he observed that "it is not certain that with this aid alone [possession of arms], they would not be able to shake off their yokes. But were the people to possess the additional advantages of local governments chosen by themselves, who could collect the national will, and direct the national force; and of officers appointed out of the militia, by these governments and attached both to them and to the militia, it may be affirmed with the greatest assurance, that the throne of every tyranny in Europe would be speedily overturned, in spite of the legions which surround it."[40] Washington, in his first substantive speech to Congress, declared: "To be prepared for war, is one of the most effectual means of preserving peace. A free people ought not only to be armed, but disciplined; to which end, a uniform and well digested plan is requisite."[41] Writing early in the nineteenth century, Dwight celebrated the right of individuals to possess arms as the hallmark of a democratic society. Then, he concluded: "The difficulty here has been to persuade the citizens to keep arms, not to prevent them from being employed for violent purposes."[42] This same lament

[38] *Ibid.*, 1 Cong., 3 sess., Dec. 16, 1790, pp. 1806–07.

[39] This is the opinion of St. George Tucker, one of the leading jurists of the day. When he edited *Blackstone's Commentaries*, Tucker noted the master's observation that the right of the people to bear arms constituted one of the essential rights necessary to protect life, liberty, and property. His footnote to this section read: "The right of the people to keep and bear arms shall not be infringed. Amendments to C.U.S. [Constitution of the United States] Art. 4, and this without any qualification as to their condition or degree as is the case in the British government." In another note Tucker observed that "whosoever examines the forest, and game laws in the British code, will readily perceive that the right of keeping arms is effectually taken away from the people of England." Blackstone himself informs us "that the prevention of popular insurrections and resistance to government by disarming the bulk of the people, is a reason oftener meant than avowed by the makers of the forest and game laws." St. George Tucker, ed., *Blackstone's Commentaries: With Notes of Reference to the Constitution and Laws, of the Federal Government of the United States; and of the Commonwealth of Virginia* (5 vols., Philadelphia, 1803), I, 144, II, 412.

[40] Madison, "Federalist No. 46 [45]," 321–22.

[41] *Annals of the Congress*, 1 Cong., 2 sess., Jan. 8, 1790, p. 969.

[42] Dwight, *Travels in New-England*, I, xiv–xv.

coursed through the observations of Story, whose *Commentaries* summed up the relationship between armed citizens and the militia as clearly as it was ever stated. In his discussion of the Second Amendment, Story wrote:

The right of the citizens to keep and bear arms has justly been considered, as the palladium of the liberties of a republic; since it offers a strong moral check against the usurpation and arbitrary power of rulers; and will generally, even if these are successful in the first instance, enable the people to resist and triumph over them. And yet, though this truth would seem so clear, and the importance of a well regulated militia would seem so undeniable, it cannot be disguised, that among the American people there is a growing indifference to any system of militia discipline, and a strong disposition, from a sense of its burthens, to be rid of all regulations. How it is practicable to keep the people duly armed without some organization, it is difficult to see. There is certainly no small danger, that indifference may lead to disgust, and disgust to contempt; and thus gradually undermine all the protection intended by this clause of our national bill of rights.[43]

The observations of Madison, Washington, Dwight, and Story reveal an interesting relationship between the armed citizen and the militia. These men firmly believed that the character and spirit of the republic rested on the freeman's possession of arms as well as his ability and willingness to defend himself and his society. This was the bedrock, the "palladium," of republican liberty. The militia was equally important in their minds. Militia laws insured that freemen would remain armed, and thus vigorous republican citizens. In addition the militia served as the means whereby the collective force of individually armed citizens became effective. It was this that would cause those in power to respect the liberties of the people and would eliminate the need to create professional armies, that greatest single threat to a republican society. Thus, the armed citizen and the militia existed as distinct, yet interrelated, elements within American republican thought.

With the passage of time, however, American republicanism placed an increasing emphasis upon the image of the armed citizen. Caught up within a dialectic between virtue and commerce, Americans struggled to preserve their Revolutionary commitment to escape from corruption. Following Harrington's reasoning that commerce could not corrupt so long as it did not overwhelm agrarian interests, Americans believed that in order to accommodate both virtue and commerce a republic must be as energetic in its search for land as it was in its search for commerce. A vast supply of land, to be occupied by an armed and self-directing yeomanry, might nurture an endless reservoir of virtue. If American virtue was threatened by the increase in commercial activity following the Constitution of 1787, it could revitalize itself on the frontier by means of the armed husbandman.[44]

[43] Joseph Story, *Commentaries on the Constitution of the United States; With a Preliminary Review of the Constitutional History of the Colonies and States before the Adoption of the Constitution* (3 vols., Boston, 1833), III, 746–47.
[44] This theme is developed in a wide range of literature. Outstanding examples include: Richard Slotkin, *Regeneration through Violence: The Mythology of the American Frontier, 1600–1860* (Middletown, Conn., 1973); Henry Nash Smith, *Virgin Land: The American West as Symbol and Myth* (Cambridge, Mass., 1950); John William Ward, *Andrew Jackson: Symbol for an Age* (New

This belief is what gave point to Jefferson's observation that "our governments will remain virtuous for many centuries; as long as they are chiefly agricultural; and this will be as long as there shall be vacant lands in any part of America." Coupled with this, however, was Jefferson's libertarian inheritance: "What country can preserve it's liberties if their rulers are not warned from time to time that their people preserve the spirit of resistance. Let them take arms."[45]

In the nearly two hundred years since the ratification of the Bill of Rights American society has undergone great transformations. As a consequence the number of people enjoying expanded civic rights and responsibilities, including the ownership of firearms, which Jefferson and others felt should be restricted to "freemen," has vastly increased. This has become the source of much controversy. Speaking for those alarmed by the presence of so many armed citizens, Sen. Edward Kennedy believes that "our complex society requires a rethinking of the proper role of firearms in modern America. Our forefathers used firearms as an integral part of their struggle for survival. But today firearms are not appropriate for daily life in the United States."[46] For his part, Edward Abbey, eloquent spokesman for individualism, fears that the measures suggested by Senator Kennedy to cope with today's "complex society" may be taking America in the direction of a worldwide drift toward totalitarianism. In his mind, throughout history whenever tyrannical governments existed and where the few ruled the many, citizens have been disarmed. "The tank, the B-52, the fighter-bomber, the state-controlled police and military are the weapons of dictatorship. The rifle is the weapon of democracy." Then, "If guns are outlawed, only the government will have guns. Only the police, the secret police, the military. The hired servants of our rulers. Only the government—and a few outlaws. I intend to be among the outlaws."[47]

Whether the armed citizen is relevant to late-twentieth-century American life is something that only the American people—through the Supreme Court, their state legislatures, and Congress—can decide. Those who advocate some measure of gun control are not without powerful arguments to advance on behalf of their position. The appalling and unforeseen destructive capability of modern weapons, the dissolving of the connection between an armed citizenry and the agrarian setting that figured so importantly in the thought of the revolutionary generation, the distinction between the right to keep arms and such measures as "registration," the general recognition of the responsibility of

York, 1955]; and Pocock, *Machiavellian Moment*, esp. 506–52. For an excellent analysis of the changing attitudes toward the militia and professional armies, see Charles Royster, *A Revolutionary People at War: The Continental Army and American Character, 1775-1783* (Chapel Hill, 1979).

[45] Thomas Jefferson to James Madison, Dec. 20, 1787, in *Papers of Jefferson*, ed. Boyd et al., XII, 442; Jefferson to William Stephens Smith, Nov. 13, 1787, *ibid.*, XII, 356.

[46] Kennedy, "Need for Gun Control Legislation," 26.

[47] For Edward Abbey's thoughts regarding the drift toward totalitarianism, see Edward Abbey, *Desert Solitaire: A Season in the Wilderness* (New York, 1968), 149–51. The quotations are drawn from Edward Abbey, "The Right to Arms," Edward Abbey, *Abbey's Road* (New York, 1979), 130–32.

succeeding generations to modify the constitutional inheritance to meet new conditions—all will be serviceable in the ongoing debate. But advocates of the control of firearms should not argue that the Second Amendment did not intend for Americans of the late eighteenth century to possess arms for their own personal defense, for the defense of their states and their nation, and for the purpose of keeping their rulers sensitive to the rights of the people.

An Armed Community: The Origins and Meaning of the Right to Bear Arms

Lawrence Delbert Cress

Military service should be the responsibility of every citizen, advised Niccolò Machiavelli in *The Art of War*, but soldiering should be the profession of none. Freedom and military might could coexist only when military service merged with the rights and responsibilities of citizenship. Machiavelli derived his insights from the past. While Rome thrived, "there was never any soldier who made war his only occupation." Citizens bore arms in defense of the state, motivated by a commitment to the common good and officered by the nation's most respected individuals. Roman liberties succumbed to tyranny only when citizens allowed professional soldiers, unmoved by a sense of the common good, to subvert the military power of the state to their own self-interest. Hence, Machiavelli concluded, "a good man [would] not make war his only profession"; nor would a "wise prince or governor . . . allow any of his subjects or citizens to do it." A well-governed commonwealth "should take care that this art of war should be practiced in time of peace only as an exercise, and in the time of war, only out of necessity and for the acquisition of glory." Most important, the military force of society should be used only in the service of the common good: "If any citizen has another end or design in following this profession [of war], he is not a good man; if any commonwealth acts otherwise, it is not well governed."[1] Some 250 years later, the people of the United States incorporated the essence of the great Florentine political theorist's ideas into the language of the Second Amendment: "A well regulated Militia, being necessary to the security of a free State, the right of the people to keep and bear Arms, shall not be infringed."

Despite the militia's poor showing during the revolutionary war, few Americans could imagine a republican government without citizens trained to arms. As the armed expression of civil authority, a militia deterred foreign aggressors while it eliminated the need for a potentially oppressive standing

Lawrence Delbert Cress is associate professor of history at Texas A&M University.

[1] Niccolò Machiavelli, *The Art of War* (Indianapolis, 1965), 14–19; J. G. A. Pocock, *The Machiavellian Moment: Florentine Political Thought and the Atlantic Republican Tradition* (Princeton, 1975), 199–212.

army. It also protected against domestic insurrection. Shays's Rebellion, the outbreak of armed insurgency in Massachusetts, had reminded all of the historic vulnerability of republican government to internal discord. The danger posed by manipulating demagogues, ambitious rulers, and foreign invaders to free institutions required the vigilance of citizen-soldiers cognizant of the common good. Thus the Second Amendment assured "the people," through the agency of "a well regulated Militia," a role in the preservation of both the external and the internal security of the Republic. It did not guarantee the right of individuals, like Daniel Shays and his followers, to closet armaments.

This view differs sharply from that offered recently by Robert E. Shalhope. He contends that the Second Amendment guaranteed individuals the right "to possess arms for their own personal defense." Shalhope concedes that the militia contributed to the political thinking that produced the amendment. Nevertheless, he argues that "Americans of the Revolutionary generation distinguished between the individual's right to *keep* arms and the need for a militia in which to *bear* them." Rather than a simple statement of the militia's place in the constitutional order, as proponents of gun control have contended, the amendment merged "two distinct, yet related rights—the individual possession of arms and the need for a militia made up of ordinary citizens." The militia may have lost its significance for modern Americans, but, concludes Shalhope, its demise has not eroded the individual's constitutional right to arms.[2]

Shalhope's essay attempts to resolve differences between opponents and proponents of gun control over the historical meaning of the Second Amendment —differences he credits correctly to a failure "to understand the origins of the amendment within the perspective of the late eighteenth, rather than that of the late twentieth, century."[3] Nevertheless, his effort to explain the aims of the amendment's authors is itself marred by anachronisms. Most important, he fails to place citizenship, especially the idea of citizens in arms, in a context compatible with the republican theory of revolutionary America. In the eighteenth century, citizenship, which was defined in part by militia service,

[2] Robert E. Shalhope, "The Ideological Origins of the Second Amendment," *Journal of American History*, 69 (Dec. 1982), 599–614. Also interpreting the Second Amendment as guaranteeing a personal right to bear arms are Robert A. Sprecher, "The Lost Amendment," *American Bar Association Journal*, 51 (June 1965), 554–57; *ibid.* (July 1965), 665–69; and Stuart R. Hays, "The Right to Bear Arms, a Study of Judicial Misinterpretation," *William and Mary Law Review*, 2 (no. 2, 1960), 381–406. Robert A. Sprecher and Stuart R. Hays focus narrowly on the legal and legislative history of the amendment. Arguing that the amendment supports the collective right of state militias to bear arms are Peter Buck Feller and Karl L. Gotting, "The Second Amendment: A Second Look," *Northwestern University Law Review*, 61 (March-April 1966), 46–70; Lucilius A. Emery, "The Constitutional Right to Keep and Bear Arms," *Harvard Law Review*, 28 (March 1915), 473–77; George I. Haight, "The Right to Keep and Bear Arms," *Bill of Rights Review*, 2 (Fall 1941), 31–42; and Ralph J. Rohner, "The Right to Bear Arms: A Phenomenon of Constitutional History," *Catholic University of America Law Review*, 16 (Sept. 1966), 53–84. Peter Beck Feller and Karl L. Gotting, Lucilius A. Emery, George I. Haight, and Ralph J. Rohner also focus their analysis on legal and constitutional issues, ignoring the ideological context out of which the Second Amendment came.

[3] Shalhope, "Ideological Origins," 600.

connoted civic virtue, a commitment to the greater public good, not an insistence on individual prerogative. Moreover, an armed citizenry by no means implied an armed population. A well-regulated militia drawn from a community's propertied yeomen and led by its most prominent citizens preserved liberty; armed individuals threatened it. Shalhope misses much, even ignoring the implications of evidence he cites himself. This essay will show that seventeenth- and eighteenth-century republican theorists understood access to arms to be a communal, rather than an individual, right.

Between the publication of Machiavelli's works in the early sixteenth century and the official addition of the Second Amendment to the Constitution on March 1, 1792, stands a corpus of political theory, constitutional law, and legislative enactments that underscores the lingering influence of the classical republican notion that arms had an acceptable function in society only in the service of the common good. Since the mid-seventeenth century, English political theorists—themselves drawing on the insights of Machiavelli—had linked the militia to the maintenance of a balanced, stable, and free constitution. James Harrington, whose *Commonwealth of Oceana* was widely read by Americans of the revolutionary generation, associated political stability with the armed, enfranchised, and propertied citizen. Land gave the individual economic independence and ultimately the leisure to serve the common good through the franchise and through membership in the militia. The citizen bore arms not to deter personal assault or to protect the limits of his freehold; for Harrington, bearing arms, like voting, symbolized the political independence that allowed for and ensured a commitment to civic virtue. The citizen militia, then, was not only an agent of national defense but also a deterrent to the ambitious nature of centralized political power.[4]

Advocates of political liberty writing during the tumultuous years before and after the Glorious Revolution of 1688 also emphasized the militia's importance as a guarantor of constitutional stability. Algernon Sidney warned of the rise of tyranny whenever the militia was allowed to decay. John Trenchard, later well known in the colonies as the coauthor with Thomas Gordon of *Cato's Letters*, began his career as a pamphleteer by chiding Parliament for providing William III with a standing army after the Treaty of Ryswick in 1697. Standing armies, he wrote, were the agents of political intrigue and corruption. Only a militia could be counted on to protect both the territory and the liberties of a free people.[5]

Sidney, Trenchard, and a host of other radical Whig essayists shared with Harrington the idea that arms were "the only true badges of liberty." In "a popular or mixed Government," wrote Sidney, "the body of the People is the

[4] S. B. Liljegren, ed., *James Harrington's Oceana* (Heidelberg, 1924), 9-10, 16, 34-35, 50-53, 176-77. My analysis follows closely that in Pocock, *Machiavellian Moment*, 386, 390-91.

[5] For a detailed analysis of the debate over the militia and standing armies in eighteenth-century thought, see Lawrence Delbert Cress, *Citizens in Arms: The Army and the Militia in American Society to the War of 1812* (Chapel Hill, 1982), 15-33; and Lawrence Delbert Cress, "Radical Whiggery on the Role of the Military: Ideological Roots of the American Revolutionary Militia," *Journal of the History of Ideas*, 40 (Jan.-March 1979), 43-60.

publick defence, and every man is arm'd and disciplin'd." No nation was secure except by relying on the military strength of its own people. Nevertheless, freedom did not depend on the armed individual. Arms guaranteed liberty only through the organization and discipline provided by the militia. More precisely, liberty was preserved "by making the Militia to consist of the same Persons as have the Property." As had Harrington, radical Whigs believed that property assured the independence of mind and action that allowed the militia to serve the common good. Calls for militia reform circulating during the first decade of William III's reign underscore the limits within which the right to bear arms was understood. Not the armed individual, but "A good militia," contended Andrew Fletcher, "is the chief part of the constitution of any free government." A rank and file well trained in the military arts and led by "persons of quality or education" will "always preserve the publick liberty." Such a military force had proven formidable in ancient times. Founding Britain's defenses on a mandatory system of militia encampments promised an opportunity to inspire a commitment to the common good and to train the citizenry at arms: "Such a [militia] camp," thought Fletcher, "would be as great a school of virtue as of military discipline."[6]

John Toland, the individual most responsible for the republication of Harrington's writings at the end of the seventeenth century, joined his friend Fletcher in drafting a militia-reform scheme intended to place arms "in the hands of sober, industrious, and understanding Freemen." "By Freemen," wrote Toland, "I understand Men of Property, or Persons that are able to live of themselves." Such men, through their awareness of and commitment to the "Publick Good," had made the armies of the Roman republic invincible. Men of lesser means lacked the leisure with which "to design the Good of the Commonwealth" and were thus unreliable defenders of the public interest. Trenchard was equally committed to building a militia structure that would bring young nobles and gentry into the field, thus providing Britain with the "best disciplin'd Troops and most excellent Souldiers in the World." In the ancient republics, "arms never lodged in the Hands of any who had not an Interest in preserving the publick Peace." To the contrary, "a general Exercise of the best of their People in the use of Arms, was the only Bulwark of their Liberties; . . . the People being secured thereby as well against the Domestick Affronts of any of their own Citizens, as against the Foreign Invasions of ambitious and unruly Neighbours." In sum, the "Sword and Soveraignty always march[ed] hand in hand." The self-interested armed individual, like universal manhood suffrage, had no place in the neo-Harringtonian thought of the radical Whigs. "Most Men do as much Mischief as lay in their Power,"

[6] Algernon Sidney, *Discourses concerning Government* (London, 1698), 155-57; [John Trenchard and Walter Moyle], *An Argument, Shewing, That a Standing Army Is Inconsistent with a Free Government, and Absolutely Destructive to the Constitution of the English Monarchy* (London, 1697), 4-5; Andrew Fletcher, *A Discourse of Government with Relation to Militia's,* in *The Political Works of Andrew Fletcher* (London, 1737), 37-65.

reminded Trenchard; it was best to "take away all Weapons by which they may do either themselves or others an Injury."[7]

Trenchard's counsel would have surprised none of his contemporaries involved in the events surrounding the Glorious Revolution. James II's use of a standing army to enforce absolute rule had contributed directly to his inglorious exile to France. He had also advanced the cause of Catholicism in England by increasing the number of Catholic officers to the exclusion of Protestants—a violation of the 1673 Test Act—and by importing Irish Catholics to fill the army's expanded ranks. As the Bill of Rights phrased it, he "did endeavour to subvert and extirpate the Protestant religion and the laws and liberties of this kingdom." He was charged in particular with "raising and keeping a standing army . . . without consent of parliament" and with "causing several good subjects being Protestants to be disarmed, at the same time when papists were both armed and employed." To correct the situation, the Bill of Rights prohibited the English monarchy from raising an army during peacetime without Parliament's consent. It also guaranteed—in language that speaks to the limited dimensions of the right to bear arms in English constitutional law—"that the subjects which are Protestants may have arms for their defence suitable to their conditions, and as allowed by law."[8]

In other words, the Bill of Rights laid down the right of a class of citizens, Protestants, to take part in the military affairs of the realm. Nowhere was an individual's right to arm in self-defense guaranteed. Protestants "may have arms for their defence," declared the revolutionary settlement, but then only as is "suitable to their conditions and as allowed by law." Those of unsuitable condition (a statute passed during the reign of Charles II disarmed anyone owning lands with an annual value of less than £100, other than the son or heir of an esquire or person of higher social rank) were not to be armed. Parliament also retained the prerogative to restrict future access to arms "by law." In sum, had Protestants not been "disarmed at the same time when papists were . . . armed," bearing arms might not have been a topic addressed by the revolutionary settlement. Guaranteeing access to arms for Protestants, which was linked in the same sentence to the prohibition against standing armies, was intended to ensure a stable government free from the disruptions caused by Catholic Jacobites and the ambitious intrigues of future monarchs. The Bill of Rights gave to Parliament the responsibility to guarantee the external and domestic security of the realm. That meant guaranteeing a place for Protestants in the military affairs of the kingdom, at least so long as that fitted the larger goal of maintaining a free and stable constitutional structure.[9]

After the Glorious Revolution, most political commentators in Britain lost interest in the militia as a guarantor of political freedom. Believing that the

[7] [John Toland], The Militia Reform'd; or, An Easy Scheme of Furnishing England with a Constant Land-Force (London, 1698), 3–66; [Trenchard and Moyle], Argument, Shewing, That a Standing Army Is Inconsistent with a Free Government, 4–5, 7, 17–18, 21–22.
[8] Bernard Schwartz, ed., The Roots of the Bill of Rights (5 vols., New York, 1980), I, 42–43.
[9] Ibid.; Emery, "Constitutional Right to Keep and Bear Arms," 473–74.

Bill of Rights had secured for Parliament the means to prevent royal misuse of the nation's military forces, men such as Daniel Defoe, John Somers, and others embraced the argument that standing armies financed by Parliament were militarily superior to the militia as well as compatible with traditional English liberties. Nevertheless, Opposition writers continued to insist that only an organized and disciplined militia composed of the landed citizenry could prevent Britain from succumbing to the same corrupting forces that had destroyed liberty in ancient Rome. Trenchard and Gordon's *Cato's Letters*, frequently reprinted in the American colonies, and the writings of Francis Hutcheson at the University of Glasgow ensured that Americans remained exposed to the neoclassical republicanism of radical Whig theory.[10]

James Burgh's *Political Disquisitions* (1774-1775), copies of which were owned by a host of prominent American leaders, provided a convenient summary of Opposition views on the relationship between the militia and the preservation of political liberty. Borrowing extensively from promilitia tracts written during the reign of William III, Burgh attacked standing armies as anathema to freedom while holding up the citizen-soldier as its only guarantor. But not just anyone should have access to the arms militia membership implied. "Men of property," Burgh insisted, "must be our only resource. . . . A militia consisting of any others than the men of *property* in a country, is no militia; but a mungrel army." The importance of placing arms only in the hands of those "whose interest is involved in that of their country" was historically undeniable. Rome succumbed to tyranny when landed citizens shed their responsibility for the republic's defense. On the other hand, liberty survived in Switzerland because arms and citizenship remained inseparable. The lessons of history were clear: "If the militia be not upon a right foot"—that is, if classical notions of the citizen in arms were violated—"the liberty of the people must perish."[11]

Burgh thought that circumstances in England and the American colonies on the eve of the American Revolution justified the position held by Opposition writers since Trenchard in 1697 wrote *An Argument, Shewing, that a Standing Army Is Inconsistent with a Free Government, and Absolutely Destructive to the Constitution of the English Monarchy*. "Our times prove Mr. Trenchard a true prophet," declared the dissident essayist. Americans concerned about the constitutional foundations of liberty in the colonies agreed. In *A Summary View of the Rights of British America*, Thomas Jefferson, indicting George III for sending "among us large bodies of armed forces, not made up of the people

[10] [John Trenchard and Thomas Gordon], *Cato's Letters: or, Essays on Liberty, Civil and Religious, and Other Important Subjects* (4 vols., London, 1755), I, 192-94, II, 278-91; Francis Hutcheson, *A System of Moral Philosophy* (3 vols., London, 1755), II, 323-25. For a discussion of the influence of these and other radical Whigs in American political circles, see Cress, "Radical Whiggery on the Role of the Military," 51-54. For an analysis of moderate Whig discussions of the militia and standing army in eighteenth-century English society, see Cress, *Citizens in Arms*, 25-33.

[11] [James Burgh], *Political Disquisitions: or, An Enquiry into Public Errors, Defects, and Abuses* (3 vols., London, 1774-1775), II, 248-49, 356-57, 359-60, 378-82, 390-92, 396-98, 400, 402-05, 425, 430-31, 434-35, 439, 463-65.

here, nor raised by the authority of our laws," reflected an American awareness of the relationship between liberty and military power. The occupation of
Boston by British soldiers in 1768 and again in 1774, to say nothing of the
Boston Massacre, left little doubt that hired soldiers could be agents of
political oppression. Important, too, was the colonial militia. In the winter
and spring of 1774–1775, colonists gathered at county assemblies and provincial conventions roundly to condemn standing armies while resolving—in
language that foreshadowed the Second Amendment—"that a well-regulated
Militia, composed of the gentlemen, freeholders, and other freemen, is the
natural strength and only stable security of a free Government." At the same
time, the Continental Congress urged provincial assemblies to "disarm all
such as will not associate to defend the American rights by arms."[12]

Such declarations merely summarized sentiment long extant in the
colonies. During the Seven Years War, Thomas Pownall reminded the officers
and men of the Massachusetts militia that "free government" depended on the
willingness of "every freeman and every freeholder" to be a soldier. "Let
therefore every man, that, appealing to his own heart, feels the least spark of
virtue or freedom there, think that it is an honour which he owes himself, and
a duty which he owes his country, to bear arms." Pownall did not have in
mind the isolated individual standing guard over his person and property. The
citizen-soldier defended life and liberty by "bear[ing] arms in the bands of his
country."[13] Sermon and pamphlet literature published in the colonies after
1768 emphasized the same point. "A well-disciplined militia is the beauty,
and under God, the security of a country," declared Samuel Stillman in 1770,
using language that would appear again and again as relations with the British
Empire worsened. The best civil constitution would be meaningless if the
people were unable to deter ambitious tyrants by force of arms. "The true
strength and safety of every commonwealth or limited monarchy," proclaimed James Lovell on the first anniversary of the Boston Massacre, "is the
bravery of its freeholders, its militia."[14]

[12] Ibid., II, 439; [Thomas Jefferson], A Summary View of the Rights of British America
(Williamsburg, [1774]), 21; Peter Force, comp., American Archives: Fourth Series. Containing a
Documentary History of the English Colonies in North America (6 vols., Washington,
1837–1846), I, 1022, 1032, II, 167–68, 399–400, III, 647–48; H. Niles, Principles and Acts of the
Revolution in America: or, An Attempt to Collect and Preserve Some of the Speeches, Orations,
and Proceedings (Baltimore, 1822), 108–10, 240, 277–78; Robert A. Rutland, ed., The Papers of
George Mason, 1725–1792 (3 vols., Chapel Hill, 1970), I, 210–11, 212, 215–16; Novanglus [John
Adams], "To the Inhabitants of the Colony of Massachusetts-Bay," Boston Gazette, Feb. 6, 1775;
Oliver Wolcott to Samuel Lyman, March 16, 1776, in Edmund C. Barnett, ed., Letters of Members
of the Continental Congress (8 vols., Washington, 1921–1936), I, 397; Cress, "Radical Whiggery
on the Role of the Military," 56–60.
[13] T. Pownall, The Exercise for the Militia of the Province of the Massachusetts-Bay, by Order of
His Excellency. Prefatory and Explanatory Instructions to the Officers and Men, in The
Remembrancer, or Impartial Repository of Public Events (17 vols., London, 1775–1784), VIII, 91.
[14] Simeon Howard, A Sermon Preached to the Ancient and Honorable Artillery-Company, in
Boston, New-England, June 7th, 1773 (Boston, 1773), 22–26, 40–41; Samuel Stillman, A Sermon
Preached to the Ancient and Honorable Artillery Company in Boston, New-England, June 4, 1770
(Boston, 1770), 28–30; Niles, Principles and Acts of the Revolution in America, 17–20; Jeremy
Belknap, A Sermon on Military Duty, Preached at Dover, November 10, 1772 (Salem, Mass.,
1773), 7–15; Elisha Fish, The Art of War Lawful, and Necessary for a Christian People, Considered

Lovell's association of freehold status with militia membership was not coincidental. A sound militia structure ensured a citizenry ably drilled in arms, but it also defined the limits of the body politic. "The sword should never be in the hands of any, but those who have an interest in the safety of the community," declared Josiah Quincy in his widely read attack on the Boston Port Bill. Landless wanderers might be pressed into military service in an emergency, but the defense of liberty depended on a "well disciplined militia, composed of men of fortunes, of education, and virtues, . . . excited to the most vigorous action, by motives infinitely superior to the expectation of spoils." The protection of family, property, and constitutional liberties motivated these individuals to serve the common good. Hence they could be relied on to return to the "enjoyment of freedom and good order" when the danger passed. Furthermore, regular training in arms had "a natural Tendency to introduce and establish good Order, and a just Subordination among the different Classes of People in the Community." As had Machiavelli, Harrington, and the radical Whigs, Americans saw the militia as an expression of the corporate unity of society. Men of rank and substance commanded the "well regulated" militia; men of lesser means filled its rank and file. In short, the parade field reinforced the deferential social and political relationships that ensured order and a respect for authority throughout society.[15]

Americans, of course, looked to the militia to protect their liberties after Great Britain returned Redcoats to American soil in the early summer of 1774. They also turned to it as new constitutions were created to replace crumbling royal authority in the late spring of 1776. Virginia's Declaration of Rights— adopted on June 12, 1776, nearly a month before the American colonies officially announced their independence—set the pattern. Article 13, drafted by George Mason and approved by a committee that included James Madison, declared "That a well-regulated Militia, composed of the body of the people, trained to arms, is the proper, natural, and safe defence of a free State." Two months later, Pennsylvania declared that "the people have a right to bear arms for the defence of themselves and the state." The language was slightly different, but the meaning was the same. Only the citizenry, trained, armed, and organized in the militia, could be depended on to preserve republican liberties for "themselves" and to ensure the constitutional stability of "the state." Both documents linked the citizen's responsibility for the defense of the state to the threat of standing armies: standing armies were "dangerous to

and Enforced (Boston, 1774), 2-17; Force, comp., *American Archives*, III, 219-21; Daniel Shute, *A Sermon Preached to the Ancient and Honorable Artillery Company in Boston, New-England, June 1, 1767* (Boston, 1767), 18-28; *Boston Gazette*, Jan. 27, 1772. For an analysis of the standing army and militia in the minds of American leaders on the eve of independence, see Cress, *Citizens in Arms*, 34-50.

[15] Howard, *Sermon Preached*, 28-29, 40-41; *Essex Gazette*, Jan. 31, 1769; Josiah Quincy, Jr., *Observations on the Act of Parliament Commonly Called the Boston Port-Bill; with Thoughts on Civil Society and Standing Armies* (Boston, 1774), 41-43; Jonas Clark, *The Importance of Military Skill, Measures for Defence and a Martial Spirit, in a Time of Peace* (Boston, 1768), 14-23; John Lathrop, *A Sermon Preached to the Ancient and Honorable Artillery-Company in Boston, New-England, June 6th 1774* (Boston, 1774), 34-39.

liberty" and must be kept "under strict subordination" to the civil government.[16]

Delaware, Maryland, and North Carolina adopted similar declarations during the first year of independence. Delaware and Maryland borrowed language from Virginia's Article 13; North Carolina, following Pennsylvania's lead, declared that "the people have a right to bear arms, for the defence of the State." Vermont, though not to become a state until 1792, quoted verbatim Pennsylvania's Article 13 in its 1777 Declaration of Rights. In the same year New York incorporated into its constitution an equally clear reminder of a militia's relationship to the success of republican government. Announcing it to be "the duty of every man who enjoys the protection of society to be prepared and willing to defend it," New Yorkers proclaimed that the "militia . . . at all times . . . shall be armed and disciplined." Several other states took a similar approach. Only Massachusetts and New Hampshire joined Virginia, Pennsylvania, Delaware, Maryland, and North Carolina in adopting a separate declaration of rights.[17]

John Adams, who was as important to the Massachusetts Declaration of Rights as Mason was to Virginia's, borrowed the style of the Quaker State's declaration when he drafted the Declaration of Rights that stood for ratification with the 1780 constitution. "The people," he wrote, "have a right to keep and to bear arms for the common defence." By "the people," John Adams meant the militia. "The public sword, without a hand to hold it, is but cold iron," he noted some years later, and "the hand which holds this sword is the militia of the nation." New Hampshire's 1783 Bill of Rights made the same point, declaring that "A well regulated militia is the proper, natural, and sure defence of a state." Both documents condemned standing armies and pronounced the subordination of military to civil authority, in the process underscoring the citizen militia's collective role as the protector of personal liberty and constitutional stability against ambitious tyrants and uncontrolled mobs.[18]

Whether it was Massachusetts' declaration that citizens had the right "to bear arms for the common defence" or Virginia's affirmation that the militia was "the proper, natural, and safe defence of a free State," the point was the same. Republicanism depended on the existence of a sound militia. Only a strong, popularly based militia could protect liberty against domestic turmoil and tyrannical intrigue.

The language of constitutional provisions protecting conscientious objectors from military service underscores the fact that for eighteenth-century Americans "to bear arms" meant militia service. Such guarantees took the form of limitations on the individual's militia obligation. Pennsylvania pro-

---

[16] Schwartz, ed., *Roots of the Bill of Rights*, II, 231, 235, 266.

[17] *Ibid.*, II, 278, 282, 287, 312, 324. For a summary of state constitutional provisions bearing on the militia and its relationship to civil authority, see Cress, *Citizens in Arms*, 60–62.

[18] Schwartz, ed., *Roots of the Bill of Rights*, II, 342, 378. John Adams quoted James Harrington's *Commonwealth of Oceana* in *A Defence of the Constitutions of Government of the United States of America.* Charles Francis Adams, ed., *The Works of John Adams, Second President of the United States* (10 vols., Boston, 1850–1856), IV, 430.

vided that no "man who is conscientiously scrupulous of bearing arms" could be "compelled" to serve in the militia, though an individual was still required to meet his obligation for the state's defense by paying an "equivalent." Delaware and Vermont adopted similar language. New York's constitution limited such exemptions only to Quakers, who "from scruples of conscience, may be averse to the bearing of arms." It, too, required conscientious objectors to "pay to the State such sums of money, in lieu of their personal service." New Hampshire's Bill of Rights was both more broadly conceived and more direct: "No person who is conscientiously scrupulous about the lawfulness of bearing arms, shall be compeled thereto, provided he will pay an equivalent."[19]

State after state guaranteed the sovereign citizenry, described collectively as "the people" or "the militia," a role in the common defense. On the other hand, the expression "man" or "person" is used to describe individual rights such as freedom of conscience. New Hampshire's Bill of Rights, the last written during the Confederation period and as such a compendium of previous thinking on the matter, provides a case in point. It declared the importance of "a well regulated militia [to the] defence of a state" while it exempted from service any "person . . . conscientiously scrupulous about the lawfulness of bearing arms." In other words, the individual right of conscience was asserted against the collective responsibility of the citizenry for the common defense. There could be no other logical reason for an exemption from "bearing arms" unless it applied to doing service in the militia. Indeed, the state assessed "equivalents" so that someone else could be hired to "bear arms" in the conscientious objector's place.[20]

The same issues that informed the states' declarations of rights—the importance of the militia to republican government, the threat of standing armies, the free exercise of conscience in matters of militia service, the subordination of military to civil authority—carried over into the debate over the new federal Constitution. Federalists and Antifederalists alike agreed that the citizenry trained in arms was the only sure guarantor of liberty. Americans, unlike peoples living under arbitrary governments, were "required by Law" to train with the militia, noted an anonymous essayist in the midst of the struggle over ratification. "This is a circumstance which encreases the power and consequence of the people; and enables them to defend their rights and privileges against every invader." Antifederalists, however, were convinced that the power granted the national government threatened the militia's place in the Republic's constitutional structure. "My great objection to this government," Patrick Henry announced to Virginia's ratification convention, "is, that it does not leave us the means of defending our rights." "Have we the means of resisting disciplined armies," he continued, "when our only defence, the militia, is put into the hands of Congress?" The author of *Letters from a Federalist Farmer* also feared Congress's power to organize and

[19] Schwartz, ed., *Roots of the Bill of Rights*, II, 265, 277, 312, 323, 377.
[20] *Ibid.*, 312, 324, 377, 378.

to train the militia. A select militia of "one fifth or one eighth part of the men capable of bearing arms, . . . and those the young and ardent part of the community, possessed of but little or no property," could be formed while propertied citizens were organized in a fashion "render[ing] them of no importance." "The former," he argued, "will answer all the purposes of [a standing] army, while the latter will be defenceless."[21]

Luther Martin, the outspoken Marylander who had left the Philadelphia Constitutional Convention in protest, also registered concern about the new government's military prerogatives. "Instead of *guarding against a standing army*, . . . which has so *often* and so *successfully* been used for the *subversion of freedom*," the Constitution gave "it an *express* and *constitutional sanction*." Congress's access to the states' militias troubled him too. Its authority over the militia, he warned, could be used "even [to] disarm" it. Worse, the militia might be abused—needlessly mobilized for service in the far reaches of the Union—so that the people would be glad to see a standing army raised in its place. "When a government wishes to deprive their citizens of freedom," he noted, "it generally makes use of a standing army . . . and leaves the militia in a situation as contemptible as possible, lest they might oppose its arbitrary designs." Pennsylvania's vocal Antifederalist minority expressed similar fears, demanding for the states the power to organize, arm, and discipline the militia as well as the power to veto a congressional call for service outside a state's borders.[22]

Mason's efforts to amend the Constitution provide a convenient summary of the sentiments that led ultimately to the Second Amendment. During the last days of the Philadelphia Constitutional Convention, Mason, having failed to secure a separate bill of rights, sought an explicit statement of the militia's place in the new government. He urged that the congressional power to arm, to organize, and to discipline the militia be prefaced by a clause identifying that prerogative as intended better to secure "the liberties of the people . . . against the danger of standing armies in time of peace." Madison, who would later

[21] *Connecticut Courant*, Jan. 7, 1788; Alexander Hamilton, "The Federalist No. 29," in *The Federalist*, ed. Jacob E. Cooke (Middletown, Conn., 1961), 184-85; James Madison, "The Federalist No. 46," in *ibid.*, 320-22; *Debates and Proceedings in the Convention of the Commonwealth of Massachusetts, Held in the Year 1788, and Which Finally Ratified the Constitution of the United States* (Boston, 1856), 349-50; [Noah Webster], *An Examination into the Leading Principles of the Federal Constitution Proposed by the Late Convention Held at Philadelphia*, in Paul Leicester Ford, ed., *Pamphlets on the Constitution of the United States, Published during Its Discussion by the People, 1787-1788* (Brooklyn, 1888), 56-57; [Tench Coxe], *An Examination of the Constitution for the United States of America*, in *ibid.*, 151; Jonathan Elliot, ed., *The Debates in the Several State Conventions on the Adoption of the Federal Constitution, as Recommended by the General Convention at Philadelphia in 1787* (5 vols., Philadelphia, 1836-1845), III, 47-48, 52; Cecelia M. Kenyon, ed., *The Antifederalists* (Indianapolis, 1966), 228-29.

[22] Paul Leicester Ford, ed., *Essays on the Constitution of the United States, Published during Its Discussion by the People, 1787-1788* (Brooklyn, 1892), 358-59; Max Farrand, ed., *The Records of the Federal Convention of 1787* (4 vols., New Haven, 1937), III, 207-08, 285; Elliot, ed., *Debates in the Several State Conventions*, I, 371-72, II, 406, 545-46, 552-53; Kenyon, ed., *Antifederalists*, 22-23, 36-37, 57-58, 361-62; John Bach McMaster and Frederick D. Stone, eds., *Pennsylvania and the Federal Constitution, 1787-1788* (Philadelphia, 1888), 180-82, 502.

draft the Bill of Rights, supported the measure, but the convention rejected the proposal. Mason subsequently declined to endorse the Constitution. As he explained in his frequently reprinted "Objections to This Constitution of Government," the document contained "no Declaration of Rights." Specifically, it lacked a "declaration of any kind . . . against the danger of standing armies."[23]

Mason became an increasingly vocal opponent of ratification during the winter of 1787–1788. On the eve of Virginia's ratification convention, he joined other Antifederalists in an effort to graft the essence of the commonwealth's Article 13—along with other parts of Virginia's Bill of Rights—to the new Constitution. Declaring that the "People have a Right to keep & to bear Arms," the proposed amendment identified "a well regulated Militia [as] the proper natural and safe Defence of a free State." It also pointed to the dangers of standing armies and to the need for the "strict Subordination" of military to civil authority. A separate amendment proposed that a person "religiously scrupulous of bearing Arms" be allowed "to employ another to bear Arms in his Stead."[24] Neither Mason nor other members of the Antifederalist caucus gathered in Richmond criticized the Constitution's failure to guarantee individual access to weapons.

For Virginia's leading Antifederalist, the issue at hand was the militia's access to arms. "The militia may be here destroyed," Mason warned Virginia's ratification convention in a lengthy speech on June 14, 1788, "by rendering them useless, by disarming them." Great Britain had entertained a scheme some forty years before "to disarm the people. . . . by totally difusing and neglecting the militia." If the new government wanted to do the same, raising a standing army in the militia's place, the states would be helpless because "congress has the exclusive right to arm them." "Why," Mason asked, "should we not provide against the danger of having our militia, our real and natural strength, destroyed?" He urged that the Constitution be amended to provide "in case the general government should neglect to arm and discipline the militia, that there should be an express declaration, that the state governments might arm and discipline them." Hence Mason backed Henry's proposal "that each State respectively shall have the Power to provide for organizing, arming and disciplining its own Militia, whensoever the Congress shall omit or neglect to provide for the Same."[25]

The notion that the individual should be guaranteed access to weapons surfaced several times during the debate over the Constitution. The minority report of the Pennsylvania ratifying convention borrowed language from the state's own Declaration of Rights to declare the people's right "to bear arms for

---

[23] Notes of Debates in the Federal Convention of 1787. Reported by James Madison (Athens, Ohio, 1966), 630, 639–40; Rutland, ed., Papers of George Mason, III, 991–93.

[24] Rutland, ed., Papers of George Mason, III, 1070–71. Concern over the Constitution's failure to protect conscientious objectors was common in Antifederalist tracts. Typical in charging that "men consciensiously scrupulous of bearing arms [are] made liable to perform military duty" was a manifesto from Albany County, N.Y., that appeared in the New York Journal. Kenyon, ed., Antifederalists, 362.

[25] Rutland, ed., Papers of George Mason, III, 1074–75, 1079–81, 1117.

the defence of themselves and their own State or the United States." But it also claimed the right to bear arms "for the purpose of killing game," adding the proviso that "no law shall be passed for disarming the people or any of them." In Massachusetts, Samuel Adams argued that the Constitution be amended so to ensure that it "never [be] construed to authorize Congress to . . . prevent the people of the United States who are peaceable citizens from keeping their own arms." He later withdrew the proposal, however, probably after reflecting on the recent revolt by armed citizens in Massachusetts. Finally, New Hampshire included a proposal that "Congress shall never disarm any citizen, unless such as are or have been in actual rebellion" among a series of amendments recommended for consideration by the First Congress.[26]

The principles evoked by those resolutions were, however, much more akin to the classical republican understanding of the armed citizenry than appears at first glance. Bearing arms was linked to the citizenry's collective responsibility for the republic's defense. Standard warnings about the threat of standing armies and the need to ensure the subordination of military to civil authority underscored that responsibility. Certainly neither Pennsylvania's dissenters nor New Hampshire's cautious supporters of the new constitutional arrangement had moved far, if they had moved at all, beyond the eighteenth-century notion that bearing arms meant militia service. That both states carefully qualified the individual's right to arms points to the same conclusion. New Hampshire recognized Congress's right to disarm individuals who "are or have been in actual rebellion." Pennsylvania's Antifederalists allowed the disarming of criminals. They also conceded that more inclusive measures could be enacted when society expected "real danger of public injury from individuals."[27] Similarly, Samuel Adams's recommendation allowed for the disarming of citizens falling outside the category of "peaceable." In other words, the order and security of society took precedence over the individual's right to arms. As in more orthodox expressions of the armed citizenry's collective relationship to the political order, constitutional stability remained the preeminent consideration.

Whatever the intention of Pennsylvania and New Hampshire, no one else followed their lead while formulating either dissenting resolutions or constitutional amendments. Jefferson's recommendation that Virginia's Constitution of 1776 guarantee that no freeman be denied the use of arms "within his own lands or tenements" represents the only other hint that Americans may have viewed bearing arms as an individual right. And, of course, that language was not incorporated into the commonwealth's constitution, probably because its framers thought that the "Militia, composed of the body of the people, trained

[26] Kenyon, ed., *Antifederalists*, 36; William V. Wells, *The Life and Public Services of Samuel Adams. Being a Narrative of His Acts and Opinions, and of His Agency in Producing and Forwarding the American Revolution* (3 vols., Boston, 1865), III, 267; Elliot, ed., *Debates in the Several State Conventions*, I, 326, II, 162.

[27] Kenyon, ed., *Antifederalists*, 36.

to arms," as Mason had phrased it in Article 13 of the Declaration of Rights, more accurately stated the armed citizenry's relationship to the body politic.[28]

The amendments proposed by state ratifying conventions reflect a determination to incorporate into the new Constitution many of the principles already embodied in existing declarations of rights. New York and North Carolina, for example, urged that Congress's power to raise a peacetime army be limited by requiring "the consent of two thirds" of the House and of the Senate. Maryland even suggested that a soldier's enlistment be restricted to four years in order to prevent Congress from having access to a permanent military force. But strong state militias remained the principal means to counter the tyrannical potential of the Constitution. Seven states expressed their commitment to the citizen's right to bear arms through the agency of a well-regulated militia either through proposed amendments, general statements of principle, or in the language of dissenting resolutions. Pennsylvania's Antifederalists were the first to act; Rhode Island's tardy ratification convention was the last. The fear that the militia would be purposely neglected gave rise to proposals guaranteeing that the states could organize, arm, and discipline their citizens if Congress failed to fulfill its responsibilities. A more common fear, though, was that Congress's right to call out the militia would prove detrimental to republican liberties. New Yorkers recommended that a state's militia not be compelled to serve outside its borders longer than six weeks "without the consent of the legislature thereof." Others worried that the subjection of the militia to martial law might lead to abuses. The Maryland convention believed that "all other provisions in favor of the rights of men would be vain and nugatory, if the power of subjecting all men, able to bear arms, to martial law at any moment should remain vested in Congress." Along with North Carolina, Maryland asked Congress to amend the Constitution so that the militia could be placed under martial law only "in time of war, invasion, or rebellion."[29] Finally, several state conventions stated firmly that no person "religiously scrupulous of bearing arms" should be compelled to do military service.[30]

Virginia's proposed amendments, which probably most directly influenced Madison's draft of the Bill of Rights, help bring into focus the concerns that ultimately produced the Second Amendment. Indeed, the changes proposed by the commonwealth's ratifying convention nicely define the issues raised during later congressional debates. Declaring that "the people have a right to keep and bear arms," Virginians asked for constitutional recognition of the principle that "a well regulated militia, composed of the body of the people trained to arms, is the proper, natural and safe defence of a free state." That

[28] Julian P. Boyd et al., eds., *The Papers of Thomas Jefferson* (20 vols., Princeton, 1950-), I, 344, 353, 363.
[29] Elliot, ed., *Debates in the Several State Conventions*, I, 328, 330-31, 334-35, II, 550-52, III, 659-60, IV, 244-47; Kenyon, ed., *Antifederalists*, 36-37. For the amendments proposed by New Hampshire, see Bernard Schwartz, ed., *The Bill of Rights: A Documentary History* (2 vols., New York, 1971), II, 760-61.
[30] Kenyon, ed., *Antifederalists*, 35, 37; Elliot, ed., *Debates in the Several State Conventions*, I, 335, II, 553, III, 659, IV, 244.

proposition addressed the fear that the new government might disarm the citizenry while raising an oppressive standing army. To reinforce the point, the convention urged that the Constitution declare that standing armies "are dangerous to liberty, and therefore ought to be avoided, as far as the circumstances and protection of the community will admit." The Constitution was also found wanting for failing to pronounce the military "in all cases" subordinate to "civil power." A separate amendment urged "That any person religiously scrupulous of bearing arms ought to be exempted, upon payment of an equivalent to employ another to bear arms in his stead." At no time did anyone express concern about the right of individuals to carry weapons.[31]

Madison had Virginia's recommendations in mind when, on June 8, 1789, he proposed to Congress that the Constitution be amended to provide that "The right of the people to keep and bear arms shall not be infringed; a well armed and well regulated militia being the best security of a free country; but no person religiously scrupulous of bearing arms shall be compelled to render military service in person." Reacting to the widely held fear that Congress's access to the militia might be misused, the Virginia representative proposed that that amendment be placed alongside the other limitations on legislative power listed in Article 1, Section 9, of the Constitution.[32]

Six weeks later, a committee of eleven, composed of Madison and representatives from each of the other states that had ratified the Constitution, began preparing a formal slate of amendments, using as a guide both Madison's recommendations and those proposed by the states. The committee revised Madison's original recommendation, stating more explicitly the armed citizenry's importance to the constitutional order. "A well regulated militia, composed of the body of the people," the new language read, "being the best security of a free state, the right of the people to keep and bear arms shall not be infringed." The use of the term *people* in the collective sense is unmistakable here. Madison's proposal to guarantee for individuals the free exercise of conscience in military matters was rewritten as well. The committee recommended that "no person religiously scrupulous shall be compelled to bear arms," removing even the obligation to pay an "equivalent" in lieu of military service.[33]

Most members of Congress found the committee's recommendation acceptable. The doubts that were raised underscore the aim of the Second Amendment to guarantee the militia's place under the new constitutional order. Elbridge Gerry commented that only the feared "mal-administration of the Government" made such an amendment necessary. He suggested that rephrasing the proposal to read "a well regulated militia, trained to arms" might better accomplish the desired end, making it "the duty of the Government to provide this security." "Whenever Governments mean to

[31] Elliot, ed., *Debates in the Several State Conventions*, III, 659–60.
[32] *Annals of Congress*, 1 Cong., 1 sess., June 8, 1789, p. 451.
[33] *Ibid.*, July 21, 1789, pp. 685–91; *ibid.*, Aug. 17, 1789, p. 778. For the Committee of Eleven Report on Proposed Amendments, July 28, 1789, see Schwartz, ed., *Roots of the Bill of Rights*, V, illustration following p. 1014.

invade the rights and liberties of the people," he reminded the House, "they always attempt to destroy the militia, in order to raise an army upon their ruins."[34]

Gerry's proposal failed to receive a second and died on the House floor, but his related concern that the exemption for conscientious objectors might seriously undermine the viability of the militia received a far more sympathetic hearing. The government might declare every citizen "religiously scrupulous, and prevent them from bearing arms," leaving the citizenry defenseless against a standing army, Gerry warned. His fear no doubt struck most in the hall as a bit farfetched. Still, the amendment's failure to link freedom of conscience to the obligation to find a substitute or to pay an "equivalent" troubled many members of the House. Requiring one part of the population to provide for the defense of the other was simply "unjust," argued Georgia's James Jackson. Others believed that matters of "religious persuasion" had no place in an amendment designed to guarantee a fundamental principle of republican government. "It is extremely injudicious," warned one congressman, "to intermix matters of doubt with fundamentals." Together those concerns caused the House to come within two votes of striking the conscientious objection clause from the proposed amendment.[35]

Yet another concern arose on the House floor before the amendment was passed on to the Senate. It spoke to a feeling, frequently expressed in state declarations of rights, that guaranteeing a place for the militia in the constitutional order would not alone prevent abuse of Congress's prerogative to raise standing armies. South Carolina's Aedanus Burke asked for a clause declaring that a "standing army . . . in time of peace is dangerous to public liberty, and such shall not be raised . . . without the consent of two-thirds of the members present of both Houses." He also asked for an explicit statement of the subordination of military to civil authority. The amendment received a second but was defeated after objections were raised to requiring more than a majority vote and amid complaints that debate had already been closed. Nevertheless, Burke's amendment underscores the context in which Congress debated the Second Amendment. The aim was to lay down a fundamental principle of republican government: that a well-regulated militia was the "best security of a free State."[36]

Little is known about the Senate's debate of the Second Amendment, though it seems to have followed a pattern similar to that in the House. The controversial conscientious objection clause failed to get Senate approval. That body, however, joined the House in rejecting a proposal to restrict Congress's power to raise armies during peacetime. Finally, the Senate rejected an amendment to insert "for the common defence"—apparently after "to bear arms"—while it agreed to rephrase the nature of the militia's relationship to the Republic's security, calling it "necessary to," rather than the "best" form of, national defense. The first change no doubt reflected

[34] *Annals of Congress*, 1 Cong., 1 sess., Aug. 17, 1789, pp. 778–80.
[35] *Ibid.*
[36] *Ibid.*, 780–81.

efforts to ensure that it was the militia that was to bear arms; its rejection reflected not the undesirability of that end but, rather, the feeling that the proposal was redundant. The decision to describe the militia as necessary to the national defense more accurately expressed the growing sentiment in America that in wartime regular soldiers also had an important role to play, even in the defense of a republic.[37]

The Senate's changes were accepted by a joint conference committee of both houses, and on September 24 and September 25, 1789, the House and Senate respectively voted their approval. Unfortunately, we know little about the Second Amendment's reception in the states. No state rejected the amendment. As a statement of republican principle already commonplace in many state declarations of rights, it probably evoked little discussion.[38] If doubts were raised, and there is no evidence that they were, they probably centered on the amendment's failure to link the militia explicitly to the dangers represented by a standing army.

Whatever the issues, when Virginia ratified the Second Amendment on December 15, 1791, "A well regulated Militia, being necessary to the security of a free State, the right of the people to keep and bear Arms, shall not be infringed" became part of the Constitution.[39] The notion that republicanism depended on a vital militia had become part of the nation's higher law. Henceforth, Congress was prohibited from taking any action that might disarm or otherwise render the militia less effective. The Second Amendment, then, stated a basic principle of American republicanism: The body politic's ability to defend the liberties of the people and the constitutional foundation of the state against an ambitious tyrant's standing army or a manipulative demagogue's armed mob could not be infringed upon.

Through the early national period, the trained militiaman remained linked to constitutional stability and to the liberty that that ensured. "A people [can] defend their territory, or resist an assuming government," reminded Thomas Barnard in a 1789 sermon addressing the importance of a well-disciplined militia, "but by arms." The members of the Ancient and Honorable Artillery Company in attendance could not have found his counsel surprising. Though frustrated by the performance of militia soldiers during the war years, few Americans—including the Continental Army's principal training officer, Friedrich von Steuben—questioned the desirability of having "a perfect knowledge of the duties of a soldier engraved on the mind of every citizen." And most would have agreed that only a well-organized militia could accomplish that end. Henry Knox, also formerly among George Washington's chief advisers, believed that the "future glory and power of the United States" depended on the establishment of a militia structure that not only trained citizens to arms but also instilled a commitment to the public good. As the last secretary at war to serve under the Articles of Confederation, he proposed such a plan—a plan he thought capable "of forming the manners of the rising

[37] Schwartz, ed., Roots of the Bill of Rights, V, 1149, 1152, 1153–54.
[38] Annals of Congress, 1 Cong., 1 sess., Sept. 24, 1789, p. 948; ibid., Sept. 25, 1789, p. 90; Schwartz, ed., Roots of the Bill of Rights, V, 1193–1203.
[39] Schwartz, ed., Roots of the Bill of Rights, V, 1202.

generation on principles of republican virtue; of infusing into their minds, that the love of their country, and the knowledge of defending it, are political duties of the most indispensible nature."[40]

At Washington's request, Knox in early 1790 submitted to Congress a revised version of his plan for militia reform, prefaced by remarks that reveal much about the assumptions behind the ratification of the Second Amendment. The United States, Knox wrote, had an "invaluable opportunity" to establish "such institutions as shall invigorate, exalt, and perpetuate, the great principles of freedom." The militia was one such institution: "an efficient military branch of Government can[not] be invented, with safety to the great principles of liberty, unless the same shall be formed of the people themselves, and supported by their habits and manners." Simply put, "an energetic national militia is to be regarded as the capital security of a free Republic; and not a standing army." In the first place, "every man . . . is firmly bound by the social compact to perform, personally, his proportion of military duty for the defence of the State." On a more practical level, however, the security of a free society depended on the people's possessing "a competent knowledge of the military art"—a knowledge that could be "attained in the present state of society" only by establishing adequate institutions for military education.[41]

Basing the "responsib[ility] for different degrees of military service" on age and physical ability, Knox proposed a classed militia intended to prepare citizens to meet both their military and their civil responsibilities. The external and internal security of the nation would be ensured by the arms of "the well-informed members of the community, actuated by the highest motives." Indeed, the citizen-soldier and the body politic would be indistinguishable under Knox's scheme. Certification of militia service would be "required as an indispensable qualification for exercising any of the rights of a free citizen." His militia plan, Knox believed, would have far-reaching consequences for America: "an energetic republican militia [would] be durably established, the invaluable principles of liberty secured and perpetuated, and a dignified national fabric erected on the solid foundation of public virtue."[42]

Knox's attempt to institutionalize, through the militia, classical perceptions of the corporate character of society as well as of the importance of public virtue proved too ambitious. Many congressmen, fearing the consequences of granting the national government extensive control over local militia units, preferred instead to establish a decentralized militia system that reflected long-standing American concerns about centralized military authority.[43] Few legislators, though, questioned the values Knox's militia plan was intended to

[40] Thomas Barnard, A Sermon. Preached at the Request of the Antient and Honourable Artillery Company. in Boston. June 1. 1789 (Boston, 1789), 25-26; Friedrich von Steuben, A Letter on the Subject of an Established Militia. and Military Arrangements. Addressed to the Inhabitants of the United States (New York, 1784), 14; [Henry Knox], A Plan for the General Arrangement of the Militia of the United States (New York, 1786), 1-6.
[41] Annals of Congress, 1 Cong., 2 sess., Jan. 18, 1790, appendix, pp. 2088-2107.
[42] Ibid.
[43] For the text of the militia act of 1792, see ibid., 2 Cong., 1 sess., May 8, 1792, appendix, pp. 1392-95. For conflicting assessments of its significance, see Cress, Citizens in Arms, 115-21; and

instill. "The security of a free State," to use the language of the Second
Amendment, depended on an armed citizenry formed into "a well regulated
Militia." Indeed, when Americans spoke of the armed citizenry's role in the
preservation of liberty, they assumed a vital militia founded on classical
notions of citizenship.

The debate over militia reform that followed on the heels of the Whisky
Rebellion is a case in point. The militia had proved less than energetic in the
face of western Pennsylvania's insurgency. More troubling was that the men
who came out were not, as Jeremiah Wadsworth put it, "the militia of the
law." They were but volunteers "influenced by their feelings, or by private
bounties." That the insurrection had been put down missed the point. A
republic must depend on its citizenry to recognize and to respond to assaults
on its security. "For any Government to rely on private, individual influence,
to protect it against its enemies, whether foreign or domestic," was dangerous.
"The same influence," advised Wadsworth, "may be turned against the
Government." William Findley, a leading Republican from Pennsylvania, also
found disconcerting the militia's reputation "as an undisciplined band of
substitutes, induced to undertake the service by the receipt of bounty and the
expectation of plunder." The mobilized militia should reflect the body politic,
each citizen "discharging [his] duty in obedience to the laws, on the same
principles with a court, jury or sheriff." After all, the militia "are as much the
representatives of the citizens, when they are called to support the laws of
their country, as the members of Congress are their Representatives to make
those laws."[44]

Similar concerns surfaced with the addition of the volunteer corps to the
American military establishment during the quasi war with France. In
Congress, Republicans charged that drawing on "men of a particular cast"—
those able to arm, to clothe, and to equip themselves—to serve at the
president's behest would undermine the constitutional balance guaranteed by
the citizen militia. Specifically, the volunteer corps reduced military service to
an expression of partisan sentiment, setting the armed force of government
apart from the body politic. The militiaman, "regulated by law," defended
liberty; but individuals united under arms by the passions of the moment
threatened the constitutional order and the freedom it preserved. As the
citizens of Louisa County, Virginia, stated the issue using language repeated
again and again by those who feared for the constitutional stability of the
Republic—"a well regulated and well organized militia, as immediately con-
necting the duties of citizens and soldiers, are the surest safeguard to the rights
and liberties of the people." If the Federalists had their way, warned one
"Humanus," the consequences would be "a well armed party-corps . . . on the
one hand; and a neglected, difused, and un-armed militia, on the other."[45]

Richard H. Kohn, *Eagle and Sword: The Federalists and the Creation of the Military Establishment
in America, 1783-1802* (New York, 1975), 128-38.
    [44] *Annals of Congress*, 3 Cong., 2 sess., Feb. 12, 1795, pp. 1217-18; *Philadelphia Aurora*, Sept. 4,
Sept. 25, Sept. 26, Sept. 27, Oct. 2, Oct. 20, Nov. 24, 1794; William Findley, *History of the
Insurrection, in the Four Western Counties of Pennsylvania* (Philadelphia, 1796), 153-68.
    [45] *Annals of Congress*, 5 Cong., 2 sess., May 16, 1798, pp. 1725-31; *Philadelphia Aurora*, Dec. 6,

The discussion evoked by John Randolph's recommendation in 1807 that Congress provide "by law, for arming and equipping the whole body of the militia of the United States" also sheds light on what contemporaries meant by "the right of the people to keep and bear Arms." "An armed people must necessarily be a free people," argued Randolph while calling for the systematic arming of all militiamen. Few in Congress disagreed. Indeed, most probably concurred with Pennsylvania's John Smilie when he observed that "it was undoubtedly a melancholy consideration, that a people enjoying the first privileges of freemen, had not yet availed themselves of one of their most important rights, that of arming themselves." Opposition that did arise centered on the practical question of cost and on the ideologically inspired fear that a militia armed by the federal government might be disarmed by the same authority. James Fisk predicted that "in the same proportion as the General Government furnished arms to the people, in the same proportion would their patriotic zeal to furnish themselves with arms be lessened." Nevertheless, his fear that Randolph's plan would jeopardize "the liberties of the people" emphasizes that for Americans the armed citizenry, "the people," were synonymous with "a well regulated Militia." "It [is] a correct principle," announced John Rhea of Tennessee, "that all the militia should be armed under a Republican Government. One of the objects of such a Government was, that the people should have arms in their hands." Roger Nelson of Maryland supported the plan to arm the militia because "he wished the people . . . to be prepared at all times to repel encroachments on their rights and liberties, whether internal or external."[46]

When discussions during the early national period turned to the preservation of liberty, then, classical assumptions about the citizen's responsibility to bear arms in the interest of the common good quickly came to the fore. "For a people who are free, and who mean to remain so," Jefferson reminded Congress in 1808 in language that summarized the republican principles embodied in the Second Amendment, "a well organized and armed militia is their best security." No one argued that the individual had a right to bear arms outside the ranks of the militia. To the contrary, bearing arms outside the framework of the established militia structure immediately provoked fears for the constitutional stability of the Republic.[47]

1798, Feb. 11, 1799, March 7, July 1, Sept. 6, 1800; *Boston Independent Chronicle*, Oct. 25, Nov. 5, Dec. 10, 1798; Joseph B. Varnum, *An Address, Delivered to the Third Division of Massachusetts, at a Review, on the Plains of Concord, 27th August, 1800* (Cambridge, Mass., 1800), 20-23. See also a song celebrating Republican election victories in Pennsylvania. *Philadelphia Aurora*, Nov. 9, 1799.

[46] *Annals of Congress*, 10 Cong., 1 sess., Dec. 1, 1807, pp. 1002-05; *ibid.*, Dec. 3, 1807, pp. 1019-56; *ibid.*, April 2, 1808, appendix, p. 2849; *ibid.*, April 9, 1808, pp. 2066-67; *ibid.*, April 16, April 18, 1808, pp. 2175-97. For discussions concerning the arming of the militia in the 1790s, see *ibid.*, 1 Cong., 3 sess., Dec. 16, Dec. 17, 1790, pp. 1804-26; *ibid.*, 5 Cong., 2 sess., June 14, 1798, pp. 1927-33; *ibid.*, July 6, 1798, appendix, pp. 3752-53.

[47] James D. Richardson, *A Compilation of the Papers of the Presidents, 1789-1897* (10 vols., Washington, 1896-1899), I, 454-55. For an analysis of thinking concerning the militia and the preservation of republicanism during the administrations of Thomas Jefferson and James Madison, see Cress, *Citizens in Arms*, 155-66.

Certainly there was no doubt in the mind of Justice Joseph Story, the great constitutional commentator of the period, that the Second Amendment was intended to guarantee "a well regulated militia." "The importance of this article will scarcely be doubted by any persons who have duly reflected upon the subject." Why? Because "the militia is the natural defence of a free country against sudden foreign invasions, domestic insurrections, and domestic usurpations of power by rulers." Citing Sir William Blackstone's *Commentaries on the Laws of England*, Story noted that "the right of the citizens to keep and bear arms has justly been considered, as the palladium of the liberties of a republic; since it offers a strong moral check against the usurpation and arbitrary power of rulers." Story's only concern was that Americans had developed an indifference to the militia that he feared would lead to contempt. If that happened, "all the protection intended by this clause of our national bill of rights" would be undermined. "The importance of a well regulated militia would seem so undeniable," argued the Supreme Court justice, that "how it is practicable to keep the people duly armed without some organization, it is difficult to see."[48]

The state and federal courts have seldom wavered from Story's interpretation of the Second Amendment. Thomas M. Cooley's 1884 edition of Blackstone's *Commentaries on the Laws of England* includes an annotation to the English jurist's comments on the right to bear arms, the annotation stating that "in the United States this right is preserved by express constitutional provisions. But it extends no further than to keep and bear those arms which are suited and proper for the general defense of the community against invasion and oppression."[49] The decision handed down by the New Jersey Supreme Court a century later is typical of what is by now nearly two centuries of constitutional opinion solidly based in the intellectual climate of the eighteenth century: "The Second Amendment, concerning the right of the people to keep and bear arms, was framed in contemplation not of individual rights but of the maintenance of the states' active, organized militias."[50]

---

[48] Joseph Story, *Commentaries on the Constitution of the United States; with a Preliminary Review of the Constitutional History of the Colonies and States, before the Adoption of the Constitution* (3 vols., Boston, 1833), III, 746–47. James Kent does not mention the right to bear arms among the individual rights guaranteed in English tradition and American law. James Kent, *Commentaries on American Law* (4 vols., New York, 1826–1830), II, 1–13.

[49] Sir William Blackstone, *Commentaries on the Laws of England*, ed. Thomas M. Cooley (2 vols., Chicago, 1884), I, 143n. See also Thomas M. Cooley, *A Treatise on the Constitutional Limitations Which Rest upon the Legislative Power of the States of the American Union* (Boston, 1868), 350.

[50] *Burton v. Sills*, 28 A.L.R. 3d 829 (1968). Important cases dealing with the meaning of the Second Amendment during the past two hundred years include *English v. State*, 35 Texas 473 (1871–72); *Andrews v. State*, 13 Heisk. 165 (Tenn. 1871); *U.S. v. Cruikshank*, 23 L. Ed. 588 (1875); *Presser v. Illinois*, 6 S. Ct. 580 (1886); *Robertson et al. v. Baldwin*, 17 S. Ct. 326 (1897); *Strickland v. State*, 72 SE 260 (Ga. 1911); *U.S. v. Miller et al.*, 59 S. Ct. 816 (1939); *U.S. v. Tot*, 131 F.2d 261 (1942). Among rare state court decisions guaranteeing individuals the constitutional right to own weapons are *Bliss v. Commonwealth*, 2 Littell 90 (Ky. 1822); and *Nunn v. State*, 1 Kelly 243 (Ga. 1846).

Article

Civic Republicanism and the Citizen Militia: The Terrifying Second Amendment

David C. Williams†

Ever since its modern rediscovery as a source of ideas for constitutional analysis, civic republicanism has not rested entirely easily in the bosoms of its principal supporters, the academic left. This discomfort may be unavoidable, because republicanism is an old belief system and carries signs of its age, while the academic left aspires to be progressive. In particular, republicans have persistently celebrated the right of citizens to keep and bear arms.[1]

This endorsement and the discomfort it causes to neorepublicans is the central theme of Sanford Levinson's recent, insightful essay, *The Embarrassing Second Amendment.*[2] Focusing on their distrust of constituted authority, Levinson argues that the republican Framers of the Second Amendment insisted

---

† Associate Professor of Law, Cornell Law School. For their many helpful comments, I would like to thank Gregory Alexander, Akhil Amar, Hendrik Hartog, James Henderson, Don Kates, Isaac Kramnick, Sanford Levinson, David Lyons, Frank Michelman, Steven Shiffrin, and Susan Williams.

1. Historically, republicanism was also at times associated with racism and slavery, *see* KENNETH S. GREENBERG, MASTERS AND STATESMEN 4 (1985), as well religious intolerance, patriarchy, and oppressive corporatism and elitism, *see* JOYCE APPLEBY, CAPITALISM AND A NEW SOCIAL ORDER: THE REPUBLICAN VISION OF THE 1790'S, at 8-19 (1984); Linda K. Kerber, *Making Republicanism Useful*, 97 YALE L.J. 1663, 1668-69 (1988). Old-style republicanism also endorsed a "natural" division of the citizenry into "the One, the Few, and the Many," *see* Frank Michelman, *The Supreme Court. 1985 Term—Foreword: Traces of Self-Government*, 100 HARV. L. REV. 4, 44-46 (1986), and an objective public good to which dissenters were required to conform, *see id.* at 22.

2. Sanford Levinson, *The Embarrassing Second Amendment*, 99 YALE L.J. 637 (1989). The Second Amendment provides: "A well regulated Militia, being necessary to the security of a free State, the right of the people to keep and bear Arms, shall not be infringed." U.S. CONST. amend. II.

on the right of all private citizens to keep arms, so as to be able to revolt.[3] Under a republican interpretation, then, the Second Amendment provides for a personal right to own firearms.[4] This reading, Levinson suggests, would be "embarrassing" to the academic left, which would prefer to prohibit private ownership of guns.[5] In a response, Wendy Brown observes that the republican right of revolution presupposed a virtuous citizenry, and as we do not now have such a populace, we should not have such a right—even if we believe in republicanism.[6] Moreover, in Brown's view, we need not today slavishly accept all aspects of early republican doctrine; instead, we should purge the tradition of its offensive elements—particularly of the sexism and violence suggested by the Second Amendment.[7]

This dialogue between Levinson and Brown has had several important consequences. It has drawn attention to the Second Amendment as a subject for scholarly analysis,[8] and it has attracted the notice of no less a popular pundit than George Will at a time when the federal government is seriously discussing nationwide gun control.[9] In addition, this dialogue explicitly addresses the concern that reviving republicanism may bring with it an acceptance, even an encouragement, of violence.[10] Levinson and Brown confront these issues with boldness, clarity, and acuity. I suggest, however, that careful examination of the intellectual context of the right to arms leads to conclusions different from both Levinson's and Brown's.

This Article addresses the meaning that the Second Amendment would bear in a modern republican interpretation. My purpose is primarily heuristic rather than prescriptive: I offer an analysis of the role of the right to bear arms in republican theory, not a judgment concerning the general attractiveness of republican theory as a whole. Such a concentration on the right to arms in the republican tradition is important for several reasons. First, the Second Amendment, perhaps more than any other provision of the Constitution, is grounded

---

3. Levinson and others commonly describe the Amendment as resting on a "right of revolution." I generally use the phrase "right of resistance" instead, because the right of revolution is so intimately associated with a Lockean framework in which citizens revolt to protect their individual rights under the social contract.

4. See Levinson, *supra* note 2, at 646-50.

5. See *id.* at 642.

6. See Wendy Brown, *Guns, Cowboys, Philadelphia Mayors, and Civic Republicanism: On Sanford Levinson's The Embarrassing Second Amendment*, 99 YALE L.J. 661, 663, 665 (1989).

7. See *id.* at 663-64, 665-66.

8. Levinson observes that the amount of academic writing on the Amendment, especially in major journals, is vastly less than that on other provisions of the Bill of Rights. See Levinson, *supra* note 2, at 639-42. Before Levinson, the only analysis in a major law journal was Don B. Kates, *Handgun Prohibition and the Original Meaning of the Second Amendment*, 82 MICH. L. REV. 204 (1983), a particularly influential piece.

9. Will recently endorsed Levinson's argument, concluding that gun control advocates—like himself—must first repeal the Amendment. See George F. Will, *The Gun Amendment Befogs a Gunfire Crisis*, ITHACA J., Mar. 22, 1991, at 8A.

10. Many commentators have noted this possibility as a concern without discussing it at any length. See, e.g., Ruth H. Bloch, *The Gendered Meanings of Virtue in Revolutionary America*, 13 SIGNS 37, 42-45 (1987); Cass R. Sunstein, *Beyond the Republican Revival*, 97 YALE L.J. 1539, 1539-40, 1564 (1988).

in the republican tradition.[11] We must therefore look principally to republicanism for illumination of the historical meaning of this particular Amendment—even if one gives a liberal reading to the rest of the document. Many
commentators have instead offered historical exegeses of the Amendment that,
in my view, miss the significance of its surrounding tradition and mistakenly
find an individual right to arms for self-defense. Second, as the dialogue
between Brown and Levinson illustrates, some neorepublicans find the Amendment embarrassing and feel the need to prune it from the republican thicket.
In contrast, I argue that the Amendment is central to the republican tradition
and perfectly consistent with its principal commitments. Finally, in a broader
sense, an analysis of the Second Amendment in the republican tradition allows
a clearer perspective on the overall advisability of a modern republican revival:
to the extent one finds the modern implications of the provision troubling,
utopian, or just not very useful, one might question the wisdom of the revival
as well.

The republican tradition that lies behind the Second Amendment is not just
embarrassing—it is terrifying. It acknowledges that humans are never wholly
in control of their own destinies. At the heart of republicanism lies a paradox
that mocks human efforts at self-government: republics can never successfully
survive unless their citizens act in a virtuous manner, eschewing private interests for the sake of the public good, but citizens will not act virtuously except
in a republic that fosters such virtuous conduct. Hence, a republic is in effect
a logical contradiction, a paradox in its very nature. Creating or maintaining
a republic against the constant risk of corruption by particularistic interests is
therefore the most difficult of tasks. Republican theory, however, offers some
structures to aid in this task, prominent among them the universal militia.

The republican framers of the Second Amendment were painfully aware
that ultimate political power would lie with those who controlled the means of
force. As a result, they sought to arm not a narrow slice of society that might
seize the government for its own end, but rather all the citizens in a state, in
the form of a universal militia, which would always act in the common good.
In republican thinking, this militia had an ambiguous status. On the one hand,
it was a creature of the state apparatus, inasmuch as the state[12] gathered it,
ensured it was universal, trained it in the use of arms, and mobilized it against
foreign invasion or domestic insurrection. On the other hand, it was composed
of all of the citizens, deriving its legitimacy from them and being virtually
synonymous with them.

---

11. I attribute significance to republicanism in explicating only this provision, not the Constitution as
a whole or late 18th-century American thinking in general.

12. For reasons explained in the next footnote, I use the term "state" throughout this Article to refer
narrowly to the state *apparatus*—the government and its ministers.

The militia, in other words, constituted a forum in which state and society met and melded,[13] and this combination offered some advantages for curbing corruption. If the evil of partiality touched a segment of the population, then the militia—constituted as an instrument of the state—could restrain any movement toward demagogic rebellion. But if the state became corrupt, then the militia—now constituted as "the people"—could resist despotism. Indeed, the line between state and people ideally disappeared in the militia, in that the militia members were both rulers and ruled.

From this republican perspective, the error of those who today seek to guarantee a private right to arms is that they would thereby consign the means of force to those who happen to possess firearms—a partial slice of society—rather than to the whole people assembled in militia. Even in the eighteenth century, literal universality was never more than a rhetorical aspiration or a regulative ideal, but it was nevertheless the prevailing ideal, and any departure from it meant failure. At a minimum, therefore, any modern version of this militia must be so inclusive that its composition offers some meaningful promise that it will not become the tool of a slice of society, as it could in the case of those who decide for private reasons to buy a gun or to become members of the national guard.[14] The militia must be the people acting together, not isolated persons acting individually.

As we today have no such universal militia and no assurance that contemporary arms-bearers will be virtuous, the Second Amendment itself is—for now—outdated. But republican theory does not, in the absence of a virtuous citizenry, give up. Through the militia ideal, republicanism offers practical guidance on how positively to engender civic virtue, in the form of disinterested self-sacrifice, amongst a nonvirtuous, self-interested populace. Although this militia ideal may seem hopelessly utopian in its conception of the redemptive possibility of politics, it is central to the historical tradition as an icon of the main theme of republicanism—empowering citizens engaged in deliberative politics in pursuit of a common good.[15] It therefore seems worthwhile to consider the present implications of the militia ideal for courts interpreting the Second Amendment, and, more importantly, for citizens seeking to realize the promise of republican government.

For courts, the great change from the 1780's is that without a universal militia it is impossible to hazard a republican reading of the Second Amend-

---

13. The melding of rulers and ruled is a characteristic republican aspiration: ideally, there should be only self-governing citizens. Indeed, there is some question whether or not before *The Federalist* Americans even had a theory of the "state" in its modern European sense. *See* Isaac Kramnick, *Editor's Introduction* to THE FEDERALIST PAPERS 67 (Isaac Krammick ed., 1987). But republicans did recognize that the state *apparatus* was separate from the people and might threaten liberty. The militia offered a place where the apparatus and society merged.

14. Neither the guard nor private gunowners reflect universality; they are distinct interest groups in the American game of pluralistic politics.

15. *Cf.* Michelman, *supra* note 1, at 74-77 (offering Supreme Court decisionmaking as icon of republican dialogue).

ment. The militia was a precondition for the right to arms. Without a militia the right is meaningless. The republican tradition thus suggests that the provision as written has become outdated. From a judicial perspective, this part of republicanism is not very useful, because the world really has changed, and republicanism cannot mean what it once did.

On the other hand, the Amendment can serve as a regulative ideal, emphasizing the importance of committing force to virtue. Despite the effective nullification of the provision by the disappearance of the militia, judges might seek other means to secure those ends. In particular, courts can give the Amendment new life by reinterpreting other constitutional provisions to serve the functions of the old militia.

The militia ideal has even greater significance for neorepublicans seeking to reconstruct society in nonjudicial fora. It suggests, in particular, that they should emphasize the populist strain of republican theory. Since the people can no longer directly participate through the militia, they need militia-surrogates, bodies that serve functions formerly served by the militia. One course would be to reactivate the universal militia itself, which would act on its own views of the commonweal to resist tyrants and demagogues. The problem with this course is the extreme danger in giving arms to citizens who are not now and may never become virtuous. That fear is rational and one that contemporary republicans should share: republican measures may be inappropriate for an unrepublican populace.

The better course is to pursue other measures that would grant the people opportunities to develop virtue, such as universal service, and to control their own lives—such as workplace democracy. At some later point, it may be appropriate to reconstitute a universal militia, and the Second Amendment would reacquire its original meaning. In the interim, the control of arms will lie with the government, not the people—a profoundly unrepublican condition—but even within a republican framework some risks are not worth taking. The suggestion of a revived militia, however, starkly poses the central difficulty faced by modern neorepublicans: How does a population characterized by selfish pursuit of discordant interests become a society in which realization of the "common good" is anything but utopian rhetoric? Neorepublicans have offered some possible answers, but they go only part of the way—and under present conditions can not go further—toward reconstructing a republican militia-surrogate.

This Article will advance two themes. First, unlike Levinson, I do not think that republicanism supplies a useful way to interpret the Second Amendment unless there are substantial changes in society. Second, unlike Brown, I do think that the Amendment's history offers an important regulative ideal in constructing a modern version of republicanism. The Article proceeds in four parts. Part I considers the extant scholarship and case law dealing with the Second Amendment, focusing on the colloquy between Levinson and Brown. Part II describes the role of the right to arms in republican thought. It first sketches the constant sense of danger that beset republicans: a republic was a fragile enterprise, always vulnerable to corruption. It then analyzes the corruption-battling functions served by the militia and the right to bear arms. Service in the militia trained one to a life of virtue, both self-sacrificing and independent; these virtuous arms-bearing citizens could block the designs of corrupt factions, whether those of demagogues among the people or despots among government ministers, and, if a corrupt faction should seize power, the citizens could resist, to restore the moral and political health of the republic.

Part III considers the implications of this tradition for a modern interpretation of the Second Amendment. In particular, I argue that because of the disappearance of the militia, the Amendment cannot have any literal meaning; at best, we can use it as a regulative ideal in interpreting other provisions. Finally, Part IV argues that the militia ideal is consistent with the rest of republicanism and discusses modern reforms based on that ideal, suggesting that universal service and measures to increase direct popular control of government can move toward serving the function of the old militia.

I. THE DEBATE

A. Before Levinson and Brown

Before the recent dialogue between Levinson and Brown, serious discussion of the Second Amendment was notably limited.[16] The Supreme Court had offered little guidance; it has decided only four significant cases under the provision, none of them recent or definitive.[17] In 1875, the Court held that the Amendment limited the actions only of government, not of private individuals.[18] Later in the century, the Court twice held that the Amendment limited the actions only of the federal government and not of the states, on the grounds

---

16. Some commentators have suggested explanations for this silence: a dissembling or timorous Supreme Court has refused to take cases that would force them to recognize the right. *See, e.g.,* Nelson L t, *The Second Amendment: Political Liberty and the Right to Self-Preservation,* 39 ALA. L. REV. 103, 103-04 (1987). Academics have abetted the judges by pretending that the Amendment does not exist, or else by willfully ignoring history and reducing the Amendment to a protection for the national guard. Similarly, Levinson explains that because the Amendment is embarrassing to the established academy, constitutional scholars dwell long on the First Amendment but then close their eyes and leap to the Fourth. *See* Levinson, *supra* note 2, at 639-42.

17. The Court did mention the Second Amendment in a fifth case, Dred Scott v. Sandford, 60 U.S. (19 How.) 393 (1857), in which Chief Justice Taney warned that if blacks were citizens, they would have the right to bear arms. *See* 60 U.S. (19 How.) at 416-17. Indeed, the right to bear arms was important to blacks in the years after the Civil War, not only symbolically, as a badge of citizenship, but practically, as a way to resist white terrorism. *See* STEPHEN HALBROOK, THAT EVERY MAN BE ARMED 107-53 (1984); Robert Cottrol & Ray Diamond, *The Second Amendment: Towards an Afro-Americanist Reconsideration,* 80 GEO. L.J. (forthcoming Dec. 1991).

18. United States v. Cruikshank, 92 U.S. 542, 553 (1875). The defendants, who had disarmed ex-slaves, were indicted under federal laws against conspiracy to deprive a citizen of constitutional rights. The Court quashed the indictment on the grounds that citizens had no constitutional right against private disarming.

that the Bill of Rights did not apply to the states.[19] The Court decided these cases, however, well before it began to incorporate the rest of the Bill of Rights into the Fourteenth Amendment, so the continuing validity of these decisions is uncertain.[20] In any event, these cases discussed only the actors against whom the right applied, not the scope of the right itself.

The Court seriously considered the scope of the right to bear arms in only one case—*United States v. Miller*, decided in 1939.[21] In *Miller*, the Court addressed a Second Amendment challenge to the National Firearms Act of 1934,[22] which prohibited, inter alia, possession of a sawed-off shotgun except in limited circumstances. The Court explained that the purpose of the Amendment was to "assure the continuation and render possible the effectiveness of [militia] forces," so that the government would not rely on standing armies.[23] But because the parties had not adduced "any evidence tending to show that possession or use of a [sawed-off shotgun] has some reasonable relationship to the preservation or efficiency of a well regulated militia," the Court could not "say that the Second Amendment guarantees the right to keep and bear such an instrument."[24] At a minimum, then, *Miller* limits the scope of the Amendment to arms suitable for use by militia.

Lower courts have suggested that *Miller* limits the right even further. If the Amendment's purpose is only to assure the "continuation" and render possible the "effectiveness" of the militia, then it may protect state governments against federal tampering with their militia, but it does not guarantee individuals any

---

19. Miller v. Texas, 153 U.S. 535, 536 (1894) (dismissing writ of error from state conviction for carrying dangerous weapons on person); Presser v. Illinois, 116 U.S. 252, 264 (1886) (dismissing writ of error from state conviction under law against organization, training, and marching of private armies).

20. Many commentators have argued that courts should assume that the Supreme Court would incorporate the Amendment today, as it has incorporated other provisions. *See, e.g.,* Kates, *supra* note 8, at 252-57; Lund, *supra* note 16, at 110. A number of courts have ignored such an invitation on the grounds that even if the Court would so rule, it has not yet done so; *Presser* and *Miller*, however old, are still the Court's last words on the subject. *See, e.g.,* Quilici v. Village of Morton Grove, 695 F.2d 261, 270 (7th Cir. 1982).

21. United States v. Miller, 307 U.S. 174 (1939).

22. Ch. 757, 48 Stat. 1236 (1934) (current version at 26 U.S.C. §§ 5801-45 (1988)).

23. 307 U.S. at 178. The Court did not explicitly say so, but it was presumably relying on the opening clause of the Amendment—"[a] well-regulated militia, being necessary to the security of a free state"—for this assertion. Actually, the Court's full analysis of this point is confusing. The Court first pointed out that Article I gives Congress the power to call forth the militia to execute the laws of the Union, suppress insurrections, and repel invaders. The Court continued: "With obvious purpose to assure the continuation and render possible the effectiveness of such forces the declaration and guarantee of the Second Amendment were made." *Id.* The Court here seems to be saying that the Second Amendment guarantees a right to arms, so that the militia will be ready for Congress' call. The provision thus protects a federal interest in the readiness of the militia. Such a reading is hard to square with the historical record. *See infra* text accompanying notes 171-86. The goal of the Amendment cannot be to protect Congress' interest in calling forth the militia, because Congress had the power to require militia readiness without the Amendment. Instead, the Amendment limits the power of Congress by providing that it may not disarm the people, even if it believed that such disarming would for some reason serve the preparedness of the militia.

24. 307 U.S. at 178.

rights at all.[25] Some of *Miller*'s language, however, is in tension with such a reading. In the eighteenth century, the Court explained, the militia "comprised all males physically capable of acting in concert for the common defense," and "when called for service these men were expected to appear bearing arms supplied by themselves."[26] In other words, the Court strongly suggested that the Amendment guarantees a private right to own guns, at least by all males of arms-bearing age, so as to be ready for militia service. But the Court did not articulate that conclusion in so many words. It was enough to conclude that a sawed-off shotgun was not appropriate for militia use.[27]

Faced with this dearth of judicial instruction, commentators fall into only two groups—often called the individual rights and states' rights positions. The latter position relies on the language of the clause explaining the Amendment's purpose: "*A well regulated Militia, being necessary to the security of a free State*, the right of the people to keep and bear Arms shall not be infringed." According to this view, the goal of the provision is thus merely to guarantee the right of the states to maintain their militias, not to guarantee any right to individuals, and Congress has adequately protected the right of the states with the National Guard system.[28]

In contrast, the individual rights' view emphasizes that the Amendment grants a right to "the people" not to the "states." Moreover, the unorganized militia in the 1790's included every male of arms-bearing age[29]—and still does.[30] The Framers emphasized the importance of the unorganized militia in the constant struggle to forestall tyranny; one could not rely on the organized or "select" militia, as that body itself could become corrupt.[31] As a last step,

---

25. *See, e.g.,* Quilici v. Village of Morton Grove, 695 F.2d 261, 270 (7th Cir. 1982); United States v. Oakes, 564 F.2d 384, 387 (10th Cir. 1977); Stevens v. United States, 440 F.2d 144, 149 (6th Cir. 1971); LAURENCE H. TRIBE, AMERICAN CONSTITUTIONAL LAW 299 n.6 (2d ed. 1988); Roy Weatherup, *Standing Armies and Armed Citizens: An Historical Analysis of the Second Amendment*, 2 HASTINGS CONST. L.Q. 961, 999 (1975).

26. 307 U.S. at 179.

27. Since *Miller*, the Court has offered only one perfunctory interpretation of the case. In Lewis v. United States, 445 U.S. 55 (1980), the Court held that a federal prohibition on the possession of firearms by a felon did not violate the Constitution because "the Second Amendment guarantees no right to keep and bear a firearm that does not have 'some reasonable relationship to the preservation or efficiency of a well regulated militia.'" *Id.* at 65-66 n.8 (quoting *Miller*, 307 U.S. at 178).

28. *See, e.g.,* JOHN H. ELY, DEMOCRACY AND DISTRUST 95, 227 n.76 (1980); TRIBE, *supra* note 25, at 299 n.6; Weatherup, *supra* note 25, at 995-96; Peter B. Feller & Karl L. Gotting, *The Second Amendment: A Second Look*, 61 NW. U. L. REV. 46, 61-62 (1966); John Levin, *The Right to Bear Arms: The Development of the American Experience*, 48 CHI.-KENT L. REV. 148, 158-59 (1971).

29. First Militia Act, Ch. 33, 1 Stat. 271 (1792) (current version at 10 U.S.C. §§ 311-12 (1988)). The Amendment does specify a "well regulated" militia, which does not sound much like an "unorganized" militia. But individual rights advocates point out that in the 18th century, "well regulated" was more likely to mean "trained" or "disciplined" than "government-controlled." *See* David T. Hardy, *Armed Citizens, Citizen Armies*, 9 HARV. J.L. & PUB. POL'Y 559, 626 n.328 (1986); Lund, *supra* note 16, at 107 n.8. As I will argue, one meaning that "well regulated" does not have is "less than universal." *See infra* note 207.

30. 10 U.S.C. § 311(a) (1988).

31. *See, e.g.,* HALBROOK, *supra* note 17, at 84-87; David I. Caplan, *Restoring the Balance: The Second Amendment Revisited*, 5 FORDHAM URB. L.J. 31, 37-40 (1976); Hardy, *supra* note 29, at 623-24; Kates, *supra* note 8, at 214-18; Joyce L. Malcolm, *The Right of the People to Keep and Bear Arms: The Common*

advocates of the individual rights view typically assert that the Amendment enshrined a right to own guns not only for revolution but also for defense of the home and perhaps for hunting and target practice as well.[32]

B. *Levinson and Brown*

Professor Levinson injects important new insights into this debate. First, he brings the recent research to bear on republican ideology. Second, he carefully distinguishes between the two rights that other commentators have merged: the Second Amendment might protect an individual right to self-defense or a "collective" right to revolution, or neither, or both. Republican ideology, Levinson suggests, supports the right to revolution, but apparently does not concern itself with the right to self-defense.[33] Moreover, Levinson himself finds the right to revolution more "interesting"[34] and apparently believes that social change may have rendered the right to self-defense, but not the right to revolution, outdated.[35]

Levinson's implicit claim that republicanism has little to say about the right to self-defense and much to say about a right of resistance is, in my view, correct.[36] If the Second Amendment does provide a right to own guns for self-defense, republicanism cannot supply the intellectual foundation for it. But if Levinson is correct to tie a right of resistance to republicanism, he is not clear about who possesses that right—the states, individuals, or some other body. On the one hand, he considers the republican right as entailing protection for private, individual ownership of guns. Defining the republican militia as "all of the people, or at least all of those treated as full citizens of the community,"[37] he attributes to that great republican James Harrington the view that liberty depends on independent citizens, and that to be independent of government, citizens must own arms. The Second Amendment thus serves to check government: "[T]he ultimate 'checking value' in a republican polity is the ability of an armed populace, presumptively motivated by a shared commitment to the common good, to resist governmental tyranny."[38] The Second Amendment thus guarantees to each citizen the ability to intimidate potentially tyrannical government with private arms.

Law Tradition, 10 HASTINGS CONST. L.Q. 285, 314 (1983).

32. *See infra* notes 198, 200.

33. Levinson's discussion of neorepublicanism occurs only in the context of his analysis of the right to revolution. *See* Levinson, *supra* note 2, at 646-50.

34. *Id.* at 646-47.

35. *See id.* at 656. Indeed, the most that Levinson has to say for the right to self-defense is that "it seems tendentious to reject out of hand the argument that one purpose of the Amendment was to recognize" it. *Id.* at 645-46.

36. *See infra* text accompanying notes 171-86.

37. Levinson, *supra* note 2, at 646-47.

38. *Id.* at 648.

On the other hand, Levinson calls the right to bear arms "collective," and he distinguishes it from an "individualist" right of self-defense. In what sense is this right collective? Levinson does not specify. It is plainly not collective in the sense that it must be exercised by the organized state militia: Levinson emphasizes that the republican militia includes every citizen, even those who are not members of the organized militia. At one point, he describes the citizenry as a "structure" that stands ready to defend liberty against those "other two structures," the state and federal governments. But he never explains how the citizens are yoked together into a "structure" rather than existing as loose atoms. The right described by Levinson seems to be collective in only two limited senses. First, it is a right held by individuals, though for the good of the whole: resistance to tyrants is service to the commonweal. Second, as a practical matter, a single individual cannot resist the government; he needs help from his friends in a collective surge of indignation. The citizenry is thus a structure only in the sense that all those atoms serve a structural role in the republican form of government: considered en masse, but not melded into any form of organization, the citizens may sufficiently frighten the government so that it will not become tyrannical.[39]

Wendy Brown launches a three-part attack on Levinson's right of revolution: it is not republican; it is no longer relevant in our changed world; and even in its original form, it is a part of republicanism better discarded. First, she maintains that the "republican argument for arming the citizenry is most powerfully elaborated not by the English thinkers Levinson cites, but in that passionate republican work, Machiavelli's *Discourses on the First Decade of Titus Livius*."[40] Focusing on Machiavelli's statist tendencies, she then claims that the "republican citizenry is not armed against the state but *as* the state—an armed citizenry is the state's heart, not its opposition or counterweight."[41] The right of revolution, on the other hand, is a product of Lockean liberalism, "in which a diffident and depoliticized populace squares off against the state, in which there is no political heart at all but only hands and feet all armed against one another."[42]

This privileging of Machiavelli over all later republicans, in reading an eighteenth-century amendment, seems unnecessary.[43] As a significant early

---

39. Second Amendment rights are thus not like the Fourteenth Amendment right of intimacy, *see, e.g.*, Griswold v. Connecticut, 381 U.S. 479 (1965) (holding that statute preventing contraceptive use violated right of marital privacy); Roberts v. United States Jaycees, 468 U.S. 609 (1984) (holding that statute compelling Jaycees to accept women as regular members does not violate male members' freedom of intimate or expressive association). They need collective action to work but are not inherently associational.

40. Brown, *supra* note 6, at 661.

41. *Id.* at 662-63.

42. *Id.* at 663.

43. Moreover, Machiavelli is susceptible to a different reading from Brown's. Machiavelli believed that a militia offered the best defense against foreign invaders; in that sense the militia was armed as the state. *See* NICCOLO MACHIAVELLI, *Discourses on the First Decade of Titus Livius*, *in* 1 THE CHIEF WORKS AND OTHERS 175, 411 (Allen Gilbert trans., 1965). But another advantage of an armed populace was that it could resist domestic tyrants. *See* NICCOLO MACHIAVELLI, *The Art of War*, *in* 2 *id.* at 561, 578. In so

republican, Machiavelli may be relevant to the Amendment, but it is difficult to discern why he is more relevant than Harrington or Trenchard and Gordon. As Brown acknowledges, those later writers endorsed a right of resistance,[44] which belonged not to a liberal "diffident and depoliticized populace" but to an intensely active citizenry, for whom self-arming was an act of concern for the health of the state.[45]

Brown's second criticism of Levinson is more persuasive: republicanism needs a virtuous citizenry, but Brown "cannot imagine a less appropriate appellation for the contemporary American citizenry, which bears a shared commitment to almost nothing, least of all a common good."[46] If the citizenry is not virtuous, we have no assurance that it will use its arms in virtuous ways. So Brown predicts pernicious results if we arm our present citizenry: gun owners are likely to use them to rape women and to murder young urban black men.[47] Whatever the need for a right of resistance by arms in the United States, there is a high probability that guns will continue to be used in the future as they have been used in the past. There is no reason to believe that current American gun owners are either virtuous or representative.[48]

The republican concept of the universal militia, however, also poses a challenge to Brown's analysis. Recognizing that republicanism relies on a virtuous populace that we lack does not end the inquiry, but only frames it: what do we do now? For Brown, the answer seems self-evident. We should abandon republicanism or at least this aspect of it: "Like Levinson, I would prefer a republican order to a liberal-capitalist one. But we do not have a

---

resisting, the citizens were still armed "as the state" in the sense that the despot had stopped representing the state and the people had stepped into the gap. But this description does not lead to Brown's conclusion. In one semantic usage, the Machiavellian citizenry cannot resist the state because it is the state; but it can resist the government. Indeed, Quentin Skinner has argued that Machiavelli's call for devotion to the common good was strictly instrumental to ensuring each citizen negative liberty from government; only if we each act as responsible citizens can any person have the freedom to order his own affairs as he wishes. See Quentin Skinner, *The Idea of Negative Liberty: Philosophical and Historical Perspectives, in* PHILOSOPHY IN HISTORY 193, 204-19 (Richard Rorty et al. eds., 1984).

44. These English writers may be more antistatist than Machiavelli because republicanism, when it crossed the English Channel, confronted a more established and monarchical state than the unstable city-states of Italy. English republicans therefore had to develop a doctrine of resistance to justify their departure from royalism. See J.G.A. POCOCK, THE MACHIAVELLIAN MOMENT 345-48, 371-75 (1975).

45. Brown seems to equate the republican right of revolution with a liberal right of autonomy. She describes the right of revolution as a "freedom that depicts man, collectively or individually, securing his autonomy, his woman, and his territory with a gun—a formulation signified in our epoch by Eugene Hasenfus flying over the forests of Central America . . . or Ollie North's good intentions." Brown, *supra* note 6, at 664. But far from the goals of republicanism, the Hasenfus and North events signify its deepest fears: members of a standing army or shadow standing army under executive direction running a secret war on private funds in distant lands against the express will of Congress. In fact, 18th-century republicans would point precisely to these events as the inevitable outcome of the failure of the private population to arm itself, leaving their defense to cowboy adventurers. Brown may mean that "redneck" gun owners (who seem to be her real target, *see id.* at 666-67) may applaud Hasenfus and North, but there is a great difference between Thomas Jefferson and North.

46. *Id.* at 663.

47. *Id.* at 665.

48. *See infra* text accompanying notes 214-25.

republican political order; we are not a republican citizenry . . . . And we cannot generate a republican order merely by interpreting our Constitution through a republican hermeneutic scheme."[49] But this imprecation is a counsel of despair. "Merely" reading the Constitution through republican lenses may not by itself create a republican order, but it may be one piece of the process. And republicanism offers us other ways by which citizens may achieve virtue: political participation, owning property independent of landlords or employers, and membership in a citizen militia.

Ultimately, Brown may discount the possibility of creating a virtuous populace through a militia because she has a deeper critique of the right to arms: "[E]ven within republicanism, we do not have to swallow it whole. The republican intellectual tradition includes a militarism, elitism, and machismo that is past due for thoughtful critique and reworking."[50] Republicanism appeals to many because it emphasizes community over separation and public dialogue over strict autonomy. In this sense, it shares many features with modern cultural feminism.[51] But contained within republicanism is this harsh "macho" kernel: the right to arms is a "bit 'gendered'. . . subduing with force, what it cannot discursively persuade, tame, or cohabit the universe with, and possessing with force what it cannot seduce."[52] Facing this apparent conflict within republicanism, Brown, like others, recommends that we wean republicanism from its objectionable elements—in this case by abandoning the right to arms.[53]

This recommendation, however, assumes that the militia is on the periphery of republicanism and in conflict with its core. Rightly understood, however, the right to arms is thoroughly consistent with republicanism's other commitments. It does contemplate that citizens may sometimes have to take up arms to defend liberty. But it vests that right in a body notable for its interactive and collective nature, to prevent the politics of interest and to encourage the politics of the

---

49. Brown, *supra* note 6, at 665.

50. *Id.* at 666.

51. *See* Suzanna Sherry, *Civic Virtue and the Feminine Voice in Constitutional Adjudication*, 72 VA. L. REV. 543, 550-54, 591 (1986); Michelman, *supra* note 1, at 17 n.68, 28-33 (1985).

52. Brown, *supra* note 6, at 663-64.

53. *Id.* at 665; *see also* Kerber, *supra* note 1, at 1665 (noting that an emphasis on arms-bearing gave republican tradition a militaristic core); Sunstein, *supra* note 10, at 1564 (classifying one strain of republicanism thought as "militaristic and heroic, and associating political behavior with warfare"). Although these writers do not directly cite it, the inspiration for this view may be Hannah Fenichel Pitkin's *Fortune Is a Woman*, which argues that much of Machiavelli's thought is misogynistic. HANNAH F. PITKIN, FORTUNE IS A WOMAN (1984). Actually, Pitkin argued that in writing about the citizenry and the militia, Machiavelli is at his least misogynistic. Machiavelli often casts the citizen and militia member as an appealing blend of those feminist virtues of interdependence, cooperation, and healthy disagreement within dialogue. *See id.* at 63-68, 90-97, 232. When Machiavelli comes to doubt the possibility of such a public-spirited dialogue, he becomes most emphatically misogynistic, conjuring up the specter of a protofascist Father/Founder to bring order, *see id.* at 75, 97-105, against the threat of Fortune, Woman, and Mother. *See id.* at 230-32, 68-73; *see also* Isaac Kramnick, *Rousseau and Women: An Alternative Reading*, in COMPARATIVE THEORY AND POLITICAL EXPERIENCE 64, 66-75 (Peter J. Katzenstein et al. eds., 1990) (although Rousseau is sometimes sexist, his true community rests on maternalized state characterized by politicized love for others).

common rood. If one believes in the bulk of republicanism, then, one should believe in the militia as well. The next part will develop this claim by putting the right to arms in context within the republican tradition.

II. THE RIGHT TO ARMS IN THE REPUBLICAN TRADITION

This part offers an historical reconstruction of the role of the right to arms in republican thinking. Fundamentally, republicans saw the militia as a response to the danger of corruption. In the first section below, I outline the nature of the republicans' fears. In the next section, I analyze the way in which the militia responded to those fears.

A republican government was thought to be one that pursued the common good rather than the private interest of a slice of society. But republics were inherently unstable, because a republican form of government depended on virtuous citizens, while citizens could be virtuous only in a republican government. As a result, corruption could arise either from a distortion of the form of government or from a public falling into self-interest.

The militia was thought to be able to restrain corruption because it was virtuous and possessed ultimate control over the means of force. It was virtuous both because it comprised the universal people and because it offered training in the habits of virtue. And as the people, it was both government and society. The state raised it and ensured that it was universal. Under state direction, the militia would repress demagogic revolts made in the interests of a few. But despite this tie to the government, the militia was a people's body. Its membership included all of the citizenry, and if the government should ever become corrupt, it could resist by arms. To offer these advantages, the militia had to be universal, not a subset of private persons or the state apparatus.

A. *The Danger of Corruption*

1. *Republican Paradoxes*

Eighteenth-century republicans shared certain views about the nature of human beings. Humans have public, political selves; they are capable of forming cooperative ventures that will benefit all. The polity itself is a universal association, "in which all types of men combine to pursue all human goods," that can achieve a universal good that is more than the realization of the private interests of a few.[54] At the same time, however, each individual has a private,

---

54. J.G.A. Pocock, *Civic Humanism and Its Role in Anglo-American Thought, in* POLITICS, LANGUAGE AND TIME: ESSAYS ON POLITICAL THOUGHT AND HISTORY 80, 86 (J.G.A. Pocock ed., 1973). The classic exposition of these ideas, and the inspiration for later republicans, is Aristotle's *Politics. See, e.g.,* POCOCK, *supra* note 44, at 66-68; Michelman, *supra* note 1, at 38.

particular self and self-interest,[55] and his public and private selves can come into conflict. A good state is one in which citizens pursue the common good; a bad state is one that has been seized by a slice of society for its own narrow ends.[56]

Republicans hoped to induce citizens to pursue the common good, but in doing so they faced a problem: the virtue of the state and of its citizens are always interdependent.[57] To be virtuous, a citizen must live in a state that enshrines the common good; otherwise he can be no more than one bit of self-serving flotsam swirling around other bits, for there is no common good to serve.[58] The state, however, will never enshrine the common good unless its citizens are virtuous—but the only way for them to be virtuous is for the state to enshrine the common good. The causation is two-way: citizens make the state, and the state makes citizens. Neither can be virtuous unless the other is.[59]

This closed circle created a republican paradox:[60] citizens are simultaneously creatures and creators of the state. That paradox gave rise to another one: the problem of creating a republic—the problem of origins. Virtuous citizens would create virtuous states, and virtuous states would create virtuous citizens, but how does one secure either of these? The paradox lies in the self-levitating quality of republics: they somehow come into being, but humans might not be able to find a patch of terra firma from which to launch one. A republic thus depends on conditions being right; a republican form of govern-

---

55. *See, e.g.,* POCOCK, *supra* note 44, at 68.

56. *See, e.g., id.* at 71, 75; GORDON S. WOOD, THE CREATION OF THE AMERICAN REPUBLIC 1776-1787, at 53-57 (1969). It should be noted that the common good was not in opposition to individual freedoms. Republicans typically believed that part of the common good was individual liberty for all, *see id.* at 18-28. and in any event, liberty was instrumentally necessary to the commonweal. *See infra* text accompanying notes 68, 71. Indeed, Machiavelli may even have valued a politics of the common good chiefly as an instrument to negative liberty against government. But the common good did not include the pursuit of self-interest as such; liberty must never be abused. *See* Skinner, *supra* note 43, at 204-19.

57. I think that this idea may be implicit in Pocock's discussion of the "Machiavellian Moment," *see supra* notes 44, 56; *infra* note 58, but I have formulated it in a somewhat more stark and direct way to emphasize the republican sense of danger.

58. *See, e.g.,* POCOCK, *supra* note 44, at 74-75.

59. *See* WOOD, *supra* note 56, at 118-119; POCOCK, *supra* note 44, at 204-05. By the same token, state and society can be mutually reinforcing if both are virtuous. For American republicans, "The relationship between government and society, in America as in England, was reciprocal, and America's healthy republican society presented the proper framework for a free government that would in turn sustain the integrity of a republican society and economy." DREW R. MCCOY, THE ELUSIVE REPUBLIC 62 (1980).

60. I speak of this tension as a paradox because at its strongest it involves logically inconsistent propositions: citizens are creatures and creators of the thing that creates them; a republic can come into being only through a citizenry that can come into being only through a republic; rights are both the precondition and product of deliberative politics. The paradox might only be apparent; indeed, for republics to exist, it would have to be. In a less stark form, the tension might more closely resemble a dialectic: a somewhat virtuous state may act on a citizenry, which would then react on the state to make it more virtuous, and so forth. But I express the tension in its strong, paradoxical form to stress the anxiety it caused: citizens must be independent of the state but also a product of it.

ment would not be viable at all times and for all peoples.[61] Those hoping for a republic might be unable to induce those conditions, and they might have to wait for history or providence to deliver a virtuous people, so that republican government becomes possible.[62] Some republican thinkers pursued the other end of the equation: they hoped for good government to make possible a virtuous people.[63]

Even if the miracle did occur, and a republican state somehow came into being, it was always in danger of slipping into corruption—the problem of maintenance. Because state and society depended on each other, if either began to lose virtue, each would quickly corrupt the other. Since neither could serve as an anchor, republicans saw the path to perdition as short, smooth, and slippery. And the world contained many hostile forces that might induce that slide; Fortuna, under various names, always lurked as a malevolent force.[64] So at the first sign of corruption, there seemed only a short time to save the republic before it was too late.[65]

This set of relationships is connected to another paradox: the complicated republican status of rights and autonomy.[66] In republican theory, citizens must, on the one hand, be independent of the state, so that they may critique it if it becomes corrupt: hence the republican denunciation of slavish subservience and praise of those brave enough to defy public ministers and even public opin-

---

61. *See* MCCOY, *supra* note 59, at 5. The vulnerability of republicanism to certain conditions is in contrast to so-called liberal individualism, which takes people as it finds them—presuming them to be self-interested—and constructs a scheme of government that tempers even their worst excesses. *See infra* text accompanying notes 96-98. Martha Nussbaum argues that vulnerability to conditions is one of the central features that distinguish the Aristotelian tradition from the liberal tradition associated with Plato and Kant. *See* MARTHA C. NUSSBAUM, THE FRAGILITY OF GOODNESS 3-7, 329-330 (1986).

62. *See, e.g.,* WOOD, *supra* note 56, at 66, 91-93, 123-24; Sherry, *supra* note 51, at 557. Some republicans sought a different way out of this difficulty: a glorious and virtuous leader might inspire or mold the citizenry to virtue. In Hannah Pitkin's view, this idea explains the fascist elements of Machiavelli's thought. In desperation at Florentine corruption, he conceived the semimythical figure of the Founder—infinitely good, powerful, and self-originating—who could mold them to virtue. *See* PITKIN, *supra* note 53, at 54-56, 75-79. By definition, the Founder is unlike ordinary mortals in that he escapes the republican paradox: he can be virtuous outside of a republican state and can therefore provide the necessary starting point for a republic. Therefore, to hope for a Founder is to hope for a miracle.

63. *See* MCCOY, *supra* note 59, at 7. John Adams, for example, ultimately concluded that virtue was the effect, not the cause, of good government. *See* JOHN P. DIGGINS, THE LOST SOUL OF AMERICAN POLITICS 69-71 (1984). Similarly, the idea that the militia can provide training in virtue, *see infra* text accompanying notes 162-70, suggests that republican government can create republican citizens. Those who chose this strategy seem to have been more activist: one could take steps to secure virtue by changing the form of governments. *See* WOOD, *supra* note 56, at 120-22.

64. *See infra* text accompanying notes 74-78, 84-87.

65. *See, e.g.,* LANCE BANNING, THE JEFFERSONIAN PERSUASION 61 (1978); POCOCK, *supra* note 44, at 205, 506-07.

66. For other descriptions of this tangled attitude, see Frank Michelman, *Law's Republic,* 97 YALE L.J. 1493 (1988); Michelman, *supra* note 1, at 42-43. For an example of a modern writer struggling with the same tension, see Jennifer Nedelsky, *Reconceiving Autonomy: Sources, Thoughts and Possibilities,* 1 YALE J.L. & FEMINISM 7, 20-36 (1989).

ion.[67] In order to attain this independence, citizens must have rights that cannot be affected by politics, so that the citizens will not be threatened by reprisals from a corrupt government.[68] This end of the paradox reflects one side of the interdependence between state and society: to have a virtuous state, there must be virtuous citizens.

At the same time, republicans believed that individuals are unable to be truly separate or fully independent, because they are products of the state. The very values that republican citizens hold are not given, but are the product of politics—hopefully deliberative, healthy politics, but politics nonetheless.[69] Citizens, moreover, must not use their rights to pursue their own self-interest ahead of the common good. Thus, the citizen cannot stand apart from the political process and use it as a mere instrument of his desires.[70] This conviction reflects the other side of the state/society equation: to have virtuous citizens, there must be a virtuous state. For republicans, then, rights are not only the precondition for good politics, but also the product of politics, not to be invoked as trumps to disrupt the deliberative dialogue.[71]

Citizens must thus have sufficient autonomy to stand against the state when it errs, but they also must be aware that their autonomy exists only for the common good and because of the self-restraining virtue of other citizens. Republican virtue includes two components: a good citizen must be prepared to sacrifice himself for the good of the whole, and he must also be independent enough to know when to resist a corrupt state. There is no inherent contradiction here. Because citizens in a republic must always act for the common good, when the state is representing that good, the citizen must sacrifice his good to that of the state. In contrast, when the state is wandering, the citizen must resist. There is, however, a deep tension in the habits of mind required: the citizen

---

67. On this side of the Atlantic, the greatest pitch of denunciation occurred just before and during the War for Independence. See CHARLES ROYSTER, A REVOLUTIONARY PEOPLE AT WAR: THE CONTINENTAL ARMY AND AMERICAN CHARACTER 1775-1783, at 6-10 (1979); WOOD, supra note 56, at 37-38, 52-53.

68. See Michelman, supra note 1, at 43.

69. See Michelman, supra note 1, at 27; Sunstein, supra note 10, at 1548-49.

70. See WOOD, supra note 56, at 61-64.

71. See Michelman, supra note 66, at 1505. This paradox may be most acute in republican ideas about property rights. On the one hand, along with arms possession, private property was the central guarantee of citizen independence from the government. See POCOCK, supra note 44, at 386-89; Gregory S. Alexander, Time and Property in the American Republican Legal Culture, 66 N.Y.U. L. REV. 273, 294-95 (1991); McCOY, supra note 59, at 62-68. On the other hand, republicans recognized that property rights were a product of collective decisions and depended on collective protection. They also knew that severe inequalities of property would bring their own form of dependence of some citizens on others. See Michelman, supra note 1, at 40-41; POCOCK, supra note 44, at 386-91; Alexander, supra, at 287, 293-94. But what if a system of private, alienable property resulted in severe inequalities of wealth through private exchange? For the state to intervene would be to acknowledge the social construction of property rights and the ephemerality of citizen independence. But for the state not to intervene would be to tolerate the very dependence that property rights were supposed to eliminate in the first place. See McCOY, supra note 59, at 72; Alexander, supra at 294-302; WOOD, supra note 56, at 64-05. In the face of this tension, republican responses differed: some recommended redistribution of property, see POCOCK, supra note 44, at 387; Michelman, supra note 1, at 41 n.214; Alexander, supra at 290; WOOD, supra note 56, at 64, some recommended a bar to redistribution, see Alexander, supra, at 291, and most conveniently ignored the problem.

of a republic is expected sometimes to be profoundly selfless, and sometimes profoundly assertive. He must have the intelligence to know when to be which and the emotional agility to shift modes when appropriate.

2. The Balance of Estates

Both problems—origin and maintenance—rested on fear of lack of popular virtue and susceptibility to corruption. As a result, republicans endlessly analyzed the causes and cures of corruption. By the eighteenth century, two primary themes had emerged from this discussion—the danger of an imbalance of estates, which emphasized corruption in government, and the danger of professionalization, which emphasized corruption in society.

Balance-of-estates theory presented society as naturally divided into three estates—the One, the Few, and the Many—each with its own political virtues and vices. Unchecked, any one of the three might misdirect the state to its own partial good; thus a republican polity should balance the estates against one another, allowing each to walk a distinct path to the universal good.[72] Maintaining that relationship, however, was never easy.[73] In the eighteenth century, concern about the balance of estates in Britain focused on the Crown. As the empire grew by trade and arms, so did the power of the Crown, through new military organizations—especially the standing army[74]—and through royal exploitation of newly developed financial institutions and techniques, notably taxes, credit, and banks.[75] The core of the fear was executive dominance of Parliament: with its expanded resources, the Crown could buy the loyalty of Members of Parliament (M.P.'s) by offering places and pensions in the royal service.[76]

During the imperial crisis, American colonials frequently expressed their grievances with Britain in similar terms: the tyrant George III had subverted Parliament, invaded historical colonial privilege, and appointed autocratic governors.[77] Upon achieving independence, the new states reacted to this fear of the executive by drafting new constitutions that curtailed executive power and expanded the power of the lower legislative house.[78] In the process, they began to alter the meaning of mixed government by insisting that the Few and

---

72. See POCOCK, supra note 44, at 71-80, 99-100, 115-16; BANNING, supra note 65, at 22-28, 33-34, 40-41; WOOD, supra note 56, at 197-202; Michelman, supra note 1, at 43-46.

73. The classical form of this problem, sometimes recited in the 18th century, was the Polybian cycle. A republic might achieve equilibrium between the three estates, but never for long; as it became more prosperous and powerful, it would become impossible to maintain the balance. It would then begin to degenerate into less healthy forms of governments in a predictable sequence. See POCOCK, supra note 44, at 79-80; BANNING, supra note 65, at 42, 47-48.

74. See, e.g., BANNING, supra note 65, at 54.

75. See id. at 65-66.

76. See id. at 42-03, 49-51; WOOD, supra note 56, at 32-34; POCOCK, supra note 44, at 406-08.

77. See BANNING, supra note 65, at 78-80, 82; WOOD, supra note 56, at 32-34, 200-02.

78. See BANNING, supra note 65, at 84-87; EDMUND S. MORGAN, INVENTING THE PEOPLE 245-47 (1988).

the One should not consist of hereditary estates.[79] They felt that the creation of hereditary orders would give the Few and the One too much power, tempting them to subvert the balance.[80] Moreover, while most republicans believed that a natural aristocracy existed in America, they viewed this aristocracy as one of talent rather than of birth,[81] which was assimilable into a broadly democratic frame of government. While the elements of government that reflected aristocratic influences might be less democratic than others, all would be directly or indirectly elected by the people.[82] In this manner, American republicans developed a system of democratic republicanism in which the One, the Few, and the Many ceased to be separate estates, and became instead distinct parts of a balanced government staffed by the people's representatives.[83]

3. *Professionalization*

In republican eyes, however, the threat of corruption was wider and deeper than the traditional language of balanced estates could accommodate. Because of the developing economy and empire, the whole fabric of English society during the eighteenth century seemed in peril of being rent into partial interests acting for their own ends. The new commercial society encouraged citizens to pursue selfish interests.[84] Perhaps more importantly, it gave them separate ends because it promoted the specialization of economic function.[85] English republican writers held up as an ideal the ancient republics in which every citizen fulfilled every function—working his own land and taking up arms to defend the republic.[86]

---

79. *See* BANNING, *supra* note 65, at 81, 86; WOOD, *supra* note 56, at 208-09; POCOCK, *supra* note 44, at 514-17.
80. *See* WOOD, *supra* note 56, at 111-30.
81. *See id.* at 70-73. On this point, Americans followed earlier republicans, especially Harrington himself. *See* POCOCK, *supra* note 44, at 394-95.
82. *See* WOOD, *supra* note 56, at 205-07; POCOCK, *supra* note 44, at 515.
83. *See* WOOD, *supra* note 56, at 237-55.
84. *See* MCCOY, *supra* note 59, at 23; POCOCK, *supra* note 44, at 444-45, 462-66. For example, Members of Parliament looked to their own income, rather than to the public welfare, by taking monarchical bribes, *see* MCCOY, *supra* note 59, at 57-58; BANNING, *supra* note 65, at 52, 59; ISAAC KRAMNICK, REPUBLICANISM AND BOURGEOIS RADICALISM 178 (1990); the standing army looked to ensure its own continued existence by fomenting and standing ready to fight foreign wars, *see* POCOCK, *supra* note 44, at 409-10, 412-14; KRAMNICK, *supra*, at 178; the monied interest, too, encouraged war, because war gave rise to public debt, which made money for men of wealth, *see* BANNING, *supra* note 65, at 65-67; POCOCK, *supra* note 44, at 409-10, 439; KRAMNICK, *supra*, at 178. Deeply complicit in this vast conspiracy was the Crown, which now possessed both money and military might, so that if any should be inclined to protest, their resistance could not be a long one. *See* BANNING, *supra* note 65, at 52-59, 65-67.
85. *See* MCCOY, *supra* note 59, at 37-38; BANNING, *supra* note 65, at 67; POCOCK, *supra* note 44, at 430-31.
86. The Court Party and its intellectual backers defended specialization as progress, since it created prosperity and culture. *See, e.g.,* POCOCK, *supra* note 44, at 459-60; MCCOY, *supra* note 59, at 25-32. The Country Party—the self-conscious expositors of republican ideas—responded that if prosperity and culture could come only with specialization, it was better to accept some coarseness and retain political morality. *See* MCCOY, *supra* note 59, at 32-33; POCOCK, *supra* note 44, at 430-31, 499-505. In the context of 18th-century England, one might describe the Country Party itself as a special interest: the party of rural,

Many American colonial writers shared these worries about Britain's social character. In their view, the English people had made their peace with tyranny and so had come to prefer luxury to liberty.[87] More broadly, the degenerative effects of social development had fractured the English populace.[88] Americans, in contrast, retained a virtue that Britons had lost. They remained poised between barbarism and effete decay—sturdy but civilized farmers, independent and unspecialized.[89]

This American concern over professionalization as a cause of corruption reflected a subtle democratic drift away from the classical ideal of mixed government. Even within the balance-of-estates structure, republicans typically cast themselves as the champions of the liberty of the Many against the One, and this posture gave their rhetoric a populist tone.[90] But in standing against specialization, republicans cast themselves not as the representatives of any particular estate, but as those virtuous souls—the mass of the American people—who stood for a commonwealth against the corrupting tide of modernity.[91]

4. The Liberal Constitution and Democratic Republican Demands for a Bill of Rights

Immediately after achieving independence, one course of reform seemed particularly desirable to many Americans. Since the threat of overreaching arose primarily from the less democratic elements of government and since the body of the American people possessed uncommon virtue, the new constitutions should increase the role of the people in government. Ultimately, this role had its limits. Few republicans claimed that direct democracy was a practicable course in any of the new states;[92] virtually all conceded that a representative democracy must balance the branches of government against one another.[93] At the same time, however, republican reformers sought to redistribute the

---

backward-looking landed wealth. See KRAMNICK, supra note 84, at 165, 177; ISAAC KRAMNICK, BOLINGBROKE AND HIS CIRCLE: THE POLITICS OF NOSTALGIA IN THE AGE OF WALPOLE (1968). They did not perceive themselves as such, however, because they believed that if all remained like themselves, Britons could share a common good—but in no imaginable order could soldiers, administrators, stockjobbers, lacemakers, factory owners, and farmers coalesce into a shared interest. See BANNING, supra note 65, at 68-69. Later, American republicans would exhibit a similar tendency by identifying the middle class with the people as a whole. See KRAMNICK, supra note 84, at 277.

87. See BANNING, supra note 65, at 80; WOOD, supra note 56, at 34.

88. See BANNING, supra note 65, at 75-76; WOOD, supra note 56, at 34-37; McCOY, supra note 59, at 57-58.

89. See BANNING, supra note 65, at 76-77; McCOY, supra note 59, at 62-70; WOOD, supra note 56, at 52-53, 57-60, 98-101, 113-14; KRAMNICK, supra note 84, at 268-69. Still others would allow for development but were concerned to stop it before it went too far. See McCOY, supra note 59, at 72-75.

90. See BANNING, supra note 65, at 63-64; WOOD, supra note 56, at 20.

91. The transition apparently was easy, since republicans often conflated the good of the whole and the good of the Many. See WOOD, supra note 56, at 20.

92. See id. at 222-24.

93. See BANNING, supra note 65, at 70, 197.

balance by limiting the authority of the executive, expanding the power of the lower house of the legislature, and increasing the dependency of the upper house on the will of the Many.[94]

The 1780's, however, brought new worries. To many, the new democratic legislatures seemed to be fora for pursuit of private interests, especially of the less affluent, rather than for discussion of the common good. America, it seemed, had entered modernity with the rest of the world, fragmented and self-interested.[95] One response to this crisis was the Federalists' embrace of liberalism. With an apparent sense of relief, they leapt off the tightrope of virtue into the chasm of appetite. Proclaiming that the bulk of the people would always be self-interested, they asserted that any sensible political system must use the structure of government not to inspire virtue but to limit the damage done by self-interest.[96] Taking the old rhetoric of mixed government and imbuing it with new meaning, the Federalists sought to remove power from local legislatures to a central government where different factions and branches of government could check one another.[97]

By the 1780's, it was too late to deny that all power derived from the people, but the Federalists gave the people a new role. The people mythically erected the Constitution that delegated power to each of the components of a distant government, and they participated from afar in the selection of their representatives. Otherwise, they essentially retired from politics; they had no direct hand in their own government. Meanwhile, their representatives carried forward the messy business of mutual limitation.[98] No longer would the people have to be virtuous for government to be just and stable.

By the early 1790's, then, many of the nation's leaders had adopted a largely liberal ideology, and the decade as a whole was one of complex interaction between new ideas and old, with both amply represented.[99] But even after

---

94. See WOOD, supra note 56, at 162-173; Kramnick, supra note 13, at 18, 21-23.

95. See WOOD, supra note 56, at 396-98, 402-06, 410-11, 414-18.

96. See, e.g., id. at 429, 612-13; POCOCK, supra note 44, at 521-23; KRAMNICK, supra note 84, at 262-64. Federalists embraced a variety of views, departing from the old republican ideal by degrees. James Madison, for example, maintained only that the bulk of the people would be self-interested, so that the goal of government was to elevate the virtuous few to office. See Cass R. Sunstein, Interest Groups in American Public Law, 38 STAN. L. REV. 29, 38-48 (1985); WOOD, supra note 56, at 505-07; KRAMNICK, supra note 84, at 270-71. Alexander Hamilton, by contrast, closely anticipated modern free market liberals by insisting that the end of government is not virtue but prosperity and that individuals best help the country by helping themselves. See, e.g., BANNING, supra note 65, at 134-40. All, however, shared a conviction that a republic pervaded by virtuous self-denial was not possible.

97. See WOOD, supra note 56, at 407, 501-05, 547-62; BANNING, supra note 65, at 87-90; POCOCK, supra note 44, at 522-23.

98. See WOOD, supra note 56, at 544-47; BANNING, supra note 65, at 97-102; POCOCK, supra note 44, at 517-21.

99. See generally KRAMNICK, supra note 84. Even Gordon Wood, who is most associated with the recovery of the republican tradition, believes that the decade was a time of transition to more liberal ideas. See, e.g., WOOD, supra note 56, at 606-15. Others, however, argue that republicanism retained a powerful hold on American thinking into the 19th century. See POCOCK, supra note 44, at 526-52. See generally BANNING, supra note 65 (arguing that Jeffersonian party platform was product of civic republican heritage); STEVEN WATTS, THE REPUBLIC REBORN: WAR AND THE MAKING OF LIBERAL AMERICA 1790-1820 (1987)

the adoption of a more liberal Constitution, some American thinkers retained old republican convictions.[100] They continued to hope that prompt action on both social and governmental fronts might preserve a truly republican America.[101]

These thinkers, predominantly Anti-Federalist republicans, feared the central government because they believed that it would be dominated by economic elites, distant from the people, acting to pursue their own self-interest. They resisted the adoption of the Constitution in order to keep power in their more egalitarian and democratic state assemblies,[102] and they urged the creation of a Bill of Rights that would limit the damage that the central government could do.[103] Thus, while over much of its history republicanism may have been associated with wealthy elites who possessed the leisure to devote themselves to politics, at this Anti-Federalist moment, republicanism belonged in large part to men with back-country accents who feared such elites.[104] The Second Amendment grew out of this reaction—a republican avatar, perhaps, in a growingly liberal age. Thus, even if liberal ideas had begun to supplant republican ones by 1792,[105] it is appropriate to read the Second Amendment in a republican light.[106]

(arguing that republicanism gave way gradually to liberalism in general culture in early 19th century). Still others argue that liberal ideas had largely replaced republican ones by the 1790's. *See generally* JOHN P. DIGGINS, THE LOST SOUL OF AMERICAN POLITICS (1984); THOMAS L. PANGLE, THE SPIRIT OF MODERN REPUBLICANISM (1988). For my purposes, the exact resolution of this debate is not critical because, regardless of whether the decade as a whole was liberal, the Second Amendment in particular was republican.

100. *See* WOOD, *supra* note 56, at 425-29; KRAMNICK, *supra* note 84, at 266-68.

101. They issued perorations to the people to return to austere republican simplicity, *see, e.g.*, WOOD, *supra* note 56, at 426-28; KRAMNICK, *supra* note 84, at 267-68, and they waited for new republican governments to mold the people to virtue. *See, e.g.*, WOOD, *supra* note 56, at 426.

102. *See* EDWARD COUNTRYMAN, A PEOPLE IN REVOLUTION 273-79 (1981); WOOD, *supra* note 56, at 519-23; Kramnick, *supra* note 53, at 15, 45-46.

103. *See, e.g.*, WOOD, *supra* note 56, at 536-38; Kramnick, *supra* note 13, at 60-61. This view of the Bill of Rights—as a democratic republican response to the text of the Constitution—is the central thesis of a recent, rich, and significant article by Akhil Amar. *See* Akhil R. Amar, *The Bill of Rights as a Constitution*, 100 YALE L.J. 1131 (1991). Professor Amar advances an interpretation of the Second Amendment that, like mine, emphasizes its populist and localist character. *See id.* at 1162-73. He also sensitively discusses the ways in which these themes underlie other provisions of the Bill of Rights.

104. Kramnick, *supra* note 53, at 23-24, 27, 62-63.

105. *See supra* text accompanying notes 95-99.

106. Commentators on both sides of the historical debate seem to agree. Pocock, for example, explains: "[T]he Second Amendment to the Constitution . . . affirms the relation between a popular militia and popular freedom in language directly descended from that of Machiavelli, which remains a potent ritual utterance in the United States to this day." POCOCK, *supra* note 44, at 528. On the other side, Kramnick connects the new comfort with a standing army with a new liberal mood, *see* KRAMNICK, *supra* note 84, at 171, 265-66; Kramnick, *supra* note 13, at 56-57, but as I will elaborate, the Second Amendment grew out of that strain of American thinking still uncomfortable with a professional army.

B. *Arms and the Militia in Republican Thought*

1. *The Problem of a Standing Army*

The Second Amendment begins with the claim that a "well regulated militia" is "necessary to the security of a free state." This language implicitly refers to an old set of republican fears and hopes: a militia could help to limit corruption, unlike a standing army, which would be part of the problem. As Elbridge Gerry stated during congressional discussion of the Amendment: "What, sir, is the use of a militia? It is to prevent the establishment of a standing army, the bane of liberty."[107] Liberals, by contrast, little feared a standing army and little valued the militia.[108]

Republicans believed that the state must arm itself to resist foreign aggression and to keep civil order. But the distribution of arms caused them great anxiety, because whoever held the weapons and real property within a republic also held ultimate control.[109] In arming itself, the state had two options: a standing professional army or a popular militia. The former posed two great threats of corruption. First, it could become a tool of executive usurpation. Second, the army posed a risk of factionalism and professionalization.

Evidence of the former threat was ample. Standing armies arose in England as a tool of the Stuart monarchs' ambitions for power, and memories of that time remained vivid in republicans' minds.[110] The standing forces were at hand to tempt the King to adopt and enforce unpopular policies; its members would follow his will rather than the common good because they depended on him for their livelihood.[111] The army was, moreover, one of the chief avenues for subversion of Parliament, as many M.P.'s held places in the army.[112]

American colonists were familiar with the consequences of executive control of the military. Throughout the eighteenth century, colonists experienced

---

107. 1 ANNALS OF CONG. 749-50 (Joseph Gales ed., 1789).

108. *See supra* note 106.

109. For example, James Burgh, the great transmitter of republican ideas to the colonies, *see* BANNING, *supra* note 65, at 60-62, made the connection between power and arms explicit: "Those, who have the command of the arms in a country, says *Aristotle*, are masters of the state, and have it in their power to make what revolutions they please." 2 JOSEPH BURGH, POLITICAL DISQUISITIONS: OR, AN ENQUIRY INTO PUBLIC ERRORS, DEFECTS, AND ABUSES 345 (London, 1775). On power following property, the classic republican source is James Harrington, who made that claim the center of his theory of government. *See* POCOCK, *supra* note 44, at 385-91.

110. *See* JOHN TRENCHARD & THOMAS GORDON, CATO'S LETTERS NO. 94, *reprinted in* THE ENGLISH LIBERTARIAN HERITAGE 222-23 (David L. Jacobson ed., 1965); Andrew Fletcher, *A Discourse of Government with Relation to Militias, in* SELECTED POLITICAL WRITINGS AND SPEECHES 1, 10 (David Daiches ed., 1979); W.A. SPECK, RELUCTANT REVOLUTIONARIES 145-46, 154-56 (1988); POCOCK, *supra* note 44, at 411-12. After the Glorious Revolution, Parliament controlled the finances of the army—a fact that assuaged the worries of many moderate Whigs.

111. *See* Fletcher, *supra* note 110, at 4, 15; LAWRENCE D. CRESS, CITIZENS IN ARMS: THE ARMY AND THE MILITIA IN AMERICAN SOCIETY TO THE WAR OF 1812, at 23-25 (1982); POCOCK, *supra* note 44, at 413.

112. *See* Fletcher, *supra* note 110, at 6; CRESS, *supra* note 111, at 20, 23-25; POCOCK, *supra* note 44, at 409-410, 412-13.

friction with the contingents of British regulars stationed near them.[113] Following the Seven Years' War, this friction increased dramatically when Britain decided that the colonists should pay for their own defense. For the first time, the imperial government levied a tax on the colonies for revenue purposes,[114] and that revenue, ominously, went to the upkeep of the standing army. When the colonists refused to pay, claiming that taxation without representation was tyranny,[115] the imperial government ordered the military occupation of Boston to enforce the policy. Perhaps most alarmingly, the occupying army was made up not only of British regulars, but also of Hessian mercenaries.[116] The colonists were experiencing a republican nightmare: an unrepresentative government was using a standing army against them to enforce an unjust policy.[117]

Like English radicals, many American republicans blamed George III for these abuses.[118] Others recognized that Parliament, controlled by conspiratorial ministers and placemen, was at least as complicitous as the King in the new policies.[119] It made little difference to American republicans, however, whether Parliament or the King controlled the standing army, since in either case it was not subject to the colonists' own legislatures.[120] After the Revolution, the framers of the new state constitutions took pains to ensure that the state military was under legislative, rather than executive, control. For some, this arrangement ameliorated the worst fears of a standing army.[121]

A standing army, however, posed a second threat: regardless of who controlled it, the very existence of a standing army provided the opportunity for social corruption through professionalization. The army was a symptom and product of modern specialization of economic function, because soldiers were trained to a particular trade—fighting—and sought to maintain their particular

---

113. *See generally* DOUGLAS E. LEACH, ROOTS OF CONFLICT: BRITISH ARMED FORCES AND COLONIAL AMERICANS, 1677-1763 (1986). The colonies never raised a standing army; they defended themselves against Indian attack first by militia and later by expeditionary forces made up of volunteers or impressed paupers, sometimes commanded by British officers. *See* CRESS, *supra* note 111, at 4-8; E. Wayne Carp, *The Problem of National Defense in the Early Wood, in* THE AMERICAN REVOLUTION: ITS CHARACTER AND LIMITS 19-20 (Jack P. Greene ed., 1987). But colonial militia served with British regulars in various conflicts and came away with sour recollections. *See generally* LEACH, *supra.* Throughout the century, moreover, there was constant tension between colonists and regulars over quartering troops and impressment. *See* CRESS, *supra* note 111, at 10-11; LEACH, *supra*, at 10-11, 87-92; PAULINE MAIER, FROM RESISTANCE TO REVOLUTION 6-7, 9-12, 20, 124-25 (1974).
114. *See* JACK P. GREENE, PERIPHERIES AND CENTER 80 (1986).
115. *See id.* at 81-82.
116. Hence the charge against George III in the Declaration of Independence that he sent "large Armies of foreign Mercenaries to compleat the works of death, destruction, and tyranny. . . ." THE DECLARATION OF INDEPENDENCE para. 27 (U.S. 1776).
117. *See* CRESS, *supra* note 111, at 11, 36-39; Carp, *supra* note 113, at 21-22; ROYSTER, *supra* note 67, at 36.
118. *See* MAIER, *supra* note 113, at 200-03, 208-11, 237-38.
119. *See id.* at 234-37.
120. *See* CRESS, *supra* note 111, at 8-9, 11, 36-38, 47; GREENE, *supra* note 114, at 83-84.
121. *See* CRESS, *supra* note 111, at 60-61; ROYSTER, *supra* note 67, at 51-53.

interests.[122] Thus, the army desired foreign wars to justify its existence, ample taxation to support it, a strong executive to collect the taxes, and docile citizens to pay the taxes.[123] The American republican Joel Barlow, in denouncing European systems of government, put the idea pithily: "Thus money is required to levy armies, and armies to levy money; and foreign wars are introduced as the pretended occupation for both."[124] Soldiers thus contributed to the breakdown of the common good in much the same way that any other professional group did. In addition, a standing army posed a special threat: it controlled the means of force.[125] As society developed and diversified, many ignominiously chose to surrender the sword to a professional army. As a consequence, those who surrendered the sword to the standing army gained a luxurious way of life but lost their moral character and their only guarantee of liberty in the bargain.[126]

2. The Militia, the Balance of Estates, and Centralization

In republican theory, the militia offered protection against all of these dangers.[127] The militia was viewed as the universal people armed—the whole people, the republic. This *armato populato* did have one limit: it included only citizens, not all residents.[128] Within this limit, however, the militia reflected the most populist strand of republican thinking. To republican thinkers, identifi-

---

122. *See* Fletcher, *supra* note 110, at 9; CRESS, *supra* note 111, at 19; POCOCK, *supra* note 44, at 430-32.

123. *See* ELBRIDGE GERRY, OBSERVATIONS ON THE NEW CONSTITUTION (1788), *reprinted in* PAMPHLETS ON THE CONSTITUTION OF THE UNITED STATES, PUBLISHED DURING ITS DISCUSSION BY THE PEOPLE, 1787-1788, at 10 (Paul L. Ford ed., Da Capo 1968) (1888); Fletcher, *supra* note 110, at 6, 12; POCOCK, *supra* note 44, at 409-13, 430.

124. JOEL BARLOW, ADVICE TO THE PRIVILEGED ORDERS IN THE SEVERAL STATES OF EUROPE 44 (1956).

125. *See* Fletcher, *supra* note 110, at 4, 9; POCOCK, *supra* note 44, at 199-200.

126. *See* Fletcher, *supra* note 110, at 6; CRESS, *supra* note 111, at 19; POCOCK, *supra* note 44, at 203-04 (Florentine origin of idea). Barlow claimed that when the people lay down their arms, they "lose at once the power of protecting themselves, and of discerning the cause of their oppression" because doing so "palsies the hand and brutalizes the mind." BARLOW, *supra* note 124, at 45.

127. Many republicans believed that the militia offered another advantage: it would be more effective against foreign enemies than would a professional army because it fought for home and hearth, rather than for lucre. *See* MORGAN, *supra* note 78, at 154-56; Fletcher, *supra* note 110, at 9, 17; CRESS, *supra* note 111, at 43-44. In fact, however, militias were never very effective, especially against trained bands and especially given the increasing sophistication of warfare in the 18th century. *See* MORGAN, *supra* note 78, at 160-62. By the 1780's most Americans had come to perceive the militia's shortcomings. *See* ROYSTER, *supra* note 67, at 37; CRESS, *supra* note 111, at 58-59. Americans still quarreled over the appropriate role of an army, but the basis of the disagreement had shifted. Opponents now argued not that an army was less effective than a militia but that it was more effective, and thus posed a threat to liberty. The militia was perhaps less proficient, but it was virtuous. *See* CRESS, *supra* note 111, at 75-93.

128. *See* Lawrence D. Cress, *An Armed Community: The Origins and Meaning of the Right to Bear Arms*, 71 J. AM. HIST. 22, 25, 29 (1984). In the 19th century, states often limited militia membership to whites, but colonial practice typically included African-American citizens. *See* Cottrol & Diamond, *supra* note 17, at 37-40. Today, the citizenry comprises a much greater proportion of the population than it did in the 1780's, and a modern analogue to the militia would thus include a vastly greater proportion of the population as well. I consider the intellectual difficulties attending such an expansion in Part IV.A.1-2.

cation of the militia and the people made the militia incomparably more attractive than a standing army.

Initially, the existence of a citizen militia was thought to limit the threat of executive usurpation. From the beginning of the tradition, theorists had closely identified the militia with the Many, to give the Many a check on the monarchical and aristocratic elements of government.[129] By the 1780's, however, the balance of estates had come to be less central to Americans. Republicans had moved toward purer democracy, and military forces had been under the control of legislatures.[130]

A new issue, however, soon replaced concern about executive usurpation: fear of the excessive concentration of power in the central government. This fear went to the heart of the debate between Federalists and Anti-Federalists over the adoption of the new Constitution. Traditionally, militia forces were local bodies, and prior to the 1790's, republicans generally believed that this proximity to the people would prevent their capture by malignant governmental actors.[131] By the 1790's, however, many had lost faith in the local militia. At times the militia had sided with the troublemakers in domestic insurrections after the Revolution. Many concluded that these insurrections were not legitimate forms of resistance, but constituted sedition against legitimate authority; it followed that the militia might also be seditious.[132] Abandoning trust in the militia[133] (and contrary to received republican wisdom),[134] the Framers of the Constitution gave Congress power to raise a standing army and to regulate state militias.[135]

The Federalist defense of this decision was even more alarming. In startlingly unrepublican fashion, Alexander Hamilton argued for the creation of a strong and modern state, distinct from its population, with sufficient means to

---

129. *See. e.g.*, Fletcher, *supra* note 110, at 16; POCOCK, *supra* note 44, at 87-91 (Leonardo Bruni); *id.* at 196-99, 202-03, 210-11 (Machiavelli); *id.* at 389-91 (Harrington).

130. *See supra* text accompanying notes 78-83. In line with the new emphasis on democracy, writers argued that popular government must depend on a popular militia. *See, e.g.*, BARLOW, *supra* note 124, at 46; Robert E. Shalhope, *The Ideological Origins of the Second Amendment*, 69 J. AM. HIST. 599, 602, 605-06 (1982) (quoting republican thinkers).

131. *See* Carp, *supra* note 113, at 19-20; *see also* CRESS, *supra* note 111, at 4-6 (specifying local nature of militia).

132. *See* CRESS, *supra* note 111, at 95-96, 128; Carp, *supra* note 113, at 32; Richard D. Brown, *Shay's Rebellion and the Ratification of the Federal Constitution in Massachusetts, in* BEYOND CONFEDERATION 113-15 (Richard Beeman et al. eds., 1987).

133. *See, e.g.*, CRESS, *supra* note 111, at 71-73.

134. *See* REGINALD C. STUART, WAR AND AMERICAN THOUGHT 50 (1982); Carp, *supra* note 113, at 33-34; CRESS, *supra* note 111, at 95-97.

135. *See* U.S. CONST. art. I, § 8, cls. 11-16; Akhil R. Amar, *Of Sovereignty and Federalism*, 96 YALE L.J. 1425, 1495-96 (1987); Carp, *supra* note 113, at 32-33; CRESS, *supra* note 111, at 97; STUART, *supra* note 134, at 59-63. In particular, Congress was given the power "[t]o provide for organizing, arming, and disciplining the Militia, and for governing such Part of them as may be employed in the Service of the United States, reserving to the States respectively, the Appointment of the Officers, and the Authority of training the militia according to the discipline prescribed by Congress." U.S. CONST. art. I, § 8, cl. 16.

carry out its will.[136] In particular, a standing army would be necessary to repel foreign invasion because "[w]ar, like most other things, is a science to be acquired and perfected by diligence, by perseverance, by time, and by practice."[137] More disturbingly, this standing army might be turned against the states themselves: "If [an] insurrection should pervade a whole State, or a principal part of it, the employment of a different [non-militia] force might become unavoidable."[138] The alternative, in Hamilton's mind, was chaos. With no firm hand from above, individual states or regions would inevitably erupt in constant civil war.[139]

For Anti-Federalist republicans, such sentiments were like a fireball in the night. They feared that the new central government would be dominated by the Few, distant from the people, and lustful for power.[140] Hamilton's writings seemed to promise that the government would use its army in repressive ways. The Anti-Federalists had not lost faith in the virtue of a people's militia,[141] and they resisted the Constitution because it would take power away from the local legislatures, which were more democratic and more devoted to the common good.[142] Even some Federalist defenses of the new government implicitly accepted the republican premise that the militia is the ultimate bulwark of virtue. Madison, for example, argued that if the federal government sought to subvert the militia, the states retained the constitutional power to protect it. So if Congress should ever use standing armies to advance tyrannical designs, they would be outnumbered and outfought by liberty-loving militia members.[143]

These reassurances were not, however, enough to allay the fears of Anti-Federalist republicans, and a number of state legislatures approved the Constitution with recommendations that Congress adopt a bill of rights. Virtually all of these proposals included some version of the right to arms, with a range of components: some sought to return complete control of the militia to the states, some sought to ban standing armies, but all sought to guarantee the right of the

---

136. Indeed, Isaac Kramnick argues that before the Federalists, American thinkers had no modern conception of the state; in that sense, Hamilton was engaged in creating an American state for the first time. *See* Kramnick, *supra* note 13, at 67-72. (The republicans did have a concept of government, and I have loosely used the term "state" to refer to their notion of government. *See supra* notes 12-13.)

137. THE FEDERALIST NO. 25 (Alexander Hamilton).

138. THE FEDERALIST NO. 28 (Alexander Hamilton).

139. *See id.*

140. *See* WOOD, *supra* note 56, at 487-96; MORGAN, *supra* note 78, at 276-87.

141. Indeed, the new republic initially saw remarkably little change in military policy. *See* Carp, *supra* note 113, at 35-37. Despite Federalist proposals for a federal select militia, Congress provided for a universal militia under state control. *Id.* at 36-37; CRESS, *supra* note 111, at 119-21. At the end of the Revolution, the Newburgh conspiracy and the Society of Cincinnati revived fears of a standing army, *see* CRESS, *supra* note 111, at 67-71; ROYSTER, *supra* note 67, at 345-57, and republicans used the old rhetoric throughout the 1790's to denounce any armed force other than a universal militia. *See* CRESS, *supra* note 111, at 127-34, 137-49.

142. *See* CRESS, *supra* note 111, at 98-102.

143. *See* THE FEDERALIST NO. 46 (James Madison); Amar, *supra* note 135, at 1496-97.

people to keep and bear arms.[144] Supporters of the Second Amendment thus inscribed faith in the local militia—not liberal concern about individual self-defense—into the Constitution: "A well regulated Militia, being necessary to the security of a free State, the right of the people to keep and bear Arms, shall not be infringed."

The Second Amendment therefore sought to protect local democracy by protecting popular, public military bodies. The states would always have an armed populace from which they could form a militia. The federal government could regulate the use of that militia, but could not disarm or disband it. As a result, state militias could always check the distant politicians in Washington.[145] On military policy, the text of the Constitution and the Bill of Rights are thus chronologically inverted compared to the general development of political ideas: the 1787 Constitution represented the new liberal mood, and the 1792 Second Amendment the older republican tradition.[146]

3. The Militia and Universality

Overconcentration of power in the central government was not, however, the only fear from which the militia offered protection. Republicans hoped that the militia would check state government as well as federal: state constitutions, too, contained right to arms provisions. Many hoped that Congress itself would rely on a militia, rather than on a standing army.[147] Even apart from its association with local governments, therefore, the militia promised virtuous control of force.

This trust in the virtue of the militia rested on its rhetorical identification with the whole of the citizenry—an equation with three significant conceptual results. The first focused on the character of the American public: because the citizenry was or could be virtuous, the militia was or could be virtuous.[148] Second, as militia members were citizens and property holders, they had a stake in the well-being of the republic—unlike mercenaries or professional soldiers, who were committed only to their own fortunes.[149]

Most important, the militia would be virtuous because it was thought to include all of the citizens of the republic. By definition, this universality

---

144. See HALBROOK, supra note 17, at 72-75; Cress, supra note 128, at 35-36; Shalhope, supra note 130, at 608-10.

145. Akhil Amar also argues that the Second Amendment provides an important linguistic gloss on Congress' military powers under Article I. In the republican tradition, an army was composed of soldiers for hire, as opposed to a militia, which was conscripted from the general public. As a result, Congress' power to raise an "army" involves authority only to enlist soldiers, not conscript them. See Amar, supra note 103, at 1163-75.

146. Cf. Carp, supra note 113, at 35 (the "passage of the Second Amendment . . . clearly reveals America's divided mind on military policy").

147. See CRESS, supra note 111, at 78-87.

148. See Henry Knox, General Knox's Militia Plan, 2 ANNALS OF CONG. 2088-89 (1790).

149. See Fletcher, supra note 110, at 9; Cress, supra note 128, at 29.

reflected the common good, rather than the good of a narrow slice of society. The militia was nothing more or less than the whole people in their military capacity.[150] Americans incessantly repeated this theme—rather than the importance of individual self-defense—in support of the militia and the Second Amendment. State proposals for the Amendment typically described the militia as "the body of the people"[151]—a phrase denoting the whole or the bulk of the community.[152] Richard Henry Lee explained: "A militia, when properly formed, are in fact the people themselves . . ."[153] Similarly, George Mason asked: "Who are the militia? They consist now of the whole people, except a few public officers."[154] In a much-quoted passage, Patrick Henry maintained: "The great object [of the Second Amendment] is, that *every* man be armed."[155]

As the people, the militia could not act against the general good because the general good and their good were one and the same. Tench Coxe declaimed: "THE POWERS OF THE SWORD ARE IN THE HANDS OF THE YEOMANRY OF AMERICA FROM SIXTEEN TO SIXTY . . . . Who are the militia? *are they not ourselves.* Is it feared, then, that we shall turn our arms *each man against his own bosom.*"[156] Samuel Adams argued: "The Militia is composed of free Citizens. There is therefore no Danger of their making use of their Power to the destruction of their own Rights, or suffering other to invade them."[157] To be universal, the militia must comprise all of the citizenry. Republican writings, of the Anti-Federalist period and before, therefore insisted that the whole people should be armed, and contrasted this universality with the partiality of a standing army or a select militia.[158]

---

150. *See* POCOCK, *supra* note 44, at 414. As I will discuss, actual Anglo-American militias were never truly universal, but the militias of republican rhetoric, theory, and aspiration nearly always were.

Recently, Elaine Scarry has connected this insistence on the universal distribution of arms with social contract rhetoric. Social contract theory requires not only the "threshold consent" to the original contract but also the "perpetual consent" of the population to government through voting, the amendment process, and willingness to go to war; the concentration of arms in a single group, however, would lead to the coercive dominance of society by that group and would destroy the possibility of a government limited by the consent of the population. *See* Elaine Scarry, *War and the Social Contract: Nuclear Policy, Distribution, and the Right to Bear Arms*, 139 U. PA. L. REV. 1257, 1276-89 (1991).

151. Cress, *supra* note 128, at 29-30, 36; *see also id.* at 29-30; Shalhope, *supra* note 130, at 608-09.

152. *See* MAIER, *supra* note 113, at 35-36.

153. RICHARD H. LEE, ADDITIONAL LETTERS FROM THE FEDERAL FARMER 169 (New York, 1788).

154. 3 DEBATES IN THE SEVERAL STATE CONVENTIONS 425-26 (Jonathan Elliot ed., B. Franklin 1968) (2d ed. 1888) [hereinafter DEBATES].

155. *See, e.g.,* HALBROOK, *supra* note 17, at 74 (emphasis added).

156. *A Pennsylvanian*, PENNSYLVANIA GAZETTE, Feb. 20, 1788, *reprinted in* 2 DOCUMENTARY HISTORY OF THE RATIFICATION OF THE CONSTITUTION (Microfilm Supp.) 1778-1780 (Kaminski & Saladino eds., 1981) [hereinafter *A Pennsylvanian*]. Decades before, an English pamphleteer made the same point: "The *Militia* must, and can never be otherwise than for *English Liberty,* because else it doth destroy *itself;* but a *standing Force* can be for nothing but *Prerogative,* by whom it hath its *idle living* and *Subsistence.*" POCOCK, *supra* note 44, at 410; *see also* CRESS, *supra* note 111, at 3, 43-45.

157. 3 SAMUEL ADAMS, WRITINGS 251 (Henry A. Cushing, ed., 1906).

158. *See* LEE, *supra* note 153, at 169; ALGERNON SIDNEY, DISCOURSES CONCERNING GOVERNMENT 155-57 (London, 1698); Fletcher, *supra* note 110, at 18-21; BARLOW, *supra* note 124, at 46; CRESS, *supra* note 111, at 100; HALBROOK, *supra* note 17, at 69-74 (1984); Cress, *supra* note 128, at 31-32. For the Anti-

The republican militia member was thus envisioned as the quintessentially unspecialized citizen, Horatio at the Plow, whose own interests reflected the general good. At one moment, he controlled policy in his enfranchised role; at another, he controlled resources in his propertied role; and at a third, he controlled force in his armed role.[159] Indeed, for some republicans the citizen's status as militia member may have been more significant than his status as voter, because it was a more direct exercise of self-government. Most American republicans conceded that direct democracy on any scale was impracticable, but understood that by foregoing such immediate citizen participation in government, they lost an important part of the republican tradition.[160] After the Federalists managed to make representation even more ephemeral, the citizen as franchise holder was left still further from the reins of governmental power. As a militia member, however, the citizen could still directly participate in politics by intimidating would-be despots and demagogues.[161]

The militia's two features—decentralization and universality—can thus be separated, and they are each independently important. But they are not in fact radically distinct, because both proceed from the same fear that a small group of powerful citizens (in an oligarchic central government) could come to dominate the republic by control of the means of coercion (held by a select militia or standing army). The solution was to vest arms in a universal body under the control of democratic local legislatures.

4. The Militia and Training in Virtue

The virtue of the militia therefore rested upon and reflected the virtue of the citizenry as a whole, because they were one and the same. But the militia

---

Federalists, the primary demon on this point was probably Hamilton, who insisted that the people should surrender liberty for wealth: a universal militia would be impracticable because "[i]t would form an [enormous] annual deduction from the annual labour of the country. . . ." THE FEDERALIST NO. 29, at 184 (Alexander Hamilton) (Clinton Rossiter ed., 1961). In the Pennsylvania Ratifying Convention, John Smilie responded: "Congress may give us a select militia which will, in fact, be a standing army . . . . When a select militia is formed; the people in general may be disarmed." A Pennsylvanian, supra note 156, at 1778-80.

159. JOHN TRENCHARD & WALTER MOYLE, AN ARGUMENT SHEWING, THAT A STANDING ARMY IS INCONSISTENT WITH A FREE GOVERNMENT, AND ABSOLUTELY DESTRUCTIVE TO THE CONSTITUTION OF THE ENGLISH MONARCHY 7 (London, 1697); CRESS, supra note 111, at 19. One of the best examples of this view was the creation of the utopian Georgia Colony by English philanthropists. They sought to prevent the development of self-interest and to promote virtue by restricting the market in land and labor. Instead of economic activity, "[t]he chief form of group participation would be military service, which was required of all adult male inhabitants." J.E. CROWLEY, THIS SHEBA, SELF: THE CONCEPTUALIZATION OF ECONOMIC LIFE IN EIGHTEENTH CENTURY AMERICA 20-21 (1974).

160. See POCOCK, supra note 44, at 517-21.

161. As Akhil Amar has demonstrated, the citizen's role as juror served much the same end by giving him a direct hand in the administration of justice. Indeed, the similarities between the jury's role and the militia's are striking. Like the militia, the jury was dialogic and deliberative in considering whether to nullify the law, especially if deemed unconstitutional, see Amar, supra note 103, at 1191-95; it provided training in virtue and self-government, see id. at 1186-87; it was populist, see id. at 1187-89, and localist, see id. at 1186; and it functioned as a protection against tyranny, see id. at 1183-85.

was more than a passive mirror of society; it also acted upon its members to
instill civic virtue. As noted before, the virtuous citizen was expected to stand
apart from the state to criticize and correct it when it began to fall into corruption. Yet, he was expected to simultaneously subordinate his particularistic
interests to the good of the state as long as the state stayed on the paths of
virtue.[162] To do so, the citizen had to judge when he could refuse the demands of the state as corrupt, but he could not let his own separate interests
cloud his judgment. Property helped the citizen to balance these conflicting
responsibilities, by giving him independence of judgment as well as a stake in
the well-being of the republic.[163] Service in the militia was yet another means
of training the citizenry to civic virtue.

The self-sacrificial aspects of militia service were obvious. Membership
was service to the state that always disrupted one's chosen round of activities
and often involved hunger, cold, disease, and danger.[164] The militia member
was expected to bear these burdens with the knowledge that he was keeping
the republic safe. The experience of working together with fellow citizens could
cement this perspective of self-sacrifice to the common good. Militia service
required cooperation among citizens and subordination to orders, stimulated a
commitment to comrades that would become a devotion to the public that they
represented, and was filled with exhortation to virtue in sermons and speeches.[165] Many veterans of the Revolution recalled military service as the emotional high point of their lives; by the 1780's they yearned for the "rage
militaire" that drew Americans together in the war.[166]

Militia service also served to engender virtue by inducing the experience
of independent self-government. In republican theory, arms and property
constituted the necessary material bases for the autonomous political personality
of the citizen, who was dependent for his safety and livelihood only on the
body of his fellow citizens, not on the state apparatus nor on particular private
individuals.[167] Conscious that they directly held the reins of coercive power,
the people would never accept that governors governed and citizens obeyed.
As Joel Barlow explained, "A people that legislate for themselves ought to be
in the habit of protecting themselves; or they will lose the spirit of both."[168]
Thus, republican commentators denounced those supine peoples who, for

---

162. *See infra* Part III.B.6.

163. *See supra* note 71; text accompanying note 149; *infra* text accompanying notes 287-288.

164. This advantage is prominent in proposals for model militias. Henry Knox, the first Secretary of
War, presented to Congress a militia plan which emphasized that the conditions of service should be dreadful
in order to accustom militia members to self-sacrifice. Knox, *supra* note 148, at 2088, 2100-01; *see also*
Fletcher, *supra* note 110, at 20-24 (suggesting use of camps to train young men to become soldiers);
POCOCK, *supra* note 44, at 201-02 (noting Machiavelli's belief that militia training induced virtue).

165. *See* Knox, *supra* note 148, at 2090, 2099-2101; Fletcher, *supra* note 110, at 20-24.

166. *See* ROYSTER, *supra* note 67, at 25, 31.

167. *See* POCOCK, *supra* note 44, at 203-04, 210-11, 385-86; CRESS, *supra* note 111, at 16-17, 23-24,
49.

168. BARLOW, *supra* note 124, at 47.

comfort and convenience, surrendered their arms—along with their liberty—to a standing army,[169] and expressed admiration for the independent, "manly," civil but not servile citizen-soldier-freeholder, committed to the common good but not enslaved to the state.[170]

5. *The Rights of Resistance and Revolution*

To entrust the means of force to the militia was thus to entrust it to the body most likely to use it in virtuous ways. This commitment of force to virtue was thought to have two important results. First, quite apart from any actual act of resistance, the knowledge that citizens possessed arms was likely to affect the behavior of both state officials and citizens. State officials would be loathe to trifle with the people's liberties, knowing that citizens had the wherewithal to defend those liberties.[171] In contrast, republicans drew from history the lesson that when despots sought to undo a republic, they began by disarming militia members.[172] Republican thinkers also believed that possession of arms changed the character of the people as well, making them more independent, more suspicious of their government, and less willing to tolerate the slightest tyranny. It was difficult and frightening to resist despots and all too easy to accept early incursions. But down that path—and not far down it—lay slavery.[173] A people armed, aware of its own empowerment, would not start down that path.

As in the case of the militia as a training ground for virtue, republicans had some first hand experience with the benefits of the militia in resisting tyranny. Traditionally, to enforce their decisions, colonial governments had to rely on the *posse comitatus* and the militia. Colonial records are full of complaints that the militia, reflecting the sentiment of the people, refused to enforce edicts perceived as unjust, or even participated in popular resistance to them.[174] Colonial culture accepted some measure of violent resistance as a normal part of life, although those in authority never ceased to complain of that fact. If the

---

169. *See id.* at 45; Fletcher, *supra* note 110, at 5-6.

170. *See* BARLOW, *supra* note 124, at 47; ROYSTER, *supra* note 67, at 28; Shalhope, *supra* note 130, at 604-07.

171. The most famous exposition of this idea is Jefferson's: "[W]hat country can preserve it's [sic] liberties, if their [sic] rulers are not warned from time to time that their people preserve the spirit of resistance? Let them take arms . . . The tree of liberty must be refreshed from time to time with the blood of patriots and tyrants." Letter from Thomas Jefferson to William S. Smith (Nov. 13, 1787), *in* JEFFERSON: WRITINGS 910, 911 (Merrill D. Peterson ed., 1984); *see also* TRENCHARD & MOYLE, *supra* note 159, at 12.

172. *See* 1 ANNALS OF CONG., *supra* note 107, at 750; NOAH WEBSTER, AN EXAMINATION INTO THE LEADING PRINCIPLES OF THE FEDERAL CONSTITUTION (1787), *reprinted in* PAMPHLETS ON THE CONSTITUTION OF THE UNITED STATES, PUBLISHED DURING ITS DISCUSSION BY THE PEOPLE, 1787-1788, at 56 (Paul L. Ford ed., B. Franklin 1971) (1888); Shalhope, *supra* note 130, at 602.

173. *See* ROYSTER, *supra* note 67, at 5-7, 16.

174. *See* MORGAN, *supra* note 78, at 164; MAIER, *supra* note 113, at 16-26; Carp, *supra* note 113, at 20.

governors had lost touch with the people or disregarded their wishes, it seemed natural to the people of the colonies to go outside normal channels so as to make their will directly felt: to riot, to burn royal ships in protest of impressment, to close down courthouses, to assault officials or to destroy their property, or any of the thousand other courses of action of which their not very obedient minds could conceive.[175]

In the end, however, if the threat of force was to have any meaningful effect, the people had to be prepared to take up arms to oust tyrannical rulers and replace them with citizens committed to the common good. This right of resistance is the second general result of entrusting force to the militia. It is the *only* purpose of the Second Amendment explicitly mentioned during its discussion in Congress. Elbridge Gerry declared: "This declaration of rights, I take it, is intended to secure the people against the mal-administration of the Government."[176] He explained that the purpose of a militia is to prevent a standing army, and that when governments intend to invade the people's liberties, they first disarm the militia.[177] No one contradicted him or suggested a different, liberal purpose for the provision.[178]

Republicans were aware of the danger implicit in vouchsafing this right of resistance in the citizenry and sensitive to the charge that they were inciting violence. They developed a number of limits on the right: It must be a product of the "body" of the people, i.e., the great majority acting by consensus; it must be a course of last resort; its inspiration must be a commitment to the common good; and its object must be a true tyrant, committed to large-scale abuse, not merely randomly unjust or sinful in private life.[179]

An uprising that failed to meet these criteria was considered an illegitimate rebellion, rather than an act of true republican resistance. The American Revolutionaries believed that they had direct experience with the distinction. The War for Independence was resistance to tyranny, but the various uprisings against the new governments—Vermont's drive for independence, the Carolina Regulation, Shay's Rebellion, New York tenant protests, the Whiskey Rebellion, and others—were all rebellions.[180] Such rebellions were no better than

---

175. The study of legitimate popular disturbances in colonial and Revolutionary society has generated a substantial and growing body of historical scholarship. *See, e.g.*, COUNTRYMAN, *supra* note 102; PAUL A. GILJE, THE ROAD TO MOBOCRACY (1987); MAIER, *supra* note 113; ALAN TAYLOR, LIBERTY MEN AND GREAT PROPRIETORS (1990).

176. 1 ANNALS OF CONG., *supra* note 107, at 749.

177. *See id.* at 749-750.

178. Even the *Federalist Papers*, written well before the adoption of the Amendment, promised that if the central government ever used a standing army to oppress the people, "[t]o these would be opposed a militia amounting to near half a million of citizens with arms in their hands, officered by men chosen from among themselves, fighting for their common liberties and united and conducted by [state] governments possessing their affections and confidence." THE FEDERALIST NO. 46, at 299 (James Madison) (Clinton Rossiter ed., 1961).

179. *See* MAIER, *supra* note 113, at 36-39; STUART, *supra* note 134, at 19-21.

180. *See* Carp, *supra* note 113, at 32; THOMAS P. SLAUGHTER, THE WHISKEY REBELLION 44-45, 48 (1986).

tyranny, and the rebel forces little different from standing armies, inasmuch as they pursued a partial interest rather than the common good.[181] This threat to the commonweal could come as easily from a demagogue as from a despot, and the universal militia was supposed to suppress insurrections by private groups as well as usurpations by public ministers.[182] In resisting a tyrant, the militia was acting against the state apparatus, and in suppressing a rebellion it was acting for the same apparatus, but in either case it was pursuing the common good.

Traditionally, the republican function of the militia may have been limited to this right of resistance, rather than to a true right of revolution. The former is characteristic of more hierarchical forms of republicanism; the people had the right, when abused, to replace tyrants or to eliminate demagogues acting against the common good.[183] By contrast, it is yet a further step to grant the people a right of revolution,[184] a right to reorder society top to bottom, "to institute new Government, laying its foundation on such principles and organizing its powers in such form, as to them shall seem most likely to effect their Safety and Happiness."[185] But in practice, the line between resistance and revolution was not sharp; once the American revolutionaries had rejected British rule, they were of necessity compelled to put a new form of government in its place, and accordingly rewrote their state constitutions to provide for democratic government in the interest of the common good.[186] Thus, by war's end, American republicans had come to embrace a right of revolution along with a right of resistance.

---

181. In particular cases, Americans disagreed whether a domestic disturbance was a rebellion or a revolution. The insurgents self-consciously saw themselves as continuing the work of the American Revolution and used republican rhetoric to describe their efforts. See SLAUGHTER, supra note 180, at 31-34, 39, 47-48, 54, 127-30. Other Americans believed that the rebels acted out of selfish, venal motives. SLAUGHTER, supra note 180, at 39, 44-45, 48, 58; see also Cress, supra note 128, at 40 (discussing popular distrust of venal motives of militia members). Still others, in rejecting the rebellions, began to modify the republicanism of the 1770's, emphasizing order over liberty, nationalism over decentralization, and hierarchy over democracy. See SLAUGHTER, supra note 180, at 133-38. All agreed, however, that some insurrections were rebellions against legitimate government.

182. See Cress, supra note 128, at 23; TRENCHARD & MOYLE, supra note 159, at 7; CRESS, supra note 111, at 9, 111; MORGAN, supra note 78, at 156; POCOCK, supra note 44, at 203-04, 210-11. New Hampshire's draft proposal for what became the Second Amendment provided: "Congress shall never disarm any Citizen unless such as are or have been in Actual Rebellion." See Shalhope, supra note 130, at 608.

183. See WOOD, supra note 56, at 20-23. Older republicans believed in the importance of revolution, but less in the sense of popular armed upheaval than in the sense of cyclical return to political health. See supra note 73.

184. I use the phrase "right to revolution" because of its common acceptance, despite the fact that a constitutional right to revolution may be nonsensical, as if the Constitution secured a right to destroy it by arms. More appropriately, perhaps, one may speak of a natural right to revolution and a constitutional right to possess the means of revolution. The Second Amendment, then, does not protect a right of revolution (with judges deciding when and how the citizenry may revolt), but does preserve the possibility of revolution (with the citizens deciding when to implement that possibility).

185. THE DECLARATION OF INDEPENDENCE para. 2 (U.S. 1776).

186. See WOOD, supra note 56, at 282-291. A 1788 letter by Anti-Federalist Luther Martin illustrates this unconscious conflation of resistance and revolution in the minds of the Anti-Federalists: "By the principles of the American revolution, arbitrary power may, and ought to, be resisted even by arms, if necessary." 1 DEBATES, supra note 154, at 382 (emphasis added).

Lockean liberals also endorsed a right of revolution, so that unadorned references to such a right in the 1780's could be either liberal or republican. In theory, a liberal right to revolution might differ substantially from a republican one. According to liberals, individuals enter the social contract for their own ends, reserving certain rights of autonomy; if the government violates those rights, citizens may take up arms to insist upon the original terms.[187] By contrast, a republican revolution is made not for a cumulation of individual ends but for a truly common good.[188] In the 1780's, however, the line between the two was not so distinct.[189] Republicans may have borrowed the ideas of the social compact and the right of revolution in part from Locke's circle[190] before converting them into an idiom of the common good. For republicans, moreover, an important part of the commonweal was the liberty of citizens to ensure their political independence.[191]

As a result, the Anti-Federalist framers of the Second Amendment may not have thought consciously about whether they were relying on liberal or republican rights of revolution. Indeed, they may have relied on both rights without worrying about inconsistency.[192] But in context, their primary loyalty seems clear. They self-consciously cast themselves as defenders of the War for Independence, a revolution made for republican principles. They gave the right to bear arms to a militia—a sacred concept in the republican tradition but one that Locke does not even mention.[193] They feared a central government created to protect Lockean accumulation of property and dominated by economic elites. And they sought to return the means of coercion to universal bodies of virtuous citizens under the direction of local democratic legislatures.

---

187. See JOHN LOCKE, Second Treatise of Government, reprinted in TWO TREATISES OF GOVERNMENT 473-77 (Peter Laslett ed., 1960).

188. For example, the Massachusetts Constitution of 1780 described itself as "a social compact, by which the whole people covenants with each Citizen, and each Citizen with the whole people, that all shall be governed by certain Laws for the common good." MASS. CONST. of 1780, pmbl., reprinted in 1 AMERICAN CONSTITUTIONS 621 (Franklin B. Hough ed., Albany, Weed, Parsons & Co., 1871).

189. Thus, Carl Becker read the Declaration of Independence as thoroughly Lockean, see CARL BECKER, THE DECLARATION OF INDEPENDENCE (1942), and Gary Wills as not at all Lockean, see GARY WILLS, INVENTING AMERICA (1978).

190. See WOOD, supra note 56, at 283.

191. Thus, Patrick Henry exhorted: "Guard with jealous attention the public liberty . . . Unfortunately, nothing will preserve it but downright force. Whenever you give up that force, you are ruined." 3 DEBATES, supra note 154, at 45.

192. The last 20 years have witnessed explosive disagreement among historians over Locke's influence on revolutionary America. For a brief review of the disagreement, see KRAMNICK, supra note 84, at 35-40.

193. Some have argued that protecting the militia may have been only one purpose of the Amendment, but I suggest that this argument rests on thin evidence. See infra Part III.A. Even if the argument is correct, however, protecting the militia is still the only purpose that the proponents of the Amendment bothered to mention—indicating that their central goal was republican.

6. Coping with the Paradox

The idea of the militia thus responds to the republican paradox that without a virtuous state there can be no virtuous citizens, but without virtuous citizens the state will not be virtuous. It does so by eliding the distinction between state and society. In republican thought, the militia had to be a body summoned, trained, and organized by the state. Without state sponsorship, the militia might not be "well regulated," nor could members gain experience in self-sacrificing service to the state. More importantly, it was critical that the militia be somehow universal; otherwise force would belong only to a slice of the population. But the state alone was truly universal and could constitute the militia as a universal organization. Without state supervision, the militia might be only a number of partial bodies—private armies asserting their private wills. Such an analysis reflected one horn of the paradox: to be moral, the citizen must exist in a virtuous state, which would constitute a universal militia. So in normal times, the militia was thought of as a state body.

But for republicans, there was danger everywhere, including state supervision of the militia. The state might become corrupt and seek to corrupt the militia—by dismantling it, by recruiting only from a slice of society, or by bribing its officers. In that case, the militia was expected to draw on other aspects of its character: its independence of mind and its capacity to take government directly into its hands. Members would remember that although the militia was gathered by the state, it was composed of, and identified with, the body of the people. The training in virtue acquired under a benign state would now stand it in good stead in resisting a corrupt one. Such a state of affairs could not last for long. Without the frame of a republic to hold them together, the pieces of a people would become disjointed, devolving into pursuit of self-interest. Republicans hoped, however, that the militia could fill the gap for the time necessary to restore political health. This analysis reflected the other horn of the paradox: without a virtuous and independent citizenry, the state itself will never be virtuous.

Lacking a state apparatus, citizens might succumb to the corruption of atomism, yet with one, they might succumb to tyranny or oligarchy. The militia, therefore, had to be ever vigilant, like pilots of a ship, trimming their sails in response to the more pressing danger. On the one hand, should a threat come from the state, the militia was to assume the character of society—independent, aggressive, suspicious of public ministers. On the other hand, should a threat arise from private groups, the militia was to bear the aspect of the state—self-sacrificing, participatory, hostile to private power.

The militia thus helped to resolve the paradox by an impaction of all the components of a republic into itself. If the state could not have virtue without virtuous citizens, then the militia would supply a virtuous citizenry; and if citizens could not have virtue without a virtuous state, then the militia would provide virtuous state supervision. The danger in a right of resistance was that the criteria were not self-applying; the line between resistance and rebellion was often in the eye of the beholder. But eighteenth-century republicans felt that the safest place to commit the right to judge was to the citizen militia.

III. THE MODERN MEANING OF THE SECOND AMENDMENT

The place of the right to arms in the republican tradition is thus central and profound. I will argue in this section, however, that a modern republican interpretation of the Second Amendment presents great difficulties. In Sections A, B, and C, I argue that the republican tradition offers no guidance for judicial mediation between the competing contemporary legal claims that the Amendment only supports the modern national guard or that it also supports a private right to arms for individual self-defense. The republican tradition justifies giving arms to a universal militia of a type which does not exist today. As a result, under modern conditions, the literal wording of the Second Amendment is meaningless. On the other hand, I argue in Section D that the Amendment can serve as a regulative ideal for courts, who could try to keep its spirit alive by reading other provisions of the Constitution to serve the same ends—by protecting property as a means to political participation or by restricting the power of the army and police. Ultimately, however, these judicial strategies can offer only limited change; in any event, in republican terms, the courts are not the best fora in which to seek reinvigorated popular control. I therefore consider in the next part other, nonjudicial options for securing the ends served by the militia.

A. *Personal Right to Self-Defense*

The republican tradition does not support a personal right to own arms for self-defense. The republicans were intensely political and saw the right to arms as a political phenomenon. The contrary vision typically espoused by the advocates of a private right to arms could hardly be more different: each man's home is his castle, and he has a natural right to defend himself, his family, and his property against threats from the outside world.[194] This vision, embracing frontier self-reliance and rugged individualism, is a deep part of American tradition,[195] but not the American *republican* tradition.[196] Whatever else may

---

194. *See, e.g.*, B. Bruce-Briggs, *The Great American Gun War*, 45 PUB. INTEREST 37, 41, 61-62 (1976); Kates, *supra* note 8, at 206; Levinson, *supra* note 2, at 643 n.37, 655-57; Lund, *supra* note 16, at 117-21.
195. *See, e.g.*, DAVID B. DAVIS, FROM HOMICIDE TO SLAVERY 41-72 (1986).
196. The frontier tradition did, however, adopt some of the cultural forms of republicanism: the republican yeoman was self-reliant, and he did have his own farm, far away from cities. But these attributes were valuable because they helped him to be a better political participant. In the 19th-century frontier tradition, that ideal slowly changed until rugged individualism became an end in itself; Americans valued those who could take care of themselves without the aid of others. *See generally* HENRY N. SMITH, VIRGIN

be laid at the door of republicans, they are not responsible for the National Rifle Association or its individualist vision.

As it is virtually impossible to prove a negative, I cannot claim that none of the proponents of the Second Amendment ever embraced a nonrepublican belief in the right to own arms for self-defense. Yet the dominance of the republican tradition in their thinking about the Amendment makes it unlikely that the primary concern of the provision was self-defense.[197] As I have argued, the discussion of the right to arms was saturated with republican concepts and rhetoric, including the language of the provision itself, with its assertion that "a well regulated militia" is "necessary to the security of a free State." The references to a popular right of resistance are countless; in contrast, the references to an individual right to arms for self-defense are quite rare.[198] I do not mean to argue that one could not construct a modern constitutional argument for a right to own arms for self-defense,[199] or that all eighteenth-century re-

LAND: THE AMERICAN WEST AS SYMBOL AND MYTH (1950). It is this image to which individual rights advocates seem to appeal.

197. Akhil Amar and Elaine Scarry have recently advanced a similar argument. See Amar, supra note 103, at 1164; Scarry, supra note 150, at 1260-86.

198. Robert Shalhope has argued that the Framers blended the right to arms for self-defense and for service in the militia. In support, he adduces a number of passages that laud the ideal of the armed citizen without specifically mentioning whether that citizen was inside the militia or outside. But, aside from the ability to resist tyranny, those passages describe only two benefits from private ownership of arms: the militia and the *posse comitatus* could help to keep order, and arms bearing was a part of a hardy, independent life that would keep Americans committed to spartan virtue, unlike the luxury-loving peoples of Europe. See Shalhope, supra note 130, at 604-12. Neither of these benefits directly supports a personal right to own arms for self-defense: the former assumes that the citizen will help to keep order, but as part of the militia or *posse comitatus*, not as a private individual; and while arms bearing may bring independent, virtuous character, that association says nothing about the use to which arms should be put—revolution or self defense. Indeed, the hope that arms bearing will produce virtue in the citizenry could as easily be part of the tradition that armed service to the state trains citizens to independence and self-sacrifice.

The other historical materials commonly claimed to demonstrate an individual right to self-defense are Pennsylvania's and Vermont's constitutions, which speak of the citizens' right to own arms "for the defence of themselves and of the state." See Shalhope, supra note 130, at 608; Hardy, supra note 29, at 595-96, 603. But other state provisions speak only of the "defence of the state," see Hardy, supra note 29, at 596-97, and the Second Amendment with its sole reference to the "militia" more resembles this category. Finally, the Senate did reject a proposal that the Amendment include the phrase "for the common defense," although it did so without explanation. Hardy, supra note 29, at 611. As the provision already included a purpose clause—providing for the militia—the Senate could readily have concluded that it did not need another redundant one.

199. Such an argument might proceed along two lines. First, as a moral matter, since we do not now have a republican society, it is important that out-groups be able to protect themselves against an oppressive state and the terrorism of in-groups. Most saliently, Professors Cottrol and Diamond have demonstrated the historical importance of a right to arms to African Americans, see Cottrol & Diamond, supra note 17, at 55-56, 77-85, and have urged that from a modern African-American perspective, courts should construe it broadly. Id. at 88-89.

Second, as a historical matter, the Framers of the 14th Amendment were more classically liberal than the Framers of the Second Amendment. See, e.g., David C. Williams, The Borders of the Equal Protection Clause: Indians as Peoples, 38 UCLA L. REV. 759, 784-85 (1991). In particular, the 1868 drafters sought to give Southern blacks the ability to protect themselves against white terrorism. See Cottrol & Diamond, supra note 177, at 64-67. As the Bill of Rights applies to the states only through the 14th, it may now be appropriate to read the early guarantees in a more individualistic light. See Amar, supra note 103, at 1201-03.

publicans rejected such a right as a matter of general philosophy. Rather, I mean to argue that that right was, for them, a peripheral issue in the debates over the Second Amendment.[200] This secondary status is critical because, as I will argue shortly, under modern conditions an individual right to arms is positively counterproductive to the goals and ideals implicit in a collective right to arms for resistance.[201] As the latter was at the center of the republicans' concern and the former on the periphery, a modern version of a republican Second Amendment would not include a private right to arms for self-defense.

The modern implications of a private right to arms differ radically, depending on whether it is a right for resistance or a right for self-defense. Modern analysts may assume that a private right to own arms automatically includes a right to own arms for self-defense, but that assumption is anachronistic.[202] The central issue in gun ownership for contemporary America is personal protection, and its discussion revolves around two sets of private rights or interests: the right of some individuals to be safe (or feel safe) by having guns, and the right of others to be safe (or feel safe) from those who should not have guns. In contrast, the central issue for the supporters of the Second Amendment was the allocation of political power, and its discussion revolved around two political actors, state and society, entwined in the militia.

B. *The Right to Resistance Outside of a Universal Militia*

Republicans believed that only a universal militia could safely hold arms, and the Second Amendment makes this assumption express: "A well regulated Militia, being necessary to the security of a free State, the right of the people

---

Both of these arguments depend on accepting the conversion to liberalism as correct or inevitable, but events in African-American history also counsel hesitance before doing so. Cottrol and Diamond point out that African Americans were successful in defending themselves against white terrorism only when they formed collective militias, not when acting as individuals. And they often felt constrained to form those militias because they could not gain admittance to the all-white—less than universal—state militia. *See* Cottrol & Diamond, *supra* note 17, at 55-57, 77-85. Guaranteeing African Americans an individual right of self-defense may be a second-best option, but the best course seems to be the creation of a truly universal militia—or its modern functional analogue.

200. Despite the introductory clause, the provision could guard the right to arms for multiple reasons, *see supra* text accompanying note 32, and the common good for republicans typically included individual liberties, *see supra* note 56. Among the more significant commentators, Don Kates and Nelson Lund have argued that the Framers based the right to revolution on the more fundamental right to self-defense: just as every individual has a right to resist aggression, so the people collectively have the right to resist tyranny. Kates, *supra* note 8, at 245; Lund, *supra* note 16, at 118-20. Yet even if the drafters did believe in a right to self-defense, it seems unlikely that they chose to protect it in the Second Amendment. The Amendment does not say "a well regulated militia being necessary to the security of a free state and the people having an innate right to self-defense against private parties, the right of the people to keep and bear arms shall not be infringed." Furthermore, this focus on government makes sense in context. The Framers were trying to hammer out the relationship between government and individuals, not between private parties. They had, after all, just completed a revolution and were concerned about keeping tyranny from rearing its head again.

201. *See infra* Part III.B. There, I argue that a private right to arms for resistance is inconsistent with the militia ideal today; it is even truer, and for the same reasons, that a private right to arms for self-defense would be inconsistent with that ideal.

202. The Supreme Court has so construed the assumption. *See supra* text accompanying notes 24-25.

to keep and bear Arms, shall not be infringed." The key issue is thus the meaning of the term "Militia." Those who support a states' rights view of the militia seek to identify the Amendment's militia with the modern national guard.[203] The guard, however, is a select body, only a fraction of the population. In contrast, as advocates of the individual rights view have maintained,[204] another meaning of militia was current in the 1780's: the unorganized militia included every male of arms-bearing age[205]—essentially all the citizenry at that time—and a vestige of that definition persists in the United States Code to this day.[206] Because the Amendment describes the right to arms as a right of "the people" it seems probable that it used "Militia" in this broader sense.

The republican tradition supports this broader reading: the militia had to be universal. Any smaller body, any "select militia," suffered from the same defects as a standing army, because it was only a segment of the citizenry. The universal militia, by contrast, was the people under another name;[207] it could not turn against the people because it was the people.[208] As the National Guard is not universal, it cannot serve as a substitute.[209]

Republicanism would also eschew any construction of the right to arms as a right only of the state government against the federal government, rather than a right of the people against all government.[210] The militia was a forum in

---

203. *See supra* text accompanying note 28.

204. *See, e.g.,* Kates, *supra* note 8, at 214-16; Levinson, *supra* note 2, at 646-47; Lund, *supra* note 16, at 106.

205. *See* Carp, *supra* note 113, at 19-20; Kates, *supra* note 8, at 215.

206. *See* 10 U.S.C. § 311(a) (1988) (unorganized militia includes all males at least 17 years of age and under 45 years of age and all female officers of National Guard).

207. Laurence Tribe seeks to avoid this conclusion by arguing that even if the Framers understood the militia to be universal, the militia was supposed to be "well regulated." *See, e.g.,* TRIBE, *supra* note 25, at 299 n.6. Presumably, Tribe means to suggest that regulation may include membership restrictions. Some regulation of the militia is consistent with republicanism: the state assembled it and supervised its training. But limiting ownership of arms to one portion of society is precisely the form of regulation that the Amendment did not contemplate; more likely, the provision contemplated a requirement of universal membership. *See supra* Part II.B.3; Amar, *supra* note 103, at 1167.

208. In line with the requirement of citizen universality, women today would have to be included in the militia because of the 19th Amendment, even if the Equal Protection Clause might not so require under current law, *cf.* Rostker v. Goldberg, 453 U.S. 57 (1981) (upholding Selective Service Act requiring male-only registration). A wholly male militia would represent only part of the citizenry.

209. The Guard is statutorily defined as that part of the organized state militia that is federally recognized and funded, and that is trained and has its officers appointed under Congress' militia powers. *See* 10 U.S.C. § 101(9)-(13) (1988). Far from universal, its present authorized strength is 600,000. *See id.* at 3225 (Supp. 1990). For some time, the guard has exhibited the characteristics of a distinct interest group. *See generally* MARTHA DERTHICK, THE NATIONAL GUARD IN POLITICS (1965). Indeed, the origin of the Guard lies in large measure in class warfare. During the great strikes of 1877, the militia had often refused to disperse strikers, so in later years the business community urged a remodeling of the militia to make it more responsive to property rights. *See* NELL I. PAINTER, STANDING AT ARMAGEDDON 15, 21-22 (1987).

210. There is no reason not to incorporate the Second Amendment against the states. The argument against incorporation, based on the collective rights theory, is that it would be incoherent to do so. Since the Second Amendment is a right of the states, it must be a restriction on the federal government, not on the states themselves. *See, e.g.,* TRIBE, *supra* note 25, at 299 n.6. But the premise is mistaken: the Amendment is a right of the people against government and against private factions. There is thus no reason to distinguish the Amendment from the other nine for incorporation purposes.

which state and people merged, in which society could check state corruption and the state could check private corruption. The right to arms is not a right of the state alone, nor a right of persons alone, but a right of the militia, which embraces both. The Amendment may give states the right to block efforts of the federal government to dismantle their militias. But it also gives the people the right to intimidate state government and ultimately to revolt.

The history of the clause supports this view: the Second Amendment was copied from right to arms provisions in state constitutions,[211] and the debates at the time reveal no suggestion that the scope of the right changed when adopted into the federal Bill of Rights. But state bills of rights were not a limit on Congress' ability to tamper with state militias; they were a limit on state governments' ability to tamper with citizens. So the state right to arms—and by implication the federal right as well—had to be a right of the people against government.[212]

By the same token, however, those who support an individual rights view of the Amendment are mistaken in equating the people's militia and the universe of private gun owners. For one thing, the militia not only may be universal; it must be, because any smaller body would reflect only a partial interest. The threat of corruption may lurk as much in insurrection by private force as in governmental tyranny. Second, while the militia must not be dominated by the state, it also must not be wholly private.

Participation in the militia gave citizens an education in civic virtue, prompting them to associate possession of weapons with service to the republic. They also learned to be independent, but as a political body devoted to the common good, not as private individuals. They were independent not from the world, but from whatever forces were seeking at the moment to corrupt the republic—whether state ministers or popular demagogues.[213]

Gun owners today do not comprise a universal militia. Not all citizens own guns. Some people in almost every demographic category own guns, but ownership is concentrated in a fairly distinctive group. American gun owners are overwhelmingly male[214] and married,[215] more Protestant than Catho-

---

211. See Cress, *supra* note 128, at 29-37; HALBROOK, *supra* note 17, at 64-66, 75-76.

212. See Hardy, *supra* note 29, at 594, 624 (making similar point from individual rights perspective).

213. Advocates of the individual rights view do not sufficiently take account of these aspects of the militia. For example, Don Kates reviews the colonial legislation that obliged all citizens to be militia members, *see* Kates, *supra* note 8, at 215, and then asserts that the right to own arms therefore belongs to every private party, *see id.* at 217-18. But we do not oblige every citizen to be a militia member today, and that change is important.

214. See U.S. DEP'T OF JUSTICE, SOURCEBOOK OF CRIMINAL JUSTICE STATISTICS—1987, at 169 tbl. 2.50 (Timothy J. Flanagan & Katherine M. Jamieson eds., 1988) [hereinafter SOURCEBOOK]; JAMES D. WRIGHT ET AL., UNDER THE GUN 109 (1983); American Firearms Industry Dealer Survey (1988) [hereinafter Industry Survey] (unpublished survey, on file with author).

215. See Industry Survey, *supra* note 214.

lic,[216] more white than black (in absolute numbers),[217] generally middle class,[218] and reside primarily in rural areas.[219] Many more people own guns in the South than elsewhere in the nation,[220] and within the South, white gun owners exhibit greater hostility to blacks than do white nonowners.[221] Americans own guns for a variety of reasons,[222] but I have observed that those who view gun owning as political expression do so for specific reasons.[223] Among themselves, such owners often wistfully talk about a revolution against the government to restore a time in which people like them—honest, self-reliant, simple people—would again have their due.[224] Such people may believe that their welfare is equivalent to the common good, but it is not.[225] If we have an armed revolution, it will be in the interests of these citizens, not of the population as a whole.

---

216. *See* WRIGHT ET AL., *supra* note 214, at 108; James D. Wright & Linda L. Marston, *The Ownership of the Means of Destruction: Weapons in the United States*, 23 SOC. PROBS. 93, 95-98 (1975); SOURCEBOOK, *supra* note 214, at 169 tbl. 2.50.

217. *See* SOURCEBOOK, *supra* note 214, at 169 tbl. 2.50; Wright & Marston, *supra* note 216, at 95, 97-98. While white gun owners may outnumber black gun owners in absolute terms, the relative rates of ownership among the two groups may be comparable. *See* WRIGHT ET AL., *supra* note 214, at 108-09. But absolute numbers, not the percentage rate, would be the critical fact should a revolution occur: more white gun owners means more white power.

218. *See* WRIGHT ET AL., *supra* note 214, at 107-08; Wright & Marston, *supra* note 216, at 95-97; Industry Survey, *supra* note 214; SOURCEBOOK, *supra* note 214, at 169 tbl. 2.50.

219. *See* WRIGHT ET AL., *supra* note 214, at 104-105; Wright & Marston, *supra* note 216, at 95.

220. *See* SOURCEBOOK, *supra* note 214, at 169 tbl. 2.50; WRIGHT, *supra* note 214, at 106-07; Wright & Marston, *supra* note 216, at 95.

221. *See* Wright & Marston, *supra* note 216, at 98 & n.8.

222. *See infra* text accompanying notes 226-28.

223. I have been unable to find statistics to support this claim, but evidence of this subculture is not difficult to find. For example, at present, my local country music station is playing a song called *A Country Boy Can Survive*: it proudly asserts that, come the revolution, rural people will be better off than now because, inter alia, they know how to use guns.

224. Some empirical work suggests that gun ownership is largely a function of early socialization into a "gun culture" that is "best typified as rural rather than urban," "heavily masculine," and that "emphasize[s] independence, self-sufficiency, mastery over nature, closeness to the land, and so on." WRIGHT, *supra* note 214, at 112-14. Bruce-Briggs, too, suggests that gun ownership reflects a deep cultural cleavage in the nation:

> [W]e are experiencing a sort of low-grade war going on between two alternative views of what America is and ought to be. On the one side are those who take bourgeois Europe as a model of civilized society . . . .
> On the other side is a group of people who do not tend to be especially articulate or literate, and whose world view is rarely expressed in print. Their model is that of the independent frontiersman who takes care of himself and his family with no interference from the state . . . .
> Manhood means responsibility and caring for your own.

Bruce-Briggs, *supra* note 194, at 61. Levinson also recognizes this cultural division and argues that good republicans should include gun owners as a "voice from the margin" in constitutional dialogue. *See* Levinson, *supra* note 2, at 658-59. But for republicans, armsbearers are never just one more voice in the dialogue; they always have the last word.

225. Their attitudes are, however, interestingly parallel to those of some in the English Country Party in the 18th century. Both pined for a past time when the citizens of the republic were homogeneous, and the public good was therefore identical to their own good. *See supra* note 86. The Country Party was wrong then, and these gun owners are wrong now: the public good must include their good, but it must also include the good of others in equal measure.

Gun owners, moreover, have not formed a militia: they have not assembled into a collective body to acquire training in virtue or the habit of associating arms bearing with dedication to the common good. Many urban dwellers probably have little experience with guns but own one for self-defense; they associate firearms with fear of their fellow citizens, not militia sorority.[226] Most gun owners use their firearms primarily for hunting,[227] and these owners may feel some bond with other hunters, but only with other hunters.[228] And then some—the "survivalists"—own guns precisely because they predict that a cataclysmic event, such as an invasion or a revolution, is in the offing. Among themselves, survivalists may display some qualities of a militia: they are trained, vigilant, and committed to each other. But they have no bond to the rest of the republic; indeed, they suspect that most others will, and perhaps should, perish in the coming conflagration. Despite the self-image of gun groups, then, a gun is not like an amulet; it does not have magical properties that convert its owner into a model republican citizen.

The eighteenth-century republicans were ready to face great risk, but they were far from insensible to danger. They believed in a right of resistance, but they gave it not to some random collection of individuals but to the people *as a whole and only as a whole*. My disagreement with a private right interpretation of the Amendment is not that it takes the provision too seriously, but that it does not take it seriously enough. The vision of the Amendment is not of a nation in which all may own arms but of one in which all are *in fact* armed. If only a small portion go armed, the hope of the Amendment will have failed as surely as if the government had prohibited arms bearing altogether. Corruption—domination of politics by a narrow slice of the public—can occur through the machinations not only of the state but of private parties as well. The undue political influence of the National Rifle Association is precisely the nightmare of all true republicans, all true believers in the Second Amendment.

Two objections might be made to this general argument. First, the literal requirement of universality may seem wooden and extreme: if even one citizen is omitted from militia service, it would seem to doom the whole enterprise. But it is hard to believe that anyone could have seriously intended the Second Amendment to rest on such an implausible background assumption. As I will consider in the next section, republicans did seem rhetorically to presuppose literal universality, but in practice they never adopted truly universal militias. We may then understand the concept of the militia as a regulative ideal or as a symbol for a political function: republicans sought to give over the control of arms to a body constituted in such a way that we should have confidence

---

226. *See* WRIGHT ET AL., *supra* note 214, at 116-17 & n.9; Wright & Marston, *supra* note 216, at 99-103.

227. *See* Bruce-Briggs, *supra* note 194, at 39; Wright & Marston, *supra* note 216, at 94 n.5.

228. *See, e.g.,* Bruce-Briggs, *supra* note 194, at 41. The "gun culture," *see supra* note 224, is one that revolves around hunting. *See* WRIGHT ET AL., *supra* note 214, at 104-06, 112-16.

that it would represent the body of the people, rather than any lesser faction. Such a body would have to be very broadly representative, potentially open to everyone, and trained in virtue. Even under these lesser requirements, private gun owners do not qualify as a militia: they still reflect particular interests[229] and are still random atoms.[230]

Second, some might argue that if some citizens fail to own arms, they have only themselves to blame: the vision of the universal militia depends on private dedication to the state, as reflected in the civic act of firearms possession. But this response would misconceive the fundamentally political nature of gun ownership by construing it as an individual right and responsibility. The argument rests on an implicit analogy to other provisions in the Bill of Rights designed as protections for the individual against acts of state abuse, such as the Fourth Amendment. The Second Amendment, in contrast, is a constitutive or structural provision: it forecasts the relationship between the state and the people as a whole. Its essential goal is not to preserve liberal rights of individual autonomy, but to ensure that ultimate power remains with the universal militia. If the militia is less than universal, the harm falls not only on those who failed to buy guns, but on the republic as a whole, because the means of force lies in the hands of a special interest.[231]

Republicans did not intend to leave the universality of the militia to the chance decision of every citizen to arm herself. The state was supposed to erect the necessary scaffolding on which the militia could build itself, to muster the militia and oblige every citizen to own a gun.[232] Some even argued that if the citizen could not afford a firearm, the state should supply one.[233] Even if every private citizen did buy a gun on her own initiative, moreover, those purchases would still not generate a militia; without training in virtue and the experience of public service, citizens would be nothing more than armed but unbonded atoms.

The identification of the militia with the National Guard is thus too state-focused, but the identification of the militia with individual gun owners is too focused on private persons. In the years since the Revolution, state and society have changed so that constitutional thinking views the government and citizens as distinct and often adversarial actors. So it may seem natural to case the Second Amendment as a simple right of liberty-loving private persons to take

---

229. Levinson is clear about this point: he casts gun owners as a particular group with particular views in a culture very different from, for example, the legal establishment. *See* Levinson, *supra* note 2, at 639-42 (Second Amendment generally ignored by legal establishment).

230. I will consider in the last section the question of what institutions might more closely fill the role of a universal militia. *See infra* Part III.D.

231. Similarly, Akhil Amar has argued that the function of the jury was to create popular control over the administration of justice. The beneficiary of the jury was thus not just the individual defendant but the whole community; accordingly, in a republican scheme, the defendant may not have the right to waive a jury trial. *See* Amar, *supra* note 103, at 1196-99.

232. *See* BARLOW, *supra* note 124, at 16; Cress, *supra* note 128, at 41.

233. 2 ANNALS OF CONG. 1804-07 (1791).

up arms against scheming government ministers. But that description is, in my view, an oversimplification. The Amendment guaranteed the right of a state/society, unified in the militia, to resist any threat of corruption, from private parties or state officials.

C. The Right to Resistance Inside a Militia

1. The Absence of a Constitutional Mandate

The militia is so central to republican thinking that it is surprising that the proponents of the Amendment did not secure a constitutional mandate for one. Republicans themselves sensed the lack, believing that the state had an obligation to constitute a militia.[234] Article I gave Congress considerable power over the composition of the militia,[235] and during the debates on its adoption, Anti-Federalists expressed fear that Congress might use its new power to raise a select militia and dismantle the state militias.[236] Before the ratification of the Bill of Rights, Richard Henry Lee maintained: "[T]he constitution ought to secure a genuine [militia] and guard against a select militia, by providing that the militia shall always be kept well organized, armed and disciplined, and include . . . all men capable of bearing arms."[237]

But although some of the amendments proposed by the state legislatures included a prohibition on standing armies—Madison ignored these in drafting his version—none included a constitutional mandate for a universal militia.[238] During Congressional discussion of the Amendment, Elbridge Gerry proposed that it be revised to mandate a federal duty to assemble a militia, but his motion failed without a second and without discussion.[239] The Second Amendment thus emerged as a guarantee that all citizens may keep and bear arms, so that the states would have the material with which to create their militias, and

---

234. See infra text accompanying notes 237, 239, and note 241.

235. See supra text accompanying notes 133-39. In particular, Congress has the power to organize, train, and discipline the militia, and to govern that part of the militia in federal service. U.S. CONST. art. 1, § 8, cl. 16. Political leaders assumed that this provision gave Congress the right to summon a select militia. During the 1790's many federal officials proposed a less than universal militia, and though these proposals were denounced as unrepublican, no one suggested that they were unconstitutional. See CRESS, supra note 111, at 116-21.

236. See supra text accompanying notes 140-44, 158-61, and note 158.

237. See LEE, supra note 153, at 169.

238. See Shalhope, supra note 130, at 608-10; Cress, supra note 128, at 29-31. One might not expect a mandate for a universal state militia in a federal constitution; such a guarantee would more naturally appear in state constitutions. But the state constitutions do not contain any such mandate. And the federal Constitution does not require that a federal militia be universal, nor does it ban federal tampering with the universality of state militias.

239. See 1 ANNALS OF CONG., supra note 107, at 750-51.

perhaps some limited, not very clear protection for those militias[240] —but no guarantee that there would be a militia.[241]

Why did the Framers fail to ensure for their posterity what they believed to be the indispensable institution of a universal militia? From early on, republicans exhibited a rather severe slippage between rhetoric and reality.[242] Many states did, in a general sense, require that all citizens own arms and serve in the militia,[243] but they also departed from this ideal in important ways. For one thing, as the frontier receded, serious military action moved away from the centers of population, and so states came to rely on expeditionary forces, which were drawn from volunteers—usually poor—and professional soldiers. The militia, in contrast, began to rust on the homefront, turning out primarily as an occasional police force.[244] When it did turn out, it did not include all, or only, citizens. Rich men could purchase exemptions by paying poor men to go in their places,[245] and even those who were not citizens of the state were subject to militia duty.[246] The states' military forces had come less and less to resemble the military incarnation of the citizenry assembled.

During all of this time, republicans continued to insist that only a universal militia was appropriate for a true republic—but they did not follow through, and did not persuade others to follow through, on the commitment. The reason seems plain: on the one hand, they were not prepared to surrender the universal militia as a necessary concept, but on the other, they could not persuade themselves or others to undergo the massive sacrifices involved in universal service.[247] As a result, they were left in a state of anxiety: they insisted that the militia must be the whole people, but they knew that in fact it was not.[248] They thus left a dual legacy: to make sense, the Second Amendment requires a universal militia but does not assure that we will have one.

Over the decades, Americans have come to exploit that discrepancy. As it became plain that the *armato populato* would never become a reality, republicans began to express their sad disappointment in a population that shirked its

---

240. See Cress, *supra* note 128, at 38; Shalhope, *supra* note 130, at 610.

241. The Republican writer Centinel complained: "It is remarkable that this article only makes the observation 'that a well-regulated militia, composed of the *body* of the people, is the best security of a free state;' it does not ordain, or constitutionally provide for, the establishment of such a one." *Centinel, Revived,* INDEPENDENT GAZETTEER, No. XXIX, Sept. 9, 1789, at 2.

242. See CRESS, *supra* note 111, at 11-14, 65; ROYSTER, *supra* note 67, at 42-45.

243. See Carp, *supra* note 113, at 19; Kates, *supra* note 8, at 215; United States v. Miller, 307 U.S. 174, 179-82 (1939).

244. See CRESS, *supra* note 111, at 5-7; Carp, *supra* note 113, at 19-20.

245. See CRESS, *supra* note 111, at 5-6, 59-60.

246. *Id.* at 6-7.

247. See *id.* at 80-81, 90-91, 117-18. As one Congressman put it, thoroughly ignoring republican orthodoxy: "As far as the whole body of the people are necessary to the general defence, they ought to be armed; but the law ought not to require more than is necessary; for that would be a just cause of complaint." 1 ANNALS OF CONG. 1806 (Joseph Gales ed., 1834) (1791).

248. Perhaps for this reason, debates over allowing exemptions from militia service on the floor of Congress tended to be simultaneously interminable and unfocused. *See, e.g.,* 2 ANNALS OF CONG. 1804-12 (1791).

civic duty to arm itself.[249] Today, only a small portion of American citizens are enrolled in the armed forces, the National Guard, or law enforcement organizations. Technically, all males aged seventeen to forty-five are members of the unorganized militia,[250] but that status has no practical legal significance. Such "militia members" are not required to own guns, to drill together, or to learn virtue. The statutory provision creating this "universal militia" is nothing more than a dim memory of a distant hope.

2. The Republican Meaninglessness of the Amendment

From the beginning, then, the republican defense of the Second Amendment sought to deny reality, because it assumed a universal militia when there was none. Advocates of the individual rights interpretation of the Amendment thus have substantial precedent for refusing to recognize that we do not have such a body. Indeed, these commentators might argue that if we really wanted to follow the example of early republicans, we would guarantee a right to arms while willfully ignoring the absence of a universal militia.

There are, however, severe problems with this approach. First, whatever the discrepancy between rhetoric and reality, republicans still clung to their insistence that the rhetoric should become reality, by the creation of universal militias. We no longer even contemplate that possibility. There is no chance that any modern legislature will impose universal militia service. Second, the gap between rhetoric and reality has grown drastically over time. In the 1780's, most citizens owned arms, but today many fewer do.[251] This change has two significant consequences: if there should be a revolution it would be for the benefit of a smaller portion of the population, and the revolution would be much less likely to be successful. The absence of a universal militia is now severe and chronic, and self-deception about its existence has become impossible.

As a result, for judges trying to interpret the Second Amendment, republicanism suggests that the Amendment, as worded, is meaningless. To make any sense, the Amendment presupposed an institution now gone. Allowing private parties to own arms would serve no republican purpose, but neither would denying them arms. For republicans, all we can really do is try to create a republic again, as I will discuss in Part IV.

---

249. See Remarks of Rep. Smilie, 18 ANNALS OF CONG. 2177, 2191-92 (1808); 3 JOSEPH STORY, COMMENTARIES ON THE CONSTITUTION OF THE UNITED STATES 746-47 (Boston, Little, Brown & Co., 3d ed. 1858).

250. See 10 U.S.C. § 311(2) (1989).

251. At most, half of all households in America have guns in them, see WRIGHT ET AL., supra note 214, at 34-35, 39; Wright & Marston, supra note 216, at 93-94; SOURCEBOOK, supra note 214, at 167 tbl. 2.47. About 29% of Americans personally own a gun, SOURCEBOOK, supra note 214, at 169 tbl. 2.50, and these owners are demographically skewed, see supra text accompanying notes 214-25.

D. *Alternative Judicial Uses of the Amendment*

In this situation, judges might be inclined to use sources other than the republican tradition to give meaning to the Amendment. This process involves issues of constitutional interpretation that are beyond the scope of this Article, but a range of options seems possible. On the one hand, following the strictures of strict constructionists, some judges might focus only on the literal language. Unfortunately, if the commentators are any guide, that device will not yield a clear result.[252] Perhaps more importantly, the literal language, standing alone, is an exceedingly narrow basis for interpretation. Even the most strict constructionists would look to the original understanding in addition to the language[253]—but again, that intent can have no meaning today. Faced with these difficulties, one might conclude that the Amendment is literally outdated, made irrelevant by events, and therefore should have no meaning at all—as if the Constitution required Congress to keep a Carolina Parrot, now extinct, as a mascot. Courts would then read the provision as a dead letter.

It is possible, however, for courts to update the Amendment in a variety of ways. This course might be the best one since the Amendment does exist and does serve a function in the scheme set up by the Constitution. One style of updating would read the Amendment, as applied to the states through the Due Process Clause, in the way that Justice Harlan read the Due Process Clause: whatever its original meaning, the Amendment has become a part of the living tradition of the American people, part of our scheme of ordered liberty.[254] In that process, the provision has taken on a new meaning, as a liberal right to arms to secure individual autonomy against private assailants

---

252. On the one hand, the provision includes a purpose clause—enshrining a "well regulated militia"—so that courts might limit the right to arms to militia members. *See* Levinson, *supra* note 2, at 644; sources cited *supra* note 29. To take that course, however, we would need to know who the militia is. Absent a "plain meaning" from the face of the provision, we would normally consult its intellectual context—but that is how we got into this mess in the first place. On the other hand, the purpose clause might not be exclusive. So, based only on its language, the provision might ensure the right of arms for many purposes. *See* Hardy, *supra* note 29, at 623, 627-28; Kates, *supra* note 8, at 217 n.53. And the provision does guarantee the right of "the people" to "keep and bear Arms," so perhaps courts could read the provision to guarantee an individual right to arms. *See* HALBROOK, *supra* note 17, at 84-85; Hardy, *supra* note 29, at 629-30; Kates, *supra* note 8, at 218; Lund, *supra* note 16, at 107. That course, too, seems troubling: the purpose clause could as easily be exclusive as nonexclusive (the Second Amendment is unusual in the Bill of Rights for having such a clause, so it seems important). Levinson, too, concludes that the literal language is obscure and then goes on to look at the republican tradition. *See* Levinson, *supra* note 2, at 643-45. Other commentators argue that the language supports one view or another, but then use historical materials to amplify their position, suggesting that the language may not be clear enough to rely on alone. *See, e.g.,* Kates, *supra* note 8, at 220.

253. *See, e.g.,* Robert H. Bork, *Neutral Principles and Some First Amendment Problems,* 47 IND. L.J. 1, 8 (1971). In the context of free speech, for instance, Judge Bork has acknowledged that text and intent together may be unclear, so that we must sometimes construct a theory of the Constitution based on principles implicit in the text and intent. *See id.* at 22-23. Some writers have, however, suggested that one can derive a meaning from the text of the Second Amendment alone. *See* HALBROOK, *supra* note 17, at 84-87; Hardy, *supra* note 29, at 622-23.

254. *See* Poe v. Ullman, 367 U.S. 497, 542-43 (1961) (Harlan, J., dissenting).

or even the government. Whatever one thinks about that vision, it is deeply embedded in large parts of the American psyche.[255]

Courts could, however, seek to update the Amendment in a more republican fashion, and that course has the dual advantage of being more true to the original context and, for some, more appealing because it is more republican. One way to do such updating would be for courts to order the kinds of reforms that I consider in the next part, reforms that would serve the same function as the old militia—a reconstituted militia, universal service, workplace democracy, and the like. But even if those reforms might be appropriate as legislation, judicial enforcement suffers from familiar problems. For one thing, courts are not the best institutions for supervising such massive and complicated social change.[256] For another, even if a court viewed originalist theories dimly, it would face great obstacles in mandating workplace democracy or even a universal militia on the basis of a provision that on its face does no more than guarantee a right to arms. Such an order might prove unenforceable, as the public would likely resist it tooth and nail as illegitimate. Such a situation is not an auspicious beginning for a plan designed to create a virtuous, public-regarding populace.

There are, on the other hand, judicially manageable ways for courts to update the Amendment. The right to arms and the universal militia were significant structural elements in the polity contemplated by the Constitution and its amendments, read as a whole. With their demise, there is a hole in the fabric of the document where they used to be. To mend that hole, courts might stretch the other fibers of the constitutional fabric to cover it, by reading other parts of the Constitution in such a way as to serve militia-like functions. An updated Second Amendment would thus have no independent content but would be a shadowy gravitational presence in interpreting the rest of the Constitution. In particular, after the demise of the Amendment, the people as a body no longer have the ability to resist government outside the normal channels. So new interpretations should seek to increase the influence of the people over their government.[257]

---

255. *See supra* text accompanying notes 194-96.

256. The logistical difficulties would be much greater than cases in which courts have declined to take over existing institutions. *See, e.g.,* Boston Pub. Hous. Tenants' Policy Council v. Lynn, 388 F. Supp. 493 (D. Mass. 1974). To take the example of the militia alone: a court would have to order revenue raised, units organized and trained, and regulations promulgated. And think of the logical test to determine whether the legislature has met the order: has the populace become virtuous? If ever there was a nonjusticiable standard, this is it.

257. I have in mind a form of constitutional interpretation similar to that proposed by Charles Black, as an "exegesis [not] of the particular textual passage considered as a directive of action . . . [but] the method of inference from the structures and relationships created by the constitution in all its parts or in some principal part." CHARLES L. BLACK, JR., STRUCTURE AND RELATIONSHIP IN CONSTITUTIONAL LAW 7 (1969). Considered as a textual directive, the Second Amendment only guarantees a right to arms; but it also is part of a relationship between government and citizens in which the latter hold power outside the normal channels. A liberal critic might respond that the Amendment really is an isolated excrescence in a liberal text, not a part of a deep structural relationship. In this view, the provision's death or transformation

Several examples may illustrate this idea. First, courts could use the gravitational pull of the Second Amendment to create constitutional space for legislation that might otherwise be suspect. Several of the neorepublican proposals that I consider in the next part—such as campaign finance reform or proportional representation[258]—might violate current law. Courts might conclude that these reforms are designed to serve some of the functions of the Second Amendment, and since the courts cannot enforce the Amendment, they should allow these reforms instead.

Second, courts might read the constitutional protections of property in new ways.[259] Like the right to arms, the republican function of property rights was to ensure independent, virtuous citizens. Also like the right to arms, republican attitudes toward property rights contained a tension: on the one hand, the state should not tinker with them, so as to allow real independence; but on the other, the distribution of property needed to be universal, so that some citizens would not dominate others.[260] If free exchange did not produce universal ownership of property, the state had to decide whether to redistribute.[261] In the case of the right to arms, the state had made that decision: it required universal membership in the militia. But in the case of property, republicans sought to avoid the conclusion that the state had a proper role in universalizing property. Instead, they hoped that the market, accompanied by geographical expansion, would take care of the matter by producing relative equality.[262]

To persist in such a belief today is self-deluding. Those with property dominate politics in a way that the republicans would find appalling,[263] and, with the practical demise of arms as a check on government, the equal distribution of property has become especially important. In particular, republicans may have been uncomfortable with a state role to ensure universal property ownership, but they were not at all uncomfortable with a state role to ensure universal

---

into a private right only brings it into line with the liberal underpinnings of the rest of the text. In fact, however, the Constitution considered in "all its parts" is a combination of republican and liberal elements, with the Bill of Rights a careful republican hedge against the liberalism of the body of the document. *See supra* text accompanying notes 103-06; Amar, *supra* note 103; James G. Pope, *Republican Moments: The Role of Direct Popular Power in the American Constitutional Order,* 139 U. PA. L. REV. 287, 341-44 (1990).

258. *See* Sunstein, *supra* note 10, at 1576-77; *infra* text accompanying notes 318-20.

259. As James Pope has argued, the Supreme Court might also read the First Amendment's right of assembly in a republican light, consistent with its heritage. *See* Pope, *supra* note 257, at 325-45. In particular, the Court might protect boycotts as a form of direct popular participation in government. *See id.* at 347-56.

260. *See* Frank I. Michelman, *Possession vs. Distribution in the Constitutional Idea of Property,* 72 IOWA L. REV. 1319, 1327-35 (1987); *supra* note 71.

261. *See* Alexander, *supra* note 71, at 300-02.

262. *See id.* at 301; Michelman, *supra* note 260, at 1333-34. The reason for the different attitudes toward the two rights may be that in the case of property, ensuring universality seemed necessarily to involve invading the property rights of some to give property to others. *See* JENNIFER NEDELSKY, PRIVATE PROPERTY AND THE LIMITS OF AMERICAN CONSTITUTIONALISM 205-07 (1990). In the case of arms, republicans seemed to sense no such tension: everyone could and should own a gun, and the more who did, the better for all. Thus, arms ownership seems a better symbol for republicanism than property rights.

263. *See* NEDELSKY, *supra* note 262, at 216-22.

ownership of the means of force. With that latter role gone, however, the state function of ensuring universal popular control of the government is more constricted than contemplated by the Bill of Rights. One natural path of reexpansion is for the state to have a larger role in ensuring universal property possession.

Thus, courts could reconceive property rights as the necessary basis for political participation, not simply as protection for private expectations.[264] That reconception would, inter alia, involve less protection against the redistribution of traditional property rights,[265] which have led to the present inequality of power,[266] and more protection for newer forms of property. As Nedelsky has elaborated, traditional "property no longer provides people with the basis for independence and autonomy in the eighteenth century sense."[267] Two centuries ago, a farmer's land or a craftsman's tools may have provided some "real independence," but the salaried employees, welfare recipients, and shareholders of today are dependent on a web of relationships.[268] Courts might therefore place less emphasis on traditional property and more on statutory welfare and other kinds of property that provide autonomy in the modern world.[269] The "new property"[270] cannot provide complete independence, because it originates in an act of the legislature, is distributed through the bureaucracy, and depends on the courts for its continuing protection.[271] But traditional property, too, has depended on state support.[272] And complete independence was never part of the paradoxical republican ideal: we must have rights in order to direct the state, but we cannot have rights without state protection.[273]

---

264. *See* Frank I. Michelman, *Property as a Constitutional Right,* 38 WASH. & LEE L. REV. 1097, 1102-03, 1109-14 (1981).
265. Others have argued that the historical roots of the Takings Clause, U.S. CONST. amend. V, are liberal, *see* RICHARD A. EPSTEIN, TAKINGS (1985), and if they are right, then the Second and Fifth Amendments are in tension, growing out of different traditions. But under the argument that I advance here, judges should import some of the Second Amendment's republican meaning into the liberal Takings Clause. We might then arrive at a "hybrid" Fifth Amendment that seeks somehow to secure property as both a collection of legitimate expectations and a source of political power.
266. *See* Michelman, *supra* note 264, at 1112-13. It would also lead to greater acceptance of legislative efforts to curtail the ability of the rich to dominate the speech marketplace. *See infra* notes 318-20 and accompanying text. Michelman, *supra* note 260, at 1343-45.
267. Nedelsky, *supra* note 66, at 19.
268. *See id.* at 19-20.
269. *See id.* at 26-28.
270. Charles A. Reich, *The New Property,* 73 YALE L.J. 733 (1964).
271. Akhil Amar has argued, however, that the 13th Amendment, with its republican underpinnings, may impose on the legislature a duty (not judicially enforceable) to provide each citizen with the modern equivalent of 40 acres and a mule—enough property to make independent political activity possible. *See* Akhil R. Amar, *Forty Acres and a Mule: A Republican Theory of Minimal Entitlements,* 13 HARV. J.L. & PUB. POL'Y 37 (1990).
272. *See* Morris R. Cohen, *Property and Sovereignty,* 13 CORNELL L.Q. 8, 11-14 (1927); Nedelsky, *supra* note 66, at 18-19.
273. *See supra* notes 66-71 and accompanying text. Michelman notes this generative tension. Michelman, *supra* note 260, at 1334; Michelman, *supra* note 264, at 1110. Nedelsky, too, notes the tension in the nature of property rights, *see* NEDELSKY, *supra* note 262, at 207-08, 272-74, but she has recently

Third, the disappearance of the militia should create a heightened constitutional suspicion'of the standing army and the police. Those bodies have, in a sense, usurped the militia's control of the means of force, and they have systematic interests in making their hold more effective at the expense of the liberties of the people. Unless we revive the militia, the republican nightmare may be inevitable, as the populace stands effectively disarmed before the might of the state. But courts can at least try to restrict that tendency by applying the Constitution stringently against the military and police.[274]

This suspicion should be at its height when the standing army and the police come into contact with the general populace and seek to restrict citizens' control over their own lives.[275] For example, the Supreme Court should not have deferred to the military's claims of necessity in the Japanese-American internment cases.[276] Similarly, criminal procedure cases that expand the discretion of the police at the expense of individual liberties represent a troubling direction for the Court.[277] On the other hand, resolving such cases from a

---

rejected constitutional property as a means to reempower the people. The Madisonian tradition of protection of private property from the contract of the majority, she thinks, is too deeply entrenched in American culture. In Nedelsky's view, Madison sought to remove the people from power precisely because they might adjust the rules of the market, so that property would be more equally distributed among them. See id. at 203-05, 207-211. Inequality is therefore a deep and integral part of the American tradition of property, and an egalitarian redefinition of property is likely to fail for that reason. See id. at 246, 261, 275-76. Nedelsky prefers to move away from property as a central concept, see id. at 265, to achieve ends that are recognizably republican, see id. at 265-76. Perhaps she is right that property rights are not the most promising route for empowerment, but they could be one useful route among many. At one point, Nedelsky argues that property rights could be positively pernicious, because the old tradition of inequality is so strong in the minds of Americans that any revival would likely be regressive. See id. at 246. But if the tradition of venerating property rights really is that strong, then it would seem that the idea of property will always be with us, and abandoning property altogether should be no easier than redefining it.

274. Elaine Scarry has gone so far as to suggest that the Supreme Court should read the Second Amendment as prohibiting nuclear war. One of the purposes of the right to arms was to give the populace direct control over the decision whether to go to war: if the government declared war and called up its armed citizenry, but no one came, no war could occur. Nuclear war, however, needs no popular ratification, as war can begin almost with a politician's push of a button. See Scarry, supra note 150, at 1297-1301, 1309-16.

275. The judiciary's deference to police and military discretion over their internal matters presents a slightly different set of concerns. The principal republican fear of a standing army was the army's tendency to dominate politics and wrest freedom from the public. But discipline within the army had a degrading effect on the citizens themselves. Many republicans were concerned that soldierhood and citizenship fostered inconsistent values as the one insisted on slavish obedience and the other fostered independent judgment. If we were to have a standing army, it should be as close to an army of citizen-soldiers as possible. See ROYSTER, supra note 67, at 38-40. Thus, the marked deference to military judgment in Goldman v. Weinberger, 475 U.S. 503 (1986) (rejecting claim that Free Exercise Clause gave Orthodox Jewish officer the right to wear a yarmulke while on duty), was inappropriate because of the military rule's effect on Goldman himself; in effect, it sought to deny him the status of an independent citizen. See Michelman, supra note 1, at 12-17; cf. Ann Scales, Militarism, Male Dominance and Law: Feminist Jurisprudence as Oxymoron?, 12 HARV. WOMEN'S L.J. 25, 42 (1989) (explaining that militarism normalizes oppression of women).

276. See Korematsu v. United States, 323 U.S. 214 (1944); Hirabayashi v. United States, 320 U.S. 81 (1943).

277. See, e.g., Illinois v. Rodriguez, 110 S. Ct. 2793 (1990) (holding that warrantless entry into home is constitutional upon permission from third party who police reasonably believed had joint authority over premises but who did not have such authority); Horton v. California, 110 S. Ct. 2301 (1990) (allowing warrantless seizure of "plain view" evidence even if discovery of evidence was not inadvertent); Maryland

republican perspective is not easy, because the police are viewed as seeking to control "rebels"—i.e., criminals seeking to disrupt the common good—and as deserving whatever discretion they need and are unlikely to abuse. For republicans, it may be better for some more truly popular body, like the militia, to control crime, but that is not currently an option. So in this imperfect world, the Court must walk a tightrope: it must allow the police, whom it cannot trust, to control crime, which detracts from the common good, but without allowing them to intimidate law-abiding citizens, which also detracts from the common good. One thing that the Court should not do, however, is what it seems to be doing: basing constitutional decisions on apparent confidence that the police generally act in good faith.[278]

IV. REPUBLICAN REFORM

A. *Advisability*

None of the interpretations of the Amendment proposed in the last part can secure all of the ends that republicans hoped that it would. Judicial strategies can ultimately offer only limited change; moreover, in republican terms, the courts are not the best forum in which to seek popular control. In this section, I will consider whether it is desirable for modern republicans to seek a contemporary surrogate for the militia outside of the courts. Any adequate substitute must serve several functions. First, the militia reflected and induced virtue. It was universal, so as to reflect the common good; and it offered training in virtue, making citizens independent and self-sacrificing. Second, the militia increased citizen control over the government. It allowed citizens to participate directly in their own self-government, not just through the process of representation, and it consigned to them ultimate control of the means of force. The two functions served by the militia were intimately linked; republicans wanted to consign force to virtue.

1. *Virtue Functions*

In the twentieth century, the first function—the militia's connection with the common good—has become more problematic, because of the diversity and

---

v. Buie, 110 S. Ct. 1093 (1990) (holding that while executing arrest warrant, police officers may execute warrantless protective sweep of entire house on reasonable suspicion of danger); Maryland v. Garrison, 480 U.S. 79 (1987) (holding that honest factual mistakes about premises, in drawing up or executing warrant, will not invalidate warrant or search); Colorado v. Bertine, 479 U.S. 367 (1987) (holding that evidence obtained during inventory search of impounded automobile may be used as basis of prosecution); United States v. Leon, 468 U.S. 897 (1984) (providing "good faith" exception to exclusionary rule).

278. *See Rodriguez*, 110 S. Ct. at 2800; *Horton*, 110 S. Ct. at 2309-2310; *Buie*, 110 S.Ct. at 1098; *Garrison*, 480 U.S. at 87-88; *Bertine*, 479 U.S. at 374-76; Tracey Maclin, *The Decline of the Right of Locomotion: The Fourth Amendment on the Streets*, 75 CORNELL L. REV. 1258, 1291-97, 1303, 1311, 1316-27 (1990).

expansion of the citizenry. Historically, some republicans expressed a desire for a homogeneous population, so that every citizen would have the same good.[279] When republicans occasionally acknowledged the fact of diversity, they offered a number of responses. Some argued teleologically that despite superficial diversity, humans shared the same essential nature—a civic personality—and should be encouraged to realize that nature. As a result, in the end, the population was ultimately homogeneous with regard to everything that mattered.[280] Other republicans argued that citizens were naturally divided into three estates; the challenge of political theory was to cause each to serve the common good in its own way, with its own virtues.[281]

But how do we define the common good today, when most are not prepared to believe in a homogeneous citizenry, ascribed *teloi*, or natural estates, when each individual has a right to be different, and when voices from the margin are praised, not denigrated?[282] Neorepublicans have tried to retain the universalism of the republican tradition while not disparaging modern diversity. They have proposed an inclusive republicanism, based on persuasive dialogue between citizens. Individuals enter this dialogue with different ends, but through conversation, they shift their self-understandings, reaching for the perspectives of others, and drawing upon a shared past of normatively authoritative recollections.[283] The hope is not for a unitary common good, but for a participatory process such that "everyone subject to a law-like utterance can actually agree that the utterance warrants being promulgated as law."[284]

If a militia-surrogate must serve this new ideal, it is more difficult to design its structure. Under the old vision of the commonweal, the task was merely to ensure that the means of power resided with the body of the people, who shared one good. Private armies might rebel against the public good, but the militia, as the rest of society, would suppress the rebellion. The situation is quite different if all of society is like the rebels, each segment with a separate interest, richly diverse and dissentient. The neorepublicans' answer is that the citizenry must be transformed through dialogic persuasion, to recognize their sameness in their difference. But that prescription is a much taller order even than giving the means of force to citizens.

It is not, however, much greater than what the older republicans, at their most optimistic, hoped of the militia. They too believed that service in the militia could transform citizens by molding them into a public-spirited, organic

---

279. *See supra* text accompanying notes 84-89, note 159.
280. *See* Michelman, *supra* note 1, at 22.
281. *See* POCOCK, *supra* note 44, at 68-80; *supra* text accompanying notes 72-76.
282. *See* Michelman, *supra* note 66.
283. *See, e.g.,* Drucilla Cornell, *Toward a Modern/Postmodern Reconstruction of Ethics*, 133 U. PA. L. REV. 291, 360-68 (1985); Michelman, *supra* note 1, at 31-33; Michelman, *supra* note 66, at 1526-28; Sunstein, *supra* note 10, at 1566-71.
284. Michelman, *supra* note 66, at 1527.

body.[285] A modern version of the militia might induce the modern version of this civic transformation: it might bring citizens together into self-revisory dialogue. The exact nature of the transformation is different, but the essential function of the militia is similar.

The primary difference between the two visions of civic transformation is that the nature of the proposed modern transformation is much more vague than the older version. The old militia was supposed to make citizens civic-minded and critical, and both of these qualities seem familiar to us today. In contrast, dialogic self-revision is a relatively new idea. Its parameters are not yet clear, and neorepublicans tend to talk about it in tentative or general terms.[286] Moreover, because it is a reformative ideal, it has no real world referents. No one can point to an example of the kind of dialogue that he would like to see, because none yet exists. As a result, conceptualizing modern analogues to the militia is difficult in part because the function that it is supposed to serve is not yet in sharp focus. This problem—of vagueness and incompletion—may be a part of all neorepublicanism and even of all new intellectual movements. As I will discuss below, however, the militia ideal makes the problem especially acute. The still-vague self-revisory dialogue is supposed to reform the people so that it would be wise to commit to them possession of the ultimate means of force.

The expansion of the citizenry creates another problem besides the simple fact of diversity: the citizenry now includes members without, perhaps, the requisite material conditions for full participation. In the 1780's, only male property-holders—in some states only white male property-holders—could be citizens and thereby militia members.[287] Today, the citizenry is vastly larger, and hence the militia would be as well. Abandoning the racial and gender based exclusivity of the militia creates no republican difficulty, because no part of republicanism affirmatively requires race or gender bias. Eliminating the property qualification, however, is not so easy. According to republican theory, only those with property can have the independent judgment necessary to be good citizens,[288] but not all citizens today have the requisite economic independence.[289] A republican politics may therefore not be possible with the present citizenry.

Again, however, it is premature to despair of remedying the situation. Property qualifications on the franchise served the same end as bearing arms: ensuring that citizens had the requisite power independently to follow the common good. As long as citizens are subject to economic tyranny by private

---

285. *See supra* text accompanying notes 162-70.

286. Michelman, for example, acknowledges: "[G]aining a secure grasp on such a possibility stretches to the limits our powers of comprehension . . . ." Michelman, *supra* note 66, at 1527.

287. *See, e.g.,* WOOD, *supra* note 56, at 168-69.

288. *See supra* note 71, text accompanying notes 259-62; EDMUND S. MORGAN, AMERICAN SLAVERY/ AMERICAN FREEDOM 381-87 (1975).

289. *See supra* text accompanying notes 263-73.

actors or governmental tyranny by public ones, they cannot be virtuous. The virtue functions of the militia thus depend on the power functions of the militia: a citizenry can be virtuous only if also powerful. By the same token, even a dramatically expanded citizenry could be virtuous if it were possible to find ways to empower them through militia[290] or property[291] surrogates.

2.   *Power Functions*

The militia ideal sought to increase the direct control of the virtuous populace over their government, outside the normal channels of representation. In its most restrictive version, the militia's right of resistance was defensive and occasional: when tyrants abused their power, the people could remove them from office and select new rulers. But by the 1780's, the concept of the militia had become part of an ideal of constant citizen involvement in government. Anti-Federalists sought to protect local militias so that the militias could protect local legislatures, because those legislatures were more democratic than Congress. Service in the militia was thought to transform members into active citizens, committed to the public good but suspicious of government, confident in their right to disagree. As a result, citizens' conduct at the polls would reflect not fear or deference, but independent assessment of the commonweal. Militia service itself, moreover, was a form of political participation, because the militia always had to appraise the decisions of the government. If those decisions departed from the commonweal, militia members should first refuse to enforce them, then resist them, and eventually either oust the persons in office or reform the government.[292]

This function may be the most terrifying aspect of the militia. Many might find it better to regularize power by surrendering it to "responsible" decisionmakers. That fear is not irrational, even in republican terms, for we are caught in the problem of origins, of how to get a republic off the ground. In republican theory, only a virtuous citizen militia can be entrusted with the means of force to resist state authority, but citizens will not be virtuous until they are already participating in policymaking under a republican form of government. The problem of origins is different from that of maintaining an ongoing republic, and the appropriate approach to the two problems may be very different. If we were already in a republic, there would be little excuse for failing to entrust the means of force into the people's hands. No course is without peril; in a republic, giving arms to the people is safer than giving arms to the government.

In nonrepublican politics, however, it is right to fear even the body of the people because they may not be virtuous. We might seek to change that situation, and opportunities for the exercise of virtue may always involve some

---

290. For possibilities, see *infra* Part IV.B.
291. For possibilities, see *supra* text accompanying notes 264-73 (discussion of "new property").
292. *See supra* Part II.B.5.

risk. There is, however, no reason to court disaster by rapid, wholesale change. It is not surprising that much neorepublicanism is incremental in its reform program. We may ultimately make dramatic changes, but more limited popular control may be appropriate for a less republican populace.

3.   The Militia Ideal and Neorepublicanism

Thus broken into its constitutive functions, the militia ideal is thoroughly consistent with the rest of republicanism: it seeks to ensure that citizens pursue more than their own self-interest, and it seeks to return power to the citizenry. The ideal stresses three particular elements of republicanism. First, it is populist: control of force should belong not to army officers, bureaucrats, or judges but to the people. Second, it has some connection to decentralization.[293] Third, it takes seriously the impact on the political arena of the distribution of power.

This collection of ideals should not be embarrassing to progressive republicans.[294] Indeed, only the last is at all troubling from a progressive perspective. In Professor Brown's words, the right to arms contemplates the people "subduing with force what [they] cannot discursively persuade."[295] She is right. Republicans recognized that sometimes reason does not work, sometimes people do evil things, and sometimes the only course is to resist with force. That view, however, does not suggest that violence should be a normal part of political life; to the contrary, for republicans, revolution was a course of last resort. Indeed, they hoped that popular arms possession would forestall the need for resistance, since demagogues or tyrants would yield in advance. Finally, since we are not in a republic, the militia ideal suggests only that we move toward

---

293.   In part, this connection is only a restatement of the first feature: the Second Amendment protected state militias because they were closer to the people. Today, the connection between the two is more complicated. The advantages of localism are still real, but decentralization also risks some reduction in universality, since localities are often demographically skewed compared to the nation as a whole. Two centuries ago, this skewing may have been less significant, because the relevant point of comparison was the state community, the location of most important decisions. With the rise of a national culture and a national government, too much decentralization could create a kind of geographically defined, select militia. The goal should therefore be to decentralize power, but to broadly inclusive bodies. For suggestions on how to do so, see BENJAMIN R. BARBER, STRONG DEMOCRACY (1984); Kathryn Abrams, Law's Republicanism, 97 YALE L.J. 1591, 1606-08 (1988).

294.   In a recent article, James Gray Pope emphasizes the populist strain of republican politics. He argues that the Constitution presupposes that in normal times, politics-as-usual consists of deals between interest groups. But in "republican moments," the people should be able to take a direct hand in their government, outside of the normal channels, to engage in serious discussion of the common good. See Pope, supra note 257, at 310-12.

Pope's vision of republican politics shares the militia ideal's dedication to popular empowerment, but differs in imagining that republican politics can occur only in "moments." Indeed, Pope suggests that even if the Second Amendment protects a right of resistance, that right "does not provide an adequate home for popular republican politics" because the people could take up arms only under the rarest of circumstances. See id. at 328. But as I have argued, the purported benefits of universal arms possession extended to politics-as-usual, not just moments of crisis: the people would never accept a passive role in government, and government would rarely become corrupt, because both knew that the people could revolt. See supra Parts II.B.5, IV.A.2.

295.   Brown, supra note 6, at 664.

some kind of popular reempowerment, not that we issue guns to potential murderers and rapists. This stance seems both realistic and hopeful.[296] Neorepublicans should celebrate the Second Amendment, not be embarrassed by it.

Have I missed something essential about the militia by reducing it to virtue and power, rather than by talking about martiality and gender? Perhaps. Republicans' use of metaphors of masculinity to describe militia members, and the centrality of guns, danger, physicality, and male-bonding themes in recollections of militia service suggest that, for many, the militia may have offered rich emotional rewards for the same reasons that hunting trips and team sports do.[297] No doubt, many republicans became attached to the militia more from these personal experiences than from any theoretical commitment. Nevertheless, the republicans did not make these experiences a part of their conscious analysis of the Second Amendment. They were, in a sense, the accidents rather than the essence of the militia in republican thought.[298] In any event, we can take what we like from the militia ideal and reject the rest. But just as we should not accept the "macho" aspects of the militia just because they cover an admirable core, so we should not reject the core because it comes wrapped in "macho" packaging.

B. *Reform Possibilities*

I discuss below several structures that might serve as militia-surrogates under modern conditions. Because of space constraints, this discussion of far-reaching, controversial reforms is necessarily sketchy and suggestive. In particular, I analyze only how well these structures might realize the old militia functions; I do not purport to consider their overall wisdom. But to the extent the militia is a worthy icon, good militia surrogates should command our attention as well.

1. *A Universal Militia*

The most obvious way to secure the functions served by the old militia would be to reconstitute a universal militia along republican lines. Conditions

---

296. Indeed, I can imagine only one group of neorepublicans who would resist this aspect of the militia ideal: those who would disarm everyone—citizenry, police, and military. But that option only pushes the analysis back a step: if we eliminate guns, the state will presumably still employ some method of force to keep order—tear gas or nightsticks or muscle—and we must still decide whether we can more safely vest the population with greater control over that use of force.

297. *See, e.g.,* ROYSTER, *supra* note 67, at 4-5, 10-13. Jean Bethke Elshtain, for example, has argued that the tradition of armed civic virtue has all too often drawn the populace together in a nationalist dream of military glory rather than in service to fellow citizens. *See* Jean B. Elshtain, *Citizenship and Armed Civic Virtue: Some Critical Questions on the Commitment to Public Life, in* COMMUNITY IN AMERICA 47, 50-55 (Charles H. Reynolds & Ralph V. Norman eds., 1988).

298. *See* Scarry, *supra* note 150, at 1289-90 n.100 ("[T]hough the vocabulary can easily be read as gendered, it would in the long run be an error to read the idiom narrowly since the language . . . belongs to 'resistance' whether . . . male or female.").

have so changed, however, that the new militia could not generate all of the benefits of the old—although it might produce some. Significantly, this new body would have to coexist, for security reasons, with a professional army. The technology of war is so advanced that exclusive reliance on an amateur force is not an option. Even many colonial republicans assumed that a small standing army could be consistent with liberty if the militia were sufficiently vigorous.[299] Modern military technology, however, would make even a vigorous militia less of a threat to an oppressive government than in the eighteenth century.[300] To make the right of resistance a real one, we would have to guarantee a private right to possess launchers and attack helicopters.

The clear objection to creating such a right builds on Brown's: it may be dangerous to give small arms to unvirtuous citizens; it seems suicidal to give them weapons of mass destruction. How then do we assure that the militia is virtuous? It would have to be universal, so that all of the interests of the people would be represented. But republicans assumed that the people would be a homogeneous group with a single set of interests, perceptions, and desires. In contrast, a modern militia would be a reflection of modern America—divided and driven by self-interest. Without some change in society, the effect of mandatory militia service is only too easy to predict. Citizens would experience service as one more demand by a distant and alienating bureaucracy, and those alienated citizens would be in possession of very dangerous weapons.

As noted before, one proposed neorepublican method of instilling virtue is citizen participation in self-revisory political dialogue. A revived militia seems to be a promising forum for such dialogue. Part of the folklore of America depicts the army as a melting pot in which young men from different backgrounds come to know and understand each other.[301] Military history suggests that the primary source of combat bravery is intense commitment to fellow soldiers[302]—a good basis for discussion and self-revision. Potentially, something of the same sort might occur in a militia. The main business of a militia is certainly not political discussion, but war and police activity. Never-

---

299. *See* CRESS, *supra* note 111, at 278-93.

300. Professor Levinson argues that even rifles in private hands can serve a checking against a modern army, because they will change government's calculus in deciding whether and how to oppress the populace. *See* Levinson, *supra* note 2, at 648-50. This checking function is a substantial advantage, but it still falls short of republican hopes that the body of the people would have the power not just to check government but to overthrow it when circumstances warranted.

301. This bit of folklore is a recurrent theme in novels and movies. For examples, see PHILIP CAPUTO, A RUMOR OF WAR (1977); SUSAN F. SCHAEFER, BUFFALO AFTERNOON (1989); and Neil Simon's film BILOXI BLUES (Universal 1988). Kenneth Karst notes the same phenomenon. Kenneth L. Karst, *The Pursuit of Manhood and the Desegregation of the Armed Forces*, 38 UCLA L. REV. 499, 501 (1991). Karst argues that the military's present exclusionary policies involve the symbolic removal of women, gays, and lesbians from power, and thereby deny them equal citizenship, *see id.* at 500, a view with which republicans would agree.

302. *See, e.g.*, GERALD F. LINDERMAN, EMBATTLED COURAGE 234-36 (1987). At this time, American combat officers are appearing every night on the evening news to explain that, in the heat of battle, soldiers do not fight for Mom and Apple Pie: "They fight for their buddies." REID MITCHELL, CIVIL WAR SOLDIERS 17-18 (1988).

theless, linking the use of arms in public service to political dialogue might remind citizens that they ultimately control the state.

A revived militia is therefore an attractive option only if it can provide an opportunity for dialogic self-government. To do so, the militia must have something to talk about, which raises the troubling question of its relationship to the civil government. During normal times, a republican militia is an arm of the state and takes its orders from elected representatives. At the same time, such a militia must exercise independent judgment in reviewing those orders: it might decline to support a tyrant, take up arms to overthrow the government, or put down civil insurrection on its own initiative. In such cases, the militia would offer great scope for dialogue; members would decide how to use the means of force for the commonweal after careful, self-revisory discussion.

That course might make many readers uneasy. The idea of a militia setting policy and enforcing it with force is terrifying. Modern citizens might feel much more comfortable with a militia trained never to question its orders from a civil government. That fear suggests how far we have come from the eighteenth-century world, but it is not an irrational fear, even within republican terms. Republican governments are not suitable for all peoples at all times, and we are not now the stuff of which republics are made. That does not mean, however, that we are paralyzed. It does mean that we must ask how we can best inculcate the values and develop the institutions essential to the vitality of a healthy republic.

A truly independent militia should be a late republican reform, if indeed conditions ever warrant one. Much of neorepublican reform is deliberately incremental. An independent militia would be a drastic and very high risk change. If other reforms first create a virtuous citizenry, it may then be time to consider a freestanding militia. In the interim, the most advisable alternative is having a militia under orders from the civil government but vested with ministerial discretion over daily operations. Such a highly "tamed" militia would closely resemble universal civic service, which I consider in the next section.

An obedient militia still leaves control over the means of force in the hands of government, and, to that extent, it falls short of the function served by the old militia. But since we do not currently have a republic, we must choose among options, none of which match the ideal. The question is thus whether it is more advisable to trust the government or the people with direct control of the means of force. The argument for trusting the government is largely prudential. Government abuses its control of the means of force, but we live with those abuses daily. In contrast, we do not know how great the abuses of an independent but unvirtuous militia might be, but they are potentially much greater. The government is subject to influence by public opinion and electoral control. To be sure, republican theory recognizes that such attenuated controls may be insufficient to resist tyranny; hence, the belief in a popular right of revolution. Nevertheless, such controls are not negligible and form a valuable check on government misconduct. If at some future point citizens habitually engage in self-modulating political discourse, we may come to trust them more than we trust the government with the means of force. Presently, however, it seems wise at first to move incrementally. Moreover, the overall purpose of the militia was to give the people the ability to control their own destiny. Vesting them with the control of force is the ultimate means to this end, but there are less extreme steps to empower the people short of giving them guns.

The militia ideal thus highlights what may be the besetting vice of neorepublicanism: its utopian, somewhat out-of-focus quality. It starkly suggests how far, if we take the intellectual inheritance seriously, we must go: reforming the character of the people so thoroughly that they should have guns so as to be able to overthrow the government. To many, even those sympathetic to neorepublicanism, that ideal may seem very utopian under present conditions. To respond that reformation will occur through self-revisory dialogue may not offer much solace given how relatively vague and incomplete that idea still is. And the intermediate steps on the way—some of which I discuss below—are really a number of separate ideas which may or may not, taken together, work a revolution in the character of the citizenry. The militia ideal thus suggests that we approach neorepublicanism carefully, not because it is violent or sexist, but because it is so hopeful.

Utopianism, however, may be the besetting sin of any new collection of ideas that seeks to change deep trends in modern social development. It may be appropriate to repeat the obvious: without some utopianism, abolitionists, women suffragists, and civil rights leaders would never have been able to get out of bed in the morning. If we do not try, we will never know.

2. Universal Service

Another alternative, currently much discussed,[303] is universal public service, not necessarily military, for a term of years in youth. The promised benefits of this course mirror some of those anticipated for the old militia. Service would bring together people from different classes, occupations, and ways of life into a common experience that could offer a basis for dialogue allowing self-revision through empathy with others.[304] And service to others and the state, such as feeding the elderly, working in disadvantaged areas, or

---

[303]. See WILLIAM F. BUCKLEY, JR., GRATITUDE (1990); CHARLES MOSKOS, A CALL TO CIVIC SERVICE (1988); NATIONAL SERVICE (Williamson M. Evers ed., 1990).

[304]. AMITAI ETZIONI, AN IMMODEST AGENDA: REBUILDING AMERICA BEFORE THE TWENTY-FIRST CENTURY 160 (1983); BUCKLEY, supra note 303, at 28-30.

rebuilding our infrastructure, might promote self-sacrifice, reduce self-absorption, and provide exposure to different folks and ways.[305]

Service plans are not without their problems, the most significant being the specter of totalitarianism if service is mandatory. None of the programs currently proposed by Congress or the Administration require service. Instead, they offer incentives like college aid, salaried jobs, or tax benefits.[306] But such financial incentive mechanisms might greatly reduce class-mixing in service, since primarily the less affluent would join.[307] A coercive service program, however, has great problems as well, and not just for liberals or libertarians. We are close to the center of the republican paradox. On the one hand, republicans endorse mandatory service. Without state supervision the militia could not be either universal or trained to virtue. On the other hand, one should be suspicious of the state as well, because state supervision could easily become indoctrination under a corrupt apparatus.[308] The ideal would be to use the state mechanism to convene the people into dialogue, but the people's judgment would then become independent of the state. At its best, universal service might capture this balance, offering opportunity for civic education from fellow citizens, not from state exhortation.[309]

As some visible politicians[310] and pundits[311] now support various service plans, we may have a chance to evaluate this option. With luck, it might provide militia-like training in virtue, and so it is probably a necessary compo-

---

305. Amitai Etzioni, *Comments*, in NATIONAL SERVICE, *supra* note 303, at 154; Tim W. Ferguson, *Comments*, in NATIONAL SERVICE, *supra* note 303, at 72-73; Don Wycliff, *Discussion*, in NATIONAL SERVICE, *supra* note 303, at 260; MOSKOS, *supra* note 303, at 4-6; BUCKLEY, *supra* note 303, at 8.

306. *See* NATIONAL SERVICE, *supra* note 303, at xix-xx.

307. *See* Benjamin R. Barber, *Discussion*, in NATIONAL SERVICE, *supra* note 303, at 80.

308. Some modern opponents of universal service stress this danger. *See* JOHN W. CHAMBERS, DRAFTEES OR VOLUNTEERS 561 (1975); Virginia Postrel, *Comments*, in NATIONAL SERVICE, *supra* note 303, at 217; BUCKLEY, *supra* note 303, at 48-49. The concern has an analogue in republican tensions over a wartime draft during the Revolution: Americans had a duty to fight for their country (part of virtue was self-sacrifice), but making them do so seemed inconsistent with their status as free citizens (another part of virtue was independence). *See* ROYSTER, *supra* note 67, at 66-69.

309. Jed Rubenfeld offers an analogy to the danger inherent in mandatory service. Privacy rights exist, he suggests, to prevent government from taking over and standardizing the lives of citizens by forcing them into certain roles and directing their daily lives. Jed Rubenfeld, *The Right of Privacy*, 102 HARV. L. REV. 737, 784 (1989). Universal service, with its avowedly educational function, poses a risk of this standardization "of treating individuals as mere instrumentalities of the state, rather than as citizens with independent minds who themselves constitute the state." *Id.* at 790. Republicanism offers, however, a more benign but more paradoxical militia, in which citizens are both creatures and creators of the state, in which education occurs not through state indoctrination but through dialogic interaction with diverse citizens. William F. Buckley captures this balance well: "The state needs at once to be used, to 'work,' and to be kept at bay; and the eternal question, of course, is, How to bind the citizen to the state without being bound by it?" BUCKLEY, *supra* note 303, at 55.

310. The roster of those on record supporting the idea in the abstract includes Senators Sam Nunn, Charles Robb, Edward Kennedy, and George Mitchell. *See* NATIONAL SERVICE, *supra* note 303, at xvii.

311. Among others, the redoubtable William F. Buckley, *see* BUCKLEY, *supra* note 303 ("taste-model for the rich"), Mickey Kaus, *First Serve*, NEW REPUBLIC, Dec. 31, 1990, at 36 (reviewing BUCKLEY, *supra* note 303), and Charles Peters, editor of *Washington Monthly*, *see* NATIONAL SERVICE, *supra* note 303, at xvii.

nent in any militia-surrogate.[312] But it has one major limitation: it would not give the people any direct control over general policy. Even if a service plan were designed to promote maximal citizen control, participants could decide only whom they served and how; they would not control the means of force and could not check the government. If the population is not virtuous, that result may be for the good, but it does not secure the functions of the old militia.

3. Direct Participation

Thus, neither a safe militia nor universal service offers the chief benefit of the old independent militia—direct control by the people of their government. But neorepublicans have offered many other options to increase direct participation by the people in their government.[313] Frank Michelman has suggested that a republican politics could occur

> in the encounters and conflicts, interactions and debates that arise in and around town meetings and local government agencies; civic and voluntary organizations; social and recreational clubs; schools public and private; managements, directorates and leadership groups of organizations of all kinds; workplaces and shop floors; public events and street life; and so on.[314]

Writing before the republican revival in the legal academy, Gerald Frug analyzed the way that liberalism historically disempowered intermediate organizations as threatening individual autonomy;[315] in recognizably republican language, he sought to reempower them in order to increase the control of citizens over their lives.[316] Professor Sunstein has offered a variety of options. Cam-

---

312. As Akhil Amar observes, public education might also offer the training in public virtue that the militia, the jury, and the church were supposed to provide, *see* Amar, *supra* note 103, at 1208-10, and I endorse that conclusion. From a republican perspective, however, public education has limits as well. Unlike universal service, public education offers little class mixing as long as neighborhoods remain fairly homogeneous; and like universal service, it offers little opportunity for direct control of government.

313. Some early neorepublican scholarship focused on opportunities for dialogue among government officials. Frank Michelman argued that the Court could engage in the kind of republican dialogue that the citizenry ideally should carry out. *See* Michelman, *supra* note 1, at 74. Cass Sunstein argued that the Court could adopt measures that would prompt republican dialogue within the legislature. *See* Sunstein, *supra* note 10, at 1576-89. The Second Amendment, in contrast, would direct the attention of republicans not to the Court or legislature, but to the people.

314. Michelman, *supra* note 66, at 1531.

315. Gerald E. Frug, *The City as a Legal Concept*, 93 HARV. L. REV. 1057, 1087-89 (1980).

316. *See id.* at 1068-73, 1120-54. Indeed, in some ways Frug's description of the medieval city is strikingly similar to the republican view of the militia. It was "neither the state nor the individual, neither political nor economic, neither public nor private, yet [it had] autonomy protected against the power of the central state." *Id.* at 1081. It "established the rights of a group that could not be distinguished from the rights of the individuals within the group . . . . [A] strict identity [had been] established between [the] individual interests and the town's interest as a whole." *Id.* at 1084. But the town was such a universal body only for a certain class: it was created by and for merchants. *See id.* at 1083-85.

paign finance reform might "improve political deliberation and . . . promote political equality and citizenship" by making it possible for people without wealth to participate in the republican dialogue.[317] Proportional representation of groups, although it may presuppose entrenched interests, might serve republican ends by ensuring that the dialogue includes voices that might not otherwise be heard.[318] These forms of popular empowerment paradoxically depend on state support, but that fact makes the analogy to the militia even closer. The state raised the militia to ensure universal access to the means of force, just as the state would regulate campaign finance to promote universal access to the means of communication. But the result of these activities was empowerment of the body of the people against both the government and private factions with disproportionate power,[319] such as corporate speakers.[320]

Any of these options might promote some of the virtues of the militia by giving the people a direct hand in their government. In toto, they may not promote popular control as fully as did the militia because none gives possession of the means of force to the people. The echo of Levinson's warning should therefore remain in our ears: one cannot trust a government that holds all the arms. But it is important to remember that the republican militia was a regulative ideal, not a practical reality. The militia was never truly universal. The young nation always had a standing army; the people were never wholly in control and perhaps never could be. Moreover, we need not adopt all of

---

More recently, Kathryn Abrams has called for "[r]ecovering the popular strain in republican theory," Abrams, *supra* note 293, at 1608, by reviving local government, *see id.* at 1604-06. Sunstein would also reinvigorate intermediate organizations, with a new federalism or workplace democracy. *See* Sunstein, *supra* note 10, at 1578.

317. Sunstein, *supra* note 10, at 1577. Similarly, Jennifer Nedelsky has suggested that a properly regulated public, rather than privately owned press, might increase the power of the people by assuring greater access. *See* Nedelsky, *supra* note 66, at 14-15.

318. *See* Sunstein, *supra* note 10, at 1588-89. Professor Levinson notes the same republican ambivalence about proportional representation but concludes that republicans would likely end up rejecting it. On the one hand, proportional representation would ensure a fairer reflection of society as a whole, *see* Sanford Levinson, *Gerrymandering and the Brooding Omnipresence of Proportional Representation: Why Won't It Go Away?*, 33 UCLA L. REV. 257, 262-63, 265, 270 (1985), but it would also produce "institutionalized selfishness and partiality," rather than a commitment to the common good, *id.* at 275.

319. In response to Professor Frug, Professor Ellickson has argued for empowering homeowner associations and not cities, on the grounds that membership in the former, but not the latter, is voluntary. Robert C. Ellickson, *Cities and Homeowners Associations*, 130 U. PA. L. REV. 1519, 1519, 1521-23 (1982). But Ellickson's objection, with its exclusive focus on individual volition, is solidly in the liberal tradition. Indeed, Ellickson gladly, if ironically, describes himself as a "Prisoner of Liberal Thought." *Id.* at 1521. For republicans, independence and rights are one horn of the dilemma in producing a healthy society, but self-sacrifice and state organization are the other. In response to Ellickson, Professor Alexander has brought this latter horn into focus. He argues that the state should intervene to prevent homeowners' associations from becoming exclusive. As they become too exclusive, such associations come to resemble—in republican terms—self-interested factions that wield disproportionate power; the state's invasion of these nodules of privilege actually promotes community and empowerment. *See* Gregory S. Alexander, *Dilemmas of Group Autonomy: Residential Associations and Community*, 75 CORNELL L. REV. 1, 4-7, 55-61 (1989).

320. In fact, from a republican perspective, the government might actually guarantee access rights to the means of communication as a means of popular empowerment, and not merely to restrain dominant speakers. The analogy to the old republican proposals to give each citizen a gun seems very close as a functional matter. *See supra* text accompanying note 233.

historical republicanism. We should seek opportunities for the people to become virtuous, but we can be discriminating in choosing among those opportunities. Empowerment can take forms other than arms bearing, and it seems wise to try those other forms first.

V. CONCLUSION

The Second Amendment is not an embarrassing relic of an outdated scheme of ideas. It guarantees a right to arms for reasons that are an integral part of neorepublicanism. Use of arms in a militia was a form of communal cooperation, characterized by self-sacrifice and independent judgment. The academic left may be uncomfortable with gun ownership in modern America, but it should not eschew the functions that the right serves.

The right to arms belonged to all, but as a collective right, a right of the universal militia and not of separate private individuals. Republicans feared government and sought to give the people ways to resist it, but they also feared the self-interest that lurked in each individual's breast. They feared the militia less than either private persons or the government because they identified the militia with the body of the people—a rhetorical construct that by definition could not betray the common good because the common good was its good. That construct was utopian and artificial even at the time. Militia members had separate and different interests, and the militia never truly represented the whole body of the people. But as a regulative ideal, the concept of the militia offers a guide to interpreting the Second Amendment.

The Amendment expresses a hope that the means of force could be vested in those who would express universal good. But with the passage of two centuries, it has become increasingly difficult to identify such a body. We have no modern analogue of the universal militia. Private gun owners represent a partial interest, and so does the National Guard. By the same token, it has become increasingly difficult to identify a "common" interest among radically heterogeneous citizens. The modern promises and problems of the Second Amendment are thus the promises and problems of neorepublicanism generally. To effectuate the Second Amendment, we must find a way to create a republican politics in a liberal state. The right to arms is no anomaly within republicanism but a reflection of its deepest commitments. And the goal of the Amendment will have been served if neorepublican reform succeeds.

The right to arms, however, should focus our attention on certain features of republicanism. Neorepublicanism dwells largely on the hope that we can do better than to pursue self-interest and to stand on our rights. But republicanism balanced hope against fear, and the Second Amendment reflects this balance. It takes seriously the idea that force lies at the root of politics. Neo-republicanism should never become so theoretical that it forgets to worry about the distribution of power, or so organicist that it forgets to fear the government, or so optimistic that it forgets to fear private persons. Republicanism insists that, in a democracy, one must at some point find a way to trust the people, but this trust must not be naively given. Eventually, the people should reacquire direct control of the means of force, but only when the right structures offer them an opportunity for virtue.

At the same time, the militia ideal itself is wildly hopeful in the long run, because it projects a time when the people hold the ultimate means of force. To some, the right to arms may therefore suggest how little relevance neorepublicanism offers to today's world. Because we do not now have a universal militia, the Amendment has little or no direct meaning for judges. At most, it can influence the interpretation of other provisions. And as a regulative ideal, the militia may seem even more specious: working toward a time when the people should hold the means of coercion may seem like working toward the impossible. Skepticism may be appropriate; it is important to be realistic about the possibility of social change. But if skepticism becomes so deep that we can no longer dream the dreams of democracy, it becomes only a prescription for paralysis. Even contemplating the militia ideal may thus depend on some measure of faith to triumph over terror, seeing the state of humankind and still hoping for republican redemption, despite our inability to control our own destinies.

THE FOURTEENTH AMENDMENT AND THE RIGHT TO KEEP AND
BEAR ARMS: THE INTENT OF THE FRAMERS

By Stephen P. Halbrook*

A well regulated militia being necessary to the security of a free state,
the right of the people to keep and bear arms shall not be infringed. —U.S.
Const. amend. II.
. . . No state shall make or enforce any law which shall abridge the
privileges or immunities of citizens of United States; nor shall any state
deprive any person of life, liberty, or property, without due process of law;
nor deny to any person within its jurisdiction the equal protection of the
laws. —U.S. Const. amend. XIV, § 1.

If African Americans were citizens, observed Chief Justice Taney
in *Dred Scott* v. *Sandford*,[1] "it would give to persons of the negro
race . . . the full liberty of speech . . .; to hold public meetings
upon political affairs, and to keep and carry arms wherever they
went."[2] If this interpretation ignores that Articles I and II of the
Bill of Rights designate the respective freedoms guaranteed therein
to "the people" and not simply the citizens (much less a select
group of orators or militia), contrariwise Dred Scott followed antebellum judicial thought in recognizing keeping and bearing arms as
an individual right[3] protected from both federal and state infringement.[4] The exception to this interpretation were cases holding that the Second Amendment only protected citizens[5] from
federal, not state,[6] infringement of the right to keep and bear
arms, to provide judicial approval of laws disarming black freemen
and slaves.

Since the Fourteenth Amendment was meant to overrule Dred
Scott by extending individual constitutional rights to black Americans and by providing protection thereof against state infringement,[7] the question arises whether the framers of Amendment
XIV and related enforcement legislation recognized keeping and
bearing arms as individual right on which no state could infringe.
The congressional intent in respect to the Fourteenth Amendment
is revealed in the debates over both Amendments XIII and XIV as
well as the Civil Rights Act of 1866, the Anti-KKK Act of 1871, and
the Civil Rights Act of 1875. Given the unanimity of opinion concerning state regulation of privately held arms by the legislators
who framed the Fourteenth Amendment and its enforcement legislation, it is surprising that judicial opinions and scholarly articles
fail to analyze the Reconstruction debates.[8]

A. ARMS AND SLAVERY

Having won their national independence from England through
armed struggle, post-Revolutionary War Americans were acutely

* J. D. 1978 Georgetown University; Ph.D. 1972 Florida State University. Member, Virginia
State Bar, various federal court bars. The author has taught legal and political philosophy at
George Mason University, Howard University and Tuskegee Institute.
This is a revision of a portion of the author's The Jurisprudence of the Second and Fourteenth
Amendments, IV GEORGE MASON L. REV. (1981).

aware that the sword and sovereignty go hand in hand, and that the firearms technology ushered in a new epoch in the human struggle for freedom. Furthermore, both proponents and opponents of slavery were cognizant that an armed black population meant the abolition of slavery, although plantation slaves were often trusted with arms for hunting.[9] This sociological fact explained not only the legal disarming of blacks but also the advocacy of a weapons culture by abolitionists. Having employed the instruments for self-defense against his pro-slavery attackers, abolitionist and Republican Party founder Cassius Marcellus Clay wrote that " 'the pistol and the Bowie knife' are to us as sacred as the gown and the pulpit."[10] And it was John Brown who argued that "the practice of carrying arms would be a good one for the colored people to adopt, as it would give them a sense of their manhood."[11]

The practical necessities of the long, bloody Civil War, demanding every human resource, led to the arming of blacks as soldiers. While originally they considered it a "white man's war," Northern authorities by 1863 were organizing black regiments on a wide scale. At the same time, black civilians were forced to arm themselves privately against mob violence. During the anti-draft riots in New York, according to a Negro newspaper of the time, "The colored men who had manhood in them armed themselves, and threw out their pickets every day and night, determined to die defending their homes. . . . Most of the colored men in Brooklyn who remained in the city were armed daily for self-defense."[12]

Toward the end of the war Southerners began to support the arming and freeing of slaves willing to fight the invaders, and the Virginia legislature, on passing a bill providing for the use of black soldiers, repealed its laws against the bearing of arms by blacks.[13] One opponent of these measures declared: "What would be the character of the returned negro soldiers, made familiar with the use of fire-arms, and taught by us, that freedom was worth fighting for?"[14] Being evident that slaves plus guns equaled abolition, the rebels were divided between those who valued nationhood to slavery and those who preferred a restored union which might not destroy the servile condition of black labor.

As the movement began before the end of the war for the complete abolition of slavery via the Thirteenth Amendment, members of the U.S. Congress recognized the key role that the bearing of arms was already playing in the freeing of the slaves. In debate over the proposed Amendment, Rep. George A. Yeaman (Unionist, Ky.) contended that whoever won the war, the abolition of slavery was inevitable due to the arming of blacks:

> Let proclamations be withdrawn, let statutes be repealed, let our armies be defeated, let the South achieve its independence, yet come out of the war . . . with an army of slaves made freemen for their service, who have been contracted with, been armed and drilled, and have seen the force of combination. Their personal status is enhanced. . . . They will not be returned to slavery.[15]

At the same time, members of the slavocracy were planning to disarm the freedmen. Arguing for speedy adoption of the Thirteenth Amendment, Rep. William D. Kelley (R., Penn.) expressed

shock at the words of an anti-secessionist planter in Mississippi
who expected the union to restore slavery. Kelley cited a letter
from a U.S. brigadier general who wrote: " 'What,'_said I, 'these
men who have had arms in their hands?' 'Yes,' he said, 'we should
take the arms away from them, of course.' "[16]

The northern government won the war only because of the
arming of the slaves, according to Sen. Charles Sumner (R., Mass.),
who argued that necessity demanded "first, that the slaves should
be declared free; and secondly, that muskets should be put into
their hands for the common defense. . . . Without emancipation,
followed by the arming of the slaves, rebel slavery would not have
been overcome."[17]

After the war was concluded, the slave codes, which limited
access of blacks to land, to arms, and to the courts, began to
reappear in the form of the black codes,[18] and United States
legislators turned their attention to the protection of the freedmen.
In support of Senate Bill No. 9, which declared as void all laws in
the rebel states which recognized inequality of rights based on
race, Sen. Henry Wilson (R., Mass.) explained in part: "In Mississippi rebel State forces, men who were in the rebel armies, are
traversing the State, visiting the freedmen disarming them, perpe-
trating murders and outrages on them. . . ."[19]

When Congress took up Senate Bill No. 61, which became the
Civil Rights Act of 1866,[20] Sen. Lyman Trumbull (R., Ill.), Chairman of the Senate Judiciary Committee, indicated that the bill was
intended to prohibit inequalities embodied in the black codes, including those provisions which "prohibit any negro or mulatto
from having fire-arms."[21] In abolishing the badges of slavery, the
bill would enforce fundamental rights against racial discrimination
in respect to civil rights, the rights to contract, sue and engage in
commerce, and equal criminal penalities. Sen. William Saulsbury
(D., Del.) added: "In my State for many years, and I presume there
are similar laws in most of the southern States, there has existed a
law of the State based upon and founded in its police power, which
declares that free negroes shall not have the possession of firearms
or ammunition. This bill proposes to take away from the States
this police power. . . ." The Delaware Democrat opposed the bill on
this basis, anticipating a time when "a numerous body of dangerous persons belonging to any distinct race" endangered the state,
for "the State shall not have the power to disarm them without
disarming the whole population."[22] Thus, the bill would have
prohibited legislative schemes which in effect disarmed blacks but
not whites. Still, supporters of the bill were soon to contend that
arms bearing was a basic right of citizenship or personhood.

In the meantime, the legislators turned their attention to the
Freedmen's Bureau Bill. Rep. Thomas D. Eloit (R., Mass.) attacked
an Opelousas, Louisiana ordinance which deprived blacks of various civil rights, including the following provision: "No freedman
who is not in the military service shall be allowed to carry firearms, or any kind of weapons, within the limits of the town of
Opelousas without the special permission of his employer . . . and

approved by the mayor or president of the board of police."[23] And Rep. Josiah B. Grinnell (R., Iowa) complained: " A white man in Kentucky may keep a gun; if a black man buys a gun he forfeits it and pays a fine of five dollars, if presuming to keep in his possession a musket which he has carried through the war."[24] Yet the right of blacks to have arms existed partly as self-defense against the state militia itself, which implied that militia needs were not the only constitutional bases for the right to bear arms. Sen. Trumbull cited a report from Vicksburg, Mississippi which stated: "Nearly all the dissatisfaction that now exists among the freedmen is caused by the abusive conduct of this militia."[25] Rather than restore order, the militia would typically "hang some freedman or search negro houses for arms."[26] As debate returned to the Civil Rights Bill, Rep. Henry J. Raymond (R., N.Y.) explained of the rights of citizenship: "Make the colored man a citizen of the United States and he has every right which you or I have as citizens of the United States under the laws and Constitution of the United States. . . . He has a defined status; he has a country and a home; a right to defend himself and his wife and children; a right to bear arms . . . ."[27] Rep. Roswell Hart (R., N.Y.) further states: "The Constitution clearly describes that to be a republican form of government for which it was expressly framed. A government . . . where 'no law shall be made prohibiting a free exercise of religion;' where 'the right of the people to keep and bear arms shall not be infringed;' . . . ."[28] He concluded that it was the duty of the United States to guarantee that the states have such a form of government.[29]

Rep. Sidney Clarke (R., Kansas) referred to an 1866 Alabama law providing: "That it shall not be lawful for any freedman, mulatto, or free person of color in this State, to own firearms, or carry about his person a pistol or other deadly weapon."[30] This same statute made it unlawful "to sell, give, or lend fire-arms to ammunition of any description whatever, to any freedman, free negro, or mulatto. . . ."[31] Clarke also attacked Mississippi, "whose rebel militia, upon the seizure of the arms of black Union Soldiers, appropriated the same to their own use."[32]

> Sir, I find in the Constitution of the United States an article which declares that "the right of the people to keep and bear arms shall not be infringed." For myself, I shall insist that the reconstructed rebels of Mississippi respect the Constitution in their local laws . . . .[33]

Emotionally referring to the disarming of black soldiers, Clarke added:

> Nearly every white man in that State that could bear arms was in the rebel ranks. Nearly all of their able-bodied colored men who could reach our lines enlisted under the old flag. Many of these brave defenders of the nation paid for the arms with which they went to battle. . . . The "reconstructed" State authorities of Mississippi were allowed to rob and disarm our veteran soldiers . . . .[34]

In sum, Clarke presupposed a constitutional right to keep privately held arms for protection against oppressive state militia.

C. THE FOURTEENTH AMENDMENT

The need for a more solid foundation for the protection of freedmen as well as white citizens was recognized, and the result was a significant new proposal—the Fourteenth Amendment. A chief exponent of the amendment, Sen. Jacob M. Howard (R., Mich.), referred to "the personal rights guaranteed and secured by the first eight amendments of the Constitution; such as freedom of speech and of the press; . . . the right to keep and to bear arms. . . ."[35] Adoption of the Fourteenth Amendment was necessary because presently these rights were not guaranteed against state legislation. "The great object of the first section of this amendment is, therefore, to restrain the power of the States and compel them at all times to respect these great fundamental guarantees."[36]

The Fourteenth Amendment was viewed as necessary to buttress the objectives of the Civil Rights Act of 1866. Rep. George W. Julian (R., Ind.) noted that the act

> Is pronounced void by the jurists and courts of the South. Florida makes it a misdemeanor for colored men to carry weapons without a license to do so from a probate judge, and the punishment of the offense is whipping and the pillory. South Carolina has the same enactments . . . Cunning legislative devices are being invented in most of the States to restore slavery in fact.[37]

It is hardly surprising that the arms question was viewed as part of a partisan struggle. "As you once needed the muskets of the colored persons, so now you need their votes," Sen. Sumner explained to his fellow Republicans in support of black suffrage in the District of Columbia.[38] At the opposite extreme, Rep. Michael C. Kerr (D., Ind.) an opponent of black suffrage and of the Fourteenth Amendment, attacked a military ordinance in Alabama that set up a volunteer militia of all males between ages 18 and 45 "without regard to race or color" on these grounds:

> Of whom will that militia consist? Mr. Speaker, it will consist only of the black men of Alabama. The white men will not degrade themselves by going into the ranks and becoming a part of the militia of the State with negroes. . . . Are the civil laws of Alabama to be enforced by this negro militia? Are white men to be disarmed by them?[39]

Kerr predicted that the disfranchisement of white voters and the above military measure would result in "a war of races."[40]

D. THE ANTI-KKK ACT

Although the Fourteenth Amendment became law in 1868, within three years the Congress was considering enforcement legislation to suppress the Ku Klux Klan. The famous report by Rep. Benjamin F. Butler (R., Mass.) on violence in the South assumed that the right to keep arms was necessary for protection against the militia but also against local law enforcement agencies. Noting instances of "armed confederates" terrorizing the negro, the report stated that "in many counties they have preceded their outrages upon him by disarming him, in violation of his right as a citizen to 'keep and bear arms,' which the Constitution expressly says shall never be infringed."[41] The congressional power based on the Fourteenth Amendment to legislate to prevent states from depriving any U.S. citizen of life, liberty, or property justified the following provision of the committee's anti-KKK bill:

> That whoever shall, without due process of law, by violence, intimidation, or threats, take away or deprive any citizen of the United States of any arms or weapons he may have in his house or possession for the defense of his person, family, or property, shall be deemed guilty of a larceny thereof, and be punished as provided in this act for a felony.[42]

Rep. Butler explained the purpose of this provision in these words:

> Section eight is intended to enforce the well-known constitutional provision guaranteeing the right in the citizen to "keep and bear arms," and provides that whoever shall take away, by force or violence, or by threats and intimidation, the arms and weapons which any person may have for his defense, shall be deemed guilty of larceny of the same. This provision seemed to your committee to be necessary, because they had observed that, before these midnight marauders made attacks upon peaceful citizens, there were very many instances in the South where the sheriff of the county had preceded them and taken away the arms of their victims. This was specially noticeable in Union County, where all the negro population were disarmed by the sheriff only a few months ago under the order of the judge . . .; and then, the sheriff having disarmed the citizens, the five hundred masked men rode at night and murdered and otherwise maltreated the ten persons who were in jail in that county.[43]

The bill was referred to the Judiciary Committee, and when later reported as H.R. No. 320 the above section was deleted—probably because its proscription extended to simple individual larceny over which Congress had no constitutional authority, and because state or conspiratorial action involving the disarming of blacks would be covered by more general provisions of the bill. Supporters of the rewritten anti-KKK bill continued to show the same concern over the disarming of freedmen. Sen. John Sherman (R., Ohio) stated the Republican position: "Wherever the negro population preponderates, there they [the KKK] hold their sway, for a few determined men . . . can carry terror among ignorant negroes . . . without arms, equipment, or discipline."[44]

Further comments clarified that the right to arms was a necessary condition for the right of free speech. Sen. Adelbert Ames (R., Miss.) averred: "In some counties it was impossible to advocate Republican principles, those attempting it being hunted like wild beasts; in other, the speakers had to be armed and supported by not a few friends."[45] Rep. William L. Stoughton (R., Mich.) exclaimed: "If political opponents can be marked for slaughter by secret bands of cowardly assassins who ride forth with impunity to execute the decrees upon the unarmed and defenseless, it will be fatal alike to the Republican party and civil liberty."[46]

Section 1 of the bill, which was taken partly from Section 2 of the Civil Rights Act of 1866 and survives today as 42 U.S.C. § 1983, was meant to enforce Section 1 of the Fourteenth Amendment by establishing a remedy for deprivation under color of state law of federal constitutional rights of all people, not only former slaves. This portion of the bill provided:

> That any person who, under color of any law, statute, ordinance, regulation, custom, or usage of any State, shall subject, or cause to be subjected, any person within the jurisdiction of the United States to the deprivation of any rights, privileges, or immunities to which . . . he is entitled under the Constitution or laws of the United States, shall . . . be liable to the party injured in an action at law, suit in equity, or other proper proceeding for redress. . . .[47]

Rep. Washington C. Whitthorne (D. Tenn.), who complained that "in having organized a negro militia, in having disarmed the white man," the Republicans had "plundered and robbed" the whites of South Carolina through "unequal laws," objected to Section 1 of the anti-KKK bill on these grounds:

> It will be noted that by the first section suits may be instituted without regard to amount or character of claim by any person within the limits of the United States who conceives that he has been deprived of any right, privilege, or immunity secured him by the Constitution of the United States, under color of any law, statute, ordinance, regulation, custom, or usage of any State. This is to say, that if a police officer of the city of Richmond or New York should find a drunken negro or white man upon the streets with a loaded pistol flourishing it, &c., and by virtue of any ordinance, law, or usage, either of city or State, he takes it away, the officer may be sued, because the right to bear arms is secured by the Constitution, and such suit brought in distant and expensive tribunals.[48]

The Tennessee Democrat assumed that the right to bear arms was absolute, deprivation of which created a cause of action against state agents under Section 1 of the anti-KKK bill. In the minds of the bill's supporters, however, the Second Amendment as incorporated in the Fourteenth Amendment recognized a right to keep and bear arms safe from state infringement, not a right to commit assault or otherwise engage in criminal conduct with arms by pointing them at people or wantonly brandishing them about so as to endanger others. Contrary to the congressman's exaggerations, the proponents of the bill had the justified fear that the opposite development would occur, i.e., that a black or white man of the wrong political party would legitimately have or possess arms and a police officer of the city of Richmond or New York who was drunken with racial prejudice or partisan politics would take it away, perhaps to ensure the success of an extremist group's attack. Significantly, none of the representative's colleagues disputed his assumption that state agents could be sued under the predecessor to § 1983 for deprivation of the right to keep arms.

Rep. William D. Kelly (R., Penn.), speaking after and in reply to Rep. Whitthorne, did not deny the argument that Section 1 allowed suit for deprivation of the right to possess arms, but emphasized the arming of the KKK. He referred to "great numbers of Winchester rifles, and a particular species of revolving pistol" coming into Charleston's ports. "Poor men, without visible means of support, whose clothes are ragged and whose lives are almost or absolutely those of vagrants, are thus armed with new and costly rifles, and wear in their belts a brace of expensive pistols."[49] These weapons were used against Southern Republicans, whose constitutional rights must thereby be guaranteed by law and arms.

However, like Congressman Whitthorne, Rep. Barbour Lewis (R., Tenn.) also decried the loss of state agent's immunity should the bill pass: "By the first section, in certain cases, the judge of a State court, though acting under oath of office, is made liable to a suit in the Federal Court and subject to damages for his decision against a suitor, however honest and conscientious that decision may be; and a ministerial officer is subject to the same pains and penalties. . . ."[50] Tennessee Republicans and Democrats alike thus agreed that what is today § 1983 provided an action for damages against state agents in general for deprivation of constitutional rights.

Debate over the anti-KKK bill naturally required exposition of Section 1 of the Fourteenth Amendment, and none was better qualified to explain that section than its draftsman, Rep. John A. Bingham (R., Ohio):

> Mr. Speaker, that the scope and meaning of the limitations imposed by the first section, fourteenth amendment of the Constitution may be more fully understood, permit me to say that the privileges and immunities of citizens of a State, are chiefly defined in the first eight amendments to the constitution of the United States. Those eight amendments are as follows:

> ARTICLE I

> Congress shall make no law respecting an establishment of religion, or prohibiting the free exercise thereof, or abridging the freedom of speech, or of the press, or the right of the people peaceably to assemble, and to petition the Government for a redress of grievances.

> ARTICLE II

> A well-regulated militia being necessary to the security of a free State, the right of the people to keep and bear arms shall not be infringed. . . . [Amendments III–VIII, also listed by Bingham, are here omitted.]

These eight articles I have shown never were limitations
upon the power of the States, until made so by the Fourteenth Amendment. The words of that amendment, "no
State shall make or enforce any law which shall abridge
the privileges or immunites of citizens of the United
States," are an express prohibition upon every State of the
Union. . . . [51]

This is a most explicit statement of the incorporation thesis by
the architect of the Fourteenth Amendment. Although he based
the incorporation on the privileges and immunities clause and not
the due process clause as did subsequent courts of selective incorporation, Rep. Bingham could hardly have anticipated the judical
metaphysics of the twentieth century in this respect. In any case,
whether based on the due process clause or on the privileges and
immunities clause, the legislative history supports the view that
the incorporation of Amendments I-VIII was clear and unmistakable in the minds of the framers of Amendment XIV.

In contrast with the above legal analysis, some comments on the
enforcement of the Fourteenth Amendment returned to discussion
of power struggle between Republicans and unreconstructed Confederates. While Republicans deplored the armed condition of
white Southerners and the unarmed state of black Southerners,
Democrats argued that the South's whites were disarmed and endangered by armed carpetbaggers and negro militia. Thus, Rep.
Ellis H. Roberts (R., N.Y.) lamented the partisan character of KKK
violence: "The victims whose property is destroyed, whose persons
are mutilated, whose lives are sacrificed, are always Republicans.
They may be black or white. . . ." Of the still rebellious whites:
"Their weapons are often new and of improved patterns; and however poor may be the individual member he never lacks for arms
or ammunition. . . . In many respects the Ku Klux Klan is an
army, organized and officered, and armed for deadly strife."[52]

Rep. Boyd Winchester (D., Ky.) set forth the contrary position,
favorably citing a letter from an ex-governor of South Carolina to
the reconstruction governor regretting the latter's "Winchester-
rifle speech" which "fiendishly proclaimed that this instrument of
death, in the hands of the negroes of South Carolina, was the most
effective means of maintaining order and quiet in the State."[53]
Calling on the governor to "disarm your militia," the letter referred to the disaster which resulted "when you organized colored
troops throughout the State, and put arms into their hands, with
powder and ball, and denied the same to the white people."[54] The
letter proceeded to cite numerous instances where the "colored
militia" murdered white people. According to Rep. Winchester, it
was the arming of blacks and disarming of whites which resulted
in white resistance. "It would seem that wherever military and
carpetbagger domination in the South has been marked by the
greatest contempt for law and right, and practiced the greatest
cruelty toward the people, Ku Klux operations have multiplied."[55]

An instance of black Republican armed resistance to agents of
the state who were in the Klan was recounted in a letter cited by
Rep. Benjamin F. Butler:

Then the Ku Klux fired on them through the window, one of the bullets striking a colored woman . . . and wounding her through the knee badly. The colored men then fired on the Ku Klux, and killed their leader or captain right there on the steps of the colored men's house. . . . There he remained until morning when he was identified, and proved to "Pat Inman," a constable and deputy sheriff. . . . [56]

By contrast, Rep. Samuel S. Cox (D., Ohio) assailed those who "arm negro militia and create a situation of terror," exclaimed that South Carolinians actually clamored for United States troops to save them from the rapacity and murder of the negro bands and their white allies," and saw the Klan as their only defense: "Is not repression the father of revolution?" The congressman compared the Klan with the French Jacobins, Italian Carbonari, and Irish Fenians.[57] Rep. John Coburn (R., Ind.) saw the situation in an opposite empirical light, deploring both state and private disarming of blacks. "How much more oppressive is the passage of a law that they shall not bear arms than the practical seizure of all arms from the hands of the colored men?"[58]

The next day Rep. Henry L. Dawes (R., Mass.) returned to a legal analysis which again asserted the incorporation thesis. Of the anti-Klan bill he argued:

The rights, privileges, and immunities of the American citizen, secured to him under the Constitution of the United States, are the subject-matter of this bill. . . .

. . . In addition to the original rights secured to him in the first article of amendments he had secured the free exercise of his religious belief, and freedom of speech and of the press. Then again he has secured to him the right to keep and bear arms in his defense. [Dawes then summarizes the remainder of the first eight amendments.] . . .

. . . And still later, sir, after the bloody sacrifice of our four years' war, we gave the most grand of all these rights, privileges, and immunities, by one single amendment to the Constitution, to four millions of American citizens. . . .

. . . [I]t is to protect and secure to him in these rights, privileges, and immunities this bill is before the House.[59]

Rep. Horatio C. Burchard (R., Ill.), while generally favoring the bill insofar as it provided against oppressive state action, rejected the interpretation by Dawes and Bingham regarding the definition of "privileges and immunities," which Burchard felt were contained only in Articles IV, V, and VI rather than I–VIII. However, Burchard still spoke in terms of "the application of their eight amendments to the States,"[60] and in any case Dawes had used the terms "*rights,* privileges and immunities." The anti-Klan bill finally was passed along partisan lines as An Act to Enforce the Provisions of the Fourteenth Amendment.[61]

E. THE CIVIL RIGHTS ACT OF 1875

After passage of the anti-Klan bill, discussion concerning arms persisted as interest developed toward what became the Civil

Rights Act of 1875, now 42 U.S.C. § 1984. A report on affairs in the South by Sen. John Scott (R., Penn.) indicated the need for further enforcement legislation: "negroes who were whipped testified that those who beat them told them they did so because they had voted the radical ticket, and in many cases made them promise that they would not do so again, and wherever they had guns took them from them."[62]

Following the introduction of the civil rights bill the debate over the meaning of the privileges and immunities clause returned. Sen. Matthew H. Carpenter (R., Wis.) cited *Cummings* v. *Missouri*,[63] a case contrasting the French legal system, which allowed deprivation of civil rights, "and among these of the right of voting, . . . of bearing arms," with the American legal system, averring that the Fourteenth Amendment prevented states from taking away the privileges of the American citizen.[64]

Sen. Allen G. Thurman (D., Ohio) argued that the "rights, privileges, and immunities of a citizen of the United States" were included in Amendments I–VIII. Reading and commenting on each of these amendments, he said of the Second: "Here is another right of a citizen of the United States, expressly declared to be his right—the right to bear arms; and this right, says the Constitution, shall not be infringed." After prodding from John A. Sherman (R., Ohio), Thurman added the Ninth Amendment to the list.[65]

The incorporationist thesis was stated succinctly by Senator Thomas M. Norwood (D., Ga.) in one of the final debates over the civil rights bill. Referring to a U.S. citizen residing in a Territory, Senator Norwood stated:

> His right to bear arms, to freedom of religious opinion, freedom of speech, and all others enumerated in the Constitution would still remain indefeasibly his, whether he remained in the Territory or removed to a State.
>
> And those and certain others are the privileges and immunities which belong to him in common with every citizen of the United States, and which no State can take away or abridge, and they are given and protected by the Constitution . . .
>
> The following are most, if not all, the privileges and immunities of a citizen of the *United States:*
>
> The right to the writ of *habeas corpus;* of peaceable assembly and of petition; . . . *to keep and bear arms* [emphasis added]; . . . from being deprived of the right to vote on account of race, color or previous condition of servitude.[66]

Arguing that the Fourteenth Amendment created no new rights but declared that "certain existing rights should not be abridged by States," the Georgia Democrat explained:

> Before its [Fourteenth Amendment] adoption any State might have established a particular religion, or restricted freedom of speech and of the press, or *the right to bear arms* [emphasis added] . . . A State could have deprived its citizens of any of the privileges and immunities contained in those eight articles, but the Federal Government could not. . .

. . . And the instant the fourteenth amendment became
a part of the Constitution, every State was at that moment
disabled from making or enforcing any law which would
deprive any citizen of a State of the benefits enjoyed by
citizens of the United States under the first eight amendments to the Federal Constitution.[67]

In sum, in the understanding of Southern Democrats and Radical
Republicans alike, the right to keep and bear arms, like other Bill
of Rights freedoms, was made applicable to the states by the Fourteenth Amendment.

The framers of the Fourteenth Amendment and of the civil
rights acts of Reconstruction, rather than predicating the right to
keep and bear arms on the needs of an organized state militia,
based it on the right of the people individually to possess arms for
protection against any oppressive force—including racist or political violence by the militia itself or by other state agents such as
sheriffs. At the same time, the militia was understood to be the
whole body of the people, including blacks. In discussion concerning the Civil Rights Act of 1875, Sen. James A Alcorn (R., Miss.)
defined the militia in these terms: "The citizens of the United
States, the Posse comitatus, or the militia if you please, and the
colored man composes part of these."[68] Every citizen, in short,
was a militiaman. With the passage of the Fourteenth Amendment,
the right and privilege individually to keep and bear arms was
protected from both state and federal infringement.[69]

REFERENCES

1. Dred Scott v. Sandford, 60 U.S. (19 How.) 393 15 L. Ed. 691 (1857).
2. 15 L. Ed. at 705 [emphasis added]. *And see id* at 719.
3. Protection of the "absolute rights of individuals" to personal security, liberty,
and private property is secured in part by "the right of bearing arms—which with
us is . . . practically enjoyed by every citizen, and is among his most valuable
privileges, since it furnishes the means of resisting as a freeman ought, the inroads
of usurpation." I Henry St. Geo. Tucker, Commentaries on the Laws of Virginia 43
(1831) (reference to U.S. Constitution). And see St. Geo. Tucker, 1 Blackstone,
Commentaries *144 n. 40 (1st ed. 1803); W. Rawle, A View of the Constitution 125-
26 (1829); 3 J. Story, Commentaries on the Constitution 746 (1833); Bliss vs. Commonwealth, 2 Litt. (Ky.) 90, 13 Am. Dec. 251 (1822); Simpson vs. State, 13 Tenn.
Reports (5 Yerg.) 356 (1833); Nunn v. State, 1 Ga. 243 (1846). Cf. State v. Buzzard, 4
Ark, 18 (1843).
4. W. Rawle, supra note 3, at 125-26, stated: The prohibition is general. No clause
in the Constitution could by any rule of construction be conceived to give to
congress a power to disarm the people. Such a flagitious attempt could be made
under some general pretence by a state legislature. But if in any blind pursuit of
inordinate power, either should attempt it, this amendment may be appealed to as a
restraint on both.
Similarly, it was stated in Nunn v. State, 1 Ga. 243, 250-51 (1846):
The language of the second amendment is broad enough to embrace both Federal
and state governments—nor is there anything in its terms which restricts its
meaning. . . . Is it not an unalienable right, which lies at the bottom of every free
government?
And see cases cited at 68 C.J. Weapons §4 n 60 (1934).
According to II J. Bishop, Criminal Law §124 (3rd ed. 1865): "Though most of the
amendments are restrictions on the general government alone, not on the States,
this one seems to be of a nature to bind both the State and National legislatures."
Approved in English v. State, 35 Tex. 473 (1872). For an analysis of U.S. Supreme
Court cases related to whether the Second and/or Fourteenth Amendments prohibit
state action which infringes on keeping and bearing arms, see S. Halbrook, The
Jurisprudence of the Second and Fourteenth Amendments, IV George Mason L.
Rev. (1981).

5. State v. Newson, 27 N.C. 203, 204 (1844); Cooper v. Savannah, 4 Ga. 72 (1848).
6. State v. Newson, 27 N.C. 203, 207 (1844). Cf. cases cited at 68 C.J. Weapons §5, n. 19, 21, 22; §8, n. 37, 40 (1934).
7. "What was the fourteenth article designed to secure? . . . [T]hat the privileges and immunities of citizens of the United States shall not be abridged or denied by the United States or by any State; defining also, what it was possible was open to some question after the Dred Scott decision, who were citizens of the United States." Sen. George F. Edmonds (R., Vt.), CONG. GLOBE, 40th Cong., 3rd. Sess., pt. 1, 1000 (Feb. 8, 1869).
8. While it "cannot turn the clock back to 1868 when the Amendment was adopted," Brown v. Board of Education of Topeka, 347 U.S. 483, 492 (1954), the Supreme Court is compelled to interpret Amendment XIV and Reconstruction legislation in accord with the Congressional intent. Lynch v. Household Finance Corp., 405 U.S. 538, 549 (1972); Monell v. Dep't. of Social Services of City of New York, 436 U.S. 658 (1978) ("fresh analyis of debate on the Civil Rights Act of 1871," id. 665, justified overruling Monroe v. Pape, 365 U.S. 167 [1961]). Cf. Fairman, Does the Fourteenth Amendment Incorporate the Bill of Rights? The Original Understanding, 2 Stanford L. Rev. 5, 44–45, 57–58, 119–20 (1949) (while contending that the Bill of Rights in general was not intended to apply to the states, cited references to the Second Amendment in congressional debates support incorporation).
Though beyond the scope of this study, the history of the prohibition of arms possession by native Americans or Indians or presents a parallel example of the use of gun control to suppress or exterminate non-white ethnic groups. While legal discrimination against blacks in respect to arms was abolished during Reconstruction, the sale of arms and ammunition to "hostile" Indians remained a prohibition. E.g., 17 stat. 457, 42nd Cong., 3rd Sess., ch. 138 (1873). See also Sioux Nation of Indians v. United States, 601 F. 2d 1571, 1166 (Ct. Cl. 1979): "Since the Army has taken from the Sioux their weapons and horses, the alternative to capitulation to the government's demands was starvation . . ." The federal government's special restrictions on selling firearms to native Americans were abolished finally in 1979. Washington Post, Jan. 6, 1979, § A, at 11, col. 1.
9. See State v. Hannibal, 51N.C. 57 (1859); State v. Harris, 51 N.C. 448 (1859); D. Hundley, Social Relations in our Southern States 361 (1860). Blacks were experienced enough in the use of arms to pay a significant, though unofficial, role as Confederate soldiers, some even as sharpshooters. H. Blackerby, Blacks in Blue and Gray 1–40 (Tusculoosa, Ala. 1979); J. Obatala, Black Confederates, Players 13 ff. (April, 1979). In Louisiana, the only state in the Union to include blacks in the militia, substantial numbers of blacks joined the rebellion furnishing their own arms. M. Berry, Negro Troops in Blue and Gray, 8 Louisiana History 165–66 (1867).
10. The Writings of Cassius Marcellus Clay 257 (H. Greeley ed. 1848).
11. DuBois, John Brown 106 (1909).
12. J. McPherson, The Negro's Civil War 72–73 (1965). While all may be fair in love and war, experiences during the conflict suggest that deprivation of one right is coupled with deprivation of others. When the secession movement began, Lincoln suspended habeas corpus and enstated the disarming of citizens and military arrests in Maryland and Missouri. In the latter state, the death penalty was enstated by union officers for those caught with arms, and after an order was issued to arm the militia by random seizures of arms, the searches provided the occasion for general looting. See 3 War of the Rebellion 466–67 (Series 1) and 13 id. at 506; R. Brownlee, Gray Ghosts of the Confederacy 37, 85, & 170 (L.S.U. 1958). The situation became so harsh for Northerners themselves that the Northern Democratic Platform of 1864 declared in its fourth resolution against the suppression of free speech and press and the denial of the right of the people to bear arms in their defense. E. Pollard, The Lost Cause 574 (1867).
13. 61 The War of the Rebellion, ser. 1, pt. 2, 1068 & 1315 (1880–1901); R. Durden, The Gray & The Black 250 (1972).
14. R. Durden, supra note 13, at 169.
15. Cong. Globe, 38th Cong., 2nd Sess., pt. 1, 171 (Jan. 9, 1865).
16. Id. 289 (Jan. 18, 1865).
17. Id., 39th Cong., 1st Sess., pt. 1, 674 (Feb. 6, 1866). But see id. at pt. 4, 3215 (June 16, 1866) (allegation by Rep. William E. Niblack (D., Ind.) that the majority of Southern blacks "either adhered from first to last to the rebellion or aided and assisted by their labor or otherwise those who did so adhere.").
18. DuBois, Black Reconstruction in America 167, 172, & 223 (New York 1962).
19. Cong. Globe, 39th Cong., 1st Sess., pt. 1, 40 (Dec. 13, 1865).
20. Civil Rights Act, 14 Stat. 27 (1866). A portion of this act survives as 42 U.S.C. § 1982: "All citizens of the United States shall have the same right, in every State

and Territory as is enjoyed by white citizens thereof to inherit, purchase, lease, sell, hold, and convey real and personal property."

21. Cong. Globe, 39th Cong., 1st Sess., pt. 1, 474 (Jan. 29, 1866).
22. *Id.* 478.
23. *Id.* 517 (Jan. 30, 1866).
24. *Id.* 651 (Feb. 5, 1866).
25. *Id.* 941 (Feb. 20, 1866).
26. *Id.*
27. *Id.*, pt. 2, 1266 (Mr. 8, 1866).
28. *Id.* 1629 (Mar. 24, 1866).
29. *Id.* 3
30. *Id.* 1838 (Ap. 7, 1866).
31. *Id.*
32. *Id.*
33. *Id.*
34. *Id.* 1839. Ironically, Clarke's home state, Kansas, adopted measures to prohibit former Confederates from possessing arms. Kennett & Anderson at 154.
35. Cong. Globe, 39th Cong., 1st Sess., pt. 3, 2765 (May 23, 1866).
36. *Id.* 2766. Italics added.
37. Id., pt. 4, 3210 (June 16, 1866).
38. Id., 2nd Sess., pt. 1, 107 (Dec. 13, 1866).
39. Id., 40th Cong., 2nd Sess. pt. 3, 2198 (Mar. 28, 1868).
40. Id.
41. 1464 H.R. REP. No. 37, 41st Cong., 3rd Sess. 3 (Feb. 20, 1871).
42. Cong. Globe, 42nd Cong., 1st Sess., pt. 1, 174 (Mar. 20, 1871). Introduced as "an act to protect loyal and peaceable citizens in the south . . .", H.R. No. 189.
43. H.R. Rep. No. 37, supra note 26, at 7-8.
44. Cong. Globe, 42nd Cong., 1st Sess., pt. 1, 154 (Mar. 18, 1871).
45. Id. 196 (Mr. 21, 1871).
46. Id. 321 (Mr. 28, 1871).
47. Id., pt. 2, Appendix, 68. Passed as the Enforcement Act, 17 Stat. 13 (1871), § 1 survives as 42 U.S.C. § 1983: "Every person who, under color of any statute, ordinance, regulation, custom, or usage, of any State or Territory, subjects, or causes to be subjected, any citizen of the United States or other person within the jurisdiction thereof to the deprivation of any rights, privileges, or immunities secured by the Constitution and laws, shall be liable to the party injured in an action at law, suit in equity, or other proper proceedings for redress." The action for conspiracy to deprive persons of rights or privileges under 42 U.S.C. § 1985 derives from the same act.
48. Cong. Globe, 42nd Cong., 1st Sess., pt. 1, 337 (Mr. 29, 1871).
49. *Id.* 339.
50. Id. 385 (Ap. 1, 1871).
51. Id., pt. 2, Appendix, 84 (Mr. 31, 1871).
52. Id., pt. 1, 413 (Ap. 3, 1871).
53. Id. 422 (Ap. 3, 1871).
54. Id.
55. Id. Nathan Bedford Forrest told Congressional investigators in 1871 that the Klan originated in Tennessee for self defense against the militia of Governor William G. Brownlow. N. Burger and J. Bettersworth, South of Appomattox 129, 132, and 137 (1959). Still, two years before, Forrest denounced Klan lawlessness because "the order was being used . . . to disarm harmless negroes having no thought of insurrectionary movements, and to whip both whites and blacks." C. Bowers, THE TRAGIC ERA 311 (1929). The outrages in turn allegedly furnished "a plausible pretext for the organization of State militias to serve the purposes of Radical politics." C. Bowers at 311. Carpetbagger controlled militias were deeply involved in political violence to influence elections, and were blamed for infringing on their opponents' constitutional rights to free speech and to keep and bear arms, among numerous other abuses. E.g., C. Bowers at 439 and passim; O. Singletary, Negro Militia and Reconstruction 35-41, 74-75 (1963).
56. Cong. Globe, 42nd Cong., 1st Sess., pt. 1, 445 (Ap. 4, 1871).
57. Id. 453.
58. Id. 459.
59. *Id.* 475-76 (Ap. 5, 1871). [Emphasis added].
60. Id., 2, Appendix, 314.
61. 17 Stat. 13, 42nd Cong., 1st Sess., ch. 22 (1871).
62. 1484 S. Rep. No. 41, 42nd Cong., 2nd Sess., pt. 1, 35 (Feb. 19, 1872).
63. *Cummings* v. *Missouri*, 71 U.S. 277, 321 (1866).
64. Cong. Globe, 42nd Cong., 2nd Sess., pt. 1, 762 (Feb. 1, 1872).

65. *Id.*, pt. 6, Appendix, 25–26 (Feb. 6, 1872). On Amendment IX as a source of an individual right to keep and bear arms, see Caplan, *Restoring the Balance: The Second Amendment Revisited,* 5 Fordham Urban L. J. 31, 49–50 (1976). See also 2 Cong. Rec. 43rd Cong., 1st Sess., pt. 1, 384–385 (Jan. 5, 1874) (statement by Rep. Robert Q. Mills (D., Tex.) that Amendment XIV adopts Bill of Rights privileges).

66. Cong. Rec., 43rd Cong., 1st Sess., pt. 6, Appendix, 241–242 (May 4, 1874). Emphasis added.

67. *Id.* 242. Italic added.

68. *Id.* (May 22, 1874). The antebellum exclusion of blacks from the armed people as militia was commented on by Sen. George Vickers (D., Md.), who recalled a 1792 law passed by Congress: "That every free able-bodied white male citizen shall be enrolled in the militia." Vickers added that as late as 1855 New Hampshire "confined the enrollment of militia to free white citizens." Cong. Globe, 41st Cong., 2nd Sess., pt. 2, 1558–59 (Feb. 25, 1870). Exclusion of a right to bear arms by blacks was further evidence of their lack of status as citizens. See 1464 H.R. Rep. No. 22, 41st Cong., 3rd Sess. 7 (Feb. 1, 1871), citing Cooper V. Savannah, 4 Ga. 72 (1848) (not entitled to bear arms or vote).

69. While unrelated to the debates over the Fourteenth Amendment, congressional deliberation over whether the federal government could abolish militias in the Southern states also gave rise to exposition of the Second Amendment. In support of repeal of a statute prohibiting the Southern militias, Sen. Charles R. Buckalew (D., Penn.) pointed out that the U.S. President favored repeal of the statute because at all times, both when it was placed upon the statute-book and every moment since, it was and is in his judgment a violation of the Constitution of the United States. One of the amendments to our fundamental law expressly provides that "the right of the people to keep and bear arms shall not be infringed"—of course by this Government; and it gives the reason that a well-regulated militia in the several divisions of the country is necessary for the protection and for the interests of the people. Cong. Globe, 40th Cong., 3rd Sess., pt. 1, 83–84.

George F. Edmunds (R., Vt.) worried that repeal of the statute "will authorize anybody and everybody in the State of Texas, under what they call its ancient militia laws . . . to organize a militia hostile to the Government," id. at 81, and thus advocated "a selected militia" chosen by State and federal governments. Id. In contrast, Garrett Davis (D. Ky.) stated: "Wherever a State organizes a government it has of its own inherent right and power authority to organize a militia for it. Congress . . . has no right to prohibit that State from the organization of its militia." *Id.* at 84. Willard Warner (R., Ala.) stressed the first clause of the Second Amendment to form militias independent of federal control: we have the right now, being restored to our full relations to the Federal Government, to organize a militia of our own, and that we could have done so at any time in the past, this law to the contrary notwithstanding. Article two of the amendments of the Constitution provides that—

"A well regulated militia being necessary to the security of a free State, the right of the people to keep and bear arms shall not be infringed." *Id.* at 85.

The prohibitionary statute was repealed, *id.* at 86. *Cf.* Houston v. Moore, 18 U.S. 1, 16–17 (1820).

Thus, while debates over the militia question suggested that the Second Amendment precluded federal legislation which prohibited the states or the people from forming militias, debates over the Fourteenth Amendment demonstrate the intent of Congress to preclude state militias or other state action from infringing on the individual right to keep and bear arms.

The Second Amendment: Toward an Afro-Americanist Reconsideration*

ROBERT J. COTTROL**
AND RAYMOND T. DIAMOND***

TABLE OF CONTENTS

* © Copyright Robert J. Cottrol and Raymond T. Diamond, 1991. This article was delivered as a paper at the 1990 annual meeting of the American Society for Legal History, at the Harvard Legal History Forum, at a faculty seminar at Northwestern University Law School, at the 1991 joint annual meeting of the Law and Society Association and the International Law and Society Association, and at the 1991 annual meeting of the American Political Science Association. The authors would like to acknowledge the helpful comments made in those forums. The authors would like to acknowledge the research assistance of Jan McNitt, Boston College Law School, 1991; Richard J. Fraher, Rutgers (Camden) School of Law, 1993; Roderick C. Sanchez, Rutgers (Camden) School of Law, 1992; Adrienne I. Logan, Tulane University School of Law, 1992; and Willie E. Shepard, Tulane University School of Law, 1992. This paper has benefitted from the criticism and helpful comments of Akhil R. Amar, Michael Les Benedict, Barbara Black, Maxwell Bloomfield, Ruth Colker, Michael Curtis, Robert Dowlut, Kermit Hall, Natalie Hull, Don B. Kates, Jr., Barbara K. Kopytoff, Sanford Levinson, Joyce Lee Malcolm, John Stick, and Robert F. Williams. The authors would also like to acknowledge summer research grants from Boston College Law School, Rutgers (Camden) School of Law, and Tulane University School of Law which contributed to the writing of this paper.
** Associate Professor, Rutgers (Camden) School of Law. A.B. 1971, Ph.D. 1978, Yale University; J.D. 1984, Georgetown University Law Center.
*** Associate Professor, Tulane University School of Law. A.B. 1973, Yale University; J.D. 1977, Yale Law School.

> It would give to persons of the negro race, who were recognized as citizens
> in any one State of the Union, the right to enter every other State whenever
> they pleased, . . . and it would give them the full liberty of speech in public
> and in private upon all subjects upon which its own citizens might speak; to
> hold public meetings upon political affairs, *and to keep and carry arms*
> *wherever they went.*[1]

INTRODUCTION

The often strident debate over the Second Amendment[2] is like few others
in American constitutional discourse and historiography. It is a constitutional debate that has taken place largely in the absence of Supreme Court
opinion.[3] It is a historical controversy where the framers' intentions have

---

1. Dred Scott v. Sanford, 60 U.S. (19 How.) 393, 417 (1857) (emphasis added).

2. "A well regulated Militia, being necessary to the security of a free State, the right of the people
to keep and bear Arms, shall not be infringed." U.S. CONST. amend. II.

3. The Supreme Court has directly ruled on Second Amendment claims in only four cases. *See*
United States v. Miller, 307 U.S. 174 (1939); Miller v. Texas, 153 U.S. 535 (1894); Presser v. Illinois, 116 U.S. 252 (1886); United States v. Cruikshank, 92 U.S. 542 (1876). Proponents of the
collective rights theory have frequently cited these cases as supportive of their views. It is more
accurate to describe the first three cases as having recognized the individual right, but also as having
construed the Second Amendment as a bar to federal, but not state or private, infringement of the
right. *See infra* Part III. *United States v. Miller* limited the Second Amendment's protection to
weapons useful for militia duty. *See infra* Part IV. Since then, a number of lower federal courts
have heard Second Amendment claims, often dismissing them on grounds that the Amendment has
not been incorporated into the Fourteenth Amendment, which would make it binding on the states.
Other courts have dismissed the claims by employing the collective rights theory. Almost all of
these cases involved persons involved in criminal activity who were also convicted of firearms
charges and thus are not really a good test of the extent to which the Second Amendment protects
the rights of the public at large. *See, e.g.,* United States v. Three Winchester 30-30 Caliber Lever
Action Carbines, 504 F.2d 1288 (7th Cir. 1974) (statute prohibiting possession of firearms by previously convicted felon does not infringe upon Second Amendment). In a recent case in which a
federal court sustained a general prohibition against handgun ownership, the Supreme Court refused to consider the case on appeal. *See* Quilici v. Village of Morton Grove, 695 F.2d 261 (7th Cir.
1982), *cert. denied,* 464 U.S. 863 (1983).

If the federal jurisprudence concerning the Second Amendment is somewhat thin, it should be
noted that there is extensive case law concerning analogous provisions in state bills of rights. Indeed it is likely, should the Supreme Court ever seriously consider the question, that it might borrow Second Amendment doctrine from the state courts. For some recent constructions of state
right to keep and bear arms provisions see, *e.g.,* Hoskins v. State, 449 So.2d 1269 (Ala. Crim. App.
1984) (statute prohibiting a person convicted of committing a crime of violence from owning or
possessing a pistol does not deny right to keep and bear arms); Rabbitt v. Leonard, 413 A.2d 489
(Conn. Super. Ct. 1979) (statute permitting revocation of pistol permit for cause and providing
notice of revocation and opportunity for de novo postrevocation hearing does not violate citizen's

best been gleaned from indirect rather than direct evidence.[4] It is a scholarly debate that members of the academy have been until recently somewhat reluctant to join,[5] leaving the field to independent scholars primarily concerned with the modern gun control controversy.[6] In short, the Second Amendment

---

right to bear arms); State v Friel, 508 A.2d 123 (Me. 1986) (statue prohibiting possession of a firearm by a convicted felon does not violate constitutional right to keep and bear arms); People v. Smelter, 437 N.W.2d 341 (Mich. Ct. App. 1989) (statute prohibiting possession of stun guns does not impermissibly infringe upon right to keep and bear arms); State v. Vlacil, 645 P.2d 677 (Utah 1982) (statute making it a Class A misdemeanor for any noncitizen to own or possess a dangerous weapon is not unconstitutional). For a historical discussion of state right to keep and bear arms provisions, see generally STEPHEN P. HALBROOK, A RIGHT TO BEAR ARMS: STATE AND FEDERAL BILLS OF RIGHTS AND CONSTITUTIONAL GUARANTEES (1989).

4. The debates in the House of Representatives over what became the Second Amendment (it was originally proposed as the Fourth Amendment) centered on a clause excepting conscientious objectors from militia duty. The original text of the Amendment read: "A well regulated militia, composed of the body of the people, being the best security of a free state, the right of the people to keep and bear arms shall not be infringed; but no person religiously scrupulous shall be compelled to bear arms." THE FOUNDERS' CONSTITUTION 210 (Phillip B. Kurland & Ralph Lerner eds., 1987). The House debate, focusing on the religious exemption, sheds little light on the individual versus collective rights debate, although the phrase "body of the people" used to describe the militia does suggest the idea of a militia of the whole. Still, the best evidence of the framers' intentions in this matter comes from the surrounding history and the comments of the constitutional framers generally with respect to the composition of the militia. See infra Part I.

5. See Sanford Levinson, The Embarrassing Second Amendment, 99 YALE L.J. 637, 639-42 (1989) (discussing the reluctance of most constitutional scholars to treat the Second Amendment as a subject worthy of serious scholarly or pedagogical consideration). Recently, however, one scholar has examined the Second Amendment within the context of the Bill of Rights as a whole. See Akhil Amar, The Bill of Rights as a Constitution, 100 YALE L.J. 1131 (1991). In Amar's view, the Bill of Rights was designed with both populist and collective concerns in mind. It was designed to protect both the right of the people and to prevent potential tyranny from an overreaching federal government. Amar sees the purpose of the Second Amendment as preventing Congress from disarming freemen, so that the populace could resist tyranny imposed by a standing army. Id. at 1162-73.

6. See, e.g., David I. Caplan, Restoring the Balance: The Second Amendment Revisited, 5 FORDHAM URB. L.J. 31 (1976) (current efforts to limit firearm possession undermine the Second Amendment's twin goals of individual and collective defense); Robert Dowlut, Federal and State Constitutional Guarantees to Arms, 15 U. DAYTON L. REV. 59 (1989) (laws seeking to disarm the people violate the Second Amendment); Robert Dowlut, The Right to Arms: Does the Constitution or the Predilection of Judges Reign?, 36 OKLA. L. REV. 65 (1983) (interpretation of the Second Amendment is controlled by the framers' intent to guarantee the individual right to keep and bear arms rather than a more narrow judicial interpretation); Keith A. Ehrman & Dennis A. Henigan, The Second Amendment in the Twentieth Century: Have You Seen Your Militia Lately?, 15 U. DAYTON L. REV. 5 (1989) (Second Amendment's historical origins erect no real barrier to federal or state laws affecting handguns); Richard E. Gardiner, To Preserve Liberty—A Look at the Right to Keep and Bear Arms, 10 N. KY. L. REV. 63 (1982) (advocates of gun control have twisted the original and plain meaning of the Second Amendment); Alan M. Gottlieb, Gun Ownership: A Constitutional Right, 10 N. KY. L. REV. 113 (1982) (modern antipathy to firearms has influenced interpretation of the Second Amendment as a collective right); David T. Hardy, The Second Amendment and the Historiography of the Bill of Rights, 4 J.L. & POL. 1 (1987) (the Second Amendment has a dual purpose stemming from the merger of the militia and the right to bear arms provisions); Maynard H. Jackson, Jr., Handgun Control: Constitutional and Critically Needed, 8 N.C. CENT. L.J. 189 (1977) (Second Amendment is central to any discussion of the legal merits of gun control); Nelson Lund, The Second Amendment, Political Liberty and the Right to Self-Preservation, 39 ALA.

is an arena of constitutional jurisprudence that still awaits its philosopher.

The debate over the Second Amendment is ultimately part of the larger debate over gun control, a debate about the extent to which the Amendment was either meant to be or should be interpreted as limiting the ability of government to prohibit or limit private ownership of firearms. Waged in the popular press,[7] in the halls of Congress,[8] and increasingly in historical and

---

L. REV. 103 (1987) (suggesting a Second Amendment jurisprudence consistent with modern treatment of the Bill of Rights such that handgun regulation be reasonably tailored to public safety); James A. McClure, *Firearms and Federalism*, 7 IDAHO L. REV. 197 (1970) (Second Amendment precludes federal interference but leaves to debate the issue of state regulation of handguns); Robert J. Riley, *Shooting to Kill the Handgun: Time to Martyr Another American "Hero,"* 51 J. URB. L. 491 (1974) (construing the Second Amendment as a surpassable barrier to handgun control by finding the handgun a weapon of marginal military utility); Jonathan A. Weiss, *A Reply to Advocates of Gun Control Law*, 52 J. URB. L. 577 (1974) (placing the Second Amendment in context of the Bill of Rights, provides an inviolable right to bear arms and an absolute bar to government restriction).

Two advocates of the individual rights theory who are outside the academy, but have nonetheless been quite instrumental in influencing the constitutional debate among law teachers and historians, are Donald B. Kates, Jr. and Stephen P. Halbrook. *See, e.g.,* Donald B. Kates, Jr., *Handgun Prohibition and the Original Meaning of the Second Amendment*, 82 MICH. L. REV. 204 (1983) (Second Amendment right to bear arms, applicable against both federal and state government, does not foreclose, but limits, gun control options); Donald B. Kates, Jr., *The Second Amendment: A Dialogue*, 49 LAW & CONTEMP. PROBS. 143 (1986) (Second Amendment substantially limits the arbitrariness of granting gun permits); Steven. P. Halbrook, THAT EVERY MAN BE ARMED: THE EVOLUTION OF A CONSTITUTIONAL RIGHT (1984) [hereinafter HALBROOK, THAT EVERY MAN BE ARMED] (the right of citizens to keep and bear arms has deep historical roots and overly restrictive interpretations of the Second Amendment are associated with reactionary concepts including elitism, militarism, and racism); Steven P. Halbrook, *The Jurisprudence of the Second and Fourteenth Amendments*, 4 GEO. MASON U. L. REV. 1 (1981) (the fundamental character of the Second Amendment and the increasingly restrictive forms of gun control legislation necessitate Supreme Court precedent on the status of the Amendment's applicability to the states); Stephen P. Halbrook, *What the Framers Intended: A Linguistic Analysis of the Right to "Bear Arms,"* 49 LAW & CONTEMP. PROBS. 151 (1986) (Second Amendment right to bear arms is incompatible with the suggestion of no right to bear arms without state or federal permission).

7. *See, e.g.,* Daniel Abrams, *What 'Right to Bear Arms'?*, N.Y. TIMES, July 20, 1989, at A23; Robert J. Cottrol, *It's Time to Enforce the Second Amendment*, PLAIN DEALER (Cleveland), Feb. 17, 1990, at 5B; Ervin N. Griswold, *Phantom Second Amendment Rights*, WASH. POST, Nov. 4, 1990, at C7; Sue Wimmershoff-Caplan, *The Founders and the AK-47*, WASH. POST, July 6, 1989, at A18. Even former Chief Justice Warren Burger has used this arena to opine on the subject. *See* Warren Burger, *The Right to Keep and Bear Arms*, PARADE MAG., Jan. 14, 1990, at 4.

For one interesting example of a writer who (reluctantly) supports the individual rights interpretation of the Second Amendment and who, as a member of the gun control group Handgun Control, Inc., is also a strong advocate of stricter gun control, see columnist Michael Kinsley, *Slicing Up the Second Amendment*, WASH. POST, Feb. 8, 1990, at A25. More recently, conservative columnist George Will, also an advocate of stricter gun control, has stated that "The National Rifle Association is perhaps correct and certainly plausible in its 'strong' reading of the Second Amendment protection for private gun ownership." Will argues for repeal of the Second Amendment on the grounds that the right is not as important as it was 200 years ago.

Will also makes the interesting observation that "The subject of gun control reveals a role reversal between liberals and conservatives that makes both sides seem tendentious. Liberals who usually argue that constitutional rights (of criminal defendants, for example) must be respected regardless of inconvenient social consequences, say that the Second Amendment right is too costly

legal journals,[9] two dominant interpretations have emerged. Advocates of stricter gun controls have tended to stress the Amendment's Militia Clause, arguing that the purpose of the Amendment was to ensure that state militias would be maintained against potential federal encroachment. This argument, embodying the collective rights theory, sees the framers' primary, indeed sole, concern as one with the concentration of military power in the hands of the federal government, and the corresponding need to ensure a decentralized military establishment largely under state control.[10]

Opponents of stricter gun controls have tended to stress the Amendment's second clause, arguing that the framers intended a militia of the whole—or at least the entire able-bodied white male—population, expected to perform its duties with privately owned weapons.[11] Advocates of this view also frequently urge that the Militia Clause should be read as an amplifying, rather than a qualifying, clause. They argue that, while maintaining a "well-regulated militia"[12] was the predominate reason for including the Second Amendment in the Bill of Rights, it should not be viewed as the sole or

---

to honor. Conservatives who frequently favor applying cost-benefit analysis to constitutional construction (of defendants' rights, for example) advocate an absolutist construction of the Second Amendment." *See* George Will, *Oh That Annoying Second Amendment: It Shows No Signs of Going Away*, PHILADELPHIA INQUIRER, March 22, 1991.

Although the Second Amendment and gun control debates involve far more than a simple liberal/conservative dichotomy, there are numerous exceptions on both sides; Will's point is well taken. If we accept the conventional view that the National Rifle Association is a predominantly conservative organization and that advocates of gun control tend to be politically liberal, we can see rather interesting role reversals. For example, the NRA has attacked firearms bans in public housing, bans which mainly affect people who are poor and black, while liberal groups have generally remained silent on the issue.

8. *See* THE RIGHT TO KEEP AND BEAR ARMS: REPORT OF THE SUBCOMM. ON THE CONSTITUTION OF THE COMM. ON THE JUDICIARY, S. REP NO. 522, 97th Cong., 2d Sess. 3 (1982) [hereinafter SUBCOMMITTEE REPORT].

9. *See id.; see also* Lawrence Delbert Cress & Robert E. Stalhope, *The Second Amendment and the Right to Bear Arms: An Exchange*, 71 J. AM. HIST. 587 (1984) (debate whether correct interpretation of Second Amendment rests on rights to bear arms or communal prerogatives implied in Militia Clause); Joyce Lee Malcolm, *The Right of the People to Keep and Bear Arms: The Common Law Tradition*, 10 HASTINGS CONST. L.Q. 285 (1983), *reprinted in* FIREARMS AND VIOLENCE: ISSUES OF PUBLIC POLICY 391-95 (Donald B. Kates, Jr. ed. 1984) (proper reading of Second Amendment extends to every citizen right to bear arms for personal defense); Robert E. Shalhope, *The Ideological Origins of the Second Amendment*, 69 J. AM. HIST. 599 (1982) (armed citizen and militia existed as distinct, yet interrelated, elements within American republican thought).

10. *See, e.g.,* Jackson, *supra* note 6, at 194 (the purpose of the Second Amendment was to maintain the militia, not to provide an individual right to bear arms); Roy G. Weatherup, *Standing Armies and Armed Citizens: An Analysis of the Second Amendment*, 2 HASTINGS CONST. L.Q. 961, 963, 995, 1000 (1975) (Second Amendment was designed solely to protect the states against the federal government, using a historical analysis of the relationship between citizens and their sovereign as evidence).

11. *See, e.g.,* Halbrook, THAT EVERY MAN BE ARMED, *supra* note 6, at 55-87; Kates, *Handgun Prohibition and the Original Meaning of the Second Amendment, supra* note 6, at 214-18, 273.

12. U.S. CONST. amend. II.

limiting reason. They argue that the framers also contemplated a right to individual and community protection.[13] This view embodies the individual rights theory.

This debate has raised often profound questions, but questions generally treated hastily, if at all, by the community of constitutional scholars.[14] For example, if one accepts the collective rights view of the Amendment, serious questions arise concerning whether the federal government's integration of the National Guard into the Army and, later, the Air Force have not in all but name destroyed the very institutional independence of the militia that is at the heart of what the collective rights theorists see as the framers' intentions.[15] Even the gun control debate is not completely resolved by an acceptance of the collective rights theory. If the Second Amendment was designed to ensure the existence of somewhat independent state militias immune from federal encroachment, then the question arises to what extent states are free to define militia membership. Could a state include as members of its militia all adult citizens, thus permitting them an exemption from federal firearms restrictions? If, instead, the federal government has plenary power to define militia membership and chooses to confine such membership to the federally controlled National Guard, does the Second Amendment become a dead letter under the collective rights theory?

If the collective rights theory raises difficult questions, the individual rights theory raises perhaps even more difficult, and perhaps more interesting ones. Some of these questions are obvious and frequently asked, such as where to draw the line between an individual's right to possess arms and the corollary right to self-defense on the one hand, and the community's interest in public safety and crime control on the other. Other questions are more elusive, more difficult to pose as well as to answer. At the heart of the individual rights view is the contention that the framers of the Second Amendment intended to protect the right to bear arms for two related purposes. The first of these was to ensure popular participation in the security of the community, an outgrowth of the English and early American reliance on posses and militias made up of the general citizenry to provide police and military forces.[16] The second purpose was to ensure an armed citizenry in order to prevent potential tyranny by a government empowered and perhaps emboldened by a monopoly of force.[17]

---

13. *See, e.g.,* Kates, *Handgun Prohibition and the Original Meaning of the Second Amendment, supra* note 6.

14. *See supra* note 5.

15. *See* Perpich v. Department of Defense, 110 S. Ct. 2418, 2422-26 (1990) (discussing the history of legislation governing the militia and the National Guard, and Congress's plenary authority over the National Guard).

16. *See* Malcolm, *supra* note 9, at 290-95.

17. *See* Stephen Halbrook's exploration of that idea within the context of classical political phi-

The second argument, that an armed populace might serve as a basis for resistance to tyranny, raises questions of its own. The framers had firsthand experience with such a phenomenon, but they lived in an age when the weapon likely to be found in private hands, the single shot musket or pistol, did not differ considerably from its military counterpart. Although the armies of the day possessed heavier weapons rarely found in private hands, battles were fought predominately by infantry or cavalry with weapons not considerably different from those employed by private citizens for personal protection or hunting.[18] Battles in which privately armed citizens vanquished regular troops, or at least gave "a good account of themselves," were not only conceivable—they happened.[19]

Modern warfare has, of course, introduced an array of weapons that no government is likely to permit ownership by the public at large[20] and that few advocates of the individual rights view would claim as part of the public domain.[21] The balance of power has shifted considerably and largely to the side of governments and their standing armies. For individual rights theorists, this shift immediately raises the question of whether, given the tremendous changes that have occurred in weapons technology, the framers' presumed intention of enabling the population to resist tyranny remains viable in the modern world.[22] Although partly a question of military tactics,

---

losophy in THAT EVERY MAN BE ARMED, *supra* note 6, at 7-35; *see also* Gardiner, *supra* note 6, at 73-82 (the history of the Second Amendment indicates that one of its purposes was to ensure the existence of an armed citizenry as a defense against domestic tyranny); Lund, *supra* note 6, at 111-16 (Second Amendment protects an individual's right to bear arms in order to secure his political freedom); Shalhope, *supra* note 9, at 610-13 (framers of the Second Amendment, motivated by their distrust of government, intended to protect the right of individuals to bear arms).

18. The American civilian of the mid-18th century was typically armed with the "Pennsylvania" rifle, later to be known as the "Kentucky" rifle. See Daniel Boorstin's discussion of the relative merits of the Pennsylvania Rifle and the muskets that British soldiers were equipped with in DANIEL J. BOORSTIN, THE AMERICANS: THE COLONIAL EXPERIENCE 350-51 (1958).

19. For one account of the battles of Lexington and Concord, see DAVID HAWKE, THE COLONIAL EXPERIENCE 573-78 (1966).

20. It should not be necessary to detail such obvious examples as stinger missiles and nuclear weapons, but even more ordinary military weapons are also unlikely to be permitted to the public at large. For example, the U.S. Army expects every soldier, regardless of military specialty, to be proficient with the M203 grenade launcher (a shoulder-fired light mortar capable of firing a 40 millimeter high explosive round 400 meters), the M72A2 light antitank weapon (LAW) (a hand-held disposable antitank weapon capable of penetrating an armored vehicle at 300 meters), the M67 fragmentation grenade, and the M18A1 Claymore antipersonnel mine. See DEPARTMENT OF THE ARMY, SOLDIER'S MANUAL OF COMMON TASKS: SKILL LEVEL 1 (1985).

21. For one of the better efforts to reconcile modern weaponry with the type of weapons the framers intended to protect, see Kates, *Handgun Prohibition and the Original Meaning of the Second Amendment, supra* note 6, at 204, 261.

22. We are putting aside for the moment the question of the utility or potential utility of an armed population as a useful auxiliary to national or local governments in maintaining either national or community security. It should be noted that during the Second World War, when the National Guard had been mobilized into the Army, impromptu home defense forces—some organized by state governments, some privately organized—patrolled beach areas and likely sabotage

and thus beyond the scope of this discussion,[23] it is also a constitutional ques-

sights. The individuals who performed this service were usually equipped with their own weapons. And while this American version of "Dad's Army" encountered no significant enemy activity—doubtless to the relief of all concerned, particularly the participants—the utility of these patrols should be noted. If such patrols were necessary, and some undoubtedly were, from the military point of view, it was probably better to have civilian auxiliaries performing this function, freeing regular military units for more pressing duties. *See id.* at 272 n.284. It should also be noted that, immediately after the attack on Pearl Harbor, the Hawaiian territorial governor ordered citizens to report with their own firearms for defense of the Islands in anticipation of Japanese invasion. Ironically, given the later treatment of Japanese Americans on the mainland, a good percentage of the men who made up the citizens' home guard in Hawaii were of Japanese descent. *See id.*

In light of our later discussion of whether or not, given the racial restriction in the Uniform Militia Act of 1792, free Negroes were considered part of the militia, *see infra* Part I.C.2, it should be noted that many of the individuals who served in these home guard organizations probably did not meet the statutory definition of militia members. By statute, membership in the militia is defined as men from 18-45. Most men in that age group were in the armed forces during the Second World War so that those performing home guard duties were probably older and younger than the statutory age limits. *See* Kates, *Handgun Prohibition and the Original Meaning of the Second Amendment, supra* note 6, at 272 n. 284 (research indicates that men between the ages of 16 and 65 served in home guard units). It is also probable that a fair number of women performed those tasks. For our purposes, what is interesting about this history is that it indicates that militia membership is even broader than the statutory definition. Perhaps the best way of viewing the issue is to regard statutory militia provisions as defining those who may be compelled to perform militia service, but to realize that the whole population might be permitted to volunteer for militia service.

23. Despite modern technological advances, the impotence of privately-armed civilians against organized armies is by no means obvious. Afghan guerrillas, to cite a recent example, were quite successful in resisting the Soviet Army largely with small arms. Harry Summers, retired Army Colonel and Professor at the Army War College, indicated in a recent column that he believed an armed population could resist a tyrannical government or at least do so better than an unarmed one. *See* Harry Summers, *Gun Collecting and Lithuania,* WASH. TIMES, Mar. 29, 1990, at F4 (public should protect its right to bear arms as a protection against government).

There are at least three ways to approach the question of an armed population resisting the government. The first is to look at what happens when actual armed conflict breaks out between a nation's military forces and the population or a segment of the population. Although modern technology weights the odds heavily in the government's favor, other considerations, including whether or not military forces are overextended, the skill of the population in general with arms (which might be influenced by the number of military veterans in the population or the number of people who regularly practice with firearms), the terrain, and the morale of military forces called upon to suppress the population, might tend to redress the technological imbalance.

The second way of viewing this question is to look at it as a question of deterrence. From this perspective, one might argue that, even if a government would ultimately win a confrontation with an armed population, the cost to the government is higher. It will endure substantially larger casualties and may have to endure large scale destruction of economically valuable infrastructure in order to achieve its objectives. This higher cost might cause a government to seek compromise, or cause a reluctance on the part of many in the military to participate, even if ultimate victory was assured. In the Soviet Union, press reports indicated great resistance on the part of citizens to sending reservists to the Azerbaijan region, in part because the population was armed and willing to resist. *See* Bill Keller, *Gorbachev Issues Emergency Decree Over Azerbaijan,* N.Y. TIMES, Jan. 16, 1990, at A1 (Azerbaijani leader threatens armed resistance against military); Bill Keller, *Moscow Dispatches 11,000 Troops to Azerbaijan,* N.Y. TIMES, Jan. 17, 1990, at A1 (Gorbachev hesitated in sending troops partly from fear of wide-scale popular resistance); Bill Keller, *Troops Seek to Calm Azerbaijan: Soviets Debate Cause of Violence,* N.Y. TIMES, Jan. 18, 1990, at A1 (one reason for hesitation before sending troops was fear of popular disapproval of sending troops to dangerous

tion. If private ownership of firearms is constitutionally protected, should this right be protected with the original military and political purposes in mind, or should the protection of firearms now be viewed as protecting only those weapons used for personal protection or recreation?[24] Or, given that all firearms are potentially multi-purpose, and that all firearms potentially may be used for military, recreational, or personal defense as well as for criminal purposes, what effect should legislatures and courts give to the framers' original military rationale? Where should the proper lines be drawn with respect to modern firearms, all of which employ technologies largely unimagined by the framers?[25]

Societal, as well as technological, changes raise questions for advocates of the individual rights view of the Second Amendment. In the eighteenth century, the chief vehicle for law enforcement was the *posse comitatus,* and the major American military force was the militia of the whole. While these institutions are still recognized by modern law,[26] they lie dormant in late twentieth-century America. Professional police forces and a standing mili-

---

area); Esther B. Fein, *Gorbachev is Backed on Azerbaijan Combat,* N.Y. TIMES, Jan. 18, 1990, at A8 (Gorbachev criticized in the past for sending troops to control civil unrest); Bill Keller, *Soviet Troops Bogged Down by Azerbaijanis Blockades of Railroads and Airfields,* N.Y. TIMES, Jan. 19, 1990, at A1 (many young Soviets not eager to be mobilized); Frances X. Clines, *Soviet Force Said to Battle With Azerbaijani Militants: Call Up of Reserves Halted,* N.Y. TIMES, Jan. 20, 1990, at A1 (Moscow ends mobilization of reservists after wide protests); Bill Keller, *Cry of Won't Give Up My Son! And Soviets End the Call-Up,* N.Y. TIMES, Jan. 20, 1990, at A6 (same).

The third consideration is the one most relevant to the Afro-American experience. Governmental oppression can occur when the state actively oppresses the population or a segment of the population. It can also occur when the state displays an active indifference to the denial of one segment of the population's rights by another. This occurred most vividly for blacks during the Jim Crow era. *See infra* Part IV.

24. The latter appears to be the view taken by former Chief Justice Burger. *See* Burger, *supra* note 7, at 4.

25. In the 18th century, when the Second Amendment was adopted, firearms were single shot devices that were reloaded very slowly. Firearms were loaded by pouring black gunpowder down the muzzle of the firearm, followed by a separate bullet (usually a lead ball); the load was then rammed down with a ramrod. By way of contrast, modern firearms are usually loaded with self-contained cartridges—cartridges where the bullet and the powder are contained in one single capsule. Almost all modern firearms, with the exception of a few firearms designed almost exclusively for target shooting or training children in the use of firearms, are repeaters: they can fire more than one bullet before the shooter has to reload. Among the types of repeating firearms that exist today are revolvers (pistols with between five and nine rotating cylinders), manually operated rifles and shotguns, firearms that require the operation of a lever or bolt between pulls of the trigger in order to make a new round of ammunition ready to fire, semiautomatic firearms (pistols, rifles, and shotguns capable of firing a new round with each pull of the trigger), and automatic firearms (weapons that will fire a new round as long as the shooter depresses the trigger). These new developments make all modern firearms much more rapid fire than those employed in the 18th century. For books that illustrate the history of firearms technology, see ROBERT HELD, THE AGE OF FIRE-ARMS, A PICTORIAL HISTORY (1957); BASIL P. HUGHES, FIREPOWER: WEAPONS EFFECTIVENESS ON THE BATTLE FIELD, 1630-1850 (1975); HAROLD L. PETERSON, THE TREASURY OF THE GUN (1962).

26. *See, e.g.,* 10 U.S.C. § 311 (1988) (unorganized militia consists of all men between the ages of

tary establishment assisted by semi-professional auxiliaries—the reserves and the National Guard—have largely assumed the roles of public protection and national security. It is possible that the concept of a militia of the armed citizenry has been largely mooted by social change.

Yet, the effect of social change on the question of the Second Amendment is a two-edged sword. If one of the motivating purposes behind the Second Amendment was to provide a popular check against potential governmental excess, then does the professionalization of national and community security make the right to keep and bear arms even more important in the modern context? Furthermore, the question remains whether the concept of a militia of the whole is worth re-examining: Did the framers, by adopting the Second Amendment, embrace a republican vision of the rights and responsibilities of free citizens that, despite the difficulties, should somehow be made to work today?

Finally, the Second Amendment debate raises important questions concerning constitutional interpretation, questions that need to be more fully addressed by legal historians and constitutional commentators. It poses important questions about notions of the living Constitution, and to what extent that doctrine can be used to limit as well as extend rights. It also poses important questions about social stratification, cultural bias, and constitutional interpretation. Do courts really protect rights explicit or implicit in the Constitution, or is the courts' interpretation of rights largely a dialogue with the elite, articulate sectors of society, with the courts enforcing those rights favored by dominant elites and ignoring those not so favored?

Many of the issues surrounding the Second Amendment debate are raised in particularly sharp relief from the perspective of African-American history. With the exception of Native Americans, no people in American history have been more influenced by violence than blacks. Private and public violence maintained slavery.[27] The nation's most destructive conflict ended the "peculiar institution."[28] That all too brief experiment in racial egalitarianism, Reconstruction, was ended by private violence[29] and abetted by Supreme Court sanction.[30] Jim Crow was sustained by private violence, often with

---

18 and 45, and females who are commissioned National Guard officers); Williams v. State, 490 S.W.2d 117, 121 (Ark. 1973) (recognizing the continued validity of the *posse comitatus* power).

27. *See* KENNETH M. STAMPP, THE PECULIAR INSTITUTION: SLAVERY IN THE ANTEBELLUM SOUTH 141-91 (1956).

28. The Civil War cost the Union and Confederate armies a combined casualty total of 498,332 deaths. By way of contrast, World War II, the nation's second bloodiest conflict, cost the United States 407,316 fatalities. *See* THE WORLD ALMANAC & BOOK OF FACTS 793 (Mark S. Hoffman ed., 1991).

29. *See generally* ERIC FONER, RECONSTRUCTION: AMERICA'S UNFINISHED REVOLUTION, 1863-1877, at 564-600 (1988); GEORGE C. RABLE, BUT THERE WAS NO PEACE: THE ROLE OF VIOLENCE IN THE POLITICS OF RECONSTRUCTION (1984).

30. *See, e.g.,* United States v. Harris, 106 U.S. 629 (1882) (holding unconstitutional a federal

public assistance.[31]

If today the memories of past interracial violence are beginning to fade, they are being quickly replaced by the frightening phenomenon of black-on-black violence, making life all too precarious for poor blacks in inner city neighborhoods.[32] Questions raised by the Second Amendment, particularly those concerning self-defense, crime, participation in the security of the community, and the wisdom or utility of relying exclusively on the state for protection, thus take on a peculiar urgency in light of the modern Afro-American experience.

This article explores Second Amendment issues in light of the Afro-American experience, concluding that the individual rights theory comports better with the history of the right to bear arms in England and Colonial and post-Revolutionary America. The article also suggests that Second Amendment issues need to be explored, not only with respect to how the right to keep and bear arms has affected American society as a whole, but also with an eye toward subcultures in American society who have been less able to rely on state protection.

The remainder of this article is divided into five parts. Part I examines the historical tension between the belief in the individual's right to bear arms and the desire to keep weapons out of the hands of "socially undesirable" groups. The English distrust of the lower classes, and then certain religious groups, was replaced in America by a distrust of two racial minorities: Native Americans and blacks. Part II examines antebellum regulations restricting black firearms ownership and participation in the militia. Part III examines the intentions of the framers of the Fourteenth Amendment with respect to the Second Amendment and how nineteenth-century Supreme Court cases limiting the scope of the Second Amendment were part of the general tendency of the courts to limit the scope of the Fourteenth Amendment. This Part also examines restrictions on firearms ownership aimed at blacks in the postbellum South and the role of private violence in reclaiming white domination in the South. Part IV examines black resistance to the violence that accompanied Jim Crow. In Part V, the article suggests directions of further inquiry regarding political access, the current specter of black-on-black crime, and the question of gun control today.

---

criminal statute designed to protect equal privileges and immunities for blacks from invasion by private persons); United States v. Cruikshank, 92 U.S. 542 (1876) (holding unconstitutional a federal criminal statute designed to prevent whites from conspiring to prevent blacks from exercising their constitutional rights).

31. *See infra* Part IV.

32. *See infra* Part V.

I. ARMED CITIZENS, FREEMEN, AND WELL-REGULATED MILITIAS: THE
BEGINNINGS OF AN AFRO-AMERICAN EXPERIENCE WITH AN
ANGLO-AMERICAN RIGHT

Any discussion of the Second Amendment should begin with the common-place observation that the framers of the Bill of Rights did not believe they were creating new rights.[33] Instead, they believed that they were simply recognizing rights already part of their English constitutional heritage and implicit in natural law.[34] In fact, many of the framers cautioned against a bill of rights, arguing that the suggested rights were inherent to a free people, and that a specific detailing of rights would suggest that the new constitution empowered the federal government to violate other traditional rights not enumerated.[35]

Thus, an analysis of the framers' intentions with respect to the Second Amendment should begin with an examination of their perception of the right to bear arms as one of the traditional rights of Englishmen, a right necessary to perform the duty of militia service. Such an analysis is in part an exercise in examining the history of arms regulation and militia service in English legal history. But a simple examination of the right to own weapons at English law combined with an analysis of the history of the militia in English society is inadequate to a full understanding of the framers' understanding of what they meant by "the right to keep and bear arms." By the time the Bill of Rights was adopted, nearly two centuries of settlement in North America had given Americans constitutional sensibilities similar to, but nonetheless distinguishable from, those of their English counterparts.[36] American settlement had created its own history with respect to the right to bear arms, a history based on English tradition, modified by the American experience, and a history that was sharply influenced by the racial climate in the American colonies.

---

33. BERNARD BAILYN, THE IDEOLOGICAL ORIGINS OF THE AMERICAN REVOLUTION 184-89, 193-94 (1967).

34. *Id.* Especially pertinent is John Philip Reid's reminder: "There are other dimensions that the standing-army controversy, when studied from the perspective of law, adds to our knowledge of the American Revolution. *One is the degree to which eighteenth-century Americans thought seventeenth-century English thoughts.*" JOHN PHILLIP REID, IN DEFIANCE OF THE LAW: THE STANDING-ARMY CONTROVERSY, THE TWO CONSTITUTIONS, AND THE COMING OF THE AMERICAN REVOLUTION 4 (1981) (emphasis added).

35. *See, e.g.,* THE FEDERALIST NO. 84 (Alexander Hamilton).

36. This can be seen with reference to the right of trial by jury. A number of scholars have noted that Americans in the late 18th century regarded the right of trial by jury as including the right to have the jury decide issues of law as well as fact. This was, of course, a departure from traditional English practice. *See* MORTON J. HOROWITZ, THE TRANSFORMATION OF AMERICAN LAW, 1780-1860, at 28-29 (1977); WILLIAM EDWARD NELSON, AMERICANIZATION OF THE COMMON LAW: THE IMPACT OF LEGAL CHANGE ON MASSACHUSETTS SOCIETY, 1760-1830, at 3-4, 8, 20-30 (1975).

A. ENGLISH LAW AND TRADITION

The English settlers who populated North America in the seventeenth century were heirs to a tradition over five centuries old governing both the right and duty to be armed. At English law, the idea of an armed citizenry responsible for the security of the community had long coexisted, perhaps somewhat uneasily, with regulation of the ownership of arms, particularly along class lines. The Assize of Arms of 1181[37] required the arming of all free men, and required free men to possess armor suitable to their condition.[38] By the thirteenth century, villeins possessing sufficient property were also expected to be armed and contribute to the security of the community.[39] Lacking both professional police forces and a standing army,[40] English law and custom dictated that the citizenry as a whole, privately equipped, assist in both law enforcement and in military matters. By law, all men between sixteen and sixty were liable to be summoned into the sheriff's *posse comitatus*. All subjects were expected to participate in the hot pursuit of criminal suspects, supplying their own arms for the occasion. There were legal penalties for failure to participate.[41]

Moreover, able-bodied men were considered part of the militia, although by the sixteenth century the general practice was to rely on select groups intensively trained for militia duty rather than to rely generally on the armed male population. This move toward a selectively trained militia was an attempt to remedy the often indifferent proficiency and motivation that occurred when relying on the population as a whole.[42]

Although English law recognized a duty to be armed, it was a duty and a right highly circumscribed by English class structure. The law often regarded the common people as a dangerous class, useful perhaps in defending shire and realm, but also capable of mischief with their weapons, mischief toward each other, toward their betters, and toward their betters' game. Restrictions on the type of arms deemed suitable for common people had long been part of English law and custom. A sixteenth-century statute designed as a crime control measure prohibited the carrying of handguns and cross-

---

37. SELECT CHARTERS & OTHER ILLUSTRATIONS OF ENGLISH CONSTITUTIONAL HISTORY FROM THE EARLIEST TIMES TO THE REIGN OF EDWARD THE FIRST 181-84 (H.W.C. Davis ed., Fred B. Cothman & Co. 1985) (1921).

38. 1 FREDERICK POLLOCK & FREDERIC W. MAITLAND, THE HISTORY OF ENGLISH LAW BEFORE THE TIME OF EDWARD I 421-42, 565 (1968).

39. *Id.*

40. Historian Joyce Lee Malcolm notes that England did not have a standing army until the late 17th century and did not have a professional police force until the nineteenth. *See* Malcolm, *supra* note 9, at 391.

41. ALAN HARDING, A SOCIAL HISTORY OF ENGLISH LAW 59 (1966); Malcolm, *supra* note 9, at 391.

42. Malcolm, *supra* note 9, at 391-92.

bows by those with incomes of less than one hundred pounds a year.[43] Catholics were also often subject to being disarmed as potential subversives after the English reformation.[44]

It took the religious and political turmoil of seventeenth-century England to bring about large scale attempts to disarm the English public and to bring the right to keep arms under English constitutional protection. Post-Restoration attempts by Charles II to disarm large portions of the population known or believed to be political opponents, and James II's efforts to disarm his Protestant opponents led, in 1689, to the adoption of the Seventh provision of the English Bill of Rights: "That the Subjects which are Protestants may have Arms for their Defence suitable to their Conditions, and as allowed by Law."[45]

By the eighteenth century, the right to possess arms, both for personal protection and as a counterbalance against state power, had come to be viewed as part of the rights of Englishmen by many on both sides of the Atlantic. Sir William Blackstone listed the right to possess arms as one of the five auxiliary rights of English subjects without which their primary rights could not be maintained.[46] He discussed the right in traditional Eng-

---

43. *Id.* at 393.

44. *Id.* at 393-94.

45. *Id.* at 408.

46. 1 WILLIAM BLACKSTONE, COMMENTARIES *143-45. Blackstone listed three primary rights—the right of personal security, the right of personal liberty, and the right of private property—all of which he regarded as natural rights recognized and protected by the common law and statutes of England. He also argued that these would be "dead letters" without the five auxiliary rights which he listed as: (1) the constitution, powers and privileges of Parliament; (2) the limitation of the king's prerogative; (3) the right to apply to the courts of justice for redress of injuries; (4) the right of petitioning the King or either house of Parliament, and for the redress of grievances; and (5) the right of subjects to have arms for their defence. *Id.* at *121-45.

Some commentators have argued that Blackstone's remarks and other evidence of English common-law and statutory rights to possess arms should be viewed in the light of the extensive regulation of firearms that traditionally existed in England and also in light of English strict gun control in the 20th century. *See, e.g.,* SUBCOMMITTEE REPORT, *supra* note 8, at 26; FRANKLIN E. ZIMRING & GORDON HAWKINS, THE CITIZEN'S GUIDE TO GUN CONTROL 142-43 (1987); Ehrman & Henigan, *supra* note 6, at 9-10. Two points should be made in that regard. First, much of English firearms regulation had an explicit class base largely inapplicable in the American context. Second, neither a common law right to keep and bear arms nor a similar statutory right such as existed in the English Bill of Rights of 1689 would, in the light of Parliamentary supremacy, be a bar to subsequent statutes repealing or modifying that right. Blackstone is cited here not as evidence that the English right, in precise form and content, became the American right; instead it is evidence that the idea of an individual right to keep and bear arms existed on both sides of the Atlantic in the 18th century.

Blackstone's importance to this discussion is twofold. His writings on the right to possess arms can be taken as partial evidence of what the framers of the Second Amendment regarded as among the rights of Englishmen that they sought to preserve. Blackstone's views greatly influenced late 18th-century American legal thought. But Blackstone's importance in this regard does not cease with the Second Amendment. Blackstone also greatly influenced 19th-century American legal thinking. One influential antebellum American jurist, Justice Joseph Story, was significantly influ-

lish terms:

> The fifth and last auxiliary right of the subject, that I shall at present mention, is that of having arms for their defence, suitable to their condition and degree, and such as are allowed by law, which is also declared by the same statute 1 W. & M. st. 2 c. 2 and is indeed a public allowance, under due restrictions, of the natural right of resistance and self-preservation, when the sanctions of society and laws are found insufficient to restrain the violence of oppression. [47]

B. ARMS AND RACE IN COLONIAL AMERICA

If the English tradition involved a right and duty to bear arms qualified by class and later religion, both the right and the duty were strengthened in the earliest American settlements. From the beginning, English settlement in North America had a quasi-military character, an obvious response to harsh frontier conditions. Governors of settlements often also held the title of militia captain, reflecting both the civil and military nature of their office. Special effort was made to ensure that white men, capable of bearing arms, were imported into the colonies.[48] Far from the security of Britain, often bordering on the colonies of other frequently hostile European powers, colonial governments viewed the arming of able-bodied white men and the requirement that they perform militia service as essential to a colony's survival.

There was another reason for the renewed emphasis on the right and duty to be armed in America: race. Britain's American colonies were home to three often antagonistic races: red, white, and black. For the settlers of Brit-

---

enced by his readings of Blackstone. *See* R. KENT NEWMYER, SUPREME COURT JUSTICE JOSEPH STORY: STATESMAN OF THE OLD REPUBLIC 40-45, 137, 246 (1985). Story viewed the Second Amendment as vitally important in maintaining a free republic. In his *Commentaries on the Constitution,* he wrote:

> The right of the citizens to keep, and bear arms has justly been considered, as the palladium of the liberties of a republic; since it offers a strong moral check against the usurpation and arbitrary power of rulers; and will generally, even if they are successful in the first instance, enable the people to resist, and triumph over them.

JOSEPH STORY, COMMENTARIES ON THE CONSTITUTION OF THE UNITED STATES 708 (Carolina Academic Press 1987) (1833).

While it would be inaccurate to attribute Story's Second Amendment views solely to his reading of Blackstone, Blackstone doubtless helped influence Story and other early 19th-century lawyers and jurists to regard the right to keep and bear arms as an important prerogative of free citizens. All of this is important for our discussion, not only with regard to antebellum opinion concerning the Second Amendment, but also in considering the cultural and legal climate that informed the framers of the Fourteenth Amendment who intended to extend what were commonly regarded as the rights of free men to the freedmen, and who also intended to extend the Bill of Rights to the states. *See infra* Part III.

47. 1 BLACKSTONE, *supra* note 46, at *143-44.

48. ABBOTT E. SMITH, COLONISTS IN BONDAGE: WHITE SERVITUDE AND CONVICT LABOR IN AMERICA, 1607-1776, at 30-34 (Norton 1971) (1947).

ish North America, an armed and universally deputized white population was necessary not only to ward off dangers from the armies of other European powers, but also to ward off attacks from the indigenous population which feared the encroachment of English settlers on their lands. An armed white population was also essential to maintain social control over blacks and Indians who toiled unwillingly as slaves and servants in English settlements.[49]

This need for racial control helped transform the traditional English right into a much broader American one. If English law had qualified the right to possess arms by class and religion, American law was much less concerned with such distinctions.[50] Initially all Englishmen, and later all white men, were expected to possess and bear arms to defend their commonwealths, both from external threats and from the internal ones posed by blacks and Indians. The statutes of many colonies specified that white men be armed at public expense.[51] In most colonies, all white men between the ages of sixteen and sixty, usually with the exception of clergy and religious objectors, were considered part of the militia and required to be armed.[52] Not only were white men required to perform traditional militia and posse duties, they were also required to serve as patrollers, a specialized posse dedicated to keeping order among the slave population, in those colonies with large slave populations.[53] This broadening of the right to keep and bear arms reflected a more general lessening of class, religious, and ethnic distinctions among whites in colonial America. The right to possess arms was, therefore, extended to classes traditionally viewed with suspicion in England, including the class of indentured servants.[54]

If there were virtually universal agreement concerning the need to arm the white population,[55] the law was much more ambivalent with respect to

---

49. BOORSTIN, *supra* note 18, at 355-56.

50. *Id.* at 353.

51. *See* A. LEON HIGGINBOTHAM, JR., IN THE MATTER OF COLOR: RACE AND THE AMERICAN LEGAL PROCESS: THE COLONIAL PERIOD 32 (1978).

It should also be added that the abundant game found in North America during the colonial period eliminated the need for the kind of game laws that had traditionally disarmed the lower classes in England. Malcolm, *supra* note 9, at 393-94.

52. *See, e.g.*, 2 LAWS OF THE ROYAL COLONY OF NEW JERSEY 15-21, 49, 96, 133, 289 (Bernard Bush ed., 1977).

53. HIGGINBOTHAM, *supra* note 51, at 260-262.

54. For a good discussion of the elevation of the rights of white indentured servants as a means of maintaining social control over the black population, see generally EDMUND S. MORGAN, AMERICAN SLAVERY, AMERICAN FREEDOM: THE ORDEAL OF COLONIAL VIRGINIA (1975).

55. Stephen Halbrook notes that Virginia's royal government in the late 17th century became very concerned that the widespread practice of carrying arms would tend to foment rebellion, and that, as a result, statutes were enacted to prevent groups of men from gathering with arms. *See* HALBROOK, THAT EVERY MAN BE ARMED, *supra* note 6, at 56-57. The sharpening of racial distinctions and the need for greater social control over slaves that occurred toward the end of the

blacks. The progress of slavery in colonial America reflected English lack of familiarity with the institution, in both law and custom.[56] In some colonies, kidnapped Africans initially were treated like other indentured servants, held for a term of years and then released from forced labor and allowed to live as free people.[57] In some colonies, the social control of slaves was one of the law's major concerns; in others, the issue was largely of private concern to the slave owner.[58]

These differences were reflected in statutes concerned with the right to possess arms and the duty to perform militia service. One colony—Virginia—provides a striking example of how social changes were reflected, over time, in restrictions concerning the right to be armed. A Virginia statute enacted in 1639 required the arming of white men at public expense.[59] The statute did not specify the arming of black men, but it also did not prohibit black men from arming themselves.[60] By 1680 a Virginia statute prohibited Negroes, slave and free, from carrying weapons, including clubs.[61] Yet, by the early eighteenth century, free Negroes who were house owners were permitted to keep one gun in their house, while blacks, slave and free, who lived on frontier plantations were able to keep guns.[62] Virginia's experience reflected three sets of concerns: the greater need to maintain social control over the black population as caste lines sharpened;[63] the need to use slaves and free blacks to help defend frontier plantations against attacks by hostile Indians; and the recognition on the part of Virginia authorities of the necessity for gun ownership for those living alone.

These concerns were mirrored in the legislation of other colonies. Massachusetts did not have general legislation prohibiting blacks from carrying arms,[64] but free Negroes in that colony were not permitted to participate in

---

seventeenth and beginning of the 18th century lessened the concern authorities had over the armed white population. See MORGAN, supra note 54, at 354-55.

56. See Raymond T. Diamond, No Call to Glory: Thurgood Marshall's Thesis on the Intent of a Pro-Slavery Constitution, 42 VAND. L. REV. 93, 101-102 (1989) (colonies dealt with slavery in an unsystematic and piecemeal fashion). See generally WINTHROP D. JORDAN, WHITE OVER BLACK: AMERICAN ATTITUDES TOWARDS THE NEGRO, 1550-1812, at 48-52 (1968).

57. HIGGINBOTHAM, supra note 51, at 21-22.

58. See HERBERT APTHEKER, AMERICAN NEGRO SLAVE REVOLTS (5th ed. 1983); Diamond, supra note 56, at 101-102, 104; Robert J. Cottrol & Raymond T. Diamond, Book Review, 56 TUL. L. REV. 1107, 1110-1112 (1982) (reviewing A. LEON HIGGINBOTHAM, JR., IN THE MATTER OF COLOR: RACE AND THE AMERICAN LEGAL PROCESS: THE COLONIAL PERIOD (1978)).

59. 1 WILLIAM W. HENING, STATUTES AT LARGE OF VIRGINIA 226 (New York, R. & W. & G. Bartow 1823); see HIGGINBOTHAM, supra note 51, at 32.

60. 1 HENING, supra note 59, at 226; see HIGGINBOTHAM, supra note 51, at 32.

61. HIGGINBOTHAM, supra note 51, at 39.

62. Id. at 58.

63. Id. at 38-40.

64. Higginbotham informs us that the Boston selectmen passed such an ordinance after some slaves had allegedly committed arson in 1724. See id. at 76.

militia drills; instead they were required to perform substitute service on public works projects.[65] New Jersey exempted blacks and Indians from militia service, though the colony permitted free Negroes to possess firearms.[66] Ironically, South Carolina, which had the harshest slave codes of this period, may have been the colony most enthusiastic about extending the right to bear arms to free Negroes. With its majority black population, that state's need to control the slave population was especially acute.[67] To secure free black assistance in controlling the slave population, South Carolina in the early eighteenth century permitted free blacks the right of suffrage, the right to keep firearms, and the right to undertake militia service.[68] As the eighteenth century unfolded, those rights were curtailed.[69]

Overall, these laws reflected the desire to maintain white supremacy and control. With respect to the right to possess arms, the colonial experience had largely eliminated class, religious, and ethnic distinctions among the white population. Those who had been part of the suspect classes in England—the poor, religious dissenters, and others who had traditionally only enjoyed a qualified right to possess arms—found the right to be considerably more robust in the American context. But blacks had come to occupy the social and legal space of the suspect classes in England. Their right to posses arms was highly dependent on white opinion of black loyalty and reliability. Their inclusion in the militia of freemen was frequently confined to times of crisis. Often, there were significant differences between the way northern and

---

65. See LORENZO J. GREENE, THE NEGRO IN COLONIAL NEW ENGLAND 127 (1968). Greene notes that blacks probably served in New England militias until the latter part of the 17th century. *Id.* It is interesting to note that, despite this prohibition on militia service, blacks served with New England forces during the French and Indian Wars. *Id.* at 188-89. Winthrop Jordan notes that in 1652 the Massachusetts General Court ordered Scotsmen, Indians, and Negroes to train with the Militia, but that, in 1656, Massachusetts and, in 1660, Connecticut excluded blacks from Militia service. See JORDAN, *supra* note 56, at 71.

66. See 2 LAWS OF THE ROYAL COLONY OF NEW JERSEY, *supra* note 52, at 49, 96, 289.

67. For a good discussion of black life in colonial South Carolina, see generally PETER H. WOOD, BLACK MAJORITY: NEGROES IN COLONIAL SOUTH CAROLINA FROM 1670 THROUGH THE STONO REBELLION (1974).

South Carolina in 1739 was the scene of the Stono Rebellion, one of the largest slave rebellions in North America. A recent study of the rebellion suggests that the presence of large numbers of African born men from the Kingdom of the Kongo played a critical role. The Kingdom, including parts of modern Zaire, Congo-Brazzaville, Gabon, and Angola, had been heavily influenced by Portuguese traders and missionaries in such areas as language, religion, and contemporary European military tactics including the use of firearms. The Stono Rebellion illustrated both the internal and external threats faced by many colonies. First, the presence of large numbers of African slaves, familiar with European military tactics and technology, posed a threat to slave society in South Carolina. Second, this threat was further enhanced by the fact that South Carolina bordered on the Spanish colony of Florida. Historical accounts of the rebellion indicate that Portugese-speaking Catholic slaves acted in concert with Spanish agents. See generally John K. Thornton, *African Dimensions of the Stono Rebellion,* 96 AM. HIST. REV. 1101 (1991)

68. See HIGGINBOTHAM, *supra* note 51, at 201-15.

69. *Id.*

southern colonies approached this question, a reflection of the very different roles that slavery played in the two regions. These differences would become sharper after the Revolution, when the northern states began to move toward the abolition of slavery and the southern states, some of which had also considered abolition,[70] began to strengthen the institution.

Ironically, while the black presence in colonial America introduced a new set of restrictions concerning the English law of arms and the militia, it helped strengthen the view that the security of the state was best achieved through the arming of all free citizens. It was this new view that was part of the cultural heritage Americans brought to the framing of the Constitution.

C. THE RIGHT OF *WHICH* PEOPLE?

1. Revolutionary Ideals

The colonial experience helped strengthen the appreciation of early Americans for the merits of an armed citizenry. That appreciation was strengthened yet further by the American Revolution. If necessity forced the early colonists to arm, the Revolution and the friction with Britain's standing army that preceded it—and in many ways precipitated it—served to revitalize Whiggish notions that standing armies were dangerous to liberty, and that militias, composed of the whole of the people, best protected both liberty and security.[71]

These notions soon found their way into the debates over the new constitution, debates which help place the language and meaning of the Second Amendment in context. Like other provisions of the proposed constitution, the clause that gave Congress the power to provide for the organizing, arming, and disciplining of the militia[72] excited fears among those who believed that the new constitution could be used to destroy both state power and individual rights.[73]

---

70. *See* Robert J. Cottrol, *Liberalism and Paternalism: Ideology, Economic Interest and the Business Law of Slavery,* 31 AM. J. LEGAL HIST. 359, 363-64 (1987).

71. *See generally* REID, *supra* note 34.

72. That clause is now found in U.S. CONST. art. I, § 8, cl. 15.

73. Elbridge Gerry of Massachusetts thought a national government which controlled the militia would be potentially despotic. James Madison's Notes on the Constitutional Convention of 1787 (Aug. 21, 1787), *in* 1 1787: DRAFTING THE U.S. CONSTITUTION 916 (Wilbowin E. Benton, ed., 1986). With this power, national government "may enslave the States." *Id.* at 846. Oliver Ellsworth of Connecticut suggested that "[t]he whole authority over the Militia ought by no means to be taken away from the States whose consequence would pine away to nothing after such a sacrifice of power." *Id.* at 909.

It is interesting, in light of the current debate, that both advocates and opponents of this increase in federal power assumed that the militia they were discussing would be one that enrolled almost all of the white male population between the ages of 16 and 60, and that that population would supply their own arms. George Mason of Virginia proposed "the idea of a select militia," but withdrew it. *Id.* at 909.

Indeed, it was the very universality of the militia that was the source of some of the objections. A number of critics of the proposed constitution feared that the proposed congressional power could subject the whole population to military discipline and a clear threat to individual liberty.[74] Others complained that the Militia Clause provided no exemptions for those with religious scruples against bearing arms.[75]

But others feared that the Militia Clause could be used to disarm the population as well as do away with the states' control of the militia. Some critics expressed fear that Congress would use its power to establish a select militia, a group of men specially trained and armed for militia duty, similar to the earlier English experience.[76] Richard Henry Lee of Virginia argued that that select militia might be used to disarm the population and that, in any event, it would pose more of a danger to individual liberty than a militia composed of the whole population. He charged that a select militia "commits the many to the mercy and the prudence of the few."[77] A number of critics objected to giving Congress the power to arm the militia, fearing that such power would likewise give Congress the power to withhold arms from the militia.[78] At the constitutional convention, Massachusetts delegate Elbridge Gerry saw such potential danger in giving the new government power over the militia, that he declared:

> This power in the United States as explained is making the states drill sergeants. He had as lief let the citizens of Massachusetts be disarmed, as to take the command from the states, and subject them to the General Legislature. It would be regarded as a system of Despotism.[79]

The fear that this new congressional authority could be used to both destroy state power over the militia and to disarm the people led delegates to state ratifying conventions to urge measures that would preserve the traditional

---

74. This was a view argued by Luther Martin before the Maryland House of Representatives. Luther Martin Before the Maryland House of Representatives (1787), *in* 3 THE RECORDS OF THE FEDERAL CONVENTION OF 1787, at 157 (Max Farrand ed., 1966) [hereinafter THE RECORDS OF THE FEDERAL CONVENTION]. Samuel Bryan, a Pennsylvania pamphleteer who argued against the proposed constitution, argued that it could subject the whole population to military discipline. Samuel Bryan, *Letter to the People of Pennsylvania*, INDEPENDENT GAZETTEER, Oct. 5, 1787, *reprinted in* THE ANTIFEDERALISTS 22-23, 27 (Cecelia M. Kenyon ed., 1966). A number of critics argued that the provision was a threat to the liberty of every man from 16 to 60. *Id.* at 57. Thus, the language of the Fifth Amendment requiring grand jury proceedings for cases arising in the militia, except when in actual service during time of war or public danger, may have been in response to this fear.

75. THE ANTIFEDERALISTS, *supra* note 74, at 57. This concern was the reason for the original language of the Second Amendment. *See supra* note 4.

76. *See supra* text accompanying note 43.

77. THE ANTIFEDERALISTS, *supra* note 74, at 228.

78. 2 THE RECORDS OF THE FEDERAL CONVENTION, *supra* note 74, at 385-87; 3 *id.* at 208-09, 272, 295.

79. 2 THE RECORDS OF THE FEDERAL CONVENTION, *supra* note 74, at 385.

right. The Virginia convention proposed language that would provide protection for the right to keep and bear arms in the federal constitution.[80]

In their efforts to defend the proposed constitution, Alexander Hamilton and James Madison addressed these charges. Hamilton's responses are interesting because he wrote as someone openly skeptical of the value of the militia of the whole. The former Revolutionary War artillery officer[81] expressed the view that, while the militia fought bravely during the Revolution, it had proven to be no match when pitted against regular troops. Hamilton, who Madison claimed initially wanted to forbid the states from controlling any land or naval forces,[82] called for uniformity in organizing and disciplining of the militia under national authority. He also urged the creation of a select militia that would be more amenable to the training and discipline he saw as necessary.[83] In what was perhaps a concession to sentiment favoring the militia of the whole, Hamilton stated: "Little more can be reasonably aimed at, with respect to the people at large, than to have them properly armed and equipped; and in order to see that this not be neglected, it will be necessary to assemble them once or twice in the course of a year."[84]

If Hamilton gave only grudging support to the concept of the militia of the whole, Madison, author of the Second Amendment, was a much more vigorous defender of the concept. He answered critics of the Militia Clause provision allowing Congress to arm the militia by stating that the term "arming" meant only that Congress's authority to arm extended only to prescribing the type of arms the militia would use, not to furnishing them.[85] But Madison's

---

80. The Virginia convention urged the adoption of the following language:

That the people have a right to keep and bear arms; that a well-regulated militia, composed of the body of the people trained to arms, is the proper, natural, and safe defence for a free state; that standing armies, in time of peace, are dangerous to liberty, and therefore ought to be avoided, as far as the circumstances and protection of the community will admit; and that in all cases, the military should be under strict subordination to, and governed by, the civil power.

3 THE DEBATES IN THE SEVERAL STATE CONVENTIONS ON THE ADOPTION OF THE FEDERAL CONSTITUTION, AS RECOMMENDED BY THE GENERAL CONVENTION AT PHILADELPHIA, IN 1787 TOGETHER WITH THE JOURNAL OF THE FEDERAL CONVENTION 657-59 (Jonathan Elliot ed., Ayer Co. 1987) (1907) [hereinafter ELLIOT'S DEBATES].

81. RICHARD B. MORRIS, SEVEN WHO SHAPED OUR DESTINY: THE FOUNDING FATHERS AS REVOLUTIONARIES 228, 237-49 (1973).

82. 1 THE RECORDS OF THE FEDERAL CONVENTION, supra note 74, at 293.

83. THE FEDERALIST No. 25, at 161 (Alexander Hamilton) (The Heritage Press 1945). For a modern study that supports Hamilton's views concerning the military ineffectiveness of the militia, see BOORSTIN, supra note 18, at 352-72.

84. THE FEDERALIST No. 29, at 183 (Alexander Hamilton) (The Heritage Press 1945). Interestingly enough, Hamilton's views anticipated the state of modern law on this subject; the National Guard has, in effect, become a select militia with a much larger reserve militia existing in the citizenry at large.

85. 5 ELLIOT'S DEBATES, supra note 80, at 464-65.

views went further. He envisioned a militia consisting of virtually the entire white male population, writing that a militia of 500,000 citizens[86] could prevent any excesses that might be perpetrated by the national government and its regular army. Madison left little doubt that he envisioned the militia of the whole as a potential counterweight to tyrannical excess on the part of the government:

> Let a regular army, fully equal to the resources of the country, be formed; and let it be entirely at the devotion of the federal government: still it would not be going too far to say, that the State governments with the people on their side, would be able to repel the danger. The highest number to which, according to the best computation, a standing army can be carried in any country does not exceed one hundredth part of the whole number of souls; or one twenty-fifth part of the number able to bear arms. This proportion would not yield, in the United States, an army more than twenty-five or thirty thousand men. To these would be opposed a militia amounting to near half a million citizens with arms in their hands, officered by men chosen among themselves, fighting for their common liberties and united and conducted by governments possessing their affections and confidence. It may well be doubted whether a militia thus circumstanced could ever be conquered by such a proportion of regular troops. Those who are best acquainted with the last successful resistance of this country against the British arms will be most inclined to deny the possibility of it. Besides the advantage of being armed, which the Americans possess over the people of almost every other nation, the existence of subordinate governments, to which the people are attached, and by which the militia officers are appointed, forms a barrier against the enterprises of ambition, more insurmountable than any which a simple government of any form can admit of. Notwithstanding the military establishments in the several kingdoms of Europe, which are carried as far as the public resources will bear, the. . . governments are afraid to trust the people with arms . . . .[87]

It is against this background that the meaning of the Second Amendment must be considered. For the revolutionary generation, the idea of the militia and an armed population were related. The principal reason for preferring a militia of the whole over either a standing army or a select militia was rooted in the idea that, whatever the inefficiency of the militia of the whole, the institution would better protect the newly won freedoms than a reliance on security provided by some more select body.

---

86. THE FEDERALIST No. 46, at 319 (James Madison) (The Heritage Press 1945). The census of 1790 listed the white male population over age 16 as 813,298. See BUREAU OF THE CENSUS, U.S. DEP'T OF COMMERCE, STATISTICAL HISTORY OF THE UNITED STATES FROM COLONIAL TIMES TO THE PRESENT 16 (1976). The census did not list the number over 60 that would have been exempt from militia duty.

87. Id.

2. Racial Limitations

One year after the ratification of the Second Amendment and the Bill of Rights, Congress passed legislation that reaffirmed the notion of the militia of the whole and explicitly introduced a racial component into the national deliberations on the subject of the militia. The Uniform Militia Act[88] called for the enrollment of every free, able-bodied *white* male citizen between the ages of eighteen and forty-five into the militia. The act further specified that every militia member was to provide himself with a musket or firelock, a bayonet, and ammunition.

This specification of a racial qualification for militia membership was somewhat at odds with general practice in the late eighteenth century. Despite its recognition and sanctioning of slavery,[89] the Constitution had no racial definition of citizenship.[90] Free Negroes voted in a majority of states.[91] A number of states had militia provisions that allowed free Negroes to participate.[92] Particularly in the northern states, many were well aware that free Negroes and former slaves had served with their state forces during the Revolution.[93] Despite the prejudices of the day, lawmakers in late eighteenth-century America were significantly less willing to write racial restrictions into constitutions and other laws guaranteeing fundamental rights than were their counterparts a generation or so later in the nineteenth century.[94] The 1792 statute restricting militia enrollment to white men was one of the earliest federal statutes to make a racial distinction.

The significance of this restriction is not altogether clear. For the South, there was a clear desire to have a militia that was reliable and could be used to suppress potential slave insurrections. But despite the fear that free Negroes might make common cause with slaves, and despite federal law, some southern states in the antebellum period enrolled free blacks as militia mem-

---

88. 1 Stat. 271.

89. *See* U.S. CONST. art. I, § 2, cl. 3 (three-fifths of slave population counted for apportionment purposes); U.S. CONST. art. I, § 9, cl. 1 (importation of slaves allowed until 1808); U.S. CONST. art. IV, § 2, cl. 3 (escaped slaves must be "delivered up" to their masters).

90. U.S. CONST. art I, § 2, cl. 3 (specifying congressional representation) is often cited for the proposition that blacks were not citizens because of the three-fifths clause. It should be noted that, under this clause, free Negroes were counted as whole persons for purposes of representation. The original wording of this provision specifically mentioned "white and other citizens," but that language was deleted by the committee on style as redundant. *See* 5 ELLIOT'S DEBATES, *supra* note 78, at 451.

91. *See infra* Part II; *see also* Robert J. Cottrol, *A Tale of Two Cultures: Or Making the Proper Connections Between Law, Social History and The Political Economy of Despair,* 25 SAN DIEGO L. REV. 989, 1004 & nn. 86-88 (1988).

92. JORDAN, *supra* note 56, at 125-26, 411-12.

93. Robert J. Cottrol, *Law, Politics and Race in Urban America: Towards a New Synthesis,* 17 RUTGERS L.J. 483, 503 & n.129 (1986).

94. Robert J. Cottrol, *The Thirteenth Amendment and the North's Overlooked Egalitarian Heritage,* 11 NAT'L BLACK L.J. 198, 202-03 (1989) (discussing racism in early 19th-century America).

bers.[95] Northern states at various times also enrolled free Negroes in the militia despite federal law and often strident prejudice.[96] States North and South employed free Negroes in state forces during times of invasion.[97] While southern states often prohibited slaves from carrying weapons and strictly regulated access to firearms by free Negroes,[98] northern states generally made no racial distinction with respect to the right to own firearms,[99] and federal law was silent on the subject.

The racial restriction in the 1792 statute indicates the unrest the revolutionary generation felt toward arming blacks and perhaps the recognition that one of the functions of the militia would indeed be to put down slave revolts. Yet, the widespread use of blacks as soldiers in time of crisis and the absence of restrictions concerning the arming of blacks in the northern states may provide another clue concerning how to read the Second Amendment. The 1792 act specified militia enrollment for white men between the ages of eighteen and forty-five.[100] Yet, while it specifically included only this limited portion of the population, *the statute excluded no one from militia service.*

The authors of the statute had experience, in the Revolution, with a militia and Continental Army considerably broad in membership. Older and younger men had served with the Revolutionary forces. Blacks had served, though their service had been an object of considerable controversy.[101] Even women had served, though, given the attitudes of the day, this was far more controversial than black service. Given this experience and the fact that the constitutional debates over the militia had constantly assumed an enrollment of the male population between sixteen and sixty, it is likely that the framers of the 1792 statute envisioned a militia even broader than the one they specified. This suggests to us how broad the term "people" in the Second Amendment was meant to be.

The 1792 statute also suggests to us also how crucial race has been in our

---

95. *See* JORDAN *supra* note 56, at 125-26, 411-12 (in varying degrees, North Carolina, South Carolina, and Georgia); BERNARD C. NALTY, STRENGTH FOR THE FIGHT: A HISTORY OF BLACK AMERICANS IN THE MILITARY 20 (1986) (same).

96. *See* JORDAN, *supra* note 56, at 125-26 ("Although [the exclusion of Negroes from the militia] lay on the statute books of all four New England colonies, Negroes served in New England forces in every colonial war." Additionally, and in varying degrees, New York, New Jersey, Pennsylvania, and Delaware included Negroes.).

97. This was particularly true during the War of 1812. *See* ROBERT J. COTTROL, THE AFRO-YANKEES: PROVIDENCE'S BLACK COMMUNITY IN THE ANTEBELLUM ERA 63 (1982); EUGENE D. GENOVESE, ROLL, JORDON, ROLL: THE WORLD THE SLAVES MADE 155 (1976); NALTY, *supra* note 95, at 24-28.

98. *See infra* Part II.A; *see also* STAMPP, *supra* note 27, at 208-28.

99. Paul Finkelman, *Prelude to the Fourteenth Amendment: Black Legal Rights in the Antebellum North,* 17 RUTGERS L.J. 415, 476 (1986).

100. *See supra* note 88.

101. NALTY, *supra* note 95, at 10-18. *See generally* BENJAMIN QUARLES, THE NEGRO IN THE AMERICAN REVOLUTION (1961).

history. If the racial distinction made in that statute was somewhat anoma-lous in the late eighteenth century, it was the kind of distinction that would become more common in the nineteenth. The story of blacks and arms would continue in the nineteenth century as racial distinctions became sharper and the defense of slavery more militant.

II. ARMS AND THE ANTEBELLUM EXPERIENCE

If, as presaged by the Uniform Militia Act of 1792,[102] racial distinctions became sharper in the nineteenth century, that development was at odds with the rhetoric of the Revolution and with developments of the immediate post-revolutionary era.[103] Flush with the precepts of egalitarian democracy, America had entered a time of recognition and expansion of rights. Eleven of the thirteen original states, as well as Vermont, passed new constitutions in the period between 1776 and 1777.[104] Five of these states rewrote their constitutions by the time of the ratification of the Bill of Rights in 1791.[105] A twelfth original state, Massachusetts, passed a new constitution in 1780.[106] Many of the new constitutions recognized the status of citizens as "free and equal" or "free and independent."[107] In Massachusetts and Vermont, these clauses were interpreted as outlawing the institution of slavery.[108] Many of the new constitutions guaranteed the right to vote regardless of race to all men who otherwise qualified,[109] and guaranteed many of the rights that

---

102. 1 Stat. 271; *see supra* note 88.

103. *See* Raymond T. Diamond & Robert J. Cottrol, *Codifying Caste: Louisiana's Racial Classification Scheme and the Fourteenth Amendment,* 29 LOY. L. REV. 255, 260-63 (1983).

104. *See* FEDERAL AND STATE CONSTITUTIONS, COLONIAL CHARTERS, AND OTHER ORGANIC LAWS OF THE UNITED STATES (Benjamin P. Poore ed., 2d ed., Washington, Government Printing Office 1878) [hereinafter FEDERAL AND STATE CONSTITUTIONS]. Massachusetts passed a new constitution in 1780. 1 *id.* at 956. Rhode Island would not do so until 1842. 2 *id.* at 1603.

105. These states were: Georgia in 1789, *see* 1 *id.* at 384; New Hampshire in 1784, *see* 2 *id.* at 1280; Pennsylvania in 1790, *see* 2 *id.* at 1548; South Carolina in 1778 and 1780, *see* 2 *id.* at 1620, 1628; and Vermont in 1786, *see* 2 *id.* at 1866.

106. 1 *id.* at 956.

107. *See* N.H. CONST. of 1784, pt. I, art. I, 2 FEDERAL AND STATE CONSTITUTIONS, *supra* note 104, at 1280; CONN. CONST. of 1776, pmbl., 1 FEDERAL AND STATE CONSTITUTIONS, *supra* note 104, at 257; MASS. CONST. of 1780, pt. I, art. I, 1 FEDERAL AND STATE CONSTITUTIONS, *supra* note 104, at 957; PA. CONST. of 1776, declaration of rights, art. I, 2 FEDERAL AND STATE CONSTITUTIONS, *supra* note 104, at 1541; PA. CONST. of 1790, § 1, 2 FEDERAL AND STATE CONSTITUTIONS, *supra* note 104, at 1554; VT. CONST. of 1786, ch. I, art. I, 2 FEDERAL AND STATE CONSTITUTIONS, *supra* note 104, at 1867; VT. CONST. of 1776, bill of rights, § 1, 2 FEDERAL AND STATE CONSTITUTIONS, *supra* note 104, at 1908.

108. *See* Diamond, *supra* note 56, at 103 nn.59-61.

109. *See, e.g.,* GA. CONST. of 1779, art. IV, § 1, 1 FEDERAL AND STATE CONSTITUTIONS, *supra* note 104, at 386; MD. CONST. OF 1776, art. II, 1 FEDERAL AND STATE CONSTITUTIONS, *supra* note 104, at 821; MASS. CONST. of 1776, pt. I, declaration of rights, art. IX, 1 FEDERAL AND STATE CONSTITUTIONS, *supra* note 104, at 958; N.H. CONST. OF 1784, pt. I, bill of rights, art. XI, 2 FEDERAL AND STATE CONSTITUTIONS, *supra* note 104, at 1281; N.J. CONST. of 1776, art. IV, 2 FEDERAL AND STATE CONSTITUTIONS, *supra* note 104, at 1311; N.C. CONST. of 1776, constitution

would later be recognized in the Bill of Rights.[110] In no instance were any of these rights limited only to the white population; several states explicitly extended rights to the entire population irrespective of race.[111]

The right to vote, perhaps the most fundamental of rights, was limited in almost all instances to men who met property restrictions, but in most states was not limited according to race.[112] Ironically, only in the nineteenth-century would black voting rights be curtailed, as Jacksonian democracy expanded voting rights for whites.[113] In its constitution of 1821, New York eliminated a one hundred dollar property requirement for white males, and concomitantly increased the requirement to two hundred fifty dollars for

---

or frame of government, art. IX, 2 FEDERAL AND STATE CONSTITUTIONS, *supra* note 104, at 1411-12; PA. CONST. of 1776, declaration of rights, art. VII, 2 FEDERAL AND STATE CONSTITUTIONS, *supra* note 104, at 1541; VT. CONST. of 1777, ch. 1, declaration of rights, art. VIII, 2 FEDERAL AND STATE CONSTITUTIONS, *supra* note 104, at 1859.

Only Georgia, under its 1776 constitution, and South Carolina, in its 1790 constitution, provided explicit racial restrictions on the right to vote. *See* GA. CONST. of 1776, art. IX, 1 FEDERAL AND STATE CONSTITUTIONS, *supra* note 104, at 379; S.C. CONST. of 1790, art. I § 4, 2 FEDERAL AND STATE CONSTITUTIONS, *supra* note 104, at 1628.

110. *See, e.g.,* GA. CONST. of 1776, art. LXI, 1 FEDERAL AND STATE CONSTITUTIONS, *supra* note 104, at 283 (freedom of the press); MASS. CONST. of 1780, pt. 1, declaration of rights, art. XVIII, 1 FEDERAL AND STATE CONSTITUTIONS, *supra* note 104, at 959 (freedom of assembly); MD. CONST. of 1776, declaration of rights, art. XXVII, 2 FEDERAL AND STATE CONSTITUTIONS, *supra* note 104, at 819 (prohibiting quartering troops in homes); N.H. CONST. of 1776, declaration of rights, art. XXIII, 1 FEDERAL AND STATE CONSTITUTIONS, *supra* note 104, at 959 (limits on searches and seizures and on general warrants); PA. CONST. of 1776, declaration of rights, art. XII, 2 FEDERAL AND STATE CONSTITUTIONS, *supra* note 104, at 1542 (freedom of speech); S.C. CONST. of 1778, art. XLI, 2 FEDERAL AND STATE CONSTITUTIONS, *supra* note 104, at 1627 (due process of law); VA. CONST. of 1776, bill of rights, § 16, 2 FEDERAL AND STATE CONSTITUTIONS, *supra* note 104, at 1909 (freedom of religion); VT. CONST. of 1786, ch. 1, declaration of rights, art. XVIII, 2 FEDERAL AND STATE CONSTITUTIONS, *supra* note 104, at 1869 (right to bear arms).

111. *See* GA. CONST. of 1776, art. LVI, 1 FEDERAL AND STATE CONSTITUTIONS, *supra* note 104, at 283; GA. CONST. of 1789, art. IV, § 5, 1 FEDERAL AND STATE CONSTITUTIONS, *supra* note 104, at 386; MD. CONST. of 1776, art. XXXIII, 1 FEDERAL AND STATE CONSTITUTIONS, *supra* note 104, at 819-20 (freedom of religion for "all persons"); N.C. CONST. of 1776, art. VIII (rights in criminal proceedings to be informed of charges, to confront witnesses, and to remain silent for "every man," and freedom of religion for "all men"), 2 FEDERAL AND STATE CONSTITUTIONS, *supra* note 104, at 1409; N.Y. CONST. of 1777, art. XIII (due process to be denied "no member of this state"), art. XXXVIII (freedom of religion "to all mankind"); PA.CONST. of 1776, art. II (freedom of religion for "all men"), art. VIII (due process for "every member of society"), 2 FEDERAL AND STATE CONSTITUTIONS, *supra* note 104, at 1541; PA. CONST. of 1790, art. XI, § 3 (freedom of religion to be denied to "no person"), art. XI, § 7 (freedom of the press for "every person" and freedom of speech for "every citizen"), art. XI, § 10 (due process to be denied to "no person"), 2 FEDERAL AND STATE CONSTITUTIONS, *supra* note 104, at 1554-55; S.C. CONST. of 1778, art. XXXVIII (freedom of religion), 2 FEDERAL AND STATE CONSTITUTIONS, *supra* note 104, at 1626-27; S.C. CONST. of 1790, art. VIII (freedom of religion "to all mankind"), 2 FEDERAL AND STATE CONSTITUTIONS, § supra note 104, at 1632.

112 *See* COTTROL, *supra* note 97, at 42-43.

113. *See* Cottrol, *supra* note 93, at 508-09. This is not to say that voting limitations were the sole measure of the failure of Jacksonian democracy to include blacks. *Id.* at 508-13.

blacks.[114] Other states would eliminate black voting rights altogether.[115] Other than Maine, no state admitted to the union in the nineteenth century's antebellum period allowed blacks to vote.[116]

This curtailment of black voting rights was part and parcel of a certain hostility toward free blacks, a hostility that ran throughout the union of states. In northern states, where slavery had been abandoned or was not a serious factor in social or economic relations, such hostility was the result of simple racism.[117] In southern states, where slavery was an integral part of the social and economic framework, this hostility was occasioned by the threat that free blacks posed to the system of Negro slavery.[118]

A. THE SOUTHERN ANTEBELLUM EXPERIENCE: CONTROL OF ARMS AS A MEANS OF RACIAL OPPRESSION

The threat that free blacks posed to southern slavery was twofold. First, free blacks were a bad example to slaves. For a slave to see free blacks enjoy the trappings of white persons—freedom of movement, expression, and association, relative freedom from fear for one's person and one's family, and freedom to own the fruits of one's labor—was to offer hope and raise desire for that which the system could not produce. A slave with horizons limited only to a continued existence in slavery was a slave who did not threaten the system,[119] whereas a slave with visions of freedom threatened rebellion.

This threat of rebellion is intimately related to the second threat that free blacks posed to the system of Negro slavery, the threat that free blacks might instigate or participate in a rebellion by their slave brethren. To forestall this threat of rebellion, southern legislatures undertook to limit the freedom of

---

114. N.Y. CONST. of 1821, art. II, *superceding* N.Y. CONST. of 1777, art. VII; *see also* Dixon R. Fox, *The Negro Vote in Old New York, in* FREE BLACKS IN AMERICA, 1800-1860, at 95, 97-112 (John H. Bracey, Jr. et. al. eds., 1970).

115. *See* COTTROL, *supra* note 97, at 42-43.

116. LEON F. LITWACK, NORTH OF SLAVERY: THE NEGRO IN THE FREE STATES, 1790-1860, at 79 (1961).

117. It is to be questioned whether racism is ever "simple." Winthrop Jordan has theorized that the English and their cultural descendants were culturally predisposed to racism. JORDAN, *supra* note 56, at 3-43. Carl Jung has suggested that for white Americans the Negro represents the part of the unconscious that requires repression. ALEXANDER THOMAS & SAMUEL SILLEN, RACISM AND PSYCHIATRY 13-14 (1972); *"America Facing its Most Tragic Moment"—Dr. Carl Jung,* N.Y. TIMES, Sept. 29, 1912, § 5, at 3. Whatever accounts for racism, it is clear that racism is capable of actuating the lawmaking process. *See generally* HIGGINBOTHAM, *supra* note 51.

118. *See* STAMPP, *supra* note 27, at 215-17.

119. Compare "Sambo," the idealized exposition of the slave psyche hypothesized by Stanley Elkins. Elkins viewed slaves as having internalized their circumstances to the point at which they became not only incapable of resisting the white masters but also actively cooperated in maintaining their own degradation. *See* STANLEY M. ELKINS, SLAVERY: A PROBLEM IN AMERICAN INSTITUTIONAL AND INTELLECTUAL LIFE 81-139 (3d ed., 1976).

movement and decision of free blacks.[120] States limited the number of free blacks who might congregate at one time;[121] they curtailed the ability of free blacks to choose their own employment,[122] and to trade and socialize with slaves.[123] Free blacks were subject to question, to search, and to summary punishment by patrols established to keep the black population, slave and free, in order.[124] To forestall the possibility that free blacks would rebel either on their own or with slaves, the southern states limited not only the right of slaves, but also the right of free blacks, to bear arms.[125]

The idea was to restrict the availability of arms to blacks, both slave and free, to the extent consistent with local conceptions of safety. At one extreme was Texas, which, between 1842 and 1850, prohibited slaves from using firearms altogether.[126] Also at this extreme was Mississippi, which forbade firearms to both free blacks and slaves after 1852.[127] At the other extreme was Kentucky, which merely provided that, should slaves or free blacks "wilfully and maliciously" shoot at a white person, or otherwise wound a free white person while attempting to kill another person, the slave or free black would suffer the death penalty.[128]

More often than not, slave state statutes restricting black access to firearms were aimed primarily at free blacks, as opposed to slaves, perhaps because the vigilant master was presumed capable of denying arms to all but the most trustworthy slaves, and would give proper supervision to the latter.[129] Thus,

---

120. GENOVESE, *supra* note 97, at 51, 399; STAMPP, *supra* note 27, at 215-217; Eugene D. Genovese, *The Slave States of North America, in* NEITHER SLAVE NOR FREE: THE FREEDMEN OF AFRICAN DESCENT IN THE SLAVE SOCIETIES OF THE NEW WORLD 258, 261-262 (David W. Cohen & Jack P. Greene eds., 1972).

121. JOHN H. FRANKLIN, FROM SLAVERY TO FREEDOM: A HISTORY OF NEGRO AMERICANS 139-40 (6th ed. 1988).

122. *Id.* at 140.

123. *Id.* at 140-41.

124. STAMPP, *supra* note 27, at 214-16.

125. *See infra* text accompanying notes 126-46.

126. An Act Concerning Slaves, § 6, 1840 Laws of Tex. 171, 172. Chapter 58 of the Texas Acts of 1850, provided penalties for violators of the 1840 statute. Act of Dec. 3, 1850, ch. 58, § 1, 1850 Laws of Tex. 42-44 (amending § 6 of An Act Concerning Slaves). Masters, overseers, or employers were to be fined between $25 and $100, and the slave was to receive not less than 39 nor more than 50 lashes. But also under the 1850 Act, slaves were allowed to carry firearms on the premises of the master, overseer, or employer, where they presumably would receive proper supervision.

127. Act of Mar. 15, 1852, ch. 206, 1852 Laws of Miss. 328 (prohibiting magistrates from issuing licenses for blacks to carry and use firearms). This act repealed Chapter 73, sections 10 and 12 of the Mississippi Acts of 1822, allowing slaves and free blacks respectively to obtain a license to carry firearms. *See* Act of June 18, 1822, ch. 73, §§ 10, 12, 1822 Laws of Miss. 179, 181-82.

128. Chapter 448, § 1, of the Kentucky Acts of 1818 was limited solely to slave offenders. Act of Feb. 10, 1819, ch. 448, § 1, 1819 Acts of Ky. 787. The Kentucky Acts of 1850 extended these provisions to free blacks as well. Act of Mar. 24, 1851, ch. 617, art. VII, § 7, 1850 Acts of Ky. 291, 300-01.

129. This presumption was not dispositive of all regulation on this subject. Sale or other delivery of firearms to slaves was forbidden by several states, among them Florida, Georgia, Louisiana, and

Louisiana provided that a slave was denied the use of firearms and all other offensive weapons,[130] unless the slave carried written permission to hunt within the boundaries of the owner's plantation.[131] South Carolina prohibited slaves outside the company of whites or without written permission from their master from using or carrying firearms unless they were hunting or guarding the master's plantation.[132] Georgia, Maryland, and Virginia did not statutorily address the question of slaves' access to firearms, perhaps because controls inherent to the system made such laws unnecessary in these states' eyes.

By contrast, free blacks, not under the close scrutiny of whites, were generally subject to tight regulation with respect to firearms. The State of Florida, which had in 1824 provided for a weekly renewable license for slaves to use firearms to hunt and for "any other necessary and lawful purpose,"[133] turned its attention to the question of free blacks in 1825. Section 8 of "An Act to Govern Patrols"[134] provided that white citizen patrols "shall enter into all negro houses and suspected places, and search for arms and other offensive or improper weapons, and may lawfully seize and take away all such arms, weapons, and ammunition . . . ." By contrast, the following section of that same statute expanded the conditions under which a slave might carry a firearm, a slave might do so under this statute either by means of the weekly renewable license or if "in the presence of some white person."[135]

Florida went back and forth on the question of licenses for free blacks[136] but, in February 1831 repealed all provision for firearm licenses for free

---

North Carolina. Act of Feb 25, 1840, no. 20, § 1, 1840 Acts of Fla. 22-23; Act of Dec. 19, 1860, no. 64, § 1, 1860 Acts of Ga. 561; Act of Apr. 8, 1811, ch. 14, 1811 Laws of La. 50, 53-54; Act of Jan. 1, 1845, ch. 87, §§ 1, 2, 1845 Acts of N.C. 124. Moreover, slave states often provided for patrols manned by local men who would be authorized to search out and confiscate firearms in the possession of free blacks as well as slaves. *See infra* text accompanying notes 133-46.

130. Black Code, ch. 33, § 19, Laws of La. 150, 160 (1806).

131. *Id.* § 20. Moreover, in 1811, Louisiana forbade peddlers from selling arms to slaves, upon a fine of $500 or one year in prison. Act of Apr. 8, 1811, ch. 14, 1811 Laws of La. 50, 53-54 (supplementing act relative to peddlers and hawkers).

132. Act of Dec. 18, 1819, 1819 Acts of S.C. 28, 31 (providing more effective performance of patrol duty).

133. An Act Concerning Slaves, § 11, Acts of Fla. 289, 291 (1824). In 1825, Florida had provided a penalty for slaves using firelight to hunt at night, but this seems to have been a police measure intended to preserve wooded land, for whites were also penalized for this offense, albeit a lesser penalty. Act of Dec. 10, 1825, § 5, 1825 Laws of Fla. 78-80. Penalties for "firehunting" were reenacted in 1827, Act of Jan. 1, 1828, 1828 Laws of Fla. 24-25, and the penalties for a slave firehunting were reenacted in 1828, Act of Nov. 21, 1828, § 46, 1828 Laws of Fla. 174, 185.

134. 1825 Acts of Fla. 52, 55.

135. *Id.* § 9.

136. In 1828, Florida twice enacted provisions providing for free blacks to carry and use firearms upon obtaining a license from a justice of the peace. Act of Nov. 17, 1828, § 9, 1828 Fla. Laws 174, 177; Act of Jan. 12, 1828, § 9, 1827 Fla. Laws 97, 100.

blacks.[137] This development predated by six months the Nat Turner slave revolt in Virginia, which was responsible for the deaths of at least fifty-seven white people[138] and which caused the legislatures of the Southern states to reinvigorate their repression of free blacks.[139] Among the measures that slave states took was to further restrict the right to carry and use firearms. In its December 1831 legislative session, Delaware for the first time required free blacks desiring to carry firearms to obtain a license from a justice of the peace.[140] In their December 1831 legislative sessions, both Maryland[141] and Virginia[142] entirely prohibited free blacks from carrying arms, Georgia followed suit in 1833, declaring that "it shall not be lawful for any free person of colour in this state, to own, use, or carry fire arms of any description whatever."[143]

Perhaps as a response to the Nat Turner rebellion, Florida in 1833 enacted another statute authorizing white citizen patrols to seize arms found in the homes of slaves and free blacks, and provided that blacks without a proper explanation for the presence of the firearms be summarily punished, without benefit of a judicial tribunal.[144] In 1846 and 1861, the Florida legislature provided once again that white citizen patrols might search the homes of blacks, both free and slave, and confiscate arms held therein.[145] Yet, searching out arms was not the only role of the white citizen patrols: these patrols were intended to enforce pass systems for both slaves and free blacks, to be sure that blacks did not possess liquor and other contraband items, and generally to terrorize blacks into accepting their subordination.[146] The patrols would meet no resistance from those who were simply unable to offer any.

---

137. Act of Jan 31, 1831, 1831 Fla. Laws 30.

138. APTHEKER, *supra* note 58, at 298. For a full account of the revolt, the bloodiest in United States history, see *id.* at 293-324. For a compilation of documentary sources on the revolt, see also HENRY I. TRAGLE, THE SOUTHAMPTON SLAVE REVOLT OF EIGHTEEN THIRTY-ONE: A COMPILATION OF SOURCE MATERIAL (1971). An account of the revolt novelized from Turner's confession can be found in WILLIAM STYRON, THE CONFESSIONS OF NAT TURNER (1967). Styron's novel has been criticized as failing to capture the power of religion to the 19th century black, and thus failing to tell the truth of the revolt. *See, e.g.,* WILLIAM F. CHEEK, BLACK RESISTANCE BEFORE THE CIVIL WAR 116-17 (1970).

139. *See* HERBERT APTHEKER, NAT TURNER'S SLAVE REBELLION 74-94 (1966).

140. *Id.* at 74-75.

141. *Id.* at 75.

142. *Id.* at 81.

143. Act of Dec 23, 1833, § 7, 1833 Ga. Laws 226, 228.

144. Act of Feb. 17, 1833, ch. 671, §§ 15, 17, 1833 Fla. Laws 26, 29. The black person offending the statute was to be "severely punished," incongruously enough "by moderate whipping," not to exceed thirty-nine strokes on the bare back. *Id.* § 17.

145. Act of Jan. 6, 1847, ch. 87, § 11, 1846 Fla. Laws 42, 44; Act of Dec. 17, 1861, ch. 1291, § 11, 1861 Fla. Laws 38, 40.

146. STAMPP, *supra* note 27, at 214-15.

B. THE NORTHERN ANTEBELLUM EXPERIENCE: USE OF FIREARMS TO COMBAT RACIALLY MOTIVATED DEPRIVATIONS OF LIBERTY

Even as northern racism defined itself in part by the curtailment of black voting rights,[147] it cumulatively amounted to what some have called a widespread "Negrophobia."[148] With notable exceptions, public schooling, if available to blacks at all, was segregated.[149] Statutory and constitutional limitations on the freedom of blacks to emigrate into northern states were a further measure of northern racism.[150] While the level of enforcement and

---

147. *See supra* text accompanying notes 112-16.

148. *See. e.g.,* RAOUL BERGER, GOVERNMENT BY JUDICIARY: THE TRANSFORMATION OF THE FOURTEENTH AMENDMENT 10 (1977).

149. After Roberts v. Boston, 59 Mass. (5 Cush.) 198 (1849), upheld the provision of segregated public education in the City of Boston, the Massachusetts legislature outlawed segregated education. Act of Mar. 24, 1855, ch. 256, 1855 Mass. Acts 256; *see* Finkelman, *supra* note 99, at 465-467. In Connecticut, most schools were integrated before 1830; only in response to a request from the Hartford black community was a separate system established in that year. *Id.* at 468. The Iowa constitution provided for integration in public schools. *See* Clark v. Board of Directors, 24 Iowa 266 (1868) (construing IOWA CONST. of 1857, art. IX, § 12).

In Ohio, blacks were excluded entirely from public schools until 1834 when the state Supreme Court ruled that children of mixed black ancestry who were more than half white might attend; not until 1848 did the legislature provide for public education of any sort for other black children. Williams v. Directors of Sch. Dist., Ohio 578 (1834); *see also* Lane v. Baker, 12 Ohio 237 (1843). In 1848, the state legislature allowed blacks to be serviced by the public schools unless whites in the community were opposed; in the alternative, the legislature provided for segregated education. Act of Feb. 24, 1848, 1848 Ohio Laws 81. The following year, the legislature provided that the choice of segregated or integrated public education lie at the option of local school districts. Act of Feb. 10, 1849, 1849 Ohio Laws 17. Cincinnati refused to comply with the mandate to educate blacks until forced to do so by a combination of statutory and judicial persuasion. Act of Mar. 14, 1853, § 31, 1853 Ohio Laws 429; Act of Apr. 18, 1854, 1854 Ohio Laws 48; Act of Apr. 8, 1856, 1856 Ohio Laws 117; State *ex rel.* Directors of the E. & W. Sch. Dist. v. City of Cincinnati, 19 Ohio 178 (1850); *see* Finkelman, *supra* note 99, at 468-470. *See generally* UNITED STATES OFFICE OF EDUCATION, HISTORY OF SCHOOLS FOR THE COLORED POPULATION (1969). In Philadelphia, public education was provided for whites in 1818, and separate education was provided for blacks in 1822. Finkelman, *supra* note 99, at 468. In Providence, public education was segregated. COTTROL, *supra* note 111, at 90. Rural schools in Rhode Island, however, were integrated. *Id.* In New York, some school districts were segregated, among them that of New York City. Finkelman, *supra* note 99, at 463, 467-68.

150. From 1807 to 1849, Ohio required blacks entering the state to post a bond. Act of Jan. 25, 1807, ch. VIII, 1807 Ohio Gen. Assem. Laws 53, *repealed by* Act of Feb. 10, 1849, 1849 Ohio Laws 17. Michigan Territory passed a similar law in 1827, though there was only one recorded attempt to enforce it. Act of Apr 13, 1827, 1827 Mich. Rev. Laws 1-10 (1st & 2d Councils). DAVID M. KATZMAN, BEFORE THE GHETTO: BLACK DETROIT IN THE NINETEENTH CENTURY 7 n.6 (1973). Indiana required a bond from 1831 until 1851, when a new constitution forbade black immigration entirely. Act of Feb. 10, 1831, 1831 Ind. Rev. Laws 375, *superseded by* IND. CONST. of 1851, art. XIII, § 1 (amended 1881). Illinois went the same route by coupling the repeal of its 1829 bond provisions with a prohibition on black immigration in its 1848 constitution. ILL. CONST. of 1848, art. XIV; Act of Jan. 17, 1832-33, Ill. Rev. Laws 463, *amended by* Act of Feb 1, 1831, 1832-33 Ill. Rev. Laws 462, *repealed by* Act of Feb. 12, 1853, 1853 Ill. Laws 57. Oregon's 1859 constitution forbade blacks to enter the state, OR. CONST. of 1859, art. XVIII (repealed 1926), and Iowa provided for a fine of two dollars a day for any black remaining in the state for more than three days. Act of Feb. 5, 1851, 1851 Iowa Laws 172.

the ultimate effect of these constitutional and statutory provisions may not have been great,[151] the very existence of these laws speaks to the level of hostility northern whites had for blacks during this period. It is against this background—if not poisonous, racist and hostile—that the black antebellum experience with the right to bear arms must be measured.

Perhaps nothing makes this point better than the race riots and mob violence against blacks that occurred in many northern cities in the antebellum period. These episodes also illustrate the uses to which firearms might be put in pursuit of self-defense and individual liberty.

A good deal of racial tension was generated by economic competition between whites and blacks during this period, and this tension accounts in part for violent attacks against blacks.[152] Moreover, whites were able to focus their attacks because blacks were segregated into distinct neighborhoods in northern states, rendering it easy for white mobs to find the objects of their hostility.[153]

Quite often, racial violence made for bloody, destructive confrontations. In July 1834, mobs in New York attacked churches, homes, and businesses of white abolitionists and blacks. These mobs were estimated at upwards of twenty thousand people and required the intervention of the militia to suppress.[154] In Boston in August of 1843, after a handful of white sailors verbally and physically assaulted four blacks who defended themselves, a mob of several hundred whites attacked and severely beat every black they could find, dispersed only by the combined efforts of police and fire personnel.[155]

The Providence Snowtown Riot of 1831 was precipitated by a fight between whites and blacks at "some houses of ill fame"[156] located in the black ghetto of Snowtown. After a mob of one hundred or so whites descended on Snowtown, and after warning shots had been fired, a black man fired into the crowd, killing a white. The mob then descended on Snowtown in earnest, destroying no fewer than seventeen black occupied dwellings across a period of four days. The mobs did not disperse until the militia fired into the crowd, killing four men and wounding fourteen others.[157]

---

151. From 1833 to 1838, Connecticut prohibited the establishment of schools for nonresident blacks. Act of May 24, 1833, ch. IX, 1833 Conn. Pub. Acts 425, *repealed by* Act of May 31, 1838, ch. XXXIV, 1838 Conn. Pub. Acts 30; *see also* Crandall v. State, 10 Conn. 339 (1834) (attempted prosecution under this statute failed due to an insufficient information). *See* Finkelman, *supra* note 99, at 430-43 (discussing the lack of enforcement of statutes regulating black immigration).

152. *See* LITWACK, *supra* note 116, at 159, 165 (in fields where blacks were allowed to compete with whites, who were often the new Irish immigrants, violence often erupted).

153. *Id.* at 153; *see also* LEONARD P. CURRY, THE FREE BLACK IN URBAN AMERICA 1800-1850: THE SHADOW OF THE DREAM 96-111 (1981).

154. CURRY, *supra* note 153, at 101.

155. *Id.* at 100.

156. *Id.* at 102.

157. *Id.* at 102-03.

Similarly, the militia in Philadelphia put down an October 1849 race riot that resulted in three deaths, injuries, and the destruction of property.[158] By contrast, in the Providence Hardscrabble Riot of October 1824, militia were not called out and the police did nothing to stop a crowd of fifty or so whites from destroying every house in the black Hardscrabble area and looting household goods.[159]

Awareness of racial hostility generally, and of incidents like these, made blacks desirous of forming militia units. The firing of the weapon in Providence in 1831 that sparked the mob to violence illustrated that blacks were willing to take up arms to protect themselves, but also illustrated the potentially counterproductive nature of individual action. The actions of the white militia in Providence and Philadelphia, as well as those of the police and fire units in Boston, proved the strength of collective armed action against mob violence. Moreover, the failure of police to take action in Providence in 1824 illustrated the vulnerability of the black community to mob violence, absent protection.

Though the Uniform Militia Act of 1792 had not specifically barred blacks from participation in the state organized militia,[160] the northern states had treated the act as such, and so the state organized militia was not an option.[161] Blacks could nonetheless form private militia groups that might serve to protect against racial violence, and did so. Free blacks in Providence formed the African Greys in 1821.[162] Oscar Handlin tells of an attempt by black Bostonians in the 1850s to form a private militia company.[163] Black members of the Pittsburgh community had no private militia but nonetheless took action against a mob expected to riot in April 1839. Instead of taking action on their own, they joined an interracial peacekeeping force proposed by the city's mayor, and were able to put a stop to the riot.[164]

It is not clear whether private black militia groups ever marched on a white mob. But that they may never have been called on to do so may be a measure of their success. The story of the July 1835 Philadelphia riot is illustrative. Precipitated when a young black man assaulted a white one, the two day riot ended without resort to military intervention when a rumor reached the streets that "fifty to sixty armed and determined black men had

---

158. *Id.* at 104.

159. *Id.* at 102.

160. *See supra* Part I.c.2.

161. JACK D. FONER, BLACKS AND THE MILITARY IN AMERICAN HISTORY: A NEW PERSPECTIVE 20-21 (1974).

162. *See* COTTROL, *supra* note 97, at 63.

163. OSCAR HANDLIN, BOSTON'S IMMIGRANTS: A STUDY IN ACCULTURATION 175 & n.110 (1959).

164. CURRY, *supra* note 153, at 100; VICTOR ULLMAN, MARTIN R. DELANY: THE BEGINNINGS OF BLACK NATIONALISM 29-31 (1971).

barricaded themselves in a building beyond the police lines."[165]

Undoubtedly, the most striking examples of the salutary use of firearms by blacks in defense of their liberty, and concurrently the disastrous results from the denial of the right to carry firearms in self-defense, lie in the same incident. In Cincinnati, in September 1841, racial hostility erupted in two nights of assaults by white mobs of up to 1500 people. On the first evening, after destroying property owned by blacks in the business district, mobs descended upon the black residential section, there to be repulsed by blacks who fired into the crowd, forcing it out of the area. The crowd returned, however, bringing with it a six-pound cannon, and the battle ensued. Two whites and two blacks were killed, and more than a dozen of both races were wounded. Eventually, the militia took control, but on the next day the blacks were disarmed at the insistence of whites, and all adult black males were taken into protective custody. On the second evening, white rioters again assaulted the black residential district, resulting in more personal injury and property damage.[166]

This history shows that if racism in the antebellum period was not limited to the southern states, neither was racial violence. Competition with and hostility toward blacks accounted for this violence in northern states, whereas the need to maintain slavery and maintain security for the white population accounted for racial violence in southern states. Another difference between the two regions is that in the southern states blacks did not have the means to protect themselves, while in northern states, blacks by and large had access to firearms and were willing to use them.

The 1841 Cincinnati riot represents the tragic, misguided irony of the city's authorities who, concerned with the safety of the black population, chose to disarm and imprison them—chose, in effect, to leave the black population of Cincinnati as southern authorities left the black population in slave states, naked to whatever indignities private parties might heap upon them, and dependent on a government either unable or unwilling to protect their rights. As a symbol for the experience of northern blacks protecting themselves against deprivations of liberty, the 1841 riot holds a vital lesson for those who would shape the content and meaning of the Fourteenth Amendment.

III. ARMS AND THE POSTBELLUM SOUTHERN ORDER

The end of the Civil War did more than simply bring about the end of

---

165. CURRY, *supra* note 153, at 105-06.
166. *Id.* at 107-08; WENDELL P. DABNEY, CINCINNATI'S COLORED CITIZENS: HISTORICAL, SOCIOLOGICAL AND BIOGRAPHICAL 48-55 (Dabney Publishing Co. 1970) (1926); *Cincinnati Riot*, NILES' NAT'L REG. (Baltimore), Sept. 11, 1841, at 32.

slavery; it brought about a sharpened conflict between two contrasting constitutional visions. One vision, largely held by northern Republicans, saw the former slaves as citizens[167] entitled to those rights long deemed as natural rights in Anglo-American society. Their's was a vision of national citizenship and national rights, rights that the federal government had the responsibility to secure for the freedmen and, indeed, for all citizens. This vision, developed during the antislavery struggle and heightened by the Civil War, caused Republicans of the Civil War and postwar generation to view the question of federalism and individual rights in a way that was significantly different from that of the original framers of the Constitution and Bill of Rights. If many who debated the original Constitution feared that the newly created national government could violate long established rights, those who changed the Constitution in the aftermath of war and slavery had firsthand experience with states violating fundamental rights. The history of the right to bear arms is, thus, inextricably linked with the efforts to reconstruct the nation and bring about a new racial order.

If the northern Republican vision was to bring the former slaves into the ranks of citizens, the concern of the defeated white South was to preserve as much of the antebellum social order as could survive northern victory and national law. The Emancipation Proclamation and the Thirteenth Amendment[168] abolished slavery; chattel slavery as it existed before the war could not survive these developments. Still, in the immediate aftermath of the war, the South was not prepared to accord the general liberties to the newly emancipated black population that northern states had allowed their free black populations.[169] Instead, while recognizing emancipation, southern states im-

---

167. Even during the Civil War, the Lincoln administration and Congress acted on the legal assumption that free blacks were citizens. Despite Chief Justice Taney's opinion in *Dred Scott* that neither free blacks nor slaves could be citizens, Dred Scott v. Sanford, 60 U.S. (15 How.) 393, 417 (1856), Lincoln's Attorney General Edward Bates issued an opinion in 1862 declaring that free blacks were citizens and entitled to be masters of an American vessel. *See* 10 Op. Atty. Gen. 382, 413 (1862). That same year, Congress amended the 1792 militia statute, striking out the restriction of militia membership to white men. *See* Act of July 17, 1862, ch. 36, § 12, 12 Stat. 597, 599. While it could be argued that these measures were in part motivated by military needs, it should be noted that the United States and various states had previously enlisted black troops during time of crisis despite the restrictions in the 1792 Act. *See supra* Part I.c.2. Thus, these measures reflected long standing Republican and antislavery beliefs concerning the citizenship of free Negroes. *See generally* Cottrol, *supra* note 91. For a good discussion of black citizenship rights in the antebellum North, see generally Finkelman, *supra* note 99.

168. Section 1. Neither slavery nor involuntary servitude, except as a punishment for crime whereof the party shall have been duly convicted, shall exist within the United States, or any place subject to their jurisdiction.

Section 2. Congress shall have power to enforce this article by appropriate legislation.

U.S. CONST. amend. XIII.

169. *See generally* Finkelman, *supra* note 99.

posed on the freedmen the legal disabilities of the antebellum free Negro population. As one North Carolina statute indicated:

> All persons of color who are now inhabitants of this state shall be entitled to the same privileges, and are subject to the same burdens and disabilities, as by the laws of the state were conferred on, or were attached to, free persons of color, prior to the ordinance of emancipation, except as the same may be changed by law.[170]

In 1865 and 1866, southern states passed a series of statutes known as the black codes. These statutes, which one historian described as "a twilight zone between slavery and freedom,"[171] were an expression of the South's determination to maintain control over the former slaves. Designed in part to ensure that traditional southern labor arrangements would be preserved, these codes were attempts " 'to put the state much in the place of the former master.' "[172] The codes often required blacks to sign labor contracts that bound black agricultural workers to their employers for a year.[173] Blacks were forbidden from serving on juries, and could not testify or act as parties against whites.[174] Vagrancy laws were used to force blacks into labor contracts and to limit freedom of movement.[175]

As further indication that the former slaves had not yet joined the ranks of free citizens, southern states passed legislation prohibiting blacks from carrying firearms without licenses, a requirement to which whites were not subjected. The Louisiana[176] and Mississippi[177] statutes were typical of the

---

170. North Carolina Black Code, ch. 40, 1866 N.C. Sess. Laws 99, *reprinted in* 1 DOCUMENTARY HISTORY OF RECONSTRUCTION: POLITICAL, MILITARY, SOCIAL, RELIGIOUS, EDUCATIONAL AND INDUSTRIAL, 1865 TO THE PRESENT TIME 291 (Walter L. Fleming, ed., 1960) [hereinafter DOCUMENTARY HISTORY OF RECONSTRUCTION].

171. KENNETH STAMPP, THE ERA OF RECONSTRUCTION, 1865-1877, at 80 (1965).

172. FONER, *supra* note 29, at 198 (1988) (quoting letter from William H. Trescot to James L. Orr, Dec. 13, 1865, South Carolina's Governor's Papers). Eugene Genovese has quoted an antebellum observer who described the free Negro as "a sort of inmate on parole." GENOVESE, *supra* note 97, at 399.

173. FONER, *supra* note 29, at 200.

174. STAMPP, *supra* note 171, at 80.

175. *Id.*

176. No Negro who is not in the military service shall be allowed to carry fire-arms, or any kind of weapons, within the parish, without the special permission of his employers, approved and indorsed by the nearest and most convenient chief of patrol. Any one violating the provisions of this section shall forfeit his weapons and pay a fine of five dollars, or in default of the payment of said fine, shall be forced to work five days on the public road, or suffer corporal punishment as hereinafter provided.

Louisiana Statute of 1865, *reprinted in* DOCUMENTARY HISTORY OF RECONSTRUCTION, *supra* note 170, at 280.

177. [N]o freedman, free negro or mulatto, not in the military service of the United States government, and not licensed so to do by the board of police of his or her county, shall keep or carry fire-arms of any kind, or any ammunition, dirk or bowie knife, and on conviction thereof in the county court shall be punished by fine, not exceeding ten dollars,

restrictions found in the codes. Alabama's[178] was even harsher.

The restrictions in the black codes caused strong concerns among northern Republicans. The charge that the South was trying to reinstitute slavery was frequently made, both in and out of Congress.[179] The news that the freedmen were being deprived of the right to bear arms was of particular concern to the champions of Negro citizenship. For them, the right of the black population to possess weapons was not merely of symbolic and theoretical importance; it was vital both as a means of maintaining the recently reunited Union and a means of preventing virtual reenslavement of those formerly held in bondage. Faced with a hostile and recalcitrant white South determined to preserve the antebellum social order by legal and extra-legal means,[180] northern Republicans were particularly alarmed at provisions of the black codes that effectively preserved the right to keep and bear arms for former Confederates while disarming blacks, the one group in the South with clear unionist sympathies.[181] This fed the determination of northern Repub-

---

and pay the cost of such proceedings, and all such arms or ammunition shall be forfeited to the informer; and it shall be the duty of every civil and military officer to arrest any freedman, free negro, or mulatto found with any such arms or ammunition, and cause him or her to be committed to trial in default of bail.

Mississippi Statute of 1865, *reprinted in* DOCUMENTARY HISTORY OF RECONSTRUCTION, *supra* note 170, at 290.

178.

1. That it shall not be lawful for any freedman, mulatto, or free person of color in this State, to own fire-arms, or carry about his person a pistol or other deadly weapon.

2. That after the 20th day of January, 1866, any person thus offending may be arrested upon the warrant of any acting justice of the peace, and upon conviction fined any sum not exceeding $100 or imprisoned in the county jail, or put to labor on the public works of any county, incorporated town, city, or village, for any term not exceeding three months.

3. That if any gun, pistol or other deadly weapon be found in the possession of any freedman, mulatto or free person of color, the same may by any justice of the peace, sheriff, or constable be taken from such freedman, mulatto, or free person of color; and if such person is proved to be the owner thereof, the same shall, upon an order of any justice of the peace, be sold, and the proceeds thereof paid over to such freedman, mulatto, or person of color owning the same.

4. That it shall not be lawful for any person to sell, give, or lend fire-arms or ammunition of any description whatever, to any freedman, free negro or mulatto; and any person so violating the provisions of this act shall be guilty of a misdemeanor, and upon conviction thereof, shall be fined in the sum of not less than fifty nor more than one hundred dollars, at the discretion of the jury trying the case.

See THE RECONSTRUCTION AMENDMENTS' DEBATES 209 (Alfred Avins ed., 1967).

179. *See* FONER, *supra* note 29, at 225-227; STAMPP, *supra* note 171, at 80-81.

180. The Ku Klux Klan was formed in 1866 and immediately launched its campaign of terror against blacks and southern white unionists. *See* FONER, *supra* note 29, at 342; *infra* text at notes 217-223.

181. During the debates over the Civil Rights Act of 1866, Republican Representative Sidney Clarke of Kansas expressed the fears of many northern Republicans who saw the clear military implications of allowing the newly formed white militias in Southern states to disarm blacks:

licans to provide national enforcement of the Bill of Rights.[182]

The efforts to disarm the freedmen were in the background when the 39th Congress debated the Fourteenth Amendment, and played an important part in convincing the 39th Congress that traditional notions concerning federalism and individual rights needed to change. While a full exploration of the incorporation controversy[183] is beyond the scope of this article, it should be noted that Jonathan Bingham, author of the Fourteenth Amendment's Privileges or Immunities Clause,[184] clearly stated that it applied the Bill of Rights to the states.[185] Others shared that same understanding.[186]

Although the history of the black codes persuaded the 39th Congress that Congress and the federal courts must be given the authority to protect citizens against state deprivations of the Bill of Rights, the Supreme Court in its earliest decisions on the Fourteenth Amendment moved to maintain much of the structure of prewar federalism. A good deal of the Court's decision-mak-

---

Who, sir, were those men? Not the present militia; but the brave black soldiers of the Union, disarmed and robbed by this wicked and despotic order. Nearly every white man in [Mississippi] that could bear arms was in the rebel ranks. Nearly all of their able-bodied colored men who could reach our lines enlisted under the old flag. Many of these brave defenders of the nation paid for their arms with which they went to battle. And I regret, sir, that justice compels me to say, to the disgrace of the Federal Government, that the "reconstructed" state authorities of Mississippi were allowed to rob and disarm our veteran soldiers and arm the rebels fresh from the field of treasonable strife. Sir, the disarmed loyalists of Alabama, Mississippi, and Louisiana are powerless today, and oppressed by the pardoned and encouraged rebels of those States.

THE RECONSTRUCTION AMENDMENTS' DEBATES, *supra* note 178, at 209.

182. Representative Roswell Hart, Republican from New York, captured those sentiments during the debates over the Civil Rights Act of 1866:

The Constitution clearly describes that to be a republican form of government for which it was expressly framed. A government which shall "establish justice, insure domestic tranquillity, provide for the common defense, promote the general welfare, and secure the blessings of liberty"; a government whose "citizens shall be entitled to all privileges and immunities of other citizens"; where "no law shall be made prohibiting the free exercise of religion"; where "the right of the people to keep and bear arms shall not be infringed"; where "the right of the people to be secure in their persons, houses, papers and effects, against unreasonable searches and seizures, shall not be violated," and where "no person shall be deprived of life, liberty, or property without due process of law."

Have these rebellious States such a form of government? If they have not, it is the duty of the United States to guaranty that they have it speedily.

THE RECONSTRUCTION AMENDMENTS' DEBATES, *supra* note 178, at 193.

183. For a good general discussion of the incorporation question, see MICHAEL K. CURTIS, NO STATE SHALL ABRIDGE: THE FOURTEENTH AMENDMENT AND THE BILL OF RIGHTS (1986). For a good discussion of the 39th Congress's views concerning the Second Amendment and its incorporation via the Fourteenth, see HALBROOK, *supra* note 6, at 107-23.

184. "No state shall make or enforce any law which shall abridge the privileges or immunities of citizens of the United States; . . . ." U.S. CONST. amend. XIV, § 1.

185. THE RECONSTRUCTION AMENDMENTS' DEBATES, *supra* note 178, at 156-60, 217-18.

186. *Id.* at 219 (remarks by Republican Sen. Jacob Howard of Michigan on privileges and immunities of citizens).

ing that weakened the effectiveness of the Second Amendment was part of the Court's overall process of eviscerating the Fourteenth Amendment soon after its enactment.

That process began with the *Slaughterhouse Cases,*[187] which dealt a severe blow to the Fourteenth Amendment's Privileges or Immunities Clause, a blow from which it has yet to recover. It was also within its early examination of the Fourteenth Amendment that the Court first heard a claim directly based on the Second Amendment. Ironically, the party first bringing an allegation before the Court concerning a Second Amendment violation was the federal government. In *United States v. Cruikshank,*[188] federal officials brought charges against William Cruikshank and others under the Enforcement Act of 1870.[189] Cruikshank had been charged with violating the rights of two black men to peaceably assemble and to bear arms. The Supreme Court held that the federal government had no power to protect citizens against private action that deprived them of their constitutional rights. The Court held that the First and Second Amendments were limitations on Congress, not on private individuals and that, for protection against private criminal action, the individual was required to look to state governments.[190]

The *Cruikshank* decision, which dealt a serious blow to Congress' ability to enforce the Fourteenth Amendment, was part of a larger campaign of the Court to ignore the original purpose of the Fourteenth Amendment—to bring about a revolution in federalism, as well as race relations.[191] While the Court in the late 1870s and 1880s was reasonably willing to strike down instances of state sponsored racial discrimination,[192] it also showed a strong concern for maintaining state prerogative and a disinclination to carry out

---

187. Butchers Benevolent Ass'n v. Crescent City Live-Stock Landing & Slaughter-House Co., 83 U.S. (16 Wall.) 36 (1872).

188. 92 U.S. 542 (1876).

189. 16 Stat. 140 (1870) (codified as amended at 18 U.S.C. §§ 241-42 (1988)). The relevant passage reads:

> That if two or more persons shall band or conspire together, or go in disguise upon the public highway, or upon the premises of another, with intent to violate any provision of this act, or to injure, oppress, threaten, or intimidate any citizen with intent to prevent or hinder his free exercise and enjoyment of any right or privilege granted or secured to him by the Constitution or laws of the United States or because of his having exercised the same, such persons shall be held guilty of a felony . . . .

Id. at 141

190. 92 U.S. at 548-59.

191. This can also be seen in the Court's reaction to the federal government's first public accommodations statute, the Civil Rights Act of 1875. With much the same reasoning, the Court held that Congress had no power to prohibit discrimination in public accommodations within states. *See* The Civil Rights Cases, 109 U.S. 3 (1883).

192. *See, e.g.,* Yick Wo v. Hopkins, 118 U.S. 356, 373 (1886) (declaring the administration of a municipal ordinance discriminatory); Strauder v. West Virginia, 100 U.S. 303, 308 (1879) (striking down a statute prohibiting blacks from serving as jurors).

the intent of the framers of the Fourteenth Amendment to make states respect national rights.

This trend was demonstrated in *Presser v. Illinois,*[193] the second case in
which the Court examined the Second Amendment. *Presser* involved an Illinois statute which prohibited individuals who were not members of the militia from parading with arms.[194] Although Justice William Woods, author of
the majority opinion, noted that the Illinois statute did not infringe upon the
right to keep and bear arms,[195] he nonetheless went on to declare that the
Second Amendment was a limitation on the federal and not the state governments. Curiously enough, Woods's opinion also contended that, despite the
nonapplicability of the Second Amendment to state action, states were forbidden from disarming their populations because such action would interfere
with the federal government's ability to maintain the sedentary militia.[196]
With its view that the statute restricting armed parading did not interfere
with the right to keep and bear arms, and its view that Congress's militia
power prevented the states from disarming its citizens, the *Presser* Court had
gone out of its way in dicta to reaffirm the old federalism and to reject the
framers' view of the Fourteenth Amendment that the Bill of Rights applied
to the states.

The rest of the story is all too well known. The Court's denial of an expanded roll for the federal government in enforcing civil rights played a crucial role in redeeming white rule. The doctrine in *Cruikshank,* that blacks
would have to look to state government for protection against criminal conspiracies, gave the green light to private forces, often with the assistance of
state and local governments, that sought to subjugate the former slaves and
their descendants. Private violence was instrumental in driving blacks from
the ranks of voters.[197] It helped force many blacks into peonage, a virtual
return to slavery,[198] and was used to force many blacks into a state of ritual-
ized subservience.[199] With the protective arm of the federal government
withdrawn, protection of black lives and property was left to largely hostile
state governments. In the Jim Crow era that would follow, the right to
posses arms would take on critical importance for many blacks. This right,
seen in the eighteenth century as a mechanism that enabled a majority to

---

193. 116 U.S. 252 (1886).
194. *Id.* at 253.
195. *Id.* at 265.
196. *Id.*
197. RABLE, *supra* note 29, at 88-90; STAMPP, *supra* note 171, at 199-204.
198. Benno C. Schmidt, Jr., *Principle and Prejudice: The Supreme Court and Race in the Progres-*
sive Era. Part 2: The Peonage Cases, 82 COLUM. L. REV. 646, 653-55 (1982).
199. GEORGE M. FREDRICKSON, WHITE SUPREMACY: A COMPARATIVE STUDY IN AMERICAN
AND SOUTH AFRICAN HISTORY 251-52 (1981); CHARLES E. SILBERMAN, CRIMINAL VIOLENCE,
CRIMINAL JUSTICE 32 (1978); JOEL WILLIAMSON, A RAGE FOR ORDER: BLACK/WHITE RELA-
TIONS IN THE AMERICAN SOUTH SINCE EMANCIPATION 124 (1986).

check the excesses of a potentially tyrannical national government, would for many blacks in the twentieth century become a means of survival in the face of private violence and state indifference.

IV. ARMS AND AFRO-AMERICAN SELF-DEFENSE IN THE TWENTIETH CENTURY: A HISTORY IGNORED

For much of the twentieth century, the black experience in this country has been one of repression. This repression has not been limited to the southern part of the country, nor is it a development divorced from the past. Born perhaps of cultural predisposition against blacks,[200] and nurtured by economic competition between blacks and whites, particularly immigrant groups and those whites at the lower rungs of the economic scale,[201] racism in the North continued after the Civil War, abated but not eliminated in its effects.[202] In the South, defeat in the Civil War and the loss of slaves as property confirmed white Southerners in their determination to degrade and dominate their black brethren.[203]

Immediately after the Civil War and the emancipation it brought, white Southerners adopted measures to keep the black population in its place.[204] Southerners saw how Northerners had utilized segregation as a means to avoid the black presence in their lives,[205] and they already had experience with segregation in southern cities before the war.[206] Southerners extended this experience of segregation to the whole of southern life through the mechanism of "Jim Crow."[207] Jim Crow was established both by the operation of

---

200. See generally JORDAN, supra note 56, at 3-43.

201. LITWACK, supra note 116, at 153-86.

202. Cottrol, supra note 91, at 1007-19.

203. C. VANN WOODWARD, THE STRANGE CAREER OF JIM CROW 22-23 (3d ed. 1974).

204. See infra text accompanying notes 169-178. See generally WOODWARD, supra note 203, at 22-29.

205. See id. at 18-21 (the Jim Crow system was born in the North where systematic segregation, with the backing of legal and extralegal codes, permeated black life in the free states by 1860); see also LITWACK, supra note 116, at 97-99 (in addition to statutes and customs that limited the political and judicial rights of blacks, extralegal codes enforced by public opinion perpetuated the North's systematic segregation of blacks from whites).

206. See RICHARD C. WADE, SLAVERY IN THE CITIES: THE SOUTH 1820-1860, at 180-208 (1964) (although more contact between blacks and whites occurred in urban areas of the South, both social standards and a legal blueprint continued the subjugation of blacks to whites).

207. See generally WOODWARD, supra note 204. Jim Crow has been said to have established

an etiquette of discrimination. It was not enough for blacks to be second class citizens, denied the franchise and consigned to inferior schools. Black subordination was reinforced by a racist punctilio dictating separate seating on public accommodations, separate water fountains and restrooms, separate seats in courthouses, and separate Bibles to swear in black witnesses about to give testimony before the law. The list of separations was ingenious and endless. Blacks became like a group of American untouchables, ritually separated from the rest of the population.

law, including the black codes and other legislation, and by an elaborate etiquette of racially restrictive social practices. The *Civil Rights Cases*[208] and *Plessy v. Ferguson*[209] gave the South freedom to pursue the task of separating black from white. The *Civil Rights Cases* went beyond *Cruikshank*, even more severely restricting congressional power to provide for the equality of blacks under Section 5 of the Fourteenth Amendment,[210] and *Plessy v. Ferguson* declared separate facilities for blacks and whites to be consonant with the Fourteenth Amendment's mandate of "equal protection of the laws."[211] In effect, states and individuals were given full freedom to effect their "social prejudices"[212] and "racial instincts"[213] to the detriment of blacks throughout the South and elsewhere.[214]

These laws and customs were given support and gruesome effect by violence. In northern cities, violence continued to threaten blacks after Reconstruction and after the turn of the century. For instance, in New York, hostility between blacks and immigrant whites ran high.[215] Negro strikebreakers were often used to break strikes of union workers.[216] Regular clashes occurred between blacks and the Irish throughout the nineteenth century,[217] until finally a major race riot broke in 1900 that lasted four days.[218]

Diamond & Cottrol, supra note 103, at 264-65 (footnote omitted).

208. 109 U.S. 3 (1883).

209. 163 U.S. 537 (1896).

210. 109 U.S. 3.

211. 163 U.S. at 548.

212. *Id.* at 551.

213. *Id.*

214. Jim Crow was not exclusively a southern experience after the Civil War. For example, at one point or another, antimiscegenation laws have been enacted by forty-one of the fifty states. Harvey M. Applebaum, *Miscegenation Statutes: A Constitutional and Social Problem*, 53 GEO. L.J. 49, 50-51 & 50 n.9 (1964). The *Adams* case, in which the federal government challenged separate university facilities throughout the union, involved the State of Pennsylvania. *See* Adams v. Richardson, 356 F. Supp. 92, 100 (D.D.C. 1973); Adams v. Richardson, 351 F. Supp. 636, 637 (D.D.C. 1972). Hansberry v. Lee, 311 U.S. 32 (1940), involved a covenant restricting the sale of property in Illinois to blacks. The set of consolidated cases that outlawed the separate but equal doctrine would later be known as Brown v. Board of Educ., 347 U.S. 483 (1954), the defendant board of education was located in Kansas, a Northern state.

215. GILBERT OSOFSKY, HARLEM: THE MAKING OF A GHETTO: NEGRO NEW YORK 1890-1930, at 46-52 (1963).

216. *Id.* at 42.

217. *Id.* at 45-46.

218. *Id.* at 46-52.

> After the riot ended, the situation nevertheless remained tense. Negroes began to arm. Revolvers and other weapons were easily purchased at local pawnshops and hard ware stores. In a survey made of [the area where the riot took place], just one day after the riot, it was found that 145 revolvers and a substantial amount of ammunition had been sold— "all had gone to negroes." Lloyd Williams, a Negro bartender, was seen leaving one store with an arsenal of weapons. When asked what he was going to do with them, he replied, "I understand they're knocking down negroes 'round here. The first man tries it on me gets this . . . ." Other Negroes warned that no white men were going to bother them. As

And in 1919, after a Chicago race riot, 38 deaths and 537 injuries were reported as a result of attacks on the black population.[219]

In the South, racism found expression, not only through the power of unorganized mobs, but also under the auspices of organized groups like the Ku Klux Klan. The Klan started in 1866 as a social organization of white Civil War veterans in Pulaski, Tennessee,[220] complete with pageantry, ritual, and opportunity for plain and innocent amusement.[221] But the group soon expanded and turned its attention to more sinister activities. The Klan's activities, primarily in the South, expanded to playing tricks on blacks and then to terroristic nightriding against them.[222] The Ku Klux Klan in this first incarnation was disbanded, possibly as early as January 1868, and no later than May 1870.[223] By that time, the Klan's activities had come to include assaults, murder, lynchings, and political repression against blacks,[224] and Klan-like activities would continue and contribute to the outcome of the federal election of 1876 that ended Reconstruction.[225] As one author has put it, "The Invisible Empire faded away, not because it had been defeated, but because it had won."[226]

The Ku Klux Klan would be revived in 1915 after the release of D.W. Griffith's film *Birth of a Nation,*[227] but, both pre- and post-dating the Klan's revival, Klan tactics would play a familiar role in the lives of black people in the South; for up to the time of the modern civil rights movement, lynching would be virtually an everyday occurrence. Between 1882 and 1968, 4,743

---

policemen patrolled the Negro blocks they were showered with bricks, bottles, and garbage, thrown from rooftops and tenement windows. They fired back with revolvers. It seems miraculous that no one was killed.

Id. at 49-50.

219. CHICAGO COMMISSION OF RACE RELATIONS, THE NEGRO IN CHICAGO: A STUDY OF RACE RELATIONS AND A RACE RIOT (1922) 595-98, 602, 640-49, *reprinted in* THE NEGRO AND THE CITY 126-33 (Richard B. Sherman ed., 1970). After World War I, an outbreak of racial violence against blacks was recorded from 1917 to 1921. Riots occurred in Chicago, Omaha, Washington, D.C., and East St. Louis, Illinois. *Id.* at 126.

220. WYN CRAIG WADE, THE FIERY CROSS: THE KU KLUX KLAN IN AMERICA 33 (1987).

221. *Id.* at 33-35.

222. *Id.* at 37.

223. STANLEY F. HORN, INVISIBLE EMPIRE: THE STORY OF THE KU KLUX KLAN 1866-1871, at 356-59 (1969).

224. *See generally* WILLIAM L. KATZ, THE INVISIBLE EMPIRE: THE KU KLUX KLAN IMPACT ON HISTORY 19-59 (1986).

225. *See* WADE, *supra* note 220, at 57, 110-11. Through the intimidation of black voters, the Democratic party in the South, with which most Klansmen were affiliated, recovered, and Republican strength waned. The Democrats captured the House of Representatives in 1874, and with the controversial compromise between Democrats and Republicans that elevated Rutherford B. Hayes to the Presidency in 1877, the end of Reconstruction was marked. *Id.*

226. KATZ, *supra* note 224, at 58.

227. WADE, *supra* note 220, at 120.

persons were lynched, the overwhelming number of these in the South;[228] 3,446 of these persons were black,[229] killed for the most part for being accused in one respect or another of not knowing their place.[230] These accusations were as widely disparate as arson,[231] theft,[232] sexual contact or even being too familiar with a white woman,[233] murdering or assaulting a white person,[234] hindering a lynch mob,[235] protecting one's legal rights,[236] not

---

228. STEPHEN J. WHITFIELD, A DEATH IN THE DELTA: THE STORY OF EMMETT TILL 5 (1988).

229. *Id.*

230. NATIONAL ASS'N FOR THE ADVANCEMENT OF COLORED PEOPLE, THIRTY YEARS OF LYNCHING IN THE UNITED STATES: 1889-1918 (1919) reported as follows:

> Among colored victims [of lynching], 35.8 per cent were accused of murder; 28.4 per cent of rape and "attacks upon women" (19 per cent of rape and 9.4 per cent of "attacks upon women"); 17.8 per cent of crimes against the person (other than those already mentioned) and against property; 12 per cent were charged with miscellaneous crimes and in 5.6 per cent no crime was charged. The 5.6 per cent. [sic] classified under "Absence of Crime" does not include a number of cases in which crime was alleged but in which it was afterwards shown conclusively that no crime had been committed.

Id. at 10.

231. *See, e.g., Negro and Wife Hanged, Suspected of Barn-Burning,* ST. PAUL PIONEER PRESS. Nov. 26, 1914, *reprinted in* RALPH GINZBURG, 100 YEARS OF LYNCHINGS 92 (1988).

232. *See, e.g., Negro Hanged as Mule Thief,* ATLANTA CONST., July 15, 1914, *reprinted in* GINZBURG, *supra* note 231, at 92; *Would be Chicken Thief,* N.Y. HERALD, Dec. 6, 1914, *reprinted in* GINZBURG, *supra* note 231, at 93 (reporting a black man having been lynched "[f]or the crime of crawling under the house of a white citizen, with the intention of stealing chickens").

233. *See, e.g.,* WHITFIELD, *supra* note 228 (Emmett Till was killed in 1955 because he was thought to have whistled at a white woman). Other major works describing individual lynchings are JAMES R. McGOVERN, ANATOMY OF A LYNCHING: THE KILLING OF CLAUDE NEAL (1982) (describing a lynching in 1934 occasioned by the rape of a white woman); HOWARD SMEAD, BLOOD JUSTICE: THE LYNCHING OF MACK CHARLES PARKER (1986) (describing another lynching of a black man for the rape of a white woman). *See also Blacks Lynched for Remark Which May Have Been 'Hello,'* PHILA. INQUIRER, Jan. 3, 1916, *reprinted in* GINZBURG, *supra* note 231, at 98; *Inter-Racial Love Affair Ended by Lynching of Man,* MEMPHIS COM. APPEAL, Jan. 14, 1922, *reprinted in* GINZBURG, *supra* note 231, at 158; *Negro Ambushed, Lynched for Writing White Girl,* MEMPHIS COM. APPEAL, Nov. 26, 1921, *reprinted in* Ginzburg, *supra* note 231, at 156; *Negro Insults White Women; Is Shot and Strung Up,* MONTGOMERY ADVERTISER, Oct. 10, 1916, *reprinted in* GINZBURG, *supra* note 231, at 111; *Negro Shot Dead for Kissing His White Girlfriend,* CHI. DEFENDER, Feb. 31, 1915, *reprinted in* GINZBURG, *supra* note 231, at 95; *Negro Youth Mutilated for Kissing White Girl,* BOSTON GUARDIAN, Apr. 30, 1914, *reprinted in* GINZBURG, *supra* note 231, at 90; *White Girl Is Jailed, Negro Friend Is Lynched,* GALVESTON TRIB. (Texas), June 21, 1934, *reprinted in* GINZBURG, *supra* note 231, at 217.

234. *See, e.g., Hoosiers Hang Negro Killer,* CHI. REC., Feb. 27, 1901, *reprinted in* GINZBURG, *supra* note 231, at 37; *Negro and White Scuffle, Negro Is Jailed, Lynched,* ATLANTA CONST., July 6, 1933, *reprinted in* GINZBURG, *supra* note 231, at 197; *Negro Shot After Striking Merchant Who Dirtied Him,* MONTGOMERY ADVERTISER, Aug. 28, 1913, *reprinted in* GINZBURG, *supra* note 231, at 88; *Negro Suspected of Slaying Bartender Is Hung by Mob,* KANSAS CITY STAR, Oct. 31, 1899, *reprinted in* GINZBURG, *supra* note 231, at 23.

235. *See, e.g., Negro Father is Lynched; Aided Son to Escape Mob,* BALT. AFRO-AM., July 6, 1923, *reprinted in* GINZBURG, *supra* note 231, at 170.

236. *See, e.g., Miss. Minister Lynched,* N.Y. AMSTERDAM NEWS, Aug. 26, 1944, *reprinted in*

showing proper respect,[237] or simply being in the wrong place at the wrong time.[238]

This is not to say that blacks went quietly or tearfully to their deaths. Oftentimes they were able to use firearms to defend themselves, though usually not with success: Jim McIlherron was lynched in Estell Springs, Tennessee, after having exchanged over one thousand rounds with his pursuers.[239] The attitude of individuals such as McIlherron is summed up by Ida B. Wells-Barnett, a black antilynching activist who wrote of her decision to carry a pistol:

> I had been warned repeatedly by my own people that something would happen if I did not cease harping on the lynching of three months before . . . . I had bought a pistol the first thing after [the lynching], because I expected some cowardly retaliation from the lynchers. I felt that one had better die fighting against injustice than to die like a dog or a rat in a trap. I had already determined to sell my life as dearly as possible if attacked. I felt if I could take one lyncher with me, this would even up the score a little bit.[240]

When blacks used firearms to protect their rights, they were often partially successful but were ultimately doomed. In 1920, two black men in Texas

---

GINZBURG, *supra* note 231, at 236 (reporting the lynching of a black man for having hired a lawyer in a property dispute).

237. *See, e.g., Impertinent Question,* BIRMINGHAM NEWS, Sept. 23, 1913, *reprinted in* GINZBURG, *supra* note 231, at 88 (relating that a black man was lynched after he asked whether a white woman's husband was home); *Insulting Remark,* MONTGOMERY ADVERTISER, Oct. 23, 1913, *reprinted in* GINZBURG, *supra* note 231, at 89 (relating that a black man was lynched for having made an insulting remark to a white woman); *Negro Half-Wit is Lynched; Threatened to Lynch Whites,* MONTGOMERY ADVERTISER, Aug. 25, 1913, *reprinted in* GINZBURG, *supra* note 231, at 87; *Negro Insults White Women; Is Shot and Strung Up,* MONTGOMERY ADVERTISER, Oct. 10, 1916, *reprinted in* GINZBURG, *supra* note 231, at 111; *Train Porter Lynched After Insult to Woman,* ATLANTA CONST., May 9, 1920, *reprinted in* GINZBURG, *supra* note 231, at 130.

238. *See, e.g., An Innocent Man Lynched,* N.Y. TIMES, June 11, 1900, *reprinted in* GINZBURG, *supra* note 231, at 31; *Boy Lynched at McGhee for No Special Cause,* ST. LOUIS ARGUS, May 27, 1921, *reprinted in* GINZBURG, *supra* note 231, at 150; *Negro Suspect Eludes Mob; Sister Lynched Instead,* N.Y. TRIB., Mar. 17, 1901, *reprinted in* GINZBURG, *supra* note 231, at 38; *Posse Lynches Innocent Man When Thwarted in Its Hunt,* WILMINGTON ADVOC., Dec. 16, 1922, *reprinted in* GINZBURG, *supra* note 231, at 166; *Texans Lynch Wrong Negro,* CHI. TRIB., Nov. 22, 1895, *reprinted in* GINZBURG, *supra* note 231, at 9; *Thwarted Mob Lynches Brother of Intended Victim,* MONTGOMERY ADVERTISER, Aug. 5, 1911, *reprinted in* GINZBURG, *supra* note 231, at 73.

239. *Blood-Curdling Lynching Witnessed by 2,000 Persons,* CHATTANOOGA TIMES, Feb. 13, 1918, *reprinted in* GINZBURG, *supra* note 231, 114-116.

240. IDA B. WELLS-BARNETT, CRUSADE FOR JUSTICE: THE AUTOBIOGRAPHY OF IDA B. WELLS 62 (Alfreda M. Duster ed., 1970). Wells-Barnett's fears for her safety, fortunately, were never realized. Born a slave in 1862, she died of natural causes in 1931. *Id.* at xxx-xxxi, 7. Eli Cooper of Caldwell, Georgia was not so lucky, however. Cooper was alleged to have said that the "Negro has been run over for fifty years, but it must stop now, and pistols and shotguns are the only weapons to stop a mob." Cooper was dragged from his home by a mob of 20 men and killed as his wife looked on. *Church Burnings Follow Negro Agitator's Lynching,* CHI. DEFENDER, Sept. 6, 1919, *reprinted in* GINZBURG, *supra* note 231, at 124.

fired on and killed two whites in self-defense. The black men were arrested and soon lynched.[241] When the sheriff of Aiken, South Carolina, came with three deputies to a black household to attempt a warrantless search and struck one female family member, three other family members used a hatchet and firearms in self-defense, killing the sheriff. The three wounded survivors were taken into custody, and after one was acquitted of murdering the sheriff, with indications of a similar verdict for the other two, all three were lynched.[242]

Although individual efforts of blacks to halt violence to their persons or property were largely unsuccessful, there were times that blacks succeeded through concerted or group activity in halting lynchings. In her autobiography, Ida Wells-Barnett reported an incident in Memphis in 1891 in which a black militia unit for two or three nights guarded approximately 100 jailed blacks who were deemed at risk of mob violence. When it seemed the crisis had passed, the militia unit ceased its work. It was only after the militia unit left that a white mob stormed the jail and lynched three black inmates.[243]

A. Philip Randolph, the longtime head of the Brotherhood of Sleeping Car Porters, and Walter White, onetime executive secretary of the National Association for the Advancement of Colored People, vividly recalled incidents in which their fathers had participated in collective efforts to use firearms to successfully forestall lynchings and other mob violence. As a thirteen-year-old, White participated in his father's experiences,[244] which, he reported, left him "gripped by the knowledge of my own identity, and in the depths of my soul, I was vaguely aware that I was glad of it."[245] After his father stood armed at a jail all night to ward off lynchers,[246] Randolph was left with a vision, not "of powerlessness, but of the 'possibilities of salvation,' which resided in unity and organization."[247]

The willingness of blacks to use firearms to protect their rights, their lives, and their property, alongside their ability to do so successfully when acting collectively, renders many gun control statutes, particularly of Southern origin, all the more worthy of condemnation. This is especially so in view of the

241. *Letter from Texas Reveals Lynching's Ironic Facts,* N.Y. NEGRO WORLD, Aug. 22, 1920, *reprinted in* GINZBURG, *supra* note 231, at 139-40.

242. *Lone Survivor of Atrocity Recounts Events of Lynching,* N.Y. AMSTERDAM NEWS, June 1, 1927, *reprinted in* GINZBURG, *supra* note 231, at 175-78.

243. WELLS-BARNETT, *supra* note 240, at 50. To forestall the occurrence of future incidents of the same nature, a Tennessee court ordered the local sheriff to take charge of the arms of the black militia unit. *Id.*

244. WALTER WHITE, A MAN CALLED WHITE 4-12 (1948), *reprinted in* THE NEGRO AND THE CITY, *supra* note 219, at 121-26.

245. *Id.* at 126.

246. JERVIS ANDERSON, A. PHILLIP RANDOLPH: A BIOGRAPHICAL PORTRAIT 41-42 (1973).

247. *Id.* at 42.

purpose of these statutes, which, like that of the gun control statutes of the black codes, was to disarm blacks.

This purpose has been recognized by some state judges. The Florida Supreme Court in 1941 refused to extend a statute forbidding the carrying of a pistol on one's person to a situation in which the pistol was found in an automobile glove compartment.[248] In a concurrence, one judge spoke of the purpose of the statute:

> I know something of the history of this legislation. The original Act of 1893 was passed when there was a great influx of negro laborers in this State drawn here for the purpose of working in the turpentine and lumber camps. The same condition existed when the Act was amended in 1901 and the Act was passed for the purpose of disarming the negro laborers and to thereby reduce the unlawful homicides that were prevalent in turpentine and saw-mill camps and to give the white citizens in sparsely settled ares a better feeling of security. The statute was never intended to be applied to the white population and in practice has never been so applied.[249]

The Ohio Supreme Court in 1920 construed the state's constitutional right of the people "to bear arms for their defense and security" not to forbid a statute outlawing the carrying of a concealed weapon.[250] In so doing, the court followed the lead of sister courts in Alabama,[251] Arkansas,[252] Georgia,[253] and Kentucky,[254] over the objections of a dissenting judge who recognized that "the race issue [in Southern states] has intensified a decisive purpose to entirely disarm the negro, and this policy is evident upon reading the opinions."[255]

That the Southern states did not prohibit firearms ownership outright is fortuitous. During the 1960s, while many blacks and white civil rights workers were threatened and even murdered by whites with guns, firearms in the hands of blacks served a useful purpose, to protect civil rights workers and blacks from white mob and terrorist activity.[256]

While the rate of lynchings in the South had slowed somewhat,[257] it was still clear by 1960 that Southerners were capable of murderous violence in

---

248. Watson v. Stone, 4 So. 2d 700 (Fla. 1941).
249. *Id.* at 703 (Buford, J., concurring).
250. State v. Nieto, 130 N.E. 663 (Ohio 1920).
251. Dunston v. State, 27 So. 333 (Ala. 1900).
252. Carroll v. State, 28 Ark. 99 (1872).
253. Brown v. State, 39 S.E. 873 (Ga. 1901).
254. Commonwealth v. Walker, 7 Ky. L. Rptr. 219 (1885) (abstract).
255. *Nieto*, 130 N.E. at 669 (Wanamaker, J., dissenting).
256. *See, e.g.*, John R. Salter, Jr. & Donald B. Kates, Jr., *The Necessity of Access to Firearms by Dissenters and Minorities Whom Government is Unwilling or Unable to Protect, in* RESTRICTING HANDGUNS: THE LIBERAL SKEPTICS SPEAK OUT, 185, 189-93 (Donald B. Kates, Jr. ed., 1979).
257. According to records kept by the Tuskeegee Institute, 4,733 lynchings occurred between 1882 and 1959. *4,733 Mob Action Victims Since '82. Tuskeegee Reports.* MONTGOMERY ADVER-

pursuit of the Southern way of life. The 1955 murder of Emmett Till, a fourteen-year-old boy killed in Money, Mississippi for wolf-whistling at a white woman, sent shock waves throughout the nation.[258] Two years later, the nation again would be shocked, this time by a riotous crowd outside Little Rock's Central High School bent on preventing nine black children from integrating the school under federal court order; President Eisenhower ordered federal troops to effectuate the court order.[259] News of yet another prominent lynching in Mississippi reached the public in 1959.[260]

In the early 1960s, Freedom Riders and protesters at sit-ins were attacked, and some suffered permanent damage at the hands of white supremacists.[261] In 1963, Medgar Evers, Mississippi secretary of the NAACP was killed.[262] Three college students were killed in Mississippi during the 1964 "Freedom Summer"; this killing would render their names—Andrew Goodman, James Chaney, and Michael Schwerner—and their sacrifice part of the public domain.[263] A church bombing in Birmingham that killed four small black children,[264] the killing of a young white housewife helping with the march from Montgomery to Selma,[265] and the destructive riot in Oxford, Mississippi,[266] that left two dead when James Meredith entered the University of Mississippi helped make clear to the nation what blacks in the South had long known: white Southerners were willing to use weapons of violence, modern equivalents of rope and faggot, to keep blacks in their place.

It struck many, then, as the height of blindness, confidence, courage, or moral certainty for the civil rights movement to adopt nonviolence as its credo, and to thus leave its adherents open to attack by terrorist elements within the white South. Yet, while nonviolence had its adherents among the mainstream civil rights organizations, many ordinary black people in the South believed in resistance and believed in the necessity of maintaining firearms for personal protection, and these people lent their assistance and their

---

TISER, April 26, 1959, *reprinted in* GINZBURG, *supra* note 231, at 244. Tuskeegee Institute's records show only ten more lynchings to have occurred by 1968. WHITFIELD, *supra* note 228, at 5.

258. *See* WHITFIELD, *supra* note 228, at 23-108; *see also Eyes on the Prize: America's Civil Rights Years, 1954-1965: Awakenings (1954-56)* (PBS television broadcast, Jan. 21, 1986).

259. *See* Cooper v. Aaron, 358 U.S. 1 (1958); *see also* TONY A. FREYER, THE LITTLE ROCK CRISIS: A CONSTITUTIONAL INTERPRETATION (1984); Raymond T. Diamond, *Confrontation as Rejoinder to Compromise: Reflections on the Little Rock Desegregation Crisis,* 11 NAT'L BLACK L.J. 151, 152-164 (1989); *Eyes on the Prize: America's Civil Rights Years, 1954-1965: Fighting Back (1957-62)* (PBS television Broadcast, Jan. 28, 1986).

260. *See generally* SMEAD, *supra* note 233.

261. RHONDA BLUMBERG, CIVIL RIGHTS: THE 1960s FREEDOM STRUGGLE 65-81 (1984).

262. CIVIL RIGHTS: 1960-66 190-91 (Lester A. Sobel ed., 1967).

263. *Id.* at 244-46.

264. *Id.* at 187-88.

265. *Id.* at 303-05.

266. *Id.* at 110-18.

protection to the civil rights movement.[267]

Daisy Bates, the leader of the Little Rock NAACP during the desegregation crisis, wrote in her memoirs that armed volunteers stood guard over her home.[268] Moreover, there are oral histories of such assistance. David Dennis, the black Congress of Racial Equality (CORE) worker who had been targeted for the fate that actually befell Goodman, Schwerner, and Chaney during the Freedom Summer,[269] has told of black Mississippi citizens with firearms who followed civil rights workers in order to keep them safe.[270]

Ad hoc efforts were not the sole means by which black Southern adherents of firearms protected workers in the civil rights movement. The Deacons for Defense and Justice were organized first in 1964 in Jonesboro, Louisiana, but received prominence in Bogalousa, Louisiana.[271] The Deacons organized in Jonesboro after their founder saw the Ku Klux Klan marching in the street and realized that the "fight against racial injustice include[d] not one but two foes: White reactionaries and police."[272] Jonesboro's Deacons obtained a charter and weapons, and vowed to shoot back if fired upon.[273] The word spread throughout the South, but most significantly to Bogalousa, where the

---

267. Donald B. Kates, Jr., recalls that:

> As a civil rights worker in a Southern State during the early 1960's, I found that the possession of firearms for self-defense was almost universally endorsed by the black community, for it could not depend on police protection from the KKK. The leading civil rights lawyer in the state (then and now a nationally prominent figure) went nowhere without a revolver on his person or in his briefcase. The black lawyer for whom I worked principally did not carry a gun all the time, but he attributed the relative quiescence of the Klan to the fact that the black community was so heavily armed. Everyone remembered an incident several years before, in which the state's Klansmen attempted to break up a civil rights meeting and were routed by return gunfire. When one of our clients (a school-teacher who had been fired for her leadership in the Movement) was threatened by the Klan, I joined the group that stood armed vigil outside her house nightly. No attack ever came—though the Klan certainly knew that the police would have done nothing to hinder or punish them.

RESTRICTING HANDGUNS: THE LIBERAL SKEPTICS SPEAK OUT, *supra* note 256, at 186.

268. DAISY BATES, THE LONG SHADOW OF LITTLE ROCK, A MEMOIR 94 (1982).

269. HOWELL RAINES, MY SOUL IS RESTED: MOVEMENT DAYS IN THE DEEP SOUTH REMEMBERED 275-76 (1977).

270. Telephone interview with David Dennis (Oct. 30, 1991).

271. Hamilton Bims, *Deacons for Defense*, EBONY, Sept. 1965, at 25, 26; *see also* Roy Reed, *The Deacons, Too, Ride by Night*, N.Y. TIMES, Aug. 15, 1965, Magazine, at 10.

272. Bims, *supra* note 271, at 25-26.

273. *Id.* at 26. Like the Deacons for Defense and Justice was the Monroe, North Carolina chapter of the NAACP, which acquired firearms and used them to deal with the Ku Klux Klan. ROBERT F. WILLIAMS, NEGROES WITH GUNS 42-49, 54-57 (1962). The Deacons for Defense and Justice are to be contrasted with the Black Panther Party for Self Defense. The Black Panther Program included the following statement:

> We believe we can end police brutality in our black community by organizing black self-defense groups that are dedicated to defending our black community from racist police oppression and brutality. The Second Amendment to the Constitution of the United

Klan was rumored to have its largest per capita membership.[274] There, a local chapter of the Deacons would grow to include "about a tenth of the Negro adult male population," or about 900 members, although the organization was deliberately secretive about exact numbers.[275] What is known, however, is that in 1965 there were fifty to sixty chapters across Louisiana, Mississippi, and Alabama.[276] In Bogalousa, as elsewhere, the Deacons' job was to protect black people from violence, and they did so by extending violence to anyone who attacked.[277]   This capability and willingness to use force to protect blacks provided a deterrent to white terroristic activity.

A prime example of how the Deacons accomplished their task lies in the experience of James Farmer, then head of (CORE), a frontline, mainstream civil rights group. Before Farmer left on a trip for Bogalousa, the Federal Bureau of Investigation informed him that he had received a death threat from the Klan. The FBI apparently also informed the state police, who met Farmer at the airport. But at the airport also were representatives of the Bogalousa chapter of the Deacons, who escorted Farmer to the town. Farmer stayed with the local head of the Deacons, and the Deacons provided close security throughout the rest of this stay and Farmer's next. Farmer later wrote in his autobiography that he was secure with the Deacons, "in the knowledge that unless a bomb were tossed . . . the Klan could only reach me if they were prepared to swap their lives for mine."[278]

Blacks in the South found the Deacons helpful because they were unable to rely upon police or other legal entities for racial justice. This provided a practical reason for a right to bear arms: In a world in which the legal system was not to be trusted, perhaps the ability of the system's victims to resist might convince the system to restrain itself.

States gives a right to bear arms. We therefore believe that all black people should arm themselves for self-defense.

Black Panther Party—Platform and Program, reprinted in REGINALD MAJOR, A PANTHER IS A BLACK CAT 286 (1971). Yet, the Black Panthers deteriorated into an ineffective group of revolutionaries, at times using arguably criminal means of effectuating their agenda. *See generally* GENE MARINE, THE BLACK PANTHERS (1969); BOBBY SEALE, SEIZE THE TIME: THE STORY OF THE BLACK PANTHER PARTY AND HUEY P. NEWTON (1968).

274. JAMES FARMER, LAY BARE THE HEART: AN AUTOBIOGRAPHY OF THE CIVIL RIGHTS MOVEMENT 287 (1985).

275. *See* Bims, *supra* note 271, at 26; *see also* Reed, *supra* note 268, at 10.

276. *See* Reed, *supra* note 271, at 10; *see also* Bims, *supra* note 268, at 26.

277. RAINES, *supra* note 269, at 417 (interview with Charles R. Sims, leader of the Bogalousa Deacons); *see* Bims, *supra* note 271, at 26; Reed, *supra* note 271, at 10-11.

278. FARMER, *supra* note 274, at 288.

CONCLUSION: SELF-DEFENSE AND THE GUN CONTROL QUESTION TODAY

There are interesting parallels between the history of African-Americans and discussion of the Second Amendment. For most of this century, the historiography of the black experience was at the periphery of the historical profession's consciousness, an area of scholarly endeavor populated by those who were either ignored or regarded with suspicion by the mainstream of the academy.[279] Not until after World War II did the insights that could be learned from the history of American race relations begin to have a major influence on the works of constitutional policy makers in courts, legislatures, and administrative bodies. Moreover, it should be stressed that, for a good portion of the twentieth century, the courts found ways to ignore the constitutional demands imposed by the reconstruction amendments.[280]

While discussion of the Second Amendment has been relegated to the margin of academic and judicial constitutional discourse, the realization that there is a racial dimension to the question, and that the right may have had greater and different significance for blacks and others less able to rely on the government's protection, has been even further on the periphery. The history of blacks and the right to bear arms, and the failure of most constitutional scholars and policymakers to seriously examine that history, is in part another instance of the difficulty of integrating the study of the black experience into larger questions of legal and social policy.[281]

Throughout American history, black and white Americans have had radically different experiences with respect to violence and state protection. Perhaps another reason the Second Amendment has not been taken very seriously by the courts and the academy is that for many of those who shape or critique constitutional policy, the state's power and inclination to protect them is a given. But for all too many black Americans, that protection historically has not been available. Nor, for many, is it readily available today. If in the past the state refused to protect black people from the horrors of white lynch mobs, today the state seems powerless in the face of the tragic black-on-black violence that plagues the mean streets of our inner cities, and

---

279. August Meir & Elliot Rudwick, *J. Franklin Jameson, Carter G. Woodson, and the Foundation of Black Historiography,* 89 AM. HIST. REV. 1005, 1005 (1984).

280. *See, e.g.,* Schmidt, *supra* note 198, at 647 (describing the way in which the Supreme Court failed to uphold the Fifteenth Amendment in the late 19th and early 20th centuries); *see also* Randall L. Kennedy, *Racial Critiques of Legal Academia,* 102 HARV. L. REV. 1745, 1753-54 (1989) (discussing the legal academia's willingness to ignore the Reconstruction Amendments in the early 20th century).

281. One scholar has criticized the failure of legal scholars with a left perspective "to incorporate the authentic experience of minority communities in America." Jose Bracamonte, *Foreword to Symposium, Minority Critiques of the Critical Legal Studies Movement,* 22 HARV. C.R.-C.L. L. REV. 297, 298 (1982).

at times seems blind to instances of unnecessary police brutality visited upon minority populations.[282]

Admittedly, the racial atmosphere in this nation today is better than at any time prior to the passage of the Voting Rights Act of 1965.[283] It must also be stressed, however, that many fear a decline in the quality of that atmosphere.

One cause for concern is the Supreme Court's assault in its 1989 Term on gains of the civil rights movement that had stood for decades.[284] Another is the prominence of former Ku Klux Klan leader David Duke, a member of the Louisiana state legislature and a defeated, but nonetheless major, candidate for the Senate in 1990.[285] In the last several years, two blacks who had entered the "wrong" neighborhood in New York City have been "lynched."[286] Is this a sign of more to come? The answer is not clear, but the question is.

Twice in this nation's history—once following the Revolution, and again after the Civil War—America has held out to blacks the promise of a nation

---

282. The beating of Rodney King on March 3, 1991, by members of the Los Angeles Police Department, captured on tape by a serendipitous amateur photographer, has focused attention recently on the problem of police brutality, though the problem predates and presumably continues beyond the incident. *See* Tracey Wood & Faye Fiore, *Beating Victim Says He Obeyed Police*, L.A. TIMES, Mar. 7, 1991, at A1.

283. Pub. L. No. 89-110, 79 Stat. 437 (codified as amended at 42 U.S.C. § 1973 (1988)).

284. *See, e.g.*, Patterson v. McLean Credit Union, 491 U.S. 164 (1989) (urging, sua sponte, not only reconsideration of Runyon v. McCrary, 427 U.S. 160 (1976), on the issue of whether the right to contract on a basis equal with whites under Civil Rights Act of 1866 includes the right to be free from discriminatory working conditions, but also overruling Runyon); Martin v. Wilkes, 490 U.S. 755 (1989) (conferring on whites claiming reverse discrimination a continuing right to challenge consent decrees involving affirmative action); Wards Cove Packing Co. v. Atonio, 490 U.S. 642 (1989) (essentially shifting the burden of proof in employment discrimination cases, such that an employee must go beyond the showing of a disparate impact on a group protected by the statute; also allowing an employer to establish a legitimate business justification as a defense, replacing the standard established in Griggs v. Duke Power Co., 401 U.S. 424 (1971), which required an employer to show that a discriminatory practice was indispensable or essential); City of Richmond v. J.A. Croson, 488 U.S. 469 (1989) (subjecting remedial measures involving affirmative action to the same standard of strict scrutiny as in cases of invidious racial discrimination).

285. *See e.g.*, Peter Applebome, *Louisiana Tally is Seen as a Sign of Voter Unrest*, N.Y. TIMES, Oct. 8, 1990, at A1; David Maraniss, *Duke Emerges from Loss Stronger Than Ever*, WASH. POST, Oct. 8, 1990, at A1; James M. Perry, *Duke's Strong Run in Louisiana Sends National Politicians a Shocking Message*, WALL. ST. J., Oct. 9, 1990, at A5. Moreover, as of the time of final editing, Duke had emerged from a field of four major candidates, including a member of Congress and the incumbent governor, to face a former governor in a runoff election. *See Ex Klan Leader in Louisiana Runoff; Primary: David Duke Will Face Former Gov. Edwin Edwards, Who Led In Ballotting*. L.A. TIMES, Oct. 20, 1991, at A1.

286. Michael Griffith, "a 23-year-old black man[,] was struck and killed by a car on a Queens highway . . . after being severely beaten twice by 9 to 12 white men who chased him and two other black men through the streets of Howard Beach in what the police called a racial attack." Robert D. McFadden, *Black Man Dies After Beating by Whites in Queens*, N.Y. TIMES, Dec. 21, 1986, § 1, at 1. Yusef Hawkins, "[a] 16-year-old black youth[,] was shot to death . . . in an attack by 10 to 30 white teenagers in the Bensonhurst section of Brooklyn . . . ." Ralph Blumenthal, *Black Youth is Killed by Whites; Brooklyn Attack Is Called Racial*, N.Y. TIMES, Aug. 25, 1989, at A1.

that would live up to its ideology of equality and of freedom. Twice the nation has reneged on that promise. The ending of separate but equal under *Brown v. Board* in 1954,[287]—the civil rights movement of the 1960s, culminating in the Civil Rights Act of 1964,[288] the Voting Rights Act of 1965,[289] and the judicial triumphs of the 1960s and early 70s—all these have held out to blacks in this century that same promise. Yet, given this history, it is not unreasonable to fear that law, politics, and societal mores will swing the pendulum of social progress in a different direction, to the potential detriment of blacks and their rights, property, and safety.

The history of blacks, firearms regulations, and the right to bear arms should cause us to ask new questions regarding the Second Amendment. These questions will pose problems both for advocates of stricter gun controls and for those who argue against them. Much of the contemporary crime that concerns Americans is in poor black neighborhoods[290] and a case can be made that greater firearms restrictions might alleviate this tragedy. But another, perhaps stronger case can be made that a society with a dismal record of protecting a people has a dubious claim on the right to disarm them. Perhaps a re-examination of this history can lead us to a modern realization of what the framers of the Second Amendment understood: that it is unwise to place the means of protection totally in the hands of the state, and that self-defense is also a civil right.

---

287. 347 U.S. 483 (1954).

288. Pub. L. No. 88-352, 78 Stat. 241 (codified as amended at 42 U.S.C. § 2000 (1988)).

289. Pub. L. No. 89-110, 79 Stat 437 (codified as amended at 42 U.S.C. § 1973 (1988)).

290. *E.g.,* SILBERMAN, supra note 199, at 160-61; Randall L. Kennedy, *McClesky v. Kemp: Race. Capital Punishment. and the Supreme Court.* 101 HARV. L. REV. 1388 (1988); Howard A. Palley & Dana A. Robinson, *Black on Black Crime.* SOCIETY, July/Aug. 1988. at 5. 59.

ACKNOWLEDGMENTS

"Aymette vs. The State." *Tennessee Reports* 21 (1842): 154–62. Courtesy of the Yale University Law Library.

"Presser v. Illinois." *United States Reports* 116 (1886): 252–69. Courtesy of the Yale University Law Library.

"United States v. Miller et al." *United States Reports* 307 (1939): 174–83. Courtesy of the Yale University Law Library.

Firearms Owners' Protection Act (Public Law 99-308) [S.49]

Brady Handgun Violence Prevention Act (Public Law 103-159)

Kates, Don B., Jr. "Handgun Prohibition and the Original Meaning of the Second Amendment." *Michigan Law Review* 82 (1983): 204–73. Reprinted with the permission of the Michigan Law Review Association. Courtesy of the Michigan Law Review Association.

Levinson, Sanford. "The Embarrassing Second Amendment." *Yale Law Journal* 99 (1989): 637–59. Reprinted by permission of The Yale Law Journal Company and Fred B. Rothman & Company. Courtesy of the Yale University Law Library.

Henigan, Dennis A. "Arms, Anarchy and the Second Amendment." *Valparaiso University Law Review* 26 (1991): 107–29. Reprinted with the permission of the author. Courtesy of the author.

Weatherup, Roy G. "Standing Armies and Armed Citizens: An Historical Analysis of the Second Amendment." *Hastings Constitutional Law Quarterly* 2 (1975): 961–1001. Reprinted with the permission of Hastings Scholarly Publications. Courtesy of the Yale University Law Library.

Malcolm, Joyce Lee. "The Right of the People to Keep and Bear Arms: The Common Law Tradition." *Hastings Constitutional Law Quarterly* 10 (1983): 285–314. Reprinted with the permission of Hastings Scholarly Publications. Courtesy of the Yale University Law Library.

Shalhope, Robert E. "The Ideological Origins of the Second Amendment." *Journal of American History* 69 (1982): 599–614. Reprinted with the permission of the *Journal of American History*. Courtesy of the Yale University Sterling Memorial Library.

Cress, Lawrence Delbert. "An Armed Community: The Origins and Meaning of the Right to Bear Arms." *Journal of American History* 71 (1984): 22–42. Reprinted with the permission of the *Journal of American History*. Courtesy of the Yale University Sterling Memorial Library.

Williams, David C. "Civic Republicanism and the Citizen Militia: The Terrifying Second Amendment." *Yale Law Journal* 101 (1991):551-615. Reprinted with the permission of the *Yale Law Journal*.

Halbrook, Stephen P. "The Fourteenth Amendment and The Right To Keep and Bear Arms: The Intent of the Framers." *Report of the Subcommittee on the Constitution of the Committee on the Judiciary United States Senate, Ninety-Seventh Congress, Second Session* (1982): 68-82. Courtesy of the Yale University Law Library.

Cottrol, Robert J., and Raymond T. Diamond. "The Second Amendment: Toward an Afro-Americanist Reconsideration." *Georgetown Law Journal* 80 (1991): 309–61. Reprinted with the permission of the publisher, copyright 1991 the Georgetown Law Journal Association and Georgetown University. Courtesy of the Yale University Law Library.